HISTORY OF SUMTER COUNTY

SUMTER COUNTY COURTHOUSE, built in 1907 on site of home of A. A. Solomons. In center is white marble memorial with names of the County's dead in World War II. (Sumter Daily Item staff photo).

HISTORY OF SUMTER COUNTY

SOUTH CAROLINA

BY
ANNE KING GREGORIE

LIBRARY BOARD OF SUMTER COUNTY
SUMTER, S. C.
1954

This volume was reproduced from
An 1954 edition located in the
Publisher's private library,
Greenville, South Carolina

All rights reserved. No part of this publication may be reproduced, stored in a retrieval system, transmitted in any form, posted on to the web in any form or by any means without the prior written permission of the publisher.

Please direct all correspondence and orders to:

www.southernhistoricalpress.com
or
SOUTHERN HISTORICAL PRESS, Inc.
PO BOX 1267
375 West Broad Street
Greenville, SC   29601
southernhistoricalpress@gmail.com

Originally published: Sumter, SC 1954
Reprinted: Southern Historical Press, Inc.
Greenville, SC
ISBN #0-89308-939-7
Printed in the United States of America

To
HUBERT GRAHAM OSTEEN
WHO HAS EXPRESSED HIS IDEALS OF CITIZENSHIP
IN SERVICE TO HIS COMMUNITY

FOREWORD

The history of Sumter County here presented is in response to a long-expressed desire of many citizens who are interested in the background of the home community of themselves and their ancestors. For years there had been talk of encouraging some qualified person to undertake the preparation of such an historical record, but nothing came of it until this Library Board was created by legislative enactment. After mature consideration, the Board decided that the sponsorship of a history of the county fell within the scope of its responsibility and authority.

This decision having been reached, the next step was to find a person qualified by experience in historical research, and to enlist the interest of that person in the undertaking. The choice fell upon Dr. Anne K. Gregorie, a curator of the South Carolina Historical Society, who had taught history at the University of South Carolina, Arkansas College and Alabama College. Trained in methods of historical research, she was selected because as author of the only full-length, factual biography of General Thomas Sumter, based upon several years work, chiefly in unpublished records, it was felt that she had already acquired good experience for work on the history of the county. At the invitation of the Board, she came to Sumter for a discussion of the project, and accepted the commission to prepare a history of the county, with no definite time set for completion of the task. The only instructions given her by the Board were that the history of the county should be an authoritative, verifiable account of the life and times of the people of Sumter County, disregarding traditions and current legends not susceptible of proof.

This goal has been achieved, in the opinion of the Library Board, who now submit to the public the well-told story of what has happened in Sumter County during the two hundred and fifty years since John Lawson passed through on his journey from Charleston to the North Carolina settlements. We are confident that it is also a valuable contribution to the history of South Carolina.

LIBRARY BOARD OF SUMTER COUNTY
H. G. Osteen, chairman; Francis M. Moise, secretary; J. A. Raffield, treasurer; James D. Blanding, I. L. Sanders, Robert Palmer, Mrs. T. D. Keels.

AUTHOR'S PREFACE

The history of any locality is necessarily a composite of the people who have lived there. During the more than two centuries since its settlement, Sumter County has had uncounted thousands of inhabitants, so a complete history cannot be given in a single volume, and inevitably, many readers will be disappointed not to find recorded here the names and deeds of their own forefathers.

The aim in this book has been to show the history of Sumter County in relation to parallel events in the state and the nation. At best, this history can be only a more or less well-balanced outline, which may be useful to those who wish to write more fully on special topics. Family histories, church histories, the county's bench and bar, the medical profession, and each of the important industries, are among the many subjects which await their historians.

In dealing with persons and events immediately following the War of Secession, I have felt that it was not within the scope of this work to re-examine evidence as to the guilt or innocence of controversial figures in public life; and the verdicts of such competent historians as David Duncan Wallace, Francis Butler Simkins, Robert Hilliard Woody, and others, have been accepted. The contemporary views of Sumter's citizens, however, as voiced in the newspaper press, have been faithfully recorded. Since the *Sumter Watchman* was subsidized by the corrupt Radical ring, its editorials during this period have not been cited.

For many reasons, it has been decided to hold the footnotes to a minimum, both in number and length, and only those of special significance have been included, chiefly with a view to indicating the character of the sources used.

Discrepancies may be noted in the spelling of local names such as Stateburg, Rafting Creek, and others. Scape Ore, Scape Hore, and Scape Hoar are among the several variants of a name which has not yet been standardized, and to which the Highway Department has now added Scape Oer. In recent years the spelling of Pedee has been accepted as Pee Dee, but Santee has not yet been broken into San Tee. Despite earnest efforts for consistency and accuracy in this book, perfection has not been achieved and is not claimed.

The work of finding material and gathering notes has brought me many happy experiences in Sumter County. The trustees of the Carnegie Public Library have been most cooperative and always ready to aid in every way. Especial acknowledgements are due the chairman of the Library Board, to whom this book is dedicated. A native of Sumter and always active in its civic affairs, he was an editor there for fifty-five years, during much of which time he was chairman of the Democratic County Committee, and served on the county school board. Later, he was a member of the city school board until his retirement. His interest in this book has been inspiring, and his knowledge indispensable. During my many sojourns at his home over the years, Miss Ruth Harrington has been the gracious hostess who has made Sumter my second home.

Acknowledgements are also due the county officials, in particular Mr. Raymond D. Blanding, clerk of court. The late Mr. Clarence Haynsworth called attention to several interesting items he had noted when indexing the county plats. While gasoline was being rationed during the war years, I was enabled to visit many parts of the county through the courtesy of Mr. Robert McLellan, county engineer, Mr. Elias W. Nettles, game warden, and Miss Elizabeth Trowell (now Mrs. Werber Bryan), home agent, when on their regular rounds of the county.

Many individuals have given access to family papers, scrapbooks, and other data: Messrs. Frank McLeod, George D. Shore, P. D. Broun, Francis Moise, Herbert Moses, H. H. Wells, H. G. Osteen, Loring Lee, Mark Reynolds, George H. Hurst, Jr., J. Nelson Frierson, and Thomas M. Stubbs; also, the Misses Emma Mood, Ruth McLaurin, Sallie Rembert, Louise Whittemore, and Emma B. Richardson; Mrs. Walter Herbert, Mrs. Shepard K. Nash, Mrs. Henry Richardson, Mr. and Mrs. Francis Marion Dwight, Jr., Mrs. F. M. Dwight, and

Mrs. Walter C. White. Others to whom acknowledgments are due but who did not live to see the completion of this book, were the late Misses Kate Moses, Edith DeLorme, and Margaret Young Logan Stancil, Florence Adams Mims of Edgefield, and Mary Hemphill Greene of Abbeville. Dr. Robert L. Meriwether, director of the South Caroliniana Library of the state university, gave every facility for use of the library's collections, in particular the invaluable files of Sumter newspapers. He also extended the privilege of using his personal notes gathered from manuscripts in the state archives. Mrs. Meriwether aided in calling attention to unpublished material which had come to light among accessions.

All photographs for the book have been donated without cost. In obtaining pictures of old homes which no longer exist, Mrs. Annie Rees Gettys and Miss Mayo Rees have given valuable help. Mr. Thomas Lee Martin traveled many miles over county roads and gave freely of his time and effort to secure the beautiful pictures which are credited to him by name. Mr. Heyward Crowson, staff photographer of the *Sumter Daily Item*, is responsible for most of the others. The pictures which have been included are not intended to show the prosperous and progressive Sumter County of today, but have been carefully selected because of their relation to the historic past, or are typical of the periods to which they belong.

Begun in the summer of 1942 and frequently interrupted, the completed manuscript of this book was submitted to the Library Board in the autumn of 1951, to be read by each member in turn, and was formally accepted in July 1952. Since then, for good reasons, publication has been delayed until now. In the dificult task of producing a book of this size and character, Mr. Joe E. Davis and his staff of printers have done everything possible to make it a success. Mr. James D. Blanding and Miss Flora B. Surles have aided generously in reading proof.

Of the natives of Sumter who have lived and become notable outside of the county, should be mentioned: William E. Mikell, dean of the Law School of the University of Pennsylvania; the Rev. A. McIver Fraser, moderator of the Synod of the Southern Presbyterian Church; Henry J. Mikell, bishop of the Diocese of Atlanta; Allen Gilbert Flowers, dean of the Law School of Baylor University; John James Monaghan, bishop of Wilmington, Delaware; Edward A. Solomons, rear admiral, United States Navy; Emile P. Moses, major general in command, Marine Corps Base, Parris Island, during the second World War. Sumter takes pride in them, but only their names can be given here. Their stories are available in other publications.

In this study, the public records in the county courthouse have been relied upon heavily. These records show that Sumter has had its share of crime. But the criminals have not shaped the history of the county and their deeds have no place here. The people of Sumter, interested in their government and abhorring corruption, have not easily followed demagogues nor run after false prophets. Their leadership generally has possessed the qualities of the people. Liberal and kind, civilized and sane, above all, tolerant, the Sumter County community in good times and bad, in famine and in plenty, has seen Jew and Gentile, Protestant and Roman Catholic, working together, with a will, for the good of all.

May their future excel their past.

ANNE KING GREGORIE

CONTENTS

CHAPTER   PART ONE   PAGE

AS IT WAS IN THE BEGINNING

I	Indians and Explorers	3
II	The Settlers	8
III	Craven County and St. Mark's Parish	22
IV	The Young Gamecock	32
V	The Revolution	36
VI	Claremont, Clarendon, and Salem Counties	55

PART TWO

SUMTER DISTRICT

VII	Sumterville	89
VIII	Cotton, Western Migration, Early Factories	108
IX	Roads, Ferries, Taverns, and the Mail	119
X	War of 1812	128
XI	Ante-Bellum Negroes	131
XII	Nullification, Fist Fights, and a Duel	146
XIII	The Sumters in the War with Mexico	154
XIV	Early Railroads	163
XV	Schools and Teachers	174
XVI	Reforms and Reformers	193
XVII	Social Patterns	204
XVIII	The Memorable Year 1855	227
XIX	The Sumter Company of Kansas Emigrants	235
XX	The Last Years of the Old Regime	241
XXI	War of Secession	251
XXII	Reconstruction	272

CONTENT

PART THREE

SUMTER COUNTY

XXIII	The New Order	307
XXIV	"Climax of Mosesism"	323
XXV	Reforms, Riots, and Red Shirts	338
XXVI	Hampton and the Conservatives	353
XXVII	The Tillman Dictatorship	370
XXVIII	Ben Tillman's Constitution	384
XXIX	Aftermath of 1895	394
XXX	Council-Manager Government, City of Sumter	402
XXXI	Old Gardens and a Bit of Gossip	410
XXXII	Painters and Paintings	423
XXXIII	Music and the Stage	431
XXXIV	Writers and Writings	440
XXXV	The Newspaper Press of Sumter	452
XXXVI	Silk Culture	462
XXXVII	The Turks	467
XXXVIII	Inventors and Inventions	471
XXXIX	An Economic Retrospect	489
XL	Recent Progress	489

ILLUSTRATIONS

Sumter County Courthouse	*Frontispiece*
A "Two Pen House"	71
Melrose House, Poinsett State Park	71
Anderson House, Black River	72
Bethel Baptist Church, Black River	72
James Bradley's House, Black River	73
Salem Presbyterian Church, Black River	74
St. Mark's Episcopal Church	75
High Hills Baptist Church	76
Rembert's Methodist Church	76
General Thomas Sumter	77
Site of Fort Watson	78
Home House, Stateburg	78
Messrs. Moore, Strange and Wright	79
Borough House, Stateburg	80
Borough House, south view	81
Marden, Stateburg	82
Woodlawn, Stateburg	82
Acton, Stateburg	83
Acton, rear view	83
Cherry Vale, near Shaw Air Force Base	84
Needwood, near Shaw Air Force Base	85
The Ruins, Stateburg	86
Sumter District Courthouse, by Robert Mills	289
Baptist Church, Sumterville	289
Presbyterian Church, Sumterville	290
Typical Small House, Sumterville	290
Home of Mrs. Buford, Sumterville	291
Home of Henry Haynsworth, Sumterville	291
Home of Dr. Josiah Haynsworth, Sumterville	292
Bethel Methodist Church, Oswego	292
Bradford Springs	293
Summer Home, Bradford Springs	293
Concord Presbyterian Church	294
Rip Raps House, Black River	294
Oakland, near Shaw Air Force Base	295

Edgehill, near Shaw Air Force Base	295
Church of the Holy Cross, Stateburg	296
Sumter Family Cemetery, Stateburg	297
Brookland, Stateburg	298
The Oaks, near Stateburg	298
Marston, Stateburg	299
Midway, Stateburg	299
The Gates at Milford	300
Gatekeeper's Lodge, Milford	300
Stable, Milford	301
Belfry, Milford	301
Milford, front view	302
Milford, side view	303
The Spring, Milford	304
General Potter	304
Confederate Monument, Sumter	499
St. Joseph's Academy, Sumter	500
Sumter, Institute, Sumter	500
Mason's Magneto Factory, Sumter	501
Washington Graded School, Sumter	501
Main Street, Sumter, before 1920	502
St. Anne's Roman Catholic Church, Sumter	503
Memorial Park, Sumter	504
Colonel Blanding's House, Sumter	505
H. L. Tilghman Forest Tree Farm	506
Rosemary Lookout Tower	507
Edmunds High School, Sumter	508
Lincoln High School, Sumter	508
Crosswell Orphanage, Sumter	509
Carnegie Public Library, Sumter	509
Temple Sinai, Sumter	510
The Sumter Hospital, now part of Tuomey Hospital	511
Tuomey Hospital, Sumter	511
The Lake, Poinsett State Park	512
Iris, Swan Lake Gardens, Sumter	513
Air View, City of Sumter	514

MAPS AND CHARTS

	PAGE
Sumter District, 1825	*front fly leaf*
Sumter County, 1954	*back fly leaf*
Plan of Stateburg about 1800	67
Jonathan Weston's Farm	207
Garden at Coldstream	419

PART ONE

HISTORY OF SUMTER COUNTY

As It Was In The Beginning

Chapter I
INDIANS AND EXPLORERS

Sumter County lies just east of the center of South Carolina within the fertile plains of the upper pine belt, and rises in the western portion to a crest of 372 feet in the picturesque sandhills that have been known since early times as the High Hills of Santee.

Settled about 1740 by the gradual infiltration of neighboring English-speaking Americans, Sumter County has a homogeneous population that is almost entirely native-born, of whom more than half is nonwhite.[1] Although the second World War has brought in citizens from other states, very few are of foreign stock. Despite its homogeneity, the population has not been stationary, and the land records attest that few if any of the early grants are now possessed by descendants of the original owners.

The region was organized as Sumter District when the legislature of South Carolina united three counties of Camden District, namely, Claremont, Clarendon, and Salem; and on the first day of January in the year 1800, the district began to function in the administration of justice through circuit courts, which were held in the centrally located farmhouse of John Gayle[2] until the courthouse could be erected. Following the fall of the Confederacy, Sumter District in 1868 became Sumter County.

The name of the county keeps alive the memory of a Revolutionary soldier, General Thomas Sumter, who, though born in Virginia, lived in South Carolina for almost seventy years, and in the vicinity of Stateburg for almost half of his life of ninety-eight years.[3]

With more than 3,000 farms, Sumter County still depends upon agriculture as the leading industry, although manufacturing is becoming increasingly important. The county-

---
[1] United States Census 1950.
[2] *Statutes at Large of South Carolina* (here cited as *Stat.*), VII, 284, 289, 292.
[3] A. K. Gregorie, *Thomas Sumter* (Columbia, 1931).

seat, Sumter, incorporated in 1845, is one of the seven largest towns of the state and is sometimes called the capital of the lumber industry. The only other incorporated communities are Mayesville and Pinewood, with populations of less than a thousand each.

The original area of the county, 1672 square miles, has been reduced to 681 square miles,[4] largely by the cutting off of Clarendon in 1855, and of Lee County in 1902. The natural boundaries on the east are Scape Hore Creek, Black River, and Lynches River; on the west are the Wateree and the Santee, two sections of one river system.

The Wateree and the Santee rivers were named for the Wateree and the Santee Indians, tribes that once lived and hunted along these streams. Both tribes were related to the Sioux Indians of the western plains, and later they united with the Catawbas, another Siouan tribe. The Catawba word *wateran*, meaning to float in the water, is said to have been the origin of the tribal name Wateree, which the Spaniards spelled *Guateri*, their *gu* being pronounced as *w*.[5]

The Waterees were first seen by a European when the Spaniard Juan de Pardo met them in 1567. The tribe then was ruled by two women chieftains, and dwelt near the hill country of the Cherokee Indians. Pardo says these women rulers of the Waterees held such absolute power that the people of the tribe were slaves rather than subjects.

A century later, in the summer of 1670, only a few months after the English settled at Charleston, John Lederer, a German explorer, found the Waterees on the upper Yadkin in North Carolina. While Lederer was there, the Wateree chief sent three warriors to kill three young women of an enemy tribe to attend his dying son into the spirit world.

In 1701 the Englishman, John Lawson, found the Waterees on the Wateree River below Camden, living on excellent lands. He described them as tall, fine-looking people, but lazy and

---

[4] R. Mills, *Statistics of South Carolina* (here cited as Mills, *Statistics*) (Charleston, 1826), p. 741; U. S. Department of Agriculture, *Soil Survey of Sumter County* (Washington, 1943), p. 1.

[5] Sources for Indians and explorers are: James Mooney, *The Siouan Tribes of the East* (Washington, 1894); Woodbury Lowery, *Spanish Settlements within the present limits of the United States* (New York and London, 1911); F. L. Harriss (ed.), *Lawson's History of North Carolina* (Richmond, 1937); D. D. Wallace, *History of South Carolina* (New York, 1934).

idle. Destitute of guns and other English goods, they were such ingenious thieves and pickpockets that they could steal even with their feet. Nevertheless, Lawson and his companions slept in their dark, smoky cabins, and found the Waterees very hospitable in supplying food. The next morning when the Englishmen of the party shaved themselves with razors, the Waterees were overcome with admiration, saying that they had never seen the like before.

Lawson also gave the earliest account of the High Hills of Santee, which he thought were mountains and described as the most amazing prospect he had seen in Carolina. The "Alp with a top like a Sugar-loaf" which he viewed across a beautiful swamp twenty miles wide, is believed to have been Cook's Mount, opposite Stateburg. These hills as well as the Santee River, derive their name from the Santee Indians, whose early history the Spanish explorers have preserved.

In 1526 Lucas d' Ayllon, a wealthy Spanish auditor of San Domingo, arrived upon the coast of what is now South Carolina, with three vessels of colonists, and entered the great river which he named the Jordan, identified by some later writers as the Santee. There are good grounds, however, for believing that it may have been the Cape Fear. There d' Ayllon died, and the wretched survivors of his settlers departed. Some eighty years afterwards, the Spanish explorer, Francisco de Ecija, reached the Jordan and found a Frenchman living among the "Sati" or Santee Indians. Ecija induced the savages to let him have the Frenchman, and from him learned the news of an English colony to the northward, perhaps Jamestown in Virginia, or Raleigh's colony on Roanoke Island. From accounts left by these Spaniards, we learn that the Santees, like the Waterees, were ruled by absolute chieftains; also that they spoke a language which was not understood by the other Indians on the Carolina coast.

When Lawson visited the Santees in 1701, he too was impressed with the absolute powers of their chief. He described the tribe as a good-humored, friendly people; and he was much interested in their vermin-proof corn cribs, which were built on supports seven or eight feet above the ground and tightly sealed with clay, both inside and out. The Indians also had a remarkable knowledge of medicinal plants, and some had amazing powers as conjurers. The chief medicine man, said Lawson, was wearing a match coat made of wild turkey feathers, which resembled the "deepest silk Shag," and other Indians had girdles, sashes and garters which they had woven from 'possum hair.

The most curious customs of the Santees, however, were concerned with their burial rites. The distinguished dead were buried on pyramids of earth, whose greater or lesser height denoted the importance of the deceased. The grave at the top of the pyramid was protected by a shed supported on nine stakes.

The corpse of an ordinary person would be laid in the sun for a day or two, then placed on crotches, covered from the rain with bark, and left until the flesh grew "mellow," when it was removed from the bones and burned. The carefully cleaned bones were then preserved in a wooden box; and with annual cleaning and oiling, skeletons remained with their respective families for generations.

During Lawson's visit he was the guest of a gigantic, well-proportioned Indian, seven feet tall, a famous hunter, who always carried with him the treated head and skin of a buck, the eyes being preserved as if still alive. Wearing this gear and imitating the motions of a deer, the hunter could approach his quarry as near as he liked. This method was not favored by populous tribes, however, for the imitations were so good that the hunter himself might be killed if another hunter happened to be in the area and mistook him for a deer.

Lawson also described the fat barbecued venison which the hospitable Santees served him, and said that his hostess tore some of it to bits with her teeth, beat it to rags in a mortar, and then boiled it to a savory stew.

At a Santee hunting camp, Lawson hired a hunter called Santee Jack as a guide and proceeded toward the High Hills. There they spent the night, but soon after falling asleep they were awakened by the hideous yells and howls of "endless Numbers of Panthers, Tigers, Wolves and other

Beasts of prey," which hunted the deer in the swamp. The next day, from immense flocks of wild turkeys, Santee Jack killed fifteen, some weighing as much as forty pounds, but for himself he chose in preference the meat of a polecat for his dinner.

A decade after Lawson made his journey, Colonel John Barnwell led a band of South Carolinians to aid the North Carolinians in their war against the Tuscarora Indians. Both the Waterees and the Santees joined him as allies, and served with the Catawbas in the companies under Captain Bull and "Esaw-Captain Jack."[6] But in 1715, when the terrible Yemassee War broke out, both the Waterees and the Santees joined the conspiracy to destroy the South Carolinians, and almost succeeded. When the war ended, however, the power of the Indians was broken, and the remnants of the Santees and Waterees who survived, went up their river and united with the Catawbas.

Thereafter, the area which is now Sumter County ceased to be the home of Indians, although it remained part of the hunting ground of the Catawbas as late as 1748, and an Indian hunting camp was near "The Raft" in the Wateree until 1750.[7] Another camp is said to have been on Camp Branch of Black River, near the present old Concord Church, where pieces of pottery have been ploughed up. Numerous Indian relics found on the Eugene W. DuRant place, indicate that an aboriginal village probably was north of the present town of Lynchburg, off the Bishopville road near Lynches River. A mound of black earth, believed to be of Indian origin, is near Salem Church, at the end of Fork Lake in Black River swamp. Its height when measured some fifty years ago was twenty-seven feet, and it covers about an acre.

[6] *The South Carolina Historical and Genealogical Magazine* (here cited as SCHGM), IX (1908), 30, 81.
[7] R. L. Meriwether, *The Expansion of South Carolina 1729-1765* (Kingsport, 1940), pp. 108, 101.

CHAPTER II

THE SETTLERS[1]

For almost thirty years after the power of the Indians was broken in the Yemassee War, the green forest which covered the future Sumter District remained the home of wild beasts, who were disturbed only occasionally by Catawba Indian hunters. Here were herds of deer and many bears, bands of wolves—not man-eaters but rather wild dogs, which later were a destructive nuisance to the settlers; and noisy panthers, a species of wildcats, which made the woods ring at night with their human-like screams.

Although there was little or no danger from hostile Indians in this section of the province after the Yemassee War, the region east of the Wateree was soon flanked by two of the nine townships which South Carolina established in the interior for the protection of the settlement at Charleston. Both of these townships were located around landmark pines. To the north, at the mouth of Pine Tree creek on the Wateree, Fredericksburg was laid out in 1734. To the south at the King's Tree on the Black, Williamsburg received its first white settlers in 1732.

Only one land route penetrated the wilderness between these two townships, a seldom-used Catawba path, which ran down the east side of the Wateree from the Catawba Indian settlements through Fredericksburg to the High Hills, where it turned westward to the Congarees. From the High Hills, the path from Fredericksburg to Charleston continued southward, paralleling the Santee, with spurs to the best places for crossing the river. The path was not made a public road until 1753, a full decade after white settlers had begun to move into the area that would become Sumter District.

[1] The use of plats and grants in the office of the secretary of state was greatly facilitated by the voluminous notes from these, the Council Journals and early newspapers, prepared by Professor Robert L. Meriwether of the University of South Carolina, for his book, *The Expansion of South Carolina, 1729-1765*. His notes and his book have been indispensable.. From citations to original grants in Sumter County conveyances, identification of some with later owners has been possible.

THE SETTLERS

These first settlers, therefore, had to look to the rivers for transportation, but found them obstructed with logs and snags, and edged with wide swamps which were frequently flooded. Nothing was done to clear the rivers until 1753, at the same time that the Catawba path was made a public road.[2] The early influx of settlers was necessarily very slow.

After Williamsburg was established, the old cattle-pens that herdsmen had already been using at the King's Tree, were ordered removed, and the privilege of having pens was reserved to residents of the township. The displaced herdsmen therefore looked to the canebrakes along Black River, and Lynches River, as pasture for their cattle, and built themselves new pens and huts in the uninhabited region between the King's Tree and Fredericksburg. In 1742, Francis Cordes and Peter Porcher, who lived south of the Santee, were advertising for sale 500 head of cattle on the north side of the river,[3] their cattle-pens being apparently in what is now Clarendon County.

As the population of the two flanking townships increased during the first decade after settlement, the overflow from them began to seek homes in the rich bottom lands along the rivers, and the future Clarendon County was settled almost as early as the townships. Some of the first settlers came from the coast near Charleston, as did John and Josiah Cantey. Captain Joseph Cantey in 1739 purchased lands near the northwest line of Williamsburg and began to develop his Mount Hope plantation. Other settlers came from Virginia, as did Richard Richardson. He married Mary Cantey, and their son Richard was born in 1742, one of a large family. As a surveyor, Richard Richardson the elder ran the lines for many of the early grants to his neighbors, but he did not petition until 1744 for his own first grant,[4] near Halfway Swamp, where he developed his plantation, Big Home. Eventually, his holdings included the fourteen miles of rich lands between Halfway Swamp and Jacks Creek, many acres of which are still owned by his numerous descendants.

[2] Work on the Wateree River and the road was authorized in the same act. Clearance of lower Black River was provided in a separate act. *Stat.* VII, 504, 503.
[3] *S. C. Gazette*, March 6, 1742.
[4] Meriwether, *op. cit.*, p. 109.

Further north, one of the first settlers on record to settle east of the Wateree was Isaac Brunson, a dissenter from New England, who, after a sojourn at Dorchester on Ashley River, had a warrant in 1740 for 200 acres adjoining lands of Peter Porcher "near a place called High Hills." Fourteen years earlier, Brunson's family when enumerated in St. George's Parish, had consisted of two white men, one white woman, seven white children, two men slaves and one woman slave. After he settled near the High Hills, Isaac Brunson was appointed in 1747 one of the board of road commissioners whose district along the waters of Black River extended up to Pine Tree Creek. Ten years later when St. Mark's Parish was established, he was one of the commissioners for building the parish church. His will, proved in Charleston in 1770, mentions his wife Mary, his seven sons, Daniel, David, Isaac, Josiah, Matthew, Moses, and Joshua; and two daughters, Mary Mellett and Susannah.[5] The map of Tacitus Gaillard and James Cook, who surveyed this area in 1770,[6] shows three "Brunston" settlements between the old Catawba path and the south fork of Black River, each of them on or near a creek.

Near the head of Black River in 1742, David Anderson, a restless man who had "been a long time in the Province, but never yet was capable of Settling himself," was living on Stony Run. When he advertised that year in the *South Carolina Gazette* for the owner of a horse which had strayed to him, he had not even applied for a land warrant, and the lands where he resided were not surveyed for him until later. He had moved on to Georgia when he died in 1784, but his family continued to own his Black River land until some of it was bought in 1813 by Robert Witherspoon and became a part of Coldstream plantation.[7]

On Rocky Bluff Swamp and Turkey Creek in 1744, John Neilson, a butcher from Charleston, had two small surveys. On one of these lived another member of his family, Samuel Neilson. The next neighbor to move in was John Hope, who then had been fifteen years in the province. Soon there were

---

[5] *Ibid.;* Gertrude Foster, MS Documentary History of Education in South Carolina, IV, 475; *Stat.* IX, 145, IV, 35.
[6] MS map in possession of South Carolina Historical Society, Charleston.
[7] Meriwether notes and *op. cit.,* p. 108; will of David Anderson and conveyances, Sumter County records.

about twenty-five settlers in the vicinity of Stony Run, including Robert Wilson, Hugh Ervin, James Bradley, James Grimes, and Henry Cassels. On Pudding Swamp, John Frierson in 1754 had a grant which his descendants probably still own. The next year Samuel Bradley obtained 250 acres near where Salem Church was built a few years later, on the east side of Black River. About thirty other settlers were then scattered along the headwaters of the river.[8]

There were enough families in the community by this time to be of some importance, and in 1758 they made their first effort to get a public road. Pleading the grievance of the lack of roads to Charleston, the nearest market for their produce, the men on the north and east side of Black River petitioned the General Assembly to appoint David Anderson, Henry Cassels, Samuel Jones, Robert Lewis and John Newman, as commissioners to lay out the necessary roads. The petition shows the names of thirty-eight citizens: William Carter, William Roberts, Charles McCoy, William McCoy, Samuel Bradley, James Bradley, Thomas Dyall, Elisha Dubose, Samuel McCoy, a Dun whose first name is illegible, Benjamin Cassels, William Wilson, John Capps, Thomas Player, John Warren, David Anderson, Thomas Keandy (Kennedy?), William Weesbury (Westberry), John McKintosh (McIntosh), Charles Storry, Thomas Abbitt, David Morgan, John Morgan, Joseph Bradley, John Frierson, Henry Sparrow, Samuel Jones, Rob Lewis, Henry Cassels, John Newman, James Armstrong, James Ross, Arthur Somsinson (Tomlinson?), Peter Mellett, Jonathan Hill, John Webb, William Cassels, and Thomas Hughs.[9]

Meanwhile, on Lynches River a number of settlers had located. One of the grantees was an erratic Charles Woodmason, an Englishman of education and intelligence, but intensely emotional, an unusual type to be found in the backwoods. In 1755 as a merchant of Craven County, he had a grant on the south side of "Lynches Creek," and later, another on Lynches Lake, as well as others on the Pedee. His wife refused to follow him to America, but Woodmason expected to develop his lands for his son, whom he planned

[8] Meriwether, *op. cit. 108.*
[9] *SCHGM*, XXVI, 122.

to bring over as a partner in his mercantile business. These plans went awry, however, and Woodmason sold his Lynches River property, some of which passed into the possession of Jared Nelson, who later sold to Thomas McFaddin.[10]

When Tacitus Gaillard and James Cook mapped the future Sumter District in 1770, the center of population was on the east side of Black River, where their map shows, going northwest from Pudding Swamp, settlements of Frierson, Gambell, Conyers, Benbow, Dees (Deas), Murray, MacKinney, Ralle, Laris, Woods, Catlie, Mitchell, Taylor, Dickey, Harvey, Anderson, Tomlinson, Bradley, Castles, Cain, Gordon, Armstrong, Wilson and Wright. On Pudding Swamp, were Taylor, Plowden, Burgess, Muckelveeny, Lowery, and Singleterry.

In the High Hills, settlement at first was retarded. In 1739 by proclamation of Lieutenant Governor Broughton, a strip ten miles wide on the east side of the Wateree and Santee Rivers, from Fredericksburg down to Jacks Creek, was reserved for two years for settlers from Scotland. For this reason it was long known as the North Britain Tract, although the Scots did not come. As late as 1743, the area must have been vacant, for the Commons House then proposed extending the time limit on the reservation.

One of the first to settle in the North Britain Tract was George Russell, who in 1749, hoping to attract a minister and perhaps a congregation, filed a request that a church glebe be reserved. Accordingly a 500-acre tract was surveyed in the High Hills for a Scotch or a Presbyterian congregation, but apparently it was never taken by any church.

Despite early restrictions upon grants, about seventy surveys in the High Hills and the sand hills were made from 1745 to 1759, between Fredericksburg and Halfway Swamp, chiefly along the Catawba path. John Dargan, with his wife Ann, two children, one servant and three Negroes, had a survey on Shanks Creek and 300 acres in the Scots' Glebe. His brother Timothy Dargan, who later became a Baptist minister, had a survey for Williams' Old Field, also on

---

[10] Plat Book 6, p. 98; Fulham Palace MSS (Library of Congress transcripts), South Carolina, No. 51; Register of mesne conveyance, Charleston, VV, 262; Sumter Conveyances, CC, 211.

Shanks Creek. John Dargan, perhaps in partnership with his brother, erected a grist mill, and improved his swamp land with dams, probably for the culture of rice. On another tract he had two sets of indigo vats.[11] An enterprising man, John prospered, and acquired slaves and other property. When he made his will in 1766, he bequeathed his Scots' Glebe tract to his daughter Mary, and his Shanks Creek land to his daughter Elizabeth Colleatt with his half of the grist mill thereon. To his daughter Alice, he left his plantation of residence, subject to the life tenancy of her mother.

In 1749 Thomas Crawford obtained a grant for 200 acres in the North Britain tract, which was still largely unoccupied, for his land was bounded on all sides by vacant land. Other early grantees in the Hills were: Thomas Abett (Abbott?), Andrew Allison, John and Bernard Beekman, Nicholas Broadway, James Brunson, Daniel Cannon, Robert Carter, Thomas Craven, John Cook, Lawrence Dully, Joseph Earl, Samuel and Thomas Elliott, William Frost, Wood Furman, Dennis Hagen, William Hilton, Henry Hunter, Henry Hyrne, Thomas Jones, Thomas Knighton, Peter Mellett, James McGirt, James McKelvey, Kenneth Mitchie, James Miles, John Mitchell, John and Robert Moses, Charles Pinckney, Roger Rees, Andrew Rutledge, George Sanders, Alexander Shepherd, Henry Sims, Christopher Singleton, James and Gilbert Stringham, John Steele, John Stuard (Stuart?), Archibald Stobo, Tunis Tebout, William Tucker, William Watson, and William Wright.

Not all of these men settled permanently on their grants, and some never came at all but held their grants for speculative profits. The Beekmans, for instance, lived in Charleston. John Beekman removed to New York, where he died, and his son John sold the High Hills grant of 750 acres to Chancellor William D. James. Daniel Cannon was a Charleston man who never became in any way identified with his High Hills property. Tunis Tebout, from the French Hugenots of Jamestown, was a Charleston blacksmith, onetime partner of William Johnson, the patriot of Liberty Tree fame. Tebout died in Beaufort before the close of the Revolution, and Wood Furman bought his grant.

[11] Meriwether, *op. cit.*, pp. 108, 109, and notes.

During the 1750's so many settlers came down from the Valley of Virginia, that by the middle of the next decade the Reverend James Harrison estimated 5000 gunmen were in St. Mark's Parish.[12] Many of the later prominent families of Sumter arrived during this period, but since most of their grants are described as bounded by vacant land, very few of their locations can now be identified.

Sherwood James, his wife Anne, and their large family came in 1753, bringing five slaves. Sherwood was too infirm to make the journey to Charleston, so Anne presented his petition for lands on the Wateree, and obtained a grant on the Catawba path in the High Hills. Their sons Sherwood, John and Francis also came down from Virginia, bringing their wives, children and slaves, and obtained grants in the High Hills.[13]

Along with the James families in 1753, came Matthew Singleton, who had married Mary, only daughter of the elder Sherwood James. Matthew obtained a grant of 500 acres on headrights for himself, his wife, two children and two slaves.[14] This grant was probably the nucleus of his Melrose plantation, now a part of Poinsett State Park.

Also from Virginia, New Kent County, came the brothers Richard and John Haynsworth, who settled in Prince Frederick's Parish, in the area which later became the southern portion of St. Mark's when that parish was created. Richard met a Swiss girl, Elizabeth Hesse, who eventually became his wife; and John married Elizabeth Davidson in 1747. Richard had already acquired property east of the Santee before he obtained his first grant in 1756, adjoining his land, which seems to have been on the path near Nelson's Ferry. After the close of the French and Indian War, Richard and Elizabeth were paid by the province for entertaining Indians. They reared a large family, and their son Henry, who married Wood Furman's daughter Sarah just before the Revolution,

---

[12] Cited by H. T. Cook, *Rambles in the Pee Dee Basin South Carolina* (Columbia, 1926), p. 142.
[13] Meriwether notes, MS Council Journals and grants.
[14] *Ibid.*, wills, Sumter County Courthouse; Virginia E. Green Singleton, *Genealogy of the Singletons* . . . (Hartsville, S. C., 1914).

is the ancestor of the several present-day Haynsworth families.[15]

Thomas Sumter, destined to become the most famous of the Virginians east of the Wateree, did not come with the great overland migration, but by way of Charleston, and he did not become a resident of the High Hills until after the Revolution.

A number of the later settlers east of the Wateree came from the Huguenot families of French Jamestown on the Santee. Peter Mellett has already been mentioned. Claudius Richbourg obtained grants in 1765, and Andrew Rembert had a grant in 1769. Other Sumter names of French origin are DuBose, DesChamps, Gaillard, Bossard, and DeLorme. The Bossards came in from Georgetown after 1800, hoping to get away from malaria. The DeLorme brothers came to Sumter, via the West Indies and Charleston, after the marriage in 1815 of their sister to John Haynsworth.

Settled three generations after the arrival of Europeans in South Carolina, Sumter County was pioneered by English-speaking Americans. As shown in the above discussion, practically all the first white inhabitants came in from other colonial settlements, and perhaps a third of them were from the coastal region of South Carolina.

In the main, the early settlers were small farmers and cattle raisers. Their grants, made on headrights of fifty acres for each member of the family including slaves, seldom totaled more than 500 acres to a family. Charles Woodmason, who came to know them well when he became their resident rector, described them as poor and illiterate, but he expressed a preference for a ministry among them because of the comparative healthfulness of the region.

Life for the pioneers was not easy. The first task for each family was to make a clearing of five or six acres by felling the great trees, a formidable task, and one that could not be accomplished until some sort of shelter had been improvised. The first shelters were probably like those at the King's Tree, mere earthen cellars, made by setting up two perpendicular

---

[15] *The Register Book for the Parish Prince Frederick Winyaw* (Baltimore, 1916); H. C. Haynsworth, *Haynsworth-Furman and Allied Families* (Sumter, 1942); *S. C. Stat.* IV, 203, 226.

forked poles, which supported a horizontal ridge-pole against which other poles were leaned at an angle. The sloping sides were covered with a matted layer of pine straw, on which was laid a layer of earth. With earthen floors, and ventilated only by the door, such dwellings had the atmosphere of a cave, and were inhabited only until the permanent log cabin could be erected. Woodmason has recorded that the first dwellings were built on the edge of the swamps, so that the planters could view their slaves at work in the rice fields. As a water supply was essential, the numerous springs and water-courses generally decided the location of the home site.

Most of the log cabins had but a single room, larger or smaller according to the size of the family, the energy of the builder, and his available man-power, for even the simplest of these homes required vast labor. Each log meant the felling of a tree. Uniformity in size was essential, so some of the logs had to be cut at some distance away and rolled to the site. For the roof, bark or split logs were used. If shingled, each clapboard or shingle had to be riven with an axe from logs sawed by hand into the desired lengths.

The floors of the cabins were sometimes the bare earth, or packed smooth with hard clay, and some were made of hewn logs. Often there were no windows, and light came from the open door in the day, and from a lightwood knot at night. Glassed windows were very rare. Chimneys were usually made on a framework of poles heavily plastered with clay. In the High Hills, however, coquina rock and field stones of hematite were available. As the chimneys were immensely large and not very high, robbers could easily enter by way of them into a locked cabin, although probably very few cabins had other than a wooden latch opened by a knotted string which could be drawn in at night. William Richardson of Bloom Hill has recorded that one of his slave women, locked in by the overseer for misconduct, escaped by climbing out through the chimney.

Regardless of the size of the cabin, it was usually the abode of a free hospitality, which turned away no traveler. The *Sumter Watchman* as late as 1858 narrated an incident which must have been typical of the social amenities in pioneer days: A stranger stopped overnight at a one-room cabin where dwelt a family of eight adults and their several Negro slaves. After a hearty supper and friendly conversation, the guest at bedtime began to wonder how he was going to retire in the presence of so many witnesses. The dogs went to sleep on the floor. The Negroes with their feet in the warm ashes, did likewise. The father and his two sons undressed and shared a single pillow. Sensing the embarrassment of the guest, the hostess tactfully said to her daughters, "Gals, turn your backs around till the stranger gits into bed." When the guest had stowed himself away, she once more spoke: "Reckon, stranger, as you ain't used to us, you'd better kiver up till the gals undress."

An improvement on the single-room log cabin was the double-room log house, known as a "two-pen house with a dog trot between", which meant that it consisted of two rooms built as separate log-pens under one roof, with a hallway between, open at both ends, through which the dogs might trot at will. To this structure a lean-to might be added at the rear and a piazza at the front, but these last were rare. In 1768 the Rev. James Harrison, who had accepted as rector of St. Mark's, said that the people of that parish were living in hovels of unhewn logs, which seldom contained more than two rooms. Three years later Charles Woodmason wrote one of his longest letters from a "Cold, open dark Logg Cabbin, in midst of Noise and People."[16]

Frame buildings with sawed planks, as in Matthew Singleton's house at Melrose, which is supposed to have been built in the 1760's, were possible only after sawmills were installed on millponds. The many flowing springs and streams were easily dammed for ponds, where wooden water-wheels were set up to turn the cornmills and to supply power for sawmills. Although no record is available for dating the first sawmills east of the Wateree, there was one in Orangeburg on the other side of the river as early as 1743. Fortunately for the builders of pioneer days, cypress timber, soft and easily worked, was found in great abundance, and unless destroyed by fire, was a very permanent material for houses. The curb for an open well was usually made from a hollow

---

[16] Cook, *Rambles in the Pee Dee*, p. 142; Fulham MSS, S. C. 62.

section of a pond cypress, and many of these curbs remained sound after fifty years of use.

Each pioneer family possessed common tools such as the axe, hatchet, and saw; as well as various hoes, which then were the chief farming implements, much more important than the crude plows. Every settlement had some blacksmith's and shoemaker's tools, and every woman possessed and knew how to use her spinning wheel and loom.

A tremendous labor for each family was the clearing of trees, underbrush and roots from the hard soil to make fields, for there were few if any abandoned fields of the Indians in this old hunting region. When necessary to save time, the settler often enlarged his first small fields by planting among the standing trees, which he killed by girdling. This mode of clearing land continued to be practiced until after the War for Southern Independence, and the timbers in the house built in Sumter on West Hampton Street by N. G. Osteen, were obtained from girdled trees. Often the trees were felled while green, and those not used in building were utilized as split rails in "worm" fences. Surplus logs were left to rot, or were burned to get them out of the way. Log-rollings combined work and fun so happily that they continued in vogue until comparatively recent times.

A log-rolling of the 1850's on the plantation of John Frierson near Mayesville has been thus described by a former slave:

> In clearing up a new ground, the undergrowth was grubbed up and burned; the oaks, maples, dogwood, and hickories were cut down, split up, and hauled to the house for firewood; and the pines were belted or cut round, and left to die. After these pines had died and partially decayed, the winter's storms, from year to year, would blow them down: hence the necessity for the annual log-rolling. These log-rollings usually took place in the spring of the year. They formed an important part of the preparations for the new crop.
>
> On the appointed day, the hands came together at the yard, and all necessary arrangements were made, the most important of which was the pairing or match-

ing of the men for the day's work. In doing this, regard was had to the height and weight of the men. They were to lift in pairs, therefore, it was necessary that they should be as nearly the same height and weight as possible. The logs have all been cut about twenty feet in length, and several good, strong hand sticks have been made ... See them as they put six handsticks under a great big log. This means twelve men—one at each end of the hand-stick. It is going to be a mighty testing of manhood. Every man is ordered to his place. The captain gives the order, 'Ready,' and every man bows to his burden, with one hand on the end of the handstick, and the other on the log to keep it from rolling. The next command given by the captain is, 'Altogether!' and up comes the big log. As they walk and stagger toward the heap, they utter a whoop like what is known as the 'Rebel yell.' If one fails to lift his part, he is said to have been 'pulled down,' and thereafter becomes the butt of ridicule for the balance of the day. When the women folks learn of his misfortune, they forever scorn him as a weakling.

At 12 o'clock the horn blows for dinner, and they all knock off, and go, and enjoy a good dinner. After a rest, for possibly two hours, they go to the field again, and finish up the work for the day. Such was the log-rolling in the 'days before the war.'

At a subsequent day the women and children gather up the bark and limbs of these fallen trees and throw or pile them on these log heaps and burn them. When fifty or seventy-five log heaps would be fully ablaze in the deepening of the evening twilight, the glare reflected from the heavens made it appear that the world was on fire.[17]

Recreation during the first hard years after settlement was a by-product of the struggle for existence, and men fished and hunted primarily for food rather than fun. But the necessity for hard work did not prevent social gatherings when a house was to be built, or a wedding celebrated;

[17] I. E. Lowery, *Life on the Old Plantation in Ante-Bellum Days* (Columbia,, 1911), pp. 89-91.

and for music to brighten these festive occasions, there were Jews harps and fiddles, as listed on several old inventories.

The usual crops were corn, wheat, and other cereals for food and fodder, some rice in the lowlands, a few staple vegetables, flax for spinning, and a little tobacco for home use. Indigo became a money crop quite early, for its small bulk made transportation to market easy, and the English bounty kept the price attractive until the Revolution.

Some cash was had from the fat cattle when rounded up from the swamps and driven the weary miles to Charleston. It is said that the Neilsons of Nelson's Ferry marked from 800 to 1,000 calves every spring, so their herd must have numbered more than 2,000 head of cattle. A neighbor of the Neilsons, Richard Haynsworth, in his will, drawn in 1756, six years before his death, bequeathed to his wife Elizabeth Hesse all his "mares and horse kind" with cattle and hogs; and he described with care his stockmarks in specifying the animals for his children.

Only two meals a day were served. After the abundant wild game of the forest dwindled, the meat supply came from domestic animals, chiefly the hog. Charles Woodmason said in 1766, there was neither beef nor butter where he lived in St. Mark's Parish, or, if any beef, it was sun-dried in the Indian manner and as hard as a board. As late as 1880 some rural families in Sumter County continued the old practice of drying beef. Mr. Woodmason found the food monotonous and unpalatable: pork in winter, bacon in summer, corn bread at all seasons, and no beer, cider, or anything better than water to drink, so it seemed to him that he was fasting for Lent throughout the year!

Sweets other than honey and sweet potatoes were virtually unknown, for sugar cane and sorghum were not planted in Sumter until the nineteenth century, and sugar in early times was imported through Charleston.

Home furnishings at first were crude and scanty. Early wills and inventories indicate that pots, pot hooks, pewter dishes, feather beds, and bed coverings were among the most prized possessions. Bear skins served as blankets and as rugs, and as late as 1826 the inventory of Dr. T. W. Wright listed a bear skin and a buffalo skin.

The favored garments of the pioneer men were homespun and buckskin shirts, and leather breeches. Little is known of what the women wore, except that their simple dresses were homespun, and they liked caps and aprons. Of his congregation in 1768, Charles Woodmason wrote, "the Females (many very pretty) come to Service in their Shifts and a short Petticoat only, barefooted and barelegged—without Caps or Handkerchiefs. . . . The Men appear in Frocks or Shirts and long Trousers—No Shoes or Stockings."

Bears and wolves were real dangers until after the close of the eighteenth century. To get rid of the wolves, the settlers trapped them in baited pits, which were dug ten or twelve feet deep and lined with poles to prevent the animal from digging out. Above the pit, fresh meat was suspended over a balanced board, which dumped the wolf into the pit when he reached for the bait. A well-known wolf pit gave its name to a branch of Black River in what was later Claremont County; and James and Samuel Reynolds' grants on Big Branch in the present Clarendon County were near a wolf pit that was long a landmark as Benbow's Pit.

Although Woodmason said the people of St. Mark's were illiterate, of the thirty-eight signatures to the petition for roads in 1758 from the settlers on the north (and east) side of Black River, only five were made by mark. There were no schools or teachers during the first years after settlement, and the children were taught by their parents, or ran wild when not at work. Even in 1766, Charles Woodmason said there was not a school or a schoolmaster among them, and he took twenty poor children free of charge to teach them writing, arithmetic, psalmody, and the principles of religion, for by this means he hoped to bring their parents into his church.

CHAPTER III

CRAVEN COUNTY AND ST. MARK'S PARISH

Early grants describe the lands east of the Wateree as lying in Craven County. In the modern sense, Craven then was not a unit of government, but merely a geographical expression for a general location. Originally, Craven County was created in 1682, on the coast, extending from Seewee Bay for twenty-three miles northeast, and inland from the shore only thirty-five miles.[1] As settlers moved into the interior, the inner and northern boundaries moved back with them and eventually the "county" extended to the North Carolina line.

Primarily, Craven County was an election district for representation in the provincial Commons House, but it had a few justices of the peace, and a sheriff and a coroner for law enforcement. Among the twenty-four justices of the peace commissioned for Craven County in 1737, was Joseph Cantey, who two years later purchased Mount Hope Plantation. He was one of the first, if not the first magistrate to be named for the region that would later be Sumter District. Another well-known magistrate was Richard Richardson of Big Home Plantation, the yard of which is said to have resembled a court of assize when he settled disputes among his neighbors.[2]

The jurisdiction of a justice of the peace varied from time to time, but during this period it extended to "small and mean" cases which involved no more than £20 currency. He could issue warrants of the peace, and warrants of hue and cry; he could commit men to prison and release them on bail, administer oaths, take depositions, attest the returns on appraised estates, and issue certificates for collect-

---

[1] A. S. Salley (ed.), *Records in the British Public Records Office relating to South Carolina*, 1663-1684 (Columbia, 1928), p. 131; *Commissions and Instructions* . . . (Columbia, 1916), p. 13.
[2] *Ibid.*, p. 14; *SCHGM*, XI, 189; *Journal of the General Assembly of S. C., 1776* (Columbia, 1906), p. 19; J. M. Burgess, *Chronicles of St. Mark's* . . . Columbia, 1888), p. 85.

ing the bounty on heads of wild beasts. He also could take charge of stray livestock, which he advertised, and, if unclaimed, sold for damages and the benefit of whoever had brought in the estray. His most extensive authority was exercised in the court of justices and freeholders, wherein two justices and three freeholders could try capital crimes committed by slaves.[3]

When the province was laid out into parishes in 1706, Craven County ceased to be an election district, and represensation was thereafter by parishes. The county thus lost all governmental significance, although the name continued in general use even after 1769, when the circuit court districts were created.

Justices of the peace were not the sole evidence of government on the frontier, for, although the pioneers were exempt from the payment of taxes for the first ten years after acquiring land, they were subject to the old militia system of universal military service.[4] As often as six times each year, every able white man between the ages of sixteen and sixty, could be summoned to the local muster field for drill with his company. Unless called for an emergency, the companies were summoned only once a year for a regimental muster.

Every freeman had to arm himself, and his white servants, if any. This meant that he had to keep in his house and take to the muster field for inspection, a serviceable gun, a cover for the lock, a cartridge box and at least four ounces of powder, a shot pouch with shot in proportion, a belt, a "ball of wax sticking to the end of his cartridge box, to defend his arms in rain, one worm and picker, four spare flints, a bayonet, sword or hatchet."

The governor or acting governor appointed and commissioned the colonels and other commissioned officers. The company commanders appointed the sergeants and corporals. Each captain had to give notice of a muster by beat of drum or some other quick method. The territory from which each company came was called a beat.

[3] *Stat.* II, 75; VII, 343, 397.
[4] For early militia laws, see *Stat.* IX, appendix; for later, VIII.

David Anderson was commissioned as captain of the company on the headwaters of the Black and Lynches rivers. Isaac Brunson was captain, and Charles Woodmason was a lieutenant, of the High Hills and upper Black River company, which enrolled 125 men.

Another evidence of government on the frontier during early days was found in the parish system, which, after 1706, when the Church of England became the established church in South Carolina, made the parish the unit of local government.[5]

The earliest settlers who came into the future Sumter County were nominally in Prince Frederick's Parish, but the parish church was many miles away on a bluff of Black River near Georgetown. Moreover, the rector, the Rev. Mr. Michael Smith, was in process of being ousted by his congregation under the leadership of Charles Woodmason, the church warden, register, and layreader of the parish.[6] During the 1750's so many new settlers came to live in the High Hills and adjacent country, that the region became of political importance. In 1757, therefore, it was made into a new parish called St. Mark's, with representation in the Commons House of Assembly. The line which separated St. Mark's from Prince Frederick's was an extension of the northwest line of Williamsburg Township to the Santee and the Pedee. St. Mark's embraced all the area between these rivers northward to the North Carolina line, and was the largest of the parishes. The first representatives elected to the Commons House were John Crawford and Joseph Poole, and upon Mr. Poole's untimely death, Richard Richardson was chosen in his place.[7]

The commissioners appointed for receiving subscriptions, building St. Mark's Church, and selling the pews, were Richard Richardson, Matthew Neilson, Isaac Brunson, James McGirt, and Joseph, William and John Cantey. Pending the erection of the parish church, the Rev. John Geissendanner of Orangeburg and Amelia townships held Episcopal services at a house in the High Hills, and at the home of Richard

---

[5] *Stat.* II, 282.
[6] *Prince Frederick's Parish Register*, pp. 130-153, *passim*.
[7] *Stat. IV*, 35. Burgess, *St. Mark's*, p. 13.

Richardson on Halfway Swamp. Before the church was built, the Rev. William Peaseley, who had come to South Carolina in 1751 from Newfoundland, became the first rector of St. Mark's. As late as November 1758, he was still officiating.[8]

In 1759 the church commissioners reported to the Commons House that with the consent of the major part of the inhabitants on the Santee and Black rivers and adjacent parts, they had selected the site for the parish church on Halfway Swamp, but by reason of the thinness of the population and the smallness of their fortunes, subscriptions for building were inadequate. In response to their petition for aid, the House committee recommended that £700 be appropriated. But still matters moved slowly. In 1764, Richard Richardson conveyed to the parish a glebe of 150 acres surrounding the church site. The next year, the province appropriated £1,000 to the building fund. The first church, said to have been built of brick and stone, was then completed.[9]

But the parsonage was not yet built. The second rector of St. Mark's, the Rev. Mr. John Evans, finding no accommodation for his family, departed in 1765 to St. Paul's. For the next two years St. Mark's church was vacant. The Rev. James Harrison of Goose Creek then accepted, but finding the rectory still unfinished at Easter, he did not stay.[10]

Finally, in 1767, the rectory was completed, a neat frame dwelling, thirty-six feet across the front, with four good rooms, a lobby and a staircase, a good kitchen, a garden, orchard, stables, and other good outbuildings. Built on the glebe, and very near the Wateree River, which abounded in fish and wild fowl, it was the kind of place, said the vestry, where a gentleman might lead an easy and comfortable, contemplative life. But they reckoned without the malaria of the river swamp. When the Rev. Thomas Morgan took charge, he died within two weeks. Once more St. Mark's church was vacant.[11]

[8] The Geissendanner Record in A. S. Salley, *The History of Orangeburg County* (Orangeburg, 1898), pp. 174, 179, *SCHGM*, XXXVIII, 105. F. Dalcho, *An Historical Account of the Protestant Episcopal Church in South Carolina* . . . (Charleston, 1820), pp. 379, 433.
[9] *Stat.* IV, 226. Burgess,*St. Mark's*, 14, 15, 12.
[10] Fulham MSS, S. C. 51; H. T. Cook, *Rambles in the Pee Dee* (Columbia, 1926), pp. 139, 142, 144.
[11] Fulham MSS, S. C. 51.

The parish was not wholly neglected however, for the Rev. John Geissendanner of Orangeburg, and the Rev. Paul Turquand of St. Matthew's, across the Wateree, made occasional visits. Also, there was now a visiting missionary, the singular Charles Woodmason, who had decided to become an Episcopal clergyman. On testimonials from St. Mark's, Woodmason had been ordained in England in 1766, and on his return, was stationed as itinerant missionary at Fredericksburg, to hold services throughout the middle and back country. Upon his journey from Charleston to Fredericksburg, he had held a service in St. Mark's, and from time to time during the next three years he returned for other services. His parish he described as 300 miles in length and 150 miles in breadth, for, he said, he was the only clergyman north of Santee River to the North Carolina line, and from the sea to the mountains. After being stationed at the Congarees for another year, Woodmason, in March 1770, became the rector of St. Mark's. Too wise to live in the rectory, he resided in the High Hills, and rode the twenty miles to the church below.[12]

The parish church was an important feature of the parish system for local government. Financed more or less by public funds, the church was a public building, and served the community for much more than religious services. On the parish church door, election notices were posted; at the church, polls for elections were set up; in the church, citations to administer on estates, proclamations and other public announcements were read. The church wardens and vestrymen were the local public officials who recorded vital statistics and administered poor relief; and, when alms were insufficient, they assessed local taxes for relief of paupers.

The democratic feature of the parish system was that the rector, the church wardens and the vestrymen were elected by the parishioners; but this was counter-balanced by the fact that only members of the Episcopal church could vote in such elections.[13]

Another unjust regulation was imposed by a law which

---

[12] Dalcho, *Episcopal Church*, p. 323; Fulham MSS, S. C. 50, 51
[13] *Stat.*, II, 288.

forbade any layman, even a magistrate, to perform a marriage ceremony. The result was that the law was not observed, and Woodmason complained in his Remonstrance that marriages were performed by magistrates and various "sectaries" in contempt of law. Apparently such "irregular" ceremonies were not recognized by the men who kept the parish registers, and pressure was brought to have ceremonies performed by the rector of the parish. A number of the early grand jury presentments cite couples for living together unlawfully, and there are some records of the christening of natural children whose parents were legally married immediately after the christening.[14]

The slight measure of local government provided by the parish system and the local justices of the peace, probably sufficed during the earliest years after settlement, for many of the first settlers were law-abiding dissenters, served by preachers of their own persuasion sent regularly from the northern colonies to teach and preach among them. Indeed the very first church known to have been built in St. Mark's Parish was Salem Black River, for which David Anderson gave land whereon the Presbyterians erected a log meetinghouse about the year 1759.[15]

But as the population increased, conditions grew worse. Villains from the older settlements infiltrated the region, and these were joined by runaway Indian and Negro slaves, as well as mestizos and mulattoes. In 1762, when Charles Woodmason was a justice of the peace, he offered a reward of £20 for the capture of one William McKay, who was believed to have contacts with a gang of outlaws on the border of the province. The disbanding of the British and French armies after the Peace of Paris in 1763, which closed the Seven Years War, is said to have released other undesirables, and a real crime wave ensued. Horses were stolen, homes were robbed, women were kidnapped, men of means were tortured to make them reveal their valuables.

Petitions for aid were sent down to Charleston, but the indifferent and uninformed officials arrested the men who

---

[14] *Ibid.*, 289. Fulham MSS, S. C. 72. *Prince Frederick's Register*, pp. 9, 12.
[15] G. Howe, *History of the Presbyterian Church in S. C.* (Columbia, 1870), I, 327.

carried them, as disturbers of the peace. Several appeals were drawn up by the country people and sent to the *Gazette*, but only one was published. So the backwoodsmen were obliged to send all the way to Virginia to have their pamphlets printed, one in particular mentioned by Woodmason, being "The Groans of the Back Settlers."

Indeed, so desperate were the victims of the outlaws, that they wished to send Woodmason and a lawyer named Carey as delegates to England to lay their grievances at the foot of the throne. But Woodmason declined, realizing the difficulties of such a course, and instead, he drafted for them a Remonstrance to the provincial government.[16]

In glowing and moving words the Remonstrance set forth the grievances of the people of St. Mark's, and prayed for remedies: the establishment of courts, the building of courthouses and jails, of churches and public schools, the codifying of the law, and the establishment of new parishes for adequate representation in the Commons House of Assembly.

Four thousand men, says Woodmason, signed the Remonstrance in the name of fifty thousand, and expected to back up their signatures by marching in a body to Charleston to deliver it to the House. But on the request of Lieutenant Governor William Bull, who asked that it be delivered in the constitutional manner by deputies, a fair copy of the Remonstrance was prepared and signed by the four deputies: Benjamin Hart, John Scott, Moses Kirkland, and Thomas Woodward, who delivered it to the House.

Great was the uproar and noise in the House, says Woodmason, on the reading of the petition, which was received as the work of four impudent fellows, who should be sent to jail and their paper burnt by the public hangman.

But wiser counsels prevailed. The deputies were admitted and allowed to speak: they had come, they said, on behalf of the people, to be led either to prison or to death, for they feared nothing. They bade the House to do nothing rashly, for the petitioners were Britons, and not to be punished for setting matters in a true light before the Assembly.

"The Firmness and Intrepidity of these Men," continues

[16] Fulham MSS, S. C. 51, 62.

Woodmason, "(be it spoken to their Everlasting Remembrance in the Annals of this Country, though their Good Deeds be forgotten), both soften'd and astonish'd the Vociferous Lawyers and Haughty Demagogues."

The petition was then examined in detail, and nothing was found to give offense but the word *infernal*. Votes were taken and copies were given to the deputies to take home, after which the town people entertained the delegates, who finally "departed with Joy and Gladness." When the good news spread through the country, the rejoicings of the people were expressed in bonfires, firings and every demonstration of joy.

But so many delays ensued before anything was done to bring relief, that a deep and abiding distrust developed in the minds of the petitioners. Eventually, fifty Rangers were sent from Charleston to deal with the outlaws, who were severely punished and finally put out of business.

In the meantime, however, the law-abiding citizens had taken matters into their own hands. About a thousand men, according to Woodmason, organized themselves as vigilantes under the name of Regulators, and were very active during the summer of 1768. They pulled down the houses of persons who had aided the outlaws, and they whipped the magistrates who had shared in the plunder. The worst criminals whom they considered worthy of death, they sent down to the provost marshal in Charleston. Petty offenders who promised to reform, they merely whipped, and the women they ducked in water. So effectual were these methods, says Woodmason, that more was accomplished in three months than executive power had effected in twenty years.

Unfortunately, the renegade magistrates and others who had been whipped, proceeded to get vengeance by means of warrants for the Regulators. The situation became so confused that law-enforcement officials in Charleston did not know who were the outlaws and who were the Regulators, and frequently they became the tools by which the outlaws wreaked vengeance. Woodmason says that many of the magistrates were tavern keepers, and worked hand in glove with the outlaws. At any rate, anarchy threatened to become the order of the day, and when writs against Thomas Sumter, Jared Neilson and William Scott were sent up to be served, the deputy was waylaid and beaten, for the Regulators had decreed that no processes should be served from Charleston in their section.[17]

In July 1768, the *Gazette* announced that 120 Regulators were expected to gather on Lynches Creek, for a band of mulattoes and free Negroes on Thompsons Creek, whom the Regulators had ordered to remove, were harboring runaway slaves. What happened further was not reported.

The enactment of the circuit court act of 1768 raised high hopes for relief, only to be dashed when the act was disallowed in London. The next year, however, a similar act was approved. The province was divided into seven judicial districts, in each of which a courthouse and a jail would be built, and the circuit court would sit.[18]

The whole of St. Mark's Parish, with the boundaries as revised in 1768, was included in Camden District, which extended from the northwest line of Williamsburg Township to the North Carolina line, and from Lynches River to the Santee-Congaree-Broad river system.

But merely to become part of a circuit court district did not bring immediately law and order, schools and churches, to the people living east of the Wateree. Some time was required for the construction of the public buildings before the courts could begin to function, and three long years were to elapse before the judges arrived in November 1772 to hold the first court in Camden.

In the meantime, when the Baptist minister, Jeremiah Dargan, preached in 1769 to the people of the High Hills in the present Stateburg section, he described it as "a wild place," a wicked, wicked neighborhood, and he despondently recorded that his efforts had been "to no purpose except provoking them to outrage."[19]

The Rev. Joseph Reese, who preached there the same year, was more successful, and alarmed many sinners. In the re-

[17] Gregorie, *T. Sumter*, p. 33.
[18] J. F. Grimke, *Public Laws, of the State of S. C.* . . . (Phila., 1790), p. 268.
[19] L. Townsend, *South Carolina Baptists 1670-1805* (Florence, 1935), p. 150.

vival which followed, Richard Furman, son of Wood Furman, was won over from the Established Church and became the most famous Baptist divine in South Carolina. Dr. Joseph Howard also was converted, and, with liberal tolerance, he donated a four-acre lot to be used for "a Meeting House for any Protestant religious Preacher to Preach in." In 1770 the meeting house was built, and later became the High Hills Baptist Church,[20] the parent of all the Baptist churches in Sumter County.

In the same year the Episcopalians of the High Hills declaring that their district was "a very populous and growing Settlement crowded with people," petitioned the Assembly for aid in building a chapel of ease for St. Mark's Church, at or near the plantation of Peter Mellett, to be under the jurisdiction of the parish vestry. The signers of the petition were: Samuel Clarke, Joseph Kershaw, John James, the elder and the younger; James Berwick, Ebenezer Hissett; Christopher, Caleb and Josiah Gayle; Peter Mellett, Abijah Rembert, Andrew Rembert, senior; Matthew Singleton, Charles Woodmason, Alexander Campbell, Robert Singleton, Isham and William Moore, Josiah Hill, Thomas Knighton, William McConnico, Richard Bradford, Arthur Richardson, Richard Howell, Daniel Ginnings [Jennings?], Edward Lane, James Clarke, Jo Terry, Samuel Cook, Matthew Robertson, John Pur[cell?], Samuel Bennett, and William Rees.[21]

The gentry of the low country now began to spend their summers in the High Hills. Formerly, said Charles Woodmason, these gentlemen had taken their families to the northern colonies for the hot months, but after the casting away of Benjamin Smith and his family on the voyage to Rhode Island in 1770, the low country men began flocking to the nearer and less perilous High Hills "to build Summer Seats and Hunting Boxes"; with the result, that the price of lands which had not been worth a shilling an acre, soared to a guinea.[22]

20 *Ibid.*
21 T. E. Richardson (pub.), broadside, "Stateburg and her Church", two documents of 1770, from papers of J. B. Moore, n. p., n. d.
22 Fulham MSS, S. C. 51.

CHAPTER IV.

THE YOUNG GAMECOCK

The world-wide Seven Years War which ended with the Peace of Paris in 1763, was fought in America as the French and Indian War, and in South Carolina as the Cherokee War. Men from east of the Wateree had a share in the fighting. In recognition of Colonel Richard Richardson's leadership, his neighbors of St. Mark's Parish presented him in 1762 with a handsome silver service.[1] Captain David Anderson also led a company into the Cherokee country; and among privates mentioned in the campaign were Peter Mellet, Sylvester Dunn, John Bradley, and Aaron Frierson.[2]

The Cherokee War, however, also brought to South Carolina a small, active young Virginian named Thomas Sumter,[3] who was destined to play a great part as the Gamecock of the Revolution. Born in Virginia in 1734, in the backwoods of Hanover County, Sergeant Sumter was among the Virginia troops sent in the autumn of 1761 to build a fort on the Holston River as a defense against the Cherokees.

Before the fort was completed, the lame Cherokee "emperor," Old Hop as he was called by the settlers, came with 400 Indians to sue for peace. This was speedily agreed upon, and as a proof of good faith, Old Hop asked that a white officer should go home with him. For this mission Lieutenant Henry Timberlake volunteered, and selected Sergeant Sumter and an interpreter to accompany him. Instead of going along with the Indians by the overland path, however, Timberlake decided to follow the rivers in a canoe, which he loaded with ten days provisions, their guns and ammunition, and a small stock of goods for trade with the Indians.

The 250-mile canoe voyage in the dead of winter through ice and snow, over shoals and rapids, required twenty-two

---

[1] Burgess, *St. Marks*, p. 85.
[2] W. W. Boddie, *History of Williamsburg*, (Columbia, 1923), p. 70.
[3] For his biography, see Gregorie, *Thomas Sumter*.

days of danger and hardship that almost cost the lives of the three adventurers. Often overboard in freezing water, the men pushed forward in clothing hung with icicles, and at night slept in wet blankets. Always in danger from prowling bears and hostile Northern Indians, they suffered a series of accidents to their guns and narrowly escaped starvation. Through it all, young Sumter showed cool courage, energy and initiative in meeting every emergency. Finally, on December 20, they arrived at Slave Catcher's house opposite the mouth of the Tellico River, where they were received hospitably and well fed. The land journey among the tribesmen was then begun.

At Tomotley town, Timberlake and his companions were welcomed by a remarkable chieftain, Otacite Ostenaco Skiagunsta, whose formidable name to the English was Judd's Friend or Man Killer. As Sumter travelled from village to village with Timberlake and the interpreter, he acquired valuable experience in Indian diplomacy and an understanding of French and English rivalry on the frontier. Several months were passed in unhurried celebrations, distributing presents, reading and translating peace terms, smoking peacepipes, and watching all-night tribal dances. Finally in early March, after elaborate farewell ceremonies, the white men began their homeward march, escorted by a retinue of released captives and Judd's Friend at the head of a hundred Indians.

When the motley host reached Williamsburg, Virginia, the governor welcomed Judd's Friend with more presents, and the Indians lingered for further leisurely celebrations. At William and Mary College one evening, Judd's Friend, when shown a picture of the recently-crowned king of England, young George the Third, was so charmed that he suddenly announced:

"Long have I wished to see the king my father; this is his resemblance, but I am determined to see himself; I am now near the sea, and never will depart from it till I have obtained my desires."

As there was no dissuading the old warrior, passage on a royal sloop was given him, his son-in-law, and an Indian attendant. Sumter, Timberlake and an interpreter joined the party on their own responsibility, and in the middle of May they sailed for England. Although the seas were calm, Sumter alone escaped seasickness, and the interpreter died. A month later the party landed at Plymouth, where Judd's Friend, in hideous ceremonial paint, chanted loud thanksgivings which brought such dense throngs to the docks that he and his escort could hardly get through to the inn.

At the inn the Americans took post for London, stopping along the way to visit famous places. The British ministry, anxious for good Indian relations, provided for Judd's Friend and his party a house, a suitable equipage, and scarlet clothes of English fashion. With Virginia's colonial agent as guide, the Indians and their friends began a round of official calls, sightseeing, and social entertainments, and a month later they were formally received by his majesty, the king.

For young Sergeant Sumter the entire adventure was a wonderful experience. Sociable fellow that he was, he made friends, fought a servant, and thoroughly enjoyed the excitment the Indians created whenever they appeared in public. The amusement places patronized by Judd's Friend were always thronged, and so great was the furor among the Londoners, that eventually the Americans were forbidden to go to public places, as productive of riots. The ministry finally decided that the uninvited guests were costing too much, and as tactfully as possible made arrangements for their departure.

After a farewell audience with the king, the Indians were placed in charge of Sumter, and in a coach with six horses, they began the return trip home by way of Portsmouth, with orders to land at Charleston. Loaded with presents of scalping knives, axes, peace pipes and belts, and stopping along the road for entertainment and sightseeing, the travellers made a sort of triumphal progress to Portsmouth, where they re-embarked on the sloop which had brought them. Setting sail immediately, they had a safe voyage, and on October 28 landed at Charleston. There they were received with every courtesy by Governor Boone, and Sumter collected £100 due for his services. Through an interpreter, Judd's Friend gave public praise to the sergeant, and begged that Sumter might be allowed to accompany him to the Cherokee towns; so the sergeant's adventure was continued through another chapter.

During his stay among the Cherokees, Sergeant Sumter took part in their games and is said to have been able to outrun, out-jump, and out-swim all but one of them, Saucy Jack. Sumter also took a hand in the frontier rivalry between the English and the French, who were maneuvering to win the continent for colonization. His most thrilling experience was the capture, single-handed, of a French emissary, the Baron des Jonnes, whom he subdued and delivered to the commander at Fort Prince George. When Sumter returned to Charleston in the spring, by request he gave the Council a full account of Indian affairs on the frontier, and the governor recommended him for compensation to the British ministry.

The young soldier then seems to have made a brief visit to Virginia, where he was promptly arrested for an old debt. But with the help of a friend, Sumter escaped from the Staunton prison, and made his way back to South Carolina, to remain for the rest of his life. Settling first within sixty miles of Charleston, he opened a crossroads store south of the Santee River on the road to Nelson's Ferry. There he proceeded to invest in lands and a few slaves the £700 he had collected from the British ministry.

In 1767 at the age of thirty-three, Thomas Sumter married Mary (Cantey) Jameson, a well-to-do widow seven years his senior, and went to live across the Santee on the Great Savannah in what is now Clarendon County. There on the road from Nelson's Ferry to Camden he opened another store, and on Jack's Creek operated a sawmill and a grist mill. As a leading citizen in the community, he was commissioned a justice of the peace. During the next few years of his busy and perhaps quiet life as a country 'squire on the Santee, the energetic man who had seen and learned so much since his boyhood days in the backwoods of Virginia gradually developed the qualities of leadership which would make him famous as the Gamecock of the fast-approaching war for American independence.

CHAPTER V

THE REVOLUTION

Many men living east of the Wateree River served in the war for American independence, but in the area which would become Sumter County, few warlike events took place, except in connection with the movement of troops over the "Great road" from Camden to Charleston.

The origin of this war goes back to the preceding Seven Years War, for after the signing of the peace terms in 1763, the British government endeavored by means of the Stamp Act to get revenue from America to defray some of the cost of the long war. The colonists objected to the idea of taxation, and their leaders stirred up high feeling over the issue of British taxation without American representation in the British Parliament. So hot was the debate in Charleston that it even reached the back country of South Carolina. The Stamp Act was repealed in 1766, but when Charles Woodmason returned from England that year as a missionary for St. Mark's Parish, he sadly wrote: "I really find not the people the same as formerly. The Stamp Act has introduced so much party rage, faction and debate that the ancient hospitality, generosity and urbanity for which these people were celebrated is destroyed."

Woodmason especially felt the suspicion with which they regarded him: "Malicious minds greatly injured me in my absence by insinuating that I . . . was a spy of the ministry and went home, not for orders, but with information and Anecdotes."[1]

By the year 1771 a whole new generation had grown up in the region east of the Wateree since the time of its settlement. The planters had prospered and built themselves homes of some dignity. Matthew Singleton's house at Melrose had a fanlight over the door and an ornamental archway in the

---
[1] Fulham MSS, S. C. 91.

THE REVOLUTION

stair hall. Life had become much easier for the people in general, so much so, that Woodmason estimated that there were 30,000 idlers in his parish, and he devised a scheme to encourage the planting of wheat, mulberry trees, vines, olives, apple and pear trees, hemp and flax, to set them to work! But, said the pessimistic parson, the only result up to that time, was "to subject the Author to every Degree of Resentment."[2]

Perhaps the idleness to which Woodmason so strongly objected was linked to horse-racing, which was then the chief amusement of his parish. As early as 1767 Richard Richardson had advertised the pedigree of *Flagatruce*, a magnificent brown stallion whose anonymous owner offered to race him against any horse, mare, or gelding, for a purse of £500. Another race horse owner was Squire Thomas Sumter of Santee. At the Charleston races in February 1773, his mare won the most coveted prize in the province, the celebrated "Charleston plate."[3]

Meanwhile, the Rev. Mr. Woodmason had added to his unpopularity by breaking off his engagement to marry a young woman who was kin to most of the St. Mark's vestrymen. Eager to leave the parish, he was delayed by difficulties in finding a successor, but finally he departed for Virginia in the spring of 1773 and was replaced by the Rev. Thomas Walker,[4] a young bachelor.

The new rector of St. Mark's made his abode with William Richardson, a young man from Charleston who was settling a plantation to which he would soon bring his wife and children. Richardson described himself as a carpenter, and his plantation in the sandhills at the entrance to the High Hills he called Bloom Hill. A portion of Bloom Hill he had inherited from his father, Edward Richardson, a bricklayer of Charleston, who in 1758 in settlement of a debt, had obtained 850 acres in the sandhills from George Snow. Later, Edward Richardson had added other tracts,[5] one being a grant for

---
[2] *Ibid.*, S. C. 51.
[3] Fairfax Harrison, *The John's Island Stud (South Carolina),* 1750-1788 (Richmond, 1931) pp. 130, 175.
[4] Fulham MSS, S. C. 51, Va. 201; Dalcho, *Episcopal Church,* p. 323.
[5] Mesne Conveyance Records, Charleston.

1,000 acres. William Richardson's letters[6] to his wife in Charleston, where she was awaiting the birth of their second child, are quite revealing of life in St Mark's on the eve of the Revolution.

Richardson wrote his wife that Parson Walker was very poor company, for he "seldom smiles but Sighs all day long, at something left in Town, the Heart ach now in Lieu of his former complaint the tooth ach." Richardson also described the St. Mark's races which he had recently attended. The dinner which followed the races, said he, was spread in the midst of a newly ploughed field, and as a high wind was blowing clouds of dust everywhere, "a Quarter of Beef Barbecuing in this dust" was "nicely browned indeed, but not with fire." The guests dined at three planks laid across some sticks for a table, which was covered not with damask, but with "Two superb Oznabrigs sheets (not white), no! they scorned to have anything so formal as to be clean) that had perhaps been laid in a month at least," and of the color of a dishclout used for a month without washing, "and you must suppose the Cook that used the Clout, a dirty bitch indeed." On the table were pewter plates with a knife at some and a half knife at others.

Of the food for the feast, Richardson said the two hogs and the quarter of beef looked like they had been "dragged thro' Charles Town streets on a very dusty day and then smoke dried." In addition there were a dish of bacon and turnip tops, a dish of beef, and "plenty of Brown loaves, their looks not inviting and in taste resembling Saw Dust." Worst of all, one of the hogs was only half roasted, "with the blood running out at every cut of the knife." To wash down the elegant repast, they had pails of water "mingled with the dust of the field" and a quantity of hair, pieces of straw, and dried leaves.

Of the company who were present, Richardson said little except that at the head of the table sat the amiable Mrs. Colonel, with "the ladies on each side arranged with appetites keen indeed, for I absolutely saw one lady devour a whole Hogs head except the bones."

[6] "Letters of William Richardson, 1765-1784," *SCHGM*, XLVII, 1-20.

Perhaps Richardson was out of sorts that day, for he was disappointed in not having received a letter from his wife; or perhaps he exaggerated somewhat, with the hope of bringing a smile to her face. At any rate, he concluded his letter by wishing that his wife, a Mrs. "D.L." and a Miss Dolly could have been with him, for "what with the dinner, quaint expressions and strange Phizes, we should have had enough to laugh at for a Month at least." He ended with a message to Mrs. D. L. "that Walker's courting the widow James" to which his wife might add "she's a great fortune. Leave out her age till you see how it works." The lovelorn Parson Walker left the parish soon after.

Richardson's neighbors in St. Mark's did not suspect that he had made fun of them, for the next year they elected him to represent them in the first Provincial Congress which met in Charleston on January 11, 1775. The other delegates from the District Eastward of Wateree River were Thomas Sumter, Richard Richardson, Joseph and Ely Kershaw, Matthew Singleton, Aaron Loocock, Robert Patton, Robert Carter, and William Wilson.[7] When the Congress met, the delegates debated and finally approved the Continental Association, an agreement to be entered into by all the colonies for the non-importation, non-consumption, and non-export of certain products which were vital to the trade with Great Britain. This Association also brought a temporary halt to the slave trade, to horse racing, and other amusements, and to the use of mourning habiliments, which were then so fashionable among the bereaved. The Association further encouraged sheep-raising and domestic manufacture.

The Committee of Thirteen to put the Association into effect in St. Mark's comprised Colonel Richard Richardson, chairman; Joseph Kershaw, Matthew Singleton, Thomas Sumter, William Richardson, Robert Patton, Robert Carter, William Wilson, Richard Richardson, Jr., John James, Sr., Samuel Little, John Marshall, and Isaac Ross. This committee among other duties had to receive and decide upon applications relative to law processes, and receive donations for the relief of the people of Boston and Massachusetts Bay.

[7] Journals of First Provincial Congress, in W. Moultrie, *Memoirs of the American Revolution*. . . . (2 vols., New York, 1802), I, 17.

When the news of the battle of Lexington was received in Charleston on May 8, 1775, the First Provincial Congress was summoned for its second session on June 1, 1775. One of the first acts of the Congress was to sign an Association for Defence, copies of which were to be sent out over the province for signatures of "the inhabitants generally." The Congress also authorized the raising of two regiments of mounted rangers. A Council of Safety of thirteen members, with Henry Laurens as president, was given full power for carrying on the government and defending the province.

The Association for Defense was sent to the District Eastward of Wateree, and 101 men signed it, solemnly uniting "under every tie of religion and honour" to defend their country; and "whenever our Continental or Provincial Councils shall decree it necessary, we will go forth and be ready to sacrifice our lives and fortunes to secure her freedom and safety. This obligation to continue in force until a reconciliation shall take place between Great Britain and America, upon constitutional principles—an event which we most ardently desire." This document with all the original 101 signatures was preserved until recent years by descendants of Matthew Singleton.[8] Two of the signers later became well-known Tories: James McCormick, who lived on the old Path north of Dr. Howard; and William Rees, who lived near the High Hill Tavern.

In the meantime, the Revolutionary party was not flourishing in the back country, and in July the Council of Safety sent William Henry Drayton and the Rev. William Tennent, accompanied by the Rev. Oliver Hart and Colonel Richard Richardson, to hold propaganda meetings and win support for the Association. To avoid civil bloodshed, Drayton on September 16, 1775, signed a treaty with Colonel Thomas Fletchall and other leading loyalists near Ninety Six. Later, when the Whigs, disguised as Indians, captured Robert Cunningham, who refused to recognize the treaty, and imprisoned him in the Charleston jail, the loyalists regarded the treaty as having been broken and laid siege to Ninety Six.

---

[8] Virginia E. (Green) Singleton, *Singletons of South Carolina*. . . . (Hartsville, 1914). A draft entitled "The Provincial Association" is in John Drayton, *Memoirs of the American Revolution*. . . . (2 vols., Charleston, 1821), I, 285.

Thus the civil war between Whig and Tory began.

On November 30, Colonel Richard Richardson marched from the Congaree against the loyalists. In this winter expedition, still called the Snow Campaign, many of his neighbors, including Thomas Sumter, took part.

Sumter was among the men who captured Colonel Fletchall at his home, where the Colonel is said to have taken refuge in a cave; and under escort of Richard Richardson, Jr., the prisoners were sent down to Henry Laurens at Charleston. Apparently the detachment crossed the Wateree River by one of the upper crossings, and proceeded south on the Camden-Charleston road east of the river. Subaltern John James, then about sixteen years of age, and on furlough at home from the Snow Campaign, having heard that Fletchall was approaching under guard, went up to meet the party. James then assisted in keeping guard over Fletchall "about where the village of Stateburg has since been built."[9]

During the Revolution the subaltern was destined to play a valorous part in the partisan brigade of General Francis Marion. Two other John Jameses were in the same brigade: John James of the Lake, one of the original settlers of Williamsburg; and his nephew, Major John James, whose son, William Dobein James, enlisted at the age of fifteen and survived to write a valuable life of Marion. The subaltern later married Martha Richardson (daughter of Richard Richardson, Jr., and his wife Dorcas Neilson); their son was Matthew James.

On March 26, 1776, the Second Provincial Congress severed all ties with Great Britain, and adopted a constitution for the independent state of South Carolina. This constitution, however, did not disestablish the Church of England in the new state, and early in the year, probably at the invitation of the young Rev. Richard Furman, a meeting of dissenter ministers of various denominations was held at the High Hills to consider the question of disestablishment.

During the summer of 1776, the combined British fleet and army were defeated in an attempt on Charleston; the

---

[9] Joseph Johnson, *Traditions and Reminiscences chiefly of the Revolution in the South.* . . . (Charleston, 1851), p. 171.

news of the signing of the Declaration of Independence arrived; a campaign of extermination was waged against the Cherokee Indians; and the state troops became part of the continental establishment.

In October Sumter's regiment returned from the Cherokee campaign to the camp on Tawcaw Swamp near his home at Nelson's Ferry, and probably were disbanded there for the winter. Soon after, at the courthouse in Camden, members of the General Assembly were elected from the District Eastward of Wateree: James Bradley, Joseph Kershaw, Aaron Loocock, William Massey, Robert Patton, Richard Richardson, William Richardson, Matthew Singleton, Thomas Sumter, and the Rev. William Tennent. William Richardson had been commissioned a captain and Thomas Sumter a lieutenant colonel in the state troops, and although neither one attended the session, the General Assembly declared that no vacancies existed by occasion of their holding dual offices.

The Rev. William Tennent however, did attend and as chairman of the committee to examine into the state of the Charleston jail and the treatment of prisoners of war, reported both as very bad, the prisoners of war being "exposed to a Treatment which if continued will not be reputable to this state."

Mr. Tennent also, on January 11, 1777, made a strong speech in the House when he presented a petition which he had drawn for the disestablishment of the Episcopal Church, and he is therefore credited with having been largely influential in bringing this to pass the next year. He did not live to see it, however, for soon after his speech, his father died in New Jersey, and he undertook the long overland journey to bring home his widowed mother. When they reached the High Hills on the return trip, Mr. Tennent became ill with fever, and died at Captain William Richardson's plantation, Bloom Hill.

The people of the District Eastward of Wateree, in obedience to a law passed at the same session of the Assembly, took the oath of allegiance to South Carolina as administered by General Richard Richardson at the head of his brigade.[10] All who refused the oath, were banished from the state with

---

[10] H. T. Cook (ed.), *A Biography of Richard Furman* (Greenville, n. d.), p. 11.

their families, and it was probably at this time that many loyalists took refuge in Florida.

In 1778 the Articles of Confederation united the American colonies, and South Carolina framed her second constitution as a sovereign state. Attention was then shifted to the election of state officers, the raising of public funds, and various civil matters. The war settled down to camp routine in and around Charleston, until in the spring, Sumter's regiment joined a four-headed expedition which once more failed to smash the power of the British in Florida. Apparently in disgust, Colonel Sumter resigned from the Continental Line, and in September returned to his mills and his indigo vats on the Santee, where he now began to operate a new ferry across the river above Nelson's Ferry. For the time being South Carolina lay in a deep peace.

But in 1779 the British were ready at last to launch their long-expected invasion from Florida, to cooperate with a combined attack by sea and land against Charleston; and after necessary preliminaries, the siege of the city began on April 1, 1780.

Refugee families fleeing from the unhappy town daily crossed the Santee. Generals Huger and McIntosh, with their carriages and wagons loaded with family baggage, were weatherbound for a rainy weekend at Sumter's own home, then proceeded to Captain Richardson's Bloom Hill, where a house was obtained for the refugees. The family of Governor Rutledge also is said to have refugeed at Bloom Hill, which appears to have been at that time a settlement with more than one dwelling.

The lines of the British rapidly closed in on Charleston, and General Lincoln was soon cut off from all communications. Governor Rutledge, realizing that civil government would perish if he were captured, quietly left the doomed capital. On May 11, 1780, Lincoln surrendered the city with all the defenders, among whom were Captain William Richardson of Bloom Hill, Captain William Rees of the High Hills militia, and many others from east of the Wateree.

The British soon fanned out over the state to complete their conquest. Lieutenant Colonel Banastre Tarleton's legion, with supporting dragoons and infantry, dashed northward with orders to cut off a detachment of Virginians under Colonel Buford, who, sent to the aid of Charleston, had reached Nelson's Ferry, heard the news of the surrender, and turned back. One of Tarleton's detachments raided Sumter's home during this expedition, but Sumter himself escaped capture. Burning for vengeance against the raiders, Sumter left his family on May 28 to enter upon the partisan career that would eventually give his name to Sumter County.

Three days later when Lord Rawdon's troops were passing through the High Hills, two boys, Kit Gayle and Sam Dinkins, fired upon them. Without regard to their youth, Gayle was hanged on a tree and Dinkins was taken in irons to the recently established post in Camden.[11]

British posts were established also at Georgetown, Cheraw, Rocky Mount, and at other strategic points for the control of the conquered state. Most of the Americans captured at Charleston were parolled to their homes. Men of military age throughout the state, thinking that the war was over, came in to the various posts and took the oath of allegiance to the king.

But the war was far from over. On June 15, 1780, a number of refugee rebels who had gathered near the Catawba reservation, had elected Sumter their general and made camp on a branch of Sugar Creek east of the Catawba; for they knew that a Continental army under the command of DeKalb was marching south to dispute the British conquest. Soon after organizing, Sumter sent John Dinkins to reconnoiter and carry letters of propaganda to stir up the Whigs in the Wateree settlements. The defeat of Captain Huyck by a detachment of Sumter's men brought many recruits into the rebel camp; and desiring to aid the approaching Continentals, Sumter sent DeKalb a report on the strength of the various British posts.

Francis Marion too was active. With some twenty ragged followers, he rode up toward Cheraw to meet the Continentals, of whom Gates, the hero of Saratoga, was now the commander, and there Marion received orders for his return to the in-

[11] T. J. Kirkland, R. M. Kennedy, *Historic Camden* (2 vols., Columbia, 1905), I, 141.

terior of the state, to remove the boats along the rivers, watch the British, and give intelligence. Marion had already won the name of Swamp Fox, and Rutledge, realizing the genius of this partisan, had commissioned him early in August as brigadier in command of all militia northeast of the Wateree-Santee Rivers. This was necessary, because General Richard Richardson, heretofore in command of this territory, having refused to join the royal standard, had been interned on John's Island. There the aged General became ill, and the British realizing that his end was near, released him on parole to his beloved Big Home, where he died in September 1780, at the age of seventy-six.[12]

The old Catawba path east of the Wateree was now a vital link in the main road from Camden to Charleston, and to safeguard their communications over this route, the British constructed a redoubt at Nelson's Ferry.

While Gates and Rawdon were facing each other in the vicinity of Camden, poised for battle, Cornwallis ordered Tarleton to join Rawdon with all the dragoons he could muster. Tarleton crossed the Santee at Lenud's ferry on August 6, and accompanied by Wemyss of the 63rd, and a band of Tories under Harrison, he moved on over the Black River to punish the inhabitants, as he said, for their "late breach of paroles and perfidious revolt." In the face of superior numbers, Marion retreated to North Carolina, and Wemyss and the Tories proceeded to utterly sack and lay waste a strip of country fifteen miles wide and seventy miles long.

Having thus removed all danger to British communications by road and river in that vicinity, Tarleton recrossed the Black River and gave out that he intended to join Rawdon by way of the main road through the Hills. But during the night he slipped back across the Black and marched rapidly northward for twenty-four hours. To get information on Gates' movements, Tarleton disguised his party as Americans, and he himself assumed the name of Colonel William Washington. James Bradley, completely deceived, welcomed the treacherous Colonel, and freely gave him all possible informa-

[12] Epitaph, *SCHGM*, XXVIII, 55.

tion. Tarleton then asked Bradley to guide him through the swamp to attack Rawdon's rear. Bradley collected some of the neighboring militia and cheerfully led the way. After passing McGirt's swamp, Tarleton felt safe, and suddenly making prisoners of his astonished guides, he delivered them to the British in Camden.[13] There, Bradley, being a member of the Assembly and a man of influence, was kept in irons throughout his imprisonment, and bore the scars on his wrists the rest of his life.

On August 16, 1780, Gates was defeated by Cornwallis at Camden, and three days later Sumter was surprised by Tarleton at Fishing Creek. Marion alone escaped the series of disasters, and did not even hear of Gates' defeat. With only sixteen men, on August 20, he intercepted a British detachment at Sumter's old field near Nelson's ferry and rescued 150 of the Continentals whom Rawdon had captured at Camden. Among the Americans hanged by the British after Gates' defeat was said to have been Josiah Gayle.[14]

The hideous war of Whig against Tory now flamed into even more murderous fury. Many people knew little of what the war was all about, and not infrequently the militia men changed sides, hoping to get protection for their families and property from the winning side. Most of the details of what happened between the Wateree and Lynches rivers have now been forgotten, but dreadful accounts have been preserved of the Whig and Tory crimes perpetrated on the other sides of those streams. Marion, however, has left a clean record of fair fighting.

In September Marion moved to chastise a Tory named Harrison, who, with his brother, had lived before the war in a log cabin near McCallum's ferry on Lynches River. Both brothers now held British commissions in the loyal militia, for Cornwallis thought them to be men of fortune and influence. Whatever influence they may have possessed, however, was lost after the murder of John Roberts, Matthew Bradley and Thomas Bradley in their own homes.[15]

[13] B. Tarleton, *A History of the Campaigns of 1780 and 1781 in the Southern Provinces of North America* (Dublin, 1787), pp. 103, 104.
[14] Kirkland and Kennedy, *op. cit.*, I, 205.
[15] Tarleton, *Campaigns*, pp. 93, 120; W. D. James, *A Sketch of the Life of Brig. Gen. Francis Marion*. . . .(Marietta, Ga., 1948), p. 45; A. Gregg, *History of the Old Cheraws*. . . . (New York, 1867), p. 308.

But before Marion found Harrison, scouts brought the news that large bodies of Tories were gathering near Salem and the forks of Black River, where a Colonel Tynes had appeared, well furnished with supplies from Charleston. Marion therefore crossed the northern fork by the lower ford on Nelson's plantation, and at midnight struck Tynes' camp on Tear Coat Swamp. The surprise was complete and there was little resistance, for Tynes had posted no sentries, and some of the Tories were playing cards, while others were eating or had gone to sleep. Amos Gaskins was killed with cards in his hand. Tynes, two other officers, and a number of men were captured, and twenty-six were killed or wounded, but most of the Tories fled into the swamp, whence some of them later returned and joined Marion. Marion did not lose a man, and he captured some sorely needed supplies. Among the prisoners he rescued was Captain James Rembert, whose arm had been broken in the skirmish.[16]

The decisive American victory at Kings Mountain in October 1780, and the retreat of Cornwallis to Winnsborough, encouraged many men to join Marion, who soon became a real threat to the British communications with Charleston. Fearing an attack on Camden, Cornwallis summoned Tarleton, then ill in Charleston, although the main body of his troops were in Camden.

Tarleton answered the summons as soon as possible, and early in November, with a small detachment, he took the road to Nelson's ferry. There Marion had hoped to capture him. But Tarleton was too quick. Having crossed the ferry and joined his main force, he turned the tables and began a search for Marion before that partisan realized what had happened. Marion crossed the Santee in pursuit, and on the night of November 10, unwittingly made his carefully hidden camp within two miles of Tarleton's.

Suddenly, Marion's camp was startled by a bright light which seemed to come from a great fire at the late General Richardson's plantation, Big Home. In a few moments, Richard Richardson, Jr., arrived with the news that Tarleton's

---

[16] James, *Marion*, pp. 60, 61; W. G. Simms, *The Life of Francis Marion* (New York, 1844), pp. 141, 142; James Jenkins, *Experience, Labours and Sufferings of*. . . . (n. p., 1842), p. 19.

entire force was at the plantation, with two field pieces. Just then Marion discovered that one of his own men had deserted to the enemy, and would probably bring the British to his hiding place.

Without delay, Marion put his men in motion and fell back six miles, across the Woodyard Swamp to Jack's Creek, while the deserter led Tarleton to the abandoned camp. The next morning Tarleton continued the chase through bewildering swamps for seven hours, and drew near enough to Marion to take a few prisoners. But the pursuit was called off by the arrival of a messenger from Cornwallis, who had urgent need for Tarleton in another quarter. Tarleton immediately began his return northward, and at Singleton's mills on Shank's Creek he met numbers of Tories, and organized a warning system for the protection of British communications along the road from Camden to Charleston.

Of the Tories on that road, Captain William Rees, who lived near the High Hill Tavern, had been highly regarded by his neighbors in the early days of the war, before he surrendered with the American garrison at Charleston. After the British paroled him to his home, Rees gave up his parole and accepted British commissions as a justice of the peace and as captain of the loyal militia. Squire Rees then used all his influence to persuade his neighbors to return to their allegiance to the King. He became so active in the British cause that he captured Patton Mahon, John Mellette and James Borough and delivered them to the enemy, who promptly hanged poor Borough. The rebel boys then swore to kill Rees, and he is said to have fled for his life to St. Augustine. The legislature of South Carolina confiscated his property and banished him and his nephew Benjamin,[17] but later the squire was pardoned and returned to the community.

Although there were many Tories east of the Wateree, the names of but few are known. James McCormick lived in the High Hills. Bill Haynsworth, according to tradition, served under Colonel Patrick Moore, and was among those who plundered the home of old Samuel McJunkin, west of the Wateree. The names of Isham Moore and William Stukes

---

[17] *SCHGM*, XXXIV, 197; "J M'K" (James McCormick?), in *Gazette of the State of South Carolina*, Apr.24, 1784.

are on the legislative list of the loyalists to be amerced 12% of the value of their estates.[18]

The most notorious of the Tories was Daniel McGirt, son of the respected settler James McGirt, who had married Priscilla Davison in Charleston in 1732, had a grant north of the Santee in 1747, was one of the commissioners of St. Mark's Parish in 1757, and later was a justice of the peace and a lieutenant colonel in Richard Richardson's regiment of militia. Daniel McGirt had married a sister of Major John James, and is said to have gone with the abortive expedition against the Tories in Florida, where he got into trouble with his officers and turned Tory himself. Many legends have come down concerning him, some good, some bad, but all of them interesting. The McGirt family appears to have been a loyalist group who removed to Florida with their possessions, but Daniel's wife remained in the High Hills with the James family.

Daniel McGirt received a British commission and headed a mongrel band of plunderers which accompanied Prevost's invasion of 1779, and gathered such rich loot that Daniel is said to have boasted that his share amounted to his own weight in gold.[19]

The year 1781 was eventful. In February Marion was warned that Major McLeroth was marching up from Nelson's ferry with a force equal to his own, and Marion promptly assailed him on the road near Halfway Swamp. Without cavalry, the British were in a plight. By skillful maneuvers McLeroth gained an open field and took refuge within an enclosure on the west side of the road, while Marion pitched camp by a cypress pond on the east side.

There McLeroth sent a flag of truce and challenged Marion to a fight in the open. Marion suggested combat between twenty picked men from each side, which was agreed to. But as the twenty Americans marched forward, the British, apparently realizing the deadly aim of the partisans, suddenly, before a shot was fired, ordered their twenty champions to retreat. When darkness came, McLeroth abandoned his bag-

[18] Seth P. Pool et al, *ibid.*, Sept. 13, 1784. E. F. Ellet, *The Women of the American Revolution* (3 vols., New York, 1850), I, 262, *SCHGM*, XXXIV, 199.
[19] Kirkland and Kennedy, *Historic Camden*, I, 297-305.

gage, left his camp fires burning, and marched rapidly towards Singleton's mill, ten miles northward.

Before daylight, Marion discovered the retreat, and sent Colonel Hugh Horry with 100 men to flank the British before they could reach the mill. Finding this impossible, Horry detached Major James with a small party of picked men on the fastest horses to cross the mill pond from above and take Singleton's house, which stood on a high hill overlooking the narrow road between the hill and the river swamp. Major James gained the house just as the British reached the foot of the hill. But James found a worse enemy than the British inside the house, for the Singleton family had smallpox.

Before James yielded the premises, one of his men mortally wounded a British officer leading the advance, an act which displeased Marion, because McLeroth was always humane in his dealings with the civil population, and seems to have hated cruelty as much as did Marion himself.[20]

Later in the same month General Sumter led an unsuccessful attack on the British post near Wright's Bluff, commonly known as Fort Watson in compliment to the commander, Colonel Watson. The post had just been reinforced by some 400 provincial light infantry and was too strong to be taken. After his repulse, Sumter encamped at Farr's on the great savannah near his own home and not far from his mills on Jack's Creek. As usual when luck was against them, his men began to leave him, and it was only at the point of the bayonet that he held the North Carolina troops for a few more days while he tried to get in touch with Marion. Then came the news that Rawdon's own regiment was hard on his heels, and, on March 1, had been quartered on Sumter's plantation at Nelson's Ferry.

Pausing only long enough to rescue his family and his servants, Sumter began his retreat through the friendly settlements towards the swamps of the Black River, expecting to by-pass Camden and reach his hideout in the Waxhaws by the Georgetown road to the east. Between Scape Hore Swamp and Radcliffe's Bridge, he encountered on March 6, a British detachment under Major Fraser of the Camden garrison,

[20] Simms, *F. Marion*, pp. 208-213.

and a sharp fight ensued. Ten of Sumter's men were killed and some forty were wounded, but Fraser lacked dragoons to pursue the mounted Americans, so Sumter continued his way northward.[21]

The British had now redoubled their efforts to crush Marion, and ordered the Tories under Harrison, and the Volunteers of Ireland under Colonel Doyle, to unite with Colonel Watson for this purpose. Before they joined forces, Marion acted, and on March 6, 1781, the very day that Sumter had his brush with Fraser, Marion attacked Watson in Wyboo Swamp, midway between Nelson's and Murray's ferries. Having only about twenty rounds of ammunition, Marion held most of his brigade in reserve and sent forward Colonel Peter Horry as a feint. When Watson's two field pieces drove Horry from the swamp, Harrison's Tory horsemen pursued, and thus fell into Marion's trap and were dispersed. In this action, Captain Conyers of Marion's cavalry, is said to have killed one of the two notorious Harrison brothers.[22]

While Marion was busy with Watson, Colonel Doyle had penetrated the swamps to Marion's hideout on Snow's Island at the mouth of Lynches Creek, and finding only a handful of the patriots on guard, he had quickly over-powered them and dumped Marion's scanty hoard of arms and ammunition into Lynches Creek. The news of this disaster brought Marion hurrying in pursuit of Doyle, who was overtaken at Witherspoon's Ferry after he had crossed and was in the act of scuttling the ferry boat. As Marion could not make the crossing, he exchanged shots and then moved up the bank of the stream, swam it fives miles above the ferry, and continued the pursuit toward Camden.

The swamps along Lynches Creek were flooded by a freshet, and several of Marion's men lost their arms. To their surprise, they found that Doyle in his haste to reach Camden, had destroyed his heavy baggage, and the route he had taken was well marked with abandoned canteens and knapsacks. According to tradition, the pursuit continued to Willow Grove, now Lynchburg, where on the afternoon of March 8, 1781, Doyle made a stand. "The battleground was marked by

[21] Gregorie, T. Sumter, p. 142.
[22] Simms, F. Marion, pp. 214-216.

a knoll of several acres covered by a thick growth of willow trees and partially surrounded by a thickly wooded stream known as the 'Big Branch.' On this knoll stood a hewn log building, previously a rum shop, and this building was used as a fort by the patriots. Doyle's men had crossed the branch on the north side. The patriots remained on the south side, taking shelter in the grove and in and behind the log fort; and, from these vantage points, the contending forces battled until night fall. At dawn it was found that Doyle had withdrawn during the night and hurried away towards Camden. The patriots, tho greatly outnumbered, had somewhat the advantage in position and very much the best marksmen, but had many wounded and one killed."[23]

As Marion's force was far inferior to Doyle's, he abandoned the pursuit and turned back for another encounter with Colonel Watson, who with fresh supplies was once more pushing toward the Peedee. General Greene had now returned to South Carolina, and sent Light Horse Harry Lee to the aid of hard-pressed Marion. On April 15, 1781, Colonel Lee and General Marion laid siege to the British post on the Santee where Colonel Watson had his headquarters.

The British had built their stockade for Fort Watson on an ancient Indian mound some forty or fifty feet high, which enabled them to overlook the surrounding terrain. Colonel Watson had not yet returned and with most of his troops was at Georgetown; and the garrison within the stockade consisted of only sixty regulars and forty Tories, under the command of Lieutenant McKay. Neither the Americans nor the British had any artillery, and the steepness of the ground precluded an attack upon the stockade by direct assault. Marion therefore cut off the garrison from their water supply in Scott's Lake, hoping that thirst would bring the enemy to a speedy surrender. McKay, however, succeeded in digging a well within the stockade.

The Americans then resorted to a classic strategem, and during the night Colonel Hezekiah Maham directed the construction of a log tower to overtop the stockade. At daylight the British were aroused by a fusillade of bullets. Soon after,

---

[23] J. A. Rhame, in A. W. Dick, G. R. McElveen, L. M. Peebles, *Lee County, Economic and Social.* Bulletin No. 156, Extension Division, University of S. C. (Columbia, 1925), p. 12.

a band of American volunteers dashed up the mound and proceeded to destroy the abatis of felled trees. Further defense was useless, for the Americans could now shoot down into the stockade, so on April 23, the British garrison surrendered. Marion immediately demolished the defenses.

This accomplished, Lee rejoined General Greene, who was now facing the British near Camden. Marion marched northward with the remnants of his force to Bloom Hill Plantation in the sandhills, from whence he could watch the roads by which Colonel Watson might march his men from Georgetown to join Lord Rawdon at Camden. Marion sent eighty of his brigade under Colonel Irvine to Rafting Creek, to cut off supplies from moving in to the British in Camden.

Meager as Marion's little force now was, his position in the High Hills was regarded as such a threat to the British in Camden, that it is said to have precipitated the battle of Hobkirk's Hill, where on April 25, 1781, General Greene was defeated by Lord Rawdon.

News of the defeat caused many desertions from Marion's depleted brigade, which was further reduced by the anxiety of the partisans to get home to their spring planting. Marion was therefore too weak to bar the roads for Colonel Watson, who soon joined Rawdon in Camden.

On May 9, however, Rawdon began to evacuate Camden, and Marion wrote to inform Sumter that the enemy would encamp the next night at Singleton's Mill, on the way to Charleston.

With this retirement of the British into the defenses of Charleston, the active phases of the war passed from the area of the future Sumter County. In July General Greene brought his depleted and hungry army into the High Hills for rest and recuperation. His "camp of repose" was on a plain known as James' Oldfield at Midway plantation "late the hospitable residence of Colonel John Singleton." He also encamped and had headquarters at Bloom Hill, Captain William Richardson's plantation.[24]

To the High Hills too came "Dictator" John Rutledge, who

[24] W. Johnson, *Sketches of the Life and Correspondence of Nathanael Green*. . . . (2 vols., Charleston, 1822), I, 178.
(2 vols., Charleston, 1822), I, 178. R. W. Gibbes, *Documentary History of the American Revolution, 1781, 1782*, (Columbia, 1853), pp. 125, 206.

established himself at Bloom Hill, where he and Greene held many consultations and matured their plans for the final expulsion of the British. In September Rutledge appointed his host, Captain William Richardson, to commandeer indigo and specie for public use, an unpopular measure but the most likely method of restoring the ruined financial credit of the state government. Apparently at Bloom Hill also was the main commissariat of the state troops.

On September 8, 1781, General Greene marched from his camp to McCord's ferry, where he crossed the river and lost a fourth of his army in the costly victory at Eutaw Springs. Immediately after, with half of the victorious survivors disabled by wounds and disease, he hastened back to recuperate his army in "his favorite encampment" in the High Hills, there to await the frosts of autumn. "At this time Gen. Greene encamped on the range of hills immediately below Stateburgh. His headquarters were at Mr. James', on the right going downwards, a beautiful spot, but now deserted."[25] There in late October he received the news of Cornwallis' surrender at Yorktown, only nine days after that event. The joyous Americans celebrated with a jubilee at headquarters, the remission of all punishments, and the release of the prisoners in custody of the provost guard.

In November Governor Rutledge sent out election writs, and again the people of Camden District elected General Sumter to represent them, this time as their state senator. The ten representatives were James Bradley, Samuel Dunlap, Wood Furman, Captain Gordon, John Gamble, Colonel John James, Joseph Kershaw, Joseph Lee, Richard Richardson, and William Welch. In January 1782, the liberation of South Carolina was signalized by the convening of the General Assembly at Jacksonborough, a village within thirty-five miles of the British-held capital, Charleston. General Sumter was among the many military leaders who attended the sessions of the "Jacksonborough Assembly," for the war in South Carolina was practically ended, although the British in Charleston did not evacuate until December of that year.

[25] Ibid., p. 138.

CLAREMONT, CLARENDON, AND SALEM COUNTIES
CHAPTER VI

After the Revolution, conditions among the people east of the Wateree, as in other parts of the devastated state, were indeed bad. Homes and barns had been burned; Negroes had been carried off; horses, cattle, and supplies of every kind, had been seized by the armies of both sides, as they passed back and forth along the old Catawba path. Camden, the nearest town, had been practically destroyed, for when the British evacuated and set fire to their military stores, many private homes and places of business were burned, along with the courthouse and jail.

William Johnson, the patriotic blacksmith of the Liberty Tree, Charleston, on his way up to Charlotte to bring home his family, travelled the road east of Black River where the country had been laid waste by Major Wemyss during the war:

> After riding until late at night, without refreshment, or a place to rest himself and his jaded horses, he stopped under a tree, tied the horses each to a bush, that they might eat the leaves, while he and his servant, Stephen, laid down on the ground, without dinner or supper, and slept soundly under the anodyne influence of fatigue. At dawn of day he awoke, and heard indistinctly the crowing of a cock. They mounted their horses, and followed the welcome sound in that dreary waste. They soon found the log-cabin, from which issued the cock's friendly invitation, and obtained the much-needed food for man and beast. He was told that this rough habitation had been constructed after the general conflagration, and at a distance from the high-road, that it might be the safer from future discovery, and that it was the only house within many miles.[1]

[1] Johnson, *Traditions*, p. 379.

To add to the difficulties of the times, the planters could no longer collect a bounty from the British government for their indigo, which soon ceased to be a money crop. The cessation of trade during the war and the tremendous losses caused by the war, had plunged everyone into debt. Francis and Cleland Kinlock estimated their indebtedness at £9,000. To protect debtors from being imprisoned, the legislature passed several stay laws which prohibited suits for the collection of debts; and some dishonest persons who were well able to pay, took advantage of those laws to defraud their creditors.[2]

To make matters worse, there was no dependable medium of exchange for the payment of debts or for any other business. The continental paper which had been issued by the Continental Congress for the prosecution of the war, was so worthless that some people actually pasted it on drafty walls to stop the cracks. The cost of the war had piled up a huge national debt as well as a state debt; no means had been devised for raising revenue; the national treasury was empty and the national credit was bankrupt.

To meet this situation, South Carolina as a sovereign power, had issued its own paper money in the form of £100,000 in interest-bearing bills of credit, which were loaned to individuals in small amounts secured by land mortgages or a deposit of family plate. The merchants had welcomed this scheme and agreed to accept the bills at par with gold and silver. Although the notes were not legal tender, and although some borrowers used the loans for luxuries instead of for the payment of debts, the scheme worked very well on the whole, and a year later the paper money of South Carolina was still supporting its credit.[3] It was not until after the federal constitution of 1789 was ratified and the financial measures of Alexander Hamilton were approved, that the national credit revived and a sound money system came into being.

The effect of the war upon the churches had been as bad as the effect upon business. St. Mark's Church, on the military highway between Charleston and Camden, was too ex-

---

[2] Felix Gilbert (ed.), "Letters of Francis Kinloch to Thomas Boone, 1782-1788," in *Journal of Southern History*, VIII, 99; *Stat.* IV, 513, 640.

[3] "Letters F. Kinloch", *loc. cit.*, p. 102.

posed to escape injury, and was burned by the British during the war. The rector, the Rev. William Davies, had died shortly before hostilities began.

Destruction must have been the fate also of the wooden church at Salem, Black River, for the pastor, the Rev. Dr. Thomas Reese, went into exile in North Carolina, and his congregation was pillaged and murdered by the Tories under the notorious Harrison brothers. The sufferings of James Bradley, one of the elders of Salem Church, have already been told.

The Rev. Richard Furman of the High Hills Baptist Church, had marched with a company to Charleston at the beginning of the Revolution, but had been sent home to win converts to the Revolutionary cause; and in 1775 he had written to the loyalists an address which General Richard Richardson distributed among them during the Snow Campaign. When Cornwallis put a price on the young preacher's head, he had to flee to North Carolina and Virginia.

Thus the war had closed all the churches and sent the ministers into exile. Moreover, as the ministers were often the schoolmasters in their communities, the schools as well as the churches had been closed during the war.

Closed too were the courts of justice. Murder, arson, robbery and other crimes which the Whigs and Tories had perpetrated upon each other during the war, had gone unpunished except for the cruelties of private vengeance. One of the most dreadful results of the war was this civil strife among neighbors, which did not end with the treaty of peace or even with the reopening of the district courts, for the circuit judges had a hard time convincing their juries that crimes of vengeance should be punished by due process of law.

With the end of military hostilities, and the new state in control of the Whigs, many of whom bore private grudges against Tory neighbors, severe laws were passed for the banishment of loyalists and the amercement or confiscation of their property. As a result, the General Assembly was flooded with petitions for the exemption of individuals whose relatives had fought against the British, or who for some other reason merited special consideration. In 1783 South

Carolina allowed seventy-seven of the banished loyalists to return, and the next year one hundred and twenty-five were exempted from penalties. Feeling still ran high, however, and many of those who ventured back were set upon by their neighbors and barbarously beaten or even murdered. From the High Hills came a letter to the *Gazette of the State of South Carolina*, saying that a whipping had been prescribed for James McCormick,[4] but nothing was said of Isham Moore and William Stukes, who had been merely amerced.

The notorious Daniel McGirt seems to have been in East Florida as late as 1793, when he sold 200 acres on the waters of Jack's Creek; but he is said to have finally returned to the High Hills, where he lived in seclusion at the home of his brother-in-law, Subaltern James, and few even knew of his presence until after his death.[5]

William Rees was among the refugees who came back from Florida in 1784. When he appeared at the High Hill Tavern, and met with Patton Mahon, Archie Henson and others, a violent quarrel began, but as Rees was the only one armed, they did not attack him. On the following Saturday, however, some seven of his neighbors, led, it is said, by General Sumter himself, went to Rees' home near the tavern, armed with hickory switches. They chased Rees to his roof, and when they found him hidden between the wall and the chimney, they administered fifty strokes on his bare back, after which they returned to the tavern and received a "treat from their friends."[6] Rees stood his ground, however, and would not again leave his home; and eventually he recovered his old place in the community and prospered.

Such disorder and lawlessness made it even harder for men to rehabilitate their ruined homes, farms and mills. The need was recognized, therefore, for the creation of counties and county courts, in which resident magistrates, sitting together as a group, might dispense a limited local justice in minor cases, and thus relieve the overcrowded dockets of the circuit courts. The idea was not new, and had been tried in South Carolina at an early date. In 1783 such a law was again

---

[4] Sept. 13, 1784.
[5] Sumter conveyances, B, p. 106; Johnson, *Traditions*, p. 174.
[6] Gregorie, *T. Sumter*, pp. 208, 309.

passed, and each of the seven great circuit court districts of the state was subdivided into counties of convenient size.

The commissioners for laying off **Camden District**, were: General Sumter, Richard Richardson, Frederick Kimball, Thomas Taylor of the Congarees, Richard Winn of Winnsboro, Edward Lacy of the New Acquisition, and John Moffatt. Assisted by surveyors, these commissioners established, largely on natural lines, the boundaries of seven counties: York, Chester, Fairfield, Richland, Lancaster, Claremont and Clarendon. The last two included the area of the future Sumter District.

Clarendon County was named for Edward Hyde, first Earl of Clarendon, one of the original lords proprietors of Carolina. The first magistrates of this county were John Cantey, John Gamble, William Martin, James Davis, William McConnico, Samuel Little, and John Lawson. They built the courthouse and jail, probably log buildings, on a branch of Ox Swamp, near the present town of Juneville. The site was owned in 1818 by the estate of Colonel Alexander Colclough, former high sheriff of Clarendon.[7]

The origin of the name Claremont is not known, but it may have been chosen by General Sumter from the name of the estate of Lord Clive, who was in England at the time of Sumter's visit to London in 1762. The name, however, was applied to more than one plantation in the region. In Claremont County near the High Hill Tavern was a Claremont Plantation owned by George Ioor and his wife Frances (Guignard), who died in 1807, and was buried there. Mary E. Huger in 1815 conveyed Clermont Plantation, 900 acres on Rafton Creek, to her son Francis, who later conveyed a part to William Sanders. In Clarendon County was another Claremont Plantation, a part of the estate of John Splatt Cripps, of Charleston. Fifteen miles north of Camden was Clermont the home of the loyalist, Colonel Henry Rugeley.

Under the constitution of 1790, Claremont and Clarendon Counties together elected one senator, but each had two representatives in the General Assembly.

Two years after the counties were authorized, the county

---

[7] Sumter conveyances, E, p. 204.

courts were set up. The first magistrates named for Claremont County were George and James Armstrong, William Murrell, William Wright, Elijah McCoy, Thomas McFadden, and William Richardson.[8] Captain Richardson served but briefly, if at all, for he was in poor health, and died at Bloom Hill in February 1786.

The county court at first was held by a quorum of at least three of the seven magistrates in each county, sitting together as a group. The sessions were held four times a year. The court had common law jurisdiction only in unimportant civil cases not exceeding £50 in the value of the property in question, and the court could not hear any cases on titles or boundaries of land. On the sites of these old county courthouses a "hangman's tree" is usually pointed out these days, but no men were ever hanged by the courts, for their jurisdiction in criminal cases did not extend to loss of life or limb. This was in a time when Christians still believed devoutly in witchcraft, and if these county court records were still in existence, they might show that witches were tried in Stateburg, as they were in Lancaster and Winnsboro.

The magistrates of the county court elected a clerk of court, sheriff, coroner, and a county attorney to prosecute criminal cases in the name of the state. The magistrates also built the courthouse and jail, set up the stocks, pillory and public whipping post; cared for paupers; supervised work on roads and bridges or appointed commissioners to do it for them; and issued licenses to taverns.

The clerk of the county court recorded local contracts and deeds for real and personal property, but such documents were required to be proved or authenticated by oath of the grantor or two witnesses before the magistrates sitting in open court.[9] Among the early clerks of the Claremont court were Wood Furman and Nathaniel Alexander.

The original county court law was amended many times, the number of magistrates varying as well as the number necessary for a quorum to hold court; the dates for court sessions and the powers of the court also were altered from time to time.

[8] Miscellaneous Records, UU, p. 278, Historical Commission of S. C.
[9] For County Court Act, see *Stat.* VII, 211 ff.

In 1787 the county court was given the powers and duties of the district ordinary, now called the judge of probate, with jurisdiction in matters testamentary, of administration, guardianship, and the settlement of estates of deceased persons. In that day of bad roads, it was a great relief to the people of the counties to be able to record wills and deeds in the local courthouses instead of taking the long journey to the district courthouse in Camden.

But the people living east of Black River found that they were still too far from a courthouse, so in 1792 Claremont and Clarendon were shorn of some of their territory to form Salem County, the part taken from Claremont being called "Upper Salem" and the part from Clarendon, "Lower Salem". The commissioners to decide upon the location and erect the courthouse and jail were James Dickey, Thomas Wilson, John Singleton, Thomas Chandler, and John McElween. The judges of the new county were Roger Wilson and John Witherspoon Jr., to whom David Reese for £5: 15 shillings conveyed from his home tract six acres on the west side of Taylors Swamp for the courthouse town of Salem. The judges in turn conveyed this to Gershon Benbow. Lots were laid out, and among the purchasers were William Anderson, James Lowery, Robert Player, and Gershon Benbow. The two principal streets of the town were designated merely as "long" and "cross" streets. The courthouse was built, and like that of Clarendon, was probably a log building. William E. Herring was clerk of court; Robert Wilson, sheriff; and Samuel Mays was appointed coroner, but must have declined, for Matthew Henderson was appointed the next day.[10]

The establishment of the counties and the county courts was only one phase of the general post-war movement toward recovery in which General Sumter was taking a leading part. He now proceeded to acquire vacant lands by paying the trifling sums required, in huge grants totaling more than 100,000 acres in various parts of Camden and Cheraw districts. Of especial interest to this narrative was his grant for 14,288 acres on Turkey Creek, waters of Black River, on a part of which now stands the present Sumter County courthouse.

[10] *Stat.* V, 216, 217; Sumter conveyances AA, p. 25.

Not only did General Sumter obtain grants for speculative purposes, but he had a part in organizing various enterprises. Among the men associated with him in the spring of 1783 were several who had fought with him during the war: Edward Lacy, one of his colonels; William Ransome Davis, a captain of the state troops; Joseph Palmer, a captain who had served as commissary under Lacy; John Sumter, who seems to have been the General's brother; and John Adair, one of the General's earliest guerrilla followers, who migrated to Kentucky in 1786 and became not only a leading citizen, but governor and United States senator. These men may have been members of the company headed by General Sumter, which purchased lands in the beautiful High Hills, and in 1783 laid out the village of Stateburg around the old High Hill tavern. The village was within a few miles of the center of the state, and the name was given in expression of the hope that it might be chosen for the state capital, which then was soon to be removed from Charleston to a more central location.

North of the old tavern, General Sumter reserved land for a public square. Although Stateburg never became the state capital, it did become the county seat of Claremont for the fifteen years that the county court functioned. A courthouse appears to have been built there, but whether the first court met in the long room of the old tavern, cannot now be ascertained, for the records have been burned, along with the house and office of John Horan,[11] first clerk of court of Sumter District.

General Sumter, meanwhile, having acquired so many interests in the High Hills, removed his residence from Clarendon County, and purchased in 1784, perhaps for his Stateburgh home the property now called The Ruins.

One of the most ambitious enterprises in the development of the new town of Stateburgh was the establishment of a newspaper. Very little is now known of this, and apparently it had but a brief existence. But in November 1786, copies of the *Claremont Gazette* were sent to Charleston by the Rev.

---

[11] *Ibid.*, BB, p. 321; J. Morse, *American Gazeteer* 1797; Sumter conveyances AA, p 50. C, p. 318.

Richard Furman, and their receipt was noted by the editor of the *Charleston Morning Post*.[12] No copies of the *Claremont Gazette* are now known to exist.

In the same year, General Sumter was one of the organizers of the Claremont Society, the others being the Rev. Richard Furman and his brother Josiah; James Rembert of Rembert Hall; Huberd Rees, Matthew Singleton of Melrose, John Macnair, Ben Young, Isham Moore, a surveyor and former loyalist; George Ioor of Claremont plantation, and William Murrell, a merchant of Stateburgh, who served as treasurer. The society opened the Claremont Academy in Stateburgh, and provided a boarding house for the pupils who came from a distance. The teaching staff was headed by William Humphries, who, while teaching at the Waxhaws previously, had had Andrew Jackson as one of his pupils. Mr. Humphries was succeeded by James Scott, a Scotchman who had tutored in Rhode Island College, now Brown University. Mr. Scott was assisted by John Horan, a young Irishman from Charleston, who taught English and mathematics, and later was General Sumter's agent while the General was absent for his duties in Congress. A separate department for girls was conducted by a Miss Stewart of Charleston. Claremont Academy did not flourish, and is said to have closed in 1788. The Claremont Society, however, did not despair, for it was incorporated in 1789 for the purpose of instituting and endowing a seminary of learning at Stateburgh.. This academy was under Dr. Patterson in 1819.[13]

In 1789, the same year that the Claremont Society was incorporated, General Sumter went to New York to take his seat on May 25 in the first Congress of the United States. In 1801 he was elected United States Senator and continued to serve until he resigned in 1810.

General Sumter and the Rev. Richard Furman at some time in their busy lives, found time to take the lead in organizing for Stateburgh a library society, which maintained a circulating library that was mentioned in 1808 as "increasing". This society was not incorporated until 1814, but

[12] C. S. Brigham, *History and Bibliography of American Newspapers, 1690-1820* (2 vols., Worcester, 1947).
[13] Cook (ed.), *Furman*, p. 15; *State Gazette of S. C.*, Apr. 24, 1786; *Camden Gazette*, Feb. 3, 1819.

at some time in its career it erected a building upon a lot in Stateburgh to which it received title in 1817 from Dr. Alexander Silliman.

Every town must have trade as its lifeblood, so the promoters of Stateburgh turned their attention to river communications. With the hope of opening water connections toward the north and eventually to the west, as well as with Charleston, General Sumter was a member of a company for opening the Catawba and Wateree rivers, which was chartered in South Carolina in 1787 and in North Carolina the following year. The plan was to connect Stateburgh with the Wateree by opening Slave Landing Creek, and extending it to the Charleston-Camden road by a canal; the rivers were to be improved by canals, dams and locks. The company purchased 500 acres at Rocky Mount, now Great Falls, and acquired title to vacant lands on both sides of the river from Camden ferry to the North Carolina line; but the project was too costly for private enterprise, and little came of it. General Sumter eventually acquired title to Rocky Mount in 1803 and conveyed it next day to President Thomas Jefferson as a site for a military establishment.

Along with general recovery had come the reopening of the churches and schools. Soon after the close of hostilities, the Rev. Thomas Reese had returned to Salem, Black River, where he opened his school and taught several boys who were being prepared for the ministry. The Rev. Richard Furman also returned to the High Hills Baptist Church, but in 1787 he accepted a call to Charleston, and was not succeeded by a full-time minister until in 1799 the Rev. John M. Roberts came, who also followed a teaching career. In 1790 the Rev. Ezra Courtney was serving at the Bethel Baptist Church of Claremont County on Black River, one of the early offshoots of the High Hills Baptist Church.

During this period a new denomination, the Methodist Church, came into being, when Bishop Francis Asbury made his first visit to South Carolina in 1785. On his way to Charleston, the Bishop stopped over with Captain James Rembert, at Rembert Hall, "the most imposing building in that part of the State," which thereafter became one of his regular stopping places on subsequent visits to South Carolina. Santee Circuit was organized the next year, 1786, and Captain Rembert erected a chapel in his community for the services. Another Methodist chapel was built through the efforts of Robert Bradford and Robert Singleton, at Bradford's plantation on Green Swamp, near the present beautiful Swan Lake Gardens at Sumter.

St. Mark's Church was not rebuilt at this time, but in the summer of 1788 the Episcopalians in the High Hills were organized, and the Rev. Matthew Tate became the rector of the Episcopal Church of Claremont at Stateburgh. There he performed services in the long room of Powell's Tavern until a frame building was erected the next year on a two-acre lot given by General Sumter. Powell's Tavern, probably the High Hill Tavern under new management, seems to have been the community center of Stateburgh, and in 1785 had been the place at which General Sumter called two meetings of the commissioners for settling the accounts of Revolutionary veterans. There too in 1787 the annual meeting of the Stateburg Jockey Club was advertised to be held.

The Stateburg races that year were announced to begin on November 24, for one of the largest purses ever run for in this state. The stewards of the jockey club at that time were Charles Myddleton, one of General Sumter's former colonels; John Mayrant, who had been a midshipman under John Paul Jones on the "Bon Homme Richard"; and Laurence Manning, a young Irishman of literary pursuits, who had come from Pennsylvania to the High Hills with Lee's Legion, and decided to stay—probably for the very good reason that he had married Susannah, daughter of General Richard Richardson.

Racing had been revived in 1785, when General Sumter's celebrated young horse *Statesburg* began his career on the Stateburg race track in the level land of the Macnairs between the village and the river. The track was reached from Stateburg by Turf Street, which entered the Charleston Road between the old Tavern and the public square. From the General's stables came other well-known racers, *Ugly* and *Plenipo*, but after he was elected to Congress, he seems to have sold his horses. Many of his neighbors were enthusiastic turfmen, among whom should be mentioned the Singletons, and the Richardsons of Clarendon County, who had their own race tracks. William Richardson of Bloom Hill was also a lover of horses, and after his death his widow auctioned off forty-three high-blooded animals.

Life in St. Mark's Parish was now changing from what it had been in the day of the Rev. Mr. Woodmason and the Regulators. In the High Hills the summer seats and shooting boxes of the gentry from the low country were giving way to spacious permanent homes, and many people now came to stay. In 1789 Thomas Hooper and his wife Mary, "of Charleston", sold their property in St. Andrew's Parish, where Hooper's Bridge near the parish church had been a landmark since 1723, and bought from General Sumter 550 acres of land near Stateburg. Apparently they then became permanent residents of Stateburg, for the next year, when they sold some Charleston property, they described themselves as "of Statesborough." Some years later they also acquired the old tavern, which is said to have become then a private residence.[14]

Artisans also came. Robert Andrews of Virginia, who described himself as a chairmaker because he built two-wheeled vehicles called riding chairs, bought from General Sumter a 26-acre farm on the highway near Stateburgh, where he erected a cottage for his large family and opened a workshop. Among those who called themselves carpenters were George Conley, Mason Spears, Jeremiah Pitts, and Josiah Furman. Joshua Hodges said he was a shoemaker.

The professional men were chiefly young lawyers, but there were also several physicians. Dr. Eli Howard had succeeded to the practice of his father, Dr. Joseph Howard. Dr. Samuel Mays purchased lands from Jared Neilson on the east side of Scape Ore Swamp. Dr. James Hartley lived in Stateburg, and Dr. Peter Keen practiced in Claremont County.

Of the lawyers, John Smyth Richardson of Bloom Hill Plantation was reading law in Charleston during the 1790's

---

[14] Deeds of 1779, 1783, 1785, 1786, 1788, and 1790, recorded in Charleston. Abstract by Mrs. Walter C. White of deed from Sumter to Hooper, 1789, in her possession. John Rutledge Sumter told the writer he had always heard that the Hooper house had been the former tavern. see plat of Stateburg, *infra*. Lands of William Hiton adjoined those of Sherwood James in Stateburg. See Sumter conveyances AA, pp. 199-200.

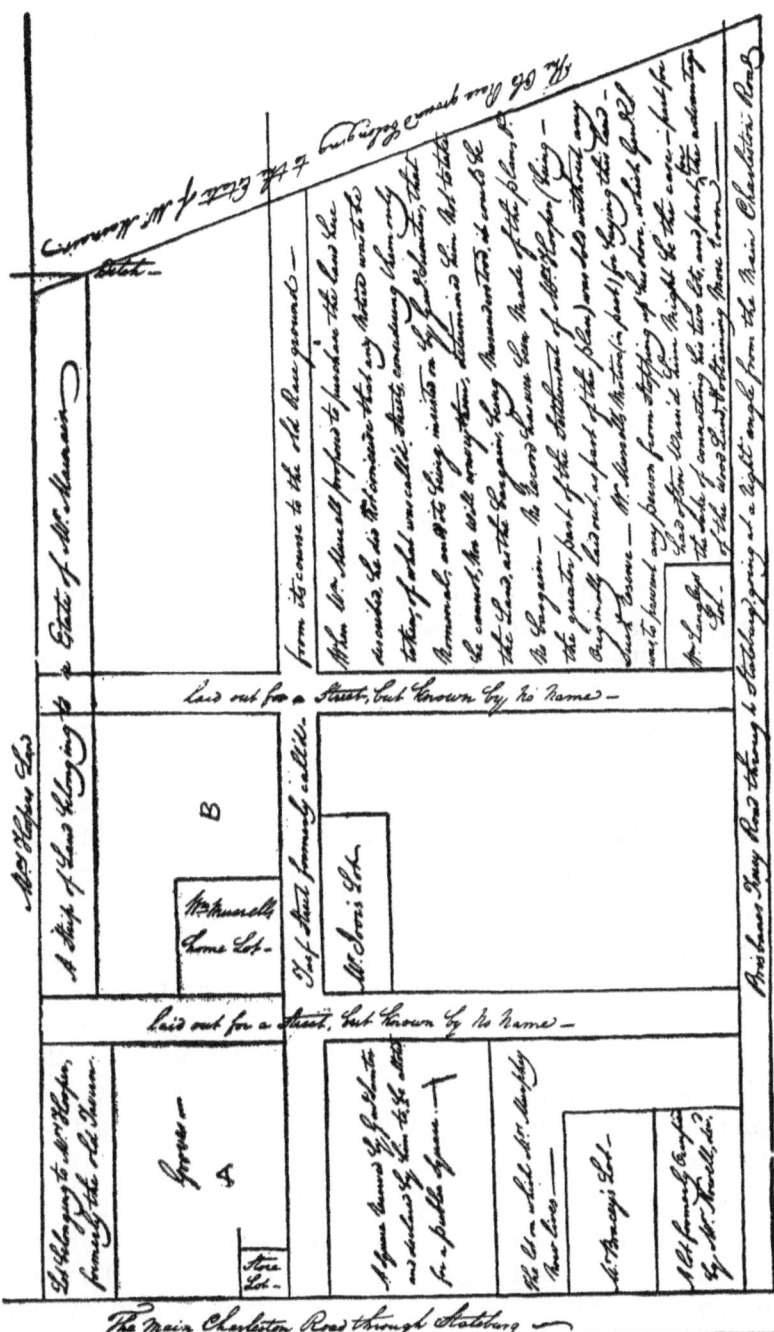

PLAN OF STATEBURG, C. 1800. From the original presented to Mrs. Walter C. White by Mrs. R. B. Furman.

and was admitted to the bar in 1799. Judge Thomas Waties of Georgetown brought his wife to settle a home which they called Marden, just outside of Stateburg. Apparently he chose the name because when he had been captured with Commodore Gillon during the Revolution, he had been paroled to Marden in Kent, England. Of the twelve children reared at Marden by Judge Waties and his wife, a son, Thomas Jr., became a physician, and a daughter Charlotte, married another local physician, Dr. Xenaphon Bracey.

During the years after the Revolution, another village, Manchester, was growing up eight miles south of Stateburg on the Charleston-Camden road. An early mention of Manchester by name occurred in 1799, when Anthony Butler, attorney at law, was married there to "the amiable and truly accomplished Miss Mary Ann James Moore, daughter of Isham Moore, esq."[15] At first the village was a summer settlement for the Moores, Ramseys, Ballards, "and other rich planters who owned lands on the Wateree River;" but from early times a tavern there had been a convenient stopping place for travellers along the old road. When cotton became the staple crop of the planters, Manchester assumed additional importance, because it was near a good landing on Beech Creek from which freight-boats could take on the cotton bales and proceed through Shanks Creek to the river, and thence to the cotton market in Charleston. The Singletons, especially, acquired wealth through their favorable proximity to the boat-landing near Manchester.

Besides the tavern at Manchester, there was also a shoe shop, two or three stores, a tailor shop, a blacksmith shop, and a log school house which also was used as a church by the Methodists. In the year 1800, this schoolhouse was the scene of a riotous religious service when the circuit-rider the Rev. James Jenkins courageously held his ground against an irreverent mob.

According to the story as told by the preacher in his memoirs, the mob had been inflamed by addresses sent from the General Conference at Richmond, on the subject of freeing the slaves. When Jenkins and another circuit rider

[15] *SCHGM*, XXVI, 46; *see also* Johnson, *Traditions*, p. 380.

arrived home from the Conference, they "found a mob raised to take Brother Garrison on his preaching day; but he took to the bushes and escaped. My time was to come next, and I expected hot work, for I was resolved to stand my ground. On riding up to the village I saw them standing in the street; I bid them good morning, and went on to the church. While I was preaching, in they came, but took their seats. I thought it was no time to be mealy mouthed, hence I poured out the law and the consequences of sin with unmeasured severity. After sermon I began to administer the sacrament, and while on my knees, one fellow took off the loaf of bread, and another touched me on the shoulder, saying 'I wish to speak with you!' When I arose, I told him, I would hear him when I was done. He then forbade my giving the sacrament to the negroes. I asked him if any of them belonged to him? He replied, 'No.' 'Yes,' said I, 'these upstarts are always the greatest opposers of religion.' He then ordered the negroes out of the house, which broke up the meeting. About this time, the fellow that had taken off the bread said, 'If you will come out here I will give you the little end of this,' holding up his whip. So I took my saddle-bags, and walked out. When I got out he said, 'I suppose you have a heap of money in your saddle-bags?' I replied, if I had, it did not belong to him. Thus after all, they did not lay violent hands on me."[16]

There is an old story that in Manchester once lived an aged blacksmith named Horne, who was not very prosperous. Not only was he long, lean, and cadaverous, but he and his wife were never known to have enough to eat. One day some skeptical fellows offered to bet with Horne's friends that he could not eat a five-foot sturgeon; and the friends accepted on condition that the fish be cooked palatably. A day was set for the contest, and Horne was asked whether he could win. Yes, he thought he could if the fish were not larger than a colt. But the skeptics sprang a surprise and cooked the sturgeon into a savory soup. Horne sat down, and happily drained bowl after bowl, until finally the last bowl was brought. Then for the first time he showed uneasiness, and turning to the jubilant skeptics, he said:

[16] Jenkins, *Experience*, pp. 96-97.

"Look here, boys! If you bring so much of this gravy, I don't recokon I kin eat that fish!"[17]

Pranks such as this, practical jokes, dancing, card playing, horse racing, cock fighting, and contests of skill and strength, were large in the life of the village for many years. The more serious history of Manchester came with the railroad era, and will be told in the chapter on early railroads.

Meanwhile, to the legal profession, the operation of the county courts was not proving satisfactory, for even in minor matters the gentlemen of the bar did not think that justice could be properly dispensed by laymen. The fact that the same magistrates did not always preside at the sessions of the county court tended to cause inequalities, inconsistencies, and irregular precedents. In 1791 therefore, the county court law was amended so as to abolish the quorum of county magistrates, and replaced them with three county court judges,[18] who should handle all business that came before the court.

Among the appointees for Claremont County under this amendment was Thomas Hooper, who had come to Stateburg from Charleston in 1789. As county judge he served with Laurence Manning in 1794, but his tenure was brief, for he was stricken with a lingering disease, and died in Charleston in 1798.

William Mayrant was a county court judge in 1796. William Murrell and Isham Moore were among the last three incumbents, for the opposition of the lawyers to lay judges had continued, and finally triumphed. The county courts were abolished effective the first day of the year 1800, when the three counties of Claremont, Clarendon, and Salem, were united into the new circuit court unit known as Sumter District.[19]

17. *Sumter Watchman*, Apr. 20, 1855.
18. *Stat.* VII, 266.
19. *Ibid.*, pp. 284, 287.

A "TWO-PEN HOUSE," showing open "dog-trot," three miles southeast of Rembert. Homestead of the Cato family, bequeathed by Alfred B. Cato, last of his family, to James Nunnery. (Photo by John S. Wilson).

MELROSE HOUSE, Poinsett State Park. Built by Matthew Singleton in the 1760's. (Library of Congress photo).

ANDERSON HOUSE, Black River, on plantation purchased in 1813 from John B. Anderson by Robert Witherspoon, who named it Coldstream. (Photo courtesy of Mrs. Shepard Nash).

BETHEL BAPTIST CHURCH, Black River, founded in 1780. (Sumter Daily Item staff photo).

JAMES BRADLEY'S HOUSE, Black River, built probably before 1776. Now owned by F. McBride Rhodes. (Sumter Daily Item staff photo).

SALEM PRESBYTERIAN CHURCH, Black River. Founded about 1759, this building, the fourth, was erected in 1846. (Sumter Daily Item staff photo).

ST. MARK'S EPISCOPAL CHURCH, near Pinewood. St. Mark's Parish was created in 1757, the first church was built about 1765. The present building, designed by Edward C. Jones, dates from 1853. (Sumter Daily Item staff photo).

HIGH HILLS BAPTIST CHURCH, founded in 1770. The present building was erected about 1803. (Photo by Thomas L. Martin).

REMBERT'S METHODIST CHURCH, founded about 1786. The present building was erected about 1835. (Sumter Daily Item staff photo).

GENERAL THOMAS SUMTER. The original in the Sumter County courthouse was painted by Charles Mason Crowson from the bust-portrait painted by Rembrandt Peale . (Sumter Daily Item staff photo).

SITE OF FORT WATSON. (From Lossing's Field Book of the Revolution).

HOME HOUSE, near Stateburg. Built by General Sumter, and later the home of Mr. and Mrs. Thomas Sumter, Jr., it no longer exists. (Photo courtesy of Mayo Rees).

MESSRS. MOORE, STRANGE AND WRIGHT. From a water color, probably by Chancellor Thomas Waites or a member of his family. (Photo courtesy of Mayo Rees).

BOROUGH HOUSE, south view. (Photo by Thomas L. Martin).

BOROUGH HOUSE, formerly Hillcrest, Stateburg. Purchased April 23, 1792, by Thomas Hooper from Adam F. Brisbane; remodeled and wings of rammed earth added in 1821 by Dr. W. W. Anderson; now owned by his great-granddaughter, Mrs. Walter C. White. (Photo by Wayne Andews, courtesy of Mrs. White).

MARDEN, near Stateburg. Home of Chancellor Thomas Waites. From old painting by Mary Hooper (Anderson), wife of Frederick L. Childs. The house no longer exists. (Photo courtesy of Mrs. Anne Rees Gettys).

WOODLAWN, near Stateburg, home of Orlando Savage Rees, later owned by the William R. Flud family. Accidentally burned in May 1891. (Photo courtesy of Miss Mattie S. Flud).

ACTON, near Stateburg. Built in 1803 by Cleland Kinloch, who devised it to his brother Francis for life. Home, 1886-1902, of Mrs. St. Julian Ravenel, the author. Accidentally destroyed by fire in 1911. (Photo courtesy of J. Nelson Frierson).

ACTON, rear view. (Photo courtesy of J. Nelson Frierson).

CHERRY VALE, near Shaw Base, acquired in 1794 by Henry Vaughan II; sold in 1836 by Henry Vaughan III to his brother-in-law, John James Frierson. Now an apartment house for families of men at Shaw Air Force Base. (Sumter Daily Item staff photo).

NEEDWOOD, on lands called Whiskey Hall by Robert F. Withers. Sold in 1827 to Frederick Wentworth Rees, who built this house, originally plastered on the exterior. Now owned by J. Frank Williams, who weatherboarded it. (Sumter Daily Item staff photo).

THE RUINS, home of John Mayrant, Stateburg. Sold in 1835 by James N. Mayrant to Willis W. Alston, who made it a seminary for young ladies. Three years later it became the property of Robert Marion Deveaux, whose descendents now own it. (Photo by Thomas L. Martin).

PART TWO

HISTORY OF SUMTER COUNTY

Sumter District

CHAPTER VII.
SUMTERVILLE (1800-1855)

Along with all other such courts in the state, the county courts of Claremont, Clarendon, and Salem were abolished, effective January 1, 1800. These counties, however, were continued as election districts, while their territories were united into a new circuit court unit called Sumter District[1] in honor of General Thomas Sumter, who was then serving in Congress.

Geographically, Sumter District was a large area, some forty-four miles long and thirty-eight miles wide, containing some 1,070,080 "square acres."[2]

Politically, Sumter District was very different from a modern county, for it was merely a unit for the administration of justice through the circuit courts of common pleas and general sessions. Sumter District was not a corporate body, and could not own property, or make contracts, or sue and be sued. It was not even an election district until the year 1857; and from 1810 until 1855, it was represented in the state Senate by the senator from Claremont and the senator from Clarendon.[3] Moreover, Sumter District did not have a treasurer, or any governing body for the administration of local government. Whatever was done in the matters of public buildings, public roads, and public welfare, was performed by various boards of commissioners appointed by the General Assembly: commissioners of public buildings looked after the courthouse and jail and provided equipment for the district offices; commissioners of roads and bridges looked after the highways in their respective road districts; and the district commissioners of the poor gave aid to the paupers. All of these boards made annual reports directly to the General Assembly. Tax collectors were appointed for the various tax districts and made their returns to the state treasurer.

[1] *Stat.* VII, 284, 287.
[2] Mills, *Statistics*, p. 741.
[3] *Stat.* V, 595.

The law which created Sumter District appointed James Davis, William Taylor, Thomas Sumter, Jr., Hubert Rees, George Cooper, John Cassels, and John Witherspoon, Jr., as commissioners to fix the location of the public buildings. It was probably on their report that a later act directed that the courthouse should be built at or near the plantation of John Gayle, and that the work should be contracted for and supervised by John Peter Richardson, Reuben Long, and John Ervin James. The sum of $5,000 was allowed by the legislature for the construction of the courthouse and jail, and until these should be ready for use, the courts were to be held in John Gayle's farmhouse,[4] a small one-story building with a piazza on the south side. Gayle's house stood until recent years in what is now the City of Sumter at the corner of Canal and Main Streets, and when it was taken down, the materials were used in the construction of the house next door, on the same lot, but fronting on Main Street.

The choice of the site for the courthouse town caused some surprise, for it was in a rather low and poorly drained section, at some distance from a navigable stream and even from a highway. But Gayle's plantation was centrally located, and eventually public roads would connect it with every part of the district. Sumterville was the name chosen for the new village which would grow up around the courthouse.

John Gayle, owner of the site, apparently was the grandson of Josiah Gayle, who in 1771 had obtained a grant of 388 acres on the High Hills, where he reared a family of some five sons and four daughters. Josiah's son Ambrose had two children, John and Sarah, who, under the will of their grandfather, inherited one-seventh of his estate. Soon after transferring the two-acre site for the public buildings, and four other lots (to John Spann, Jacob Boatner, John McLelland and John McDonald), John Gayle seems to have removed to Edgefield, where in 1804, he sold the remainder of his 850-acre plantation to Richard Harvin.[5]

When the November term of court in the year 1800 was held in John Gayle's house, two of the civil cases heard were

---

[4] *Stat.* VII, 289, 292, 298.
[5] Sumter wills, book AA, p. 459; conveyances, I, p. 248.

Thomas Nightingale Johnson v. Thomas Coulliette; and *Peter Gaillard executor of Peter Sinkler* v. *Redden McCoy administrator of John Tucker deceased.*[6]

The first clerk of court was John Horan, a native of Ireland, who had come to Stateburg from Charleston soon after the Revolution as a teacher in Claremont Academy, and he had been General Sumter's agent during the years the General was absent in Washington. As Horan retained his home and office in Stateburg, he had to ride back and forth to Sumterville.

The first ordinary was William Taylor, who had charge of the probate of wills and matters testamentary. The first sheriff, Huberd Rees, was "heir at law" of the John Rees who had received a grant in Craven County in 1770. Robert Bradford probably was the first coroner, and later he became sheriff.

All cases which had been pending in the courts of Claremont, Clarendon and Salem were transferred to Sumter District, and the records were delivered to Clerk of Court Horan. Unfortunately, when his house and office in Stateburg were destroyed by fire on November 27, 1800, most of the records were consumed. Later, many persons who retained their original deeds and other documents, brought them to Sumterville and had them re-recorded.

After the courthouse was erected on the public square at the intersection of the only two streets, Liberty and Broad (now Main) Sumterville grew slowly. The materials in the courthouse must have been poor, for it needed repairs before it was finally completed in 1806. The first store in the new cross-roads village was operated by John Spann, just west of the courthouse, and already had been built when he received in January 1802, the deed from John Gayle for the half-acre lot on which it stood.

The tavern, a busy place during court week, was kept by one Scott, whose wife was the daughter of William Anderson of Salem, Black River.[7] There the lawyers, the judge, and all who had business in court, found food, drink and shelter during the quarterly sessions.

[6] Sumter deeds, book A, pp. 69, 313.
[7] E. J. Scott, *Random Recollections of a Long Life* (Columbia, 1884), p. 9.

Perhaps because of malaria, dwelling houses were slow in appearing, and twelve years after settlement, Sumterville was still so small that a lady who passed through, mistook the village for "a well-settled plantation and was much surprised to learn that it really was Sumterville."[8] Two years later, an early plat showed the names of the lot owners: Peter Mellett, a carpenter of Huguenot descent; John McDonnell, a surveyor; Daniel Rose, a storekeeper, naturalized in 1807, who later married Elizabeth, daughter of Major John Singleton of Midway Plantation; Charles Miller, brother of Stephen D. Miller, later governor, congressman, and United States senator; Hartwell Macon, a veteran of the Revolution and an early sheriff; James Caldwell; Angus N. Bethune, a physician; Robert Bradford, sheriff; Charles and John A. Spears; Miss Sarah Harvin; John S. Richardson of Bloom Hill, state attorney-general, and in 1818 to become resident circuit judge; Miss Jane McCants; William Magee; and John B. Miller.[9]

John Blount Miller eventually became one of the most useful and influential citizens of Sumterville. Born in Charleston during the Revolution, and brought up to become a retail merchant, he decided to study law and was admitted to the bar in 1805, the year he settled in Sumterville. Three years later he married Mary C. Murrell, of Stateburg, and together they reared a family of seven daughters and two sons. Active in church affairs, and respected for his sound judgment and reliability, he was named in 1812 as one of the first eight commissioners of free schools for Sumter District. When the court of equity was established in Sumter District, he became in 1817 the first commissioner in equity, in charge of the local office, which he held until his death in 1851.

One of the most systematic and accurate of men, Miller made his office a model of efficiency. As no equipment was available for the filing and protection of his public records, he, at his own expense, provided his office with hand-woven cotton bags, in which he kept the loose papers in clean, neat packages, all papers pertaining to each case in one package.

---

[8] *Black River Watchman*, May 20, 1853.

[9] Sumter conveyances, D, p. 297.

These he arranged, labeled and indexed so systematically, that any paper could be found instantly when called for.

Twenty-three years after John Blount Miller had set up his excellent system of filing, the state legislature passed a law which required the commissioners in equity to classify the case papers, and to file separately each kind of document after indexing it on a general index. All bills of complaint were to be filed together, as were the petitions, the decrees, the writs, etc., each classification under its own heading. This meant that when the papers for any case were needed, they would have to be collected from several different places.

Commissioner in Equity Miller was too busy a man to go back over twenty-three years' accumulation of papers, which were in order, and re-file them by a cumbersome new method which was not as good as his, so he merely filed new papers according to the new law. When he was reported by the solicitor for neglecting to obey the law, he apparently convinced that gentleman that no change should be made. At any rate, Mr. Miller never did re-file the old records of his office, and in 1850, the year before his death, his system of filing records was adopted by law for all equity offices in the state.[10]

At an early date the residents of Sumterville showed an interest in library facilities, and in the summer of 1809, some thirty-five men and women formed the Sumterville Circulating Library Society. After drawing up fourteen rules, several of which were truly formidable, they elected John B. Miller, president; Daniel Rose, treasurer and librarian; and William L. Brunson, secretary. The first purchase of books was made from John Hoff, apparently in Charleston, although the freight charge of only one dollar on the bill seems very small for such a distance. The ten titles included four on history: Rollins' *Ancient History*, Ramsay's *South Carolina* and *Life of Washington;* and Russell's *Ancient and Modern Europe;* three poems: Milton's *Paradise Lost,* Young's *Night Thoughts,* and Thompson's *Seasons;* one reference work, *The Domestic Encyclopedia;* and a two-volume work entitled *Thornton Ab-*

---

[10] *Stat.* XI, 117; XII, 60; *S. C. Reports and Resolutions, 1844,* p. 193. For sketch, see J. B. O'Neall, *Bench and Bar of South Carolina* (2 vols., Charleston, 1859), II, 272

bey. These were supplemented by a gift of nine more books from Mr. and Mrs. Miller.

The last entry in the extant minutes of this long-defunct society was made in February 1810, when the treasurer was ordered to sue in a magistrate's court for collection of unpaid dues! This did not break up the society, however, for the next year it was chartered, with power to own real and personal property not to exceed the yearly value of $2,000.[11]

On an early list of books to be purchased by the Library Society, was a history of New England, possibly because some families in or near Sumterville had New England connections. Among the early New Englanders to arrive was Sarah Elizabeth Morse, born in Connecticut the year that Sumter District was organized, who came to Stateburg as a young girl with her father's family, and later married William Haynsworth of Sumterville. The good Methodist Jesse Morgan, who had the tanyard many years, had been born in Maine in 1798. Freeman Hoyt, a young journeyman watchmaker of New Hampshire, rode a horse to Sumterville in 1831, opened a jewelry shop, prospered, married, and eventually died there. Henrietta Elizabeth, the only child of Daniel Rose, in 1838 married Samuel L. Hinckley of Massachusetts. The Rev. Julius Lyman Bartlett, of Massachusetts, who had a school in Sumterville, and whose brother Edward was a tutor in the family of Dr. T. M. Dick at Glenwood, married and eventually died in Sumter.

Besides the New Englanders, there were other outsiders coming to Sumterville, notably the Jews. Soon after the close of the war of 1812, Sephardic Jews from Spain and Portugal began to arrive in Sumterville from Charleston. When Daniel Rose died in 1818, his store was purchased by Moses Lopez, who, with Esdaile P. Cohen, carried on business there until they dissolved partnership two years later. Mark Solomons, the first Jew to remain permanently, began business in Sumterville about this time, purchased two slaves in 1822, and became a naturalized citizen seven years later. Young Israel Franklin Moses, from Charleston, settled in Sumterville in 1825, at the suggestion of Judge Richardson,

[11] Minutes Sumterville Library Society; *Stat.* VIII, 262.

and began to practice law with John L. Wilson. Five years later, Moses purchased two lots on the north side of Republican (now East Hampton) Street between Harvin and Main, for his residence. There his wife, Jane McLellan, a devoted Methodist, developed a garden that became famous for its roses, and there was born their only son, Franklin Israel Moses, Jr. Why the father reversed the order of the first two names is unknown, but the middle initial soon became confused with "J", and both father and son are now known as "F. J. Moses." In 1832 Montgomery Moses, brother of the elder Moses, became his law partner practicing as the firm of F. I. and M. Moses, in Chesterfield, Marlboro, Marion, Darlington, Kershaw, Sumter, and Lancaster.[12]

A few of Sumterville's citizens came directly from across the seas, among them being two Scots, James McKellar of Argyle, naturalized in 1811, and John Dow of Moray, the next year. Of the Irish, John Horan already has been mentioned. His nephew and heir, Thomas Muleedy from County Roscommon, was naturalized in 1812, as was James Coskrey of County Down; and Lucas Creydon from County Sligo, the previous year. Later, about thirty Irish settled around Providence, where the first Roman Catholic Church in the district was organized in 1838 under the patronage of the Blessed Virgin Mary. Natalie Delage, widow of Thomas Sumter, the younger, was a devout member of this congregation, and at her death in 1841 she bequeathed to it 160 acres of land surrounding the church. Mrs. Charles Spann was another devoted member of the little congregation. Mary de Coursay was the first to be buried there. Eventually this church was abandoned, when the congregation moved into Sumterville.[13]

There was no church of any denomination in Sumterville during the first twenty years of its existence, but from time to time religious services were held in the courthouse. By the year 1824, the tiny village of only a dozen houses, could point

[12] Barnett A. Elzas, *The Jews of South Carolina* (Philadelphia, 1905), pp. 197-199, 247-253; H. A. Moses, *The Early Minutes of the Sumter Society of Israelites* (Sumter, 1936); U. R. Brooks, *South Carolina Bench and Bar* (Columbia, 1908), pp. 33-35; Sumter County records and newspapers, and Moses family letters owned by Mr. H. A. Moses of Sumter.

[13] Sumter naturalization records; *Sumter Item*, Nov. 13, 1943; will and diary of Natalie Sumter.

with pride to two churches, the Baptist, dedicated in 1820, and the Presbyterian, organized in 1823. The Reverend James Jenkins, who began to ride the Santee circuit in 1794, has recorded that the Methodist Society met with opposition in Sumterville from the beginning, but that unlike the mob who persecuted him in Manchester, the people of Sumterville were respectful hearers of the word, if not doers of the work! Because of this opposition, perhaps, the congregation of the Green Swamp Church, near the present Swan Lake, did not move into the village until 1827, when a lot on the north side of West Liberty Street was purchased from the Frierson estate and a building was erected. Later, when a new site and building were acquired on the opposite side of the street, the Methodists sold their old church to the Roman Catholics, who remodeled, and dedicated it in 1849 under the patronage of St. Lawrence Martyr.[14]

In 1820, the same year that the Baptists built the first church in Sumterville, the State Board of Public Works decided to erect a new courthouse for Sumter District. This Sumter's second courthouse, was built of brick, from plans by Robert Mills, state engineer and architect,[15] who loved the classics and designed his courthouses as "temples of justice." On the ground floor were the offices of the clerk of court, sheriff, and judge of probate (then called ordinary). On the second floor were the jury rooms, and the courtroom opening upon a classic portico overlooking Main Street and reached by a double flight of curving stone steps with iron banisters. This solid old Mills' courthouse still stands on Main Street, but the portico and steps have been removed, and it has been remodeled into the National Bank of South Carolina Building and the South Carolina Power and Light offices. Only from an aerial view can its identity now be recognized.

For the early schools of Sumterville, little is available. In 1827 Major W. R. Theus opened the Sumter Military, Gymnastic and Classical School on Harvin Street, next door to Dr. James Haynsworth, who with Thomas Dugan, Thomas Baker, and John Mayrant, seems to have had a share in the enter-

---

[14] D. James Winn, *An Historical Sketch of Methodism* . . . (Sumter, 1918); *Sumter Item*, Nov. 13, 1943.
[15] B. St. J. Ravenel, *Architects of Charleston* (Charleston, 1945), pp. 108-109.

prise. The academy building, sixty feet long, consisted only of classrooms, for Theus advertised that board could be had for 200 or more students in the village, the boys "of tender age" to be taken into the most respectable families. The cost for board, laundry, medical care, candles, wood for fuel, the use of books, stationery, uniforms and arms, was not to exceed $300 a year, one-half payable in advance. For every 25 students, Theus promised at least one teacher, and, to procure his staff, he immediately would visit West Point, "Mr. Partridge's" school in Middletown, Connecticut, as well as other well-known schools in the North. To provide for the girls, Mrs. J. Chester, formerly of New London, Connecticut, announced the same year the opening of her Young Ladies' Seminary in Sumterville.[16] What is known of later schools will be given in other chapters.

By 1832, when the Nullification excitement was at its height, the number of dwellings in Sumterville had grown to twenty,[17] and two newspapers were being published. Despite the meagerness of their news columns, these early newspapers did much to enlarge the mental horizon of the village community. The history of the newspaper press will be given later.

During the 1840's a number of dwellings were built. The present home of Mr. Loring Lee dates from 1844. When State Senator F. I. Moses built his new house in 1847, he placed the date on the chimney, but this homestead no longer exists. Of the old houses which still survive, most have been rolled to new sites and have been remodeled.

In 1845 Sumterville was incorporated, the official boundary being the sides of a square each measuring ¾ of a mile from the courthouse and paralleling the cardinal points of the compass. The designated government was by a council of an intendant and four wardens.[18] Who was the first intendant is not known, but in 1847 the name of William Clark is mentioned.

Two years later and many times thereafter, the people of Sumterville elected as intendant the popular and witty Irish-

---
[16] *Camden Journal*, Jan. 6, Feb. 17, 1827.
[17] T. P. Lockwood, *A Geography of South Carolina* . . . (Charleston, 1832), p. 49.
[18] *Stat.*, XI, 336.

man, Thomas Jefferson Coghlan, born in 1803 upon the high seas, while his parents were migrating to Charleston. For this reason, he always said he was not a native of any country. Orphaned in boyhood, Coghlan had been apprenticed at the age of fourteen to a Charleston blacksmith named Hughs, and at the end of his seven years' service he had come to Sumter District in the employ of John Frierson of Cherry Vale. There in 1830 he had courted and married a seventeen-year-old girl, Penelope Sledge, and removed to Sumterville. In 1832 Coghlan was advertising to do both blacksmith and whitesmith work at his shop on Republican (now Hampton) Street near the Baptist Church, of which his wife and his mother-in-law were devoted members. Although Coghlan himself was a devout Roman Catholic, minutes of the Baptist Church for 1836 show that he was present at almost every business meeting of the congregation.

Throughout his life Coghlan advertised regularly his many enterprises. When engaged in the lumber business, in 1849, he built a steam sawmill a mile from town, and used the same power for grinding corn. For three years the mills continued in operation and then came tragedy, when the three boilers exploded simultaneously, demolishing the two-story mill and killing three Negroes, besides injuring seriously four other men.

Later, Coghlan added a gun shop and a locksmith shop to his blacksmith and whitesmith shops near the depot, and in 1858 he advertised a foundry where could be cast the iron for any type of fixture. Like other business men of the antebellum era, he had difficulty in collecting his bills, but he dealt with the problem on lines all his own, and advertised:

> To my far Seeing Customers. Excellent Friends: How strikingly apparent now is your wisdom and firmness. For the last five, nay—even seven years, have some of you from time to time visited my presumptive importunities for payment of your small bills and with that highminded and lofty indifference to *small matters*, which always distinguish men of sound judgment, deep penetration and a proper regard for the rights of others —you have invariably silenced me with the simple words

SUMTERVILLE (1800-1855)

"wait till I sell my cotton," and for the life of me I could not account for your holding back from market, the crops of so many years, but now the mystery is revealed; here is 1849; the year you were looking to for cotton to rise—and cotton has risen, and I am convinced from the pleasing aspect of your ancient bills (as we have an interview once a year) that this is the time you were waiting for, to dispose of your large accumulations of cotton, and at one fell swoop, to write in the Book of every Blacksmith those electrifying words, which will cause our anvils to discourse most elegant music.

"Come on gentlemen, we are prepared for the shock".[19]

Probably because of this rise in the price of cotton, Sumterville experienced something of a boom, but some observers thought it was due to the incorporation of the town. Said the editor of the *Banner*, F. M. Adams, a schoolmaster and an attorney at law, the incorporation of 1845 "produced beneficial results. Previous to that time, no public spirit was manifested; and the place was known as the theatre of much dissipation." He then pointed to the improved morals of the people and appearance of the village; the elevation of the sidewalks and rounding of the streets, the planting of shade trees, the night police, and the enlarging of the courthouse to practically double its size. The boom continued during 1849. The Presbyterians and the Catholics were collecting liberal contributions for church buildings, new houses were being built, old warehouses improved, and the "hammer of the carpenter and the trowel of the mason may be heard in every direction."[20]

The fact that a railroad into Sumterville was being seriously planned, must have had much to do with inciting all this hustle and progress, and as a result the village in 1850 could boast of having ninety houses and a population of 840 persons, of whom 330 were slaves.[21] This was the year that the beloved Methodist minister, the Reverend William W. Mood first passed through Sumterville "as a wearied traveller with a tired horse." It was about this time, too, that William

[19] From Sumter newspapers and from Miss Louise Whittemore, daughter of Coghlan's adopted daughter.
[20] *Sumter Banner*, May 31, 1848; Aug. 29, 1849.
[21] *Black River Watchman*, Jan. 4, 1851.

J. Brunson moved his family from the old Isaac Brunson grant near Manchester, to educate his children in Sumterville. His little son Joel, then a very small boy, later recorded his memories of the place and the people:[22]

Sumterville! Why do I write of Sumterville? It certainly is not with the hope of worldly gain, for I am old enough to know better. It is not with the hope of pleasing the people and thereby winning their favor, for the present generation care little about the past and less about the future. They live absorbed with the deceptive Now and the almighty Dollar. The most popular creed is "Do your brother before he has time to do you. Every man for himself and the Devil take the hindermost." But why do I write of Sumterville? It is because I know when you are worn out with the bitter struggle and are seeking rest for your weary spirits you will find much pleasure in reading this little sketch, just as it gives me pleasure to recall the scenes and incidents of the long ago. . . .

Stand with me, in fact you might take my hand . . . in the Cross Streets, and you must not forget that there is only one place in the village called "Cross Street" and that place is where Main and Liberty Streets now cross.

Now turn your face to rising sun. That house on the right on the corner is the Fed Myers Inn, quite a large wooden building with a few slats nailed around the piazza for a ballustrade. Almost by the time you look for it again, it will have been removed. Let us go east and look at the houses on the right hand side. Next to the Fed Myers tavern stands a long single story building with a bright blue sign about six feet square over the door and the gilt letters on that sign read "William Webb's New York Store". Not quite half way on the block, and this low frame building will be occupied in the course of a few years by Friendly Bird, while out back of it stand a lot of old carriage sheds, and the old worn-out vehicles, still showing the comfortable way our grandmothers had to get out of a carriage: the door was opened by the footman, the steps, Yes, real steps, were let down to the ground, and she didn't jump two feet like a modern, but gracefully walked down like a lady.

Now, that square building with the big door and two forges, a lot of charcoal, vices and other blacksmith tools, two strikers, and two blacksmiths just a heating and hammering for life, making "twisters," that's Webb's blacksmith shop, where they made plows, put shoes on fine horses, made steel scrapers, none of your two-for-four-pence, Yankee-cut, thin scrapers that would turn back as soon as it struck a root, but good scrapers that would run nicely through the season.

[22] After Mr. Brunson's death, his daughter Margaret found on his desk this unfinished sketch.

Sumterville (1800-1855)

This is the corner of Liberty and Broad, now called Harvin, and this two-story house will soon be occupied by Michael Welch. The upper part serves as living rooms, and downstairs is the store. But cross the street, and this is the home of Major Billy Haynsworth. You see the part next to Broad Street is single story, and the eastern part is of two-story design, so coming from the lower part of the piazza you must go up about six feet to reach the little portico in front of the eastern part. It is some distance to the next house, a dwelling, and at some time later occupied by the Gilberts. But it is this two story, with its big front door, that holds special interest for me. Here, on each side are work benches with vices and tools of all kinds, while the centre of the building is filled with new carriage bodies, spokes, hubs, tongues, etc.; and that tall thin man there is Mr. Tom Flowers, the owner of the shop. Jim Flowers (I don't know that he is any kin to the owner) is upstairs, painting and trimming a carriage; and those boys moving about in the shop are Bill, Tom and Sam.

That next house is the home of D. B. McLaurin. Then that little house with about four rooms and a little piazza, and standing well back from the road in a modest way, is the home of Mrs. Garden. Hugh and Ally and Miss Fanny live there with their mother. We will go on now down by this big ditch to the last house in the Village. He lives Mr. Tim Norton and his wife Susan and their two daughters; and that negro boy in the yard is named George. This building here on the road is Mr. Norton's wheelwright shop, and just behind it, right side the ditch, is "Norton's well", known to every boy and girl in the village as supplying the coolest, sweetest water in the whole world. Nothing more now until we get to Turkey Creek bridge, where we fish and catch maw-mouth and cats. You see, the stream south of the road has never been ditched, and it is good fishing all the way round to Dingle's mill.

This is the village limit, but we must go further to see some things. It is just about two hundred yards back to the bridge, and those rails so nicely adjusted on the top of the fence, mark the place where Judge William Lewis, County Ordinary, gets over the fence. He frequently sits here for hours and talks with people who pass along the road. That negro coming round the path from his house is named Shady; he can make music on a tin horn as long as a rail; it will bring all the raccoons in the Creek out to dance.

This is the avenue leading up to Judge Lewis' home. You see from his house (two stories, four large columns, the roof painted red) the beautiful shade trees, the wide flower garden (well kept), and the numerous negro servants about the place, that he is in easy circumstances. We go now about a hundred yards, and that little road twelve feet wide leads to the home of William Chancellor Duncan. His sons are named Tom and George. The stable, as you see, stands nearer the road and off toward Lewis avenue. Mr. Duncan had one peculiar passion and that was to own all the blind horses in the State—he bought every blind horse offered for sale, if he could. Whether it was because they were easier to keep, or couldn't run away, or couldn't see how much corn was in the barn, I shouldn't like to say. We've come now nearly a quarter of a mile and here, just a mile and a half from the village courthouse begins the race track. That ditch on our side of the road furnished the clay to cover it and there is not enough travel over it to cut it up, so you see it is a hard level road for a mile. Here Mr. James, a Kentuckian, comes with his horses once a year. None of your shabby shuffling scrubs, but clean-limbed pure blooded racers, to carry home with him a pocket full of Sumterville tin.

Let's go back to the village, and keep an eye on the right side of the road. This house is Mrs. Baker's and her boys are named George and Bill and Abner, and they have a good time eating nuts from those two large hickory trees by the house. That is the extension of Lewis avenue and now we are at the outer edge of O. C. Hulburt's brick yard. Mr. Hulburt came from the North, where they didn't have any negroes he could bring with him, so he has to hire some of ours. He is mighty smart and smarts every hand he hires. Now that square box has four rows of long hickory pegs inside; the shaft turning in the center has four lines of pegs, so arranged that as it turns around, the pegs lap and must pass between each other to grind the clay. That negro boy throwing the clay in the box is named Isaac and belongs to Mrs. Lansdell. As the horse goes round and turns the shaft, you see the ground clay pushing out of that little hole at the bottom, and banking itself on the little platform. That little man with the muddy clothes you see moving with the regularity of clock-work, taking the ground clay with his hands and putting it in the moulds, striking it with a straight edge and sliding it to the man with the wheelbarrow to take it away, that's Mr. Hulburt himself. He hasn't any boys but he has the only brick house in the village to live in. They say he makes good brick and at the same time makes good money.

No more houses now until we reach Rev. Mr. [Jesse] Morgan's, just across the street from Mr. Norton's woods on the right; and as we cross the creek bridge, a small triangle is cleared and said to belong to Judge Lewis. He plants rice here every year, and you just ought to see the red wing rice birds that come in, and have to be shot by the village boys. All woods now to Mr. Morgan's. Go right through the house, a single story with four rooms and a piazza in front. The biggest boy is named Henry, next Alonzo, then Eddie, and that bright-eyed girl is Caroline; but we'll go on down to the tanyard. This little branch drains the water from near the Baptist church graveyard. This pool over which

Sumterville (1800-1855) 103

this boardway lies, you see, is full of hides with the hair taken off and those two round loglike benches, with one end higher than the other, is where Mr. Morgan pulls out his hides and with a currying knife rubs off all the flesh spots and other things to make them even and smooth. Just up on the hill in front of us, stands Mr. Morgan's leather house, where he worked, cut out shoes, and told yarns to the little boys who came to see him. This little foot path leads up to his shoe shop, where old Archie is pegging away making common, coarse, cow belly shoes, and singing as he pegs:

>Cornwallis muster ole and young,
>Hosstief and nigger-traders.
>Huzzah, huzzah my jolly brave boys,
>Lord Wallace in the morning
>Rit me rue de dol da dit
>Rit me rue de dol.

But here on our right is Mr. Morgan's bark mill, where he grinds red-oak bark to put in these vats on the left, with the hides after cleaning them in the pool behind us. And here under this cottonwood tree is his lime vat, where he puts the hides to loosen the hair so he can curry it off. Brother William put his bird dog, Bob, in here to cure him of the mange, he did and it did. Let's go on by the shoe shop now so you can hear Archie sing, and as there is no house between Mr. Morgan's and Jim Flowers', we can go straight out to the road.

Now this is Jim Flowers' home, and just across the street stands Tom Flowers' carriage shop, where he trims and paints, as I told you. Here is the house where Bowen Clarkson lives. He is a lively black-haired boy, but I know nothing about his people.

We cross this little indistinct road, and go about sixty yards, and we stand in front of the Baptist Church. They say that little old building, with doors on each side and in front, its staircase leading up to the gallery where fifty negroes could be seated, its twenty-odd pews on the lower floor where one hundred of the white villagers could sit and worship while Dr. [Roberts] preached, is the first house of worship Sumterville ever had, built by Anderson Spears, carpenter, in 1818-20, dedicated (in 1820), and now more than thirty years old. That last pew in the northeast corner is the one occupied by William Mitchell Lansdell and his bride, Emilie Brumby, soon after it was built. And here in this open space where all the seats come, aisles cross, Major Billy Haynsworth and Miss Maria Morse were united in the holy bands of matrimony Nov. 16, 1823.

That house on the corner of Liberty and Broad [Harvin], with steps running down both ways from the piazza in front, and a semicircular hole through the brick work, is the home of Montgomery Moses. Lawyer Moses' wife is named Catherine Esther and their boys are named Myre, Minie, Frank, Claremont and Altamont. Altamont is a little bits of a boy like me.

This store on the corner across the street belongs to Mrs. O'Brian, she owns the next store also. She is a very fat lady of 200 lbs., or more, about 4 ft. 6 in. high and has two daughters, Catherine and Johannah. Her brother Ned and John Kinney work at carpenter. The next building after Mrs. O'Brian's is a little 16' by 20' single story store sometime without occupants. And then nearly half way to Main Street stands the two-story building some eight or ten feet from the line of the street. Here Abram and Ransom, two negro carpenters are making doors under the direction of their master, Bill Hoyt. About twenty feet from the Hoyt building is another little 20'x30' store without an occupant. Two feet from this begins a rough large store, and you see the sign extending across the pavement reads "P Bligh's Cheap Variety Store." Pat Bligh, his mother, sister Bridget and John Bligh do business within. The next, another little 16' x 20' shop is occupied by Mrs. McGhee, quite an old lady, and now we reach the storeroom of L. B. Hanks, whose store fronts on Main street. This building has an old appearance even now, and may have been used as a residence by some one in the past. The piazza, running the whole length of the building comes out to the street and the house is about three feet from the ground. That mulatto boy in there is named Dave. Fifteen or twenty feet from this and fronting on the street we have a store about 25' x 40' in which Washington Black is merchandising. Between it and the corner house there is an old well.

And now this last building fronts on Main street, and while I can't tell you who is doing business in it, you see it is just a plain old wooden store. We are at Cross Street and I must rest before we go south on Main Street.

That large wooden building on the south-west corner of Main and Liberty holds the merchandise of Mr. James Barrett. He, as you see, is of a literary turn of mind, and though he is nearsighted and wears glasses, whenever you meet him he is reading some select work. Whenever he is out, his wife, with a big motherly heart, waits on the customers.

And now comes Freeman Hoyt's jewelry store, about twenty feet in front on Main and forty feet deep. Mr. Hoyt is a northern man and they say he is an excellent hand with a watch. Next is a building of like size and occupied by John Thompson as a drug store, another northern man, a good druggist, low in stature, shrewd in business and without kith or kin in the village. The store we are now coming to is owned and the business is conducted by

Mr. C. T. Mason. He repairs anything and everything in the line of watches, jewelry, clocks—a workman of fine ability and pleasing address. If he can't fix your watch throw it in the bushes; and if he can't sell you a new one, go home, for nobody else can.

That little store there, 18' x 20', three feet off the ground is the milinery shop of Annette Hulburt. She is the wife of O. C. Hulburt, whom we saw over the creek making brick. While he makes the brick, she makes the hats; that is no evidence that either has a brick in his or her hat; for she is a most lovable woman, helping to trim the sails of her neighbors so that they may drift into seas of peace and prosperity. This next store, fifty yards this side of the home of John F. Haynsworth, is one of those little stores sometimes with and sometimes without a keeper and I do not know to whom it belongs. This two-story house here fronting on Dugan street and about thirty feet from the street with the end even on the line of Main street

Here ends unfinished, Joel Brunson's story of the Sumterville he knew in 1850.

In 1852 the railroad entered Sumterville, and so stimulated the boom, that a lady who made a visit there "was so struck with the size and imposing aspect of our Churches, Hotels and numerous Stores" she thought she had "missed her road and had got into Camden."[23]

But despite the growth of the village, domestic animals still continued to roam the streets at will, although an ordinance in 1850 had prohibited this. An indignant letter in the *Banner*, signed "A Sufferer," said:

> I have been a serious sufferer from the hog-law, it having cost me a pretty gang of hogs, which I preferred to send off to the country to a friend rather than keep them here as the cause of constant annoyance. . . . But I cannot do without cows nor can they be kept out of the street, . . . so that I have before me the pleasant anticipation of constant annoyance and constant extortion. And for what?[24]

Another who signed himself "Forecast" declared that a stranger might think the geography of Sumterville was like that of "Auld Ireland," which he described in this catechism:

[23] *Black River Watchman,* May 13, 1853.
[24] *Banner,* June 18, 1851.

What is the nature of the soil? Bogs.
What is the nature of the climate? Fogs.
What is the chief animal? Dogs.
What is the principal production? Frogs.
What is the chief article of food? Hogs.
What is the chief drink? Grogs.
What are the chief import? Logs.

So annoyed was "Forecast" by the dogs, that he thought the town fathers should purchase strychnine and order its use. "But," he continued, "there lie the Hogs . . .[and] every citizen [is] liable to ride on a Hog an indefinite distance because the Town Fathers neither light the Streets nor compel the hogs to keep indoors." He found it an intolerable nuisance when hurrying home to bed, to be pitched headlong into a bed of pigs in the middle of the pavement! And on Main Street near Mr. Hulbert's, the hogs had two or three times rooted down the pavement.[25]

Nevertheless, the little town was being beautified. When "Scribbler" passed through in 1853, after noting the wide streets lined with oaks, he wrote: "A taste for flowers obtains among the residents," and he declared that in a few years Sumterville would well deserve the appellation of the 'Town of Roses'."[26]

The erection of so many wooden buildings during the Sumterville boom of 1845-48, had brought a realization of the need for fire protection. An editorial in *The Banner* pointed out that a fire would probably destroy a fourth of the village; and urged "Let not our village smoulder in ashes as soon as it has awoke to enterprise," especially when a well for a water supply could be dug and bricked for a small amount, and an engine and hose could be procured for $1,000.

But the villagers were not yet ready to tax themselves for such a purpose, and nothing seems to have been done until after a tragic night in May 1855, when a kitchen in the jail yard caught fire and burned to death a slave woman, Sophy, and her three children—the property of Dr. James L. Haynsworth. The town guard arrived in time to hear the screams

---
[25] *Watchman*, March 17, 1854.
[26] *Watchman*, Sept. 30, 1853.

of the victims, but without engine, ladders or buckets, could give no aid. All that saved the village from destruction that night was the providential fact that there was no wind. The tragedy, however, accomplished what editorials had failed to do, and the villagers awoke to their danger. An order was placed in Newark for a thirdclass, piano-style, 7-inch-cylinder fire engine, to be built by J. & L. Allen. The ladies of Sumterville were appealed to, to help raise funds to pay for it, and in response, "A Lady" in a letter to the *Watchman* offered the practical suggestion that Town Council might confiscate and sell at public auction the cows and hogs running at large in the streets.[27]

At the fall session of the legislature that year, Representative James D. Blanding presented the petition of the Sumter Fire Engine Company for incorporation; and in the spring of 1856, when the engine had been delivered, the company paraded in full uniform, and then took a vote on whether to accept the engine.[28]

State Senator Franklin I. Moses at the same session of 1855, introduced a bill to extend the expiring town charter and to change the name of Sumterville to Sumter, which was duly enacted into law.[29]

[27] *Banner*, Jan. 12, 1848; *Watchman*, May 11, Oct. 10, 1855.
[28] *Stat.* XII, 385; *Watchman*, Dec. 5, 1855; March 12, 1856.
[29] *Watchman*, Dec. 5, 1855; *Stat.* XII, 406.

CHAPTER VIII

COTTON, WESTERN MIGRATION AND
EARLY FACTORIES

Cotton for home use on the spinning-wheel and hand-loom probably was raised in Sumter County from the beginning, but if so, the quantity was small, for each seed had to be pulled from the fibre by hand. As early as 1768 the people of the neighboring St. David's Parish had found that cotton, as well as hemp and flax, could be raised there, and that from a pound of cotton might be made twelve yards of cloth. In the High Hills of Santee the black-seed, long staple variety of cotton, usually called sea island, was cultivated as a garden plant for its blossoms.

The Revolutionary War, by cutting off the importation of cloth, is said to have stimulated the growing of cotton for domestic manufacture, and by 1790 "home spun" cloth was in general use throughout South Carolina. Usually the cotton yarn was spun at home and then sent to a local weaver to be made into cloth. In 1789, John Macnair, in association with others, built a cotton factory near Stateburg on the plantation of Benjamin Waring. Macnair was probably the "gentleman of great mechanical knowledge and instructed in most branches of cotton manufactures in Europe" who was referred to in 1790 as having already "fixed and completed a mill now at work in the high hills of the Santee (river) near Stateburg." This cotton mill was run by water power; and besides carding and spinning machines, with 84 spindles, it had "several other useful implements for manufacturing every necessary article in cotton." Its "corduroys and other Manchester cotton stuffs" were said to have been excellent. For a time the enterprise promised to be a great success, but a "want of public patronage" and the high cost of labor, made it too costly to compete with the low-priced English goods. Benjamin Waring died unmarried in 1791, and the machinery of his factory is said to have been sold in Lincolnton, North Carolina.[1]

Mary Murrell, who in later years remembered the beginning of the commercial planting of black-seed cotton in the High Hills, said that at General Sumter's home, the Negro children would be assembled during the long winter evenings, and set to the task of removing the seed, which did not adhere to the fibre as firmly as did the green seed of the short-staple variety. In the midst of the children would be Mrs. Sumter, "picking more than any two of them, though one of her hands was crippled and almost useless. The pickaninnies too small to be trusted with the precious staple carried round the gourds that received the seed."

The problem of finding a quicker method of removing the seed was studied by many. In 1788 Captain John Hart had petitioned the legislature of South Carolina for a patent on a machine of his own invention for ginning cotton. In the spring of 1794 Eli Whitney patented his cotton gin, a crude affair with wire teeth set in a wooden cylinder. The next year Captain James Kincaid set up the first saw gin in South Carolina in his grist mill on Mill Creek in Fairfield County. A year later, cotton was being planted in the High Hills for commercial use, although probably no gins were there as yet. William Murrell, a merchant of Stateburg at that time, wrote in 1796 that his neighbors were planting some cotton to test the market and in 1797 he sent some samples of saw-ginned cotton to Charleston and to England. John Mayrant has been credited with having planted the following year the first real cotton crop in Sumter District.

With the general use of the gin, came the knowledge that green-seed cotton was more profitable in the uplands than black-seed cotton. At last a staple money-crop had been found that could be grown in practically all parts of the South.

The old staples, rice and indigo, had required large outlays of capital, and great plantations with slave gangs for the laborious work. Cotton, however, was a poor man's crop, and

[1] John Drayton, *A View of South Carolina* . . . (Charleston 1802), p. 139; Henry Lesesne, citing *The American Museum*, VIII, appendix IV, in *Sumter Daily Item*, March 14, 1947; SCHGM XXIV (1923), 91.

could be raised by white families that did not own even a single slave. But the profits of the crop in its early years, stirred ambitions in even the poorest farmers to buy more land and to acquire slaves. Mechanics, too, invested their earnings in land, and began to plant cotton. Soon the farms grew into plantations, and the Southern sentiment for freeing the slaves, which had become evident after the Revolution, gave way to an ardent belief in the righteousness of slavery. The plantation system spread into every part of South Carolina and to every state in the South.

The enormous profits of the first years of the new staple soon stimulated over-production, and by 1806 the price of cotton had fallen from the 44 cents of 1799 to only 20 cents a pound. The news of the declaration of war on Great Britain in 1812 caused the price to fall from 9½ cents to 4½ cents. Besides the problem of falling prices, the cotton planters faced the worse problem of exhausted lands, for at that time few men understood the value of fertilizer, and cultivation with a steel plow was believed to poison the land. Great as was the labor of clearing new fields, many planters had found it the only way to maintain a profitable yield. Eventually, of course, the limit of what might be cleared was reached, and then the alternative was to join the great migration which was moving to the inexhaustibly rich lands of the new southwestern territories.

The people of Sumter District saw endless caravans of the pioneers moving down the old Charleston road along the Wateree to the ferries and heading for Alabama, Mississippi, Louisiana, and other new territories of the southwest. Most of the emigrants crossed the river at Camden; others, at Brisbane's ferry, later called Garner's; some others went on down to Wright's Bluff. In 1810, Mrs. Thomas Sumter, Jr., in one of her letters refers to the great migration of people in the Stateburg neighborhood who had gone to Mississippi Territory.

Many of these Sumter emigrants had left in November 1809 under the leadership of John Gaulden Richardson, who, born on February 28, 1785, was the son of Francis and Martha (Gaulden) Richardson, and had grown up in the

Richardson homestead near Stateburg. When the price of cotton fell and the crop became less profitable on the worn and unfertilized lands, a meeting of neighboring planters was called to consider the question of going to the rich new lands of Mississippi. After much discussion, it was finally agreed that young John Gaulden Richardson should go ahead as a pioneer and remain for a year, during which he should make a crop of corn and cotton, and then return home with a report on the venture.

Accompanied by two stalwart Negro servants, Caesar and Pina, who drove a covered wagon loaded with necessities, Richardson rode horseback across Georgia and Alabama to the settlement now called Woodville in the southwestern corner of Mississippi Territory. Arriving in January 1809, he acquired 160 acres of land covered with a canebrake, which he and the Negroes cut down, burned off, and planted. In the fall he sold his crops at a good profit, and returned to his father's home in Sumter District with such a glowing report of success that most of the Richardson community decided to migrate with all their Negroes, livestock and moveable possessions. No time could be lost, even though winter was at hand, for the new lands must be made ready to produce crops the first year.

The business of first importance for John Gaulden Richardson was a quiet marriage to his sweetheart, Margaret DuBose of Camden, whom he took to his father's house for a busy honeymoon of two weeks, while preparations for the journey were being hurried through. On the last Monday in November 1809, "family after family fell into line, each with wagon, teams and equipment. Negro boys generally rode mules, while the women and children were stowed away in the wagons. A long line of family carriages followed in the rear and completed this army of emigrants numbering over a thousand grown persons besides children." Couriers were sent a day's journey ahead "to select camping grounds, arrange ferriage, inspect bridges, and detect as far as possible any lurking danger" from Indians or other perils. Leading the great caravan was John Gaulden Richardson with his young bride.[2]

---

[2] *Memoirs of Francis D. Richardson* . . . (Friars Point, Miss., 1930).

The land records of Sumter show that many others besides the Richardsons joined the great movement of population to the southwest. William Bracey had already settled in Laurence County, Mississippi, in the fall of 1820, when he sold his Sumter lands near Manchester to Robert H. Brumby. Some of the Brumby family lie buried in the plantation cemetery near Wedgefield, but modern generations of the family are citizens of Georgia, Florida, Texas, Mississippi, California, and perhaps other states.

A deed of 1823 shows the wide scattering of a single family that migrated from Sumter District, all of them members of the Conyers family. Mary, formerly the widow of Daniel Conyers, with her new husband Michael Freeman, went to Kentucky. Leah, a daughter of Daniel Conyers, with her husband Alexander Dobbin, settled in Alabama. Sarah, another daughter of Daniel Conyers, went with her husband John M. Frierson to make their new home in Tennessee.

Among those who went very early from Sumter District to Alabama, were Daniel Loring of Massachusetts, and his young wife Rebecca, of Stateburg. According to the family story, the young Lorings left their little son Lucius with her parents, Jeremiah and Valentine Pitts, until they could get settled in their new home. When the Lorings were ready for their child to come, the grandparents made ready to take him. With a wagon for their baggage, and a riding horse for emergencies, Jeremiah and Valentine Pitts set forth on the long journey in their riding chair, which had been newly painted for the trip. But when on their way through Georgia, Valentine was seized with a violent illness, and suddenly died. The cause of her death was supposed to have been "painter's colic," a poisoning from the new paint on the riding chair. The shocked and grief-stricken husband immediately gave up the trip and turned back home. Later, Daniel Loring died, and his widow Rebecca married a Lane. After Lane's death, she married for the third time, Lemuel B. Davis. Her son, Lucius P. Loring, grew up as a citizen of Sumter, where some of his descendants still reside.

During these restless years, Samuel Maverick, a Charleston merchant, in the winter of 1816 bought a lot in Stateburg next to Stephen D. Miller's, at the intersection of the old Garner's Ferry and Charleston roads. Eventually, Maverick took his family to the red clay hills of Anderson County, and his son, Samuel Augustus Maverick, a lawyer, in 1835 settled in Texas. There young Maverick received three hundred cows in payment of a debt, and, as he could not sell them, he turned them over to his Negroes to be looked after. As the Negroes were not trained cowboys, the calves strayed away without being branded. Ranchers began to speak of unmarked cattle as Maverick's, and eventually the name came to be applied to such cattle throughout the West. Writing his son in Texas in 1841, old Samuel Maverick said:

> I wish you were all here with me in this poor country and healthy climate. You must not do as my father done to stay in a feverish place Charleston, James Island &c, and bury 10 children, and as I have done in the same place. . . . I staid untill I was bailed up in flannels to keep Soul and body together and had turned yellow with the climate. . . . Of what use is all the lands in Texas or the figures on a Bank book to a dead man. I lost a great estate by leaving of Charleston, but I gained a hundred times as much by saving my children and my own life. Praises be to God that I had sence enough to leave it we have here all that is necessary and useful in the world, and good health in the bargain.[3]

During the great migration of the 1830's, a distinguished citizen to leave Stateburg was ex-Governor Stephen D. Miller, who settled in Mississippi as a cotton planter. Among the many others who went from Sumter District were Dr. Robert Lowry and Isaac R. Harris, who filed an agreement that they would go to western Tennessee, traveling together and sharing expenses; and, as the doctor was unskilled in planting, that Harris would oversee their combined agricultural forces.

John Croswell, desiring to remove to the West, advertised for sale his farm three miles from Bishopville, with a new framed dwelling and outhouses, a ginhouse, and a fine well of water. James Coulter, whose wife Susannah refused to

[3] U. B. Phillips, *Life and Labor in the Old South* (Boston, 1930), p. 105.

accompany him to the western country, advertised a caution to the public against extending to her any credit. John F. Chester gave public notice of his going West, and placed his notes and books of account in the hands of William Haynsworth for settlement.

Agur T. Morse, innkeeper, and his wife Grace, sold their tavern in Sumterville to Archibald Ruffin and went to Montgomery, Alabama. Later, Morse settled in Mississippi, where he, his father Josiah, and his mother Nancy, eventually died and were buried.

Camden in 1834 reported as many as eight hundred persons passing through in a single week, three hundred of whom were in a single party, many being South Carolinians. They rode on horseback, in carryalls and in riding chairs, carts, and covered wagons, piled high with everything from household articles, poultry and pets, to old folks and babies. Trudging along in the dust and mud of the abominable roads were long lines of Negroes, and lowing cattle with tinkling bells. In time of freshet, the caravans camped at the ferries and waited until the floods subsided. The drain on South Carolina's population was so great in the decade from 1830 to 1840, that there was no increase in population.

Many emigrants failed to find success in their new homes, and a tragic note was sounded in the case of Joseph F. Rhame, who in December 1836 left his family near Bradford Springs to seek his fortune. An advertisement on February 17, 1838, stated that the last letter received from him had been written from New Orleans on New Year's Day 1837, when he was about to embark on a warship for Texas; and pathetically added that Ellen S. Rhame, at Reynold's Store, would be thankful for news of him. Obituaries in the Sumterville newspapers chronicled the fate of others who had gone.

During the 1840's and 1850's the migration continued. In March 1848 Thomas E. Dickey offered for sale his plantation in the fork of Black River, 3,100 acres with 900 acres under fence, his own dwelling of eight upright rooms each with fireplace; and, besides the usual outbuilding, a log house with piazza and shedrooms, where his son James lived. William G. O'Cain, "being anxious to move Westward," offered his summer residence of 350 acres near the head of Rafting Creek. Dr. J. I. Miller, druggist for many years "at the Sign of the Golden Mortar" in Sumterville, joined the western tide, leaving on sale his valuable collection of "Good Books," some of which "could be found in no book store in the country." J. Sinkler Moore advertised his Bells Mill plantation (now owned by Tuomey Hospital), 3327 acres ideally located on the Wilmington and Manchester railroad, with 800 acres under cultivation, a new dwelling just completed, overseer's house, stables and barns in complete order. But in that day of free land and scarce money, plantations were not easily sold except on long-term credit, an arrangement not suited to the needs of a man about to begin life in a new country. L. T. Smith's advertisement of his 819½ level acres at the base of the High Hills, ran for at least four years.

During the gold rush to California, when 6,000 gold-seekers on the Isthmus of Panama were awaiting passage, an editorial in the Sumter *Banner* called attention to the ship "Othello," a "very fast sailer" of 370 tons, as a safe, comfortable ship which would sail from Charleston for the gold region on a six months voyage around Cape Horn. The cost was only $200 a person, if a sufficient number took passage. On December 27, 1848, the steamer "Isabel" sailed from Charleston "for the golden shores of California," taking 385 whites and 55 slaves from the mountains of North Carolina and Georgia, who were accustomed to mining operations. Several Sumter men went to California, and some journeyed thence on across the Pacific to the gold fields of Australia. George B. Morse, a brother of Agur T. Morse, is said to have prospered in that far away continent, and young Leonard White also went there, never to return.

Although so many of the adventurous-minded sought their fortunes in the West, many others were firmly rooted in Sumter District. Intendant Thomas Jefferson Coghlan of Sumterville and his partner G. C. Jones, believed in putting their money into home enterprises, and when they were advertising to build new houses in and around the town, they expressed a determination "to wipe off the reproach attached to the noble old South Carolina—and arouse her from her Rip

Van Winkle slumbers, and leave California to take care of herself."

Coghlan and Jones were probably wise, for a Sumter emigrant, signing himself "W. W. W.", wrote from the mines on the Yuber River that he was making ten or twelve dollars a day, but he had never worked so hard in his life; that flour was $60 a barrel, and pork $1 a pound, with the prices of everything else in proportion; and that he expected to return home in a year. Perhaps he was the man who did return from California in 1852, with "six thousand dollars worth of —experience, and two cents in money."

During the years, as the price of cotton rose and fell from time to time, several enterprising men attempted to introduce manufacturing as an alternative to emigration. The same year that Macnair built the cotton factory on Benjamin Waring's plantation, a nail and hoe-making shop was started near Stateburg.

A much more ambitious project was undertaken in 1815 by Congressman William Mayrant of Stateburg, who left Washington that year for New York to purchase machinery for his cotton factory on "Mine Hill," which later became the property of H. W. McLauren. The machinery had to be shipped by water to Charleston, and transported thence by the Santee Canal and the river to Rafting Creek landing near Stateburg. Although Mayrant's business transactions, as he confided to his wife, had been with "commercial rascals whose only object was selfish gain," he arranged to bring with his machinery a Mr. Wardle as general director of the factory, and two men, McKnight and Holaday, to manage the two "mules" of 180 spindles each, and to do the "switching." Waring believed that his own Negroes could be taught to "attend the throstles." Once in operation, Waring expected the factory to net him $500 a week.

His hopes were not realized, however, and he sold his machinery to the Rev. Thomas Hutchings and John M. Courcier, on May 2, 1821, for $8,251, taking a mortgage on the 307 acres of land where the new mill was to be established in Greenville County.[4]

[4] *S. C. Historical Magazine*, LIII (Jan. 1953), 1.

In 1816, John W. Rees bought lands on Hatchet Creek from James Mellette, apparently for some sort of manufacturing project, but after making a number of improvements on the property, he agreed to let Mellette take "possession of said factory" on payment of $1800 for the improvements.

About the same time, William and Christopher McConnico, who had migrated to Mississippi Territory, sold their lands in Sumter District to Jeptha Dyson, a young surveyor from Abbeville District, who married Martha, daughter of Colonel Laurence Manning, and became a planter. Some years later, in the 1840's, Jeptha Dyson built a large cotton factory near Fulton, only a few miles from the present town of Pinewood.

In 1848 the brick building of the factory was destroyed by fire at a loss of $30,000, and "many poor workers" were thrown out of employment. The Bank of the State of South Carolina held a mortgage on the property, and immediately offered it for sale, with a plantation of 800 acres and 40 select Negroes, some of whom had worked in the factory. Presumably the sale was not made, for Dyson the next month was making bricks to rebuild his factory. Two months later he received a patent for an important invention to clean the teeth of the main card cylinder as it revolved. Formerly, these teeth had clogged, and four times a day the machinery had to be stopped for fifteen minutes while they were being cleaned.

Dyson never completed the rebuilding of his factory, for on Christmas Day 1850, the *Sumter Banner* carried a notice that he was offering the factory for sale, with the new building as nearly fireproof as any in the South, almost ready for machinery to use 3,000 spindles, consuming from 1500 to 2000 bales of cotton a year. The machinery was evidently to be run by water power, for the property was fully equipped with dams and raceways with waterwheels, which required but slight repairs, and had a water supply that was unfailing even in the driest seasons.

Perhaps it was family tragedy that caused Dyson to sell his factory. His son Richard Manning Dyson, who had graduated from the South Carolina College in 1844, and was practicing law in Sumterville, had had an unfortunate difficulty the preceding spring with C. D. Gayle in the latter's home in Clarendon, and had killed him. The published account of the affair stated that "We are credibly informed by one who witnessed the act, that Mr. Dyson acted strictly on the defensive."

Nevertheless, young Dyson was arraigned for murder. Tried at the fall term of court in Sumterville, he was found guilty of man-slaughter with a recommendation to "the Clemency of the Court." No doubt the trial was a costly affair for the young man's family, and coming so soon after the ruinous fire of 1848 and the rebuilding which ensued, little wonder that Jeptha Dyson had to put his factory on the market.

Tradition affirms that another result came from the trial of Richard Manning Dyson, namely, that his influential family connections at once began a movement for the separation of Clarendon from Sumter District, and its erection into a separate judicial district. This was successfully accomplished in 1855.

Jeptha Dyson survived until June 13, 1881, when, at the age of ninety-three years, he died in Columbia and was buried in Trinity churchyard, in a grave "previously occupied by Gen. Winder." His obituary stated that although Dyson had formerly been affluent, he died "indigent", the patent for his great invention that so improved the manufacture of cotton having been infringed upon in England, he lost its benefits.[5]

In 1850, the same year that Dyson placed his Fulton factory on the market, an unsuccessful effort was launched in Sumterville to charter a cotton factory. At that time there were only sixteen cotton factories in South Carolina. Capitalized at $1,000,000, they employed 1600 operatives, and consumed 15,000 bales of cotton a year.

[5] Sumter deeds, E, p. 165; F, pp. 533, 587; *Banner*, Nov. 15, Dec. 27, 1848; Dec. 25, 1850; *True Southron*, June 14, 1881.

Chapter IX
ROADS, FERRIES, TAVERNS AND THE MAIL

The oldest road in Sumter District, as has been said, developed from the ancient Catawba path east of the Wateree, and became a public road in 1753. Throughout colonial times it was shown on plats and referred to in the records as the "Broad Road", and the "Great Road", or the Charleston Road. In recent years it has been called the King's Highway.

Much travel flowed over this road, for it was the artery between Camden and Charleston, and linked those towns with the northern colonies. Before the Revolution, the settlers in St. Mark's Parish traded over this road with the Moravians of North Carolina, receiving from them flour, earthen ware, peach brandy, whiskey, iron tools, copper utensils, and woodenware. During the Revolution, British and American armies marched over it. In April 1793, Citizen Genet, minister from revolutionary France, having landed at Charleston, traveled over it enroute to the national capital at Philadelphia, and spent the night at Stateburg, where, as he was entering his carriage next morning, a group of the citizens presented him with "a short though warm testimony of American esteem."

Over this road, too, moved painfully great trains of fifteen or twenty loaded wagons carrying two or three tons each on narrow wheels that cut deep into the road bed, drawn by teams of straining, emaciated horses. In 1812, Robert W. Andrews of Stateburg, then a lad in his teens, substituted for an ill teamster, and drove a load of New England shoes, cheap jewelry, and carding tools to Charleston, where the wagon was loaded with cotton and furs for the return trip to Boston.[1]

The Catawba Indians continued to use this road during the ante-bellum era when on their journeys to Charleston,

[1] *The Life and Adventures of Capt. Robert W. Andrews, of Sumter, South Carolina.* (Boston, 1887) pp. 9, 10.

camping by the roadside, and selling their clay pots and pans to plantations along the way.

The most prosperous plantations of Sumter District lay on both sides of this road. In 1830 Mrs. Anne Royall travelled over it by stage coach to Camden, leaving us her delightful description of Colonel Richard Singleton's Home plantation, with its roadside rose hedges, which she passed through near Manchester. It was over this road, too, that Robert W. Andrews walked the 103 miles from Charleston to Stateburg in thirty-two hours of walking time, leaving Charleston at ten o'clock in the morning, and arriving home at six o'clock on the afternoon of the following day.[2]

The next oldest road in Sumter District was laid out in 1762 along the north side of Black River and down to Murray's Ferry on the Santee, in response to a petition of 1758 from the then newly settled communities between Black River and Lynches Creek.[3] Over this road too, in later years, rumbled heavy wagons in the Charleston trade, for until the railroad era, practically all the commerce of Sumter District was with Charleston.

William Elias Mills, born near Salem Black River in 1816, recalled that as a boy of twelve years, he was sent on several wagon trips to Charleston with Daddy Ben, a trusted teamster. "The trip would often take four weeks, sometimes much longer, if the Santee River was in flood, or if the swamp there was muddy." Often they would pry the great wagon out of one mud-hole only to have it fall into another, and in the course of a day so little progress would be made, that at nightfall they would return to the camp of the previous evening for live coals to start their campfire, there being no matches in those days. "Wagons were camped for weeks sometimes at the Staggers place below Greelyville on the Murray's Ferry Road, waiting their turn" to cross the ferry in flood time. They were usually drawn by four horses, and the teamsters were skilful, one especially, who would set four short pins in the ground at an incline, then start his horses

---

[2] Andrews, *Life*, p. 12.
[3] *Stat.*, IX, 200; *SCHGM*, XXVI, 122.

ROADS, FERRIES, TAVERNS AND THE MAIL

at a trot, and drive all the pins into the ground, two with the front wheels, and two with the hind wheels.[4]

The map of 1770 by Tacitus Gaillard and James Cook shows this Black River road and the Great Road as the only two in the future Sumter District. Finley's map of 1827 shows a third north and south road through the center of the District, passing north from Nelson's Ferry through Jamesville and Sumterville, and dividing at Scape Hore crossing, to reach Camden and Darlington.

Many new public roads came into being during the ensuing years, notably with the establishment of each new ferry over the several rivers. On the Santee River, Nelson's ferry, the oldest, was begun privately by James Beard, became a public ferry in 1756, and before 1762 was vested in Jared Neilson. Wright's ferry was made a public crossing in 1766. When General Sumter's home was in what is now Clarendon County, he operated a ferry between Gaillard's ferry and Nelson's ferry. In later years, he seems to have had an interest in a ferry at Sumter's Landing on the Wateree.

The most important ferry on the Wateree, however, to the people of Sumter District, was Brisbane's ferry, which linked them as well as the people of the eastern districts with the new capital at Columbia, only forty-five miles from Sumterville. The road to this ferry had developed from a branch of the old Catawba path, which led to the Congarees from the High Hills. The crossing over the Wateree became known as Simmons' ferry, but in 1783 received its new name when it was vested in Adam Fowler Brisbane and the heirs of Wood Furman. Colonel Brisbane had been born in Charleston in in 1754, married in Georgia on the eve of the Revolution, and located in Camden during the war. In 1781 he had purchased six tracts, totalling nearly a thousand acres, in the High Hills and Wateree Swamp. Later he acquired title to the lands on both sides of his ferry and made his home in Richland District, where he died in the summer of 1799.[5]

The early taverns of Sumter District, as elsewhere, were located usually at the ferries or cross roads. The first of

---

[4] MS on Mills family, by Professor W. H. Mills, in possession of Miss Margaret Brunson.
[5] For ferries, see index, *Stat.*, IX; for Brisbane, *SCHGM*, XIV, 187, 188.

several grants to the elder Sherwood James, "tavern keeper", who came to the High Hills in 1753, was on both sides of the old Catawba path, south of Howard's and Freeman's settlements and near the head of Beech creek. There James' High Hill tavern became a landmark. When Sherwood James made his will in 1763, among other legacies to his children, he bequeathed his land and buildings in the High Hills to his son John. When John made his will in 1778 (proved in 1784), he bequeathed to his son John "the old plantation always called and known by [the name of] the high hill tavern."[6] John Stuart's map of 1780 shows that James's Tavern was "now Williams". In later years, 1785-1788, the tavern may have been the well-known Powell's Tavern of Stateburg, the center for community gatherings, from meetings of the Jockey Club to assemblies for church services.

In 1797 Ward's tavern in Stateburg is mentioned. Later, Thomas Sumter, Jr., owned a hotel there, and William Middleton Brooks operated Brooks' Inn. In the great hailstorm of March 1824, when the hailstones were from four to eleven inches in circumference, Brooks lost 175 window-panes. Brooks' Inn for a time was taken over by Robert W. Andrews. In 1832 Brooks sold it to William Sanders, and later the sheriff sold it to Alfred China, who carried on the business for many years.[7]

A distinction should be noted between two uses of the term "tavern". When Robert Mills in 1826 wrote that in taverns Sumter District "unfortunately abounds; almost every store presents one," he was referring to "groggeries" where intoxicating liquors were sold to be drunk on the premises. When he enumerated the taverns "for entertainment", he meant inns or hotels where bed and board might be obtained. Of these he says there were two in Stateburg, two in Sumterville, two at Bradford Springs, and one in Manchester.

The tavern at Manchester was from an early date a well-known stopping place for travelers. Between 1806 and 1811 it was Scott's Tavern, kept by the same man who had opened

---

[6] Will of the elder Sherwood James is recorded in Charleston; that of John James, in Sumter.

[7] *City Gazette*, Charleston, Feb. 10, 1797; Camden *Gazette*, March 13, 1817; *Southern Chronicle and Camden AEgis*, Apr. 21, 1824. Sumter conveyances, HH, p. 398; II, pp. 7, 543.

the first tavern in Sumterville. Watson's Inn in Manchester during the 1830's is mentioned by Robert W. Andrews. In 1839, by order of the court, the "tavern house of the late Mrs. Jane Compton" was sold to Thomas J. Monk.

Further south on the same road during the Revolution were once two very old taverns near Jacks Creek, Cantey's Tavern on the north side and Dennis' Tavern on the south side. Their history is unknown.

The inns of Sumterville had a complicated chain of successive proprietors. On the west side of Main Street at Liberty, adjoining the old courthouse square, stood Warner Macon's hotel. This was taken over in 1832 by James Watson, and a little later by D. B. McLaurin. In March 1836, when fire destroyed all the offices in the rear of the courthouse, only by the greatest exertions was McLaurin's hotel saved. In 1841 Alfred China took possession of the hotel, and he was succeeded by John China, who refitted and enlarged it. The spacious lot was equipped with stables for 52 horses, and was subdivided into wagon and horse lots for drovers. In 1856, however, this well-known hostelry was in custody of the sheriff for debt, and soon W. K. Bell was advertising as the new proprietor, with W. J. Norris and John M. James in charge. Apparently Bell did not prosper, and two years later the hotel was bought by Noah Graham and Son.[8]

Diagonally opposite, on the east side of Main Street at Liberty, before the year 1825, stood the Agur T. Morse tavern. When Morse migrated to Alabama, he sold the property to Archibald R. Ruffin. Two years later Ruffin sold it to Tyre J. Dinkins. During the 1840's it was Windham's Hotel, the headquarters of the drum that was beaten nightly to mark the beginning and the end of the town watchmen's patrol duty. Later a bell was rung there as a substitute for the drum-beating. In 1850 Windham's Hotel became the Sumter House, kept by Fed Meyers, and a few years later the name was changed to Meyers' Hotel.[9]

The old roadside inns and taverns were favorite lounging

---

8 *Southern Whig*, Feb. 23, 1832. Conveyances, II, pp. 26, 427, *Camden Journal*, March 28, 1836, July 21, 1841. Sumter *Banner*, Dec. 16, 1846; *Watchman*, Jan. 23, Feb. 27, 1856; Oct. 26, 1858.

9 Conveyances G, pp. 130, 147; I, pp. 47, 349, 354, 413. *Camden Journal*, Jan. 31, 1835. *Banner*, Nov. 15, 1848; March 28, 1849. *Watchman*, July 13, 1850; March 4, 1853.

places, and became lively indeed when the stage coaches arrived, bringing talkative passengers and eagerly welcomed mails from the outside world.

The letters written by settlers in colonial days were sent only when a chance opportunity offered, for the few postoffices were all at the seaports. Even in 1789, six years after the founding of Stateburg, there were only 75 postoffices in the whole United States. By the year 1800, however, when Sumter District came into existence, the number had increased to 903, and Stateburg was already a post town, getting mail by the Charleston-Camden mail service passing through. Manchester, on the same post road, also enjoyed a very early mail service; and in the summer of 1816 a postoffice was established at Fulton, eleven miles below Manchester.

Mail service for Sumterville was authorized on February 25, 1801, when John Gayle was appointed postmaster, and the postmaster-general of the United States wrote to Tyre Jennings, mail contractor at Stateburg:

> General Sumpter wishes to have a post office established at Mr. John Gale's on your route for the accommodation of the people in that neighborhood. He represents that the distance of your ride will not be increased by calling at Mr. Gale's, which will be designated Sumpterville, being in the district of that name.

In 1816, the *Camden Gazette* announced that it had established a private weekly mail route, leaving Camden every Friday morning and returning by Black River on Saturday. On the way down, places of deposit were at Swift Creek, Mrs. Diggs', Dr. Eli Howard's, Major Lyon's store, and at Mr. Wm Taylor's store in Sumterville; on the return trip, at Dr. Samuel M. Cummings' and Mr. Henry Young's. A little later the post-rider deposited his papers at Mr. Pierson's, Bradford Springs.[10]

The mail as announced in 1823, ran once a week from Charleston by Monck's Corner, Nelson's Ferry, Jamesville and Stateburg, to Camden, 120 miles, leaving Charleston at

---

[10] Official records of United States postoffice, in *The Sumter Daily Item*, Sept. 23, 1953; *Camden Gazette*, Nov. 14, 16, 1816.

8 A. M. every Wednesday and arriving in Camden at 2 P. M. on Friday. On the return, it left Camden at 4 A. M. every Sunday, arriving in Charleston at 2 P. M. on Tuesday. Ten years later the stages began a daily schedule; and Mr. Henry Haynsworth became postmaster in Sumterville, to continue in office for thirty-one years. At that time the regular mail route from Charleston to Camden had been passing through Sumterville for some three years, a service to which it was entitled under the federal law of 1825, as a courthouse town. As Mr. Haynsworth was the sole employee at the office, his hours daily, except Sunday, were from 8 A.M. to 1 P.M.; from 2:30 to 5 P.M.; and from 8:30 to 9:30 P.M.[11]

Not infrequently perils along the route caused the loss of the mail. During the winter of 1831 when the Santee was in flood, the mail stage from Camden to Charleston attempted to cross the river at Vance's ferry about sunrise. But the swift current swept the heavily-loaded flat boat against a tree, causing the flat to careen, and throwing overboard both horses, still attached to the stage, which rolled in after them. The three passengers, Mr. Waites and two Misses Waites, escaped just before the plunge, and one of the ladies was painfully though not dangerously injured. "The horses, stage and mail, were all lost."[12]

There were no registry service in the early post offices. In March 1835, M. J. Blackwell of Trenton, West Tennessee, advertised a reward of $10 for "the right hand halves" of a list of notes on the Bank of the United States, which had been mailed to him the previous May by John C. Blackwell at Jacksonville post office, Sumter District, and had never arrived.[13]

In 1801 the postage on a single-sheet letter was eight cents for forty miles or less, and increased with the distance up to twenty-five cents for five hundred miles or more. From time to time the rates were changed.

Until 1846 the amount of postage was three cents for distances up to 300 miles, and ten cents for all distances in ex-

---

[11] *Southern Chronicle*, Jan. 8, 1823. *Camden Journal*, Apr. 10, 1830; Jan. 12, Nov. 17, 1833. *Watchman*, May 1, 1850.
[12] Camden *Journal*, Feb. 19, 1831.
[13] *Camden Journal and Southern Whig*, March 14, 1835.

cess. Postage was not required to be prepaid, and four times a year each postmaster published the lists of letters uncalled for at his office. The next year adhesive stamps were authorized, but not required. In 1855 prepayment of postage was required, and the next year the prepayment by stamps became compulsory.

The Sumterville post office at different times was located in various stores, and in 1849 it was removed from the store of A. White to that of A. J. and P. Moses.

The daily trains of the Camden Branch were by this time having an effect upon the mail service, and Captain P. M. Butler, the mail contractor, who in 1847 had opened his Darlington and Gadsden line of stages, as well as a two-horse hack service between Sumterville and Darlington, began to advertise that his stage would leave Sumterville daily at 3 A.M. for Claremont Depot, returning in the afternoon upon the arrival of the cars from the junction. This meant that his passengers had to leave their beds soon after midnight, and travel over the heavy roads at a snail's pace for four hours, waiting at Stateburg from one to two hours while the postmaster opened and closed the mail. A Sumterville merchant, who was a constant traveller, wrote an open letter suggesting that Captain Butler's schedule might be improved, and some hours saved, by driving the stage directly to Middleton, while a boy and a horse took care of the Stateburg mail. This was so well received that a meeting of the citizens was called to consider the schedule. Even the stage horses seem to have felt that matters could be bettered, and one day while their driver and the one passenger were waiting by the fire at the Stateburg post office, the intelligent animals "quietly trotted off on their journey. Thus without a driver they travelled until they reached the Rail Road Depot, more than 2 miles, when they halled up to deliver the mail, after having passed harmless, a gate and several wagons which were in the yard."[14]

But the stage horses were not always so efficient. During the time that the Wateree trestle was being re-built after its collapse in 1850, the South Carolina Railroad arranged with Captain Butler to carry the mail daily in four-horse coaches

[14] *Banner*, Nov. 3, 1847; July 18, Nov. 7, 1849; Jan. 23, 30, 1850.

from Sumterville across the Wateree to Gadsden. One day on the return trip, when the stage was descending the long hill to the river, the horses became frightened and overturned the coach, injuring the driver, Lewis D. Hope, severely in the leg. Nevertheless, he took the stage on to Stateburg, but the leg became infected, and he died. A native of Germany, Hope had been a member of the Sumter Brass Band.[15]

At this time, 1850, Sumter District had twenty post offices: Sumterville, Bishopville, Bradford Institute, Bradleyville, Brewington, Clarendon, Friendship, Fulton, Lodibar, Manchester, Mechanicsville, Mill Grove, Mount Clio, Plowden's Mills, Privateer, Providence, Salem, Stateburg, Willow Grove, Wright's Bluff.[16]

Moreover, in the autumn of that year, a new mail route was authorized between Sumterville and Wilmington, which would mean that the northern mails could reach Sumter District much sooner than by the old route from Charleston. The plan was amended in 1851 to extend the line to Manchester, by a tri-weekly line of stages; but the Postmaster General estimated that it would operate at a deficit of $4,412, superceding a service that cost only $1,230 a year, so the line was not put into operation. Bitter was the editorial cry of the *Banner*: "While Congress is annually squandering millions on objects useless, and often detrimental to the public interests, the Post Master General objects to hazarding four thousand dollars, though a large portion of the country is thereby left almost without communication." The next year, however, when the Wilmington and Manchester Railroad was running as far as Mayesville, a daily line of stages began carrying United States mail through Darlington and Cheraw to Fayetteville, where it made railroad connection with Wilmington and the northern states.[17]

The railroads had not yet conquered the rivers, however, and when the floods came down, the mails had to wait. In September 1852, the editor of the *Watchman* lamented going to press without having seen a northern or southern mail in a week; and that, in a day of no telegraph, telephone, or radio, must have meant no news!

---

15 *Watchman*, Nov. 2, 1850.
16 *Ibid.*, Apr. 27, 1850.
17 *Ibid.*, Apr. 17, 1852.

Chapter X
WAR OF 1812

During the early decades after the American Revolution, the great struggle between Napoleon and Great Britain was keenly felt in the seaboard cities of the United States, whose foreign trade suffered heavy losses. President Jefferson tried to deal with the problem by an embargo which forbade American vessels to leave port. But this was unpopular and hurt American pride. The younger statesmen then in Congress, with only dim ideas of the realities of war, began to talk of another war with Britain, this time for American liberty and independence on the high seas.

When Congress adjourned in the summer of 1809, General Sumter, who was then in the Senate, came back to his Home House, near Stateburg. At that time, young William Capers, whose family then resided at Woodland plantation nearby, was studying law under John Smyth Richardson of Bloom Hill, whose law office was in Stateburg. Shortly after General Sumter's return, young Capers was surprised to receive a note inviting him to dinner at Home House. A postscript to the note was even more surprising: "None but gentlemen invited." The mystery was solved when on arrival at the General's house, Capers found some twenty other unmarried young men, of whom he was the youngest.

After dinner when the cloth had been removed and Mrs. Sumter had withdrawn, General Sumter told his young guests of the difficulties with England and the approach of war, which certainly would bring immortal fame and honor to the heroes of great deeds. Promotion, he said, would come fast to officers in the first enlistment, which Congress had now ordered; and he had been authorized by President Madison to promise officers' commissions to any of those present who would volunteer for service. He believed their futures would be assured by acceptance of these commissions.

The General's talk made a deep impression. Young Capers

was eager to drop the law and become a soldier; but his father, a veteran of the Revolution, disagreed, and angrily refused permission: "Our liberties are not in danger; and the government is strong enough to take care of itself."[1]

So William Capers had to forget his dreams of military glory, and return to his law books. But in July he went to another camp-meeting at Rembert's, and eventually he became, not a lawyer, but a bishop of the Methodist church.

Four years after General Sumter's dinner party, the United States on June 18, 1812, declared war on Great Britain, and the War of 1812 began. At the request of the federal government, South Carolina undertook to defend herself. The militia was called up for six months service, and the quota of 5,000 state troops was promptly raised. Moreover, the state paid in advance her direct federal taxes, appropriated $500,000 for defense, and even furnished some arms and equipment to federal troops. For these expenditures, South Carolina had to wait almost a hundred years for federal reimbursement.

Major General Thomas Pinckney was placed in command of Southeastern United States, and David R. Williams of Society Hill ended his congressional career by becoming a brigadier general. Several privateers were built in Charleston for sea duty.

Although the war was fought far from Sumter District, mainly on the Great Lakes and on the seacoast, men of Sumter District were in service. General Sumter is said to have been offered a general's commission by President Madison. But the old soldier was now long past his three-score years and ten, and, shortly after his re-election to the Senate in December 1810, he had resigned his seat because of an old wound in his thigh which had abcessed. When in the fall of 1812, a committee urged him to accept nomination for governor of the state, he declined to emerge from his retirement in the High Hills.

William Sumter, the General's grandson, having been graduated from West Point early in 1812 and commissioned as a second lieutenant, was already in service when war began,

---

[1] William Capers, autobiography, in W. M. Wightman, *Life of William Capers* (Nashville, Tenn., 1858), pp. 70, 71.

and served in the campaign on the New York frontier. Promoted to first lieutenant upon the capture of Fort George, he was honorably discharged at the end of the war. Later he reentered the regular army and became a captain.[2]

Mark Johnson and Wiley Fort were two of the privates from Sumter District who served in the army and came home safely after the war. Johnson recorded his certificate of service at the courthouse in 1831, and Fort's obituary appeared in 1860 in the *Watchman*.[3]

During the war, British vessels infested the coast of South Carolina, where they looted plantations, especially on the islands, and preyed upon ships entering and leaving the ports. This danger to the coastwise trade, stimulated the overland wagon trade between the North and the South, and was one of the reasons that Robert W. Andrews of Stateburg began his adventures in October 1812, as a teamster of a five-horse wagon in the Charleston-Boston trade.

Perhaps the nearest physical approach of the war to Sumter District was at Fort Dearborn, an arsenal on the Catawba River near the great falls. This was built in 1803 on the 500-acre site which General Sumter sold to Thomas Jefferson as president of the United States. The last soldiers marched away from the arsenal in 1817, and thereafter it fell into ruin. South Carolina in 1839 appropriated $2,615 for the purchase of the site from the federal government.[4]

For Sumter District as well as for all of the agricultural South, the War of 1812 was felt most in its economic effects, primarily in the impact upon the price of cotton. When the news of the declaration of war reached the great cotton market of New Orleans on July 8, 1812, the price of cotton fell from 9½ cents a pound to 4½ cents. The return of peace in 1815 sent the price up to 30 cents, and two years later it was even higher.

---

[2] Gregorie, *T. Sumter*, pp. 265, 266.

[3] Sumter conveyances, II, p. 108. *Watchman*, Feb. 22, 1860.

[4] Wallace, *South Carolina*, p. 366. Fort Dearborn was also called Mount Dearborn. The tract of 523 acres was bought by General Sumter for $100 from Isham Moore, Nov. 12, 1802, and sold by him the next day for $200 to Thomas Jefferson and his successors in the presidency. Conveyances AA, pp. 77-81, Sumter Courthouse.

CHAPTER XI

ANTE-BELLUM NEGROES

The early settlers of Sumter County possessed very few slaves. The first federal census in 1790, shows for Claremont County a total of 2,000 slaves owned by 389 families, an average of five slaves for each family. Isham Moore is listed as the largest slaveholder, with 145; Benjamin Waring came next, with 110; John Singleton, Sr., had 81, Samuel Boykin 76, John Mayrant and William Ransome Davis 60 each. In Clarendon County the total was 910 slaves, averaging three for each family. James Bradley had 48, the largest gang. The census figures, however, are of limited value, for General Sumter of Stateburg and the Richardsons of Bloom Hill, who owned many slaves, are not listed in the census of Claremont County; and the Richard Richardson families are omitted from the census of Clarendon County.

At the time of the American Revolution, there was a strong sentiment in South Carolina for emancipation. From 1787 until 1801, a series of state laws forbade the importation of slaves from beyond the seas and from other states. Henry Laurens was not the only large slaveholder who expressed a hope for general emancipation by the state.

East of the Wateree, as elsewhere, there were a number of manumissions. William Pearson of Wyboo Swamp, Clarendon, by his will of 1783 bequeathed freedom and a life-interest in twenty acres of land to his trusty Negro fellow Jem. Known as Black Jamey Pearson, this freedman seems to have prospered, for a few years later he purchased a slave woman, Judy, and her child. In 1791 he emancipated her and her two children. Charles Richardson at Bloom Hill gave his Charlotte a certificate that she might "act as she pleases" under his protection, and deeded to her for life the ownership of a slave Bess, who was to be freed at Charlotte's death. James Lowry, a merchant of Salem County, by his will of 1799 emancipated a Negro wench, Bella.[1]

[1] Sumter wills; conveyances A, pp. 122, 123; B, p. 325.

Some irresponsible and conscienceless slaveholders had made a practice of freeing their most vicious and troublesome slaves and those who were too old or infirm to make a living. A law of 1800 therefore required that a master wishing to emancipate, must signify his intention to a justice of the quorum, who should summon five freeholders. When they convened with the justice, the master had to bring before them his slave for examination. If the slave was found to be of good character and capable of self-support, the justice and freeholders signed a certificate of his fitness, and the master signed a deed of emancipation, both of which documents the master was to have recorded at the courthouse within six months.[2]

A number of these certificates and deeds are on record at Sumter courthouse. Henry Jennings thus freed his Judy, Keziah, Peter, and Epsey. Pumpkin, a free man of color, gave freedom to Grace and her child Anthony. Perhaps the largest single manumission was that by Leonora Gamble Montgomery, who by deed in the spring of 1816 set free eleven slaves.[3]

Although emancipation by will had become illegal under the law of 1800 requiring a deed, as late as 1811 Henry Vaughan bequeathed freedom to six young slaves, with the provision that two, Edmond and Merryman, should be apprenticed to a good trade until reaching the age of eighteen or twenty years; if necessary, they were to be supported until that time out of the estate. The mothers of these slaves, Peg and Thisby, were "not to be put in the field or to any laborious work," and were directed to be freed at the death of Mrs. Vaughan, who survived her husband for many years. Although it would seem that the administrators and the surviving members of the family might have carried out the spirit of the will by executing deeds, there were several reasons why this was not done. Slave children could not be given deeds of freedom, and the Vaughan heirs were minors. All the slaves, therefore, were retained in "protective" custody, and none was freed.[4]

[2] *Stat.* VII, 443.
[3] Conveyances C, p. 25; CC, p. 22; DD, pp. 278, 279.
[4] Sumter wills, A, p. 121, and information from J. Nelson Frierson.

Alarmed by the great increase in free Negroes through emancipation and by their migration into the state, the legislature in 1820 banned the entry into the state of all free persons of color, and prohibited any further manumissions by individuals, vesting such power solely in the legislature.[5]

During the administration of Governor James B. Richardson, of Sumter District, the demand for field labor after the invention of the cotton gin resulted in an act of 1803, which forbade importation of slaves from the Bahamas, the West Indies and South America, and even required a certificate of good character for the entry of slaves from sister states, but repealed all restrictions on the African slave trade. During the next four years nearly 40,000 Africans were brought over to South Carolina. In 1808 a federal law prohibited the African trade, but the demand for laborers continued so great, that an estimated 30,000 slaves a year were brought into the state illegally from Maryland and Virginia. Not until 1818 was the ban removed from interstate importations of slaves.[6]

The tremendous increase in the black population caused anxiety to many thoughtful people, for they dreaded slave insurrections. A slave plot in Camden in 1816 brought increased demands for more strict controls, and the patrol act of 1819 made several changes in the system of policing the Negroes. The attempted insurrection in Charleston under Denmark Vesey, resulted in stringent laws for their control. A tax of $50 a year was laid upon every free male Negro who was not a native of the state. Furthermore, every free male Negro above the age of fifteen years was required to have as guardian a respectable white freeholder of the district. The guardian had to signify his acceptance of the trust before the clerk of court, and file at the same time a certificate of the good character and correct habits for his ward. When this law went into effect in 1823, only twenty guardianships in Sumter District were recorded, indicating that the district then had few free Negro men.[7]

---

[5] *Stat.* VII, 459.
[6] *Stat.* VII, 449, 450. D. D. Wallace, *South Carolina: A Short History 1520-1948* (Chapel Hill, 1951), pp. 365, 366.
[7] *Stat.* VII, 461. H. M. Henry, *The Police Control of the Slave in South Carolina* (Emory, Va., 1914), p. 179.

In 1831 the antislavery paper, *The Liberator*, began to excite the abolitionists of the North. After a decade of their fanatical attacks upon the South, the legislature of South Carolina became so alarmed by the potential danger from free Negroes that it prohibited all further manumission.[8]

Although a state census of free Negroes was taken each year, the figures show such variation that it is impossible to say how many actually were living in Claremont County. In 1840 there were 21; three years later they had almost tripled, showing 61; then for the next three years there were 40, 31, 25; after 1847 they began to increase again: in 1848, there were 31; in 1849, 44. In 1850 there were 35, and in 1851, only 30. If these erratic figures were accurate, the explanation may have been the removal of free Negroes to other places, such as Charleston, which had a large and prosperous colony of them. A few may have migrated to Liberia, which had been founded in 1817 by the American Colonization Society. Undoubtedly, some free Negroes were kidnapped by slave-stealers such as the notorious Murrell gang, and sold back into slavery in other states.

The most remarkable free Negro to reside in Sumter District was William Ellison, a ginwright. His advertisement in the *Camden Gazette,* February 1, 1817, stated that having served a regular apprenticeship with Captain McCreight of Winnsboro, he had established himself at Stateburg to make and repair gins on McCreight's plan at a charge of $3 a saw.

During his apprenticeship, Ellison is said to have bought his freedom with money earned in his own time by extra work. His gins were well liked by the planters and Ellison prospered. Soon he was able to buy his wife Matilda, and their daughter Eliza Ann. He also bought land from General Sumter, and in 1838 purchased the Stateburg house of Governor Stephen D. Miller, which remained the home of the Ellisons for three generations. In a letter to the *Saturday Evening Post* in 1856, W. H. Bowen stated that by 1848 William Ellison had owned 40 or 50 slaves, a large cotton plantation, and nearly half of the village of Stateburg. At the time of writing, Bowen supposed that Ellison was probably worth

---

[8] *Stat.* XI, 154, 155.

from eighty to a hundred thousand dollars. Best of all, declared Bowen, "William Ellison is respected by all classes of citizens and is honorable in all his dealings."[9]

According to the floor plan of Claremont Episcopal Church at Stateburg, William Ellison had pew number 30, and the members of his family were communicants of that church as long as they lived in Stateburg.

In ante-bellum times, it was customary for slaves to worship in the same church with their masters, the Negroes being seated in the rear or in the gallery. The Rev. A. L. Converse, rector of Claremont Episcopal Church at Stateburg, in 1841 reported 25 white members of the church and 41 Negroes. The Rev. Jeptha Dyson, rector of St. Mark's, reported in 1845 that one clergyman and one catechist were giving religious instruction to Negroes. The catechist made weekly visits to ten plantations, where he regularly catechised 420 adult Negroes and 160 children. Every Sunday afternoon the rector delivered a sermon to the Negroes. The Rev. W. W. Mood of Sumter Circuit, reported in the 1850's that at Rembert's Church, which enrolled 81 whites and about 500 Negroes, Willis Spann and James W. Rembert, the class leaders, were most attentive to the Negro members.

William Ellison was so much respected that he was sometimes accorded the title of "Mr." Robert W. Andrews in his reminiscences speaks of "Mr. Ellison" in recounting his own journey to Virginia to bring back one of Ellison's most valuable slaves who had run away. Not infrequently Ellison advertised for runaways from his shop and farm, and tradition says that his slaves were the worst-clad and the worst-fed in Sumter District. In 1858 one of his advertisements offered a $20-reward for the return of his man Gabriel.

Through his guardian, Dr. W. W. Anderson of Stateburg, Ellison placed on record in the clerk of court's office in the courthouse, the birth dates of all of his children as he had recorded them in his family Bible. His three sons were educated in Canada; and William, the second son, married a convent-educated white Canadian named Patricia. Their son, Billy John, looked like a white man and also married a white

[9] *Watchman*, May 7, 1856.

Canadian. The ginwright's son Reuben, however, to the great displeasure of William Ellison, married a slave woman, and their descendants have remained Negroes, the best-known, perhaps, being the Rev. J. McKenzie Harrison, whose mother was the maid of "old Mrs. Rees."[10]

Ellison's will was drawn in 1851 but was not probated until December 15, 1861, at the end of the first year of the great war, so he died without knowing of the heavy losses which would come to his estate in the fall of the Confederacy.

The slavery system operated in Sumter District very much as it did in other parts of the state, and was better or worse according to the master or slave concerned. In many homes, the house-servants were beloved though subordinate members of the household. When Antrim, slave of Mrs. Leah McFaddin, died in 1858, she published his obituary in the *Watchman*, paying him tribute as a good Christian and a most faithful old servant who had died perfectly resigned to the will of God.[11]

Robert Witherspoon of Coldstream plantation on Black River, in 1837 added a codicil to his will: "Let only a sober, steady and humane man be employed to oversee my poor helpless slaves who I hope will always when there is opportunity attend the teachings of the Church." The Witherspoon slaves did attend the teachings of the church and were among those who communed at Salem Black River. Each slave in good standing was given a "token", an oblong piece of metal inscribed with the words, "Do this in remembrance of me." On communion Sundays, the elders stood at the north and south doors of the church, to receive these tokens, which admitted the owners to the communion table in front of the pulpit.[12]

Not infrequently the house-servants were taught to read and write, and in 1829 the Sumter grand jury presented as a grievance the liberty allowed slaveholders to teach their Negroes. The great fear was that education might enable them to write letters and organize a widespread conspiracy

---

[10] Conveyances K, p. 167, and information from H. G. Osteen.
[11] *Watchman*, April 28, 1858.
[12] Hamilton Witherspoon, "An Old Plantation Garden", in *The Century Magazine*, Aug. 1909.

to destroy the greatly-outnumbered whites. In 1834 South Carolina prohibited the teaching of slaves, and penalized the employment of any person of color as a clerk. The manuscript journal of John Witherspoon Ervin, a schoolmaster of ante-bellum Sumter, reveals that he was taught to read by his Negro nurse before he was of school age.[13]

The ceaseless petty annoyances and even hardships which beset the prosperous and unprosperous slaveholders alike, will surprise the people of today who imagine that the master and mistress enjoyed lives of idleness and ease.

The diary of Natalie Delage Sumter, the widow of Thomas Sumter, Jr., gives a contemporary picture of almost intolerable burdens borne by that most gentle and conscientious plantation mistress of many slaves. During the summer, she arose at four o'clock in the morning for what was often a 20-hour day with the problems of her servants. She had to remove Dennis, the slave "driver" who was foreman of field work, because he disobeyed her in making the Negroes work in the heat of the day, although she had told him that "it was his master's last orders that they should not work when it was hot." She ministered to the sick and "gave Venus a fine wedding."

After going to services in the Catholic Church at Providence, Mrs. Sumter taught the catechism to twenty-two Negroes, then sent them home with a good dinner of soup, meat, baked apples and peaches. She also gave apples and peaches to all the plantation slaves.

When the first railroad to approach Sumter District was under construction in 1840 near Kingville, across the Wateree, Mrs. Sumter had an opportunity to hire her slaves to the company, but first she discussed the matter with the Negroes and made sure that they were willing to go. Then, having given orders for them to have new outfits of shoes and clothing, she made a personal visit to the railroad.

Although Mrs. Sumter was in frail health, she seldom retired to rest until midnight, and even later when the maid Delia neglected to make up her bed. The diary has allusions to Delia's disobedience and impudence, and once "Delia kept

---

[13] Henry, *Police Control*, p. 166. *SCHGM*, XLVI, 166.

me again awake all night—she will drive me out of the house." Priscilla, the other maid, was a different type: sometimes she was not to be found at bedtime, and everyone had to turn out to look for her. When she did go to bed, Priscilla snored so loudly that one night her mistress had to open the door five times and awaken her. More than once Mrs. Sumter was alarmed to find Delia and Priscilla asleep with a lighted candle between them.

The problem of the cook was equal to that of the maids: for Dr. Anderson forbade Diana to cook; Caty said she could not cook; and Sally forgot to get vegetables and prepared a miserable dinner! In despair, Mrs. Sumter wrote to her neighbor, Ann Rutledge, to try to hire a cook. When the poor lady inspected her kitchen and cellars, she "found everything in very bad order." Anna and Hampton had kept the pickled pork out of pickle for fifteen days; the cows had not been put out to pasture.

One night at eleven o'clock Mrs. Sumter went to the cowhouse and found it had been left open so that sneak thieves could climb into the stables and steal the corn from the horses. Then she discovered that her house-doors were being left open every night! Again, at a late hour when all of the horses were out, she had to find Mingo and Hampton to go bring them in.

On another memorable night when Mrs. Sumter had overnight guests, a great fight at bedtime, between Mr. Nelson's Caesar and Mrs. Spann's Edmund, kept the household up until one o'clock in the morning. While the exhausted hostess lay in bed next morning, the trial of the culprits was held in her chamber from eight o'clock until eleven. On another occasion an uproar involved Anna and Henry, and when Anna broke Henry's head, Dr. Anderson had to be summoned. Not once in the diary is there any mention of punishment. Eventually Mrs. Sumter found she had to have help, and employed as overseer a Mr. Cox, at a salary of $250 a year.

Another conscientious slaveholder of whom record was found was John Frierson, whose plantation on Pudding Swamp about twenty miles east of Sumterville had been granted in 1754 to his ancestor, John Frierson. The Rev. I.

E. Lowery, Frierson's onetime slave, says in his book of recollections:[14]

> Mr. Frierson always looked carefully after the morals of his slaves, . . . he did not allow them to steal if he could possibly help it. He did everything he could to teach them to be truthful, to be honest, and to be morally upright. He had it understood on his plantation that there should be no little bastard slaves there . . . When the boys and girls reached a marriageable age he advised them to marry, but marry some one on the plantation, and he would see to it that they should not be separated. But if they married some one from the adjoining plantations, they might be separated eventually by the 'nigger traders' . . . But Mr. Frierson was never known to separate a man and his wife by sale or by trading. Nor was he ever known to separate mother and child.

Monthly religious services by a Negro preacher were held under the oaks in the large yard around the Frierson home, for the slaves on his and the neighboring plantation; about 300 Negroes sat on comfortable seats in the yard facing the east, and the white people sat to listen on the long front piazza. In the afternoon, Sunday school was conducted for them at nearby Shiloh Methodist Church.

Around the Friersons lived other good slaveholders. To the north dwelt Isaac Keels and his father William; to the east lived Alexander Lemon; on the south was Cris Player, who kept a store and the local postoffice; and on the west were his brother Jack Player and the family of the late [James?] Fullwood. Lowery recalled that "none of them were cruel to their slaves."[15]

Nevertheless, there were cruel slaveholders, and the Sumter sessions docket, 1827-1854, lists thirteen cases of cruelty to slaves. Of these, two pleaded guilty, five were convicted, six were dropped. Apparently the only punishment on record was a fine of one dollar. During the same years, the grand jury had eleven bills for murder of slaves by white men, one of whom was a wellborn, wealthy planter, whose family had

[14] *Life on the Old Plantation*, p. 42.
[15] *Ibid.*, pp. 71, 72, 85.

included more than one governor. The grand jury returned three bills as "no bill", and one as "bad treatment not intentional murder"; the six that went to trial were found not guilty. Of two others tried, one pleaded guilty, the other was found "true bill on second count."[16]

As a check on runaways, no slave was permitted to leave his master's plantation without a written permit called a ticket, unless he was accompanied by a white person. The patrol system which policed the ante-bellum Negroes was really a part of the militia system. The commanding officer of each militia-beat was required to divide his beat into convenient patrol districts; to make up a roll of the free white men residing in each district; and to select therefrom the men who should ride patrol until the next muster. He also named the commander or captain of each patrol, whose duty it was to call up his men at least once in every two weeks and ride through his district in search of contraband arms, and runaway slaves. As the slaves did not work on Sunday, the afternoon of that day was generally the time chosen for the ride, and if any slave was found away from his master's plantation under suspicious circumstances or without his ticket, the patrol had to administer a moderate whipping.[17] The Negroes made a song about the patrol, which began:

"Run, nigger, run, or the pateroll will git you!"

Every owner of a settled plantation was required to have on his or her plantation a white man capable of performing patrol duty. Not infrequently, therefore, patrol warrants were sent to widows or spinsters, who then had to send an overseer or some other substitute to perform the duty for them. The following is such a warrant:

PATROL WARRANT

To Miss Catherine Suggs:

You are hereby commanded to take under your command Mr. George Calder and Mrs. Mary Cawley and regularly perform Patrol duty in your beat and return this warrant on the first Saturday in October next on oath.

Apr. 2d. 1855.   SIMON PLATT, *Capt. Beat No. 2.*

[16] Henry, *Police Control*, pp. 71, 75, 76.
[17] *Stat.* VII, 371 ff; VIII, 538 ff; IX, 639.

This warrant was sent to the *Watchman* by a correspondent signing himself "Don Q", who, in the name of Miss Suggs, asked the editor's advice: "She desires to know if she must really take her horse and whip and ride over the country, on Sunday afternoons in search of stray negroes, or appear before Court Martial and submit to the penalties..."[18]

One of the common causes of trouble with the slaves was the traffic in stolen articles which unscrupulous persons carried on with the Negroes, who thus were encouraged to pilfer salable articles of every kind. In 1828 the Sumter grand jury presented as a grievance the permitting of trade with Negroes after dark, even when the slave carried a ticket from his owner. The traffic was so profitable to the purchasers as well as to the Negroes, that it was very difficult to control, despite the many laws prohibiting it. In a presentment of 1834 the grand jury declared that Negro-trading had become the chief object of pursuit and the chief source of gain to many persons, and appealed to good citizens to put it down.

Another appeal to the citizens of Sumter District, signed "Black River," declared that the social evil of selling liquor to slaves in exchange for stolen articles, was not confined to towns, villages, and country stores, nor was it limited to shops of the lowest grade, for in almost every community there were persons who were ready to barter.

In some localities the citizens organized themselves to ferret out the evidence for conviction of Negro-traders, and formed the Salem Vigilant Association, and the Clarendon Vigilante Society.

Between 1827 and 1860 convictions were had in 48% of the cases of Negro-trading in Sumter District. In the fourteen cases brought to trial between 1827 and 1831, there were ten convictions. The heaviest sentence imposed was a fine of $500 and four months in prison, but the fine was remitted. In other cases there was a fine of $200 and varying terms of imprisonment. When Governor John L. Manning extended clemency to a duly convicted Negro-trader, the Clarendon Vigilante Society published resolutions of censure

[18] *Watchman,*...Apr. 13, 1855.

against him as having abused his power and forfeited confidence.[19]

The harboring of slaves, that is, giving them shelter when they were in hiding, was punishable by a maximum fine of $1000 and imprisonment at the discretion of the court. Eight such cases were tried in Sumter District in 1827, but only three of the accused were convicted.[20]

The stealing of a slave from his master was a felony in South Carolina, punishable by death,[21] but nevertheless slaves were stolen. An interesting case developed near Manchester in 1838, when three slaves were stolen, one each from Willis Spann, W. L. Brunson, and John Watson.

The accused was Mina [Minor?] McCoy, a skilled mechanic, by trade a gin-maker who sometimes worked as a house carpenter. At the April term of court, the grand jury found true bills against him, and while awaiting trial, he was confined in one of the rooms reserved for debtors, on the second floor of the jail. Detected with two augers, after he had bored through the floor, he was removed to the second debtor's room. On June 25, McCoy's wife and their twelve-year-old son came to see him, and were locked in with him for most of the day. Sheriff W. E. Richardson, fearing a second attempt at escape, called in Robert Lansdell, a carpenter, and John D. Jones, and with an iron hammer, they tested every iron bar and every plank in the walls and floor. On June 29, the sheriff left town for the night. At supper time, the jailer, Briant Bateman, who lived below, made a minute examination of the room, and then he too left home for the night. Before daylight the next morning, McCoy with a thin instrument, not a file, had cut through an 1½-inch iron bar and lowered himself to the ground with one of the ropes which supported the mattress on his bed.

Six years later Mina McCoy was caught and arraigned. On the indictment prosecuted by Willis Spann, he was found guilty with recommendation to mercy. The other two cases against him were continued until the following year, when,

19 *Ibid.*, June 13, 1855. Henry, *Police Control*, pp. 83, 86, 87. *Watchman*, Apr. 7, 1854.
20 Henry, *Police Control*, p. 114.
21 *Stat.* VII, 426.

on one or both, he was found guilty and sentenced to be hanged.

Tradition says that McCoy was a Free Mason, and that his brother Masons arranged for his escape. Be that as it may, at the spring term of court in 1846, Alexander Watson was brought to trial by Sheriff Henry S. Eveleigh for the "Voluntary Escape of Mina McCoy under sentence of death." Watson pleaded guilty, was tried the same day, and was cleared of the charge![22]

At the spring term of court in Sumter in 1856, William Friendly Byrd was arraigned on a charge of Negro stealing. The traverse docket records that on the eve of his trial, "The Prisoner hung himself in jail Sunday night April 13, 1856."

Not infrequently, slaves and even free Negroes were enticed away from their homes by professional thieves, such as the notorious Murrell Gang, who carried on an organized interstate traffic for several years, until broken up in 1844 when the leaders were captured and brought to trial.[23]

But greater than the fear of the Murrell Gang, was the dread with which the South regarded travelling abolitionists from the northern states; for not only did these rabid reformers often aid the slaves to escape into free states, but the more fanatical among them preached insurrection to the Negroes. As a result, every stranger who did not give a reasonable explanation of himself, was regarded with suspicion. At best, the agents of the abolitionists distributed copies of *The Liberator* and other "incendiary" publications, among whites as well as Negroes, hoping to win converts. But they also used other techniques, as in the case of a Dr. L. Major, a suspected emissary, who was said to have been in the habit of "possum hunting with Negroes in order to deliver philosophical lectures on freedom;" and was further accused of having brought to the Negroes a chemical for changing the color of their skins, so that they might pass for whites.[24] Usually these emissaries were given a hearing and then sent back to their homes. Later, relying on southern

---
[22] Sessions journal 1827-1840, fall term, 1838. Traverse docket, spring term, 1844, 1846.
[23] Phillips, *Life and Labor*, p. 108.
[24] *Banner*, May 24, 1848.

gallantry, the abolitionists were said to have screened themselves behind women emissaries who gave lectures and distributed pamphlets.

Fugitive slaves did not always try to reach the free soil of the northern states when they ran away from their masters. Sometimes they took refuge in the dense swamps along the rivers, where they lived in camps, tribal fashion, with their wives and children. One of the most notorious of these outlaw bands, known as Joe's Gang, lived in the fork between the Wateree and the Congaree, and plundered the east banks of the rivers from Manchester to Nelson's Ferry. Apparently Joe began his murderous career in 1820 by the killing of a Mr. Ford of Georgetown, and despite the Governor's offer of a reward, he escaped to become the leader of the fugitives he found in the swamps. Some three years later, Joe and four of his followers appeared in a field where the slaves of Colonel J. B. Richardson were at work, and shot down a valuable man against whom Joe had a personal grudge.

A manhunt was immediately begun, and a week later the Charleston post-rider reported that Colonel Manning's party had killed four of the gang, including Joe, whose "head was cut off and stuck on a pole at the mouth of the creek, as a solemn warning to vicious slaves." The final chapter was written with the capture in St. Stephen's Parish of two men and three women. Joe's wife, who was wearing a man's coat, was shot, and probably died later. A child also was accidentally shot and died. The captured men were tried before a court of magistrates and freeholders, and one was sentenced to be hanged.[25]

Much has been written of old customs, strange beliefs, and weird practices among ante-bellum Negroes, which need not be repeated here. Irving E. Lowery, who was a slave boy on the Frierson plantation on Pudding Swamp, has published his recollections of log-rolling, corn-shucking, 'possum-hunting, weddings, funerals, and Christmas frolics.

From Lowery comes also the story of a black girl named Mary, who was conjured by a rival in a lovescrape. Mary wasted away, and her master called in the family doctor, a

[25] *Southern Chronicle*, Sept. 17, Oct. 8, 22, 29, 1823.

graduate of the Philadelphia medical college, but Mary's family secretly employed a voodoo doctor, and Mary died. The torch-lighted funeral procession that followed her body to the grave was the longest ever known on the plantation. Beside the open grave a strange ceremony took place, when Mary's baby "was passed from one person to another across the coffin. The slaves believed that if this was not done it would be impossible to raise the infant. The mother's spirit would come back for her baby and take it to herself. This belief is held by many of the descendants of these slaves, who practice the same thing at the present day."[26]

[26] *Life on the Old Plantation*, pp. 83-86.

CHAPTER XII

NULLIFICATION, FIST-FIGHTS, AND A DUEL

As early as the year 1820 the question of federal tariffs on imports from foreign countries had aroused serious alarm in the South. Four years later, when the first truly protective tariff was imposed for the benefit of Northern manufacturers, Southern planters felt deep resentment that they were forced to pay artificially high prices for clothing and other necessities which they were buying from the North for themselves and their Negroes, especially since the revenue derived from the tariff was being used to build roads and canals in the West. Stephen D. Miller, state senator from Claremont, drafted resolutions which were passed by the South Carolina Senate, declaring that Congress had no right to adopt a system of internal improvements, nor to tax the citizens of one state to pay for roads and canals in another, and that federal protective tariffs were unconstitutional. These resolutions became the platform of the States Rights Party, later known as the Nullifiers.

In Sumterville early in August 1827, at an anti-tariff meeting, James G. Spann in the chair, and young Franklin I. Moses secretary, speakers voiced opposition to the pending tariff bill which would protect woolens, and discussed the adoption of measures to prevent its passage. At the adjourned session the following month, more than a thousand citizens heard a report from Senator Miller, and drafted a memorial and resolutions in opposition to the woolens bill.[1]

These measures had no effect, and the tariff act of 1828 was so oppressive to the agricultural South, that it is known to this day as the Tariff of Abominations. South Carolina flamed with anger, and Governor John Taylor in a message to the legislature advised that the tariff act be declared unconstitutional. The report of the committee on the governor's

[1] *Camden Journal*, Aug. 18, Oct. 6, 1827. *The Memorial and Resolutions adopted at the Anti-Tariff Meeting . . . 3rd of September, 1827.*

message was drafted by the great Calhoun himself, and was printed by order of the legislature. This report and Calhoun's famous "Exposition" set forth the doctrine of Nullification, namely, that South Carolina as a sovereign state could nullify within its borders an unconstitutional law of its agent, the federal government.

Many people urged a boycott of all goods manufactured in the North, and when Stephen D. Miller was inaugurated governor in the winter of 1828, he wore a full suit of home-spun. Congressman George McDuffie, son-in-law of Colonel Richard Singleton of Sumter District, gave his broadcloth coat of Northern make to his servant, saying that it was a livery fit only for a slave.

The great debates in Congress between Hayne and Webster were eagerly read and argued all over again in every part of South Carolina, and the entire population took sides either as Nullifiers or as Unionists. Nowhere was interest keener than in Sumter District, where Nullification was debated in the courthouse, along the highways, at the militia musters, and probably at the church doors. Even the school children are said to have taken sides.

The Nullifiers added color to the times by wearing cockades of blue ribbon, with palmetto trees on the gold centers. In general, sentiment in Sumter District is said to have been almost evenly divided, and a north-south line through the courthouse would have separated the Nullifiers in the east of the district from the Unionists in the west. When a convention was being agitated for in 1830 to deal with the question, a poll of a muster at Bishopville showed 106 Nullifiers for the convention, and 11 Unionists against it. At Captain Belser's muster-ground, only 2 Nullifiers were for, and 45 were against. At Captain Levy Rhame's muster, two-thirds were opposed. Manchester was Unionist, but Sumterville and Stateburg were practically solid for Nullification. So were the Scotch-Irish families, the Bradleys, the McFaddins, and the Muldrows; and the Huguenot families of Rembert, Deschamps, Dubose, and LaCoste.[2]

As their official organ, the Nullifiers founded the *Sumter-*

---

[2] *Camden Journal*, Sept. 11, 1830. Letter from J. D. Blanding to J. J. Hemphill, Oct. 22, 1905, owned by Mrs. Mary Hemphill Greene.

ville Gazette, published at Sumterville by James S. Bowen. Almost the whole of one of its early issues was devoted to proceedings at Stateburg in August 1830, when a public dinner was attended by nearly a thousand citizens from Kershaw, Richland, and Darlington, as well as Sumter. General Sumter was invited, but was among those notables who did not attend, for he was now too old to take an active part in politics. His grandsons, however, were ardent Nullifiers; and his granddaughter, Mrs. Louisa Murrell, is said to have continued to argue the question some years after it had been settled! At the Stateburg dinner, with no disorder and to thundering applause, speeches were made by Governor Miller, a Nullifier, and by three Unionists, Judge Richardson, Colonel Manning, and John Peter Richardson,[3] who eventually carried the whole of Clarendon into the Unionist fold. George McDuffie, who became a Nullifier after going to Congress, probably carried the Singletons with him.

Both Nullifiers and Unionists felt that a word from General Sumter as a survivor of the men who had made the Union and guided its early years, would be as the voice of an oracle to public opinion. Each party, therefore, made strenuous efforts to win his endorsement. The General was living alone on his South Mount plantation, a solitary place where he apparently saw few people except his grandsons when they rode over to see how he was getting along; and he probably was not in very close touch with the politics of the times. Near the end of October 1830, he answered a request for his views by urging the people of the state to "endeavor to change a system of usurpations no longer in harmony with the spirit of our constitution." He advocated calling a popular convention which would issue an appeal to other states for regional action in opposition to the tariff: "There is no danger of a convention proceeding to nullification, since it is not for this purpose they are convened. What is the use of creating a new power to nullify, when the Legislature can of itself do it?"[4] He believed in states' rights!

Published in full in newspapers of the state and given national publicity in *Niles' Weekly Register*, General Sum-

---

[3] *Ibid.*, and *Camden Journal*, Aug. 14, Sept. 30, 1830.
[4] Gregorie, *T. Sumter*, p. 277.

ter's letter was jubilantly toasted by Nullifiers everywhere. Typical was the sentiment of Waddy Thompson: "The South Carolina Game Cock—not too old to flap his wings and crow. As the old cock crows may the young ones learn."

Stung to action by the Nullifiers' victory, the Unionists sought to counteract the General's letter by an interview with him, and the *Camden Journal's* sensational article on "General Sumter's Opinions" stated that he had changed his views. The General's grandson, Thomas Delage Sumter, a hot Nullifier, at once carried the paper to the old man and asked for an open letter to himself that would leave no doubt as to his grandfather's stand. The General complied in a long letter, published in the Charleston *Mercury*, September 2, 1831, in which he ridiculed the *Camden Journal's* article, declared his views unchanged, and called attention to his famous letter of October 28, 1830, which had expressed his states' rights opinions in full.[5]

At the end of his term, Governor Miller was elected to the United States Senate, where he spoke and voted against the protective tariff of 1832. One of his most widely quoted statements offered three ways to reform bad congressional legislation, namely the ballot box, the jury box, and the cartridge box.

The whole of the year 1832 in South Carolina was devoted to the campaign to elect a two-thirds majority of the legislators in favor of calling a convention, and public excitement reached a new high. The Nullifiers were now calling the Unionists "submissionists," and the Unionists were calling the Nullifiers "traitors", and many bloody noses and black eyes resulted.

At the height of the campaign, it is said that a public meeting convened in the Sumter Courthouse to name a ticket of delegates to the state convention. The courthouse was jammed with both Unionists and Nullifiers, and feeling ran so high that the meeting could not even elect a chairman.

"To prevent a general melee in the Court House," wrote an old citizen, "the leaders of the factions called upon their adherents to rally at certain points in the street, to which

[5] *Ibid.*, p. 278. *Camden Journal*, Aug. 20, 1831.

a rush was made down the steps on different sides of the Court House door. They formed on the pavements on opposite sides of the street facing each other, then with cockades and banners flung to the breeze, one marched Northward and the other Southward. But increasing distance produced oozing out of patriotism, so both factions countermarched and when opposite each other at the corner of Main and Liberty Streets, halted and glared at each other."[6]

One story is that William ("Buck") Miller then advanced from the Nullifiers and "dared any Union man to meet him in the middle of the street and he would whip him in a fair fight." Maynard Richardson, son of Judge Richardson, accepted the challenge; each champion chose two seconds "to see that there was a fair fist and skull fight, no interference from anyone, no biting nor gouging and no knife nor knucks." The fight was to last until one or the other could not stand up.

Buck Miller chose John Furman and William Furman Baker as his seconds. Richardson chose Samuel Mayrant and Mike Spann. The four seconds then drew a circle around the champions and stood guard. Each faction-leader ordered that no follower should break ranks, and posted two sentinels to march up and down the lines to keep order.

At the words "Fall to! pop away!" the fight began, and on the unpaved street, according to Dr. Witherspoon, "the dust began to rise like a four-mule waggon running away on a sandy road during a drought."

The champions fought until they fell together in the ring and neither was able to rise, when the seconds decided that it was a drawn battle and carried them home—after which to the end of their brief young lives, Miller and Richardson were intimate friends.

As soon as ranks were broken, it is said that there were fist-and-skull fights all along the lines. Each Unionist who was knocked down and dragged out, was carried to the public pump and washed in the horse trough; while each defeated Nullifier was taken to the public well and doused from the chained tin bucket.

[6] Blanding to Hemphill, Oct. 22, 1905.

NULLIFICATION, FIST-FIGHTS, AND A DUEL

To conclude the day, the Unionists gathered at Morse's Tavern, on the southeast corner of Main and Liberty, while the Nullifiers made for China's Tavern next door to the Courthouse Square. On the piazza of each hostelry stood a barrel of North Carolina corn whiskey "lately brought by wagon fresh from the Still," each with tin cups hanging near. The one-man police force of the village, probably a deputy sheriff, is said to have carried the resulting drunks to the two debtors' rooms on the second floor of the jail, and by nightfall he had laid them two courses deep upon the floor.[7]

The Sumter Unionists at this time had an official organ in the *Southern Whig*, owned and edited by Maynard Davis Richardson, who was following in his father's footsteps both as a lawyer and a Unionist. The *Sumterville Gazette* was now being edited for the Nullifiers by John Hemphill, another young lawyer, who had come to Sumterville from Chester District. The two young editors became bitter adversaries, personal as well as political, and their opposing editorials did not cool the inflamed passions of their respective factions. During a near-riot in Sumterville, Maynard Richardson is said to have been set upon by the mob, but was rescued by his father, the judge, who unarmed, "rushed into the crowd and used his umbrella right and left most dextrously and effectively."[8]

On the first day of June in that summer of 1832, the people of Sumter District were saddened by news of the sudden death of their venerable fellow citizen, General Thomas Sumter. In the morning he is said to have been pruning some apple trees; about noon he had gone into the house and called his servant to help him to bed, but before help could come, he died in his chair. So at long last, after ninety-eight wonderful years, his active and adventurous life ended as he himself would have chosen, with his boots on, busy to the end.

The campaign of 1832 resulted in a sweeping victory for the Nullifiers, and at a special session of the legislature, the Convention was called to meet in November. As the inevitable result, the Ordinance of Nullification was passed. The

---
[7] Ibid.
[8] B. F. Perry, *Reminiscences of Public Men* (Philadelphia, 1883), p. 200.

Unionists had President Andrew Jackson as their champion in the White House, for he had sided with the federal government against the sovereignty of his native state. Calhoun resigned the vice-Presidency and came home to stand with his beloved state. So intense was popular feeling, that South Carolina stood upon the brink of civil war between its own citizens, as well as with the United States.

The fiery Jackson, however, while pushing through Congress the Force Bill for the coercion of South Carolina, had also used his great influence to have objectionable tariffs reduced. Both sides eagerly welcomed a compromise, and in 1833 South Carolina rescinded the Ordinance of Nullification.

Before the compromise was reached, young Maynard Richardson suddenly died, on October 12, 1832, at the untimely age of only twenty years. A memorial volume of his life and work prepared by his friend William Gilmore Simms has kept alive his memory.[9]

His rival, John Hemphill, had a much longer career, and in the summer of 1833 was a principal in a duel. An article which Hemphill had printed in the *Sumterville Gazette* gave offense to Captain Mordecai M. Levy, a merchant of Camden, who, signing himself "A Jew" published in the *Camden Journal* a communication containing these offensive words: "Thus it seems that J. Hemphill has become the voluntary bully for Mr. Johnstone; and has played the blackguard for the mere love of the fame. . . ."

Quick to resent the insult, Hemphill dispatched to Captain Levy the following challenge:

Camden, Aug. 20, 1833

Sir—

As you are the avowed author of the article over the signature "A Jew", in the Camden Journal of the 24th instant, of you I demand satisfaction. Mr. J. D. Cooke is authorized on my part to make the necessary arrangements for our meeting.

Yours & c

JOHN HEMPHILL.

---

[9] *The Remains of Maynard Davis Richardson with a Memoir of his Life* (Charleston, 1833).

Captain Levy chose as his second Colonel Chapman Levy, who, with Mr. Cooke, drew up nineteen appalling articles for conducting the mortal combat. The principals were to use smoothbore pistols at twelve yards distance, and the seconds were to be armed with pistols "to shoot down, at discretion, either of the parties violating any of the rules."

The encounter took place at Carter's Mill, near Camden. John Hemphill was shot in the pistol hand, and the blow of the bullet let down the hammer so that his pistol could not be fired. Both parties then withdrew the offensive words which brought on the duel, and the affair was adjusted honorably to all concerned.[10]

After the duel, Hemphill remained in Sumterville practicing law for five more years. In the great depression following the bank panic of 1837, he joined the migration which had been moving westward through Sumter District ever since the Revolution, and settled himself in Texas, where he became the first chief justice and later United States senator from that state.

[10] From family papers owned by Mrs. Mary Hemphill Greene. *Camden Journal*, Aug. 24, Sept. 7, 1833. For a sketch, see *Dictionary of American Biography*.

Chapter XIII

THE SUMTERS IN THE WAR WITH MEXICO

When the War with Mexico began in the summer of 1846, the abolitionists of the North developed bitter opposition, for they feared that annexation of conquered territory would only extend slavery. In the South, however, despite disapproval from the great Calhoun, the President's call for volunteers was answered by eager young men who dreamed of high adventure in the land of the montezumas, little knowing what it would cost them. The freesoil states sent 22,136 soldiers, while the slave states contributed 43,232.

South Carolina raised the Palmetto Regiment. In Sumter District on June 6, was organized a volunteer company which officially became Company A of that regiment, but was known at home as The Sumters. Enlisted for the duration of the war, the original company numbered only about forty, among whom were boys from sixteen to eighteen years of age, several having left college to volunteer. A young lawyer, Francis Sumter, grandson of General Sumter, was elected captain, with a stipend of $70 a month. A comrade later said of Captain Sumter that all the dictionaries in the language could not give him "the faintest conception of what fear means." Captain Sumter's younger brother, Sebastian, a sergeant major, was described by the same comrade as a "young game cock of the South, worthy of his great ancestor." Albertus C. Spain was first lieutenant, at $69 a month; C. S. Mellet was second lieutenant, at $64 a month. Later, James D. Blanding was chosen an additional second lieutenant, and was succeeded as orderly sergeant by Thomas M. Baker. From their salaries the officers were expected to pay all official as well as personal expenses, and there was no provision for the families of men in service.

In November 1846 the various companies of the Palmetto Regiment received orders to rendezvous in Charleston for immediate service in Mexico. The following Saturday The Sumters paraded through Sumterville. A week later, after a final business meeting, they dined together at China's Hotel, and on the afternoon of December 7, they assembled at the courthouse to begin the journey to Charleston. On the same day a mass meeting was held at the courthouse to take steps for relief of the destitute families at home, but it was not until after the war that the state made an appropriation for the widows, orphans and disabled survivors. Even before Captain Sumter reached Mexico, the sheriff of Sumter District was advertising a distress sale of his 126-acre property near Stateburg, at the suit of A. Anderson, S. Allen, F. I. Moses, and Thomas D. Condy.

Without uniforms and almost destitute of equipment, The Sumters marched away from the courthouse and bivouacked the first night at Shot Pouch Camp, two miles from Sumterville. The next day they resumed their march and reached Camp Sumter, within a mile of Stateburg. During the night the little company suffered its first casualty, for Moses Grooms while on guard was kicked severely by a mule, and had two ribs broken. However, said the news dispatch, "The spirited old man continued his round of duty." With daylight came better luck, for the Stateburg people brought out their wagon teams and took the footsore company by ferry across the Wateree to Gadsden Depot, where the men entrained for Charleston on the South Carolina Railroad.

Arriving safely the next day, The Sumters were met at the Charleston depot by the Chester Company, the Hammond Guards of Barnwell, and the Ninety-Six Boys of Edgefield. Together they marched to headquarters at Magnolia Farm on Charleston Neck, which they reached about five o'clock in the afternoon and were escorted to their tents by a detachment detailed from the Charleston Volunteers, the Moultrie Guards, and the Washington Light Infantry.

While at Magnolia, The Sumters, in an impressive afternoon ceremony, received their company flag, the gift of the ladies of Sumterville. Presented by Lieutenant Spain, the flag bearer A. F. Allen received it on his knees, "in token of his devotion to the cause and his respect for the fair donors." The flag was made of blue silk, having on one side a gaffed gamecock, and the motto "We have come"; on the other side was a palmetto, with two United States flags borne crosswise over the trunk and the state motto, *"Animis Opibusque Parati"*.

As The Sumters still numbered only about forty men, they now brought their company to full strength by recruiting a motley assortment of "borough" toughs and some recently arrived emigrants from Ireland.

Late in December the camp was removed from Magnolia to the Washington Race Course, whence on December 21, the left wing of the Palmetto Regiment broke camp and marched away on the first leg of the long journey to Mexico. On Christmas Eve a regimental detachment followed by rail to prepare a camp for the marchers on Horse Creek, about five miles from the rail terminus at Hamburg, opposite Augusta. On Christmas morning The Sumters followed in the right wing of the regiment. Moses Grooms, however, was still lying disabled in the Citadel Hospital, and had to be left behind, so the good people of Charleston made up a "liberal purse" for him to return home when he could travel. Little did Grooms realize how lucky he was, and his disappointment would have become inexpressible relief had he known what was ahead of his comrades.

For never did any group of brave men suffer more grievously from the ignorance, neglect, and general inefficiency of their government!

A moving account of their experiences has been left by one of the few survivors of the Palmetto Regiment, Ben Lane Posey, then an eighteen-year-old from the sophomore class of the South Carolina College:

> The government had not furnished tents or equipage, or given us a dollar of money. We had no government officers with us with funds or credit to supply us even with provisions. The State of South Carolina lent us the few tents we had, and also our arms. At our own expense, and with our own private funds we supplied ourselves. It rained nearly every day . . . we laid down at night upon damp ground and wet blankets. Pneumonia and other diseases decimated the ranks of the regiment.

Most of us were boys, inexperienced in hardships, tenderly raised. . . .

The regiment left home-soil at Hamburg, and proceeded across Georgia to Atlanta, the western terminus of the Georgia Railroad, and at that time a new village of about a hundred shacks with a population of 300 people. "The Georgians," says Posey, "treated us generously and hospitably . . . . many gentlemen hearing of our coming had large quantities of provisions cooked which were freely given to us."

The worst hardships of the regiment came after it left Georgia. Averaging about twenty miles a day, it marched the 150 miles from Atlanta to Notasulga, which was then the terminus of the Alabama Railroad. There the weary marchers happily boarded open cars, which carried them in a few hours to Montgomery, where they arrived in the afternoon to the noisy but thrilling welcome of a salute from the Montgomery Artillery. After standing in line to receive the visits and congratulations of the citizens, they marched to the river, where they were crowded aboard the small steamboat, "William Bradstreet", hardly a third large enough to accommodate them.

For two hideous days, as they moved down the river toward Mobile, the men were without food. At the same time they were suffering from such intense cold that they had to crowd around the steam-boilers to keep life in their stiffening bodies. "It was a sad and pitiful sight to look upon them" says Posey. "Boys who had been reared in luxury and splendor—who had never done a day's work in their lives and had never suffered a hardship, were suddenly reduced to gnawing hunger, to the bitterest blasts of winter, and to quarters hideously loathsome to refined feelings."

For undisciplined troops it was too much to be borne, and open mutiny broke out. About forty of the men, chiefly from the Hammond Guards of Barnwell, fixed bayonets, stopped the steamer, and went ashore. When the officers ordered them arrested, no one obeyed the order, and the mutineers had their way. Realizing the provocation, the officers yielded, and the matter was hushed up.

Finally, on a bright sunny morning, Mobile was reached,

the regiment was comfortably quartered in a large warehouse on the bay, and for the first time the men were "decently fed." Indeed it was time that they were, for they were in sorry shape. From Mobile a member of the DeKalb Guards from Kershaw wrote home on January 19 a cautious appraisal: "Our men are generally well, except colds and mumps . . . Captain Sumter reported ten cases in his company this morning. The men generally look well and *thriving*, though not *clean* or *handsome*—if they were, they would not be soldiers."

The colonel of the regiment, meanwhile, had gone ahead to New Orleans to procure vessels for the voyage from Mobile to Mexico, which would require at least seven days. When en route across the Gulf, one of the vessels, the "Alhambra", ran into a storm, "the hatches were nailed down upon the suffocating sea-sick soldiers, who, tumbled together in a common pile with the barrels of mess pork and pilot bread, were rolled from side to side. . . . On deck the horses—broken from their stalls, and frantic with fright, were only saved from trampling each other to death by being swept together into the deep". After narrowly escaping shipwreck, the "Alhambra" was blown so near the Mexican coast that it could be seen distinctly.

Finally the ships reached the rendezvous fixed by General Winfield Scott, at Lebos, a beautiful but waterless little island a hundred miles from Vera Cruz. There the men suffered agonies of thirst, for they could not drink the foul water which had been brought on the ships, it having been put into unwashed meat-casks. They therefore dug holes on the beach and found for themselves a nauseating brackish fluid, which aggravated the cases of dysentery. There died and was buried, John Hall of Abbeville; and not long after The Sumters lost Scarborough Drake. While on the island, the ragged men bought themselves coarse, heavy shirts of red flannel and blue striped cotton, which reached down nearly to their knees. These they belted at the waist and wore as gaudy frock coats over their trousers.

From Lobos the army proceeded by sailing vessels to Lizardo, and there on March 9, died young Sergeant M. J. M.

Murphy of The Sumters, from inflamation of the bowels, caused by bad food. He was a young lawyer of Sumterville, and the only son of his parents.

When the Palmetto Regiment finally arrived on Mexican soil, most of the sick had either died or recovered, and only some three or four members were still in the hospital. As one man grimly wrote: "The few of them left can only be killed by bullets."

Of their further sufferings on the field of battle, and their incredible valor, the record may be read in many histories. Suffice it for us to say, that after the storming and capture of Chapultepec, The Sumters, headed by Captain James D. Blanding in command, marched among the first to enter Mexico City, and the Palmetto flag was the first to be planted on the walls.

When the war was over, the first member of The Sumters to reach home, early in March 1848, was John S. Brumby, his health injured. In April Captain Francis Sumter appeared at the courthouse, his wounded arm still in a sling, but he was hopeful of recovering its use. In June the *Sumter Banner* reported that of the original company, only a fourth of The Sumters remained. In July an editorial announced the safe return of Captain James D. Blanding, who had been in all the battles, and even been knocked down by a bullet which struck his coin purse, but he had come out unscathed, one of the few survivors to live to old age without some form of permanent injury. Among the few mementoes the Captain brought home was a Mexican gold coin, bought from a looter. This coin he had made into a wedding ring for his young sweetheart, Leonora McFaddin, to whom he was soon happily married.

Almost immediately after his arrival, Captain Blanding had a card in the *Banner*, saying that he would be in Washington during the month of August to procure the land warrants for 160 acres or government script for $100 in lieu thereof, due each member of The Sumters or his heir at law. Throughout his long life Captain Blanding was destined to have many public services thrust upon him, for he was always a man of action. When South Carolina awarded medals to members of the Palmetto Regiment, Captain Blanding was named to make the distribution.

In July 1848, when news reached Sumterville that the survivors of The Sumters would soon be home, a public meeting of the citizens was called at the courthouse to arrange for their reception. The Honorable F. I. Moses offered four resolutions, which were promptly adopted; a committee of sixteen was appointed to meet The Sumters on arrival in Charleston; another committee of thirty (later expanded to fifty) was named to arrange for a public dinner in Sumterville in their honor, to which Governor David Johnson and his staff, Lieutenant-Governor Cain, and other dignitaries were invited.

Finally in mid-August, the heroes came home. A ball was given for them in the new house of Mr. Andrew Jackson Moses, who generously loaned it for the occasion. Said the *Banner*, "Everything went as merry as a marriage." The dinner was served at China's Hotel, and was highlighted by two innovations: the next to the last toast was offered "By a Lady"; and another by Master Z. P. Moses, captain in the boys' Temperance Cold Water Army, who offered "Cold Water."

But a week later there was a sorrowful note when the Chairman of Arrangements published in the *Banner* a plea to the Dinner Committee "to come forward and pay up, as there is considerable deficiency, and Mr. China is in want of his money." In November he gave public notice once more that $200 was still due Mr. China. But apparently few responded, and at the end of February 1849, Mr. John China himself published a request that the Committee of Fifty pay the $175.61 yet due him.[1]

A few days before Mexico signed the treaty of peace ceding to the United States the vast domains of California and New Mexico, some lumps of gold were picked up in California. When the news appeared some months later in the eastern newspapers, a sensational gold-rush ensued, which, within a year swelled the population of the territory by more than a

---

[1] The story of The Sumters is from the files of the Sumter *Banner*, Nov. 25, 1846—Feb. 28, 1849. Posey's narrative is in the *Watchman*, Nov. 1857—Jan. 1858. In 1852 he was editing the *Independent Press* at Abbeville, and later he was an editor in Alabama.

hundred thousand. The fortune hunters included men of every class and condition, and many outlaws. In dire need for law and order, the Californians adopted a constitution and applied for statehood. As the new constitution excluded slavery, the South realized that the admission of California would give the North a majority in Congress, and Southerners deeply resented the injustice of excluding slaveholders from territory which had been won largely by Southern blood and sacrifice. In Washington, Henry Clay put through his last great Compromise of 1850, admitting California without slavery, and providing for a rigorous Fugitive Slave Law.

Intense excitement prevailed in South Carolina, and Calhoun believed the time had come for secession. The people of Sumter District formed a Committee of Safety headed by John L. Manning; and a Committee of Vigilance, each member of which was to organize in his neighborhood a corps of minutemen, with arms. These committees merged their efforts into Associations for the Defense of Southern Rights. The published roll of the Claremont Association shows 546 names.

In December 1850, the legislature of South Carolina prepared for secession and increased taxes by 50% to put the state on a war footing. Governor Means recommended the expulsion from the state of every free Negro who did not own land or slaves, but his recommendation was rejected.

Sumter newspapers took part in the editorial debate of the issues. The *Banner* answered with spirit a letter from Joel R. Poinsett counselling "abject submission" to Congress. The *Watchman* reprinted with a rebuttal a submissionist letter from Sumterville, which had been published in B. F. Perry's *Southern Patriot*. Public sentiment in Sumter District crystalized into a few Submissionists, some Secessionists who believed that South Carolina should secede alone, and many Cooperationists who wanted secession only if other Southern states would cooperate in leaving the Union with South Carolina.

When the state Southern Rights Convention met in Charleston in May 1851, some forty associations were represented. Claremont sent Dr. W. W. Anderson, Sebastian Sumter,

William Nettles, Ezra Pugh, F. I. Moses, Montgomery Moses, Albertus C. Spain, T. B. Fraser, William Harris, Thomas R. English, Sr., and J. W. Brownfield. Clarendon sent W. L. Reynolds, Dr. James McCauley, Dr. Robert R. Durant, Jared J. Nelson, R. C. Richardson, Richard P. Haynsworth, and Dr. Samuel W. Witherspoon. Ex-Governor John Peter Richardson, of Sumter District, was chosen president, and made a "temperate and forcible speech."

Sentiment in the convention was overwhelmingly for secession, but, as an unofficial body, it could not take such a step. In the meantime Virginia, Alabama, Mississippi and Georgia made plain their opposition to secession. When the official Convention of the People of South Carolina, met in April 1852 to decide the question, the members realized that independent secession was impracticable, and side-stepped the issue.

Peace among the state factions came with the election in December 1852, of amiable warm-hearted John L. Manning as governor, the fourth man from Sumter District to be chosen to that office.

CHAPTER XIV
EARLY RAILROADS

Although at the time of the War with Mexico there was no railroad in Sumter District, ever since that Christmas Day in 1830, when the "Best Friend" locomotive went into regular service between Charleston and Hamburg, the progressive citizens of Sumterville had begun to think about plans for getting railway connection with Charleston. The next year many people had an opportunity to ride on a miniature circular steam-railway, which was exhibited in Camden in the old Methodist Church. By 1834 the people of Sumter District generally, realized that a railroad would be their best friend also; and in August the *Camden Journal and Southern Whig* published a notice that the citizens of Claremont, Salem, and Clarendon, would apply at the next session of the legislature for the incorporation of a company to lay a railroad from Sumterville to Charleston.

The staggering cost, however, must have caused the plan to be amended; and, when the citizens met at Sumter Courthouse in October 1835, they unanimously adopted a resolution offered by C. W. Miller that a railroad from Sumterville to the Santee River, either to cross, or to meet a steamboat for Charleston, would be both practicable and profitable; and a committee was appointed to confer with the legislative delegation of Sumter District in regard to chartering a company.

At the December session of the legislature in 1836, a company was chartered for building a railroad from Darlington via Bishopville, Mechanicsville, and Sumterville, to the north bank of the Santee between the fork of the Wateree and Congaree, and a point five miles below Vance's Ferry. The following March the company opened subscription books, and offered shares at $100, only $10 down.[1]

But money was scarce and the time was not favorable. The

[1] *Stat.*, VIII, 440. *Camden Journal and Southern Whig*, Mch. 18, 1837.

merchants and planters who had survived the financial panic of 1819 and the economic depression of 1825, were beginning to feel the pinch of the worst and longest of all ante-bellum depressions, which lasted from 1837 until 1845. Texas had begun to produce more cotton than the Atlantic states, and many Sumter planters were planning to leave their exhausted lands and remove westward. So the railroad project languished for ten long years, while plodding teams on wretched roads continued to haul their heavy loads to the steamboat landings along the Wateree.

Two railroads, however, were destined to serve ante-bellum Sumter District, the Camden Branch of the South Carolina Railroad, and the Wilmington and Manchester Railroad.

Although a railroad from Camden to Charleston had been agitated in 1833-34, and the surveys had been made, nothing came of it until 1842, when a branch line from Charleston to Columbia was completed for freight and passenger service. The northern portion of the Columbia branch line ran between the fork of the Congaree and Wateree Rivers, and was, therefore, less than forty miles from Camden, and only a few miles from Manchester, Stateburg and Sumterville. A Camden branch was now practicable, and by 1845, acceptable plans had been completed, rights of way were obtained, contracts were let, and work was begun. The projected line was to cross the Wateree near Manchester, turn north toward Camden and follow the edge of Wateree swamp within a mile of Stateburg.

By February 1848, the trestle over the Wateree had been built and the grading of the roadbed completed. As in the case of the Columbia branch, contracts were let to planters for slave labor, for it was hoped that in addition to other benefits brought by the railroad, profitable employment for the slaves would enable hard-pressed planters to rest their worn lands, and prevent further migration westward.

By April, cars were crossing the river and taking passengers to connect with the South Carolina Railroad's trains at the junction (now Kingville) in Richland District. On the Sumter side of the river, a station between Stateburg and Manchester completed early in April, was called Clarendon

Depot, but in August the name was changed to Middleton.

North of Manchester, the station called Claremontville or Claremont Depot, was expected to cause the abandonment of Stateburg as a place of business, but although it flourished briefly, it never developed into a town.

By September 1848 the Camden Branch had reached Boykins, and by November it was running a regular schedule into Camden. The thirty-eight miles of track had been completed at a cost of $606,060.53, financed on a fifty-fifty basis by the stockholders and the South Carolina Railroad. In the construction, heavy T-rails had been used, which gave such strength, that, for the first time, crossties had been laid directly on the roadbed, without the costly underlying mudsills.[2]

The other early railroad which served Sumter district had its origin in 1846, when plans were made for connecting Manchester with Wilmington, North Carolina, where the projected line would meet the Wilmington and Roanoke Railroad; and charters were obtained from both North and South Carolina for the Wilmington and Manchester Railroad Company. In January 1847, the favorable report of the surveyors of the proposed route to connect with Camden Branch, was published, and in February books for subscriptions were opened at Darlington, Marion and other towns. In Sumterville the books were in charge of Wm. Haynsworth, M. Moses, J. D. Blanding, L. White, J. Dyson, J. L. Manning, S. E. Wilson, J. E. Dennis, S. McBride, and J. O. Durant.

The time was favorable, for the long depression which had paralyzed business since 1837 was at last ending. Cotton was selling for 10½ and 12½ cents in Charleston, and although the market was uncertain, and at times even gloomy, the planters now had better prospects. At Sumterville in April, 300 shares of Wilmington and Manchester railroad stock were taken at $30,000, to be paid in installments. In August, W. W. Harllee, president of the railroad, announced that the engineers would begin work on both ends of the line and work toward a meeting. In November 1848 contracts were let for grading the roadbed between Sumter and Lynches Creek. But

---

[2] S. M. Derrick, *Centennial History of South Carolina Railroad* (Columbia, 1930), pp. 195-197.

in the same month when cotton fell again to 6½ and 8 cents, the collections from purchasers of shares were disappointing, and work was retarded.

New hope came in May of the next year with the announcement that directors of both the Wilmington and Manchester, and the South Carolina railroad, had at last agreed on a junction of the two roads, and had chosen Rocky Mount, a mile and a half below Middleton, where the Camden Branch entered Wateree swamp. Simultaneously came the announcement that stockholders had accepted contracts for grading the entire route, which would be paid for in stock. The *Banner* in February 1849, carried an invitation to the public to witness on Washington's birthday the breaking of ground at Wilmington, the northern end of the line.

But in July 1849, the heavens opened and floods of rain descended, drowning the crops of cotton and corn, and washing away the embankments of the roadbed. Trains on the Camden Branch were held up for hours because of sand which had washed over the rails. Milldams overflowed and were washed away. The heat of summer changed suddenly to the chill of December, and stayed there until after the *Banner* went to press. The mail from Darlington to Sumter could proceed no further than White's Mills, and, attempting to return to Bishopville, had to swim for it. Thus the great railroad project was hampered by a discouraging series of disasters and disappointments, which were faithfully chronicled in the columns of the *Banner*. But despite everything, the work continued.

The advertisement of T. J. Coghlan announced to railroad contractors that he could furnish a few dozen railroad carts, with three-inch tires, at $300 a dozen, and "Recollect," said Mr. Coghlan, "the carts will not be built of green pine, but of the best Riverswamp oak, ash and hickory, and will be suitable for plantation purposes when the road is completed."

In September contractors advertised for a hundred hands to work in the pine woods until after frost should end the malarial season; then they would work on the edge of the river swamp; "the hands will be supplied with an abundance of wholesome food and dry tents. Wages are good, and paid in *Cash* monthly." Interested persons were to apply to C. S. Mellet near Manchester, or to D. B. McLaurin in Sumterville.

All of the next year the work proceeded slowly, with discouraging delays that brought doubts to the investors. In a stirring appeal to the disheartened stockholders, the year 1851 was declared by "A Stockholder" to be the year of crisis. The lowest estimate for the 162-mile railroad, was $1,550,000, and, if completed, would be the cheapest ever built. Of this sum, individuals had subscribed $760,000; and the State of South Carolina, $200,000; the remaining $600,000 must be provided by the company before the road could go into operation. There had been no mismanagement, but the company had exhausted all funds from subscriptions. Was the road to be completed? or abandoned with all its costly investment? Once more the stockholders rallied, the crisis was passed, and the work went forward.

By January 1852, the whistle of the locomotive on the other side of Green Swamp could be heard in Sumterville, and numbers of people would walk out from the town to see the wonder. The Rev. William W. Mood has preserved the story of such an afternoon trip with a party from his congregation: Mr. and Mrs. James Harvey Dingle, Mrs. Watson and her daughter Mag; Ellen and Mary Anderson; and last but not least, an old Mrs. Terry, and the Dingle's little maid servant Ann, neither of whom had ever seen a locomotive. The long walk across the swamp brought them finally to the scene, and Mr. Mood began to point out to Mrs. Terry the parts of the strange machine. S. S. Solomons, who was superintending the road, was on the engine, and for fun blew the whistle. All were startled, but when Mr. Solomons, continuing the joke, let out a longer blast, the old lady and the little maid took to their heels in panic, scrambled up the sides of the cut, and made for the woods. In vain were they called back, and, too terrified to heed, they had to be pursued and overtaken. In utter exhaustion, the old lady was literally carried back to the cars. They finally made the return trip through the swamp by starlight, getting their feet wet and having a rough passage. The repentant Mr. Solomons did everything possible to make amends, and saw that Mrs. Terry got safely home, but for several days she kept her bed.[3]

A little later, L. J. Fleming, resident engineer, advertised that on and after March 8, 1852, a passenger train would run daily except Sunday from Sumterville to the junction at 6:30 A. M., and the freight rate on cotton from Sumterville to Camden Branch would be 25 cents a bale. In April, service was extended to Mayes Station, now Mayesville. By December, the following was the schedule for the down train:

Leave	Hills	3:40 A. M.
"	Timmonsville	4:00 A. M.
"	Lynchburg	4:40 A. M.
"	Mayesville	5:20 A. M.
"	Sumterville	6:00 A. M.
"	Manchester	6:50 A. M.
Ar.	Junction	7:15 A. M.

The station at the junction, often called Sumter Junction and sometimes Camden Junction but now Foxville, has been described as a "very small room, in Wateree Swamp, surrounded by water." The unhurried agent there for many years was sociable Henry J. Haynsworth, who married Vermelle Arthur, a sister of President Arthur.

In April 1853, the Wilmington and Manchester reached Darlington Depot[4], now Florence; and receipts at Sumterville averaged $100 a day for the month. When the road was completed in 1854, it proved to be profitable, and the nominal net profit the next year was $213,824. Unfortunately, more than two-thirds of the profit had to be spent immediately for repairs and improvements.

Crude and flimsy as they were, the Camden Branch and the Wilmington and Manchester railroads were among the best of their day. Their speed was perhaps from twelve to twenty miles an hour, and the wood-burning engines threw so many sparks into the cars that the passengers had to watch their clothes for fires. Another annoyance was from free-ranging cows on the tracks. Conductor Fowler of the Charlotte Railway used the plan of placing a man with a gun on the front of the engine to clear the tracks by shooting the

---

[3] W. W. Mood, in *Southern Christian Advocate*, Sept. 12, 1889.

[4] Darlington Depot, ten miles south of Darlington, was at Ebenezer Church. The town of Florence then did not exist.

cattle with small shot, and thus he was relieved of having to stop every mile or two to drive off stock.

Accidents were not infrequent, especially on the Wateree trestle of the Camden Branch. In October 1850, three miles of the trestle collapsed, "due to grossly erroneous plan of construction." The estimated time for repairs was set variously at three, six, or even nine months; and this too at the time of year when the bulk of the cotton crop was yet to be moved to market. Furthermore, although the steamboat "Robert Martin" was expected at Sumter's Landing, the river was so low that there was doubt if Camden could be reached. Two years later, while the train was passing over the swamp, the trestle again collapsed, and completely demolished the cars. Among the dead were Colonel Richard Singleton of "Home" plantation (and White Sulphur Springs), and his young grandson. Charles Mayrant and Samuel J. Bradley were seriously injured, several others were slightly hurt, and one was reported missing. The next year, there was a freight tie-up at the trestle, when the bridge was cut away to allow Captain L. H. Belser's boat to pass up the river to Camden. The legislature therefore ordered the railroad to rebuild the bridge thirty-five feet high, and to pay the expense of having smoke-stacks of steamboats hinged so that they might be lowered to pass under the bridge.

The advent of railroad transportation brought the question, should the trains run on Sunday? At the December session of the legislature in 1859, Senator Moses presented a petition from the citizens of Claremont election district, asking that operation cease on the Sabbath. It was referred to the Committee on College, Education, and Religion.

The effect of the railroad upon the villages which had become stations was spectacular. Manchester, the old wayside community, where men and boys had lazed away the summers with all-day card games, fist fights, feats of strength, and match games at the ball battery, now had all the prestige of a railroad terminus, and suddenly became a busy town. As soon as Camden Branch was opened to Manchester, Alexander Campbell began advertising his inn, two and a half miles from the depot, as a place where breakfast could be had at five o'clock in the morning or earlier, and horses might be left in his care until the owners returned from Charleston. A. Loryea of the Sumterville Bakery was one of the first to move in and open up a new general store, where he offered to sell at low prices for either cash or country produce.

Indeed, Manchester grew so rapidly under the impetus of the railroad, that by the time the line to Wilmington was completed, the once sleepy old village was being referred to as a city. But on the night of January 25, 1855, disaster struck the budding young metropolis, when a fire, believed to be of incendiary origin, was discovered in a wooden tenement occupied by Mrs. Leonora Bartlett and her family. The fire department under Chief Kolb, assisted by the mayor and many volunteers, worked valiantly, but the entire town below Depot Lane was consumed. The block north of this might have gone too, but at the critical moment the wind shifted and sent the flames toward the Belser and McLaurin residences. Fortunately, these were saved by the fire department. Still more fortunately, no lives were lost, although the widow of Peter Bogart was found unconscious on the steps of a burning building, and had a narrow escape. To quote some of the highlights of the news story as related by "Syksey" in the *Watchman*, the citizens were "under great obligations to the distinguished strangers who were on a visit to the city at the time and who rendered the most efficient aid." "Amid the crackling of flames, the crash of falling timbers and all the horrors of such a conflagration, one of the principal sufferers was observed seated upon the small remnant of furniture preserved, quietly smoking and viewing the awful scene with a calmness which won . . . admiration from all observers." Although a fifth of the town was destroyed and there was no insurance, Manchester was rebuilt and continued to prosper for many years. In 1856 Dr. W. A. Ramsay was advertising from Manchester for a teacher to take charge of a small school, capable of preparing students to enter college. Two years later N. E. Venable was advertising the second session of his select school, limited to twenty pupils, near Manchester Depot.

Eight miles to the north, the effect of the railroad upon Stateburg was negligible. For a time the depot at Claremont, a mile away, enjoyed prosperity, and tended to draw away most of the business which remained at Stateburg after Sumterville took the courts. But Stateburg continued to be pre-eminently the residential section of the District, for the name was applied to the entire community of spacious homes in the surrounding hills.

At Sumterville, the boom which was in progress in 1848 continued unchecked. So urban had it become that when the town was re-incorporated in 1855, "ville" was dropped from the name. Said patriotic printer, T. P. McQueen, who gloried in being a native of the Game Cock District: "We have lawyers enough to get everybody a fighting. Doctors enough to cure every body"; from the two good newspapers, "we know every thing that is going on in the world"; walk to the depot and you will find a steam mill and a machine shop carried on by Coghlan and Gay: "There you will hear the sons of Vulcan at their anvils; and perhaps . . . the snorting of the iron horse." The passengers who arrived on the cars of the "iron horse" were now met at the depot and carried to their homes by an omnibus operated by Robert W. Andrews, who had traded some horses for it in Charleston. Apparently the "bus" was not profitable, for in 1855 the sheriff offered it for sale with the four horses and harness, levied on at the suit of Samuel Bradley.

Indeed there were many improvements in the town of Sumter, for by 1857 the streets had been drained; and several stores were being built of brick. White, Haynsworth and Company's brick store was a hundred feet long, with a semicircular glass front, receding from iron columns sustained above and below by granite. Adjoining it, the brick grocery store of Lafar and Dick was being erected. A few hundred feet further up, on the same side of the street, was rising the large dwelling of A. A. Solomons, which, said the *Watchman,* "justly ranks as a superb city residence." A new brick jail, three stories high, was also under construction, and the old jail was being considered as a possible bank, or an engine house and post office. Two years later, a large brick freight-depot was being built, and the town council agreed that thereafter the railroad, which had brought so much good to Sumter, should have no taxes levied on its property within the town limits.

Although the town had grown beyond all expectations, its citizens still had many wants, the first being a bank. A charter had been obtained in 1852. The commissioners W. F. B. Haynsworth, T. D. Frierson and A. J. Moses were to sell the stock in the store of Mr. Frierson at $25 a share, $5 down. But the money could not be raised, for the railroad was then absorbing all surplus capital, and the bank charter expired. Another charter was issued in 1856, with like result. The second vital need of Sumter was a telegraph. When the line from Wilmington was being constructed through the town, an office could have been opened if the citizens had agreed to pay the operator's salary, but the condition was not met, and the office did not open.

Eight miles to the northeast of Sumter was the next station, Mayesville, named for Matthew Peterson Mayes, known as Squire Mayes. Born in Virginia in 1794, he had settled in Sumter District because of his marriage to Martha Bradley of Salem, whom he had met as a schoolgirl in Raleigh. After her untimely death, he had married Henrietta Shaw and built a house on the plantation, where later was to develop the village of Mayesville around the railroad station. Their eldest son, Junius Alcaeus Mayes, was born there, and became an influential physician in the community.[5] T. B. Taylor of the Charleston firm of Ketchum, Taylor and Company, opened a store at the station in 1857; and the next year Chandler, Mayes and Company were advertising their business.

Before the advent of the railroad, Lynchburg, the next station, had begun existence as Murphrey's Cross Roads, "marked by one solitary dwelling of revolutionary memory, and one store of a more recent date, occupied at times, and at others not." Later it was known as English's Cross Roads.[6] But the place was to have other changes of name. Elisha Spencer, whose store was there, noted in his daybook on December 19, 1850, "This place hitherto called Five Forks will from this time forward be called Willow Grove." On August 15, 1851, he entered another change: "A post office having

---

[5] From family records owned by Miss Margaret Brunson.
[6] "Pro Patria", in the *Watchman*, Jan. 17, 1860.

been established at this place by the name of Lynchburg the place from this time forward will be called Lynchburg instead of Willow Grove."[7] When the railroad station was built a mile north of the crossroads, it was given the name Lynchburg, in harmony with the recently established post office. In 1853, R. G. Potts had a carriage and buggy shop at Lynchburg and was advertising for a blacksmith to forge the irons. Soon after, W. H. DeBerry and W. J. McLeod, in partnership, were advertising their well-selected stock of dry goods.

The Lynchburg Academy for boys was opened in 1856 under R. Diston, a teacher of ability, long experience, and the highest testimonials, according to the trustees, James G. McIntosh, Elisha Spencer, W. H. DeBerry, R. W. Durant and David Cole. The next year the Lynchburg Female School opened with Miss C. R. Crockeroft in charge.

Lynchburg and its business soon outgrew the station's "parasol of a building", which, wrote a facetious citizen to the *Watchman*, was not only unable to hold the freight, but in cold or rain was utterly unfit to shelter the passengers, who too often found it necessary to intrude on the privacies of the neighborhood, or to take to the Tank, or to the "house that Jack built."[8] So rapidly did the village grow that at the close of 1859 it was incorporated, the limits to "extend one-half of a mile in the direction of the cardinal points from the cross roads . . . and form a square."[9] At the first town election, Elisha Spencer was chosen intendant; and W. J. McLeod, A. W. Durant, Dr. S. H. Miller, and S. P. Durant, wardens. At that time, Lynchburg had two churches, Presbyterian and Methodist; three stores, one for groceries and two for dry goods; a wagon factory, a blacksmith shop, and an academy. Within its corporate limits, continued "Pro Patria," lived twenty-four voters, and "nearly an equal number of as pretty ladies as can be seen in any 'burg'."[10]

[7] I am indebted to Frank A. McLeod for use of Spencer's daybook.
[8] *Watchman*, Mch. 4, 1857.
[9] *Stat.*, XII, 680.
[10] *Watchman*, Jan. 7, 1860.

CHAPTER XV

EARLY SCHOOLS AND TEACHERS

The first schoolmasters of Sumter District were generally the ministers of the gospel, such as the Rev. Charles Woodmason of St. Mark's, and Dr. Thomas Reese of Salem Black River, whose schools already have been mentioned. An exception was Wood Furman, a surveyor, who in the 1770's, was teaching in the High Hills. The first school buildings were the old log cabins on abandoned fields, the "old-field schools", or log churches, such as the meetinghouse in Manchester, where Father Jenkins preached when he was almost mobbed by hecklers.

Many early wills on record in Sumter contain instructions for the education of the testator's sons. James Conyers in 1783 directed that his eldest son, John, should begin school at the age of eight years, and, if the estate's funds sufficed, should be sent to college. Conyers' younger son, James, also was to enter school at the age of eight, but should remain only until he mastered languages, and then, if a commission could be obtained, he should enter the Continental Army.

Several inventories of estates show lists of books—fiction, history, biography, drama, and poetry, as well as books on military and religious subjects. Hiram Tomlin of Salem, at the time of his death in 1822, had a library which included all of the above categories as well as music, mathematics and geography, a dictionary and an English grammar, three volumes of lectures, *The Spectator,* and *The Monthly Register.* Robert McKnight, who died the same year, had among his books an encyclopedia and four volumes of *The Rambler.* Charles Osborne's estate in 1826 had fifty-seven volumes valued at forty dollars. Robert Brailsford's inventory of 1828 listed more than a hundred books and a lot of pamphlets. James Grier White in 1833 left, with some three dozen other books, a set of "American Biography" valued at twelve dollars.

The education of children in these and earlier times was the responsibility of their parents, and if the parents were too poor or indifferent, the children grew up illiterate. To protect helpless orphans from such a fate, the Clarendon Orphan Society was chartered in 1798 to establish a public school, financed from escheated property in the county, and to be managed by seven trustees: Richard Richardson, James Davis, Thomas Nightingale Johnson, John Peter Richardson, Samuel Montgomery, Matthew James, and James Burchell Richardson. The school functioned, but in 1812, Mark Moore, a former teacher of the Clarendon Orphan Academy, stated that its location rendered it unsafe to health during the summer.

South Carolina undertook to relieve the children of the poor in 1811, and enacted a free-school law which provided for their elementary education. John B. Miller was one of the first Board of seven Free School Commissioners for Claremont election district. The annual report of W. F. B. Haynsworth, secretary-treasurer of the Board, shows for the year 1857, a total of 589 pupils, and 52 free schools in Sumter District, each with one teacher. Eight of these schools were in the town of Sumter, the largest enrollment being thirty-seven pupils taught by C[aroline] Morgan. The next largest was thirty pupils in a school near Cato's Spring, taught by A. J. McFarland. Each pupil was listed to pay 5 cents a day, or $3 a quarter, or $6 a session. The state had appropriated $1,800 and the patrons paid $796.91, so the total free-school fund for Sumter District in 1857, was less than $2600. Little wonder that a country schoolmaster that year sent the following to the *Watchman:*

> Dear Sir:
> I here present my school account,
> I wish from you the full amount,
>   That's due me!
> My creditors must all be paid
> Or I perhaps in jail be laid,
>   To suffer there!
> To have a widower lodged in jail
> 'Twould be a most heart rending tale,

> To tell the girls!
> I am just and honest, though a fool,
> I wish the amount of my free school,
> To pay my debts!
> You know my friend, what I'm about,
> And in this matter help me out,
> I'll thank you sir!

Mr. Haynsworth's report of 1857 shows how little popular support was being given to free schools. This is understandable, for the parents generally felt that to send their children to the free schools was a stigma upon both themselves and their children. Colonel G. S. C. DesChamps was so disturbed by the inadequacy of the free schools, that he advocated that year the founding of a college for the children of the poor. Thus, since the public schools lacked both patrons and proficiency, the private schools remained throughout the antebellum era the mainstay of general education, and were found in every community.

On isolated plantations, well-to-do parents employed a tutor or a governess. In more populous areas, private schools were very numerous. Some were owned by the teacher in charge, who set aside a schoolroom in his residence or built a schoolhouse nearby. Other schools were the result of cooperation among parents, who formed a society and contributed to a common fund to employ a teacher and perhaps erect a schoolhouse. A school which prepared for college entrance was sometimes called a high school, and a girls' finishing school was frequently an institute or a seminary, but the name most generally favored for every school which taught more than the "three R's," was academy.

The names and teachers of all these academies will never be known. The Sandville Academy, between Stateburg and Pinckney's Ferry, was being taught in 1812 by Mark Moore, the former preceptor of the Clarendon Orphan Academy. About the same time, Lodebar Academy had a Mrs. Langley as a teacher, who left there to find pupils in Camden. Incorporated in 1817, with Thomas Humphries, Gabriel Capers and perhaps other trustees, Lodebar Academy was advertised the following spring as being in full operation under teachers of learning and exceptional moral character. Chartered at the same time as Lodebar, was Mount Clio Academy, to whose trustees, James C. Postell, John J. Muldrow, and others, in 1815, Matthew Meeks had conveyed an acre of land for the school. The building was erected, and, as authorized in the charter, a lottery was advertised to raise funds for equipment, with prizes ranging from $100 to $2000. Apparently the Academy must have been burned, for the next year the trustees sold the one-acre site to Eli Lee, who, in 1820 conveyed it to Dr. Jacques Bishop as the acre on which Mount Clio Academy had formerly stood. At the academy near Salem Black River in 1812, were the teachers Joseph B. Cook and George C. MacWhorter, and some twenty years later, William Banks. A schoolmaster, John Parker, in 1824 bought a farm in that neighborhood.

The trustees of Bishopville Academy, Dr. Jacques Bishop, James Rembert, Jonathan Miller, A. G. Crosswell, Edward Barrett, and William H. Bowen, announced its opening early in 1835 under Mrs. Frances Bowen, who had engaged Mrs. Catherine Ladd as an assistant. Four years later, Bishopville Academy was chartered, with Dr. James Durant, John E. Dennis, A. G. Cockerell, James McCullum, Hardy Stuckey, Robert Fraser, and J. W. English, as trustees. In 1848, the Rev. W. W. Wilson was in charge. The Academy evidently was not continuous, for ten years later, the trustees announced that the fifth session would commence on the second Monday in January, under the supervision of J. M. Dennis, A. M., a graduate of the University of North Carolina, who had been managing the school during the previous two years, apparently to their entire satisfaction.

Rembert settlement too, had its academy, and in 1834, L. L. Fraser, secretary of the Board of Trustees, was advertising for a teacher. During the 1850's Sumter newspapers carried many other advertisements of local schools, such as William T. Capers' school at Providence; W. H. and George E. Coit's High School at Mayesville; the Swimming Pens and the Plowden Mills schools. Among the Clarendon institutions were St. Paul's Academy, taught by Thomas Waties, witty and popular son of Judge Waties; Friendship Academy, and

Summerton Academy, both of which flourished under the successive administrations of R. K. Rutledge.

Although private schools were found in every part of Sumter District, there were three localities which were especially favored, particularly for boarding schools, and these were Stateburg, Bradford Springs, and Sumterville.

The reputation of the High Hills for healthfulness was the chief factor that caused several excellent academies to be located near Stateburg. Claremont Academy already has been mentioned. Dr. John M. Robert's Academy nearby, received funds from the Baptist State Convention for the education of ministerial students, and after his tragic death, Furman Academy was established in Edgefield to continue such work. Furman Academy soon was relocated in the High Hills, then went to Fairfield, and finally was chartered in 1850 as Furman University at Greenville.

About seven miles northeast of Stateburg was Woodville Academy, a cooperative project of a group of neighbors, Reuben Long, John Monk, Thomas Baker and others, who purchased a ten-acre site from John Darrington in the High Hills and erected a building. In December 1816, Thomas Baker and W. R. Theus began advertising for a teacher capable of teaching English, Latin and Greek, to which they added a statement that "this Academy is intended to be liberal and permanent." A year later the sponsors were incorporated as "The Associated Supporters of the Woodville Academy," and authorized to raise funds up to ten thousand dollars by lottery. In April 1819, the secretary was advertising for an assistant teacher. The Academy was still in existence in 1821, when S. H. Boykin made his survey of Sumter District for Mills' *Atlas*.

Another well-known boys' school in the Stateburg neighborhood, was Edgehill Academy, incorporated near the close of 1834. The Academy had opened the previous year in charge of Willard Richardson, who had come to Sumter in 1818 from Massachusetts as a lad of sixteen years, and ten years later had been graduated from the South Carolina College. He and some of his pupils boarded near the Academy with Mrs. Louisa Murrell, granddaughter of General Sumter, and late in life he married Louisa Blanche Murrell. A kind and patient man, Richardson was known among the boys as Old Bull. After the Nullification era, he joined the migration to the West, and in 1837 opened a school for young men in Houston, Texas.

Perhaps the last teacher at Edgehill Academy was William Keating Stuart, who in 1845, married Susanna Marion Heriot. Her marriage settlement indicates that she was an heiress, with an income in her own right. They resided at Edgehill Academy, where Mr. Stuart had a boarding and day school at least as late as 1848. From Edgehill they removed to Fulton, in the sandhills. Four years later, planning another move, Stuart offered for sale his carriage-horses and all of his household possessions, including a shower bath and a Chickering piano.

Among other schools near Stateburg, was Thornton Academy, advertised by its teacher of that name to open at his residence in November 1821, for young ladies and gentlemen. His promised discipline was to be *"mild* but *decisive,"* and the girls were to be taught music and other branches of ornamental education by an "eminently qualified" lady. Shortly before the War of Secession, "Rafton Creek Academy" was being conducted under the tutorship of William M. Gay, in the home of Isaac N. Lenoir near Sumter's Landing. In 1859, the "examination exercises" in Latin, history, geography, arithmetic, and declamation, were attended by many of the patrons, and lasted from 11 A. M. to 4 P. M., after which some of the twenty-odd boys exhibited their horsemanship in a tournament. The only girl enrolled in the school appears to have been chosen the Queen of Love and Beauty.

The Hawthorndean Seminary for young ladies was in Stateburg, in the very large house now called The Ruins, which had been the residence of the elder John Mayrant. The schoolmaster, Willis W. Alston, purchased the property in 1835 and opened his seminary, but three years later he sold it, apparently at a profit, and purchased another site, which he called Cottage Level, ten miles northeast of Sumterville on the Mechanicsville road. There he conducted a boarding school for boys. Later, he and his wife were in charge of the

Sumterville Academy, and eventually he removed to Louisiana, where he died in 1858, near Mansfield.

Bradford Springs because of its reputation as a health resort, became also a center for schools. The springs took their name from Nathaniel Bradford, who in 1785 had a grant there for 600 acres of vacant land. In 1806 Bradford sold a one-acre lot to John Smyth Richardson, and an adjoining four-acre lot to Dr. James Hartley, with the privilege to both of using and drinking the waters of the mineral spring and other springs nearby. Dr. Hartley was probably the pioneer promoter of Bradford Springs as a health resort, for at this time, mineral springs were favored by doctors and eagerly sought by many despairing invalids.

Ten years later, a Mrs. Campbell opened at the springs a young ladies' school, where she advertised to teach in addition to the three R's, English grammar, geography, elementary astronomy, natural and civil history, drawing, map-work, and embroidery as well as useful and ornamental needlework. Genteel board for her pupils was to be had "at Mrs. Pearson's." The following December, Benjamin Pierson published a notice that his boarding-house at Bradford Springs would be fitted in a suitable manner with bathing-houses. During Mr. Pierson's absence in August in 1817, Mrs. Pierson appears to have continued the business at the springs. Rates for board at the springs in 1818, as offered by S. Rembert, were one dollar a day or twenty dollars a month, with servants at half price; and rates for a horse the same as for his master.

The next year an academy was opened within a mile of the springs, in charge of Dr. Patterson of North Carolina. The trustees were General Sumter, Caleb Rembert, James R. Carter, Joseph S. Bossard, W. H. Capers, James and Samuel Dwyer, Sinclair Limbaker, Zachariah Cantey, and John Perry, the first two of whom in 1786 had been among the founders of Claremont Academy at Stateburg. Board for the pupils could be had "in decent houses convenient to the Academy" by paying half in advance. The career of this school appears to have been brief.

The resort business at Bradford Springs, meanwhile, had

EARLY SCHOOLS AND TEACHERS

not flourished and the buildings had fallen into ruinous condition, but under the management of Horace W. Bronson, according to his announcement, they were now put into good condition and were again ready for the accommodation of the delicate and infirm as well as those in search of pleasure. At the time of Boykin's survey in 1821, Miss Jane McCants had a tavern near the springs.

The Nullification controvery brought another academy to Bradford Springs. The Rev. R. W. Bailey, a Northern man, who had been conducting a military school near Columbia, had his school broken up because local sentiment opposed having a Southern military institution in charge of a Northerner. Mr. Bailey, therefore, taking with him N. D. Welch, his mathematics teacher, reopened his school at the springs, where public sentiment was more friendly, and the next year he began preaching every alternate Sunday at the Presbyterian church in Sumterville. A real estate advertisement of 1850 referred to the school as having been "most profitable", but it then had been closed for some years.

In the vicinity of Bradford Springs were a number of schools for girls. In 1837 Mrs. Honoria Richbourg advertised she would open a school at her residence near the springs. Four years later Mrs. Charles Spann announced the opening of a Female Seminary at her residence, Orange Grove, in association with three ladies of wide teaching experience, recently arrived from Europe. French was to be the mode of communication; music, painting and needlework were prominent in the curriculum.

After changing owners several times, the Bradford Springs property was purchased in 1835 by Henry Britton, whose inn there is said to have been well patronized. After Britton's death, the Rev. Julius J. DuBose, a Presbyterian minister from Darlington, who had totally lost his voice some years before, converted the inn into a girls' school which became well known as the Bradford Springs Female Academy. Encouraged by the interest manifested in his enterprise, Mr. DuBose advertised in 1846 that he had decided to purchase the property, which he was then improving. The faculty, besides Mr. DuBose and his wife, Mrs. M. E. DuBose, included Dr. Isaac Auld, M. D., who lectured on chemistry, and Miss Mary Hort, an English lady from Bristol. To quote the modest notice in the *Sumter Banner*, "Delicacy forbids the Principal to speak of the competency of himself and Mrs. DuBose to conduct such an institution." The fees for the ten-months' session were equally modest: tuition and board, with fuel, lights and laundry, $150.00; for the extras: music, $50.00; drawing and painting, $30.00; modern languages, $40.00. Vacations were from November 27, through the first two weeks in January; and from the first to the middle of May.

In the early spring of 1847, a most sensational incident occurred at the Academy, when the Rev. J. A. Bachouse, a former Baptist minister, made an unsuccessful attempt upon the life of Mr. DuBose. The incident might have escaped publicity, for Mr. DuBose merely inserted a notice in the *Banner* that the Academy would not be closed because of his "indisposition." But Dr. Auld was less discreet, and published the whole story in the *Banner*. Mr. Bachouse was tried at the spring term of court, found to be insane, and was committed to the Asylum.

A year later the Academy was advertised for sale, for Mr. DuBose had recovered his voice and wished to return to preaching. Of the 1246 acres in the property, 250 acres were under fence and 400 acres were cleared. The main building, 120 feet long, had twenty-five or thirty spacious rooms with lofty ceilings, and, in the Spartan manner of the times, was heated by only ten fireplaces. Besides the wide passages and a handsome basement, the structure had a piazza the full length of the front, and a 60-foot balcony. Among the many outbuildings were two cabins, each with five rooms, two fireplaces and a piazza; and a residence suitable for a family. The whole property, offered as a resort hotel, or an academy, or "a summer retreat for a gentleman of fortune," was priced at only $6000, with $1000 down, and the remainder in five annual payments.

Under local leadership, the Bradford Female Institute Company was quickly organized and agreed to purchase the property for $5,600. The following May the trustees advertised for a principal at $1,000 a year, and two female teachers and a bursar at $350 each, no applications to be considered "without the highest testimonials." Sargent and Miller, a Sumterville firm, having underbid competitors in Charleston and Columbia, was awarded the contract for furnishings.

The Institute opened in July 1849, with the Rev. Edwin Cater, principal; Madame Hummel and Miss E. Spain assistants. Mr. and Mrs. Jenkins were the first to manage the bursar's department, but the position was difficult and there were frequent changes in personnel. After the resignation of the Rev. Noah Graham, Mr. and Mrs. Cater took over the work for a time. By August thirty girls were enrolled. Two years later there were a hundred, and the faculty was enlarged. The increased enrollment perhaps was due to the bargain rates offered the parents of many daughters, for when five from one family enrolled the fifth received board and tuition free.

The Institute reached out into the community as a cultural influence, and Mr. Cater frequently advertised invitations to the public to attend his lectures. When he installed an hydraulic ram for conveying water from the spring into the school buildings, the *Watchman* carried an editorial.

Apparently the Institute was not a financial success, for in May 1853, by order of the stockholders, the real and personal property of the company went on sale in Sumter, and was purchased by the Rev. Gilbert Morgan of North Carolina. He immediately reopened the school as Harmony Female College, with himself, his wife, their son Gilbert, their daughter Margaret, and a Miss Wasserman as faculty. These were ample for the twenty-four boarding and seven day pupils. The unique schedule of recitations, called for one hour before breakfast, two and a half hours before dinner, and two hours in the afternoon. Parents and friends were invited to the public examinations held from time to time by a board of visitors.

Harmony College was an immediate success. By 1856 the faculty numbered eight full-time experienced teachers, of whom Oswald E. Melicher, a successful musician of New York, had led "the chorus at the White House"; and Miss

Heiti, a pretty and accomplished lady from Germany, was "a rare bird and a singing one." The college commencement in November that year was described as a brilliant affair that attracted people from Camden, Cheraw, Marion, Darlington, Sumter and Charleston.

Although the depression of 1857 cut down student enrollment to fifty, and the faculty to seven, Harmony College operated successfully until it was closed by the War of Secession. The Italian teacher, Miss Ronzoni, who probably could not return to Italy because of the federal blockade of the coast, remained at the college with the Morgan family. In 1863, when burning some old papers in her fireplace, she is said to have accidentally set fire to the main building, which was completely destroyed, and the college never again reopened.

In Sumterville, which was important as the courthouse town, the earliest educational institutions of which record has been found by this writer, were the Sumter Military, Gymnastic, and Classical School, headed by Major W. R. Theus, and the Young Ladies' Seminary taught by Mrs. J. Chester, both of which opened in 1827, and already have been mentioned. Theus's Academy was on Harvin Street near the corner of Republican, now Hampton.

A few years later, James H. Thornwell, a recent graduate of the South Carolina College, was advertising in Sumterville in May 1832, to prepare young men in the classics and all other branches required for admission into college. While in Sumter, he became deeply religious, and later was a distinguished preacher in the Presbyterian church.

In January 1832, The Sumterville Female Academy opened, in charge of Mrs. Frances Bowen, late of Raleigh, North Carolina, and formerly prinicipal of the Fayette Female Academy. She had only one assistant, but the list of the academy's trustees was truly impressive, for it included Dr. James Haynsworth as president, William L. Brunson, treasurer; Thomas Williams, secretary; Thomas Dugan, Rev. James Parsons, John B. Miller, Thomas J. Wilder, Dr. J. B. Witherspoon, Robert Bradford, Charles Mayrant, John J. Potts, and John Hemphill—all of whose names were appended to the announcement of the opening of the academy. The music department was in charge of Mr. and Mrs. Samuel Weir, the latter described as a highly distinguished teacher, well known in South Carolina and Georgia. In the spring they enlivened the village by giving a concert at the courthouse, in a program of overtures, rondos, duetts, and songs, some sentimental and others comic. The admission fee was only fifty cents, so they probably had a good audience.

The beginning of a more permanent institution for education is found in the gift by John B. Miller in 1837, of a one-acre site for an academy, to the Sumterville Academical Society. This acre, on the west side of Washington Street between Republican (now Hampton) and Liberty streets, was long known as the Academy Square or the Academy Grove, and is now the site of the Confederate monument and the Washington Graded School. The Academical Society held its first meting on February 4, 1837, in the "long room of the Tavern lately occupied by Mr. Stuckey", and elected John B. Miller president, Dr. James Haynsworth vice-president, and C. W. Miller secretary and treasurer; also as trustees, F. I. Moses, Rev. John S. Richardson, Alester Garden, Rev. James DuPre, and William Haynsworth. The trustees met immediately afterwards and organized, with Mr. DuPre as president, and C. W. Miller as secretary.

After advertising for a man and wife to take charge "of a promiscuous academy of males and females," the trustees elected as teachers James M. Fenn, his wife, and a Miss Proctor; and notified Mr. Fenn to be present to open the Academy on the first Monday in July 1837, or they would elect some one else. They also agreed to rent "Mr. Barrett's old school house" temporarily at $35 a year, and appointed a committee to get estimates of the cost of building a schoolhouse on the Academy lot. The school apparently opened at the designated time, but in September the trustees allowed Fenn to close the school for three weeks on condition that he send a circular to the pupils' parents giving his reasons. When the legislature convened that year, the Society was incorporated, and empowered to possess escheated property within Claremont election district not to exceed $10,000.

Mr. Fenn was re-elected for the year 1838, and was requested to have a public examination of his school at the end of the second quarter; also, he was asked to procure a music and French teacher as soon as practicable. In March Mr. Fenn announced in the *Commercial Courier* that arrangements had been made to increase the number of pupils from eighty to one hundred; that he was in charge of the department of the classics and mathematics; that the English department was under Mr. W. J. O'Hara, assisted by Mr. W. Bronson; that the female department was under Miss H. O'Hara, assisted by Miss A. Holt; that a few boarders could be accommodated in the family of the principal; and that a professor of music and French was expected soon.

The new "professor" proved to be a talented young couple, Mr. and Mrs. George Kellogg of Massachusetts. Mrs. Kellogg took charge of the music department, greatly to the satisfaction of the trustees, who recorded in their minutes the following October, that, having lately witnessed the progress of the pupils in the musical department under Mrs. Kellogg, they expressed their warm satisfaction at the proficiency displayed.

The minutes also reveal some of the troubles that now beset the young Academy. One was the playing of billiards, a game "highly injurious to habits of industry of the scholars." The Board therefore resolved that pupils should be prohibited from playing without the written consent of their parents or guardians, and that the owners of billiard tables in the village should be requested "to preclude scholars of the school from the use thereof."

A more serious trouble was the friction that seems to have developed between the trustees and the principal. The Board had set the hours of tuition between March and October, from 8 A. M. to 12:30 P. M., and from 3 P. M. to 6 P. M., to be "strictly kept." The trustees also asked Mr. Fenn to give them a report on the number of classes in the school and the "routine of studies pursued by each." Mr. Fenn refused to comply with the schedule of hours, and seems to have sent out a circular to the patrons asking the withdrawal of the pupils to a school of his own. The Board then resolved that under the circumstances, it must refuse Mr. Fenn's request for a conference. When the Rev. Mr. Richardson informed Mr. Fenn of this action, he sent the Board a note stating that "he would teach 7½ hours per day if left to his own election." On this concession, the Board decided to suspend for the present proceedings against him.

Apparently Mr. Fenn had some pressing business elsewhere which needed his attention, for he requested permission to set the 1838 vacation period from July 1 to October, 1, during which he wanted a two-months' leave of absence. He also asked that he be re-elected for a term that would terminate on April 1, 1839. When both of these requests were refused, he left without permission early in October, and the Academy was closed for the remainder of that year. One of his admirers later wrote in the *Sumter News* that the loss of Mr. Fenn, who was a teacher of extraordinary ability, was severely felt when he relinquished the position.

Later in the autumn of 1838, the Board elected as teachers for the ensuing year, John A. Inglis for the boys' department and George Kellogg for the girls' department. Mr. Inglis was a young lawyer who later became chancellor of the court of equity. The Board also appropriated $1,000 to build a "plain one story wooden house" on the lot given by John B. Miller as the site for the academy.

The Sumterville Academy opened in 1839, however, in rented quarters. At a meeting of the Academical Society in the courthouse the following July, several alterations were agreed upon in the construction of the academy building, and each member of the Society was urged to use his best efforts to raise the balance of the money due the contractor for his work.

Another event of more than ordinary interest occurred that same month, for on July 12, 1839, a daughter was born to Mr. and Mrs. Kellogg at their Sumterville home on the northwest corner of Main and Dugan streets. Named for an "excellent lady" of the village, the child grew up to make her debut as a dramatic soprano in London in 1867, and became the famous prima donna, Clara Louise Kellogg.

For the 1840 session of the Academy, the trustees elected Mr. Kellogg principal of the Female Academy and Mrs. Kellogg instructress of the music department. Fley Coleman was principal of the Male Academy. The Board also set up two committees to inspect the work of the two schools during the ensuing six months, whereupon an irregularity was discovered, and the trustees came to the opinion "that instruction by the principal of the Female Academy in any Branches required by the teacher of the Male Academy is against the spirit of the contract made with the teacher of the Female Academy." Apparently Mr. Kellogg was doing some of the teaching in the boys' school, and the trustees straightway appointed a committee of two to wait on Mr. George Kellogg and inform him of their opinion. The Kelloggs seem to have remained in Sumterville until some time during the year 1841, and then returned to the North, where Mr. Kellogg became an inventor and manufacturer of surgical instruments.

During the ensuing years of its existence, the Academy saw many other teachers come and go. In 1846, when Thomas B. Russell was principal of the boys' department, the semi-annual public examinations closed with a program of public speaking by the pupils. The first speaker was little Claremont Moses, then a tot of some four or five years, with the subject "The Good Little Boy." Said the *Sumter Banner*, "he sweetly lisped his well-committed piece to the admiration of all." Others on the program were M. A. Brunson, Joseph and Thomas Waties Dinkins; Meyer, Zalegman and Franklin Moses, Jr.; Joseph Wilder, William Clarke, William DeLorme, Grier White, Franklin Folsom, and Preston Gayle. Among the advanced pupils mentioned were James McDowell, Edward and John Conyers, Joseph Lewis, and John Nelson.

In July 1850, the Academy was in charge of John Witherspoon Ervin, a literary young man who during the preceding winter had moved his family to Sumterville from his Black River farm. Before his election to the Academy, Ervin had taught his own school and in his spare time had edited *The Black River Watchman*. Unhappily, a feud soon developed between Trustee F. I. Moses and Mr. Ervin, which resulted in the latter's return to his own school. Apparently

Willis W. Alston and his wife were the next two principals of the Academy, but they remained only a year, then opened a girls school of their own. In 1853, Frank Moses, Jr., as secretary of the Sumter Juvenile Debating Society, advertised that a public debate would be held at the Academy upon the question, "Was Coriolanus justifiable in making war upon his country?" It seems probable that about this time the Academy may have been without a teacher.

W. B. Leary was the next principal, assisted by D. D. Rosa, elected at the close of the year 1854. These two men were acclaimed in the *Watchman* as rare teachers, who charmed their pupils along the toilsome road of learning. But in November 1855 Mr. Leary appeared before the Board, handed in his report, and resigned. Financial dificulties appear to have closed the school during the next year, but later the trustees were advertising for a qualified teacher at $1,000 a year. In February 1856 they elected the Rev. Julius J. Fleming, a Methodist minister, who was then in a violent controversy that was shared by his congregation. He remained in charge until the spring of 1858, when suddenly the Academy was closed, and Mr. Fleming was ordained to the Baptist ministry.

Theodore McGowan, an honor graduate of Princeton, was elected principal early in 1859, and the Academy was advertised to open on the first of February. Two months later his salary was increased to $1200 on condition that he employ a competent assistant. In May 1860, Joseph H. Long was given a contract to alter and enlarge the Academy, for $850; and C. G. Memminger of Charleston was invited to make an address on public education on the Fourth of July, a church to be borrowed for the occasion in the event of his acceptance. But secession and war were now at hand. Mr. Memminger had just returned from a mission to Virginia, and he was soon to be a leader in the Secession Convention. The pressure of public affairs probably prevented his acceptance of the trustees' invitation.

The outbreak of the war may have been a factor in terminating Theodore McGowan's work at the Academy. On August 29, 1861, the trustees resolved that Mr. McGowan had dissolved connection with the Board as principal by leaving school before the end of the year without proper notice to the Board or its consent, and they then elected J. J. McCants principal of the Male Academy for the remainder of the year. Mr. McCants was re-elected for the year 1862 without any guaranty of salary. In the summer of 1864, the Academy building seems to have been occupied by J. R. Kendrick as a dwelling, so the war had closed the Academy. Although the trustees received an application from a Mr. Strong that year, there is no indication that the school was re-opened.

After the war, S. M. Richardson and W. H. Johnson were elected principals in November 1866, and were authorized to spend a hundred dollars on repairs, which the trustees agreed to refund. Mr. Richardson resigned the following August, but Mr. Johnson remained through the term. The trustees then requested the Post commander to remove federal troops from the Academy lot and vicinity, and advertised for teachers. As no applications were received, they agreed on December 28, 1867, their last meeting, to allow George Edward Haynsworth and Thomas P. McQueen the use of the Academy on condition that they expend twenty-five dollars on repairs and use the building as a schoolhouse. Shortly afterwards the Academy was destroyed by fire.

Thus ended after thirty years of more or less precarious existence, a cultural institution which had meant much in the community life of Sumter. The minutes of the Board show that although the trustees had been on the alert for escheated property, they never succeeded in building up sufficient capital.

Throughout its existence, the Sumterville Academy was always in competition with numerous private schools. Francis M. Adams, who seems to have come to Sumter from Pendleton to practice law, and for a time edited the *Sumter Banner*, advertised for twenty pupils for his "English School." He probably did not get them, for a few months later he put his school desks and benches on sale, and in the spring of 1849 he left Sumter.

William G. Barrett, a native of the District who united with the Sumterville Baptist Church in 1842, built a "snug frame" school house a mile and a half from the village and enlarged his home for boarding pupils. But he failed to attract patronage, and in 1849, having rented a room in Sumter, he pathetically published a plea to his old friends to give him "something to do." Two years later he removed his family to Clarke County, Georgia.

Schools for girls were also numerous. Miss Mary Hort, the English lady, when Bradford Springs Female Academy closed in 1848, erected her own commodious schoolhouse in Sumterville where she opened a "High School for Young Ladies," and the next year she became a naturalized American. Her school must have been a success, for eight years later Miss Hort had taken a partner, Miss Lawton of Philadelphia.

A younger schoolmistress who taught for a lifetime in Sumter was Miss Hortensia Haynsworth, whose school in 1855 had as assistant Miss S. M. Wells.

In the same year "Copeland Stiles with his Lady and Daughter" opened a school for boys and girls, five to fourteen years of age, in his new residence in the northeastern part of the village, "remote from all the busy scenes and noise of town." Later, Mr. Stiles taught the older boys; his wife, Amelia Rosamond, took charge of the older girls; and their daughter Sarah, the little tots.

The Rev. Julius Lyman Bartlett, who came from Massachusetts and married Agnes, daughter of Captain Leonard White, advertised in 1857 that he would open a Female Academy at his residence.

The next year the Sumter Collegiate Institute was beginning its second session with Thomas Waites Dinkins as principal, and J. R. Manget as teacher of French.

Indeed, the ante-bellum teachers of Sumterville were so numerous that only a few can be named here, but mention should be made of H. E. Bowles, W. H. Brunson, Susan E. Brunson, Mrs. J. B. N. Hammett, Mr. and Mrs. C. M. Hurst, J. R. Kendrick, Caroline Morgan, Mrs. E. Owens and her Zoar Academy, Mrs. Rice and her Seminary, Mrs. S. K. Smith; and the Rev. Hartwell Spain, who, with his daughter Aimee, kept a "female school" to which boys under twelve years of age were admitted.

In addition to these resident teachers, there were from time to time a number of itinerant teachers of specialties, who came to Sumter and recruited classes for short courses in commercial subjects, penmanship, French, and dancing.

The published reminiscences of the pupils of some early schools, agree that the teachers did not spare the rod, and that standard equipment for the schoolrooms was a bundle of switches, preferably the tough chinquapin variety. Floggings were a daily routine that was supposed to stimulate the dullards, and some teachers even reduced the outer garments to shreds and flayed the flesh beneath. Happily, no reminiscences of such extreme cruelty have as yet been discovered for the schools of Sumter.

Much of the teacher's effort was devoted to spelling, which then was considered a requisite for learning to read, and the small children were required to "chime through the ba's bla's, bra's, spla's, spra's with a chanting voice, giving a cadence at the end of each." Perhaps such early training may account for the great number of rhymes and verses that were contributed to their local newspapers by Sumter citizens.

This chapter, as may be seen in the text, has been compiled chiefly from the public records of Sumter, the *S. C. Statutes* and the contemporary newspapers.

Existence of MS Minutes of the Sumterville Academical Society, in the office of the superintendent of Sumter city schools, was learned from seeing at the University of S. C. a thesis by Miss Thelma M. Gaston. Printed sources included, E. J. Scott, *Random Recollections of a Long Life;* S. D. McGill, *Narrative of Reminiscences* (Columbia, 1897); and John Furman Thomason, *The Foundations of the Public Schools of South Carolina* (Columbia, 1925).

CHAPTER XVI

REFORMS AND REFORMERS

Edwin J. Scott, whose father kept the earliest known tavern in Sumterville, states in his recollections that when he was a very small child, every morning before breakfast he and his brothers were given a small quantity of whiskey for their health's sake. Dr. Samuel McGill in his *Narrative of Reminiscences* also mentions this family custom of having a tumbler full of a sweetened morning dram, from which the mother took the first sip before passing it on to each child. He further says the dram was supposed to keep down worms in children and to prevent malarial chills and fever, each plantation having as its yearly allowance at least one barrel of whiskey to be used for the morning dram, snake bites, Christmas eggnogs, bitters, sick horses, and other singular but then common purposes.[1] Everywhere the people drank alcoholic beverages constantly and freely, at an ever increasing rate. In 1792 the average per capita consumed was 2½ gallons; in 1810, 4½ gallons; and in 1823, 7½ gallons.

Because of the conditions resulting from excessive drinking, the first "Temperate Society" was organized in New York in 1808, the members agreeing not to consume alcoholic beverages except at public dinners, and then to avoid intoxication. In his *History of South Carolina* published that year, Dr. David Ramsay said "Drunkenness may be called an endemic vice of Carolina", and as a physician he wrote rather strongly against the supposed medicinal virtues of intoxicants. The Methodist Church, as its first step towards temperance, undertook to stop its ministers from distilling and selling alcoholic liquors.

In Sumter District, the good old Methodist circuit rider, the Rev. James Jenkins, known to his friends as Father Jenkins, and to others as Bawling Jenkins because of his

[1] Scott, *Random Recollections*, p. 13; McGill, *Reminiscences*, p. 45.

stentorian voice, was so courageously active, that bibulous wags began to call their whiskey "Jenkins' Devil." In his memoirs, Father Jenkins tells of conditions in the neighborhood now called Wisacky, but then known as Cooterboro, because the drunken patrons of the local Weeks' groggery were said to have crawled home on all-fours like cooters. At the nearby crossroads which has since become the town of Bishopville, was the groggery of a notorious Mrs. Singleton. "As I passed one Sunday morning," says Jenkins, "I saw the drunken men lying about like dead hogs; some in the road and others on the piazza. I continued to preach and pray against these places, amidst abuses and cursing, until tippling shops were broken up in the neighborhood."[2]

A deeply moving event took place in the State House in January 1828, when that gallant old soldier of the Revolution, Judge William D. James, of Brookland, Stateburg, was impeached and removed from the bench for habitual drunkenness. The Senate sat in silence behind closed doors, in an atmosphere charged with emotion. After the evidence was in, each senator was called by name to give his vote, and as he arose, the President put the question, "What say you? Guilty or not guilty?" One by one, each placed his right hand upon his breast, and answered, "Guilty (or not guilty) on my honor." The vote was overwhelmingly guilty, but even the sternest man could not keep back his tears.[3]

About this time, two other jurists, the tender-hearted Judge Richard Gantt, and the Quaker-Baptist Judge John Belton O'Neall, moved by the miseries of cases which came before them in court, began to work for reform. Under their leadership, the temperance movement began in South Carolina.

The Rembert Settlement Temperance Society, formed in 1832, appears to have been the first organized group for reform in Sumter District.[4]

The next year at the November session of court, the Sumter grand jury presented as "a grievance of alarming character,

---

[2] Jenkins, *Experience*, pp. 172, 173.
[3] O'Neall, *Bench and Bar* I, 236-240.
[4] *Commercial Courier*, Dec. 23, 1837, has an account of its fifth anniversary.

the intemperate use of Ardent Spirits . . . in producing crimes and misdemeanors, involving the severest penalties of positive Law, as well as vice and immorality, debasing to the guilty, and disgusting to the Spectator. The grand jury would not advise the adoption of sumptuary laws but they respectfully suggests to the Legislature the propriety of utterly withholding the power of granting licenses." Signing this document were H. Hollyman, *foreman;* Giles M. Herrington, Wiley Fort, John Dority, Ripley Copeland, R. G. McLeod, Samuel P. Taylor, William H. Bochat, William N. Harvin, John S. Richbourg, Hopkin Daniels, Burrel Dunn, Charles Brock, Jacob Giddens, and Joseph Sprott.

In 1840 the Baptists endeavored to organize temperance societies in all the churches of the Sumter Union. By 1847 temperance societies had been formed at Sumterville and Lodibar, and the next year the children of Sumterville were organized into the cold Water Army, with Zalegman P. Moses as president. Declining reelection, he was succeeded by Master W. J. Clark.[5]

The heyday of the temperance movement in Sumterville began in September of the same year with the organizing of Sumter Division No. 12, of the Sons of Temperance, a nation-wide secret fraternal order. Torchlight processions with banners and brass bands, sumptuous costumes, grandiose titles of office, and impressive public meetings at which scores were initiated, gave the organization a wide appeal for the masses, and the movement spread rapidly in Sumter District.

The editor of the *Sumter Banner*, however, saw dangerous tendencies in the movement, and sounded a note of warning: "Mr. Bowman . . . editor of the *Temperance Advocate*, writing from our midst, gives a glowing account of Sumterville, enumerating all our business firms, trades and professions, but, very significantly points out the 'Sons' in preference to all others . . . thus verging on partisanship . . . the time will soon reach us when a Son will be instructed by his Order when, how and with whom he must trade etc., and then the glorious principles will sink to the ground and the Order,

[5] C. C. Brown, *History of the First Baptist Church of Sumter* (Sumter, 1938). *Banner*, March 19, 1847; April 12, Aug. 26, 1848.

disturbed by intestine quarrels, break up. This is the monster that injures the cause of Temperance and we verily believe is the actuating motive of the joining of one half the members of this charitable Order."[6]

It should be remembered that in those days, drunkards were regarded as stubborn sinners, to be punished, and in some states they were offered for sale at the courthouse door for several months of servitude. The *Watchman* carried the story of a blacksmith who was auctioned in Rushville, Illinois, to serve for four months.[7]

When the Grand Division of the State held its quarterly celebration in Sumterville in 1850, it was escorted from Town Hall to the Methodist Church in an "imposing and gorgeous procession", the rich velvet collars and handsome emblems of office contrasting effectively with the white collars and variegated rosettes of the Sons. At the April meeting the Sons marched in torch-light procession to the church, where they listened to an "appropriate, humorous and effective speech" from the "W. P.", Worthy Patriarch T. J. Coghlan, and "strongly manifested their approval of the speaker's sentiment." On this occasion the martial music of the Sumter Brass Band was supplemented with an ode sung by an "Amateur Band"; the *Banner* does not make clear to which of the two it referred in saying "music again disturbed the silence."

These spectacular methods of the reformers brought the desired results, and before the close of 1850, Judge William Lewis, sometime Methodist preacher, wrote the *Banner* that there were six powerful and efficient organizations for the suppression of intemperance in Sumter District.

A year later Temperance Hall in Sumterville was dedicated, the old Presbyterian Church having been remodeled for the Sons of Temperance "by the intrepid Father of Temperance," Judge Lewis. At the impresive ceremonies, a "beautiful address on very short notice," was delivered by the Rev. John S. Richardson, son of Judge Richardson. As usual, the Sumter Band was in evidence, and was tendered thanks for "in-

[6] Nov. 28, 1849.
[7] *Watchman*, April 5, 1851.

terest added to the occasion by their music." The officers of the Division at that time were Montgomery Moses, Judge Lewis, T. B. Fraser, W. F. B. Haynsworth, P. McRoy, and Richard M. Dyson.[8]

Temperance Hall was also the meeting place in 1853 of the Knights of Jericho, who seem to have offered little competition to the Sons of Temperance. Title to the hall was transferred by Montgomery Moses, William Lewis, and W. F. B. Haynsworth in the memorable year 1855, when the temperance movement was at its peak, to Sumter Division No. 12 of the Sons of Temperance. It was in the same year that an Ohio woman came to Sumterville to deliver a temperance lecture. The idea of a woman speaking in public so shocked one of her listeners that he wrote a letter to the *Watchman*, saying that although the lecture was a good one, it should have been given by a man.

Other contributors to the *Watchman* that year were two physicians, "Dr. Patrick" and "Medicus," who in verses and essays, anonymously supported the temperance cause.

The *Watchman* itself carried many editorials on the subject during these years. One, headed "Death of Messrs Brandy, Rum and Whiskey," credited the newly-elected intendant, T. J. Coghlan, with "some pretty savage thrusts at the above named ancient firm in our town." Another editorial pointed out the paradox that although the quantity of liquor then being consumed was less than in former years, the amount being manufactured had gone on increasing; and while a favorable change might be expected, "it will not be due to the efforts of temperance organizations, which have ceased to have any decided effect upon social habits." The distillers, said the editor, had received their greatest encouragement from the reformers, whose efforts to stop importation of intoxicants had influenced Congress to impose a 100% tariff upon foreign liquors. As a result of this tariff wall, old distilleries here were being refitted, new ones were built, and a second paradox developed. For the distillers, not content with the profits they enjoyed under the protection of the tariff, sought to increase their profits by the wholesale

[8] *Banner*, Oct. 14, 1851.

adulteration of their product with fusil oil, copper, sulphuric acid, prussic acid, and strychnine. Adulterants were openly advertised in the *Charleston Mercury*. The result was to make total abstainers of all who valued health and life, and thus the distillers themselves had done more than the reformers to promote abstainers.[9]

Paralleling the temperance movement were less colorful but important efforts for reform in dealing with poverty, crime, and insanity, social evils which often have accompanied intemperance.

From ancient times prisons had been dreadful places, used not for the reform of criminals, but for detaining accused persons, poor debtors, runaway slaves, or the dangerously insane. Debtors were virtually classed with criminals, because failure to pay a debt was regarded as a form of stealing. During the 1760's the Charleston jail, which then served the whole of South Carolina, was described by the Rev. Charles Woodmason as a small house hired by the provost marshal containing five or six rooms about twelve feet square each, and in one of these rooms had sixteen debtors been crowded. They often had to take turns at lying down for want of space, and in the intolerable heat of the Charlestown summer, one was suffocated. In winter the jail was unheated. Sanitation was unknown and there was no provision for feeding the prisoners.

After the Revolution, to discourage imprisonment for debts of trivial amounts, each creditor who prosecuted, was required to pay for the support in prison of his insolvent debtor. Three years later, debtor prisoners were relieved from the rigors of imprisonment by being kept in custody of the sheriff within "prison bounds" which were fixed by law as 350 yards in a direct line from each side of the prison walls. After 1841, when prison bounds were extended to the boundaries of the judicial districts, imprisonment virtually ceased, although not abolished until after the War of Secession.[10]

In Sumter District the debtors were assigned to two rooms on the second floor of the jail. The most distinguished debtor

---

[9] *Watchman*, Feb. 4, Oct. 7, 1857.
[10] *Stat.*, VII, 231; V, 78; XI, 153; Constitution 1868, Art. I, sec. 20.

of Sumter District was General Thomas Sumter, who in his old age was so beset by creditors that he is said to have gone into hiding on one of his outlying plantations. As his chief creditor was the Bank of the State of South Carolina, the citizens of Sumter and Kershaw Districts petitioned the legislature for the relief of the old hero. In Columbia too, his friends were active, and as a result, the bank was directed by law to grant the general "indulgence, free of interest" for the remainder of his life.[11]

Punishments for crimes were barbarous. In Sumter at the November term of court in 1831, a man was convicted of both grand and petit larceny. His sentence for the first was to be branded next morning with a hot iron in the palm of his hand; for the second, he was to receive at noon on the following Saturday, thirty lashes on the bare back at the common whipping post. At the spring term in 1833, a Sumter man found guilty of manslaughter was sentenced to be confined in jail until the first Monday after the fourth Monday in the ensuing October, then he was to be branded with the letter M on the left thumb, and remanded to jail for another year. He may have been among the last to suffer branding, for in December 1833, fine and imprisonment were substituted for that barbarous punishment, in the case of free white persons.[12]

As late as 1813, the laws of South Carolina prescribed death for 165 offenses. In 1850 there were still 22 capital crimes on the statute books, and in 1857, death was mandatory even for a convicted pickpocket. The flogging of seamen in the United States Navy was not abolished until 1850. In early days women as well as men were publicly flogged on the bare back through the streets, or even nailed by their ears in the pillory. The cropping of ears was a common punishment and because of this, there are a number of affidavits on the Sumter records explaining how non-criminals came to lose their ears accidentally. John T. Wilson deposed that he was present at the house of Augustin Wilson when Joseph Ellis fought Jesse Wilson and bit off part of his ear. Colonel John R. Spann certified that Jacob Garrot, who had always

[11] Gregorie, *T. Sumter*, p. 273; *Stat.* VI, 350.
[12] Sumter court records: *Stat.* VI, 489.

sustained a good character, got into an affray in Manchester with one Bartlette, who bit off Garrot's ear. Commissioner in Equity John Blount Miller testified that his slave Scipio had lost his right ear when beaten by W. R. Lenoir's slave Tom.

The wretched jails were generally used for the confinement of accused persons awaiting trial. Offenders remanded to jail after trial were usually those who were sentenced to pay fines and were too poor to pay them. Governor Stephen D. Miller was horrified to find that some judges permitted pauper criminals to take an oath of insolvency and go free, while denying the same privilege to non-criminals imprisoned for debt.[13]

Little wonder then that the reformers turned their attention to prisons and prisoners. Gradually during these years the idea of reforming criminals began to take shape. The objects of all Law, wrote "A Plain Man" of Lynchburg to the *Watchman*, were first, to protect the innocent; and second, to make the offender feel that he has done evil; and third, to make a bad man or woman a better citizen. These objects, he said, could not be attained by putting the lash on the offender's bare back, for that merely degraded him; nor could it be attained by merely shutting him in jail, for time was lost, expense incurred, health was ruined and the convict was made worse. "Plain Man's" solution of the problem was to build a penitentiary to serve the whole state.[14] Plans were advanced for a state penitentiary, but in 1850 war clouds were threatening, and Governor Seabrook opposed spending money for a penitentiary because he feared all the resources of the state would be needed for defense.

Reform had been effected, however, in the field of the neglected and often brutally treated victims of mental disorders. Their sufferings stirred the public conscience early in the nineteenth century, and in 1828 the State Hospital for the Insane was opened in Columbia. A near tragic incident that occurred at Bradford Springs was told in the preceding chapter.

[13] Wallace, *History of S. C.*, II, 465.
[14] *Watchman*, Dec. 13, 1859.

In lighter vein, tradition still tells of the amazing and fantastic projects of a certain wealthy but mentally unbalanced citizen, whose career has not yet been forgotten in Sumter. After several exciting episodes, his family realized that he needed hospitalization, and placed him in custody of the sheriff for committal to the State Hospital. On the way, however, the erratic gentleman got possession of the committal papers, and upon arriving at the hospital he committed the sheriff's deputy!

Other governmental reforms were also desired by thoughtful citizens. "A Plain Man" of Lynchburg pointed out several abuses which the legislature should remedy: (1) the election system, which was unfair and invited fraudulent voting by keeping open the town polls for two days, while the country polls were open but one day; (2) the system of road duty, which was onerous, unjust and defective, because an energetic community which put its own roads in order was penalized by being called out to help a lazy community; (3) the free school system, which was a failure, not because of the plan, but because of its execution, for the legislature appointed the school commissioners; and he urged "let the people elect their own commissioners and the resulting change would be gratifying."[15]

The militia system was another ancient evil which cried out in vain for reform. "A Patriot" of Clarendon wrote the *Watchman* that a recent parade at "Timmons Town" had been but "splendid nonsense," featured by sundry carts surmounted with whiskey barrels, on one of which a lad of fourteen years dealt out drinks to the crowd of motley customers. In contrast, "Patriot" pointed to the newly-raised volunteer troop of Black River Cavalry, under the command of Captain E. B. Davis, which paraded in fine uniforms at June and Walker's store, and performed well. Ladies had been present and there was no drinking and no fighting; and the young troopers had returned home with their certificates in their pockets, well pleased. "Patriot" thought the militia should be abolished and volunteer companies encouraged.[16]

Apparently "Patriot" was not alone in his sentiments, for

[15] *Ibid.*
[16] *Watchman*, Oct. 14, 1853.

at the April term of court in the memorable year 1855, the Sumter grand jury presented the militia system as "odious and oppressive in its operations *and a nuisance.*" Presiding Judge O'Neall agreed, and declared that the time had come when a radical change was necessary. The militia system, commented the *Watchman*, compelled a poor man to leave his little crop in the busiest season, and walk from 15 to 30 miles to a review; or if sick and unable to attend, to walk 20 or 30 miles to be tried by court martial.

Militia laws were frequently changed, notably in 1857, when the system was improved if not reformed. Volunteer companies became even more popular The oldest was the Claremont Troop of cavalry, which was electing officers in Stateburg in May 1816, and probably much earlier. To be captain of the Troop was a coveted honor, and among those who enjoyed it more than once was Franklin Israel Moses. The Clarendon Troop was chartered in 1834, but little of its history is known. Organized somewhat later were the Salem Troop and the Knights of Clarendon. Among the best known was the Sumter Riflemen, incorporated in 1848.[17] All of these added color and gaiety to the social life of Sumter District, with their parades, military balls, dinners, jousts and tournaments. Washington's Birthday and the Fourth of July were the two great days of their calendar, and the former was usually celebrated with an all-day program, which included a full-dress parade, in white pants and gloves, a speech at the courthouse, a dinner, with many toasts, and an evening ball, to which were invited all the uniformed companies in the District.

Perhaps the temperance reformers did not reach all the members of these volunteer companies, for sometimes they got out of hand. At the celebration of the Riflemen's anniversary in Sumterville in January 1855, in which other companies participated, five fights followed each other in close succession, and "unhappy scenes closed the day." Said the *Watchman*, "this is the second time our peaceful and quiet streets have been scandalized—a law-abiding community may

[17] *Stat.*, XII, 578; VIII, 392; XI, 519; *Camden Gazette*, May 30, 1816.

not brook it a third time." For this reason, on the ensuing Fourth of July, when the Sumter Riflemen and the Claremont Troop gave a public dinner at the Academy Grove, the members were ordered to dispense with their guns and sidearms, and ladies were particularly urged to be present. When these two companies celebrated Washington's Birthday in 1857, at the public meeting in the Courthouse, Franklin Moses, Jr., made his first public speech as orator of the day. Afterwards, the companies jousted in an old field for a handsome saddle, which was won by R. M. Jones, who successfully bore off the elusive ring on the point of his sword.[18]

[18] *Watchman*, Jan. 12, May 4, 1855; Feb. 25, 1857.

CHAPTER XVII

SOCIAL PATTERNS

In the days of hand-woven and hand-stitched garments, fashions changed slowly, and clothing was handed down in bequests from one generation to another, like other heirlooms. Suits, cloaks and dresses were not to be discarded until completely worn out.

When Sumter District was organized in the year 1800, fashionable ladies were wearing the styles of the Napoleonic Empire, high-waisted dresses with slim, scanty skirts, low neck, and long or short puffed sleeves. Men were still wearing wigs, three-cornered cocked hats or the newer high hats, long-tailed coats with big pockets, knee breeches and buckled shoes. By 1805, however, short hair for men had been introduced, and when two young carpenters, Sam and John McGill, who had been building houses in Sumter District, appeared at a dance in Kingstree, shorn of their queues, the whisper went around "What shave pate men are they?"[1]

Edwin J. Scott, then a very small child living at the first Sumterville tavern, recalls that, at dances, the young ladies "wore sharp-toed moroco slippers of all colors of the rainbow, and gentlemen looked particularly neat and genteel in fair-topped boots, worn with knee breeches, and having a band of smooth yellow leather four or five inches wide at the top." Although powdered hair had lost favor in 1794, Scott says that gentlemen of Sumterville still "wore white powder in their hair on public occasions."[2]

By 1820, most men had replaced their knee breeches with long pantaloons, and were wearing blue coats and high hats that enjoyed a long popularity. The lost-and-found columns of local newspapers throw light from time to time on what well-dressed people were wearing in Sumter District. The *Southern Whig* in February 1832, carried the following:

[1] McGill, *Reminiscences*, p. 289.
[2] *Random Recollections*, p. 11.

Lost, a few days since, between Camden and Sumterville, a SKY BLUE BOX-COAT, Velvet collar. In the side pocket was a red morocco Clasp Pocket-Book. . . .

A generation later, The *Watchman* in January 1853, advertised the loss of a band box "containing a blue-black sattin cloak trimmed with velvet, marked Mrs. Mary Birch care of General S. R. Candler. . . ."

Hoopskirts became fashionable in 1854, and soon masculine objection to them was raging in private and in the press. But the men had adopted an equally grotesque fashion in turning out enormous mustaches, so a lady who signed herself "Hoopiana," set the woolly fellows in their places:

> We'll wear just what we please
> For every lady doth need
> Protection from the woolly breed
> If she regards her ease. . . .

Fashions in houses varied as widely as other fashions. Along the eastern rivers, swamps that were impassable all winter, isolated the people there from interstate traffic and from markets for their produce. Also, these people suffered more from malaria than did the planters who enjoyed summer homes in the Sandhills. Hence the farmers on the Black and Lynches rivers did not prosper as early as did those on the Great Road along the Wateree, but were held back until they acquired drainage, roads, bridges, and ferries. The homes therefore were less costly, and needs had to be self-supplied.

Each family raised its own food, spun and wove its own clothing, performed its own mechanical tasks, and built its own simple home with the aid of neighbors. William Elias Mills of Salem, who as a boy had made some of the early trips by wagon to Charleston, said he was born on a dirt floor. Before his twentieth birthday, he married on March 9, 1836, Martha Elmira Wilson of the Mt. Zion Church community. Together they bought a farm near the present St. Charles. Mills was strong, and so active that in three standing jumps he could cover thirty-three feet. He farmed so well that he made his farm self-subsisting, and he used to say that he never had to buy butter but once in his life, when he traded his entire supply of seventy-two pounds for a "Vermont (Morgan) colt." [3]

Jonathan Weston was an equally thrifty and hardworking farmer, who had come from North Carolina as a young man and married Mary Pringle, daughter of William and Elizabeth Pringle of Salem. In 1811 he began purchasing land on Camp Branch of Rocky Bluff Swamp, north of Concord Church. His one-story farmhouse had a living-room which occupied half of the main structure, and two bedrooms in the other half. At the rear were two shedrooms, separated by a hall. The attic was reached by an enclosed stair which took part of the back bedroom, with a door on the living-room. A chimney was at each end of the house. Under the three main rooms was a clay-plastered basement, used for storage. A piazza was across the front of the house, and hand-riven shingles, pegged to slats on the rafters, formed the roof of the dwelling. Directly behind the house, about forty feet away, was a two-room building with a clay floor, used for the kitchen and the loom-room. To the left of the house was the wheat house, where the grain was threshed. To the right of the house stood a workshop, which contained a still, two cobbler-benches, and a hand-gin for extracting the seeds from sea island cotton. Behind the workshop were the smokehouse for curing meat, and the tanning vats for making leather.

The really remarkable feature of the Weston settlement was the L-shaped string of log buildings, all under one continuous loft, which surrounded two sides of the barnyard, and had alternating open and closed sections which served various purposes, such as cattle-shed, fodder-room, unloading shed, and gear-room. Through one of the open sections passed the roadway from the house-grounds out to the avenue, which led to the Sumter highway. This log structure in plan was not unlike the stone buildings which enclose the old farmyards of Europe, and was a pioneer adaptation of an ancient design which had developed from a need for protection.

West of the barnyard near the gate was a well-equipped blacksmith shop. Here, too, were the Negro quarters. In the

---

[3] W. H. Mills, MS on Mills family.

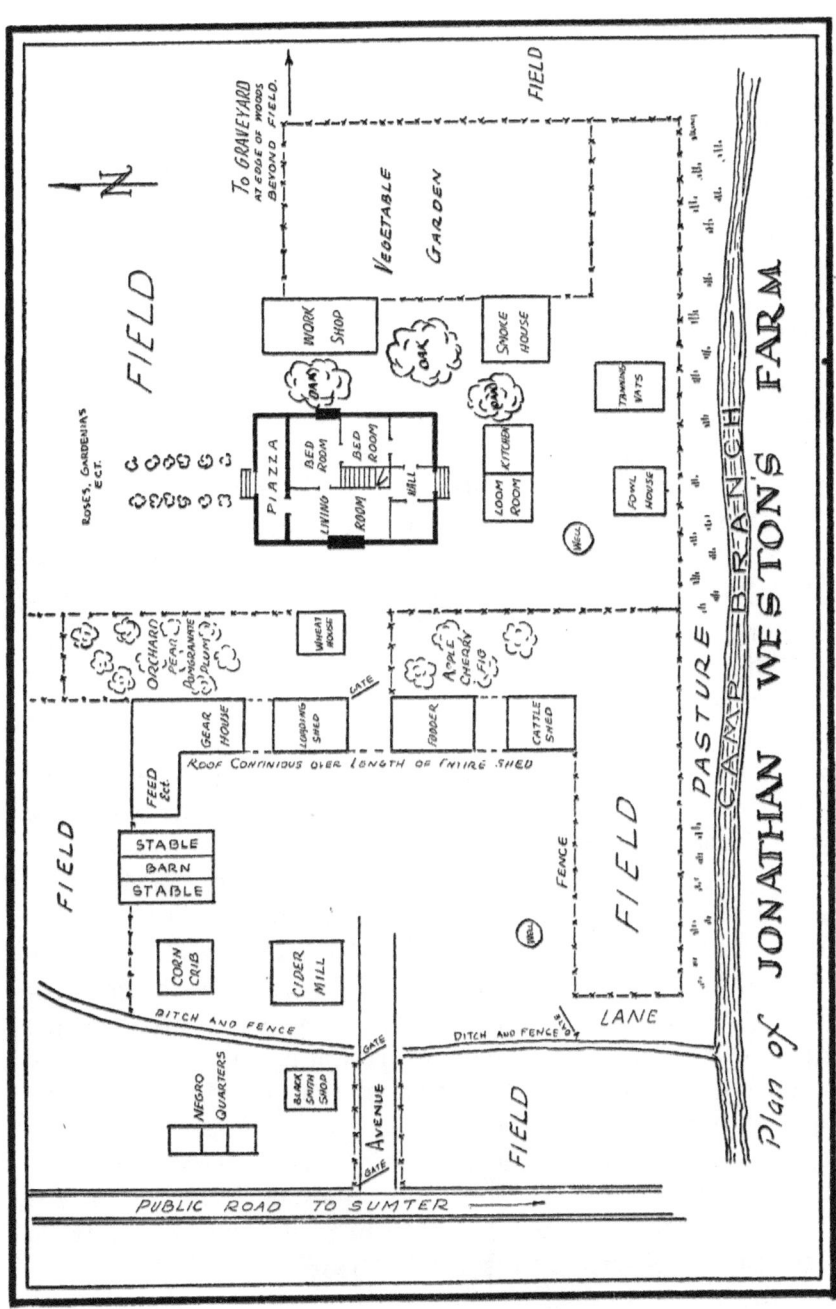

barnyard were the barn and stables, a corncrib, a cider mill, and a corn mill. East of the dwelling, behind the workshop and the smokehouse, was the garden where grew the vegetables. Beehives for the busy bees supplied honey. Near the house were fig, apple, and cherry trees, and an orchard of pears, plums, and pomegranates; and Jonathan Weston made barrels of cider and vinegar from his fruit. Indeed, his farm supplied all the necessities of his family. But he owned few slaves, and the labor of carrying on the farm and the innumerable other tasks, was so severe, that two of his three sons ran away from home before they were twenty-one.[4]

The large plantations usually had very large two-story houses, such as those at James McBride's Rip Raps plantation, the Witherspoons' Cold Stream, the George W. Coopers' Rollindale, and the McFaddin and DuRant homes on Brewington road, but these seem to have been built after the pioneer days, when prosperity from cotton made them possible.

On the Great Road along the Wateree where the planters prospered earlier, the small houses were of the type that Matthew Singleton had built before the Revolution on his Melrose plantation: a story-and-a-half frame building, lathed and plastered, with paneled wainscoating and a sloping shingled roof with dormors. From a piazza the length of the house, twin doors open into two large rooms connected by a paneled door. Each room has two large windows on the piazza, and on the gable ends, two half-width windows flanking the chimneys. Each of these rooms has a paneled door opening on the central stair-hall, which has two small rooms on each side. The feature of the hall is a graceful arch beyond the stair, where three steps the width of the hall descend to the fanlighted door. The half-story contains only one finished room, and is lighted by windows in the gables, for the dormors were removed when the house was re-shingled. Although the house is now in ruinous condition, it still shows evidence of good workmanship, for the original weather boards mitred and fitted at the corners without stylings, are finished under the eaves with an inset, wide board that once may have been topped by a molding.

[4] Plan and description of Weston's farm are from H. G. Osteen, who frequently stayed there in boyhood.

Further south on the Great Road, near Halfway Swamp, was Big Home of the Richard Richardson family, approached by an avenue of live oaks more than a mile long. This house was probably the second or third on the site, for the Richardsons lost many houses besides the one burned by Tarleton. The central portion had a portico with large pillars. In one wing was the dining room, and above it was a great ballroom, with its polished floor resting on springs to undulate with the rhythm of the dancers. In the other wing were the two immense bedrooms of the four daughters of the family, each room having a dresing room opening on a side piazza.

Elizabeth Allen Sinkler, a cousin who often visited Big Home, says that the parties there were "exciting but quite medieval in some ways." The Richardsons' "hospitality was unbounded, but their practical jokes almost barbaric, such as being awakened after a very short night, by the loud crowing of a cock that had been placed in a basket under the bed." Each of the four sisters had "her own maid, whose manners and morals she was supposed to take care of, as well as cutting out their clothes, etc., and tending them when sick."

The butler at Big Home, a tall mulatto, "domineered frightfully over his young mistresses as well as over the troops of servants. The girls used to humbly beg him to send supper to our rooms by the maids, and if he were in a good humor there would be cold turkey, salads and many nice things; but sometimes a pot of hominy and greens would be our portion."

Before breakfast, trays were arranged by Nannie, the eldest sister, and sent to the guests in their rooms: "eggnog or mint julips for the most favored, delicious coffee or tumblers of cream, down to glasses of buttermilk for us young girls."

Breakfast was served at eleven o'clock in the dining room "at a long table covered with great dishes of chickens, ducks, pigeons and sausages and great tureens of tomato catsup, while hominy and hot breads were handed by dozens of men servants, and small boys stood around waving peacock-tail brushes to keep off flies."

Elizabeth Allen Sinkler also visited the deVeaux family in

Stateburg at The Ruins, which she described as one of the most beautiful and luxurious homes in the South: "the mode of life was, it seemed to me, quite like a great French chateau."[5]

In the early days, the fare of the poor was very plain. When the future Bishop William Capers attended Dr. Roberts' Academy near Stateburg in 1801, he boarded with a Mrs. Jefferson, and carried his dinner to school in a large tin bucket. Invariably it consisted of corn bread and bacon. He says his usual practice was to throw away the bacon and make his meal on the pone of bread, washed down by pure spring water cupped in a hickory leaf.

The other facilities of Mrs. Jefferson's home were equally plain, for her boarders slept on a mattress on the floor, and covered with osnaburg sheets. Later, little William Capers and his brother were sent to board with Mr. Roberts' family, where they had much better fare.[6]

Samuel McGill attended Edgehill Academy near Stateburg, in 1835, in the home of General Sumter's granddaughter, Mrs. Louisa Murrell. He describes it as an antique building in a dilapidated condition, but large and commodious, resting on pillars eight or ten feet above the ground. Some ten of the school boys slept in a large room upstairs on single and double cots, and four other boys were lodged in a partitioned-off part of the room. The boys nicknamed this house "the old castle," and in the cold winter of 1835, they suffered in their unheated dormitory with its broken-paned windows. After supper every evening, each boy was provided with a little brass lamp and studied his lessons in the large dining hall, under the supervision of kindly Mr. Willard Richardson, the schoolmaster.[7]

At the time that Sumterville was founded, Jedediah Morse in his *American Universal Geography*, criticised the funerals of the rich in South Carolina, as sumptuous entertainments, with splendid decorations, and pompous ceremonies, which no persons attended unless particularly invited; "Wine, punch

---

[5] Elizabeth Allen (Sinkler) Coxe, *Memoirs of a South Carolina Plantation During the War* (Privately printed, 1912), pp. 77-81.
[6] "Recollections," Wightman, *Life*, pp. 39-41, 44.
[7] *Reminiscences*, pp. 97, 98.

Social Patterns 211

and all kinds of liquors, tea, coffee, cake, &c in profusions, are handed round on these solemn occasions. . . . It would be difficult to distinguish a house of mourning from a house of feasting."

Weddings, too, were as lavish as the means of the parties permitted. The most exciting, perhaps, was the wedding at Home plantation in November 1833, when Sarah Angelica, daughter of Colonel Richard Singleton, was married to Abraham Van Buren, son and secretary of the President of the United States. On their honeymoon, the young couple went abroad, and were received in London in the style of visiting royalty by Queen Victoria, and at Saint Cloud by King Louis Philippe. They returned in time for Angelica to receive as "first lady" at the New Year's reception at the White House, where she became the official hostess for the widower President.

Only a brief formal notice of this wedding appeared in the Charleston newspapers, and there was no mention anywhere that the President had attended as his son's best man. But Martin Van Buren did visit Colonel Singleton for several weeks in 1842. [8]

A very picturesque double wedding, long remembered, took place in St. Mark's Church when two Richardson sisters were married: Eleanor, to her cousin John Peter Richardson; and Julia, to Major A. Moultrie Brailsford. As the wedding was at night, the bridal procession was escorted by Negroes on horseback carrying torches; and when the church was reached, each Negro rode to an open window and illuminated the ceremony with his torch. [9]

In 1849, the *Sumter Banner* carried this unusual marriage notice:

> Married. on the 26th inst. [August], by the Rev. John B. Hicks, Miss E. Lemon, aged 15 to Mr. Daniel Hardy, aged 17, all of this District. May the shoots of the grafted Hardy-Lemon, prove numerous and prolific and

---

[8] Denis T. Lynch, *An Epoch and a Man: Martin Van Buren and His Times* (New York, 1929), p. 436; American Historical Association *Annual Report* 1918, II, 394.

[9] Mrs. Elizabeth Sinkler (Manning) Richardson, MS Recollections, courtesy of Miss Eleanor S. Richardson.

the rara avis of a hardy lemon bloom long on the soil of Sumter.

Sometimes bachelors advertised for wives, as witness the following from Sumterville, in June 1835, signed "C.D.":

> Circumstances ... having prevented the advertiser from mingling much in female society, he takes this method of appealing to the heart, and soliciting the hand of any young lady, who, like himself, possesses a good temper, and a disposition to be happy. If the partiality of private friendship has not exaggerated his personal appearance ... no lady, however fastidious ... will be dissatisfied ... the former are perfectly unexceptionable, and the latter of the most amiable and affectionate kind. In fine ... it is extremely seldom that any young lady ... has such an opportunity presented her. . . .

Although divorce was not provided for by South Carolina law in ante-bellum days, there were broken marriages. Usually in such cases a legal separation was arranged, the husband conveying to trustees a portion of his property for the support of his wife and children. But sometimes an unhappy couple made unique arrangements of their own. At the Sumter courthouse in 1805, a "Release from the Bond of Marriage" was recorded in two curious documents. The first set forth that Jesse Mitchum of Clarendon County, released Eleonor Mitchum "from all right and claim of any duty of a wife to him, at her request." Sworn to before J. Ridgill, justice of the peace, the release was witnessed by Hezekiah Nettles. The wife in turn gave her husband the accompanying document, releasing Jesse Mitchum from "all right and claim of any duty of a husband to her at her request." By mutual consent, the parties gave each other freedom to marry again.

Snuff taking, so fashionable in colonial times, was succeeded by tobacco chewing. The Rev. James H. Thornwell, who was born in 1812, commenced "to chew at eleven years of age, and a little later, to smoke." [10] A German writer was credited by the *Watchman* with the statement that the people of the United States could burst more steamboats and chew

---

[10] B. M. Palmer, *The Life and Letters of James Henley Thornwell* . . . Richmond, 1876, p. 23.

more tobacco than any other five nations in the world; and an anonymous wit recommended portable spittoons with gold screw-caps "for gentlemen who chew tobacco in churches, concert rooms, parlors and such places."

The newspapers of Sumterville gave their readers many pointers on good breeding. The *Sumter Banner* declared that:

> No perfect gentleman will pick his teeth at the table . . . Nor will he use his nose in company, as if playing second to a bugle. . . .
>
> A perfect gentleman does not wipe his mouth upon the table cloth, nor spit upon the carpet. . . .

There was a prescribed code of etiquette, too, for behavior in church. The perfect gentleman "if he must yawn, whether in or out of Church, will be very shy about it.—Nor will he lie down in his pew."

By custom in many churches, the end seat farthest from the aisle, belonged to the elder lady of the household, and if she arrived late, a whole pew full of men might have to arise and file out into the aisle until she was seated. An annoyed editor suggested that she preferably might take the seat by the door of the pew; and if not, that the customary confusion might be replaced by a military evolution: the lady to advance a pace beyond the pew door, halt, about face, and salute, while the pew was being vacated in a flank movement by the occupying squad, who should arise simultaneously and deploy into the aisle, the leader facing the lady, while the others passed to the right rear. The lady then should complete her salute and advance to position in the pew, after which the gentlemen might break off by files and resume their places.

There was also a "Rule for Wearing Rings," quoted by the *Banner*:

> When a lady is *not* engaged she wears a ring on her first finger; if engaged, on her second; if married, on her third; and if she intends to remain unmarried, she wears the ring on her fourth finger.

In the field of sports, Robert W. Andrews mentions hunting wild cattle in Wateree Swamp. A letter from "Old Rifle" at Sumterville in 1825 tells of a three-day competitive squirrel-hunt for a barbecue, by citizens in the fork of Black River. The hunters were organized into two teams of twenty men each, and on the third day when the scalps were counted, the winners had 2844; the losers 2726, a total of 5570. Allowing a quart of corn saved to each squirrel, "Old Rifle" estimated that 174 bushels had been saved to the neighborhood. [11]

In 1856 the *Watchman* carried the story of a mid-summer "Camp Hunt" by a party of men from Bishopville. Taking along their dogs, guns and supplies, the hunters went up Lynches Creek into Chesterfield, where they were joined by men from Chesterfield and Darlington. At sunset they erected tents at Camp Gardner on the head of Cedar Creek, and cooked supper. Next morning, having breakfasted before dawn, they took stands, entered the drive, and brought down a fine buck. Because of the intense heat and drought, they stayed in camp until mid-afternoon, but on the second drive they had no luck. That night a mock court martial was held for those who had violated hunting rules, and fines were imposed to furnish powder and shot for the next camp hunt.

Next morning the hunters moved on about six miles through the sand hills, and across "the old Tory Road," into country where there was not a settlement within thirty miles. By noon they reached Camp Alligator at the head of lower Alligator creek, where they rested until the cool of the day, and killed another deer. On the third day, as some illness had developed, several of the party went home, but those who remained killed another deer. This ended the sport, and next morning they packed equipment, collected their dogs, and took the nearest road to Tillers ferry and home.

Horse racing continued in favor as a sport. The Stateburg Jockey Club regularly advertised its races for half a century or more, and its members raced their horses on many tracks. During the 1830's there were notices of races by the Fulton and the Sumterville jockey clubs. Robert W. Andrews has put on record a notorious horse thief called Black Jack, who was active in Sumter District during these years, and stole from Mr. and Mrs. Rees a magnificent black stallion, which

---

[11] *Southern Chronicle and Camden Literary and Political Register*, June 4, 1825.

Andrews was luckily able to recover on Richard Dickey's plantation, to the gratification of the owners.

In 1826, *Bertrand,* bred by John R. Spann of Churchill plantation, was the most celebrated racer in South Carolina and "one of the best horses that ever gave character to the American Turf." Colonel Spann sold him to a Kentuckian for $3,250, and regretted it the rest of his life. [12]

James B. Richardson, the father-in-law of Colonel Spann, also had a famous racing stable, including *Bertrand Jr., Little Venus,* and other winners. Although he lost many races with unruffled sweetness of temper, in 1833 at one race he won all the jockey club purses in Charleston. [13]

Colonel Richard Singleton, another great racing sportsman, imported a number of his horses from England, several of which were yearlings from the King's own stud. The Singleton stud is authoritatively said to have bred "more High Mettled Racers than almost any other in the Union." His oval racetrack in front of the pillared residence measured a mile, and passed so close to the portico that from the top of the steps, where concrete lions crouched, the Colonel could call his orders to his jockeys. [14]

During the 1850's tournaments became popular, and were carried through with heralds, brass bands, and charging knights in costume, who showed their fine horsemanship by tilting with wooden lances for a suspended ring. At the Sumterville tournament in 1851, the Knight of Snowden [Rev. James McDowell] took the ring in every charge, and as victor, crowned Rosalie Moses the Queen of Love and Beauty.

At Momus Hall, the Sandhill home of James B. Richardson, even more memorable horsemanship was displayed, when eight young riders in fancy costume guided their horses through the figures of a quadrille to the music of "The Lancers."[15]

No evidence has been found of any ante-bellum prize fights in Sumter District, but there must have been some interest

---

[12] John B. Irving, *The South Carolina Jockey Club* (Charleston, 1857), p. 176.
[13] *Ibid.,* p. 174.
[14] Perceval Reniers, *The Springs of Virginia* (Chapel Hill, 1941), pp. 51, 168.
[15] Mrs. Elizabeth Richardson, MS Recollections.

in them, for the *Watchman* carried stories of fearful fights elsewhere. In one of these in 1858, a pugilist named McCoy died in the one-hundred-and-twentieth round.

Cockfighting, however, was favorably regarded in early days, and the District was not inappropriately named for the Gamecock of the Revolution. As late as 1825, cockfighting was regretfully admitted to be still in vogue among some citizens of Sumter District; and billiards and card-playing were said to be carried to excess.[16]

An odd suit in chancery, growing out of a card game and involving a race horse, was brought in 1827 by William H. James, J. G. Frierson, Henry Vaughan, William M. Myers, and Matthew S. Moore. James set forth in his bill that in 1825 he had played cards with Myers and lost $750, which he paid by a note payable to Frierson. Frierson explained this by the statement that he had bet with Myers and won $750 of the money lost by James, of which he had relinquished $200 and accepted a note from James for $500. Before the note matured, it was endorsed by Vaughan and transferred by Frierson to Moore in payment for a race horse. Moore then brought suit. James, "acting from a false notion of honor," confessed judgment, and Moore proceeded to sell James' property to satisfy the judgment. James, alleging fraud and collusion in the card game, then appealed to the court of chancery to cancel all the proceedings. As the allegation of cheating was not sustained, the question for the chancellor to decide was whether the court of chancery could give relief to James after he had confessed judgment in a court of law. In handing down his decree, Chancellor deSaussure summarized the laws which made gambling debts uncollectible, thus proving that the note was void. He therefore ordered a perpetual injunction to restrain the defendants from enforcing the judgment at law against James.[17]

Although tennis, baseball, football and basketball were unknown in Sumter District, a very popular ball game, called fives, attracted people there from all over the state when match games were played, and sometimes considerable sums

---

[16] Mills, *Statistics*, p. 749.
[17] Mr. Clarence Haynsworth called my attention to this case, MS Report Book B, pp. 415-419.

were staked on the outcome. Fives required a ball battery and an alley. As described by Edwin J. Scott:

> The battery was a smooth wooden wall, perhaps forty feet long by thirty in height, with the alley of corresponding length and breadth, carefully leveled, tightly packed, and swept clean.

A famous ball alley was at Manchester, a short distance south of the village. According to L. R. Moore, son of John Moore who removed to Alabama in 1821, the game was played by two teams of from five to twenty or more players, arranged in two rows:

> The ball was thrown up by one in the first Row. It was then that someone in the second struck it up against the Battery with open hand. This was done alternately from one party to the other, each man trying to strike it so hard against the battery as to prevent the others from striking the ball. . . .

When either team "failed to strike the ball against the battery, it counted one," and the game continued until a score of five was made by one side or the other. The game required great exertion in running after the ball, and although simple, it was never short—"the ball was kept moving for a long time so as to tire the strongest of them before the game was ended."

Samuel DuBose of Blueford plantation on the south side of Santee, who watched many games at a ball alley nearby, regarded the game as "the most manly of all others," and says that General Sumter, who often played there, "was unrivalled as a ball-player." In 1820, when the General was eighty-six years old, L. R. Moore watched him play an entire game at Manchester, and says the old man "ran after the ball with as much activity as the young men did."

Scott says that young Stephen D. Miller was one of the best players in the state.[18]

The people of Sumter District did not lack for other amuse-

---

[18] Scott, *Random Recollections*, pp. 12, 13; L. R. Moore to L. C. Draper, Draper MSS, 2VV74; Samuel DuBose, "Reminiscences of St. Stephen's Parish," in *A Contribution to the History of the Huguenots* (New York, 1887), p. 69.

ments. In the 1830's "The American Fire King," W. C. Houghton, excited wonder if not pleasure by remaining in an oven at 500 degrees "long enough to cook a beef steer," and performing other disagreeable tricks. The original Siamese Twins were exhibited in Stateburg and Sumterville. The ladies of the village, too, were giving fairs to raise money for benevolent purposes.

As early as 1827, taxes were being collected in Sumterville from circuses. During the 1840's circuses were stopping over in Stateburg and Sumterville for performances that disturbed the consciences of some church members, and caused the disciplining of others who dared to attend; but the tents were thronged, and little wonder; Raymond and Waring's Great Zoological Exhibition from the City of New York, had in its grand cavalcade the New York Brass Band, a music chariot drawn by eight gray horses of the largest size, and twenty carriages drawn by seventy-five horses. In the arena, John Shaffer, the daring lion tamer, drove a large African lion harnessed to a car, and "his equally intrepid Lady" entered the den of lions. But on the day of the show the weather was cold and rainy, and the public was disappointed "in the fewness of the beasts," and in the smallness of the boa constrictor, which was only twelve or fifteen feet long and but two feet around. Worst of all, "The excessive impoliteness of several persons, in refusing to give place to the ladies," said the editor of the *Banner*, "was a subject of general remark."

Robinson and Eldred's Circus the next year played afternoon and evening performances to large crowds, who so enjoyed the clown, that when the show returned, it brought two clowns. In 1859 Yankee Robinson advertised a double feature on the Academy Green in Sumterville, the circus and a drama.

Medical shows also came. "Dr." Trotter sought a class in "Phrenology, Pychology [sic], and Human Magnetism" at five dollars a student; offered his batteries for rheumatism, St. Vitus dance and deafness; and cured headache and toothache with his mesmerising hands. Professor Hale of New Orleans lectured and performed experiments in "Electro-Biology (not Mesmerism)", free to clergymen, and front seats reserved for ladies, who were promised they should "laugh, Wonder and be

Amused." For two nights the Magic Oil men amused the town with a free show and John Thompson of Sumter accepted the agency for their medicine.

Among itinerant entertainers Mr. Everett performed sleight of hand tricks; Mr. Beale brought a Panoramic Exhibition to Town Hall, showing Niagra Falls and Mammoth Cave; and The Estelle Troupe for four nights performed with "favor and success" a series of plays of which "The Drunkard" received favorable comment.

Despite the lack of a concert hall, concerts were always in season. Professors VanHouten and Cutler, blind pianist and violinist, made their first and last public appearances in Sumterville, before locating in a female seminary at Decatur. Picayune Butler gave his grand concert in the dining room of the Sumter Hotel. Rumsey and Newcomb's "world renowned and only Campbell Minstrels, and Brass Band" had a three-night engagement at Temperance Hall. Mr. Huntley, a blind vocalist, pleased a large audience at Town Hall.

Among local individuals there was always an interest in music. Dr. James Haynsworth and others possessed pianos, and in 1848 Joseph Frey began coming twice a year to keep them in tune. Perry Moses was agent for Newman and Brothers, whose "Piano Fortes" manufactured in Baltimore, were warranted to stand the southern climate.

When music was had at a party, said the Sumter *Banner*, the playing should always be by a professional or a member of the family, for it "is not delicate to invite any of the guests to go to the piano, and to tax their efforts for the entertainment of the circle."

The churches organized choirs, and the Methodists apparently sang anthems, judging from the following letter in The *Watchman* of July 22, 1953, signed "A. * * * *":

> I preached in T[rinity?] Church last Sabbath, and had ... the deep mortification of listening to their far-famed choir. No wonder old Brother J[enkins?] found it, while he lived, a rock of offense ... Shades of Piel and Handel! Something between the roar of a storm, the braying of an ass, and the breathing of an asthmatic elephant. ...

Then, having bidden his readers to imagine twenty or thirty voices performing in squads of five or six, the reverend critic concluded, "great drops of sweat stood out on my face in spite of myself."

Four years later J. C. Witherspoon was instructing a class embracing most of the Presbyterian, Baptist and Methodist congregations, who were "learning to sing scientifically; and "Jordanus R" wrote the *Watchman* that there was a great improvement in the singing at the Methodist Church. In December that year the Baptist Church gave a concert.

During these years Sumter audiences were thrilled by concerts from young Ellen Brennan, the "Carolina Mocking Bird" of Columbia, who several times visited friends in the village. The editor of the *Watchman* who had "enjoyed the rare pleasure of meeting her at several very brilliant parties," appeared to have been captivated by "the magic intonations and deep modulated cadences of her finely cultivated voice." Miss Brennan afterward married her music teacher and together they conducted a well-known school of music in Columbia.

The Sumterville Brass Band, prominent during the temperance movement, already has been mentioned.

Perhaps the most widely-known band in Sumter District was Colonel James B. Richardson's "Lilliputian" Negro band at Momus Hall, composed of five little boys, who, after drawing large crowds in Charleston, went on a Southern tour. Their performances were said to have pleased "even a musically fastidious audience."

The leader, Robin, a full-blooded Negro, aged thirteen, had the habits and disposition of an uncivilized African. When a small child, he made the corn-stalk fiddles and reed flutes so common to plantation children, but attracted attention when he manufactured for himself from cypress shingles, a violin with horse-hair strings, and a bass string of waxed twine. A Charleston visitor was so impressed that he persuaded Colonel Richardson to send the child to the city for instruction. In four months Robin learned to play the violin very well, understood the notes in music and could read a little. When he returned to Momus Hall, he began to instruct Sanders, who in a month learned the notes and how to play the second violin. Later Sanders studied the flute. A mild and submissive child, except to members of his own race, Sanders was "a prime boy" with the hoe, and even when cotton was light, he could pick 150 pounds a day.

Robin tried to train several other boys, but with little success. Edward, aged nine, and Henry, aged eight, a half brother of Robin, progressed so slowly that Colonel Richardson sent them to the music master in Charleston, who gave them up after two months. Robin then made both of them very good violinists and taught Edward the guitar in a month. Henry was so unruly that it was said that no human being could control him except his master. March, the youngest, aged seven, performed admirably on the triangle and was learning the violin.[19]

These little musicians played for many dances at Momus Hall and perhaps, too, in the ballroom of Big Home, for the numerous families descended from the first Richard Richardson, lived in a perpetual round of big house-parties and nightly home dances. On the other hand, the descendants of William Richardson of Bloom Hill, no kin to the dancing Richardsons, generally studied law. As Judge John Smyth Richardson wittily put it: "*They* are the *foot* Richardsons; I belong to the *head* Richardsons."[20] The social graces of the "foot Richardsons" apparently were assets, for three of the family became governors, as also did three of their cousins, the Mannings.

As regards dancing there were two schools of thought in Sumter District. The Episcopalians saw no harm in such a pastime, but the Dissenter congregations thought it scandalous. "Thalia" of Manchester, writing to the *Camden Gazette* in 1818, said:

> Let him be easy, free and gay,
> Of dancing never tired,
> Have something always smart to say,
> Yet silent when required.

Eight years later the Sumterville Baptist Church inquired

[19] *Watchman*, Dec. 10, 1856.
[20] Wallace, *History of S. C.*, II, 458n.

of a member why she had gone to a ball in Manchester, and as her reply was unsatisfactory, good Deacon John B. Miller was delegated to reason with her, with the result that she apologized to the church. She soon relapsed, however, was suspended, and finally excluded from the Baptist church.[21]

By 1849 less austere ideas seem to have prevailed in Sumterville, for Monsieur A. Berger, a native of Paris, who had taught dancing for eight years in the first families of Charleston, opened a dancing academy, to teach quadrilles, cotillions, the waltz, polka, mazurka and fancy dances. To allure beginners, who, he warranted, would dance in eighteen lessons, he advertised two soirees at Town Hall, where his 'teen age daughter Octavia, the "best Dancer in America," and her eight-year-old sister Amelia, would perform twelve beautiful and difficult opera dances, all in character.

For those persons who were averse to dancing, Monsieur Berger offered a "School for Mantien or Mainners" where he would teach "all that is quite indispensable to be known to move with grace and unembarrassed in general or exalted society." Berger apparently met with success for in 1854 his school was open and he was teaching his classes everything from walking steps to the most difficult opera dancing.[22]

Other dancing teachers were "Messers Black and Williams," Professor Antonio, Mr. P. O. Coolican, "late of New Orleans," and Mr. Henry J. Brissenden. Cotillions became very popular in Sumterville and were frequently advertised, with lists of junior and senior managers.

The people of Sumter District were organized into a number of social and fraternal orders. The oldest of these was probably the Claremont Lodge No. 64 of Ancient Free Masons, organized at Manchester in 1809, and removed to Sumterville in 1825. The Grand Lodge of South Carolina Masons had purchased a lot on the north side of the Sumter jail in 1814, but sold it five years later to Daniel Rose. In 1822, Stephen D. Miller, executor of Charles Miller, sold a lot near the jail to James Caldwell, Worshipful Master, for the use of Lodge No. 52, but it, too, soon passed into private hands.

[21] Brown, *First Baptist Church*, pp. 25, 26.
[22] Berger was still advertising in Sumter newspapers in 1893.

In 1853 the Sumter Lodge No. 23 of Odd Fellows was organized and began to hold its regular weekly meetings. In 1847 notices of metings of the Sumterville Mechanics Association were appearing in the *Banner*, W. Lewis, secretary. The officers in 1849 were T. J. Coghlan, president; Freeman Hoyt, vice president; A. Conway, secretary and treasurer; John Brunson, librarian; W. S. Hudson, J. L. Haynsworth and Noah Crane, executive committee. Honorary members, J. B. Miller, T. B. Fraser and Albertus C. Spain, donated books to the Mechanics' library as did also several ladies of Sumterville.

Besides there were several debating societies. Mechanicsville had one in the 1840's. The Sumterville society held public debates at the courthouse on such questions as "Whether has the Enthusiast or Matter of Fact Man been of most benefit to the World"; and "Have man's inherent capacities a greater share in the formation of his character, than external circumstances." In this instance, the affirmative was upheld by L L. Fraser, Jr., J. A. Clark, Dr. C. H. Richardson, and John Richardson Logan; the negative, by J. B. N. Hammet, W. B. Richardson, John Witherspoon Ervin, and John S. Richardson. Sometimes the subject was not announced until the meeting; again, the exercises might begin with an oration, as when C. W. Wolfe was announced to give one "On the Pursuit of Knowledge."

Some of the organizations are not easily classified, such as the Brick Bat Club, whose order to meet for practice was signed "B.B.B." The Sumter Fantastic Company elected Angus Rightangle captain; Wootehangkaifonggangtsekiang, first lieutenant; Bob Ridley, second lieutenant; Robert Wicklesquashe, third lieutenant; and staged a Fourth of July parade in 1859.

During the 1850's, the Sumter Bible Society held anniversary meetings on the second Sabbath in May.

The most thrilling experiences, however, for the people of old Sumter District were the annual Methodist camp-meetings, which lasted five or six days at a time and were attended by entire families, many from other denominations. There were many camp grounds in the District, but perhaps the oldest was Lodibar near the present Oswego. Another was at Providence

Springs near Dalzell, for many years the scene of annual state meetings.

Young William Capers, the future Bishop, attended camp-meetings in 1802, 1803, and 1806, and was converted at the last, which was held in Rembert's settlement. He says in his autobiography that at the two earlier meetings the tents were small and few, most people using their wagons, and shelters made from blankets and quilts. At daybreak the camps were awakened by a horn, which was sounded again before sunrise. Beyond that there was little organization and no routine. Very little cooking was attempted and most people lived on cold food brought from home. The two preaching stands were about six hundred feet apart, and when used simultaneously, as sometimes happened, there was great confusion, with people running from one to the other, especially when a sinner was seized with one of the customary strange manifestations called "exercises."

Under the preaching of an eloquent exhorter, men, women and children fell violently to the ground as though shot, and lay unconscious, sometimes for hours. This was called being "struck down." When they professed religion, they were said to have "come through." One of the strangest of the exercises was "the jerks," when the head was jerked spasmodically back and forth so rapidly that a woman's plaits would snap like a whip, and the throat uttered yelps like a dog. When the arms and clenched fists jerked in opposite directions, and the legs and body contorted into strange positions, they were as uncontrollable as wild horses. When a woman was thus affected, the other women joined hands and kept her in a protecting circle; but the men jerked "at large through the congregation, over benches, over logs, and even over fences." Sometimes sinners were seized with jumping exercises, "in which several persons might be seen standing perfectly erect, and springing upward without seeming to bend a joint of their bodies."

At the meeting in 1806, there were more people, larger tents, and much better organization. Also, there were few or no exercises, but there were many conversions.[23]

The well-known Tabernacle camp ground on Lynches River

---

[23] "Recollections," Wightman, *Life*, pp. 51-54; A. M. Shipp, *The History of Methodism in South Carolina* (Nashville, 1884), pp. 274.

was about four miles below the old site of Lynchburg, on two acres deeded in 1829 by Arthur Smith to Bartlett Sanders, Daniel Chandler; George, Henry and William Laws, Thomas Gordon McLeod, and John Kirby, with the privilege of getting timbers to build a meeting-house.

At that time the tents of earlier days had been replaced by a circle of small wooden cottages called "tents," each with several rooms and a piazza on the front. In the center of the circle, stood the tabernacle, illuminated at night from a number of small platforms, each about three feet square, covered with a layer of earth on which lightwood fires blazed. These platforms were sometimes called "lanterns." More light came from bonfires which blazed on the ground at the front and rear of each cottage. Families here customarily cooked at the rear fires.

The annual camp-meetings in the autumn were great occasions for the whole countryside, and when the horn sounded, the tabernacle was filled. Some farmers were regular "tent-holders," bringing their families year after year to the same cottage, with the same neighbors on either side. Thus the camp-meetings were not only religious revivals, but great family outings, and community gatherings, where crops were discussed, business was transacted, and young people found opportunity for courtship. The camp ground served, too, as a clearing house for settling disputes among neighbors, and the preachers took a hand in arranging their differences. There is still in existence a little note written to Thomas McLeod by S. Proctor Taylor, dated "campground 11 o'clock at night" beginning, "Dear Bro: I have succeeded in settling the affairs between you and Bro: Guild. . . ."[24]

Rural life in Sumter District also had another ally in the agricultural fairs and associations. Early in the 1820's an agricultural association had existed at Stateburg, but its history is unknown to this writer.

On October 3, 1852, the Sumter Agricultural Association was organized at the courthouse, adopted a constitution, and elected as officers: president, John J. Moore; eight vice-presidents, William Harris, James E. Rembert, Samuel Rembert, Samuel

[24] Family papers of Frank A. McLeod, Sumter.

R. Chandler, John Ballard, J. J. Rembert, and E. J. Pugh; secretary, J. D. Blanding; corresponding secretary and treasurer, T. B. Fraser.

In November 1853 the Association held the first Sumter Agricultural Fair, and awarded premiums for a lengthy list of entries. One of the most notable was 220 yards of mixed cotton-and-wool cloth from his own loom, exhibited by D. J. M. Pitts, with six counterpanes of different designs. Of four quilts, the best was entered by the Rev. G. C. Gregg. Among other winners were: Samuel R. Chandler, largest yield of cotton; William Harris, largest yield of corn on pine land and A. G. Witherspoon, largest on ditched swamp land; William Elias Mills, the best specimen of vegetables and also seven bales of the best hay, with his statement of the process by which it was produced.

A year later, the second Sumter Fair was held at Temperance Hall, which, with the enclosed lot, had been offered by the Sons. Among the many winners were: W. S. Hudson, the best full-blooded cow and calf, and Elijah Pringle the best cow and calf of common stock; S. R. Chandler, the best home-made soap; R. B. Cain, the best brandy peaches; H. N. Bradford, the best quilt. One suspects that the gentlemen who were named for quilt entries, were shielding their wives from unbecoming publicity!

In July 1855 the Association sent delegates to Greenwood, where the State Agricultural Association was organized. At the third and last ante-bellum Sumter Fair, held in November of that year, the orator was the Rev. John Smyth Richardson. Like his father, he had studied law, but he was deeply interested in agriculture as attested by his articles in the *Watchman* on the "Use of Lime and Ashes as Fertilizers" and "Conversations on Agricultural Chemistry."

Nothing further is available on the Sumter Association until October 1859, when a letter from R. M. Stokes, proprietor of the *Farmer and Planter*, appeared in the *Watchman*, urging the reorganization of the Association: "Its good effects were palpable during its continuation, and traces . . . are yet to be seen."

CHAPTER XVIII

THE MEMORABLE YEAR 1855

After the failure of the States Rights movement in South Carolina in 1850, local matters seem to have occupied public attention in Sumter District. Politics there for some years had centered largely around Franklin I. Moses, who from 1841 to 1866 served continuously as state senator from Claremont election district—which in 1855 became the same as Sumter District. In partnership with his brother Montgomery, the Senator enjoyed a large and successful law practice, and politically dominated the District. His chief political opponent appears to have been Major Albertus C. Spain, who, having survived service in Mexico with "The Sumters," upon his return had acquired property in and near Sumterville and opened a law office. The details of his rivalry with Moses are now lost in the mists of time, but it continued until some fifteen years later, when Major Spain sold his Sumter property and removed to Darlington.

Another opponent of Senator Moses was John Witherspoon Ervin, the young schoolmaster who edited the *Black River Watchman* (1850-1851) and taught a private school in Sumterville until he removed to Manning in 1857 to take charge of the Clarendon Grammar School and edit the *Clarendon Banner*. Said Ervin: "The majority of the trustees of the Sumterville Academy are under the direct control of Col. F. Moses against whom I assumed a hostile attitude as soon as I knew him. He and his political friends have in secret used their utmost influence against me. I have prevented them from employing any teacher in their Academy and they in turn have prevented me from having a full school." Ervin further declared his intention to attack editorially "without stint or mercy, those politicians, wherever they may be found who have sacrificed honesty and principle to popularity. We have but two such in Sumter, Moses and Green."[1]

---
[1] MS letter to E. B. Cash, Nov. 14, 1856, courtesy of South Caroliniana Library.

The Green to whom Ervin referred was a young Unionist from near Mechanicsville plantation, John T. Green, who had read law in the office of the Moses brothers, and been admitted to the bar in 1849. More will be said of him later.

The **congressional campaign of 1853** was marked in Sumterville by the usual parade, and political speeches at the courthouse by the candidates, W. W. Boyce and F. I. Moses. There was no excitement, and the *Watchman* commented that the candidates' remarks "were necessarily general, there being no questions of special interest now agitating the public mind."

But this was only the calm before the storm, for in 1854 the militant Republican Party was founded in the North and opened an active attack upon slavery. The next year the Know Nothing or American Party, had a spectacular rise to power, and is said to have organized a powerful following in Sumter District. Letters in the *Watchman* signed "Hampden" and "Warwick" expressed opposition to the party as a secret political organization, for they felt that public evils should be corrected always by public means. The party very soon came under the control of Southerners, adopted resolutions favorable to slavery, and thereby lost its hold in the North. Said the *Watchman* in facetious vein:

> The Masons, Odd-Fellows, Sons of Temperance and Knights of Jerico have in times past, occupied much of public attention. Lately rumors of 'Know Nothings' have been rife in our town. We have heard, too, of the 'Know Somethings,' and it is said that the 'Pay Nothings' have become alarmingly popular in certain portions of the country. We also have heard upon the streets today, some hints of an order of 'Do Nothings'.

The year 1855 had opened with the price of cotton down as low as $5\frac{1}{4}$ cents, and the depressing effect upon business moved the *Watchman* to speak sharply of travelling salesmen: "that chameleon tribe, which makes its appearance . . . with smiling faces in the spring, happy to serve you, then known as *drummers*. Again in the fall, with sharp features and savage look, as *dunners*. Some lately have spoken so saucily here will win title of *runners*."

THE MEMORABLE YEAR 1855

As a melancholy evidence of the hard times in Sumter District there were 1200 suits for debt upon the docket for the spring term of court, and the *Watchman* laid the blame upon the unreasonable demands of the Charleston and Northern merchants, declaring that the tightness of the times was a sufficient excuse to put in suit the notes of the best men of the community. The same issue carried more than a column of sheriff's sales.

In addition to the financial depression, there was a notable series of disastrous fires. The story of the great fire in the city of Manchester already has been told. The Manchester fire was followed three weeks later by a fire in Sumterville, which consumed the buildings and stock in the tanyard of the Rev. Jesse Morgan, who also lost his account books, and notes which had been given in payment for shoes. So depressed were people by these events, that when the Claremont Troop had its customary celebration of Washington's birthday, ending with a ball at Town Hall, the *Watchman* remarked that dancing seemed to have gone out of vogue, for the Troop "failed to secure the attendance of a sufficient number of ladies to make it interesting."

The following month came a conflagration that flamed across three states, with appalling injury to man and beast. There had been a wide-spread drought during the winter, and the fields and forests had become parched. When these ignited, the fires spread rapidly, and on March ninth the whole of Sumter District became a vast blaze which carried all before it—Negro houses, fences, barns, stables, gin houses and dwellings. Hundreds of thousands of acres were enveloped in flames, said the *Watchman*.

> Fire on hill; fire in vale; fire to the left—surging and rolling and spreading and heaving and roaring, like the great ocean when the spirit of the storm is abroad. Dense clouds of smoke . . . in a moment scattered . . . so that a murky, hazy, veil everywhere obscures the sun . . . . Fire clapping its hands in the grand old woods, which have braved the tempests ever since the red man sculked . . . through their dim aisles . . . And when it comes to the lake or river, do you think that its frolic is at an end?

Not a bit of it. Running up the trunk of a resinous pine, as swiftly as the flying squirrel which scuds before it, it runs out upon the crackling branches and, spreading its wings, is borne to the other side.

In Richland District several persons met death in fighting the fire. In Fairfield the daughter of Mr. J. Mabry was killed, and the homes of seven gentlemen were burned. The loss in Lexington District was estimated at $150,000. The *Marion Star* reported thirty families burned out west of the Pedee. Kershaw, Darlington, Newberry, Orangeburg and Charleston suffered immense damage, and the newspaper of Georgia and North Carolina carried full accounts of direful devastation.

But a week later came the rain, and the *Watchman's* editor, perhaps John Witherspoon Ervin, wrote in whimsical vein:

No doubt the storm cloud was very sorry that it was so tardy: for, as it hung over the land and beheld the blackened fields and charred forests, it wept long and looked very gloomily upon the scene, and then went off slowly towards the Atlantic .... This morning

> Flowers are blooming,
> Seeds are springing,
> Buds are bursting,
> Birds are singing.

As has been told, another tragic fire occurred in Sumterville in May, when poor Sophy and her three children were burned to death in the jail yard, and the town was shocked into the purchase of its first fire engine.

During the spring days a telegraph line was under construction along the Wilmington and Manchester Railroad, and from the *Watchman* came an announcement that a telegraph office would be established in Sumterville if the citizens would agree to pay the salary of the operator. The suggestion met with no success.

The weather, meanwhile, was not yet through with its antics, and on June 13, the town of Sumterville was visited by the first tornado it had ever known. Lasting only a moment and striking nowhere else, the wind left the streets blocked with trees in every direction, but apparently did no other damage.

The summer of this year also saw the opening of the first book store in Sumterville, when, on July fourth, J. T. Munds announced his "New Book Store" next door to Clarkson and Brunson's Clothing House. Said Mr. Munds, "Sumter is certainly intelligent and wealthy enough to support a Book Store, and ought to have one of her own." He then enumerated as on hand, a variety of medical, agricultural, theological, architectural, historical and poetical works, as well as school and blank books; gold and steel pens as well as quills; ink stands, sealing wax, sand boxes, diaries, writing desks, pictures, picture frames, albums, spy glasses, perfumery, fans, guitars, banjos, violins, accordions, fifes, etc. The *Watchman's* editor, under the heading "A Good Book Store," declared that Mr. Munds, late of Wilmington, had supplied a long-felt want.

The long-felt want, however, was quickly satisfied, for the next year Munds advertised a consignment of clocks and watches at his "Book Store," which was now "prepared to feed and clothe the body as well as furnish the mind," for he had added a large stock of clothing, shoes and groceries.

A year later, Munds announced that having disposed of his entire stock of old books, he now offered new school books and *Russels Magazine*, as well as meal, hominy and first-rate lard. In 1859 his list of new books named the Methodist Discipline and Hymns, Livington's *Missionary Travels in South Africa*, Lorenza Dow's *Works*, and various denominational histories.

During this series of events, cotton, which had dropped so low on the Charleston market in January, began slowly to rise, until in June and July it reached a top of $12\frac{1}{4}$ cents. With economic prospects thus brightening, although the depression was far from over, the planters could turn their thoughts to local politics. This they promptly did.

The greatest local political excitement in the summer of 1855, was the agitation by the citizens of old Clarendon County for separation from Sumter District. The lawyers of Sumterville fought the plan, for it would mean the diversion of a large share of their business to the new courthouse. But at the December session, the legislature voted for the creation of

Clarendon District, with the same boundaries as old Clarendon county.

Said the *Watchman*, "the Legislature have granted a bill of divorce between Clarendon and Claremont." Ignoring superstition, thirteen men were named as commissioners to select and acquire from six to sixty acres on which to lay out the new courthouse village: R. C. Baker, L. F. Rhame, J. C. Brock, W. W. Owens, Joseph Sprott, J. C. Burgess, M. T. Brogdon, J. J. Nelson, Samuel A. Burgess, J. J. McFadden, Jesse Hill, R. R. Haynsworth, and P. S. Worsham. Five other commissioners, R. I. Manning, L. F. Rhame, J. B. Brogdon, J. J. Conyers, and William A. Burgess, were named for erecting the courthouse and jail from a state appropriation of $18,000, plus whatever funds might be realized from the sale of lots. The new village was named Manning, in honor of former Governor John Laurence Manning. The site for the village was presented to the state by Joseph C. Burgess, and work was begun at once. On the second Monday of the following October, the new district officers were elected, and Clarendon began its separate existence from Sumter District.[2]

At the same session of 1855, the legislature shortened the name of Sumterville to Sumter.[3]

Out in the world at large during this memorable year, the World's Fair was about to open in Paris; an American named William Walker was scheming to checkmate the British in Central America by a coup in Nicaragua; the United States was showing a touchy nationalism and an aggressive interest in the Pacific and the Caribbean; and a certain notorious confidence man of Sumter was now widely known by his most respectable alias of "Dr." David Hines. Commenting upon these matters with fine sarcasm, said the editor of the *Watchman*:

> A schooner of onions can scarcely be hailed at sea but forthwith we have 'an outrage upon the American flag,' and a claim of indemnity for damages. If a pickpocket of American origin is arrested abroad, it is an outrage upon the rights of American citizens, that cries to heaven for

[2] *Stat.* XII, 364-366.
[3] *Ibid.*, 406.

vengeance, and gives the President and his Cabinet matter of discussion for a month. We trust that . . . Dr. David Hines may consent to remain at home during the approaching Worlds' Fair in Paris, and spare his country the contingency of a war in defending his rights.

In the United States, relations between the North and the South had not improved, and there were dark forbodings of approaching tragedy. The Fugitive Slave Law as a hope of peace was now an acknowledged failure, for it did not protect the Southern slaveholder, and the *Watchman* declared it had only given "a great intensity to those feelings of hostility which we fear will eventually vent themselves in the blood of thousands. All confidence is gone between the North and the South . . . never to return."

In December Joseph S. Bossard of the Bradford Springs community, wrote an open letter to a committee of the Sumter Agricultural Association, inviting the attention of planters to a scheme for confederating the slaveholding states. Bossard believed that such a Confederation would not only be a remedy for political evils, but, by uniting the "aggrieved portions of the republic, the Union might be preserved." Among the main purposes of the plan were: to fix a fair and permanent price upon cotton below which it should not fluctuate, and to insure this price to the planter immediately upon delivery of his cotton to a shipping port; thus transferring the power of price-fixing from foreign dealers and manufacturers to the planters. The result would be to enlarge the profits of the planter and to counteract the effects of the deadly national tariff which had been established by Northern interests for the protection of Northern manufacturers. But Bossard's most radical suggestion was to institute a currency for the Confederation based upon its agricultural credits; and no plantation products of the Confederation would be sold except for specie or its own paper. Bossard estimated that this would put into circulation a safe, sound and uniform currency equal in value to the cotton and tobacco crops, amounting at least to $100,000,000. The first duty of the president of the Confederation would be to establish warehouse offices at each seaport and other proper places, at each of which would be a manager and clerks to store the produce, and offer or hold it, at the price to be fixed once a year by the president and state directors of the Confederation.[4]

Perhaps if Bossard's plan had been given a fair trial, the course of history might have been changed!

On somewhat similar lines were letters in the *Watchman* two years later, on Balance of Power, signed by "Peep of Day," written, said he, not to enlighten experienced statesmen, but to arouse the attention of farmers, mechanics, merchants and laborers, to the all important question How Can the South be Saved? A voluntary association of the plantation states, he believed, was "their only safety, in or out of the Union." Condemning the old Missouri Compromise as a fatal congressional error, he declared that to set up any political boundaries to the extension of slavery was futile, for the laws of God had already set geographical boundaries beyond which slavery was unprofitable; and only a confederation of planters, acting in concert, could hope to maintain their legitimate rights in Kansas and other new states.[5]

But there were many who did not share these temperate views, and from "W.R.B." of Providence came "An Appeal to the South" which shouted a battle cry:

> Children of the South arise!
> Hoist your standards to the skies!
> Dangers, distance, death despise,
> Our Southern flag must wave.

[4] *Watchman*, Dec. 19, 1855.
[5] *Watchman*, Feb. 18, Mar. 18, 1857.

Chapter XIX

THE SUMTER COMPANY OF KANSAS EMIGRANTS

When the North and the South had come to the parting of the ways in 1850, the Rev. R. B. Cater well expressed the feeling of many Southerners when he wrote:

I can go to England, Scotland, or Ireland, and [with] my credentials, that I am a minister of the Gospel, of the Presbyterian order . . . I will have Christian courtesy extended to me, so far as to invite me to preach in their pulpits. But if I go to Boston, and some other cities North, and let it be known I hail from this slaveholding State, and am a slaveholder, I will not be permitted to sit down to the communion table with them.

Now this is a specimen of the Union we are commanded to preserve, and to which, if we do not submit, we are to be branded with treason . . . .[1]

Had the South seceded in 1850, as Calhoun desired, she might have gone her way in peace. But too many Southerners then preferred to remain in the Union which the South had so largely helped to establish, and the opportune moment passed. Calhoun, prophet of secession, died, and Clay's Compromise of 1850 brought only a temporary hope for peace, which was rudely shattered by Northern fury against the fugitive slave law, a fury which seemed righteous to the many readers of *Uncle Tom's Cabin.*

When the Kansas-Nebraska bill was signed by President Pierce in 1854, most people assumed that Nebraska would enter the Union as a free-soil state, and Kansas would come in with slavery, thus preserving the political *status quo* of the North and the South in the national government.

But the abolitionists were not willing for this, and within two months a party of emigrants left Massachusetts for Kansas

[1] *Watchman,* Oct. 5, 1850.

Territory. Under the Kansas-Nebraska Act, the question of slavery within those territories would be decided by the citizens themselves, who would draft their own state constitutions. If enough Northern emigrants should settle in Kansas, that territory as well as Nebraska would vote to exclude slavery. The New England Emigrant Aid Society immediately sent 750 emigrants, and the next year, 635 more; while innumerable other organizations raised money to keep a stream of Northern migration moving into the rich Kansas territory.

At first the South did not realize what was happening. But in 1856 Major Jefferson Buford of Alabama stirred such interest in the situation that he raised $14,000 in contributions and sent an unarmed expedition of 400 young men from Alabama, Georgia and South Carolina to the aid of the Border Ruffians, as the Southerners in Kansas were called. Buford's expedition arrived at Westport, across the river from Kansas, late in April 1856. He returned South to raise more recruits, for in the fall would be held the election for delegates to frame the constitution of Kansas.

On May 5, 1856, a lively meeting was held at the Sumter Courthouse, Senator F. I. Moses presiding, to form a Kansas Association of Sumter District. Major Albertus Spain reviewed the recent events in Kansas. Colonel Blanding then introduced eighteen young men who desired to migrate to Kansas as Border Ruffians. Captain J. B. N. Hammet announced that, having no son old enough, he, with the consent of his wife, would go himself. Other volunteers were Mr. Charles DeLorme, and the two sons of Mr. Jared Law. Three other men decided to go at their own expense, so that they might be free to return at their own discretion, J. M. Dennis, and his two friends James McClendon and John Luckey. Ex-Governor John Peter Richardson was elected president of the Association, and a committee of forty-seven was named to solicit funds.[2]

At the July meeting of the Association twenty-four persons pledged $100 each, among whom was William Ellison, the free mulatto ginwright of Stateburg. The Kershaw Kansas Association contributed $200.

[2] *Watchman*, May 7, 1856.

The Kansas Emigrants on the last night of July attended a Kansas Ball at the Sumter Town Hall. The following Monday, the day of departure, they were present at the meeting of the Association at the courthouse, and heard the report of General P. H. Nelson, chairman of the executive committee. He said that the zeal of the District had not been equal to the importance of the cause, and the $2,615.55 in hand was not enough to send all the many volunteers. The committee, therefore, had selected twelve young men in whose keeping the honor of the State and the District would be safe. Among these was Charles Pinckney Townsend of Bennettsville, a graduate of the South Carolina College but then teaching in Clarendon. In addition to the twelve, there was one "emigrant" from Walterboro, and another from Darlington. The committee recommended that $2400 be confided to Major John W. Dargan, who should have large discretionary powers, and with the advice of his first and second assistants, J. Joseph Harvin and Charles Pinckney Townsend, should pay the expenses of the trip to Kansas, and for residence there until after the election in October. Major Dargan and his assistants were also to enter claims for 40-acre homesteads in the names of those young men who should decide to become bona-fide residents. The remaining money was to be equally divided, provided the leader and his assistants were satisfied the young men would use it to carry out the intention of the Association. After Major Dargan had expressed his appreciation, the Rev. Samuel Furman "in an address full of tender sentiment and wise council," presented each volunteer with a beautiful Bible.

The meeting then adjourned to the depot, where the members of the Sumter Kansas Company boarded the three o'clock train; and, feeling dedicated to high purpose, they set forth like crusaders of old, to do or die in a far country.

At Nashville, Tennessee, the Emigrants boarded an open flat boat, and, exposed to the weather, with no bedding save a blanket apiece, they floated down the Cumberland River toward the Ohio. Their only food was "strong bacon" and cornbread, until one day they spied a churn of buttermilk in a spring, and eagerly drank it, but good fellows that they were, they left money in its place. At length the current of the river carried them down to Paducah, Kentucky, where "H.G." mailed home a letter recounting their adventures.

Five days later they were steaming up the Missouri River on board the "Australia," which ran in connection with the Pacific Railroad from Jefferson City to Weston, across the river from Kansas. Apparently the "Australia" had a woman for a captain, for the Sumter boys held a formal meeting and resolved that their thanks were especially due Captain Baker of the "Australia" and "her clerk" Mr. Morris. The "her," however, may have referred to the boat. They also passed resolutions thanking the officers of the Pacific Railroad and the owners of the "Australia" for having reduced their fares.

On Sunday, August 24, exactly three weeks after their departure from home, the Sumter Emigrants arrived at Leavenworth City, Kansas. The next day they marched out to camp and reported for duty. "C.D.O." wrote home that "the crowd" at the camp had formed a company and elected Major Dargan captain, Buchanan of Winnsboro first lieutenant, and Townsend second lieutenant; that the next day, Dargan had been elected major of the regiment, and was succeeded by Buchanan as captain. "Some of our boys," he continued, "had a brush and killed a couple of Free-soilers"; and the week before they had taken ten wagons and twenty-five prisoners; "We are in the right and pray that the God of battles may give us the victory."

Later, when near Lecompton, W. F. Nail of Chester was elected third lieutenant of the company, all fifty of whom were from South Carolina. W. J. Norris, one of the original twelve, wrote home that Kansas was the most beautiful country he had ever seen; that many murders were being committed, but no murderer was ever found.

In October the Kansas elections were duly held, but the Free Soilers refused to vote, so only Southern men were elected as delegates to the constitutional convention held at Lecompton. But further developments in Kansas do not concern this narrative, for the Sumter Emigrants, "weary of hardships and perils," having done their part, began to make their way home. The first to arrive, early in November, was W. J. Norris, "looking well and bearing little impress of toil and hardship." A little later the *Watchman* having received through General P. H. Nelson a letter from Major Dargan, giving an account of his stewardship, commented that the Major evidently designed to make Kansas his home.[3] Two years later John W. Dargan was still there; but in July 1859, he had accepted an appointment as conductor on the Wilmington and Manchester Railroad, and announced for the office of tax collector. Apparently he had not prospered, for his open letter to the voters of the Sumter District stated that his motive in announcing himself as candidate was the same that prompted him "to follow the plow in the first of the year—viz: NECESSITY." Charles Townsend returned and later became a circuit judge.

One Emigrant who did not return was C. L. Tisdale, who decided to go on to the gold mines of Montana, and later to Evanston, Wyoming. From there in 1871, he wrote to the *Sumter News* that if any young man cared to join him, "by going two miles from this town he will be in Utah, where he can have all the wives he wants." In 1873, the *True Southern* announced that Tisdale had been elected to the Wyoming legislature by a handsome majority.

The efforts of the Kansas Emigrants did not succeed in making Kansas a state open to slavery, but the Sumter Association could feel well satisfied with the young men it had sent there as its representatives.

One other episode of the year 1856 grew out of the Kansas affair and shows the ever widening breach between the North and the South.

In Washington late in May, Senator Sumner of Massachusetts, in a bitter speech on "The Crime Against Kansas," had coarsely attacked Senator Andrew P. Butler, the senior senator from South Carolina, in language "befitting only the barroom." Senator Cass of Michigan expressed the general reaction when he called the speech 'the most un-American and unpatriotic that ever grated on the ears of the members of this high body." Congressman Brooks of Edgefield, nephew of Senator Butler, demanded but did not get, an apology from

---

[3] The remainder of the story of the Emigrants is from the file of the *Watchman* for 1856.

Sumner. Two days later, after the adjournment of the Senate, Brooks found Sumner writing at his desk in the Senate, and chastised him with fifty blows from a gutta percha cane.

Never has any caning caused such violent nation-wide excitement. The North regarded Sumner as a martyr who had suffered at the hands of a barbarian. The South felt that the chivalrous Brooks had met only the requirements of honor.

Bishopville held a Brooks Demonstration, of which Thomas H. Muldrow was chairman, and purchased a gold-mounted black cane from a jeweler in Charleston, for presentation to Mr. Brooks. In the classical manner of the day, it was suitably inscribed *"Absenten qui non defendi."*

A postscript to the story of the Kansas Emigrants appeared in the *Watchman* of July 1, 1857, when the editor announced that he had received six well-written chapters entitled "Our trip to Kansas, by a Sumter Boy." As it was unaccompanied by the real name of the contributor, it could not be published.

CHAPTER XX

LAST YEARS OF THE OLD REGIME

During the last few years before secession, the people of Sumter District were concerned with many other interests besides politics.

The Sumterville boom of 1848 had brought demands for a local bank to facilitate the rapidly increasing business of the town, for the nearest financial institution was a branch bank in Camden, thirty miles away. In the fall of 1849, the *Banner* carried a notice that application for a bank charter would be made to the ensuing session of the legislature, but apparently the movement failed. In December the president of the Bank of Wilmington declined to open in Sumterville a branch similar to one in Marion.[1]

A year later, however, the Bank of the State of South Carolina established a Sumterville agency in the office of Montgomery Moses, the agent. Meanwhile, efforts for a local bank continued, and in December 1852, the Bank of Sumterville was chartered with an authorized capital of $300,000. Commissioners for subscriptions were named for Charleston, Columbia, Camden, Lancaster, Cheraw, Marion, Darlington, and Kingstree; and in Sumterville, the subscription books were in the store of Captain T. D. Frierson, who with W. F. B. Haynsworth and Andrew Jackson Moses, advertised shares at $25 each, with only $5 down. But the capital was not subscribed and the charter lapsed.[2]

In 1856 the movement for a bank was revived, and the *Watchman* pointed out that the old jail on Main Street could be converted into a secure and convenient bank at a cost of only $2500. Another charter was obtained, and early in 1857 commissioners were appointed[3] who probably would have met with complete success but for an unexpected and wholly unnecessary disaster.

1 *Banner*, Nev. 7, Dec. 19, 1849.
2 *Watchman*, Dec. 14, 1850; *Stat.* XII, 193; *Watchman*, Mch. 18, 1853.
3 *Watchman*, June 25, 1856; Feb. 18, 1857; *Stat.* XII, 441.

During the summer of 1857, a great financial institution in Ohio failed, thus starting a money panic which spread over the United States and was felt even in Great Britain.- The banks of New York and Philadelphia, although holding more than enough gold reserves to take care of all their obligations, suspended specie payments and refused to cash checks. Many industries had to shut down and thousands of people were thrown out of work, in Louisville alone some 3000 men being idle. With the approach of winter, Northern workmen began to hold meetings, at some of which the cry of "Bread or Blood" was raised.

The *Sumter Watchman*, with understandable local pride, announced that so far as trade in Sumter was concerned, the effects of the monetary pressure were scarcely visible, and the merchants were doing a heavy fall business.

But the report of the state comptroller general, John D. Ashmore, of Sumter District, showed that twelve of the twenty banks in South Carolina had suspended specie payments. As remedy, Ashmore recommended that no bank should be allowed to issue notes of less than $20 denomination, and that any bank, which, for more than thirty consecutive days, had a circulation of more than three times its specie reserve, should be penalized by a 10% fine. With modifications, the legislature adopted his recommendations. Mr. Ashmore particularly deplored the current practice among the banks of "shaving paper" under the name of domestic exchange, that is, of buying notes at a discount greater than the legal rate of interest. As to the recently chartered Bank of Sumter, for which no returns had reached him, Mr. Ashmore, assuming that efforts to raise the capital had failed, declared: "The Legislature, the citizens of the State, and particularly those of Sumter, should congratulate themselves upon the failure, lest it should have added another shaving shop institution to the State."[4]

As a result of the panic, according to C. G. Memminger, chairman of the ways and means committee, the cotton crop of South Carolina, worth $20,000,000 before the suspensions, had lost a third of its market value or $7,000,000.[5]

This was bad indeed for the planters of the state, but the

---

[4] *Reports and Resolutions to General Assembly* 1857.
[5] *Watchman*, Dec. 23, 1857.

legislature made matters far worse by refusing to accept the notes of the suspended banks in payment of taxes, although those notes had to be accepted as legal tender for obligations among the citizens. Said the *Watchman* in righteous indignation:

> The State is willing to palm off upon her citizens that which she herself will not receive into her treasury. *The planter must receive that in payment for his cotton with which he cannot pay his dues to the State. Two currencies—one for the State* and the other for *the people of the State.*[6]

G. W. Bradford of Sumter District however, who had endorsed many notes for his borrowing friends, had something more personal to say about the banker-made depression. For more than a year he ran an advertisement in the *Watchman* "To all persons Concerned," stating with wry humor, that after more than once paying the debts of others, he now informs his friends and the public in general "that he has resigned" and "quit the business."

In another quarter the chronic debtors had been discouraged, for the *Watchman* announced that it would enforce "The Cash System" in the newspaper business. This included payment for marriage notices, which would be inserted only when accompanied by a dollar or "a liberal share of the cake."

After some months the banks reopened, business recovered, and even the hard-pressed South enjoyed a season of prosperity. In the autumn of 1858, most of the merchants of Sumter visited New York to purchase large and varied stocks of goods. As an even better sign of easing times, the spring term of court in Sumter had only 250 civil cases in 1859, compared with 1200 of 1855, and the *Watchman* reported that Sumter planters not only were emerging from debt, but many of them had money to invest.

Meanwhile, in addition to financial troubles, the town of Sumter had been having some very unwelcome visitors. An editorial in the *Watchman* declared that the town was "infested with a legion of wandering, pilfering, begging, dirty and

---

6 Jan. 27, 1858.

squalid Gypsies, who appear in town during the day, and practice . . . impertinent mendicancy and falacious prophecy. . . ."

A more alarming visitor had preceded the Gypsies, in the person of a woman abolitionist. In the spring of 1857, a Mrs. Emerson arrived in Sumter under highly suspicious circumstances. For Mrs. Emerson not only travelled alone with her own horse and buggy, but she carried a lantern and a side saddle, and she announced that she would give a public lecture.

The town council sent a committee headed by Charles Wesley Wolfe to investigate Mrs. Emerson's character and motives. At the conclusion of her lecture, which was a "tirade of abuse against Southern ladies," the committee, on the grounds that she had come from a hostile section, asked her to state and prove her reasons for having come, and in a "respectful manner asked she would allow them to search her baggage," offering recompense if the search should establish her innocence. The search, however, confirmed their darkest suspicions, and showed that Mrs. Emerson came, not from Virginia, as she claimed, but from Ohio; and that she was collecting notes on Negro burnings, and insurrections, for a book similar to *Uncle Tom's Cabin.*

Convinced of her guilt, the committee went no further with the search. After rejecting a motion to sell her possessions and send her home by public conveyance, the weary gentlemen allowed her to depart in peace, but published their report in the *Watchman.* The publication proved to be effective, for when Mrs. Emerson attempted to lecture in the courthouse at Bennettsville, a citizens' committee blew out the lights; and at Cheraw she failed to get even a lecture room; and sensing the hostility, she departed for Wadesboro "without having her horse taken from the vehicle."[7]

A more welcome visitor was General William Walker, the American adventurer whose fantastic career in Nicaragua may be read elsewhere in history. Dressed in civilian clothes, and accompanied by a uniformed attendant, he arrived one winter day in 1858 at the Sumter depot, on his way back to Nicaragua by way of Mobile. The citizens of Sumter, who gloried in his

[7] *Watchman*, Mch. 25, Apr. 8, 1857.

exploits, quickly organized a committee to extend him the hospitalities of the town and invite him to make an address on Nicaragua. But the General begged off on the plea of engagements, and a few days later the *Watchman* carried the story of his address in Mobile to an enthusiastic Nicaragua meeting.

A restrained but none the less sensational editorial appeared in the *Watchman* in the autumn of 1857, giving an account of a duel in Sumter between unnamed parties, the first such encounter of which mention has been found since the Hemphill-Levy duel of a generation earlier:

AN AFFAIR OF HONOR

Our quiet town was the scene of some little excitement on Friday morning last, by the intelligence that an affair of "honor" had taken place at an early hour on that morning. We do not give the names of the principals . . . nor do we intend to enter into details. It might be sufficient to express our unqualified condemnation of the transaction. . . . Two persons, whose occupations are unknown, had some cause of difference . . . on the morning mentioned. A friend of each was chosen, and pistols obtained. The party repaired to the stable lot attached to the Sumter Hotel, the place chosen for the fight . . . . Unknown to the principals, the two first rounds were composed of blank cartridges. One of the principals making the discovery, charged his own weapon for the third fire, and demanded that they should fight from the ends of a handkerchief, which would have been well nigh muzzle to breast. This was not agreed to, and five paces was demanded, which was likewise rejected. Ten paces . . . . was decided upon, and the shots fired. One of the combatants fired first, when the other advanced two or three paces and fired one shot, taking slight effect in the leg, and another passing through the coat, grazing the breast. He who had fired first then advanced and inflicted several severe wounds upon the head of his antagonist, when the matter ended. (The pistols were loaded with large shot, we learn.) The principal actors, and the most culpable, we presume, have fled from the grasp of the law. Intemperance had doubtless much to do with the occurrence. It is needless to add that all good citizens frown upon the action, and raise their voice in condemnation thereof.[8]

Nothing more has been found concerning this mysterious affair.

Meanwhile, despite such depressing ideas of honor, and the ever-growing hostility between North and South, a new influence for peace and international brotherhood had come into a troubled world: the Young Men's Christian Association had been founded in Canada; and three years later the first YMCA in the South was organized in Charleston in 1854. The town of Sumter, closely associated with Charleston, soon formed one of the earliest YMCA's in the state, and when in April 1858, the international Confederation of YMCA's of the United States and British Provinces met in Charleston, Sumter sent two delegates: "A.A.G.", the initials of Allan A. Gilbert, editor of the Sumter *Watchman*, and John S. Richardson, Jr., grandson of Judge Richardson. "A.A.G." has left a vivid account of the convention in four letters published in the *Watchman*.

Leaving Sumter on the midday train, and reaching Orangeburg at dusk, said he, they saw young girls of the Orangeburg Female College strolling among the "mansion-like" buildings on the picturesque campus. Upon arriving in Charleston at midnight, they went to the "palacious" Charleston Hotel, and next morning were assigned to Mr. John Drummond at 57 Broad Street.

The highlight of the convention was the evening session in Institute Hall, when the Governor, the delegates, the clergymen, and honored citizens sat on the stage, and Dr. James H. Thornwell, "that Theological giant," addressed an audience of perhaps 3,000 persons, who then united in singing "Before Jehovah's Awful Throne." An important item on the agenda of the convention was the appointment of delegates to the second Universal Conference in Geneva, Switzerland, scheduled for the following August.

Next day the Sumter delegates asked information as to their relation to the convention and to the Confederation, and were told that, not having ratified the Confederation articles, they

[8] *Watchman*, Oct. 28, 1857.

were a distinct body, but, as delegates, they might participate in discussions without the privilege of voting.

In the closing hours of this "interesting, virtuous, intelligent and warm-hearted assemblage of young men," says their chronicler, the "most intense brotherly and fraternal love seemed to pervade every heart. They knew no North, no South, no East, and no West, no Presbyterian, Baptist, Episcopalian or Methodist—they knew nothing but a common Lord and Master."

In the same year, the skyline of the town of Sumter showed a new church steeple, for the Episcopalians had erected the Church of the Holy Comforter on the southeast corner of South Main and Bartlett streets. The little Gothic structure could seat only 250 persons, but it had a 105-foot spire that soared above all others in the village, and was a landmark for many miles. In the steeple hung a 650-pound bell, given by Mrs. Elizabeth Buford, who also gave the site for the church. One of the first marriages solemnized in the new church was that of its architect and builder, Joseph H. Long of Charleston, to Susan E. Darr of Sumter, and thereafter Mr. Long was a citizen of Sumter. The following summer, two handsome gifts to the church were exhibited at the drugstore of John Thomson, one of the vestrymen: a baptismal font of the best Italian marble, presented by the ladies of St. Philip's Church, Charleston; and a five-piece communion set of heavy silver lined with gold, two cups and three plates, inscribed as the gift of the ladies of St. Michael's Church, Charleston.

The year 1859 saw another event of local importance, when Sumter's first nurseryman, Christian Sanders of Charleston, bought from William Haynsworth, eleven acres of land between the Rev. Jesse Morgan's tanyard and the lot of State Senator Moses. Here Mr. Sanders developed a nursery for fruit trees, shrubbery, rose trees, and flowering shrubs of all kinds. Here too, he built his house and kitchen, and here he and his wife Louise settled themselves in what they expected would be their permanent home. But war clouds were gathering fast, and the time was not propitious for a new venture.

For it was in the summer of 1859 that the most fanatical of Northern abolitionists reached the climax of their frenzy, and

John Brown made his raid on Harper's Ferry arsenal. There he seized arms from the United States in an incredible attempt to arm the slaves against their masters. When the outlaw was hanged for his crime, and the North acclaimed him as a saint and a martyr, feeling in the South ran higher than ever before. Public meetings were held all over Sumter District to alert the white population against transients who might be abolitionist spies and emissaries in the guise of book agents, medicine salesmen or lecturers.

In a speech in the State House, Senator Moses, credited with spirited remarks, said: "Sir, there is a unanimity of sentiment from the mountain to the seaboard. The eyes of the Union are looking to this Legislature . . . let us move . . . let us act." In Columbia an alleged abolitionist was taken from the guardhouse by a mob, given a coat of tar and feathers, and driven out of town.

At the meeting in the town hall of Sumter, presided over by G. S. C. Des Champs,, resolutions called upon the Town Council for rigid surveillance of transients, and prompt action to eject all who might be dangerous.

At a public meeting in Clarendon, R. A. Chandler, chairman, reported that William Bodiford, although exciting sympathy because of having a wife and four children, had been ordered off, and had left Sumter for Kingville saying he was going to Columbia.

W. B. Burgess, chairman of a meeting held at R. E. Wheeler's near the Sumter-Clarendon line, reported that a committee of three had escorted one Thomas W. Barfield to Wilmington and put him on the Weldon train to leave the state. The same committee made similar disposition of Eli Vassar and Bryant Howell. At a meeting in the Bethel neighborhood near Privateer, the Privateer Rifle and Vigilance Company was formed. Meetings were held at Stateburg, Providence and Springhill.

The fateful year of 1860 found the people of Sumter expecting the worst, but carrying on the routines of daily life. Late in January, a new newspaper, *The Sumter Despatch*, [sic] made its first appearance, edited by Thomas Waties Dinkins for the owners and printers, W. J. Francis and W. M. DeLorme, Jr. Young editor Dinkins, who had taught in the Sumter Collegiate Institute in 1858, was now an attorney at law and a solicitor in equity. Like Sanders' nursery, this newspaper had begun at a bad time.

Early in May a memorable tragedy occurred when twenty-five happy picnickers were drowned in Boykin's Millpond. They had crowded upon a flat boat to cross the pond, but when near the middle, in water twenty feet deep, the boat struck a snag which pierced the bottom, and in a few minutes it sank. Fireman Jones, on the Camden train, which was near the pond at the time, rushed into the water and by herioic efforts rescued three of the party. Among those who died were a sister and a brother of Isaac McKagen, who had a drugstore in Sumter. The *Watchman* issued an *Extra* when the news reached Sumter.

The national Democratic Convention met in Charleston in the spring of 1860, but the Northern delegates dominated the proceedings. The Southern delegates, therefore, withdrew to meet later in a convention which nominated John C. Breckenridge for president. The Northern Democrats nominated Stephen A. Douglas. A third conglomerate group nominated what was called a Kangaroo ticket, headed by John Bell of Tennessee.

The three-way split among the Democrats left the field open to the Republicans, who nominated Abraham Lincoln as "the man who can split rails and maul Democrats," a slogan which proved prophetic, for when the elections were held in the fall, Lincoln, although polling a million less votes than his combined opponents, was duly elected as a minority president.

The South, believing that the election of Lincoln meant not merely the destruction of slavery but also the Africanizing of the South with a numerically superior horde of freedmen, determined upon immediate secession. In every district of South Carolina, secret associations of Minute Men pledged themselves to march with arms on a minute's notice, if ordered, to prevent the inauguration of Lincoln. The legislature unanimously called a convention of the people for December 17, to consider the value of the Union and to take action on the question of secession.

When the call for the convention was issued, Edmund Ruffin, leader of secession sentiment in Virginia, realized that South Carolina would lead the way, and came to Columbia, where he joined the Minute Men.

Throughout South Carolina, preparations were made with prayerful care, to elect the convention delegates from the best leadership. Sumter District called a public meeting at the courthouse for the election of delegates, and invited Edmund Ruffin to make the principal address. When he arrived at the Sumter depot on November 14, he found 150 Minute Men waiting to receive him, with a brass band and a salute of artillery.

The next day the courthouse was crowded, and even the ladies were out. Ruffin spoke for almost an hour to the applauding throng, who passed solemn resolutions binding the delegates to support secession. That night the cannon, fired twelve times, once more voiced the intense excitement of the people.

Sumter's delegates to the convention were Matthew Peterson Mayes, Albertus Chambers Spain, the Rev. Thomas Reese English, and Dr. Henry D. Green. The convention met in Columbia, and then, because of smallpox, adjourned to Charleston. In the words of the Rev. James H. Thornwell, the membership "embraced the wisdom, moderation and integrity of the bench; the learning and prudence of the bar; and the eloquence and learning of the pulpit." In the character of its members, he continued, it deserved Milton's tribute to the Parliament of Great Britain, "which taught the nations of the earth that resistance to tyrants was obedience to God."[9]

On December 20, 1860, the Convention unanimously adopted the Ordinance of Secession. In the afternoon, before crowded galleries, the members for two hours were filing forward to reverently affix their names to the momentous document, and when the last name was in place ex-Governor John Laurence Manning waved the parchment over his head amid a pandemonium of applause.

South Carolina, as a sovereign state, had resumed her delegated powers and left the Union.

[9] Wallace, *History of S. C.*, III, 153, 154.

CHAPTER XXI
WAR OF SECESSION

The war began slowly, so slowly that many people in the North and the South believed there would be no war. Confederate "peace" commissioners went to Washington to negotiate terms for peaceful evacuation of Southern forts. State Senator Franklin Moses was one of the secession commissioners sent to North Carolina to assist that state in leaving the Union. Later, he served a brief term in West Virginia on the staff of General Wise. His son, Franklin Jr., became private secretary to Governor Francis Pickens in Columbia, where apparently he was known as "Little Moses."[1]

In Charleston harbor, a defensive sand-battery manned by Citadel cadets was erected on Morris Island. Early in January 1861, when the "Star of the West" attempted to bring in supplies for the federal troops in Fort Sumter, the shot which splashed the waves before her bow and turned her back, was fired from that sand-battery by a Sumter youth, Cadet George E. Haynsworth.[2]

After that the *status quo* continued until Lincoln's inauguration in March, for on him rested the burden of the great decision of whether there should be peace or war. When he refused to communicate in any way with the Confederate commissioners, and gave orders for an expedition to reinforce Sumter, the South realized that he had decided on war.

In Sumter District as elsewhere, everyone felt the strain of the long suspense, and when on the evening of March 12, the first Sumter telegraph office was opened, State Senator Moses sent the first telegram to the publishers of the *Charleston Mercury*, asking for news of Fort Sumter. Promptly the reply came back, delivered to him neatly written in long-hand on embossed paper: "We congratulate you on the success of

---
[1] Brooks, *Bench and Bar*, p. 34; Mary B. Chestnut, *A Diary from Dixie*, edited by Ben Ames Williams (Boston, 1949), 193, 213, *passim*.
[2] Haynsworth, *Haynesworth-Furman and Allied Families*, pp. 69, 70; *Sumter Herald*, Jan. 13, 1939; *Citadel Cadets; The Journal of Cadet Tom Law*, (Clinton, 1941), p. 311.

your enterprise. Nothing new about Sumter. A. S. Willington & Co."[3]

A month later, at daybreak on the morning of April 12, 1861, the people of the Charleston area were awakened by the roar of cannon which rattled their window glasses, as the Confederates opened fire upon the fort. After a defense of thirty-three hours in which not a man was killed, Major Anderson surrendered the fort at noon the next day. Both the Confederate and the Palmetto flags were raised over the fort. Governor Pickens could not attend the ceremonies, but he sent an officer, R. B. Johnson, to raise the South Carolina flag, which he did. According to Johnson, soon after the flag had been raised, Frank Moses, the governor's secretary, arrived to claim the flag-raising honor. Greatly disappointed to find himself too late, Moses asked Johnson to let him have the credit for having officiated and immediately circulated the report that he actually had done so.[4] After the war, this claim, accepted as his chief war service, proved embarrassing to his career. In November 1862, young Moses was commissioned as a second lieutenant in Captain Thomas M. Baker's company, and later was assigned to Colonel Alfred Rhett's artillery regiment at Charleston. As his nerves were said to be "not especially suited to the music of battle," Lieutenant Moses was transferred to the recruiting service, and later held a colonel's commission as enrolling officer of conscripts, who, it was said, for a price could "get any sort of certificate of disability required."[5]

In response to Governor Pickens' call for ten regiments of volunteers from the militia, the Second Palmetto Regiment had been organized, and was mustered into state service on April 9, 1861. Company D of this regiment was organized at Sumter by James D. Blanding on January 7, as the Sumter Volunteers, with John S. Richardson, Jr., captain, and was among those which volunteered for Confederate service. After two weeks on Morris Island, the Sumter Volunteers were transferred to Virginia.[6]

[3] Original in possession of Herbert E. Moses, Sumter.
[4] *SCHGM*, VI, 134; Wallace, *History of S. C.*, III 167, note.
[5] A. S. Sally (ed.), *South Carolina Troops in Confederate Service*, (Columbia, 1913), p. 125; *The True Southron*, July 30, 1874, quoting *Louisville Courier Journal*, "a gentleman who has known him from a child."
[6] *S. C. Troops in Confed. Service*, II, 3, 92.

When General Beauregard was ordered to Virginia, he was replaced at Charleston by Colonel Richard H. Anderson of Stateburg, he having resigned from the United States army to serve his state. In July 1861, Colonel Anderson was made a brigadier, and soon after, was sent to Florida. Later, he saw much service in Virginia, and eventually he became a lieutenant general.

Besides the soldiers who went into battle from Sumter District, there were many physicians and surgeons who served the Confederacy, both in local hospitals and in the field with the armies. Dr. Matthew S. Moore, of James Hill, Stateburg, and Dr. J. J. Bossard of Sumter, served through the war with the medical corps. Dr. William W. Anderson in 1861 resigned from the United States medical corps to enter Confederate service. Eventually he became medical inspector of the camps, armies and hospitals of the Confederacy. Dr. Junius Alcaeus Mayes of Mayesville, for his skill and courage in the service, received the thanks of the Confederate government. Like Dr. Francis Peyre Porcher of Charleston, with whom he actively corresponded, he made useful discoveries in medical botany, notably in the sedative properties of native plants which might be used as substitutes for the anesthetics which were shut out by the federal blockade.[7]

Among the few physicians who remained at home to care for civilians, were Dr. Robert Sydney Mellett, a veteran of the Mexican War, and Dr. Marcus Reynolds, a native of County Armagh, Ireland, who, in 1844, had become a naturalized citizen of the United States, and was opposed to secession.

Sumter's ministers of the Gospel, too, felt the impact of the war. Rev. John Smyth Richardson, Sr., is said to have "spent most of his time praying for the Confederacy and planning torpedo boats to blow up Yankee warships in Charleston harbor and send Yankee seamen to a better world."[8] The Rev. John Leighton Wilson, a veteran missionary, resigned his position in New York as secretary of the Presbyterian Board of Foreign Misions, and came home to Sumter District to cast his lot with his state. He carried on evangelistic work in the Confederate armies, and for a time served as a chaplain. When

---

[7] "S. C. Birthday," *Charleston News and Courier*, June 23, 1949.
[8] Winn, *Methodism, Sumter*, p. 52.

254   HISTORY OF SUMTER COUNTY

the Presbyterian Church in the Confederate States was organized, he took charge of its foreign and domestic missions.[9]

The inertia of the "Hundred Days" following the capture of Fort Sumter, ended on Sunday, July 21, 1861, in the spectacular Confederate victory at Manassas. The share of the Sumter Volunteers in that battle plunged their homes in gloom, for neither the young men nor their homes were ready for the shock of battle. Early in the action, Captain John S. Richardson "having received a slight flesh wound left the field," according to the official report of Second Lieutenant Thomas M. Durant, who took command after the first lieutenant had been 'taken sick whilst marching to the field."[10] The next morning, a telegram which had been sent early in the battle by an inexperienced officer of the Volunteers, reached Sumter, and the *Watchman* issued a dismal *Extra*: "Captain Richardson is wounded, his men cut up, but few or none known to be dead." In the words of Mrs. Octavia Harby Moses, the eldest of whose six enlisted sons was wounded, the news of the battle of Manassas came to the families at home "like a stroke of lightning over the land."

Colonel James D. Blanding, in command of the Ninth South Carolina Regiment, reached Manassas on the evening of the battle and was disabled. Later, the full scope of the victory, which was not realized immediately, revealed the South's lost opportunity to have captured Washington.

Conditions during the ensuing months are revealed in the following letter from Colonel Blanding[11] in Virginia to William F. B. Haynsworth in Sumter:

> Head Quarters 9th Regiment South Carolina Volunteers
> McLean's Ford, (Virginia) October 25th, 1861

Dear Bill

I hardly know how to begin writing without beginning with "Pursuant to order No." et cetera. But I must write you a few lines on business and add a few more hastily about ourselves, but not movements.

Please withdraw the appearance of Blanding and Richardson in the Case of "T. I. and C. H. Nevise vs. Dr. F. L. Green" on note for $357.78, Sumter and Dinkins plaintiff's Attorneys. I have just received a letter

---

[9] H. C. DuBose, *Memoirs of Rev. John Leighton Wilson, D.D.*, (Richmond, 1895), *passim*.

[10] MS report of T. M. Durant in possession of H. G. Osteen.

[11] See sketch of Colonel Blanding in J. C. Garlington, *Men of the Time*, (Spartanburg, 1902), p. 33; his original letter is in the South Carolinian Library.

from Dinkins on the subject and have not had time to answer—do say to him that I am much obliged for reminding me of the matter. I am only surprised that Green has not long since paid the balance although he has not probably thought of the $200.00 I advanced out of my pocket for him on the note. Is there any use to ask anybody for money at home — The profession of arms is about as lucrative as Law. Government don't pay— 4 months hard service and no pay, has reduced us to nothing. If however you think there is any chance, do take my private notes and attempt some collection and if possible send my wife two or three hundred dollars and as much more as you collect. If you have any funds in your office coming to me now or during the winter, do pay it over to Capt. McFaddin for me. Ought there not be a good fee and probably some costs for me in the two Sanders cases? I send authority to pay to Capt. McFaddin.

We have had an exceedingly hard time during the last month. We scarcely get off of one tour of picket duty before they move the Regiment on another, it is the hardest duty we have to perform. To describe it may best be done by telling you what my orders are tonight. The Regiment will start at daylight tomorrow morning with one blanket each, without tents or covering, with three days cooked provisions in haversack, with one waggon, march about 7 miles and relieve Winders Regiment on the Winchester Road where we were relieved last Sunday evening—and there bivouac with the ground for our beds and the open heavens for our canopy and is our certain fortune, have a wet bed and wet canopy. We will be relieved Tuesday, Wednesday or Thursday, dependent upon circumstances in front and rear. These picket posts are our nearest forces to the enemy, requiring the utmost vigilance over every road and hog path, and hence 1/3 of the Regiment have to be on duty at a time and for 24 hours duration, the other 2/3d sleep with one eye open. No fires are allowed at all at the picket posts, and at the Regimental Reserve only in the day time. Many of the men at night sleep sitting against a tree to avoid the wet ground and sleep in the day. I was amused with Joe Wilder on last picket saying he slept across a gully in order that the water might run under him without wetting his back. You can well conceive that to me, particularly at this time, it is a duty entailing even more anxiety than hardship. There is as much danger of being shot or shooting our own picket and scouting parties as from the enemy.

Last week I was posted at night without knowing anything of the country or that there was any force on my right, and my right picket of 4 men was fired upon by 4 Rifles, shot 50 yards off, and just as I had posted a Company 100 yards in their rear to support them, we were fired upon with a volly of 18 or 20 guns. I carried out Wylie's Harrington's, Canty's and Foster's Companies, and posted so as to surround the party on three sides, and with the last company to surround on the 4th side at daylight. As day dawned Wylie captured a Lieutenant and party of 8 or 10, and Harrington's took two officers, when Lo! they proved to be Georgians of the 20th Regiment. It came near being a sad affair, as both Regiments were under arms facing each other all night. But God in merciful providence ruled otherwise.

The health of the Regiment has decidedly improved, altho' we have 187 convalescent back in the Hospitals at Richmond and Charlottesville. The spirit of the Regiment is at its highest point, as you would expect every South Carolina Regiment to be when under expectation that the enemy are about to advance. We are ready, and as General Beauregard says he is ready, we only wish that the enemy would give us the opportunity of deciding in battle (the mode he has forced upon us) a contest which keeps us from all we hold dear, and changes the comforts of home for the hardships of camp, altho many of us in Gods Providence may have to go to our long homes, and never again on earth see those most dear to us. Would to God the war was over, but so long as it lasts, here is my post and here I shall remain cheerfully.

I remain as ever with high esteem your attached friend.

J. D. BLANDING

I cannot say anything of future movements even if I knew them. I have determined not even to write any opinions about them and camp rumors are the most unreliable kind of rumors.

Do present my kindest regards to your father and his family and to your lady. I would be glad to be remembered to Dr. Haynsworth, Mr. McQueen, Frierson, and such other friends as inquire after me. I would like to name more, but remember me to one and all.

Fraser has entirely recovered—and Dick and Bossard are both well.

In the military reorganization of the following year, James D. Graham became captain of the Sumter Volunteers; and Hugh R. Garden was authorized to raise and equip an artillery company to be called the Palmetto Battery. Young Captain Garden was without experience, but he met the emergency by giving John Alexander, foundryman of Columbia, a contract to cast six field guns. He gave another contract to a country saddler to make a hundred sets of artillery harness, and a third contract to a sash-and-blind manufacturer to construct the gun-carriages and caisons. Garden's command was assigned to duty under General Longstreet, and appropriately the Palmetto Battery became known as Garden's Battery.

While the young men of Sumter District were leaving for service on the frontiers of the Confederacy, the older men were being organized into the Home Guard, and many were stationed on the coast. Soon there were few except the women and children at home, and on the women fell the responsibility for raising food and maintaining order among the slaves. To the slaves' credit, most of them responded with loyalty, many of them with devotion, and the work of seedtime and harvest went forward much as usual.

The women of Stateburg and Sumter formed themselves into Soldier's Relief Associations, and knitted socks, ravelled lint for dressing wounds, rolled bandages, and sent boxes of supplies to the larger centers at Charleston and Columbia. They also sent contributions of food to the Wayside Homes which were organized by women for the soldiers at all important railroad centers.

At the depot in Sumter, the ladies set up a long table beside the tracks, where in fair weather, hot food was served to soldiers on the crowded troop-trains passing through. In bad weather, they used the dining-room of the Rev. Noah Graham's hotel. Later in the war, when hurrying soldiers did not have time to stop, the ladies handed out packaged lunches, while their little daughters filled the canteens with fresh water. Even in the small hours after midnight, Mrs. Octavia Moses and other devoted women would walk to the depot, taking food for the soldiers.

With the help of their servants, the busy women of Sumter spun, wove, knitted, dyed, and stitched by hand, the garments for their families as well as for the soldiers. They made imitation coffee from okra seeds and parched peanuts, and dim, evil-smelling candles from tallow and myrtle berries. They devised hats from corn shucks, and new dresses from old window curtains. They sent their silver to the Confederate government, the church bells to the foundries to be cast into cannon, and cut their carpets into blankets for the soldiers. They held fairs and bazaars to raise money for the various war activities.

During the second year of the war, Sumter District lost one of its wealthiest and most public-spirited citizens, the former brigadier general of the fifth brigade of militia, Samuel Rembert Chandler, whose wealth in slaves and other property he disposed of in a will of more than ordinary interest. In trust of the executor, Thomas Boone Fraser, he provided liberally for his young wife, Mary Jacqueline, who was free to marry again, and to live with her husband in the

Chandler home, enjoying his many legacies to her, including his "fine colt called Jeff Davis," and half the net revenue of the estate. He also left legacies to his brother Isaac James Chandler; to his sisters, Mrs. Jane Taylor, Eliza Chandler, Louisa Spann, and Agnes D. McLaurin; and to Concord Church, where he was buried.

General Chandler's will further directed that upon the death of Mary Jacqueline, the executor should sell the estate and pay half the proceeds to her surviving child or children, if any; and the other half into a permanent, public trust-fund. All the trustees of this fund were public officials: the state senator and representatives from Sumter District, the commissioner in equity, and the ordinary—now called the judge of probate. These trustees were charged to establish and maintain in the town of Sumter, a college for young men, to be called Sumter Institute, on the "most liberal plan which the fund . . . will warrant, having in view the attainment of a high order of scholarship." In the event that Mary Jacqueline should leave no issue, the entire proceeds from the sale of the Chandler estate were to go into the trust fund for the Sumter Institute.

This will was made at the time the Confederacy was winning brilliant victories on the battlefield, and prospects were bright for Southern independence, so General Chandler could not foresee what fate held in store for his country.

Mary Jacqueline did marry again, and had a daughter whom she named for herself, and a son whom she named for General Chandler. The executor of the will, Judge Fraser, died near the close of the year 1900, and Mary Jacqueline survived until 1908, almost twenty-eight years after the death of her second husband, a physician. Their son, Samuel Chandler Baker, followed in his father's footsteps and also became a Sumter physician.

Meanwhile, the weary war years lengthened, and wounded soldiers from distant battlefields came by train to be nursed and healed in the peace and security of Sumter. Hospitals were set up in the Baptist and Presbyterian churches, in the hotel, and in the courthouse. Many convalescent soldiers were taken into private homes and tenderly cared for.

Civilian refugees, too, sought safety in Sumter. From bombarded Charleston came old Mr. Robert Bee and his daughters, who took a house just outside of the village at the fork of the Charleston-Savannah and Manning roads; and also the daughters of Dr. Joseph Johnson, Jane and Hannah. The Sisters of Mercy transferred their convent from the beleaguered old city and opened St. Joseph's Academy in Sumter. The Mellichamp family came from James Island, the Whildens from Christ Church Parish, and the Venning family from Mount Pleasant. The McKagen family left Camden to be under the protection of Dr. Isaac McKagen, the Sumter druggist. From Virginia in 1863 came a party of ladies, one of whom, young Martha Wright Thomas, was married to Thomas Murritt DeLorme in 1866, and lived the rest of her life in Sumter. To the High Hills came other non-combatant refugees. Midway, the historic home of John Singleton near Manchester, was occupied by the J. J. Pringle Smiths of Charleston, during whose occupancy it was destroyed accidentally by fire.

Once more, as in the days of the Revolution, Sumter District became a center for army stores. Hundreds of freight cars loaded with war supplies rolled northward on the Camden Branch. Many others carrying munitions, lumber and food, passed eastward through Mayesville on the Wilmington and Manchester railroad.

While the war progressed from bad to worse, and news from the battle fronts grew more grim, the people of Sumter worked and hoped, even when, in February 1865, Charleston fell to the enemy. While Sherman marched north from the sea, they sorrowfully heard of the sack and destruction of Columbia, and watched the night skies reflect the glare of burning homes along his route to Camden. The tracks from Columbia toward Kingville had been sabotaged by federal troops, and trains from Sumter could not proceed west beyond Kingville. From Cheraw, Sherman destroyed the railroad trestles southward as far as Darlington. The Confederates had burned the railroad bridge across the Pedee, so an immense amount of rolling stock, loaded with war materials, became immobilized on the tracks between Florence, Manchester and Camden.

Sherman determined to destroy these supplies, and ordered Brigadier General Edward E. Potter to lead an expedition for that purpose from Charleston by way of Georgetown. Soon rumors came to Sumter of another march from the sea, even more to be dreaded than Sherman's, for armed Negroes made up a large part of Potter's expeditionary force.[12]

On April 5, 1865, Potter left Georgetown with three regiments of Negro troops, two regiments of white soldiers, two pieces of artillery, and a cavalry unit, a total of about 2,700 fighting-men. He followed the river road, then branched off to Kingstree, broke the Northeastern Railroad, and moved down to Manning, meeting very little opposition. His supplies had been sent up the Santee River to Wright's Bluff, and as he moved through the rich, peaceful country, burning mills, ginhouses and cotton, his foragers denuded the plantations of food, carried off the livestock, and gathered up an ever-increasing horde of excited Negroes.

For the first time since the Revolution, war and its horrors were advancing upon the people of Sumter in their own homes.

The only hope of protection from the invaders, lay in the remnants of local militia, from which most of the able bodied men had long since been drawn away. Nevertheless, Colonel G. W. Lee issued Order No. 2 from headquarters in Sumter: "The Regiment will assemble at this place immediately with three days' cooked rations to repel a threatened raid of the enemy. The men are earnestly requested to mount themselves if possible . . . ." signed by T. B. Fraser, *adjutant.*

In response to this order, came old men, 'teen-age boys, and

[12] The account of Potter's Raid which follows is based upon *Official Records of the Union and Confederate Armies*, (Washington, 1880-1901), Series I, XLVII, Part 1, Reports, 1026-1032; L. F. Emilio, *History of the Fifty-Fourth Regiment of Massachusetts Volunteer Infantry*, 1863-1865, (Boston, 1894), pp. 289-309; *Life and Adventures of Capt. Robert W. Andrews;* narratives by Rev. W. W. Mood, in *Watchman and Southron*, reprinted in *Manning Enterprise* in 1886 and in the *Southern Christian Advocate* in 1895—all in a scrapbook of Rev. Mr. Mood, now owned by Miss Emma Mood, Sumter; MS recollections of Catherine Louise McLauren and Mrs. Mary McKagen Clarke; printed recollections of Mrs. Octavia Harby Moses and others in *South Carolina Women in the Confederacy*, (Columbia, 1907); conversations with Mrs. W. H. Pate, Mrs. Margaret Y. L. Stancill; address by S. H. Edmunds at unveiling of marker at Dingle's Mill, April 9, 1918; "The Battle of Dingle's Mill" by D. J. Winn, undated clippings from *Sumter Daily Item*, 1920; letter from Mrs. Catsy Spain Woods, Durlington, Feb. 21, 1948, to Anne K. Gregorie; *The Sumter News*, June 21, 1866.

convalescent soldiers from the hospitals. The remnants of neighboring militia companies joined them. Colonel Lee had 80 men; Colonel Connors of Clarendon, about 40 men, a few of whom were mounted; Colonel James F. Pressley, with his arm in a sling from a wound received in a western campaign, reached Sumter late on Saturday afternoon, April 8, with 100 men. Colonel Caldwell of Kentucky, came from across the Santee with 120, including a few cavalrymen from General Lewis' command; Lieutenant Colonel Brown brought 60, and Captain Alex Colclough, 100. A convalescent French artilleryman from Louisiana, Lieutenant Pamperya, left a hospital to help, and with 15 men was assigned to a small cannon, a brass twelve-pounder; Lieutenant W. A. McQueen, son of Sumter's Presbyterian pastor, was in charge of another old fieldpiece, an iron gun, with 15 men. Lieutenant McGregor had 30 men, and Sergeant Dunbar 15 more. The total force of 575 men was under the command of Colonel Caldwell, the senior officer.

Although the people of Sumter had only heard of the war heretofore, there was little or no panic at Potter's approach, but excitement ran high as scouts galloped back and forth, and rumors flew from mouth to mouth. The commissioners of public buildings who were responsible for the courthouse and its contents, saved the public records by having them sent ten miles into the country and hidden. Some people left town.

Everyone was busy, hiding food, clothing and valuables in unexpected places. Mrs. McKagen, who lived in a two-story house at the corner of Liberty and Washington, concealed her meat supplies in the loft of the chicken house, her silver and linen in holes under the house, and much of the family's clothing in a large piano-box, which had been made into a couch for Fannie, her daughter-in-law, who was then just recovering from pneumonia. Most people dressed themselves in as many suits and dresses as they could squeeze into, and the ladies made good use of their voluminous skirts.

Andrew Jackson Moses loaded a four-mule wagon with food, and placed it in charge of his faithful servant, Dick Moore, who hid it safely in the woods until all danger had passed. Robert W. Andrews, who had just reached home from service as a veterinarian with Garden's Battery, did not care to join in a fight, so he told his wife to say he had gone fishing. He then took charge of Dr. China's carriage and horses, and a four-horse wagon loaded with valuables, and assisted by three of the doctor's Negroes, he secreted them all successfully in Cedar Bay, where he, too, remained until danger had passed.

Potter, meanwhile, had left Manning, and on Sunday morning, April 9, the day of General Lee's surrender at Appomatox, though no one in Sumter then knew it, Potter took the road to Sumter.

The defenders marched out on the road to Manning to meet him, and through three miles of deep sand they dragged their little cannon to Dingle's Mill, where they had decided to make a stand. The creek which crossed the road at this point had been dammed to form a wide millpond, too deep and miry to ford. The bridge over the creek was burned. The only crossing then was by a narrow causeway about two hundred feet long, flanked by woods and dense thickets. The mill-building stood on the defenders' right, a few yards from the bank where the waste water spilled into a thicket. To command the causeway, the defenders quickly threw up a small earthwork, and here Lieutenant McQueen placed his gun, while Lieutenant Pamperya mounted his gun a few yards further to the right. A third old gun, in charge of Sergeant Dunbar, proved useless because the primers did not fit. Pamperya masked the little battery with pine tops and saplings, and pickets were posted on the left side of the road to watch for the approach of the enemy. On Paperya's battery rested the success or failure of his plan to hold the causeway with an enfilading fire.

One of the very young defenders, D. James Winn, stationed in a trench, has recorded that the ladies of Sumter sent out a nice basket dinner to Pamperya and others, who spread it out near his gun and enjoyed it while they waited. Winn's old uncle, Charles DeLorme, sent for the lad to join the party, and noting his hungry zest, said, "Help yourself, son. If we must die, die with a full stomach." On his way back to his post, says Winn, he passed Lieutenant McQueen sitting on his gun carriage, twirling his glasses and laughingly chatting with his men.

About two o'clock in the afternoon, the enemy came within range, and the little battery opened fire. Two boys, Andrew Buchanan, nephew of Dr. J. J. Bossard, and J. Blanding Jones, ran to a Negro cabin for some pieces of burning wood, and tried desperately to shoot Dunbar's gun without the primers, but it merely flashed and did not fire a shot. Potter soon located the position of the battery, and ordered his men to charge it, but they were driven back by the defending riflemen. Colonel Pressly now ordered the mill-building burned, to keep it from giving cover to the enemy. Potter's artillery soon arrived, and one of the first rounds killed Lieutenant McQueen with a ball through the body, and silenced his gun. When Potter's second charge was driven back, he sent a New York regiment to turn the defender's left by wading the swamp below, led by the old Negro miller.

This was successful, and a volley from the flanking party killed Lieutenant Pamperya with a Minie ball through the head. John Thompson, an Englishman who had a drugstore in Sumter, also was killed. Mr. C. N. Harbun of the Reserves, and young William Reeder of the Siege Train, fell mortally wounded. Sergeant Joseph H. Long, going to Reeder's assistance, was instantly killed. William Harrel, also assisting Reeder, was wounded and captured. Others among the wounded were Wade Newman, Potts Davis, William Wingate, William Baker, and Charles McCoy. H. D. Lincoln and one Wooten, both of the Twentieth South Carolina Regiment, were captured. G. C. Fabib of the Twenty-second Georgia Regiment, was wounded in the arm and leg, which Potter's surgeons amputated. Private Fahm was another Georgian wounded in the battle.

With the silencing of Pamperya's gun, further resistance was impossible, and a general retreat under cover of Caldwell's cavalry was ordered. The fifty men under Colonel Lee, who had been flanked by the enemy, came very near being captured, and during their retreat up the road toward Sumter, they were exposed to the enemy's fire across the fields for almost a mile from the battlefield.

Potter did not pursue, for he knew that the road into Sumter was now open. Moreover, his men were weary, and he had to dispose of the dead and wounded. His own dead he placed in large pits in mass burial, which he concealed by burning fence rails heaped over them, presumably to dry the damp earth and destroy the scent of blood which might attract animals to dig out the bodies.

The bad news was not long in reaching Sumter. Donald McQueen, one of the youngest of the defenders, galloped back into town with the sash and hat from his dead brother's body, screaming, "They have killed my brother!"

Mothers closed the shutters of their homes and sat inside with their children, waiting quietly for what fate might bring. Young Alberta Spain, eldest daughter of Albertus Spain, was so terrified of reprisal from the enemy, that she carried into the yard and burned her father's copy of the Ordinance of Secession showing his signature.

Late in the afternoon of that dreadful Sabbath, Potter's cavalry rode up Main Street into Liberty, and then back to the depot, where they encamped with the Negro troops. The white infantry bivouacked on Liberty Street in the Catholic grove; and a third camp was made on the road to Providence. Some say that General Potter and his staff made headquarters in the Solomons' house on Main Street, but it was at the Altamont Moses house on Washington Street that Mrs. McKagen and other anxious women applied for, and obtained guards for their homes during the terrible night. In many homes not even children were undressed for bed.

One of the first acts of the invaders was to round up all the Negroes in town, men, women, and children, who were taken to the depot and kept under guard with the Negro rabble which was following the expeditionary force.

Fires soon broke out. The depot, railroad shops, and the cotton warehouses of Mr. Bogin and Mr. A. J. Moses were among the first to be set afire, and the flames soon spread to the rows of one- and two-room houses where the railroad employees lived. In the field next to the A. J. Moses house, 196 bales of his cotton were burned.

Party after party of Union soldiers, white and Negro, went

from house, to house, ostensibly searching for contraband weapons and hidden Confederate soldiers, but also taking away food, clothing, and valuables of every kind which they could find.

At Mrs. McKagen's, late in the evening, before the guard arrived, one of the final pair of looters horrified the children by shoving his gun-barrel into the open mouth of their sleeping nurse. When the same man asked if any of the family had fought that day at Dingle's Mill, Fannie, the sick wife of Dr. McKagen, answered,

"Yes, my husband."

Then, in her terrible anxiety for news of him, she described her husband, and asked if the soldier had seen him. Laughing, the man replied,

"Yes, I saw him. He was lying on his stomach and I stuck my bayonet through him and turned him over."

The shock to the sick woman was too much, and although her husband soon sent a note telling her of his safety, Fannie died the following Friday. In the words of Mrs. Mary McKagen Clark in later years, "That soldier had as truly killed her as if he had stuck his bayonet through her."

The next day the systematic destruction went on. Some of the Negro troops moved along the railroad to Mayesville, and there destroyed seven cars and a bridge. Another detachment of Negro troops went three miles toward Manchester, and burned a long, covered railroad-bridge, four cars, 200 bales of cotton, a ginhouse, and a mill filled with corn. In Sumter, details of the 54th Massachusetts Negro Infantry, destroyed four locomotives, twenty cars, the well-equipped railroad machine-shops, and the tracks and trestles for six miles on each side of the town. Both the new jail and the old one which had been remodeled into the town hall, were burned. The courthouse, although in use as a hospital, was damaged, for some of the public records which had not been moved, were dumped and the furniture was destroyed. Dr. China's residence and some other homes are said to have been burned, possibly set on fire by flames from the burning cotton and public buildings.

The merchants of the town suffered, for their shops were

broken into and denuded. The office of the *Watchman* was seized, and the printing presses of Gilbert and Darr were used by the soldier-printers to publish a sheet which they called *The Banner of Freedom*. Before leaving town, they wrecked all the printing machinery and scrambled the type.

On Tuesday morning, April 11, 1865, Potter's army left Sumter, the soldiers singing John Brown's hymn as they marched along the bed of the Wilmington and Manchester railroad, the twelve miles to Manchester.

With the raiders out of town, the people of Sumter opened their shuttered windows and went forth to discover how each other had fared. Most families found themselves without servants, for they had gone with Potter's horde. Only four Negro men are said to have been left in town: two house carpenters, Andrew Spann and Ransom Hoyt, and two preachers, James White and Stephen Haynsworth, who had managed to slip away from the guards.

Although the occupation by the enemy had not been as terrible as expected, there had been tragedy. Old Mr. Robert Bee was found hanging from the rafters of his attic, tortured and murdered by drunken soldiers, who were said to have raped his daughter. Mr. Harmon DeLeon of Charleston, saw to his burial.

Mr. Augustus Solomons and Mr. A. J. Moses went out to Dingle's Mill to take care of the Confederate dead. Young Reeder, who had been taken to a hospital, where he died, was buried in the burial plot of N. G. Osteen, but later his body was removed to the Confederate plot in the cemetery on Oakland Avenue, where many of the soldiers who died in Sumter hospitals were buried.

Potter, meanwhile, had reached Manchester, and on Tuesday night, April 11, he established headquarters in the Richard Singleton mansion, where his First Brigade encamped in the beautiful grove. Other regiments bivouacked north of Manchester along the road to Stateburg. On the Singleton plantation, a young Confederate soldier, said to have been from Kentucky, was captured, and when he steadfastly refused to take the oath of allegiance to the United States, he was killed and buried at the corner of the Singleton house.

Three miles away to the north, the D. B. McLaurin family was at Argyle plantation, the former Ararat of the William Mayrant family. "Our anxiety may be imagined," wrote Catherine Louisa, one of the daughters, "as we sat on the piazza, watching the smoke arising from the burning depots, dwellings, gin-houses, barns, cotton, etc., in the country around." Mrs. S. J. C. Elliott's handsome old home about a mile from Manchester, was completely destroyed, with her gin-house, barns and all outbuildings. The James M. Caldwell home, which stood where the Manchester road entered Stateburg, also was burned.

The worst tragedy occurred at the home of Mrs. E. S. Campbell, the seventy-six year old widow of Alexander Campbell, whose daughter and invalid son lived with her. When the Negro troops came, the son met them, and, failing to understand one of their orders, was instantly shot. His body was left in the dust for a day and a night, while the house was being completely stripped of food, clothing and valuables. Spurred on by the accusations of a vindictive old servant who had always been a run-away, the troops probably would have burned the house, and might even have done worse. But when the storehouse was set on fire, an eighteen-year-old Negro girl extinguished the blaze, and then she pleaded so affectionately and eloquently for her old mistress, that the officers set a guard to protect Mrs. Campbell and her daughter from further injury.

Potter's mission, meanwhile, was being accomplished, and the railroad, rolling stock, and military stores, were being systematically blown up and rendered useless. At Wateree Junction, five miles west of Manchester, the invaders set fire to the trestle and destroyed 5 engines, 13 cars, a quantity of lumber, the turn-table, and the water tanks. Three miles further west in the swamp, they blasted 3 more locomotives, and 35 cars loaded with supplies estimated to have "a total value of $300,000." The rails of the track were thrown and looped in every direction, and, until recently, the iron wheels of a car could be seen in a tree top.

Potter's first incomplete report on his work showed the destruction of 32 locomotives, 250 cars, 100 cotton gins and presses, 5,000 bales of cotton, more than 1,000,000 feet of lumber, and vast government stores. In addition, he took innumerable vehicles such as wagons, carts, etc., and between 300 and 500 horses and mules. He estimated the number of Negroes following his column at 5,000. On April 12, Potter sent his wounded soldiers and several thousand Negroes to Wright's Bluff, twenty-five miles below, where the wounded, and the women and children, were placed aboard light-draft vessels for the trip to Georgetown. The Negro men were armed with 200 captured muskets and sent overland on foot.

Next day, April 13, Potter sent a detachment to Stateburg and destroyed some stores. On the afternoon of the 14th, he had a brush with a score of Confederate pickets in that neighborhood. On the 15th, another skirmish took place near Stateburg.

Near Bradford Springs on April 16, a sharp skirmish was fought with the Confederates under Colonel Pressley at Spring Hill, the handsome old Davis home which stood on a solid brick basement, and was then occupied by the Barfield family. On Colonel Pressley's orders, Mrs. Barfield's mother, Mrs. Lowder, old and ill, was taken to the basement for the protection of the brick walls, and was being taken care of there by her young granddaughters. The invaders soon flanked the position and Pressley evacuated the premises. Yelling Negro troops swarmed into the house upon the family. Fortunately General Potter arrived, and after a cautious reconnaissance for Confederate stragglers, cleared the house of his noisy troops. He also had his field surgeon examine and prescribe for the sick woman, but she refused all medicine and would take only a little food from the hand of the enemy.

While at Spring Hill, the surgeon amputated the leg of a wounded soldier, using a door from one of the out-buildings for an operating table; the leg was wrapped in a white window curtain and buried in the garden. The only prisoner taken at Spring Hill was Augustus Capell, who was captured in the Methodist graveyard near the house. That night Potter rested at Spring Hill, where his wounded men were put to bed, and the Negro soldiers made camp outside. Before leaving the next morning, the General offered the family whatever food the sick woman might require. Strange to say, after such humanity, his soldiers carried away many of the family's possessions, including the bedclothes.

Although Camden already had been sacked by Sherman, Potter arrived there on April 17, but finding nothing further to destroy, he turned back the next morning toward Stateburg. The few Confederates still in the field tried vainly to check his progress, and fought skirmishes on April 18, at Boykin's Mill and Bradford Springs; and on April 19 at Dinkins' Mill and Beach Creek near Stateburg.

The entire day of April 20 was devoted by the enemy to the destruction of rolling stock and supplies at Middleton Depot on the Camden Branch, where, within the space of two miles, were 16 locomotives and 245 cars loaded with ordnance, machinery, and quartermaster's stores. The next day Potter began his return march to Georgetown through Manchester and Fulton.

Meanwhile, many unprotected families had sought refuge at Milford, the magnificent home of former Governor John Laurence Manning in the Sandhills near St. Mark's Church. A thrilling account of the dramatic events which took place there on Friday, April 21, 1865, has been recorded by the Rev. William W. Mood, who wrote it down as dictated to him by Governor Manning himself.

The Governor had a prominent part in those events, for he had recently returned from a tour of the western states, under a commission from Governor Magrath. During the morning of that fateful day, the anxious refugees at Milford had watched columns of smoke arising four miles away, from the 700 bales of blazing cotton belonging to Mrs. Richard I. Manning, a widow whose husband had died at the beginning of the war, and whose oldest child was only twelve years old. The smoke meant that Potter was nearing Milford, making his way back to the boats at Wright's Bluff for the return to Georgetown.

Soon a noisy mob of black soldiers surged into the beautiful hall of Milford from the rear, and a sergeant in the lead shouted, "Have you any protection for this house?"

"Our only protection," replied Manning, "is from the army of the Confederate States."

Raising his gun, the angered Negro aimed at the elderly gentleman and said, "You are a dead man!"

Just then a Negro officer shouted, "Halt! The General is at the front door."

Turning his back upon the mob in the hall, Manning walked out on the portico to greet his uninvited guests, and saw Potter and his officers on horseback.

"I suppose," said the Governor, "This is the commander of the United States army?"

"Yes sir," replied the General, "and I have come to protect your family and house from injury."

"I ask no protection but for the ladies under my roof," was the answer, "and that is always granted in civilized warfare."

"That is my object in coming here," said General Potter, "and I'll carry out my purpose." He then dismounted, and followed by his officers, entered the portico.

"This is a fine structure," said the General.

"Yes," said the Governor, "it was built by a man from New England by the name of Potter, and I suppose a man from New York by the name of Potter will destroy it."

"No sir," said Potter, "that is not my intention. Your place shall be protected." He then asked if Manning had had any news of the fall of the Confederacy, and receiving a negative reply, he said it was imminent. Then he issued orders that everything on the premises should be protected, and when two soldiers tried to lasso a horse, he threatened to hang them. The General then proceeded into the hall, and as he crossed the threshold, the Governor announced, "The commander of the United States army."

In tones that all could hear, the General said, "There shall be no injury done to your estate, Governor, and the ladies shall be protected."

In the drawingroom and the library, the General and his officers were presented to the ladies. As both he and his staff were courteous, there was a general conversation for some hours until the army had passed, leaving no stragglers. All of the officers were taken on a tour of the mansion, one of the finest in the South. Built on a sandhill, the mere foundations are said to have required 300,000 bricks and great quantities of granite.

About four o'clock in the afternoon, after a six-hour stay, the General and his retinue rode away. They had been gone only about twenty minutes, when a Confederate courier, Lieutenant Rhett, arrived with the news of the armistice signed by Sherman and Johnston. Exhausted by his ride, the young officer fell asleep almost immediately upon a divan in the hall. But in a few minutes, the Governor awoke him and asked that he carry the news to Potter under a flag of truce. The Lieutenant overtook Potter only about a mile away, and the General at once sent him back with one of his own aides to convey his compliments and good wishes to the Governor. As the news had spread rapidly, a number of Confederates converged upon Milford and filled the hall, so Potter's aide arrived to deliver his message in the presence of some sixty or more of his late enemies.

Potter continued his course slowly toward Wright's Bluff, and on April 22, when he received the news of General Lee's surrender, he ceased to lay waste the country. But in the two terrible weeks of his occupation,[12] Sumter District already had been ruined, and Potter's Raid had become a saga of the final days of the Confederacy.

CHAPTER XXII

RECONSTRUCTION

After the surrender of the Confederate armies, the soldiers made their way home as best they might, some on foot, and some on horses as thin and weak as themselves. Major Edwin Warren Moise, who had commanded a regiment though not commissioned as Colonel, came to join his wife and children in Sumter, riding a wounded horse which he later sold to pay their board.[1]

Tragedy attended some of the homecomings. One Sumter soldier, released from a Northern prison, deafened by cold and exposure, arrived home one midnight and tried to get in at the front door. His father, who had given up the son for dead, called out but received no answer. A little later, hearing a noise at a window which the son was trying to open, the father fired, and felt the house shaken by a fall. He had killed his only son.[2]

For a time the state was without a civil government, for in May Governor Magrath was removed from office and imprisoned in Fort Pulaski. Not until July did Benjamin F. Perry, the respected Unionist of Greenville, take office as provisional governor, appointed by President Andrew Johnson.

During the summer the town of Sumter was garrisoned by a Massachusetts regiment quartered in the courthouse. This military occupation was a cloud which proved to have a silver lining, for when the soldiers were paid, greenbacks became plentiful and stimulated business. Freeman Hoyt, the watchmaker, reopened his Main Street shop and with the help of his young son Oliver, did a good business repairing the watches of the soldiers.[3]

---

[1] Elzas, *Jews of S. C.*, p. 249.

[2] Mary Boykin Chesnut, *A Diary from Dixie*, (New York, 1929), p. 401.

[3] Freeman Hoyt, Aug. 10, 1865, to Mary French Hoyt, in possession of T. A. Stubbs, Sumter.

The mere fact that bloodshed had ceased and the survivors had come home, caused the spirits of the people to revive. In the fall a tournament described as the grandest the country had ever witnessed, was held at Sumter, where "some thirty knights, in splendid attire and magnificently mounted, contended for the prize in the presence of several thousand spectators."[4]

But thoughtful people were anxious. No one knew what to expect. Would the homes and plantations in Sumter District be confiscated as they had been on the coast? In every community there were helpless people, widows and orphans, without the necessities of life. How were they to be relieved? The slaves who had behaved so well during the war were now in great part idle and demoralized, happy in the belief that emancipation meant freedom from work for life. Old Shady Lewis, "notorious and venerable colored sinner," was typical of his race as he happily walked the streets of Sumter, making sweet music and reciting strange "examples of elocution and rhetoric."[5] How were the freedmen to be induced to return to the fields and produce the food so necessary to all?

Some of these questions were answered by the Freedmen's Bureau, created shortly before Lee's surrender. General Saxton, its first chief in South Carolina, largely originated the idea that every freedman would get forty acres and a mule. At the town of Sumter was one of the ten centers of the Bureau in the state. Until it was inactivated in 1868, many starving people of both races were helped by the Bureau; and although it organized some gigantic land-frauds, only 454 acres at a cost of $2,000 were purchased in the district of Sumter.[6]

Perhaps the absence of scandal in the Sumter office of the Bureau may have been because the local post commanders were superior officers. The garrison and the Bureau were closely associated, especially in court matters, for at first the post commander was judge of the provost court set up at

---

[4] F. B. Simpkins and R. H. Woody, *South Carolina During Reconstruction* (Chapel Hill, 1932), p. 345. This excellent study is one of the two chief sources for this chapter.
[5] *Ibid.*, p. 363; *The True Southron*, Sept. 25, 1874.
[6] James S. Pike, *The Prostrate State* (New York, 1935), 153.

Sumter for the combined districts of Sumter, Clarendon and Kershaw. In 1866, John T. Green, a lawyer of Sumter, was "president" of the provost court, and apparently held the office until the civil courts reopened. Thomas E. Richardson, clerk of the provost court, advertised in the *Sumter News* in August 1867, that under the rules of the court, civil actions would be begun by petition addressed to the post commander, stating the cause of complaint; and criminal actions would be brought merely by information lodged with the post commander. The purpose in establishing the court was to protect the freedmen from injustices. Frank Moses, Jr., is said to have served a brief term as provost judge; and it was in the provost court that Major Edwin W. Moise found a beginning for the resumption of his law practice.[7]

In order that crops might be planted, the general in command of the state directed the landowners and Negroes to enter into temporary labor contracts on a sharecrop basis. The signing of these contracts on John Frierson's plantation on Pudding Swamp, as described in later years by a Negro who was present, probably was typical of the signings on other plantations. Mr. Frierson had sent out a call for all hands to come to his house, and soon the yard was crowded with Negroes, facing toward the piazza where he stood with a labor contract in his hand. Beside him stood his son Adolphus, recently returned from the war. His son Rush had been killed.

Mr. Frierson made a brief speech: "My Servants: I call you together today, to read this contract to you, and have you all to sign it." Then he explained that they were free, and might go if they wished, but he hoped that they would stay. "You all have been taught to work and to behave yourselves," he went on, "and I hope you will continue to lead such lives in the future." He then read aloud and explained the contract, which stated that if they remained on the plantation and produced the crops, a sharing of the harvest would be had on January 1, 1866. When he had finished "the older heads of these ex-slaves filed in one by one and touched the pen in

---

[7] For Moses, see the *True Southron*, May 7, 1874; for Moise, see Elzas, *Jews of S. C.*, 249.

the hand of Mr. Adolphus, and made their mark. Then they left the yard and returned to their work."[8]

From the Mount Zion community near Mayesville, good Dr. John Leighton Wilson, the missionary who had devoted his life in Africa and America to the advancement of the Negro race, was summoned before Provost Judge Boyen to explain a supposed breach of a labor contract with his house servant, and received the following letter:

> H.Q.U.S. Forces, Sumter, S. C. June 14, 1866.
>
> Dr. Wilson:
>
> Sir,—The Freedman Harrison English Complains at this office that you have accused his wife Julia, of thieving without cause, and turned her out of your employ, paying no regard to your contract with her. this conduct is rong, the woman says she wants to work for you till Janry next. if she has done any rong, prosecute her, and the court, if she is found guilty, will relieve you from the contract. otherways if you do not permit her to return to work, will hold you responsible for her wages and Board. M. BOYEN, *Provost Judge.*

When Dr. Wilson went to see the provost judge and explained the affair, he had no further trouble.[9]

In the meantime, President Johnson had directed Governor Perry to enroll the citizens who had been eligible to vote under prewar state law, and who, since then, had taken the oath of allegiance to the United States. After the enrollment, those who qualified elected delegates to a constitutional convention, which met in Columbia in September 1865, and, having repealed the ordinance of secession, framed a new government for the state. Sumter's delegates to the convention were, J. N. Frierson of Cherry Vale plantation, Thomas W. Muldrow, and Franklin Israel Moses. Under the constitution of 1865, James L. Orr of Anderson was elected governor in October, and a goodly proportion of excellent men was sent to the legislature. The legislative delegation from Sumter was headed by Franklin I. Moses as state senator.

---

[8] Lowery, *Life on the Old Plantation*, 120-124.
[9] DuBose, *John Leighton Wilson*, p. 290.

Faced with the appalling problems of a newly emancipated black population which outnumbered the whites, and was completely unprepared for political responsibility, the legislature of 1865 did not enfranchise the Negroes. On the contrary, it enacted a so-called "Black Code" for their control, and set up a system of constitutional "district courts" to handle civil and criminal cases in which Negroes were parties. These measures, realistic and necessary from the Southern view, were highly provocative to Northern radicals, and gave them an excuse for measures which would prove to be as disastrous as the war.

Unaware of danger, however, the legislature ratified the Thirteenth Amendment to the federal constitution, elected B. F. Perry and John L. Manning to the United States Senate, and named the judges for the courts. State Senator Franklin I. Moses was among the judges of the circuit court, and Major Thomas Boone Fraser, an honest and competent lawyer, became judge of the new "district court" to handle Negro cases in Sumter. Mr. Fraser soon resigned, however, and was succeeded by Captain Charles Mayrant.

With the machinery of civil government thus restored, President Johnson on April 2, 1866, declared the late "rebellion" at an end, and civil government reinstated. Military taxes were abolished, and jails were returned to civil officers. During the year the federal garrisons in the state were gradually reduced from 7,408 men to 2,747; but military courts continued to function, often in conflict with the state courts.

Without money, it was very difficult for the state to restore the public buildings necessary to the functioning of civil government. In Sumter the commissioners of public buildings, of which Montgomery Moses was chairman and W. F. B. Haynsworth secretary-treasurer, were allotted one thousand dollars by the legislature for the construction of a log jail to replace the one burned by General Potter. But the lowest bid was for $2,500, and they had to devise an alternative. As the federal garrison had evacuated the courthouse, the commissioners installed iron bars on the windows of the grand jury room, to serve as a temporary prison. The first prisoners promptly escaped, and thus, said the *Sumter News*, not only was the expense of a new building saved, but also the additional expense of feeding the prisoners!

The commissioners had other problems. When the public records were brought back from their hiding place in the country, the sheriff's records were found so badly injured from exposure, that they had to be transcribed into new books. In the clerk of court's office the papers were in utter confusion; and the federal troops, when departing, had carried off some record books there, and also from the commissioner in equity, as well as most of the furniture from the offices. To refit and repair the "interior appurtenances," the commissioners employed J. D. Craig, the cabinet maker, who had come to Sumter three years before the war. As all funds had been exhausted, they had to levy a local tax to raise the additional seven hundred dollars found to be needed.

It was not until the summer of 1868 that the commissioners of public buildings finally completed a new jail,[10] a sturdy structure, framed from heart-timbers ten inches thick. The plans were drawn by Edwin W. Moise, one of the commissioners, and the construction was done by Andrew J. Moses.

As the invading armies had destroyed all bridges and railroads, for a time there were no trains, no mails, and no newspapers. Occasionally letters would be brought by a man on horseback. To get supplies, men drove wagon-teams to Columbia and Charleston over bad roads, and ferried over rivers. Everywhere, men were eager for work of any kind, and accepted whatever they could get, no matter if menial or dangerous. Lieutenant General Richard H. Anderson did not scorn to work as a railroad-yard laborer. Even the rich had nothing left but their lands and their debts. Frank Moses, Jr., is said to have tried his hand at dealing in eggs and chickens for a time, and to have written in desperation to a relative in New York for help in getting a theatrical job as a stock actor, for, he said, there is not a dollar in the country and "starvation is at my door."[11]

---

[10] For jail, see *Stat*, XIII, 243, 373, 383; *Sumter News*, Nov. 8, Dec. 6, 1866, June 27, 1868.

[11] Wallace, *History of S. C.*, III, 222; Moses' letter is in *Sumter News*, May 29, 1873.

Allan A. Gilbert came home from war service as a captain of artillery, to find the printing office of the *Sumter Watchman*, of which he had been editor and co-owner, a wreck and a shambles, just as it had been left by Potter's soldiers. The presses were repaired at the railroad shop, and the types were finally assorted. In partnership with his brother-in-law, T. E. Flowers, who bought H. L. Darr's share of the paper, Mr. Gilbert resumed publication of the *Watchman*, and his old vocation of editor. When he had to be absent, his editorial duties were committed to "the able pen and the strong mind" of Edwin W. Moise, who had decided to settle in Sumter.[12]

The dissolution of the old Gilbert and Darr partnership soon led to competition, for in June 1866, Mr. Darr began to publish a rival weekly, the *Sumter News*, "Devoted to Literature, Morality, and General Intelligence," with Frank Moses, Jr., as the first editor. Three months later, Noah G. Osteen, the young printer, bought a half interest in the paper, which thereafter was issued by the firm of Darr and Osteen.

In spite of the hard times, or, perhaps, in desperation, the French dancing-master from Charleston, "the irrepressible Monsieur Berger," arrived in Sumter that summer to resume his long-interrupted classes in the social graces.

In the meantime, the system of labor contracts was failing to solve the problem of free labor. The crops of 1866 were a failure, the estimated yield of corn being only from two to five bushels per acre. The cotton crop was rated fair,[13] and was the sole hope of the stricken people.

Because of the general destitution, General Sickles, on appeal from Governor Orr, abolished imprisonment for debt, extended the amount of homestead exemption, suspended executions for judgments that had been rendered during the war, and banned foreclosures for a year, it being feared that desperate men, if prosecuted, might destroy court records and mob the sheriffs. Also, on the Governor's suggestion, some juries scaled down prewar debts to a third of their original

---

[12] Address of N. G. Osteen to Rotary Club, Sumter, about 1911; *Sumter News*, Dec. 6, 1866.
[13] Lieut. E. P. Doherty, *Sumter News*, Oct. 18, 1866.

sums. During Orr's administration, the state penitentiary was put into operation, but he made liberal use of the pardoning power, for all available man-power was needed for rehabilitating the ruined state. The sufferings of the South stirred sympathy even in the North, and the Rev. William W. Mood served on a relief committee that distributed three thousand dollars from a mid-western state to the widows and orphans of Confederate soldiers in Williamsburg District.[14]

In the fall of 1866, John Smyth Richardson, Jr., sponsored a bill in the legislature to authorize a tax to raise $75,000 for relief purposes. From this fund, $50,000 was to be spent for corn to be distributed among the boards of commissioners of the poor in proportion to the representation in the legislature from the respective districts. It also provided that the governor should appoint a commission of three men to confer with grain merchants of the West. In November, the *Sumter News* carried a card from Hugh Richardson Garden, commander of Garden's Battery during the war, announcing that he had been authorized to purchase 50,000 bushels of corn for the planters of Sumter District, and would depart the ensuing week for the corn-growing regions. He expected to be able to deliver corn to any mid-portion of the state at $1.15 a bushel.[15] The men of Sumter were not passively waiting for public relief!

At the same session of the legislature, an appropriation of $10,000 was provided for obtaining artificial limbs for veterans who had been maimed in the service of the Confederacy. Through the efforts of the Sumter delegation, July Holliday, a Negro who had lost an arm and a leg when working on Fort Sumter during the war, was awarded fifty dollars and an order for artificial limbs.[16]

The post commander in Sumter at this time was Lieutenant E. C. Doherty of the Fifth Cavalry, an officer who after the assassination of Lincoln, had participated in the capture of the assassin. Fresh from four months service on the Sumter post, Doherty was interviewed in Washington by a cor-

---
[14] *Southern Christian Advocate*, Aug. 22, 1890.
[15] *Sumter News*, Nov. 15, Dec. 13, 20, 1866. Apparently Richardson's bill did not pass.
[16] *Sumter News*, Jan. 10, 1867; *Stat.* XIII, 401.

respondent of the *New York Herald,* and expressed himself not only as in favor of abolishing the provost courts, but as "decidedly of the opinion that the labor question would soon adjust itself to the advantage of all concerned if left to itself."[17]

The Radical Republican members of Congress, however, were not willing to let the South settle its problems. The fact that South Carolina had not enfranchised the freedmen was regarded as continued "rebellion," and the "Black Code" was pointed to as evidence of a sinister conspiracy to hold the Negroes in peonage. In the face of these antagonistic elements, the South almost unanimously rejected the Fourteenth Amendment, which conferred citizenship upon the freedmen, and imposed political disability upon civil and military officers of the Confederacy. Congress, therefore, refused to seat the senators and representatives from South Carolina, despite the President's proclamation of the end of hostilities. Indeed, the President was suspected of treasonable intentions in having given the South too soft a reconstruction, and he came into increasingly sharp conflict with Congress.

Commenting on this situation, Editor Moses of the *Sumter News,* on October 4, 1866, declared that if Congress by unconstitutional majorities was determined to rule in defiance of the President and the constitution, "the President has the example of Louis Napoleon. He must make a *coup d'etat,* and like Cromwell with Barebone's Parliament, dissolve it by the soldiery"—a suggestion which, to say the least, was incendiary!

Early in March 1867, the radical Congress passed the first of a series of vindictive reconstruction acts which divided the South into five military districts, uniting North and South Carolina into District Two, and prescribing the steps whereby statehood and seats in Congress might be recovered.

In the same month, the citizens of Sumter gathered at the courthouse to consider the alarming state of the public debt. Speeches were made by J. N. Frierson, A. A. Gilbert, J. S. Richardson, Jr., F. H. Kennedy (who vacated the chair to

[17] Note 13, *supra.*

speak), J. A. Carnes, and J. B. White. Three resolutions were passed, prefaced by the moving preamble:

... Our county is groaning under a load of affliction and distress unparalleled in its history, involving not only political oppression and difficulty, social disruption and disorganization of our industrial system, but stern, absolute and pressing want of bread. ...

The Rev. Thomas R. English and Allan A. Gilbert were named as a committee to prepare and publish an address[18]— a measure which seems hardly adequate for such grievous woes!

Indicative of the changing times, a mixed assemblage of Negroes and whites gathered in Sumter one night in late April, to hear an address from General Robert K. Scott, the kindly but weak head of the Freedmen's Bureau in South Carolina. Born in Pennsylvania, Scott had mined in California, visited in Mexico and South America, and then settled in Ohio to practice medicine. The war had brought him to the South with Ohio infantry, and he arrived in Charleston as a prisoner of war. His address was followed by brief remarks from Judge Franklin Moses, Editor Frank Moses, John S. Richardson, and Allen A. Gilbert. Three other whites, Dr. J. B. Witherspoon, T. J. Coghlan, and Captain Samuel Place of the Freedmen's Bureau, excused themselves from speaking. Then came talks by three Negro preachers, Ben Lawson, Jack Witherspoon, and Jim White. The occasion, said the *Sumter News* cryptically, was one of great interest and pleasure.[19]

A week later, an even more sensational event occurred at the courthouse, when Mrs. Frances Ellen Watkins Harper, a Northern Negro, addressed the Sumter freedmen. As reported by Editor Moses in the May 9 issue of the *News*, she advised them that labor must be their watchword; that they should now learn the machinery of government; she did not desire social equality for herself or her race, and believed that no attempt should be made to enforce it by law, for certain things regulate themselves; the Northern states should not

[18] *Sumter News*, Mch. 7, 1867.
[19] *Sumter News*, July 6, 1867.

demand suffrage for blacks in the South as long as suffrage was being denied to blacks in the North. She warned against improper use of the ballot; and she advised uniting with the Republican party, but cautioned against trusting it too far, because politicians work only for themselves.

In June, orders for the registration of citizens were published, directing military commanders to enroll all adult males, except felons and men who were disqualified for having had a part in the "rebellion." Meetings were organized throughout the county to give freedmen instructions for registering and voting. In a beautiful grove near Stateburg, W. Warren Ramsey, a Negro whose wife was in the employ of Dr. Marcus Reynolds, presided at a meeting which was addressed by T. J. Coghlan, J. N. Frierson, Dr. W. W. Anderson, Potter Withers, and J. H. Ferriter, the last a newcomer from the Bureau of Internal Revenue. The colored speakers were the Rev. Burwell James, who urged the Negroes to stand by the Republicans; and the Rev. William E. Johnson, a free octoroon from Charleston who had settled in Sumter. Tall, handsome, well-educated, and possessed of courteous manners, Johnson was an oratorical spell-binder, and became a political power in Sumter County. He also founded an offshoot of the Methodist Church of which he became Bishop. The secretary of the meeting was Sam Lee, a young and almost-white native of Sumter, the son of Malvina, a former slave in the family of Judge Franklin Moses. Able and ambitious, Lee had been encouraged to study by Mrs. Moses, and eventually became a prominent local politician.[20]

When the Union Republican party held its state convention in Columbia in July, the Sumter delegates were T. J. Coghlan, chairman of the group; two colored preachers, William E. Johnson and J. B. Burrows; and one James Smiley, a "Red Bones" who became the magistrate of Paxville. Eventually, he returned to North Carolina, where his children could be placed in a school for Croatans. Presiding at the convention was Richard Howell Gleaves, a mulatto from

[20] Information on Ramsey, Johnson and Lee is from H. G. Osteen, who knew them.

Pennsylvania, well-versed in parliamentary tactics.[21] The events of this convention influenced the state for a decade, not only because of the candidates whom it named, but because the delegates returned home to organize the notorious Union Leagues which would elect those candidates through control of the Negro vote.

Registrars for Sumter County appointed by General Sickles for the great enrollment were T. J. Coghlan, Ezekiel Keels, W. C. Bruce, Hosea Wilson, James I. Dean, C. M. Hurst, J. J. McKellar, and two Negroes, J. W. Westberry and James M. Johnson. On the fateful day of registration, August 15, 1867, the registrars enrolled for Sumter County 3,288 Negroes and 1,191 whites.[22] In the state at large, nearly twice as many Negroes as whites were registered, and South Carolina passed under nominal Negro control. The real control, however, was to be in the white men, scalawags and carpetbaggers, who manipulated the Negro vote through the Union League.

With weird ceremonies, the League in secret night sessions set up altars where its chaplains swore the initiates amid mysterious sounds, to vote always as members of the Radical Republican Party. The four sacred words of the League were Liberty, Lincoln, Loyal, and League. Members were threatened that failure to keep their oaths would bring prosecution for perjury and a term in the penitentiary; or, worse still, a report to the president of the United States, who would put them back into slavery.

Another powerful organization for control of the black vote, was the Freedmen's Bureau, which had become a frankly political agency. Until it was inactivated, the Bureau convinced the Negroes that the whites were trying to restore slavery, and drilled the freedmen to oppose every measure favored by their former masters.

Meanwhile, Editor Frank Moses, Jr., was experiencing a change of heart, and had begun editorial attacks on the antebellum leadership which had carried the state into secession. His editorial "Adversity Teaches Many Lessons," declared

---

[21] *Sumter News*, July 27, 1867; H. G. Osteen; Simkins and Woody, *Reconstruction*, p. 130.

[22] *Sumter News*, July 27, Aug. 3, 10, Sept. 28, 1867.

that the right of suffrage in South Carolina had been a mockery, and the South had never "enjoyed the blessings and privileges of a Republican Government." Under the heading "Truth" he wrote that in 1860, "not a single paper in South Carolina would consent to publish an editorial against the prevailing insanity." In the next issue, his valedictory explained that his "political sentiments have not been in accord with the large majority of the patrons of the News"[23] —a statement which certainly was the "Truth." He was succeeded by W. H. Johnson, principal of the Academy. When Mr. Johnson went to the Peabody school in Mount Pleasant at the end of the year, the editorship was assumed by Thomas Waties Dinkins, who had edited the *Sumter Despatch* during its brief career. His talented wife, the former Sarah Ann Moise, took charge of the "News and Belle Letters" contents.

In the plebiscite of November 1867, the voters approved the calling of a convention to frame a new state constitution. The delegates included seventy-six Negroes and forty-eight whites, of whom fifty-nine Negroes and twenty-three whites paid no taxes. Only twenty-three of the white delegates were natives of the state, and of them the *New York Times* correspondent declared there was scarcely one "whose character would keep him out of the penitentiary." The president of the convention was Dr. Albert Gallatin Mackey, an able and upright Unionist of Charleston, who contributed firm discipline and enlightened leadership to the proceedings.

Sumter sent to the Constitutional Convention of 1868, which met in Charleston on January 14, Frank Moses, Jr., T. J. Coghlan, and the octoroons Sam Lee and the Rev. W. E. Johnson. They unanimously voted for the ordinance to nullify old contracts and liabilities for the purchase of slaves. Able in debate, and a good parliamentarian, Moses took an active part in debates, and became chairman of an important committee. He opposed the confiscation of lands, and proposed diversion of relief funds from the Freedmen's Bureau to buy lands for the ex-slaves: "Give them lands; give them houses. They deserve it for protecting the families of those

---

[23] *Sumter News*, Aug. 31, Sept. 14, 21, 1867.

who were away from their homes during the late war." He opposed payment of the poll tax as a requirement for voting. He led a fight to have juries restricted to passing only upon matters of fact, not law. But his eloquence failed to win adequate support for many of his proposals. Coghlan served on the credentials committee; and proposed that the convention should take steps to "expunge forever from the vocabulary of South Carolina the epithets 'negro,' 'nigger,' and 'yankee' as used in the opprobrious sense," but his resolution was tabled.[24]

The native Negro delegates for the most part were too uninformed and timid to have a place in the proceedings. Except for President Mackey, T. J. Robertson, and a few other respectable natives, the leaders were a small group of adventurers: preachers, teachers, army officers and lawyers, both black and white, some of whom were idealists, but others, venal politicians. Nevertheless, within fifty-three days, they had fashioned a remarkably just and liberal constitution, most of whose provisions are still in force in the present constitution of Ben Tillman, which is based upon it.

A week before adjournment, many of the delegates took their seats in the state convention of the Republican party to nominate candidates for office. At the head of the ticket was General Robert K. Scott for governor, with Lemuel Boozer of Lexington for lieutenant-governor, and Frank Moses, Jr., for adjutant and inspector general of militia. The latter also announced himself as a candidate for the House from Berkeley County.[25]

Sumter's delegates to the Republican convention were T. J. Coghlan, chairman of the group, Frank Moses, Jr., and the two octoroons, Sam Lee and the Rev. W. E. Johnson. Thousands of Negroes gathered at Sumter to hear their report on the convention and to nominate the county candidates. These were T. J. Coghlan for state senator; J. H. Ferriter, Burrell James, William E. Johnson, and James E. Smiley for the House; J. J. McKellar for judge of probate; G. W. Reardon,

[24] Simkins and Woody, *Reconstruction*, 94, 95, 98, 99; *Proceedings of the Constitutional Convention of South Carolina* . . . . 1868, Charleston, 1868, *passim*.
[25] *Sumter News*, April 11, 1868.

an Irish stonecutter from Massachusetts, who had come before the war to work on the State House, for clerk of court; D. J. Robertson for tax collector; and J. H. Ferriter for sheriff.[26]

Stung to action by the outlook, the Democrats of Sumter had organized on March 30, with the appeal, "Fellow citizens of Sumter District, arouse from your lethargy. Think of your wives and children. Let the love of them stimulate you to action!" J. N. Frierson was chairman, Altamont Moses secretary, and Montgomery Moses chairman of the nominating committee. After eloquent speeches by Edwin W. Moise, John S. Richardson, and James D. Blanding, the delegates unanimously elected to the state convention were, John N. Frierson, E. W. Moise, Charles Mayrant, T. J. McCants, J. S. Richardson, T. B. Fraser, and Altamont Moses. Early in April the state convention met in Columbia to nominate congressional and state tickets, and also delegates to the national convention, to which they still pinned some hope.[27]

The Democrats did not approve of the new constitution, which conferred unlimited suffrage upon illiterate mases of freedmen unprepared for citizenship. But in April the constitution was approved by a plebiscite composed largely of those voters, and in June the elections under the constitution were held. The Radical Republicans elected congressional and state tickets, and in the counties they carried all except Horry and the nine predominantly-white counties in the piedmont. The only failure of the party was in not obtaining control of the executive branch of the federal government, for shortly before the elections, after impeachment proceedings of more than two months, President Andrew Johnson was acquitted by one vote.

Elected to the first legislature under the new constitution were eighty-eight Negroes and sixty-seven whites. By order of General Canby, the new officials-elect were directed to take over the government in July, and ratify the Fourteenth Amendment, for only after that ratification would South Carolina be permitted to resume statehood in the Union.

[26] *Sumter News*, Apr. 4, 1868.
[27] *Ibid.*

In an editorial on "The Government which is to be," by Edwin W. Moise, the *Sumter News* expressed the feelings of the South:

> Whatever is the law, we must respect, and as good citizens, we are bound to obey all laws and respect all officers who derive their authority from the duly constituted powers of the land. It behooves us then to yield gracefully to the yoke and to submit ourselves in no grudging spirit to the severe ordeal which is before us . . . . true it may have the authority of law . . . . But it has not and never can have the moral sanction of right, truth or justice. . . .[28]

[28] *Sumter News*, June 27, 1868. Editor Dinkins died on June 11, 1868, and the *News* announced on June 20 that political articles would be prepared by E. W. Moise, "who has kindly consented to contribute to our columns for the benefit of the widow and orphans of our late Editor." Mrs. Dinkins continued to manage the news and fiction until she removed to Charleston.

SUMTER DISTRICT COURTHOUSE, completed in 1821, Robert Mills, architect. Sold in 1905; portico removed, and now used by National Bank of S. C.

BAPTIST CHURCH, Sumterville, constituted August 7, 1813. This, the second building, erected in 1854 and razed in 1901.

PRESBYTERIAN CHURCH, Sumterville, organized in 1823. This, the first building, erected in 1823 and replaced in 1850

TYPICAL SMALL HOUSE, Sumterville. Home of Horatio L. Darr. Built before 1850. (Sumter Daily Item staff photo).

HOME OF MRS. BUFORD, Sumterville, buit around 1840. Bequeathed to the Presbyterian Church, it was the manse during the 1860's, and later sold to N. G. Osteen. Now owned by Frank McLeod. (Sumter Daily Item staff photo).

HOME OF HENRY HAYNSWORTH, Sumterville postmaster, 1823-1865. Typical large house, built before 1850. Now owned by Dr. Robert Bland Bultman. (Sumter Daily Item staff photo).

HOME OF DR. JOSIAH C. HAYNSWORTH, Sumterville. Built before 1850. (Sumter Daily Item staff photo).

BETHEL METHODIST CHURCH, Oswego. Organized 1856 by union of Clark's Meeting-house, Sardis Chapel and Lodebar Camp Ground. Gallery removed 1887; modernized 1949. (Sumter Daily Item staff photo).

BRADFORD SPRINGS. (Photo by Thomas L. Martin).

"SUMMER HOME", Bradford Springs. Built about 1840 by James Gaillard, planter of Charleston District, later Berkeley County. Now owned by Porcher Gaillard Rembert. (Sumter Daily Item staff photo).

CONCORD PRESBYTERIAN CHURCH, eight miles east of Sumter on road to Turberville. Organized 1808. Present building was "new" in 1841. (Sumter Daily Item staff photo).

RIP RAPS HOUSE, Black River. Named from the sound of rain in the gutters. Built by James McBride about 1860, on grant of 1751 to Peter Mellett. Now owned by James McBride Dabbs. (Photo courtesy of Mrs. Dabbs).

OAKLAND, formerly Churchill of Colonel James G. Spann; later, Holmesley of Wyndham M. Manning. (Library of Congress photo).

EDGEHILL, near Shaw Base. A very old house, used during 1830's as a boys' school. (Sumter Daily Item staff photo).

CHURCH OF THE HOLY CROSS, Stateburg. Originated about 1770 as chapel of ease for St. Mark's, and chartered in 1788 as Episcopal Church of Claremont. Present building of rammed earth erected 1850, Edward C. Jones, architect. (Sumter Daily Item staff photo).

SUMTER FAMILY CEMETERY. Monument to General Sumter erected by the state in 1907. Chapel over grave of Mrs. Thomas Sumter, Jr., erected by her children as requested in her will. (Photo by Thomas L. Martin).

BROOKLAND, built about 1804 by Judge William D. James, and bequeathed to daughter Sarah. Sold in 1836 to John Bradley. During 1860's and later occupied by Edward Holmes family, refugees from siege of Charleston. Now owned by William Wilson. (Library of Congress photo).

THE OAKS, formerly James Hill. Granted 1753 to Sherwood James, sold 1808 to William Bracey, advertised 1852 for sale as property of Thomas Bracey, deceased. (Library of Congress photo).

MARSTON, Stateburg. P. H. Nelson purchased Acton in 1837, and later built Marston house on part which became share of P. H. Nelson, Jr. Now owned by Mrs. S. O. Plowden.

MIDWAY. Half way between Woodlawn, home of O. S. Rees, and Oakley, home of William J. Rees. Built 1851 by Orlando S. Rees as wedding gift to son Wilson Waites Rees. Destroyed by fire in 1930.

THE GATES AT MILFORD. (Photo by Thomas L. Martin).

GATEKEEPER'S LODGE, Milford. (Photo by Thomas L. Martin).

STABLE at Milford. (Photo by Thomas L. Martin).

BELFRY at Milford. (Photo by Thomas L. Martin).

MILFORD, near Pinewood. Built by John Laurence Manning about 1840. Now owned by Emory W. Clark. (Photo by Thomas L. Martin).

MILFORD, side view. (Photo by Thomas L. Martin).

THE SPRING, Milford. (Photo by Thomas L. Martin).

BRIGADIER GENERAL EDWARD E. POTTER, U. S. A.
(Photo by Matthew B. Brady, gift of Mrs. Hermine M. Baumhofer, National Archives).

PART THREE

HISTORY OF SUMTER COUNTY

Sumter County

Chapter XXIII
THE NEW ORDER[1]

The restoration of South Carolina to the Union did not end the sufferings of her people. "I hope the Good One may bless us with a good fruit year," wrote Freeman Hoyt to his New England sister, "as there are many that used to live in affluence now so poor that they cannot get enough to eat of common food." But it was not to be a good year for fruit or any other food, and in the spring, floods of rain began to descend. "It not only rained all last week," said the Sumter correspondent of the *Courier*, "but the week before, and the week before that. During the preceding week there was a rain that lasted seven days, and was the continuation of a rain storm that had been raining, day and night for the past three or six anterior months. . . ." He then quoted a farmer who had prepared his field for a crop of watermelons: "I have half the crop already secured; my land is well covered with water, and all it lacks is the melons."

After the elections in April 1868, this correspondent sarcastically expressed the sentiments of the Democrats: "What a joy it is to know that we live 'in the government'—a government which relieves the white population of all care or participation in its management, fills all the offices by machinery, and regularly compliments the taxpayers by emptying their pockets to feed its hungry host of followers. What an honor to have the privilege of feeding and clothing the many charming adventurers, who, unable to get bread, or make bread, in their own States, are devoting themselves to the . . . . work of reconstructing the South."

The Northern adventurers who were in power through their control of the Negro voters, realized the advantage of

---

[1] Sources for this chapter were: MS letters of Freeman Hoyt, owned by Thomas M. Stubbs; MS address of Harmon D. Moïse, undated, before the Fortnightly Club; files of the *Sumter News*; Brooks, *Bench and Bar*; Simkins and Woody, *S. C. Reconstruction*; Wallace, *History of S. C.*

having also some native white support, and readily found the men they wanted, for political patronage was a powerful argument in making converts. Two new words, therefore, *carpetbagger* and *scalawag*, came into general use to express the disgust and bitterness in the hearts of the Southerners. The carpetbagger was a non-native Republican, who arrived after the war with all his worldly goods in a carpetbag, to make his fortune from the conquered South. The scalawag was a white native or prewar citizen, who joined the Republicans and worked with them for the control of the Negro vote in order to obtain office and to share in the plunder.

One of the most prominent South Carolinians to join the Republicans was ex-Governor James L. Orr, who rationalized his apostasy by saying he hoped to exert some measure of control from within the party. He was elected circuit judge under the new constitution of 1868, and later he become United States minister to Russia, but editorially in the *Sumter News*, he became the "Buzzard in Columbia."

On the day before the new legislature elected the judiciary, the *Courier's* correspondent wrote from Columbia that David T. Corbin, although a lawyer from Vermont, stood the best chance for getting the chief justiceship, but Judge Franklin I. Moses was working very hard for the place: "He made a speech to a caucus this afternoon in which he said he was fully and heartily in accordance with the Republican party, and was willing to devote the rest of his life to its success." On the third ballot, Judge Moses was elected, receiving seventy votes. He could not take his seat, however, until December, when Congress removed the political disability caused by his brief service with the Confederacy.

Friends of the Chief Justice were shocked that he should have joined the Republicans to obtain office, and they shunned him. "A Jew" writing from Sumter to the *Courier* said:

> Judge Moses many years ago placed himself outside of Judiasm. . . . the Jews of Charleston, where Judge Moses was born, and the Jews of Sumter, where he has lived since manhood, alike disclaim any responsibility for his political conduct, and . . . . thoroughly condemn his

recent betrayal of his State and party .... What the "Chief Justice's" religion is we do not know; but judging from his recent conduct, we presume he is a devout worshipper at the shrine of Mamon.

Montgomery Moses, brother and partner of the Chief Justice, also became a Republican, and was appointed collector of internal revenue, from which office Samuel Mayrant had been removed. Later, when the legislature elected Mr. Moses a circuit judge in 1871, he went to live in Newberry, where he remained until his death in 1886. Frank Moses, Jr., duly elected adjutant general of militia and also a member of the House, was chosen speaker by the House.

Sometimes necessity forced men of no prominence to join the Republican ranks. Such a man had come to Sumter from Florida as a teacher before the war. Afterwards, with a large family and no pupils, he joined the Radicals and received a magistrate's commission, which enabled him to support his family. As some two hundred of the men who received magistrate's commissions were unable to read, this ex-teacher probably rendered his community a real service in warding off one appointment of an illiterate!

Knowing full well that only by force could the new governments survive in the South, the Radical Republicans in Washington continued the army posts in many places, although civil government had been restored. Fortunately for Sumter, the officers at the local post were "men whose intercourse and companionship are always desirable." The personnel of men and officers was shifted often, but always the *Sumter News* found something favorable to say of them; and the money spent by the garrison was eagerly welcomed by the merchants. So scarce was money at this time as a medium of exchange that the town of Sumter had to issue its own scrip as currency for local use.

The general misery that engulfed the people was expressed by Freeman Hoyt in a letter of August 8, 1868, to his sister:

> Mary, you at the North have no conception of how we at the South are living. Many that were rich before the war are now poor, and one-half of them have nothing to

eat. . . . The Negroes are stealing everything they can lay their hands on. If the Northern people do not help us to select a good Democratic President, it will not be long before there will be a war of races.

Governor Scott's administration of the new government gave no assurance of better times. During his first year in office, he issued pardons at the rate of one a day. With the full knowledge of Attorney-General Chamberlain, cultured and well-educated lawyer from Massachusetts, a corrupt "Ring" which included the Governor, and probably the attorney-general himself, was fraudulently enriching its members by manipulation of public contracts, bond issues, and the ante-bellum railroad securities owned by the state.

The legislature under the new order, with its Negro majority and its scalawags and carpetbaggers, was brazenly corrupt. Bribery was open and unashamed. Votes for desirable legislation affecting business had to be bought from legislators at high prices, and Governor Scott declared that even the Saviour would be crucified again if on trial before the lawmakers, unless the members were bought off by bribes!

In the State House, the legislature at public expense, opened a free barroom for members and their friends, furnished their own homes and lodgings with fine furniture, and supplied themselves with costly clothing, jewelry, horses, mules, carriages, and whatever else they fancied. The House even adjourned to attend a horse race, and then voted Speaker Moses a thousand dollars to pay the bet he had lost to W. J. Whipper, a Negro member of the House.

Speaker Moses lavishly approved in fantastic sums the fraudulent pay-certificates for these and like purposes. Some corruptionists profited by purchasing the certificates at a discount, and then collecting in full from the state treasurer. The Speaker also, in his capacity as adjutant general of militia, misappropriated to himself the funds allocated by the state for the purchase of arms.

The rule of the Republicans also brought great changes in local government. Under the constitution of 1868 the change from *"Sumter District"* to *"Sumter County"* had meant much more than a change of name. For the first time local administration was vested in a constitutional board of three county commissioners, who had jurisdiction not only over roads, bridges, and ferries, but also over all matters relating to taxes and disbursements of money for county purposes. For the first time there was a county treasurer to collect the taxes and to pay the claims which were approved by the board of county commissioners. For the first time there was a county auditor to make up the tax books, and a county school commissioner to superintend the county schools. The county had become a corporate body which could own property, and its government had been streamlined.

The first board of county commissioners consisted of Captain Samuel Place of the Freedmen's Bureau, Captain Thomas Brent Johnston of the garrison, a native of Massachusetts; and John H. Ferriter, assistant assessor of internal revenue, a native of County Cork, Ireland, who had come to Sumter from Boston in 1865, and became a naturalized citizen a year later.

Dual office-holding was the order of the day. State Senator Thomas Jefferson Coghlan had resigned from the Senate soon after it met, but he still held the offices of county treasurer, sheriff, and United States deputy marshal. J. N. Corbett the county auditor, was also the county school commissioner and clerk of the board of county commissioners.

Streamlining the constitution did not mean that the government had become more efficient, for the increase of crime among the Negroes was alarming. At the November 1867 term of the district court in Sumter for the trial of Negro cases, the jurors had been discharged for the lack of any business, but in 1868 almost every issue of the newspapers told of robberies and violence. Near Bradford Springs the barn of Joseph S. Bossard was entered from above, and his bacon, sugar, coffee and corn were carried away. Two Negroes were jailed for stealing cattle from James Booth; and three others for robbing the smokehouse of Mr. Childs at Stateburg. In Sumter the stores of J. E. Suares, Thomas Feeny, and others were broken into. The residence of the Rev. H. B. McCallum was entered. Even the postoffice was looted of small change.

The Negroes of Mechanicsville plantation published an appeal to the colored people of the county for law and order, signed by J. W. Westberry and eleven others. But crime continued, and cases of arson and murder were reported, as well as robbery and whipping.

A carpetbagger who squirmed under the lash of the *Sumter News*' editorials, hired a Negro woman to set fire to the home of N. G. Osteen, one of the owners of the paper. Fortunately, she was seen from the printing office before harm was done. She was not punished.

But there were also some less distressing items in the news. In the spring of 1869 the town of Sumter was enlivened when A. W. Suder received by express from Charleston a new machine called a velocipede, "one of the fast novelties of a fast age!" The *Sumter News* reported that several young men were learning to ride, and one Saturday afternoon when the May term of court was in session, the velocipede "propelled at a swift speed" caused such excitement on Main street that the judge had to "request an abatement of the noise."

When the end of Governor Scott's term approached in 1870, the corrupt Radicals, characterizing his administration as "wise, economical, and honest," nominated him for a second term, with Alonzo J. Ransier, an almost-white native freedman, as running mate. The platform cynically asked for "a continuance of the strict and close economy in all departments . . . . to maintain the happy financial condition which our State has attained under our Republican rule."

Hoping that the year 1870 might prove to be the "Year of Deliverance" the Democrats united with a group of Republican reformers and formed the Union Reform party to oppose the Radical ticket. For governor the coalition nominated Judge Richard Brinsley Carpenter, a respected Republican from Kentucky. General M. C. Butler of Edgefield was named to second place after two Negroes had withdrawn in his favor.

Scott refused to take the stump, but both parties waged an energetic campaign. The Radicals, however, held a trump card in the Negro militia which they had organized during the spring and summer. Judge Carpenter estimated that more than 20,000 Negroes had been armed by election day.

The records of the adjutant general's office, however, show less than half this number of arms issued. Scott had another trump in the active aid of the Union League, as well as the state constabulary, and in the fall elections he polled some 85,000 votes to Carpenter's 51,537. On both sides there was evidence of fraud.

The arming of Negroes in the guise of militia companies had stirred the whites to counter measures for self-protection, and the Ku-Klux Klan began to operate in the state. Sumter County rejected the bloody excesses of this formidable secret organization, and comparatively few Klan activities there have been recorded.

On an October night in 1870, Klansmen burned the store of David G. Robertson, a brother of United States Senator Thomas J. Robertson. The Senator, an alumnus of the South Carolina College, and a wealthy business man, had been one of the first prominent South Carolinians to join the Republicans. On the same night, masked men went to the home of John J. Neason, another storekeeper about five miles away on the Bishopville road, some ten miles from Sumter. Neason was a Republican hailing from Savannah, who had served in the Confederate army, and, having married a Sumter girl, had settled in the county. The masked men warned Neason to stop buying seed-cotton from Negroes, and he replied that if the order were general for all stores, he would stop. The leader said that the order was general, and the masked men departed without violence.

The reason for the order was that most of the county Negroes were planting very small fields of cotton, which did not yield enough to gin into a bale. It was not unusual, therefore, for some of them to pick cotton from white planters' fields by moonlight, with the result that such Negroes generally had more cotton from a half-acre than anyone else from two acres. When unginned cotton was sold at country stores, the chances were that it had been stolen. In any event, traffic in seed-cotton placed temptation in a vulnerable quarter, and white planters wanted it stopped.

The following March some thirty or forty men armed with double-barrel guns and dressed in calico, homespun, and paper hats, called Neason from his bed at midnight. "Tell your wife," said the leader, "we do not intend to harm you." They then took him to his store nearby, and threatened to whip him, but he begged off. In silence, the weird company began to dance around him, poking their fingers at him and making various signs. By their gestures, Neason thought he recognized some of his neighbors, "the young bloods of the county," Mose McLeod, John Lem Brown, John Joe Brown, William Frazier, E. Holloman, R. L. Heriot, and C. Williamson. Some of the men named by Neason were arrested later on the complaint of David Robertson.

Soon after this second visit of the Ku-Klux to Neason, he was summoned to testify before a Congressional committee; for after the election of 1870, the federal government had moved to suppress the Ku-Klux "conspiracy," and, in the spring of 1871, had enacted a drastic law which gave the President extraordinary powers.

In May the *Sumter News* described a monster in human form, about thirty feet tall, which walked through the night near Bishopville, plucking fence rails from the roadside to scratch its head. Around the neck was an iron chain from which hung a blacksmith's anvil and sledge hammers, jangling as it moved, breathing like the wind in the tree tops, and at intervals, emitting sounds like the loud pouring of liquid from a bottle. Consternation was said to reign among the Negroes, who believed it to be the King of the Ku-Klux.

A week later the Bishopville giant was reported to have appeared in Manning about ten o'clock at night and moved into the courthouse square, where it disappeared into the well. A frightened Negro declared that its ice-cold hand had touched him. About the same time a respectable Negro man was reported as having seen a huge cow or ox near Jordan, some thirty feet high, with fifteen-foot horns, switching an enormous tail.

A rumor went around that H. Ryttenburg, a storekeeper about fifteen miles from Sumter, was whipped by the Klan; but he published a denial saying that the Klansmen had merely asked him to stop buying seed-cotton, that he had complied, and there had been no violence.

THE NEW ORDER 315

In October 1871, President Grant suspended the writ of *habeas corpus* in nine counties of South Carolina, but Sumter was not among them. That martial law should be declared in a time of profound peace, when state courts were in full operation, aroused the *Sumter News,* which declared that respectable citizens were being arrested by constables who refused to show warrants, that the "homes of our people are invaded by soldiers and constables in the dead hours of night, women and children frightened and insulted, citizens dragged to jail, who could have been arrested at any time of the day in the public streets or on the highway."

When the Ku-Klux trials began in Columbia, the *News* carried a letter from James D. Blanding in regard to raising a thousand dollars, the county's quota of a $15,000-fund for employing Northern lawyers to defend the prosecuted men. This quota must have seemed very large then, for times were hard. The scarcity of money was evidenced by the dull bidding at Sheriff Coghlan's distress sales. On the June sales day, Chief Justice Moses lost some of his property; and on the last sales day of the year, the furniture and other personal property of Adjutant and Inspector General Frank Moses, Jr., were auctioned at the courthouse, at "fair prices," said the *Sumter News,* "for these days of general impecuniosity."

To Sheriff Coghlan, in his capacity of United States deputy marshal, the *Sumter News* gave the title of "Ku-Klux Exterminator." What part he actually played in the prosecutions has not been traced. The federal government's drastic measures, however, effectively broke up the Klan, and there were no further manifestations of its presence in Sumter county.

During the summer of 1871, a pathetic story of a Negro woman's death appeared in the *Sumter News.* After becoming a church member, she "backslided" into sin; when she became ill, none of her friends came to her aid, and she died, probably from neglect. Her Negro pastor then directed that she be placed in her grave, head downwards, because she was going to Hell; and his order was carried out.

Soon after this, the soldiers of the garrison had a clash with the civilians of the town, when for some unknown reason the soldiers opened fire on a crowd at the corner of Main and Liberty streets. Two Negroes were wounded. The next day another Negro was brought in, who had been shot in the head, and in terror had fled into the country. The following spring, the soldiers had a bloody battle with the town police, who not only held their ground but took two of them as prisoners to jail.

On the last day of November in 1871, the *Sumter News* carried an obituary of its editor, Lemuel Bingham Gay, who was found dead in his room. A native of Massachusetts, he had come South in early life, studied law and been admitted to the bar. He soon became a teacher, however, first in the school of the Rev. J. L. Bartlett, in Charleston, and later with the Rev. Mr. Legare in the Orangeburg Female Seminary. Throughout the war, he was a Confederate soldier, and at the end, he came to Sumter as a teacher. A fearless and independent editor, he became well known throughout the state.

Editor Gay was succeeded by William G. Kennedy, a lawyer who had been a member of the class of 1848 at the South Carolina College but did not graduate. During the four years of Mr. Kennedy's editorship of the *News*, his Irish wit, literary vocabulary, and genius for name-calling and invective, made his editorials the delight of his readers and the torment of the Radicals. The racial mixture in the legislature at Columbia, became in Editor Kennedy's words, the "Menagerie;" Frank Moses, Jr., when not "Count Bond-Swindleinski" was "Scalawag Moses, the younger of the distinguished triplet of law-givers of that ilk;" and the Chief Justice and son, were designated "the elder and the younger Moses, namesakes and descendants perhaps of the great Lawgiver of Israel."

Fortunately for the people of Sumter, better business conditions became possible in 1871 with the opening of the Wilmington, Columbia and Augusta railroad, which gave a direct line to Columbia through a new station on Wedgefield plantation, a few miles north of Manchester. This meant that the old railroad from Sumter to Columbia by way of Manchester and Kingville was abandoned. Manchester was deserted, and soon disappeared, most of its business following the railroad to Wedgefield.

The railroads of the state had now generally recovered from the ruin of war, and were expanding their lines and services. The Camden Branch of the South Carolina railroad had been reopened to traffic in May of 1867. During the construction of the Wilmington, Columbia and Augusta line, the "Isis," an iron steamer of shallow draft, with excellent accommodations for freight and passengers, had plied in connection with the railroad, up to Camden. The South Carolina railroad also announced it would build a new track into Sumter to give improved connection with Charleston.

Good railroad service had a share in making the town of Sumter grow, and by 1872 there was not a vacant house in Sumter. A wave of building followed, and as soon as the foundations of a house were laid, someone applied for it. Active in this work was Edwin W. Moise, who is said to have had more houses built in the town than any other man of the time. This busy lawyer was also active in his profession, and sometimes he is said to have used unique methods in winning cases. On one occasion, after exasperating delay of the railroad in settling a just case for one of his clients, he took action that brought results. With a powerful chain and lock, he met one of the trains at the depot, and "with his own hands chained and locked the locomotive to the track."

With the revival of business came also a necessity for banks. The banks in general, however, had had a sorry time at the hands of the corrupt state government, and as a result, men of means were cautious about risking capital. By 1870, a number of banks throughout the state had begun operation, and the following year the Citizens' Savings Bank opened a branch in Sumter, with Major John William Dargan in charge as the assistant cashier—a man who enjoyed the entire confidence of the community.

Sumter County, meanwhile, was in better condition than some other counties. In January 1872, County Treasurer Coghlan announced that, with all taxes collected for 1868, 1869, and 1870, and the teachers paid in full up to January 1 of that year, the county was solvent. The *Sumter News*, however, had an unpaid claim against the county on which, after ten months of effort, it could get no action from the county commissioners. The *News* therefore asked some pointed questions: If the county was solvent, why didn't it pay its debts? Was it a mark of solvency to pay only seventy-five cents on the dollar? Does a "shave" of 25% discount on a claim go into the pocket of the county treasurer? Whose fault is it when the treasurer refused to pay anything on a claim?

During the ensuing months, attacks on the management of the county's finances continued, with embarrassing accusations: Taxpayers were paying $20,000 a year for county purposes, but roads were impassable, bridges dangerous, and trade from the east was being diverted to Camden because the county commissioners refused to bridge Lynches Creek. Taxes were being frittered away in paying bills for worthless officials, of whom the trial justices were "the most insatiable moths" that preyed on the county treasury.

In September 1872, the county commissioners' account with the county treasurer showed total expenditures $13,672.40; total indebtedness $2,525.00; and total due the county $950.00 —figures that soon would look quite handsome compared with the figures to come!

Because the lawlessness which continued among the freedmen was often in emulation of the lawlessness of the Columbia Ring, local thieves were referred to by the *Sumter News* as Ring-worms and Ring doves. These troublesome people seldom were punished, for even when convicted, an executive pardon soon turned them loose.

In 1872, however, one Taylor Wilson, a Negro, was publicly executed in Sumter for the murder of Tom Keith, another Negro. A tremendous crowd gathered to see the spectacle, and had the added thrill of hearing the murderer confess on the gallows. As principal in the crime, he accused John D. Frierson, who had been arrested along with Wilson as a suspect.

Not long afterward, a party of disguised Negroes seized another Negro on the streets of Sumter and cowhided him unmercifully. The victim identified his attackers and had them arrested the next morning, but when they were brought to trial, the jury of the trial justice's court turned them loose.

Editor Kennedy usually referred to this magistrate as "Judge Dogberry."

When Governor Scott's second term was drawing to a close, with a record on a par with that of his first, the political pot once more began to boil furiously. At the Radical county convention in Sumter, the "flower of the Grant party" held a stormy session at which Sam Lee and his friends made desperate but vain efforts to block the election of Frank Moses, Jr., and his supporters, as delegates to the state convention.

At the state convention, the corruptionists, led by Robert Brown Elliott, the Negro congressman, and aided by money from the notorious Senator "Honest" John Patterson, nominated Frank Moses, Jr., as Scott's successor. Richard Howell Gleaves, an intelligent mulatto of pleasing appearance, from Pennsylvania, was the nominee for lieutenant governor.

A minority of the delegates, however, headed by Judge James L. Orr of Anderson, refused to accept these nominations, and bolted the party, nominating as governor the former state auditor, Reuben Tomlinson, a carpetbagger from Pennsylvania, who had come South as a missionary, and had served as superintendent of education for the Freedmen's Bureau. This split in the party was not altogether new, for a move had begun earlier to impeach Governor Scott. He had quashed it, however, by bribing the legislators with $48,645 which he obtained by fictitious warrants on the state treasury, from which sum, Speaker Frank Moses, Jr., received $15,000 as his share.

Referring to the carpetbaggers, the *New York Nation* asked, "What service have these persons rendered the country that we should grant them the monopoly of robbing the rebels?" and the *Sumter News* replied: "They certainly rendered the North a very great service by leaving it."

Discouraged by defeat in the two previous campaigns, the conservative Democrats declined to call a state convention. To most of them the campaign of 1872 merely offered the choice between "a black dog and a monkey." The *Sumter News* called it a dog-fight, and declared the difference between the two Republican tickets was merely the difference between "Buzzard and biled Crow."

The Democratic executive committee of Sumter County, Thomas Boone Fraser, Edwin Warren Moise, and James Douglas Blanding, met at the courthouse with other citizens, and passed resolutions stating that they did not endorse any set of candidates for state or county offices; that they recognized in the ballot the right of a citizen to do what he could to alleviate the evils under which the country was suffering; and that they recommended every man should make for himself the best choice his judgment might suggest.

David T. Corbin, legislator, trained lawyer, and perhaps the ablest carpetbagger in the state, in his Fourth of July speech at Greenville, gave some plain facts on Frank Moses' record in public life: As adjutant and inspector general, he had spent $110,000 and made no report; as speaker of the House, with the duty of signing pay certificates to cover actual expenses (totalling $143,808), he had signed more than $1,000,000 worth, with the bland admission, "I admit I have been extravagant in this matter, but I am a candidate for office against Scott, Parker and the rest of them, who have the State Treasury at their backs. . . . They will use the Funds of the Treasury to secure their re-election, and I must use my pay certificates."

Early in the campaign, the *Sumter News* reprinted a report from the *Beaufort Republican* that a fine pair of mules had been sent by Frank Moses to Robert Smalls, the Negro state senator, to be used in hauling campaign speakers around Beaufort County: "The mules are too honest-looking for such work. One is named Validating Bill and the other Certifi Kate. Their tails are appropriately shaved to indicate the condition of the State treasury."

A few days later, the *News* announced that "Pay Certificate Moses and his distinguished parent," aided by two Negroes, had held a grand pow-wow on Academy Green in Sumter, but unfortunately, while they were instructing their constituents, the barbecue disappeared!

Although Sumter was the home county of Candidate Moses, many local officeholders worked for the Bolters' ticket headed by Tomlinson. In late September at a political meeting on Mechanicsville plantation, Sheriff Coghlan denounced young Moses as the greatest robber known to him, and as proof, exhibited some of the fraudulent pay certificates. Other speakers were, Julius J. Fleming, now a lawyer; J. Wiley, J. Johnston Knox; Judge John T. Green, who had read law in the office of Chief Justice Moses; and Sam Lee. Warren W. Ramsey, candidate for the House on the Moses ticket, agreed that everything said against Moses was true, but declared that he himself was not a party to, nor a beneficiary from, any of the Moses frauds.

The mere fact that this meeting had an audience was significant, for on the previous night, the Moses party had sent out runners telling the people not to go to Mechanicsville, but to assemble at the store of John J. Neason. As inducements for the meeting at Neason's store, those who attended would find two barbecued beeves, free whiskey, and a brass band. But when the Rev. William E. Johnson and the brass band arrived at Neason's store, they found so few people, that he went on over to Mechanicsville to bring off an audience. He did not succeed, however, and when the Tomlinson faction invited him to speak, he departed.

On Saturday night before the election, a typical campaign meeting at the courthouse was reported by the *Sumter News* as "The 87th and Last Pow-wow." Proceedings opened with the Rev. W. E. Johnson speaking from the balcony, while Sheriff Coghlan at the top of his lungs shouted an opposition speech downstairs. Pandemonium reigned, but finally was quelled when Sam Lee got the floor. The lion of the evening, who spoke in support of Moses, was Congressman Robert Brown Elliott. A college-bred lawyer from Massachusetts, Elliott was very black but of commanding presence, and reputed one of the best Negro orators in the South. Prominent in the applause was Chief Justice Moses. From time to time, Sam Lee interrupted the speaker with "simple, gentlemanly questions," which invariably brought upon him storms of abuse from the crowd.

On election day, October 16, 1872, the Chief Justice electioneered for the straight Radical ticket headed by his son. At Bishopville, for a time, there was not a single manager at a box—all were out electioneering! One was reported as reviling or ridiculing everyone who cast a vote for Tomlinson.

Like many other disheartened Democrats, Editor Kennedy of the *Sumter News* did not vote in the general election, but most of the white votes that were cast, went to Tomlinson. Frank Moses, however, polled 69,838 votes to Tomlinson's 36,533, and once more a native son of Sumter became governor of South Carolina.

Sheriff Coghlan did not fare well in his race for re-election to the sheriff's office, and was defeated by Major John M. Tindall. Worse still for Mr. Coghlan, Governor Scott, as one of the last acts of his disgraceful administration, although hitherto he had complimented Coghlan as the best collector of taxes in the state, now removed him as county treasurer and appointed in his place W. H. Gardner.

The howl over this appointment was appalling, wrote the *Charleston Courier's* correspondent from Sumter, for Mr. Coghlan was "an old, well-known and highly respected citizen, whereas Gardner, who had come to Sumter with the first federal garrison, enjoyed no enviable reputation."

Perhaps it was to Governor Scott that a witty Negro offered this toast, "De Gubernor of our State. He come in wid very little oppostion—he go out wid none at all."

When the new legislature met, the *Sumter News* expressed sarcastic concern as to whether that body could "survive the loss of its master-spirit, that Hydra-headed genius and modern Pericles, the distinguished Herr Van Lengel Pay Certificate Moses, the Blackstone of America, the eminent Provost Judge, the redoubtable warrior, able Enrolling Officer and lucid Commentator and Lecturer on Religion, who has been translated to a higher and nobler sphere of usefulness."

Chapter XXIV

CLIMAX OF "MOSESISM", 1872-1874

Sworn in by his father the Chief Justice, Franklin Israel Moses, Jr., was inaugurated as governor on Tuesday, December 3, 1872, at the age of thirty-four years. His inaugural address laid the blame for past corruption upon the Conservatives, and he alluded to making reforms. Among his recommendations were: the appointment of three lawyers to simplify the code of law; and "that the salaries of the Supreme Court and Circuit Court Judges of the State be proportionately increased respectively. They are the hardest worked and poorest paid officers in any department."

In view of Governor Moses' past record, few people expected reform. The Columbia Ring of corruptionists knew that with him in Columbia as governor, and General Grant in Washington as president, there was nothing to fear. The *Colleton Gazette* commented that, "if the salaries paid the Governor's relatives are not princely enough," they should resign until the state could support them becomingly. Eventually, when the bill to increase judicial salaries reached the floor of the House, *The South Carolinian* reported a mortifying scene, for the judges "soiled their judicial ermine" by lobbying for its passage. It failed to pass.

The State's printing bill, however, jumped to almost half a million dollars. The Columbia correspondent of the *New York Tribune* announced that much of this money went to muzzle the free press of South Carolina, an installment of $75,000 having gone to twenty-five newspapers in sums ranging from $1,000 to $7,000. This statement was supported by State Treasurer Cardoza's official list of recipients, published by order of the legislature. Small weekly journals could almost be kept going on such subsidies. Governor Moses himself, for not vetoing the bill, was said to have blackmailed its instigators for ten percent of the total amount, but by his own sworn statement, he received only $15,000.[1]

Although the state had provided the governor with an executive mansion in 1868, Governor Moses declined to live in it. After finding temporary quarters in an hotel suite of six rooms, at $750 a week, he used his share of the printing-bill plunder as first payment on the Preston mansion, better known as "Hampton Gardens," which he agreed to buy for $40,000. The *Colleton Gazette* soon christened this residence the "Chateau de Plunderville." While elaborate changes were being made there, the Governor was accused of having entertained lavishly elsewhere, with dinners, soirees, balls and parties, exclusively for whites who were not officials. The Governor's wife, it was said, did not share his political ideas of social equality.

His Negro friends, however, were not totally neglected. The Governor chose as his private secretary C. J. Houston, a Negro. An eyewitness has recorded that in Columbia on several occasions he saw a handsome landeau drawn by a pair of high-stepping Kentucky horses, "and containing four Negro wenches arrayed in low-neck and short-sleeve dresses, their black bosoms and arms covered with real jewels in the middle of the day, draw up in front of a barroom on Main Street. .... Out of the saloon would come the governor, accompanied by several high state officials, followed by a servant bearing a waiter on which was champagne and glasses, and right there in the public sidewalk enter into a perfect orgy with the dusky belles."[2]

Work on the Preston mansion dragged along through much of the Governor's first year in office. Contractors bought the best materials, but were halted when the plumber refused to complete his work until paid. When this was adjusted and the contractors returned, they found their materials being "cobbled by penitentiary hands" which His Excellency had resourcefully set to work. The magnificent mirrors, pearl-mounted piano, and other costly furnishings which arrived from the North, also received unfavorable mention in the

---

[1] *Sumter News*, Feb. 20, Mch. 27, 1873; Wallace, *History S. C.*, III, 290.

[2] James Morris Morgan, *Recollections of a Rebel Reefer*, (Boston, 1917), p. 328.

news. When the Governor moved in, he is said to have established there social headquarters for official society, and entertained sumptuously in a series of receptions which accorded social equality to gorgeously dressed Negroes.

The home in Sumter which the Governor's father had built for him during the war, was a large two-story frame house, set back in the square at the southwest corner of the present Broad and Church streets. The spacious, elaborately landscaped grounds were tended by an imported gardener, who lived in the cottage which still stands there, and the entire square was surrounded by a handsome iron fence, with large iron gates. A two-story office was equipped with a bar, a billiard table, and bedrooms where Negro friends might be accommodated overnight without embarrassment to the family. The large stables on the west side of the spacious grounds had living quarters on the second floor for the coachman. The furnishings of the drawing-room, library, dining room, halls, the "Crimson Room," the "Family Room," the "Blue Room," and the "Oak Room," were said by the *Colleton Gazette* to have been purchased at state expense. Before he became governor, Frank Moses had tried to safeguard this place from creditors by conveying it to his wife in trusteeship of her brother.[3] His real estate holdings had further been extended in 1870 when he purchased from William G. Kennedy of the *Sumter News,* one of the finest plantations in Sumter County, Rose Hill, 2,791 acres, on the headwaters of Black River.[4]

On an official salary of $3,500 a year, Governor Moses could not maintain his extravagant scale of living, and he supplemented his income by the sale of pardons and appointments,[5] as well as from bribes for withholding vetoes on legislation. Indicative of the tone of his administration, a news item told that a watchman, who had been at the State House ever since its erection, had caught one Jim Washington in the act of stealing carpets through one of the windows. The Governor was said to have at once discharged the watchman and given the job to the thief.

---

[3] Plat and description of premises, Sumter conveyances; *Sumter News* May 1, 1873, recollections of H. G. Osteeen.

[4] Sumter conveyances.

[5] Wallace, *History S. C.*, III, 292; Simkins and Woody, *S. C. Reconstruction*, p. 127.

In April 1873, after the legislature had adjourned, Governor Moses turned his attention to the Sumter municipal election, and was said to have allocated $500 to secure the success of J. E. Suares, candidate for intendant. On the eve of the election, according to the *Sumter News*, the Governor reached Sumter by the light of the midnight moon, and marched to the courthouse amid drum-beating, fife-blowing, and the deafening shouts of his admirers. Mounting the rostrum, he and Ellis C. Green, former intendant, who supported A. W. Suder, spoke until daylight on the relative merits of the rival candidates, and many voters went from the all-night meeting to the polls. The voting, however, was quiet until afternoon, when a fight broke out among the Negroes.

The result of the election was hardly to the Governor's liking, for Suder was elected intendant; and E. W. Moise, J. T. Solomons, Dr. J. B. Witherspoon, and W. H. Girardeau, wardens. In the words of the *Sumter News*, "Green knocked the native humbug off his pony."

The Governor also took a hand in county affairs, and removed George W. Reardon as jury commissioner, replacing him with Zach Walker, a Negro. Deputy Sheriff E. H. Bateman already had been removed, suspiciously soon after levying a town execution upon the Governor's roan horse. According to Bateman, he witnessed the opening of the box containing Reardon's jury list, in the office of County Treasurer Gardner, in the presence of Sheriff Tindall, Auditor Corbett, and Zach Walker, who, as the new jury commissioner, tore up Reardon's list. In drawing the new jury list, declared Bateman, whenever the names of respectable white men were drawn, the sheriff destroyed them; other names considered more suitable, and made in duplicate to insure being drawn, sometimes were drawn twice; the name of the Rev. Prince Dickerson was thrown out because he was a preacher, but the name of the Rev. William E. Johnson was retained.

At this time Governor Moses was *ex officio* chairman of the Board of Trustees of the state University, and when the Board conferred an honorary L.L.D. degree upon Chief Justice Moses, Editor Kennedy commented that Columbia's generosity in bestowing titles, especially upon Sumter people, almost tempted him to go for his! He then listed members of the Moses family who had received titles: *Chief Justice and Doctor of Laws,* Franklin I. Moses; *Circuit Judge,* Montgomery Moses; *Trial Justice,* M. B. Moses; *General of Militia,* Z. P. Moses; *Major of Militia,* H. C. Moses; and "Lord-knows-what, 'our native young Governor.'"

Samuel J. Lee of Aiken, first Negro to be speaker of the House, and sometimes confused with Sam Lee of Sumter, was only one of the many Negroes who held office in the Moses administration. The Senate was presided over by Lieutenant-Governor R. Howell Gleaves, a mulatto. Henry E. Hayne was secretary of state; F. L. Cardoza, state treasurer, and H. W. Purvis, adjutant general of militia. When General McDowel of the Union army, invited the Governor to join him on an inspection, expecting the courtesy to be declined, the Governor not only accepted but brought with him General Purvis, who, cigar in hand, inspected too; and for once, soldiers of the regular army were inspected by a militia officer!

Many stories concerning the Moses regime were published by George F. McIntyre, editor of the *Colleton Gazette,* a weekly newspaper on the official subsidized list. Born in Charleston in 1844, McIntyre had served in the Confederate army, and afterwards joined the Republicans. As a member of the House and later of the Senate from Colleton, where he was known as "Captain of the Forty Thieves," he had been intimate with Frank Moses until an over-due debt from Moses caused McIntyre to sue and obtain judgment. Some of the *Gazette's* stories were shocking, some were funny, but all were interesting, and Editor Kennedy reprinted them in the *Sumter News.* Usually, McIntyre referred to the Governor as "Franklin Judas Moses" or "Judas Moses." One story was concerned with the Hibernian Society of Charleston, an organization which by ancient custom had always invited the chief executive to the annual dinner. In 1873, however, the officers and members threatened to resign if Governor Moses were invited. Hoping to avoid, if possible, a public slight, the Governor availed himself of an unofficial invitation from a member who was unaware of the situation. When the Governor appeared at the dinner, there was no little embarrassment. To compensate for not according him the customary courtesy of replying to the toast to the state, he was "allowed the slight privilege of remarking how much he loved poor Ireland," in the course of which, he revealed that he was born on St. Patrick's Day. The applause was so great, said the *Gazette*, "You could hear a pin fall."[6]

In May the *Colleton Gazette* reported that although the Governor already had spent $185,000 from various contingent funds, he was so hard-pressed for money that he tried to borrow from a bank, offering as security his salary and his Masonic word of honor. As neither was acceptable security to the bank, he then sold two costly gold watches, and tried to sell his even more costly horses. "We sketch our Judas as he goes," said Editor McIntyre.[7] Soon after this revelation, Governor Moses cashiered McIntyre from his colonelcy in the militia. The *Gazette* already had suspended publication the previous week.

The financial standing of Sumter County at this time was just about as bad as the Governor's. In February 1873, County Treasurer Gardner had announced that $50,000 had been collected, but in April J. N. Corbett, county auditor and school commissioner, suspended specie and currency payments, and some of the county schools were closed. In May the Sumter Bar Association found that fraud was being practiced in the drawing of juries, and unanimously offered the grand jury whatever legal aid it might desire in an investigation of the county affairs for the past four years.

The ensuing presentment of the grand jury indicated that only a superficial examination had been made of current conditions. The office of the clerk of court was reported in good order, except that fees were sometimes too high. The sheriff's office was commended. The treasurer was censured for not having made any report since the previous February. The board of county commissioners was reprimanded for irregularities in vouchers, and for having paid some claims in preference to others. Of the trial justices, only one was

---

[6] *Sumter News*, Aug. 24, 1873.
[7] *Sumter News*, May 8, 1873.

found to have turned in any fines to the county treasurer. All the county schools were closed.

For the time being, the town of Sumter seems to have escaped the general financial wreck. The carefully itemized report of John F. Haynsworth, clerk and treasurer, in April 1873, showed receipts and expenditures in balance at $15,544.74, and the indebtedness reduced from $3,492.76 to $1,365.76. Bad times were around the corner, however, and apparently for a non-political reason, for its was the project of a new town hall which brought trouble.

Near the close of the year 1871, an enterprising group of townsmen had undertaken the ambitious scheme of building a town hall and market, to be financed as a private enterprise by the sale of stock. Estimated to cost only $4,363.45, the plans called for a two-story structure, one hundred feet long and forty feet wide, with a twelve-foot ceiling downstairs, and a fourteen-foot ceiling above. Although only $2,307.45 was subscribed, the corner stone was laid on January 14, 1872, with Masonic ceremonies. The contractors were T. J. Toumey for the masonry, and Hiram Phillips for the carpentry. By June the exterior had been completed and given a coat of white paint, but the interior was unfinished, and all the money had been spent.

The promoters, however, obtained credit, and A. J. Moses completed the building, with a new guardhouse in the rear. When the house-warming ball was held in December, the total cost of Town Hall had reached $9,936.02. At some time in the course of these transactions, the town seems to have issued bonds for the deficit, and as a result got into serious financial difficulties.

The large hall on the upper floor of the new Town Hall became an "elegant little Theatre" when the town council purchased a set of handsome scenery painted in Wilmington. For a few weeks called the Sumter Opera House, it soon became Music Hall, and was the scene of many entertainments. The local performances featured the Sumter Orchestra and the Sumter Brass Band, both of which were trained by H. M. C. Kopff, a German music teacher. At Music Hall, too, were held the regular monthly lecturers of the Sumter

Lyceum, organized in 1872 by the Rev. Dr. McQueen at the Presbyterian Session House. Among the lecturers were Professor William James Rivers of the state university and Dr. James Carlisle of Wofford College. Here too Monsieur Berger, ageless high priest of the dance "for the last forty years," taught his classes for many more years. In his pocket he carried a phial containing what he called the elixir of life, which he drank many times a day and to which he attributed his youthful agility.

Few realized then that Town Hall would become a financial burden, and Sumter enjoyed it as a much-needed community center. The real anxiety of the time to taxpayers, was the condition of the state's finances under the administration of Governor Moses, but that anxiety did not cause Sumter to cease normal activities.

Worldly-minded citizens found recreation in the sport of horse racing, which had been revived early in 1872 on an improvised course near the town. Here R. G. Ellerbe's *Belle of York*, W. P. Burch's roan horse *Wild Arab*, J. H. Bracy's chestnut horse *Rabbit Hash*, J. H. Ferriter's gray mare *Molly*, and other well-known racers contended for purses ranging from one hundred to a thousand dollars. In later years Mr. Burch became the head of the famous Belmont stables.

The sportsmen of Sumter also resumed their camp hunts up in Chesterfield county. For those religiously inclined, camp meetings were enjoyed at the new camp ground near Providence. In December 1873, the South Carolina Conference of the Methodist Church met in Sumter, presided over by Bishop McTyeire, who later became chancellor of Vanderbilt University.

That energetic old Sumter citizen, Thomas Jefferson Coghlan, was once more in the news of the day. After Governor Scott deprived him of the county treasurer's office, he went into the lumber business. As his timber was five miles from town, he undertook to build a wooden tramway from his sawmill to the Sumter depot. By September, 1873, it was completed. The cars on the tramway were drawn by two oxen, working tandem, and they were said to be able to do the work of from twelve to fourteen oxen on an ordinary road. Afterwards he replaced the oxen with mules. He also planned to build a wooden track on the deep sand of Main street, to haul cotton to the depot and to bring freight to the merchants, but this was never finished. He then reopened his blacksmith shop on the south side of West Liberty street between Main and Sumter, where he carried his old trade.

On Liberty Street were other changes. M. F. Hewson had opened a tenpin alley next door to the oyster saloon of James Lassiter. On East Liberty in the block next to Main were Tom Feeny, Myles Moran, who had a grist mill worked by horse-power, George Reardon, Pat and Dennis O'Donnell, the Croghans, and their mother, Mrs. Harney, who was married several times but ran a bakery. On West Liberty in the block next to Main, were the O'Connor, Bogan, and Barrett business establishments, and nearby on Main were Dick and R. P. Monaghan. Indeed, so many Irish were in the blocks at the intersection of Main and Liberty, that it was sometimes called "Little Dublin."[8]

Some changes were on Main Street. J. H. Ferriter had his office for the collection of internal revenue in the Ricker and Ferriter Building, upstairs in the rear of the *Sumter News* office. The furniture warerooms of J. E. Suares were next to the C. T. Mason watch and jewelry shop. W. J. Andrews, a prosperous Negro who had served in the legislature, ran a restaurant. He was not a trouble-maker and was well thought of.

At the corner of Sumter and Dugan streets was Hauser's steam mill, grinding corn, and ginning and packing cotton on a new plan, for its two steam cylinders and pistons were adjusted to act on "the driving-shaft at an angle to each other" that overcame the dead-center, thus insuring a regularity which could not be had with a single cylinder. Made at the iron works of John Alexander in Columbia, the engine developed ten horse-power and was said to be the only one in the United States.

Meanwhile arson, robbery and murder were flourishing. When Mrs. E. S. Campbell's inn at Manchester was burned,

[8] H. G. Osteen.

she removed to Sumter, but eighteen months later the new building erected on the same site met the same fate. The *Sumter News* declared that the Ku-Klux was needed, or "better still, Judge Lynch."

In Sumter the jail was set afire, and the whole upper story burned before the fire engines arrived, the prisoners being released barely in time. Jake Singleton, the jailer, then had to keep the prisoners in the "hole in the wall" only eight feet by four, under the portico of the courthouse, thus depriving the sheriff of his wood house, until new quarters for the lawbreakers could be found. The $4,000 insurance on the jail was collected promptly by County Treasurer Gardner, but ten weeks after the fire, he was reported to be "traveling among the hills and valleys of his native land" in the North, and nothing had been done about providing a new jail. It was almost a year later that the *True Southron* published the welcome news that "Jake Singleton's new and commodious Dove-cote," on the corner of Canal and Sumter streets, "for the accommodation of the meek-eyed . . . Ring-doves," had been finished.

Some months after the jail fire, Gardner's own new and handsomely furnished home on Main street was completely destroyed by an incendiary fire, the family barely escaping with their lives. The rope of the fire bell on the Market House had been cut, and when the fire companies arrived, they could save only the surrounding houses. The loss was estimated at double the insurance, but Mr. Gardner immediately cleared the lot and rebuilt.

During the summer of 1873, Editor Kennedy persuaded Darr and Osteen, publishers of the *Sumter News,* to change its name, and on August 14, *The True Southron,* "organ, exponent and champion of the White people of the South," made its appearance. Like its former self, the *Sumter News,* it would be "the zealous guardian and defender of their honor and reputation, the fearless, independent and incorruptible champion of their rights and liberties, and the uncompromising and implacable foe of carpet-baggers and renegades—of imported and domestic, official and unofficial corruption, venality and fraud." Soon after, an attempt was made to silence the paper, when an emmissary from the State House Ring came to Sumter with an offer of $4,000 for the plant (three times what it was worth), with the privilege to the owners of keeping it, provided that it not be used anywhere in the state for one year. The offer was promptly rejected.[9]

It was well that the new jail was commodious, said the *True Southron,* for "Sumter was ahead of all competitors in the race of crime." Good citizens were appalled and disheartened by conditions. Editor Kennedy himself decided to remove to the southwest, and advertised for sale his home in Sumter, an eight-room residence with hallways twelve feet wide, upstairs and down, a piazza on every side, a kitchen and "bathing room" attached, and a smokehouse and storeroom in the yard. As the market was slow, he later advertised to sell all his real estate in the town "at panic prices", with only one-fourth in cash.

One reason for Mr. Kennedy's desire to depart was the incendiary loss of a new cottage he had recently built on Warren street. Another reason probably was that he had been haled into court by Judge Carpenter, the Republican from Kentucky, who had run for governor against Scott in 1870 on the Union Reform ticket. When the judge disbarred a member of the Columbia bar, Editor Kennedy, as usual, had expressed his opinions freely, and the judge issued a rule to show cause why Mr. Kennedy should not be committed for contempt of court. The case came before Judge Carpenter at May term in 1874. Mr. Kennedy was defended by Thomas Boone Fraser and the learned James S. G. Richardson. The plea of the latter argued that his client could not be punished because of the constitutional guarantee of freedom of the press; furthermore, that Judge Carpenter was not eligible to decide the case, because under the common law, no man may be judge of his own cause.

The trial did not curb Mr. Kennedy's use of his talents for invective. In reporting the wave of robberies and incendiary fires which plagued Sumter during Governor Moses' administration, he wrote: "Thus progresses Mosesism in South Carolina, and in Sumter County, the native home of his Lowness,

[9] *Watchman and Southron,* Aug. 10, 1892.

Tatterdemalion 1st, Commander in Chief of the Colored 'Melish' of the State." The editor was never prosecuted for libel by his target. But this may be explained, perhaps, by the Governor's boast that newspaper attacks could not injure him, as his constituents could not read.[10]

While governmental corruption consumed more and more of the tax revenue, good citizens desperately sought for a remedy. Early in the year 1874, the taxpayers of Sumter held a mass meeting at the courthouse, well attended by both whites and Negroes, who heard addresses on the situation from John S. Richardson, James D. Blanding, and Edwin W. Moise. The Rev. William E. Johnson, state senator from Sumter County, attacked resolutions offered by Mr. Blanding, and sought to array the Negroes against the whites. He succeeded in starting a fight, but the resolutions were adopted and plans were laid for the formation of tax unions throughout the county.

These tax unions resulted from a statewide movement which had begun two years before, and had been devised by the taxpayers' convention held in Columbia in February 1874. The aims were to have taxes fairly assessed and collected, and to prosecute dishonest officials who misused county funds. By August almost two hundred county and subordinate unions had been organized. Although no direct relief resulted, taxpayers were encouraged to struggle against their oppressors by the slogan, "Old men in the Tax Unions and young men in the Rifle Clubs."

At the May term of court in 1874, the Sumter grand jury presented County Treasurer Gardner for malfeasance in office, and found a true bill against him for failure to make monthly returns. In open court, Judge Mackey declared from the bench he had been informed that during the two preceding months Gardner had bought for himself more than $4,000 worth of county scrip at a heavy discount, and then collected it from the county at face value. Gardner was not the only county official in trouble, for the grand jury had also presented J. N. Corbett for malfeasance in his office of school commissioner.

[10] *True Southron*, Aug. 20, July 2, 1874.

Their malfeasance, however, was insignificant compared with the Governor's. When his financial difficulties reached a new crisis, he had applied to the Negro treasurer of Orangeburg County for a substantial loan, accompanied by a threat of dismissal if refused. As security for the loan, His Excellency gave the unfortunate Treasurer Humbert a draft on the executive contingent fund, ignoring the fact that he already had spent the fund. When State Treasuer Cardoza declined to honor the draft, Humbert was removed from office for delfaction.

Humbert went on trial at the May term of court in Orangeburg. The grand jury also presented the Governor and found a true bill against him. Judge Graham issued a bench warrant, and on May 19 sent Sheriff Cain to arrest the Chief Executive, who had the customary privilege of giving bail for his appearance in court. The Governor, however, called out the Negro militia, telegraphed for his father the chief justice, and declared that he neither would be arrested nor give bail, unless impeached and removed from office by the legislature.

The comic opera aspects of the situation were presented in a dispatch by Tim Hurley, the irrespressible Irish wit of the radicals:

> Seat of War, Preston Mansion
> Columbia, midnight, May 19, 1874
>
> .... Moses still inside, holding a council of war .... They have agreed to declare martial law, and blockade .... Richland, sending forces to the Orangeburg line .... The roads leading to the city are filled with volunteers .... cheering the Penitentiary .... The entrie Moses family are here, all having been called to serve as quartermasters, some eighty of them ....

When Sheriff Cain returned the bench warrant to the court, the solicitor asked Judge Graham what steps to take, and his honor replied that for the present the court "did not see its way to a successful fight with the State militia, and further action would be held under advisement."

On May 28, the day preceding the trial, Coroner Coleman of Orangeburg issued his warrant for the arrest of Sheriff Cain, charging the attempted "illegal arrest of the Governor." At the trial, counsel for the Governor pleaded that even as the king can do no wrong, neither can a governor while still in office, and no warrant of law can reach his person, a plea which was upheld by Judge Graham.[11] Newspapers throughout the state printed columns of comment, but the case was closed.

The Governor's champion in Sumter was State Senator W. E. Johnson, who, said Editor Kennedy, preached "Mosesism through the week and African Methodism" on Sundays.

While these sensational events were in progress, Governor Moses appointed his former critic, George F. McIntyre, then state senator from Colleton, as major general of the Fourth Division of militia. Soon after, the *New York Sun* announced that His Excellency had removed the treasurer of Colleton County and replaced him with McIntyre. The office of county treasurer, explained the *Sun,* is a lucrative position in South Carolina, for the incumbents although "alert in making collections, only occasionally deem it necessary to make any returns."

When the campaign of 1874 opened, Governor Moses had alienated so many members of his party that his name was not even offered in nomination at the state convention, and Daniel H. Chamberlain was named as the Radical condidate for governor.

Although Chamberlain based his campaign on a platform of reform, his running mate was R. H. Gleaves, the same corrupt mulatto who had served as lieutenant-governor with Moses. Hence, few white citizens had any faith in Chamberlain's sincerity. The Independent Republicans, therefore, who really desired reform, bolted the party and nominated Judge John T. Green, a native of Sumter County who had studied law in the office of the Moses brothers, and was generally believed to be a man of honesty and fair ability. On this ticket, Major Martin R. Delany, the Negro explorer, scientist, newspaper editor, and former army officer, was the nominee for lieutenant-governor. Of him, after eight years observation, Benjamin F. Perry said, that his speeches exhibited "more wisdom and prudence, more honor and pa-

[11] *True Southron,* May 28, 1874.

triotism, than any other Republican in South Carolina, white or black."

The campaign was disappointing, for Judge Green was an ill man and could not take the stump. Sumter County gave him a majority, however, and in the state he was the choice of all Democrats as well as Independent Republicans, polling almost as many votes as had put Moses in office in the previous election. But once again the Radicals had a victory, and Chamberlain and Gleaves were elected with a majority of 11,585 votes.

During his last days in office, Governor Moses was energetic in trying to relieve his financial difficulties, and was said by Chamberlain to have sold the appointments of the commissioners of election for $30,000, half in cash and the remainder contingent upon the defeat of Chamberlain. The last hour of his term was spent by his Excellency in signing fifty-seven pardons, bringing to 457 the total for his two years as governor. Despite these measures, however, he went into bankruptcy[12] very soon after leaving office, and never returned to live in Sumter.

[12] Walter Allen, *Governor Chamberlain's Administration in South Carolina*, (New York, 1888), pp. 232, 253; Wallace, *History S. C.*, III, 293, 297.

CHAPTER XXV

REFORMS, RIOTS, AND RED SHIRTS

In his inaugural address, Governor Chamberlain declared that "freedom and justice will bear sway in South Carolina," and though those who knew his record doubted him, his words proved to be sincere. To the surprise of his supporters as well as the doubters, he took immediate steps for economy and against fraud, enforcing his reforms by a series of nineteen vetoes, all of which were sustained. He secured relief for taxpayers by equitable reductions in assessed values of property and tax levies. The outrageous state printing bill was reduced to $50,000, little more than a tenth of what it had been. He refused to sell pardons, signing only seventy-three in the first eighteen months of his term. He even disbanded the disorderly Negro militia in Edgefield County. In Sumter, he appointed John B. Johnston, brother of Thomas Brent Johnston, to succeed Gardner as county treasurer. But, although C. J. Houston, ex-Governor Moses' Negro private secretary, was arrested for breach of trust, in not accounting for $13,000 in pay certificates which he had cashed with the state treasurer, neither he nor other corrupt officials were brought to trial.

Nor could Chamberlain reform his party, and he soon admitted that if he had foreseen the pressure it would bring upon him for performing these acts of public duty, he would not have dared to accept office. "Honest John" Patterson, the carpet-bagger from Pennsylvania who was then United States senator from South Carolina, was quoted by Judge Mackey as saying: "Are you going to let Chamberlain frighten you off with his cry of reform and economy? Why, gentlemen, there are five years of good stealing in South Carolina yet."

The first blow against the Governor's plans had been the election of the notorious Negro R. B. Elliott as speaker of the House, but Chamberlain's firmness and eloquence did much to hold the legislature in line. The next year, however, his hopes for a reform record which might have redeemed his party, were blasted. Taking advantage of his absence in Greenville for a day, the legislature in December 1875, elected the Negro W. J. Whipper, an adventurer from Michigan, as judge of the First circuit, which included Charleston; and Frank Moses, Jr., as judge of the Third circuit, which included Sumter. Chamberlain met the disaster by declaring the incumbent judges, Reed and Shaw, had been elected the previous year for four-year terms, not to fill unexpired terms, and he refused to issue commissions to Whipper and Moses.

When news of the election of Whipper and Moses reached Sumter, the *True Southron* came out on December 23, with a vitriolic editorial,[1] which declared that Frank Moses was "by nature, by education and by practice, a thief, a liar and a libertine. . . . And yet our Legislature is mad enough to suppose we will allow this dirty, venal, ignorant wretch, to serve us as Judge."

From Florence "An Old Citizen" wrote the *Southron* some words of advice for the Sumter bar: "Work against Moses, gentlemen, work long, work strong, for if ever little Frank gets on the Bench, your clients will cease to fee you . . . and instead fee the Bench."[2]

The citizens of Sumter were already at work, and had circulated handbills through the county calling a mass meeting. In answer to the call, on January 3, 1876, some two thousand Negroes joined the throng around Music Hall, to break up the meeting, but careful preparation forestalled trouble and prevented bloodshed. From a front window John S. Richardson invited in all who opposed Moses and Whipper as judges and favored sustaining the Governor. The doors were then opened, and about five hundred whites and two hundred Negroes surged up the stairs. The meeting was organized with Thomas Boone Fraser as president, twenty vice-presidents, and two secretaries.

In a calm brief speech, the president urged all citizens to

[1] John J. Dargan was then editor, having succeeded W. G. Kennedy in July 1875; In poor health, Kennedy had to walk with two canes; besides his incendiary losses, his life was being threatened.
[2] *True Southron*, Jan. 6, 1876.

unite in an effort to "cleanse out these Augean stables," and declared that young Moses should never hold court in Sumter unless seated there by federal power.

Edwin W. Moise offered eight resolutions and made an eloquent address: "Were the venerable Chief Justice to appear on our streets, grinding an organ, whilst his son Frank danced like the monkey, it would be no more farcial than his escorting him before our eyes to the Judicial tripod."

Charles H. Moise, "a plain merchant," called for the formation of a courthouse guard, declaring that if the younger Moses by any legal trickery should gain access to the courthouse steps and attempt to ascend them, he "Charles H. Moise, forty-six years old, with a wife and ten children to support," was ready to stand with the guards and "with muskets on our shoulders, guard that Temple of Justice from desecration."

James D. Blanding, "from an overflowing heart," said that he had determined to take no further part in political affairs, and his self-respect forbade him to defile his mouth with vituperation of that puppy Frank Moses; that he had prepared to remove to Texas, but he would not leave while such a calamity threatened his state, and he pledged his best abilities as a lawyer to prevent by peaceful means this outrage upon civilization.

After adoption of the eight resolutions offered by E. W. Moise, a motion was passed to publish them, because "we want the whole State to know what we are doing."

Good citizens of the state already realized that a reforming governor was not a sufficient remedy for the political evils under which they lived. As Chamberlain himself had foreseen, the election of Whipper and Moses was an act so flagrant that it meant the revival and reorganization of the Democratic party in South Carolina. Some Radical newspapers admitted that the legislature by this action had signed the death warrant of the Republican party in the state, and Governor Chamberlain in a telegram to the New England Society of Charleston said that the civilization of the Cavalier and the Puritan, of the Roundhead and the Huguenot, was in peril.

From the *New York Tribune* came a suggestion that the plight of South Carolina was due to too many Moses in the government, for ever since Reconstruction, "You couldn't fire into any kind of a ring where thieving was going on, without bringing down a Moses. . . . The South Carolina House of Representatives impeached one of these Moseses on Tuesday . . . . a judge of the Circuit Court . . . the brother of Chief-Justice Moses and the uncle of ex-Governor Moses . . . They seem to be leaders, law-givers and deliverers—stand-and-deliverers."[3]

Attacks such as this caused some members of the Moses family to drop the name, and to take their mother's maiden name of Harby. The Chief Justice himself found the loss of his old friends deeply painful, and the previous year he had tried to help matters by calling for a reunion of the members of the Claremont Troop on Washington's birthday. But the call was unheeded. The *True Southron* branded it a first step in a flank movement back towards the Democrats from whom he had seceded, and bluntly said "If the Chief Justice is disgusted with South Carolina Radicalism, as we believe he is, and desires to retrace his steps, let him do so openly . . . . If he will acknowledge, in a manly way, that he committed a grave error . . . and express regret for his mistake, we will take him by the hand and welcome him back . . . ."[4]

Chamberlain's reforms had won support for him among many Democrats who believed that the only hope of escaping ruin lay in a compromise that would re-elect him for a second term. Even the Sumter County Democratic Committee recognized in Governor Chamberlain "a Republican of the first class." This however, was not the general sentiment. Dr. Mark Reynolds, cautious and conservative, declared himself against passivity, compromise, cooperation and concessions: "A party composed of the mixed elements of two great parties, will never carry an election *here*."[5] On May 24, the *True Southron* took its stand against Chamberlain, because "a Demcrat and a better man than Chamberlain can be elected . . . . We say keep the party pure and straight—make no compromise with thieves, their aiders, abetters, or candidates."[6]

[3] Feb. 17, 1876, quoted in *True Southron*, Mch. 2, 1876.
[4] *True Southron*, Feb. 4, 1875.
[5] *Ibid.*, Jan. 13, 1876.
[6] N. G. Osteen was acting as editor, J. J. Dargan having resigned early in March for "strictly private reasons."

To some patriots the year 1876, centennial of American independence, seemed symbolic of hope. On June 28, when Charleston celebrated the hundredth anniversary of the battle of Fort Moultrie, Wade Hampton and other Confederate leaders rode in the parade as well as Governor Chamberlain. Afterwards, on the train leaving Charleston, Hampton was approached by General Mart Gary and asked if he would accept the Democratic nomination for governor: "With General Butler and myself on your flanks, we could win this battle as we won others in the war.". Hampton replied that he had no political ambitions, but if the convention nominated him he would accept.[7] He then proceeded to his summer home in North Carolina, and his friends began to lay plans for the campaign of 1876.

By a coincidence, in Aiken county on Independence Day, July 4, 1876, a Negro militia company, drilling in the public highway which passed through Hamburg, had refused to let two white men pass, and thus set in motion a series of fateful events, which resulted in race riots and the death four days later of young McKie Meriwether and seven Negroes. These race riots aroused a storm of excitement that welded the Democrats of the state into an invincible force.

While the excitement over the Hamburg riots was at its height, Whipper appeared before Chief Justice Moses on July 12, took the oath of office as judge, and announced that he would hold court in Charleston without the Governor's commission. Chamberlain issued a proclamation that such an attempt would be unlawful and riotous, and would be prevented by whatever force might be required.

Frank Moses claimed that his father could issue a mandamus from the Supreme Court and compel the Governor to issue the commission, but the Chief Justice seems to have held that the commissions were non-essentials. Following Chamberlain's lead, Judge Shaw announced that he intended to retain his seat for a full term, and would hold court in Sumter at the proper time.

Three days after Whipper was sworn in, the state Demo-

---

[7] Manly A. Wellman, *Giant in Gray: A Biography of Wade Hampton of South Carolina*, (New York, 1940), pp. 240-248; Simkins and Woody, *S. C. Reconstruction*, p. 490, note.

cratic Committee issued a call for the state convention to reconvene in Columbia on August 15. But Hampton's campaign was already under way: "Old Confederate cavalrymen began to shout along the roads and in the streets of courthouse towns that with somebody like Wade Hampton to lead them they could and would storm Hell." Sumter county felt the same way, and on August 10, five days before the state convention met, four political meetings were held, at one of which Abram Ruffin, a Negro contractor, former slave of Freeman Hoyt, declared himself a Democrat. After dark there was a stirring torchlight procession, with mottoes on transparencies, such as "1776-1876," and "What we did in 1776 we will do in 1876." Among the speakers of the exciting day were Joseph H. Earle, James D. Blanding, John J. Dargan, R. D. Lee, Edwin W. Moise, and Dr. Henry D. Green.[8]

When the Democratic convention met at the State House on August 15, there was still some sentiment for the support of Chamberlain on a fusion ticket. But the next day, when General Butler nominated Hampton, his former commander, no other candidate would accept and Wade Hampton was nominated by acclamation. The "Straight-Out" ticket he headed included Edwin W. Moise of Sumter as candidate for adjutant general. The platform was brief, simple and clear. Urging a peaceful, fair election, it pledged the party to Reform, Retrenchment and Relief, and asked the help of every man, regardless of race, color or party affiliation.

After the Hamburg riots, Governor Chamberlain asked that more federal troops be sent into the state. When two new companies arrived in Edgefield, the citizens tried a novel technique and went joyously out to meet them with an uproarous welcome. The astonished soldiers soon caught the idea and became their fast friends, while the bewildered Radicals who had asked for their protection, got little cooperation. Other communities followed similar tactics, and soon the Republican newspapers were saying: "Sending troops does no good. They like troops. The more troops they get the better they are pleased."

In the North a great hue and cry had been raised over the

[8] A. B. Williams, *Hampton and his Red Shirts*, (Charleston, 1935), pp. 38, 63.

race riots. United States Senator Oliver P. Morton, Republican from Indiana, delivered a violent speech and displayed a bloody shirt, which he said was from the body of an abused Louisiana Negro. Thereafter the expression "Waving the bloody shirt" became the slang phrase which was applied to all political appeals to sectional prejudice.

In derision of such appeals, Charleston in August showed a red shirt on one of the fifty transparencies in its Hampton parade. At Aiken in a torchlight procession honoring Edgefield, the company of A. P. Butler appeared in homespun shirts painted red. The idea caught popular fancy, and soon the women of the state were buying yards and yards of red flannel to make the famous red shirts which became the spectacular uniform of Hampton's supporters, in parades all over the state.

Only four days after the Democratic state convention, the Hampton club in the town of Sumter had 236 white members and 116 Negroes; and four townships had been fully organized for the campaign. Varied measures were used to win the Negroes from their Republican leaders, and soon the changing of party affiliation came to be known as "crossing Jordan." One of the most prominent Republicans to cross Jordan was Judge Thomas Jefferson Mackey, who decided to campaign for Hampton, and whose effective speeches all over the state were widely quoted for their wit. His brother, E. W. M. Mackey, who married Victoria Alice Sumter, a pretty, well-educated octoroon from Sumter county, remained a Republican. Major Martin F. Delany, the idealistic Negro leader, declared himself for Hampton on the grounds that it was his duty to unite the races "in one common interest."

Returning from Manning late in August, Governor Chamberlain spent the night in Sumter as the guest of Sheriff Tindall, and held a strategy council with William E. Johnson and the courthouse ring. They were reported to have decided to remove magistrates M. B. Moses and C. M. Hurst, and to replace them with only one trial justice, T. J. Coghlan, a "mighty man in the past," who had done valiant service for the Republicans in Reconstruction days but had retained the respect of many Democrats.

Early in September the Sumter Radical convention met with T. J. Coghlan in the chair. With nice impartiality, it elected as delegates to the state convention Thomas Brent Johnston, white; Sam Lee, "nearly white;" William E. Johnson, "bright yellow;" and young lawyer Thomas McCants Stewart, "black." So, said the *True Southron*, "all complexions had representation." Sam Lee was the only one of the four delegates who was opposed to Chamberlain. The campaign speech of the evening was made by Benjamin Franklin Whittemore, a notorious carpetbagger who hated Chamberlain for his reforms. Thomas McCants Stewart, the first Negro graduate of the University of South Carolina, is said to have done much to nullify Whittemore's influence in Sumter.

Bloody race riots in Charleston at this time focused national attention on the state. These riots and Chamberlain's prestige with the Northern press, made the gubernatorial campaign of 1876 in South Carolina national news on a par with the Hayes-Tilden presidential campaign.

In Sumter the meetings of the Radicals at the courthouse, and the Democrats at Music Hall, were held almost every night with multitudes of speeches. One favorably noticed speech was made by John J. Dargan, the Democratic candidate for solicitor, a young lawyer who had come from Darlington in 1874 to practice in Sumter. Pointing to the courthouse, he said: "Over yonder is a race contending against another race—over here the two races sit together in peace—over yonder is weakness—over here is strength—over yonder is hatred—over here is friendship—over yonder is defeat—over here is victory."

Hampton's tour of the state began on September 2, opening a contest which Tim Hurley, Irish wit of the radicals, characterized as a fight between Huguenots and Pineknots, "the chivalry and the shovelry."

A big powerful man and a superb horseman, Hampton was literally the "man on horseback" to lead his state in the hour of need. Always he traveled unarmed. His quiet voice was distinct and far-reaching, and his speeches were full of good sense, calm, brief and free from oratory. Invariably he appealed to the Negroes with a kind, frank and friendly reasoning, without condescension, and every promise he made to them was faithfully kept. His slogan embodied threee R's, Reconciliation, Retrenchment and Reform. Late in September when Hampton passed through Sumter at eleven o'clock on a rainy night, the citizens marched to the depot in procession, with music and banners, and greeted him in the glare of brilliant bonfires.

Hampton Day in Sumter was on October 7, exactly one month before the election, and more than six thousand wildly excited people witnessed one of the greatest celebrations ever held in the state. A detachment went to meet Hampton at the county line, and a magnificent parade formed at the depot. Hampton and General Connor rode in a handsome carriage drawn by four "noble grays" driven by old Robert W. Andrews. John W. Dargan, chief marshal, and his twenty-one assistant marshals, wore red, white, or blue sashes across their shoulders, and carried white batons trimmed with red, white and blue. The long line of marchers on foot moved with military precision to the music of bands from Columbia, Timmonsville, Darlington and Stateburg. Last came the thrilling sight of more than two thousand mounted Red Shirts, including some three hundred Negroes. Flowers, flags and banners decorated the line of march, and at the intersection of Main and Liberty, a great arch had been erected. A second arch was in front of the *True Southron* office, and a third was before the home of Charles H. Moise.

When Hampton advanced to the steps of the speaker's stand, "a bowed figure draped in robes of dense black and wrapped with chains stepped to the platform above and before him. As he ascended, the chains were cast aside with a clang, the mourning robes were thrown off, and a radiant young woman in pure white stood tall and stately, head up-lifted and eyes shining like stars with excitement and pleasure, a golden coronet on her hair—'South Carolina.' "[9]

Chairman Thomas B. Fraser introduced Hampton, who as usual spoke briefly but effectively. Speeches also were made

---

[9] *Ibid.*, p. 244. The beautiful young woman is said to have been Margaret Young Logan, later Mrs. Charles Stancill.

by M. P. O'Connor, James Chesnut and J. B. Kershaw. Chief Justice Moses was among those present, and when the orators spoke of the evils besetting the state, he is said to have wept freely, but he did not commit himself in words. Everyone knew that it was in his power to help or hinder the outcome of the campaign, and any legal questions which might arise from it, for he was said to control the vote of Associate Justice Wright, a Negro from Massachusetts, whose adherence gave the Chief Justice two of the court's three votes.[10]

At the barbecue which followed the speeches, special provision was made for the Negroes, but because of a malicious rumor that the food was poisoned, many of them stayed away. A torchlight procession and more speeches at the courthouse, concluded this memorable Hampton Day.

Alfred Williams, a young reporter who spent that night in a Sumter hotel, has recorded that the meaning of the day was summed up for him in three words, which he heard in the midnight stillness as a lone horseman, galloping homeward, shouted just once, "Hampton or Hell!" The Democrats felt that Chamberlain favored the latter, when, that same day, he declared Aiken and Barnwell under martial law, and ordered the almost three hundred white rifle clubs to disband, a move which the whites interpreted as leaving them at the mercy of the armed Negro militia. General Hampton was at dinner in Judge Fraser's house on North Main street in Sumter, when the telegram came announcing the Governor's proclamation. After dinner, the gentlemen adjourned to the shade of a chestnut oak in the yard, and made plans to checkmate the move. As a result, the rifle clubs met promptly, disbanded, and immediately reorganized under the names of brass bands, church sewing circles, baseball clubs, and "Mother's Little Helpers."[11]

The increasing strength of the Democrats was now like a rolling snowball, and the Radicals knew it. Some began to take cover. On October 9, former Governor Robert K. Scott

---

[10] Letter from *"Caucasian"* in *True Southron,* Jan. 13, 1878, said the Chief Justice had told the writer that Wright "never decides any point except as he (Old Moses) tells him."

[11] Williams, *Hampton and Red Shirts,* p. 246; Allen, *Chamberlain,* p. 389; letter from Rev. McIver Fraser, son of Judge Fraser, in *Sumter Daily Item,* May 17, 1950. The Fraser home was later Governor R. I. Manning's, and is now owned by A. T. Heath.

hesitantly "crossed Jordan"; and Frank Moses, Jr., announced his "resignation" as circuit judge. That night 370 breech-loading rifles stored in the Edgefield jail, mysteriously disappeared within a hundred yards of a federal sentry, who saw and heard nothing. Neither the Democrats nor the Republicans demanded an investigation.

Two days later in Aiken, a United States marshal began wholesale arrests of Democrats on general charges of "conspiracy." Adding horror to the tense situation, on October 16, came the Cainhoy massacre near Charleston, when secretly armed Negroes at a political rally opened a murderous fire on the whites. Incendiary fires were reported from all over the state. In answer to Chamberlain's call, came more and more federal troops. The Hampton forces realized the importance of avoiding all justification for their presence, and Hampton's stern orders to avoid incidents were scrupulously observed. To veterans of the Confederacy, discipline was easy, and Hampton rallies were managed like Sunday-school picnics. Ladies came to them in throngs, bringing tons of flowers to their hero, who gently left the tributes to wither in secluded spots along his way.

Five days before the election, United States troops arrived in peaceful Sumter to maintain order. As had Edgefield and other towns, Sumter received them cordially and won their friendship. When the troops departed a week later, a party of citizens headed by the Democratic brass band, went to see them off at the depot, where the officers expressed themselves well pleased with their brief visit. Major Kelly even went so far as to say that the Sumter people could take care of themselves and did not need any troops!

Happily, the election day all over the state was bloodless, but a few days later there were riots in Charleston and Beaufort. The vote had been heavy, and the returns were slow and conflicting. In some counties, the census figures for the population were exceeded by the Negro vote, in others by the white vote, so there were many contested returns that went to the state board of canvassers, all of whom were Radicals.

Under the constitution, each house of the legislature had the sole right to accept or reject its members. The Democrats, therefore, appealed to the Supreme Court to have the state canvassers merely certify the returns which they received from the county boards, without passing upon the validity. As Justice Wright later said, if the state board could throw out the returns of one or two counties, it could throw out all, and thus abolish the legislature! The Radical board, however, paid no attention to the court, and refused to certify the returns of Edgefield and Laurens, where Hampton had heavy majorities.

At midnight on November 27, Chamberlain secretly placed federal troops in the State House. When the members-elect assembled next morning to organize the legislature, the troops excluded the delegations from Edgefield and Laurens, thus giving the Radicals a majority. The indignant Democrats as a whole then refused to enter, and were joined by a Republican, W. H. Reeish of Orangeburg, who could not stomach the sight of federal soldiers barring South Carolinians from their own hall. The Republicans, all of whom were Negro except E. M. W. Mackey of Charleston, Thomas Brent Johnston and J. H. Ferriter of Sumter, claiming a bare quorum, proceeded to organize and elected Mackey as speaker.

At Carolina Hall the Democrats were sworn in by Judge Cooke. Then came a dramatic surprise, as J. W. Wesbury, of Sumter, deserted the Mackey House, leaving it without a quorum, and joined the Democrats amid a storm of applause. With a legal quorum, the Democrats organized and unanimously elected W. H. Wallace of Union as speaker. The next day, however, Wesbury was discovered back at his desk in the Mackey House, where he had gone to get his election certificate, and was forcibly detained. Using him to make a quorum, the Mackey House seated the Republican delegation from Barnwell, whose seats were contested by the Democrats, and then allowed Wesbury to leave.

By the count of the Republicans themselves, under the eyes of Democratic watchers, Hampton received 92,261 votes, to Chamberlain's 91,127, giving Hampton a majority of 1,134 which he could not have won without the Negro Democrats, whose vote he estimated at 17,000. Before inauguration, however, it was necessary that the election of the governor and the lieutenant governor be confirmed by the legislature.

On December 5, the Mackey House declared Chamberlain elected, and two days later amid gloomy surroundings, he was inaugurated. At his home and at his office, he kept himself closely guarded by United States soldiers.

On the night of Chamberlain's inauguration, some five thousand Red Shirts assembled around Hampton's office, ready to tear down the State House with their bare hands. Hampton quieted them in a famous speech which counseled patience and peace: "The people have elected me governor, and, by the eternal God, I will be governor, or we shall have a military governor." When he concluded, the men quietly dispersed.

The state supreme court on December 6, formally recognized the Wallace House as the legal legislative body, and on December 14, Hampton was inaugurated with brilliant ceremonies, sworn in by Judge Thomas Jefferson Mackey, brother of the speaker of the Mackey House.

South Carolina thus had two organized governments, each recognized by its constituents. During the months that the dual government continued, there were many tense moments when bloodshed might have touched off another civil war. Hampton, however, was determined that this should not happen, and he held complete control over his followers.

In January 1877, mass meetings in Sumter and fifteen other counties followed the lead of Charleston, and adopted resolutions to pay no taxes to the Chamberlain government, but to pay immediately the ten per cent of the tax levy called for by Hampton. Both state governments were without funds, for the state treasury was empty.

Meanwhile, Sumter County also was having a period of dual government in some of its county offices. In the general election of 1876, the county had cast 6,260 votes, of which Hampton had received 2,382. The Republican ticket of county officers had been elected: county commissioners, T. J. Coghlan, Z. Walker, and Rufus Westberry; sheriff J. M. Tindall, incumbent; probate judge, Samuel Lee; clerk of court, G. W. Reardon; school commissioner, T. J. Tuomey.

The new board of county commissioners appointed F. A. M. Teicher, clerk, but the old board retained office, pending a decision on the legality of the election. This old board, however, made no annual report, because the clerk claimed that the office safe in which the records were kept, could not be opened.

In the treasurer's office, John Brent Johnston, Chamberlain's respected appointee, advertised that he would receive county taxes then due. But W. F. B. Haysworth, Hampton's "special agent", persuasively advertised "Pay Your Tax Ransom", an invitation to property owners to pay him Hampton's allotted ten per cent of the tax levy, and soon he had $3,000 in hand. By the end of the month, Hampton's government had $62,000 at his disposal.

The most spectacular collision between rival claimants in Sumter occurred in the judge of probate's office, where C. M. Hurst, the Republican incumbent, decided not to vacate until the legality of Sam Lee's election was decided. But early on the morning of January 19, Sam Lee took possession of the office, and when Hurst appeared, he found Alberry L. Singleton, deputy United States marshal, on hand to protect Lee. A noisy row ensued, during which a pistol was fired, and Hurst was ejected. He soon returned with friends who, in turn, ejected Lee. An excited crowd soon gathered. Sheriff Tindall commanded the peace, but no one heeded, and a riot seemed inevitable. Luckily, court was in session, and Judge Shaw appeared on the scene. He dispersed the crowd, locked the probate office, and placed it in custody of the sheriff.

At the January term of court in Chester, Judge Thomas Jefferson Mackey served notice that any court official who read a Chamberlain commission dated after Hampton's inauguration, would be jailed for contempt of court. All other circuit judges in the state, except one, took similar action. Gradually but surely the Hampton government was gaining upon Chamberlain's.

In February Hampton began removing the corrupt county treasurers. Adjutant and Inspector General Moise began to reorganize the militia. Late in the month, while Chief Justice Moses lay ill, Associate Justices Willard and Wright recognized a pardon issued by Hampton and the prisoner was released.

Honest officials had nothing to fear, for Hampton had pledged his victory to good government, not to party or race. After the death of Chief Justice Moses on March 6, 1877, Hampton, despite opposition, backed Associate Justice Willard for the chief justiceship, although Willard was a Republican from New York, who had come South with federal Negro troops.

Soon after the inauguration of President Hayes, Hampton requested the withdrawal of federal troops, and the President invited both Hampton and Chamberlain to confer with him. On April 10, 1877, the troops were withdrawn, almost on the anniversary of the firing on Fort Sumter, and twelve years after Lee's surrender at Appomatox!

The next morning at eleven o'clock, Chamberlain left the governor's office, and his secretary handed the keys to Wade Hampton Manning, Governor Hampton's private secretary. The government of South Carolina had been returned to South Carolinians.

CHAPTER XXVI

HAMPTON AND THE CONSERVATIVES

With the departure of the federal troops in 1877, many of the worst Radicals left the state. Some of those who remained became forgotten men, and a few were prosecuted. The rise of the Democrats to power did not bring a millenium, for the effects of the radical decade would endure for generations. Much of the so-called "reconstruction" had to be undone, and Wade Hampton was the man to guide the work, for he was magnanimous, free from race hatred, and felt in honor bound to fulfill his campaign promises.[1]

In Sumter County, Hampton appointed Charles W. Moise as auditor, W. F. B. Haynsworth treasurer, and J. N. Frierson jury commissioner. Chamberlain's "Late County Treasurer", John B. Johnston, advertised in July that he would be at the treasurer's office for ten days, to refund the 1877 tax payments which had been made to him. The duly elected Republican officials quietly took offices in the courthouse, and Sam Lee became the undisputed probate judge.

The new Board of County Commissioners found itself unable to function properly without the office records, which were still locked in the unopened safe. Chairman T. J. Coghlan, therefore, had the safe carried to his blacksmith shop and cut off the hinges and bolts. True to his promise not to open the safe except in the presence of the ex-Board members, he sent for them. Evidently they had their own reasons for being present, and while Coghlan was busy, they suddenly emptied the safe and hastily departed with all the records. The *True Southron* indignantly declared that here was work for the grand jury. In August Governor Hampton appointed Charles Mayrant, R. J. Brownfield, and J. A. Mills to examine into the indebtedness of Sumter County. When the fiscal year ended on October 31, 1877, the annual report of the county

---

[1] Hampton M. Jarrell, *Wade Hampton and the Negro* (Columbia, 1949), pp. 73, 149-150, and *passim*.

commissioners could not include any statement of past indebtedness, for the committee was still at work. The former Board and clerk were slated for trial at the next term of court.[2]

In the probate court, records are still extant which indicate that Sam Lee kept better looking records than did some other incumbents of the office; but evidently they are incomplete, being entered only from February 27, to September 3, 1877. During the year 1878, there were complaints that Lee had turned his office into "a Radical Club Room," and was neglecting his duties. Lee did actually close his office and go to Washington; and while he was there, northern newspapers quoted him as saying there was a reign of terror in Sumter County, where the bloody leaders of oppression were Joseph Haynsworth Earle and John Julius Dargan. Lee's accusations did not pass unheard, for President Hayes directed the attorney general to look into the matter, and report what federal action might be taken against the accused.

When Lee returned from Washington, he was arrested and jailed on the charge of having closed his office and neglected its duties. Alberry Singleton, Lee's brother-in-law, attempted unsuccessfully to protect him, claiming immunity for Lee as a federal witness in a pending action. Singleton then went to Charleston, obtained a federal warrant, arrested Sheriff Tindall and deputy Watson, and took them to Charleston, where they were held without bail. Lee was released from jail and went to Charleston as a witness, but at the hearing, for reasons not stated, no witnesses appeared, and Tindall and Watson were released.[3]

The Democratic campaign of 1878 in Sumter County was noteworthy, because, for the first time, nominations were made in party primary elections, instead of county conventions. An editorial in the *True Southron* explained the new plan, and in the first primary on September 7, the precinct clubs polled a total of 1,636 votes for the following candidates: state senator, T. B. Fraser, 1,489; representatives, J. J. Dargan, 1,126 and J. W. Westberry, 941; county com-

[2] *True Southron*, May 8, Aug. 7, Nov. 27, 1877.
[3] *Ibid.*, Oct. 15, Nov. 17, 1876.

missioners, J. M. Wilder, 1,375 and John Durant, 908. When the second primary was held a week later, Joseph H. Earle received 700 of the 850 cast and was nominated to the House. In October the Democratic nominations also included W. D. Scarborough for the House, Jacob Keels for the Board of Commissioners, T. V. Walsh for judge of probate, and William F. Rhame for county school commissioner.

When Judge A. J. Shaw died in the fall of 1878, he was succeeded by Thomas Boone Fraser, and in a primary in April 1879, J. J. Bossard, the most popular physician in the county, was nominated to succeed Judge Fraser in the state senate.

In the scandalously corrupt elections of 1878, the Democrats elected their entire ticket, headed again by Wade Hampton. Although Sam Lee was defeated for the probate judgeship in Sumter, he continued active among the Republicans and early in 1879 was nominated by President Hayes as postmaster. Two weeks later, Lee was convicted in the circuit court of having closed his probate office, and Judge Mackey filed a sealed sentence, Lee being absent. Soon after, the President withdrew Lee's nomination.[4]

Hampton did not serve his second term as governor, for in December 1878, although not a candidate, he was elected to the United States Senate.

Among the new members of the legislature which elected him were Joseph H. Earle and John J. Dargan. During the session a serious quarrel arose between them, which reached a climax in September 1879, when Dargan challenged Earle to a duel. Both men as lawyers were fully aware of the laws against dueling, so they agreed to quietly leave the state and shoot it out in Georgia.

Before they could leave Sumter, however, someone notified the Sumter sheriff, who promptly arrested them. Dargan was compelled to give a peace bond, but Earle escaped, and with his second W. D. Blanding, arrived on Thursday night at Augusta, where they registered as Joseph Hayne of Macon, and William DeSaussure of Savannah.

Having signed his bond, Dargan was released and took a train for Augusta by way of Florence, Charleston and Branch-

[4] *Ibid.*, Feb. 4, 18, Mch. 4, 1879.

ville, and was joined by his second, Guignard Richardson. The intendant of Sumter had word of their departure, and immediately sent telegrams to the chief of police in Augusta, giving descriptions of the antagonists and requesting their arrest. As soon as their train rolled into Augusta, Dargan and Richardson were taken into custody. A policeman went to the Planters' Hotel for Earle, but Earle warned him off so ominously, that the officer decided to get a warrant from city hall, and left a guard to keep an eye on Earle.

But Earle was a man of action, and before anyone realized what he was going to do, he leaped into a buggy in front of the hotel, seized the reins from the Negro driver, and headed at a gallop for the Savannah River Bridge. Having reached South Carolina soil, he sent back the buggy and driver, and disappeared. When the officer arrived with the warrant, Earle could not be found.

The next morning Dargan was taken into court and required to post a $1,000 peace-bond. In the afternoon, he and his second boarded a train for Columbia, but once more the authorities had been alerted, and Dargan was arrested as soon as he reached the city.

Earle and Blanding, meanwhile, had boarded a freight train for Charlotte, where they took the precaution of registering separately as Baylis Wilmot of Greenville and William Braddy of Marion. There for twelve hours they awaited word from Dargan and Richardson. As no word came, they consulted with some of the prominent gentlemen of Charlotte, and by their advice decided to return home. Shortly after midnight on Tuesday, Earle and Blanding left the hotel by the front exit, went to the Charlotte, Columbia and Augusta Railroad, and took the 12:35 train for Sumter, where they arrived the following night. In the morning Earle was arrested, and his friends voluntarily put up $5,000 bond, for he refused to ask aid. When Dargan and Richardson arrived on Thursday, Dargan was again arrested and gave bail for $5,000.

At the request of J. D. Kennedy, T. W. Woodward, and H. A. Gaillard, the two seconds then adjusted matters between the antagonists "honorably and satisfactorily to all parties."

Thus ended a week of tension and excitement, which made conversation for many years to come.

But there was no real reconciliation between Earle and Dargan. The following June when court was in session, they had a "rumpus" in the courthouse. Judge Aldrich ruled both gentlemen for contempt of court, sentenced each to pay a fine of fifty dollars, and suspended them from practice in the probate and the circuit courts until the ensuing January.

In October Senator Hampton made a personal appeal to Earle and Dargan to end their feud. They agreed to place the matter in the capable hands of Hampton, John Bratton, and Johnson Hagood, who succeeded in making an adjustment which both Earle and Dargan publicly accepted. When the fall term of court opened in Sumter, Judge Pressley reinstated the belligerent gentlemen to practice in the courts.[5]

The end of duelling in South Carolina came soon after, when the Cash-Shannon duel of July 1880, aroused such a storm of popular indignation that the practice ceased to be tolerated.

Meanwhile, other changes were taking place, and Democratic promises to Negro voters were being disregarded, especially after Senator Hampton went to Washington and his direct influence was removed from state politics. In mortal fear of a return of Negro Republican rule, politicians were seeking means to cut down the alarming Negro majorities. In 1878 the number of polling places in the predominantly Negro counties had been reduced, so that only by great effort could Negro voters reach the polls. In 1880 the Democrats of Sumter and other counties were prosecuted for violation of federal election laws.[6] The Republicans printed their ballot with a plaid back, a "calico ticket," for the illiterates. T. J. Coghlan, a candidate that year for sheriff on a fusion ticket of Republicans and independents, was defeated. Bloc voting by the whites became an accepted policy. "An independent is worse than a Republican" became the slogan of the Democrats, whose usual answer to criticism was "Hush, or you will split

---

[5] *Ibid.*, Sept. 23, 1879; June 15, Oct. 12, Oct. 19, 1880.
[6] Wallace, *History of S. C.*, III, 330.

the Democratic Party." The white voters of the state solidly held to the party line.

In 1882 the "eight box election law" disfranchised many Negroes, for it required a separate ballot and a separate but plainly marked ballot box at the polls for each office to be filled.[7] Voters who could not read usually invalidated their ballots by placing them in the wrong box.

A curious "deal" was made that year by the Sumter Democrats with Sam Lee, who was a candidate against E. W. M. Mackey for Congress. On the eve of the election, James D. Blanding, in charge of the county congressional boxes, sent confidential instructions to the poll managers: "Samuel Lee has agreed that his friends will not vote for the Greenback ticket or any other State or County ticket; and I have agreed that if they do not, then the Democrats will vote for him instead of Mackey for Congress. You are appointed to carry out at your polls this agreement." As a result, Lee polled 5,281 votes in Sumter county, and Mackey only 744. The deal was ineffective, however, for Mackey had majorities in other counties of the congressional district. Lee contested Mackey's election, resulting in a congressional deadlock. The House committee on elections gave Lee permission to withdraw, and he then applied for a clerkship, which Mackey endorsed.[8]

Lee was again mentioned as a Republican candidate for Congress in 1890, but did not win. He received an appointment in Washington, but later he is said to have lost his mind, and died in an asylum. His daughter's son is said to have graduated from Columbia University and been elected to the New York legislature.[9]

While the threat of a return of radical rule was being lessened by the various restraints upon the Negro vote, the white Democrats were becoming proportionately freer to voice their criticisms, especially during the politically stormy years which were now at hand when the Democratic party was to be split into embittered factions.

The events of that period have often been described as the

[7] *Stat.* XVII, 1117-1118.
[8] *Watchman and Southron*, Jan. 2, 16, Mch. 13, 1883; Nov. 21, 1882.
[9] H. G. Osteen.

farmers' revolt, therefore mention should be made of the Grange, or Patrons of Husbandry, a national farmers' organization which entered the state in 1871 and helped to prepare the way for the revolt. The aim was to organize the farmers for the improvement of rural life and to establish cooperative trading. In Sumter County it was well under way in 1873, and among the local Granges in 1880 were Concord, Lynchburg, Sumter, Manchester, Bishopville, Bethel No. 3, and Pomona No. 11. In 1882 officers of Concord No. 39 and Manchester No. 17 were listed in the news. Although the Grange debarred politics from its program, it is said to have been effective in the Hampton campaign of 1876. Undoubtedly, it helped during the 1880's to lay the foundations for the farmers' movement, which culminated at the close of the decade and swept the Hampton regime from power.

The decade of the 1880's was profoundly affected by economic conditions. The crops of 1880 were good, and Sumter farmers were said to have shown little interest in politics. But the next year, drought ruined the cereal crops, the army worm wrought havoc in the cotton fields, and men long remembered "the year of calamity." In January 1882, a petition to the legislature signed by J. E. Rembert and fifty-nine others, declared that people of Mechanicsville were in actual want of bread, and asked that the state come to their aid, taking a lien on the crops. Although the farmers made their largest cotton crop that fall, it did not bring prosperity. In October, when the Sumter Park and Agricultural Association held its third annual fair, it was not a success. Three years later, the discouraged directors announced that no fair would be held.

And again in 1883, the crops around Wedgefield were reported as failures. Conditions did not improve in 1884, and people found themselves slipping deeper into debt with each passing year. Continuing hard times affected the rising generation as well as their elders, and in June 1884, the good citizens of Sumter were shocked to discover that the young sons of respected parents had organized themselves into a sneak-thieving gang. For several weeks the boys had been robbing tills, stealing watches, and making off with miscellaneous articles. "Invest twenty-five cents in a cowhide, if switches are scarce," advised the *Watchman and Southron*. The horrified parents took prompt and effective action, and not only was the gang broken up, but several of its members in later years became outstanding citizens of national reputation.

Hard times brought political discontent, and throughout the state, talk was heard of a "New Deal" which would throw out of public office the very men who had thrown out the Republicans. "The State is too poor to indulge in the luxury of dead-beat officials whose duties outside of drawing their salaries and getting drunk whenever free champagne is set up, are purely ornamental," warned the *Watchman and Southron*. "We have good officers but there are plenty others just as good," and the editor advocated rotation in office, because it would tend "to relieve the office holders of any idea that they have a life tenure."

Vainly seeking a cure for economic ills, the hard-pressed farmers of Sumter again organized, this time as the Sumter Farmers' Association, with Dr. J. H. Furman as president, and Henry Ragin Thomas of Wedgefield as secretary.

But it was a burly farmer of Edgefield County, Ben Tillman,[10] whose aggressive leadership gave the "New Deal" idea its impetus.

Tillman captured attention by fanning the widespread discontent of the times into a blaze. Announcing himself as a reformer, he savagely attacked the gentlemen of the old regime who were conducting the government of the state. He hinted at political rottenness, which he did not specify or prove. His raucus voice harped on the "robbery" of the farmers by greedy money-lenders, and his rugged eloquence lashed his adherents into a frenzy that howled down his opponents. Capitalizing animosity, he set whites against Negroes, plain men against aristocrats, upcountrymen against lowcountrymen, and farm people against city dwellers. Heaping abuse upon the South Carolina College as a place whose very atmosphere was "tainted with contempt for

---

[10] The standard biography of Tillman is Francis B. Simkins, *Pitchfork Ben Tillman, South Carolinian* (Baton Rouge, 1944).

farming," and scoring the Citadel as a military dude factory, he demanded a separate agricultural college for farmers' sons. He argued for the reduction of taxes and cutting of officials' salaries. He called for repeal of the lien law, which bound the farmers to the merchants who financed their crops, and he advocated a convention to make a new state constitution.

In April 1886 Tillman got his program under way at a Farmers' Convention in the state agricultural building in Columbia. Sumter's delegates were R. I. Manning, E. M. Cooper, J. H. Wilson, R. M. Cooper, and H. R. Thomas. It was agreed that the Farmers' Association should have an annual convention every November, from which a committee headed by Tillman would carry to the legislature the farmers' program. Heretofore, the farmers' numerical majority in the legislature had availed them little, for they lacked organization. This was now to be supplied by Tillman.

The *Watchman and Southron's* diagnosis of the cause of the farmers' plight varied somewhat from Tillman's. Admitting that the farmers were poor and getting poorer, the editor declared that they should not ascribe all their troubles to the lien law, high taxes, and incompetent office-holders; the true cause was the credit system: "Planting all cotton and keeping one's smokehouse and corncrib in the West is bad enough, but cannot compare in evil with buying on credit."[11]

A more extended analysis was made that summer by Dr. Edward J. Rembert before the joint meeting of the State Grange and the State Agricultural and Mechanical Society. Dr. Rembert, a large landowner, after taking degrees in the liberal arts and medicine, had spent several years of advanced study in Paris. Beginning with the maelstrom of the Civil War which had left the South "nothing but penury, sorrow and want," he showed how the enormous federal war expenditures and greenback issues had enriched the North, where capital had been swollen further by military pensions and high tariffs. So abundant was capital there, that interest was only three per cent, whereas in the South it was nominally ten per cent and actually many times greater. This crushing interest was protected by law; furthermore, while the na-

[11] *Watchman and Southron*, Mch. 2, 1886.

tional banks were untaxed, the state banks were taxed ten per cent. Calling for a speedy change in the banking and financial system, he declared that the Southern farmer also was throttled by the treatment of silver, and under existing conditions the debts of producers could not be liquidated.[12]

In Sumter County the most active exponent of Tillman's program was Henry Ragin Thomas, a native of Summerton but then planting near Wedgefield. His name originally was Henry Lawrence Ragin, but in 1877 by act of the legislature, his surname was changed to Thomas.[13] During Reconstruction he was alleged to have killed a Negro, and to have fled to Canada, where he married a Canadian. A man of ability, he became president of the Sumter Farmers' Association in 1886, and, seeing the possibilities of the Tillman movement, he climbed on the Tillman bandwagon.

The most able antagonist of Tillmanism in the county was Joseph H. Earle, who, elected state senator in 1882, became in 1886 the state attorney general. Orphaned early in life, Earle had grown up in Sumter County at the plantation of his maternal aunt. In 1880 he had purchased and made his home in the handsome residence in Sumter which Chief Justice Moses had built with such high hopes for his son Frank. Earle, born in 1847, had been a young soldier of the Confederacy, and his fearlessness combined with his handsome person, legal experience, and ready wit, to make him a formidable adversary in debate. As Tillman himself later admitted, "He never relaxed his grasp upon my throat . . . . He pressed his arguments home with powerful logic and subtle reasoning."[14]

The impact of Tillmanism upon the state was in some respects not unlike the great earthquake which struck Charleston in the night during the closing hours of August 1886, killing ninety-two persons and damaging property in excess of $5,000,000. Although the earth tremors were felt in Wisconsin, nearly a thousand miles away, the disaster did little harm in Sumter County, except to cause great alarm. At

---

[12] Address, Aug. 14, 1886, in *Watchman and Southron*, Jan. 4, 1887.
[13] *Stat.* XVI, 284.
[14] *Memorial Addresses on the Life and Character of Joseph H. Earle*, (Washington, 1898), p. 58.

Privateer, chimneys were badly cracked and the tops of several fell. In Sumter, several chimneys were demolished. At Stateburg, thirteen shocks were reported, but little or no damage.

On November 30, 1886, Governor John Peter Richardson of the Clarendon family of many governors, was inaugurated. A typical representative of the ante-bellum regime which had been restored to power in 1876, he was destined to witness, during two stormy administrations, a furious struggle for political power between the conservatives of his class, and the vociferous supporters of Tillman.

On the floor of the legislature during the session of 1886, four Tillmanite members championed the farmers' program, while Tillman himself headed the lobbyists. His violent speech and manners antagonized many, who otherwise might have considered the program on its merits, and it met little success. At the session of 1887 also, little was achieved. Discouraged, Tillman issued his "Farewell Letter" and went into retirement on his Edgefield farm.

A tragedy in Sumter at the end of the year drew local attention completely away from politics, when George E. Haynsworth was shot to death in the peaceable discharge of his duties as trial justice. As a Citadel cadet, "Tuck" Haynsworth had fired from Morris Island the first gun in the War of Secession, and had rendered valiant service in that conflict until the last battle at Bentonville. Returning to Sumter, he had taught school, studied law, married, and was universally respected in the community as a quiet, modest gentleman. His death orphaned two small sons, and aroused deep feeling. Under the headline, "Sumter's Black Friday," the *Watchman and Southron* called his untimely end the "blackest stigma that has befallen this county for generations."

The shooting had its origin in a quarrel between two young men some time before in Bishopville, when Peyton G. Bowman, Jr., then teaching in Bishopville, and John R. Keels, a lawyer of Sumter, had words about the charges for some legal papers drawn by Keels, and Bowman was slightly wounded in the leg by a pistol shot. Not long after, Bowman's brother-in-law, a cousin of the same name as his, a lawyer in Sumter, met Keels in Rosendorf's saloon and another quarrel grew out of the first, but ended without shooting. It touched off, however, a feud between the two families, and some days later the Keels clan, represented by D. E. Keels (father of John R.), Kenneth Pennington, and some others, came from Lynchburg to Sumter, armed and looking for trouble, and went to John R. Keels' office on Main Street. Awaiting them in the street were the elder Peyton G. Bowman, W. A. Bowman, Walter I. Harby, and others of the Bowman clan, all armed. To head off further trouble, several citizens swore out warrants, had both factions arrested and taken before Mr. Haynsworth to be put under peace bonds. Unfortunately, and inexplicably, the prisoners were not disarmed. While Mr. Haynsworth was writing the bonds, someone fired a shot, a fusillade broke loose, and the magistrate sprang to his feet "just in time to intercept a badly aimed bullet."

Three of the prisoners were wounded and could not be taken to jail but were placed under guard, the elder Peyton Bowman at his home, the elder Keels at his son's house in Lynchburg, and Pennington at the Jervey House in Sumter.

After taking testimony for two days, the coroner's jury brought in a verdict that the deceased came to his death during a riot by P. G. Bowman, W. I. Harby, K. Pennington, and J. R. Keels, from a shot fired from a pistol in the hand of one of them, the others aiding and abetting.

When the rioters were put on trial, they were defended by Moise and Lee, W. C. Benet, and Robert Aldrich, son of the presiding judge. At the end of a week, after an all night deliberation, the jury, shortly before sunrise on Sunday morning, brought in a verdict of acquittal for Bowman and Harby. When the court re-convened the following Wednesday, the charge against Keels was *nol prossed*.

Meanwhile, in the state at large, Tillmanism received a new impetus. In the spring of 1888, Thomas G. Clemson died, and bequeathed to the state his plantation and an endowment for the establishing of an agricultural college. Among the seven life trustees for the bequest, he named Ben Tillman. Elated by this turn of events, Tillman immediately emerged from retirement, and resumed his propaganda against the well-mannered men in public office, deriding them as broken-down aristocrats and Bourbons. Even when Tillman's accusations of corruption were shown to be false, he continued to repeat them for their vote-getting value. To his not well-informed admirers, he had became an idolized leader, to be followed with blind devotion, and they cherished a corresponding hatred and suspicion toward all who opposed him.

As yet Tillman had not been able to obtain control of the state Democratic Convention, and, as a result, had never succeeded in naming a candidate for the governorship. In the Convention of 1888, the Tillmanites, still outnumbered by Conservative delegates, decided to cast their votes for a Conservative, Joseph H. Earle of Sumter. With the Tillmanites' support, Earle might easily have had the nomination for governor. But as a Conservative, he felt in honor bound to support the re-nomination of Governor Richardson, and he refused to be a candidate.

Tillman, knowing full well his own popularity with the masses, then advocated a direct primary instead of the convention for the nomination of candidates for state offices. "Give me a state primary," he said, "and I'll run for governor myself." But the proposal was voted down, although the primary had been used in Sumter and other counties ever since 1878, for the selection of candidates for county offices. The Convention of 1888, however, did approve the innovation of the county-to-county joint debate by state candidates, which has remained ever since a regular feature of the party campaigns.

Although Tillman had not been nominated as a candidate for any office, he entered the campaign debates, and was with the candidates when they appeared in Sumter. The crowd that came to see and hear him was so large, that many people were reminded of Hampton Day in 1876. This audience, however, was not friendly to Tillman, and he got some heckling. He began his speech, "Some come here to see what sort of an animal I am. I have neither hoofs nor horns, but I am a plain, simple farmer like yourself." He then reprimanded the voters of Sumter for having chosen their own delegates to the nominating convention before they had heard him.

When he launched his customary accusations against the office-holders, Earle refuted his statements, and Tillman was forced "to take water."

The campaign, nevertheless, served to increase Tillman's personal popularity. But his program was still so far from being accomplished, that he did not even attend the listless Farmers' Association Convention in November, and once more he went into a brooding retirement on his farm.

An issue in the campaign of 1888 was acceptance of the Clemson bequest. In May 1889, the federal court of appeals declared the contested Clemson will was valid, and at the opening of the legislature in November, Governor Richardson signed the act for acceptance. The legislature then passed the other measures for bringing into existence the proposed Clemson College.

In the meantime, the rival Farmers' Alliance had come into the state. In September 1888, J. E. Pettigrew of Florence, lecturer of the Alliance, began to organize Sumter farmers into sub-alliances. The organization claimed to be non-political, and concerned solely with the farmers' economic protection. Unlike the Association, which was Democratic in membership, the Alliance included both Republicans and Democrats.

The Red Land Alliance was organized near Gaillard's Cross Roads, and apparently was made up entirely of white farmers. The colored Farmers' Alliance had a barbecue at Stateburg in the summer of 1889, which was attended by almost a thousand persons. They were addressed by several speakers, including John J. Dargan; George Washington Murray, "the most intellectual negro in the county"; W. W. Anderson; and the Negro postmaster from Wedgefield. Organized in almost every county in the state, the Alliance in 1890 numbered about 60,000 members. The organization soon became a political machine, and after Tillman joined forces with it, the Alliance proved to be an effective aid in his successful campaign for the governorship.

While the Democratic party was being split into factions, the Sumter County Republicans were being held together by Thomas Brent Johnson and Timothy J. Tuomey, two white men of wealth and intelligence. F. A. M. Teicher is said to have been the only other white member of the local party. The young Negro lawyer, T. McCants Stewart, had settled in New York to practice, but the Negro West Pointer, M. F. Stewart, was active in the party. The real Negro leader, however, was George Washington Murray, a hardworking teacher and farmer of the Rafting Creek section, who was acquiring lands in that neighborhood.

Tillman and his supporters, knowing that he again might fail to win the nomination in the Democratic state convention, laid careful plans to avoid disappointment, and decided to call a farmers' convention early in the spring of 1890. In January, the executive committee of the Farmers' Association published a policy statement, which, written by Tillman but named for G. W. Shell, president of the Association, became known as the Shell Manifesto. The Manifesto called for election of delegates to the proposed farmers' convention, which would meet and select a slate of candidates. More important, the convention would lay plans for the adoption of the slate by the Democratic state convention.

On Saturday, March 1, 1890, the farmers of Sumter County met at the courthouse. Although many were suspicious of Tillman's plans, all the speakers agreed that redress must be sought only within the Democratic party, and the following delegates were elected: J. J. Dargan, J. H. Wilson, E. M. Cooper, R. M. Wilson, W. A. James, Jr., H. G. Shaw, O. C. Scarborough, H. R. Thomas, D. E. Keels, and John Singleton.

Most of the Sumter delegates were known to oppose Tillman vigorously, but they were seated when the Convention met. Despite the expressions of party loyalty in the Shell Manifesto, many delegates were opposed to the idea of making nominations outside of a party convention, realizing a break in party solidarity might bring back into power the organized Negro majority. So many anti-Tillman delegates were seated, that when the vote to "suggest" candidates was taken, there were 117 against and 116 for. But the Tillmanites were equal to this unexpected result. While the chairman withheld announcement of the vote, John L. Manning Irby managed to get enough votes changed to announce a few minutes later a victory for Tillman. Headed by Tillman for governor, a full ticket of generally respected men was named to run on his platform, including J. E. Tindal, who owned a large plantation near Pinewood, for secretary of state. In his speech of acceptance, Tillman was quoted as saying, "you will have at your head *the only man* who has the brain and the nerve and the ability to organize the common people against the aristocracy."

The county-to-county canvass got under way in May 1890, with barbecues, flower-decked rostrums, and Tillman, the "One-Eyed Plowboy" seated in a farm wagon drawn by the "wool hat and one-gallus boys."

In June, Joseph H. Earle announced he would be a candidate for governor, and was endorsed by the citizens of Sumter County generally, with the exception of H. R. Thomas and John J. Dargan. General John Bratton was another Conservative candidate. The campaign grew in ferocity with each passing day. At Laurens, Earle and Bratton were howled down without a hearing. At Aiken, Senator Hampton himself was forced to sit down. At Winnsboro there was near-violence, and Tillman was howled down. But all the while the Tillman forces were gathering strength. The noisy crowds paid little heed to issues, but roared their enjoyment of Tillman's coarse ridicule of his opponents. Sumter, however, remained one of the few counties in the state where Tillmanites did not obtain control of the local party organization.

When the state Democratic Convention met in August to formulate party rules, the only anti-Tillman delegations were those from Sumter, Beaufort, Richland and Charleston. Outnumbered, they withdrew. The Tillmanites created a new executive committee, supplanting old leaders with men from their own ranks.

When the nominating state Convention met in September, the contested delegations from Sumter and Fairfield were not seated, and Tillman and his ticken were nominated. The indignant Conservative minority refused to recognize the legality of the Convention, and called a "Straightout" Convention to meet in October. The address of the Straightouts to the democracy of South Carolina gave the reasons for the withdrawal, and was signed for Sumter by J. D. Blanding, J. D. Graham, W. D. Scarborough, John S. Hughson, and Frank Mellett.

To the Straightout Convention in October, Sumter elected as delegates J. D. Blanding, John Singleton, and Ellison D. Smith, but Smith did not go. A full Straightout ticket was nominated, headed by Alexander C. Haskell, a distinguished Confederate veteran, banker, and lawyer, whose sincere religious convictions had been shocked by the profane Tillman. The Straightouts became known as Haskellites for their leader, whose manifesto had declared: "Legally, I should not vote for Mr. Tillman. From self-respect I will not vote for him. Morally, I cannot vote for him." The Convention concluded its work with a published address which solemnly alleged that "B. R. Tillman and his associates ... have done more harm and brought greater sorrow on the State than the sword or fire or the hand of man in any shape has ever before effected."

Although Tillman was not the choice of the conservative Democrats, many of them felt bound to support him as the choice of the majority. Even Senator Hampton signified that he would vote for Tillman.

Returns from the November elections gave Tillman nearly 60,000 votes to Haskell's less than 15,000. In Sumter County the final tally was 882 for Tillman and 751 for Haskell. The Tillmanites threw out the box from Rafting Creek, and thus unseated all the representatives from Sumter County except Altamont Moses, whose majority was too large to be manipulated. For the state Senate, a long drawn-out legal battle ensued between W. D. Scarborough and Dr. Henry T. Abbott, which finally was ended by the Tillmanite Senate seating Dr. Abbott.

With the close of Governor John Peter Richardson's second administration, he went out of office as the last of the antebellum ruling class, and the government of South Carolina passed into control of the Tillman dictatorship.

CHAPTER XXVII

THE TILLMAN DICTATORSHIP

Ben Tillman, boss of his triumphant faction, on December 4, 1890, was sworn in as governor. Although his inaugural demanded that Negroes be segregated, and that a constitutional convention be called to disfranchise them, he asked for authority to remove sheriffs who failed to protect prisoners from lynchers. He recommended reforms in taxation, remedies for educational "retrogression," the abolition of useless offices, and improvements in the administration of state institutions; and he voiced an "imperative need for an industrial school for girls."

Tillman worked hard to put through his program, and in legislative halls he became known as "the boss downstairs." But enactment of his suggestions did not always bring the best results. When the legislators doubled the state's royalties on phosphate mining, that already enfeebled industry went into bankruptcy. When the legislature reorganized the state University as the South Carolina College, transferred the agricultural and mechanical departments with their appropriations, and cut the teaching staff in half, the institution all but perished. He won applause, however, when provisions were made for removing the Winthrop Training School, founded in 1886, from Columbia to Rock Hill, to become the state "Industrial and Winthrop Normal College" for young women. Many have questioned, however, whether it might better have remained in Columbia as the woman's college of the University.

No corruption was found in the state government as administered by the Bourbons. Nor was the reform Governor able to reduce state expenses, which Hampton and his successors had so carefully held to about half those of the Republicans. Perhaps the greatest disillusionment came to Tillman's admirers when he accepted a free pass from the railroads, a current practice among officials which he had attacked savagely in his campaign.

The greed of the Tillmanites for public office far exceeded that of the "broken-down aristocrats" whom Tillman had criticized on that score. Although none of the "common people" were honored with office, the lawyers and other professional men of his faction scrambled for places, as a Tillmanite said, like "ravenous lions over the carcass of a zebra." John L. Manning Irby became speaker of the House, and when the election was held by the legislature for United States Senator, he replaced Wade Hampton. For refusing to vote against Hampton in the caucus, Frank Mellett and A. K. Sanders, long the honored representatives from Sumter, lost their seats in the House. Nepotism was rife and shameless. Five relatives of Mart Gary secured positions. Even the most insignificant clerks of the old regime were turned out in favor of loyal Tillmanites.

Henry Ragin Thomas of Wedgefield was telegraphed for by Tillman and given a place on the Railroad Commission. While he was in Columbia, Thomas was credited with having obtained a place on the Sinking Fund Commission for his friend, J. M. Cooper, with a salary and a travel allowance. In the recent election, Cooper had been a candidate on the Tillman ticket for county school commissioner.

After two sessions, however, the legislature had not called a constitutional convention, nor had it enacted many other favored items of the Tillman program, though it had passed an act to prohibit public officials from accepting free passes. Tillman's bullying tactics had antagonized some of his friends, and he had done nothing to win recruits from the "curs" of the Haskell faction. But the "common people" still idolized him, and he knew it. When, at the close of 1891, he announced his candidacy for reelection, he demanded that they rid him of the "dead driftwood" legislature, and elect one that would do his will.

Meanwhile, Joseph H. Earle, whose Sumter home burned in 1889, had removed to Greenville in 1891, and was practicing law. Realizing that the hold of Tillman upon the farmers was as strong as ever, Earle advised the Conservatives not to nominate a candidate: "Give me a Tillman a thousand times before a Scott or a Moses. When the Convention meets let him be nominated .... let him be elected without opposition so far as any Democrat is concerned." Many people took this to mean that Earle had made his peace with Tillman. "Col. Earle's former political friends," said the *Watchman and Southron,* "are greatly disgusted—disgust hardly expresses the feeling."

In Sumter County the people were still divided into two bitter factions, the county Executive Committee of the Tillmanites being the one that was recognized by the state Executive Committee. When the time came to reorganize the party clubs, W. F. B. Haynsworth issued a call to both factions for a mass meeting to devise a plan for amicable settlement. "I make this call," he said, "in the interest of neither faction." H. R. Thomas opposed the mass meeting: "Neither Mr. Keels nor myself," said he, "care for the (party) offices and I propose to step down after reorganization and use my influence for a conservative man like Mr. Haynsworth." Despite his opposition, the mass meeting was held, and it elected as delegates to the state convention: W. F. B. Haynsworth, Altamont Moses, Edwin W. Moise, W. H. Commander, R. I. Manning, Joseph C. Scott, N. S. McLeod, Frank Mellett, W. D. Scarborough, F. J. Mayes, B. F. Jones, and J. M. Ross. Apparently it was not a mass meeting of Tillmanites.

The Conservatives' "Peace and Harmony" Convention met in Columbia in March 1892, with 272 delegates, and nominated ex-Governor Sheppard to head the ticket, with James L. Orr, law-partner of Joseph H. Earle, in second place, and L. W. Youmans for secretary of state. In every county the Conservatives built strong organizations.

The campaign opened in Greenville in April, with yells and counter-yells, which consumed much time; and more time had to be spent in "dislodging Citizen Josh Ashley and other noisy Tillmanites from the roof of the speakers' stand." As Tillman had accepted the entire program of the Farmers' Alliance for his platform, he enjoyed in return the effective support of that organization.

The Conservative candidates, said Editor Osteen of the *Watchman and Southron,* "are leaving out vituperation, demagogical appeals to class prejudice, and unfounded charges, which are the weapons of Tillman and crew. They are using the record of the Administration during the past two years, and it is a record that even Tillman is ashamed of, for he blames the Legislature . . . for all the blunders, all the failures, all the unredeemed pledges . . . The Legislature is the scapegoat."

The county-to-county canvass reached Sumter on June 20. As many of the preceding meetings had been near-riots, the town took precautions. Business places and saloons were closed, special police were appointed, and every political club delegated at least one man to help keep order.

General Edwin W. Moise, Democratic candidate for Congress, spoke first, introduced by Chairman Keels, although the General needed no introduction to the people of Sumter. To oppose him, the Republicans later in the summer nominated George Washington Murray, the Negro landowner of Rafting Creek, who at that time was serving as inspector of customs in Charleston. The Congressional race, therefore, was the one in which the people of Sumter came to be the most deeply concerned.

Introduced by R. M. Wilson, Governor Tillman spoke next, and received some cheers, but a hand-primary showed that only a fourth of the audience were for him.

In August a speaker before the Darlington County Alliance declared that the newspaper press in the state was being bribed by the Tillman administration for its influence in the campaign. The *Watchman and Southron* confirmed this accusation. Recalling the days of Reconstruction, when the Columbia Ring had tried to bribe the *True Southron* with an offer of three times its value to keep silent for a year, the editor said: "Within the past year this paper has been approached more than once by members of the present dominant element with offers of material and substantial support, if, in return, this paper would discontinue its active opposition to Tillmanism. They did not stipulate that Tillman should be supported or defended. We rejected, as the course of this paper testifies, the proposition with as great decision and promptness as the proposition of the Radicals in 1873 . . . It is such things that give us grounds for opposition to Tillmanism, and an abiding contempt for its leaders."[1]

James E. Tindal of Pinewood, secretary of state in the Tillman administration, was campaigning for reelection on his past record as a Confederate soldier and a good Democrat during Reconstruction, notably in the campaign of 1876. Tindal really was a superior candidate. A graduate of Furman before the war, he had continued his studies at the University of Bonn in Germany, until South Carolina left the Union. He then came home, enlisted, and served the Confederacy until the surrender at Appomattox, having been wounded more than once. But there were rumors that Mr. Tindal had consorted with Negroes and Republicans during Reconstruction. *The Watchman and Southron* investigated, and received a letter saying, "What you have heard is strictly true ... When E. W. M. Mackey of the Mackey House was billed for his Clarendon crusade, Mr. Tindal .... *entertained him at his own house.*" This letter was published by the newspaper, and other letters to similar effect. What made the accusation so devastating to Tindal was that Mackey had married Victoria Sumter, a pretty, well-educated octoroon, whom the Sumter family had reared as a lady's maid.[2]

In justice to Tindal, the *Watchman and Southron* published his defense: "As to giving a night's lodging to Mackey, I did, and would do it again under the circumstances .... Our County then had no railroads or hotels, and I was brought up ... to entertain strangers, to give hospitality, to give food and shelter even to one's enemy."[3]

But the Tillmanites and Conservatives alike could not tolerate the idea of a candidate who had entertained in his home "the most noted miscegenator of the South", and Tindal was not elected.

A note of humor brightened and relieved the grim bitterness of the campaign during that summer. Merrick Reid, who was seeking nomination as county commissioner, in his speech at Privateer, took the word *ability* for his text, and then

---
[1] *Watchman and Southron*, Aug. 10, 1892.
[2] *Ibid.*, May 4, 1892; Emma E. Holmes to Mrs. T. Sumter Means, Draper MSS, 18VV4, Wisconsin Historical Society.
[3] *Watchman and Southron*, May 11, 1892.

adopted it as his campaign slogan. He promised to plank all the sandy roads to the best of his ability; to trestle and bridge all quagmires to the best of his ability; to grade the hills to the best of his ability; and to see that a steady stream of money should be flowing through the county treasury to the best of his ability. Reid was well known as a humorist to readers of the newspapers, where his letters appeared over the signature "Gov." No one took his campaign seriously, and after the election, "The Defeated Philosopher" came out in a long letter: "To the people of Sumter County we'd say that we regret they have lost our valuable services, for we should certainly have served them 'to the best of our ability'."

The census of 1890 had credited Sumter County with 2730 white voters. Official returns after the first primary in 1892 gave the Conservatives 1345 votes and the Tillmanites 1261. In the state, Tillman defeated the Conservatives by 22,000 votes, and the "driftwood" legislature was replaced by obedient Tillmanites. Due to the Negro vote, the congressional race between General Moise and George Washington Murray was close, and although returns from November elections announced the election of General Moise, the state Board of Canvassers gave the certificate of election to Murray. As loyal Tillmanites, members of the Board preferred a Negro to a Conservative. Everyone knew that if the General contested the election in Washington, the Republican Congress would seat the Republican candidate. In December the General announced that he would not contest the election; and the following March, Murray took his seat in Congress. Five of the seven Congressmen elected from the state were Tillmanites. George Tillman, the Governor's elder brother, after long service in Congress, was defeated because he refused to accept the program of the Alliance. He was succeeded by W. Jasper Talbert of Edgefield, who had been chairman of the March Convention of 1890, which had placed Ben Tillman's name at the head of the farmers' ticket.

During his second term as governor, Tillman reversed his stand against lynching, and that crime increased from five in his first term to thirteen in his second. His program in general fared well. The new legislature provided for a referendum on calling a constitutional convention. A Railroad Commission with rate-fixing and other powers, was created. Labor in cotton mills was limited to sixty-four hours a week. The state debt was refunded at a lower rate of interest. The governor's salary of $3,500 was cut by $500, and with comparable reductions for other salaries, a saving of $7,000 was effected.

The most spectacular achievement, however, was the establishment of the state Dispensary, a public monopoly of the alcoholic liquor trade, on a plan patterned after a modification of the Swedish system, which was then being tried in Athens, Georgia.

Although during the campaign of 1892, none of the candidates had raised the liquor question, separate ballot boxes were provided in the August primary for those who wished to vote on state prohibition. The resulting vote showed that 68,515 ballots out of 88,474, were cast on the issue, with a majority of almost 10,000 favoring prohibition.

In the closing days of the legislative session of 1892, the Senate was in the process of passing a House-approved bill for prohibition, when a new bill providing for a state dispensary arrived from Tillman, with orders for immediate enactment. As there was no time for debate, to avoid the necessity for three readings of the bill on three separate days, the new bill was hastily passed as an amendment to the prohibition bill, and in effect virtually superseded it. A few minutes before adjournment on December 24, 1892, the House accepted the amendment, almost without consideration.

On Christmas morning 1892, the people of South Carolina read with astonishment the news that they were committed to an experiment in state socialism. Tillman called the dispensary a compromise between the whiskey traffic and prohibition, and like many compromises, it satisfied no one—except Tillman.

To operate the new system, Tillman appointed a commissioner who would act under a state Board of Control consisting of the governor, the comptroller-general, and the attorney-general. This state Board appointed the county Boards of Control, which in turn appointed a dispenser, who would operate at the county seat, a dispensary for the retail sale of alcoholic liquors. Columbia, however, was to have three dispensaries, and Charleston, ten. Towns other than county seats might have a dispensary on petition of a majority of the town's freeholders and approval of the county Board of Control.

Profits from the wholesale business of the state Dispensary were to go into the state treasury. Profits from the retail sales of local dispensaries were to be shared equally by the respective counties and municipalities.

Enforcement of the new law was to be in the hands of a state constabulary directly under the control of the governor, and this was perhaps the most unpopular feature of the entire plan, as events would soon show. The dispensary law was to go in to effect on July 1, 1893.

All through the month of June, in anticipation of the closing of the saloons, people were purchasing large quantities of alcoholic liquors. On the last two days of the month, the town of Sumter was as crowded with visitors as during a week before Christmas. Negroes swarmed in from the country with eggs, fruit and chickens to sell, and the saloons did a land-office business. On the evening of the last day of June, E. P. Ricker & Co. had sold out and closed up before six o'clock. Weinberg & Co. on Liberty Street closed soon after; Strauss & Co. shut their doors at nine o'clock, and Dave Morris an hour later, with a small stock left.

Although there was comparatively little disturbance, towards midnight some citizens were holding to lamp-posts; and one was seen embracing the barber pole in front of Julius Edwards' shop. At midnight only three saloons were still open, Gallagher Brothers, with a small stock; O'Donnell's, and Manheim's, both with considerable amounts. The Sumter Negro band serenaded the new era of the state Dispensary with a few tunes, and thus the old order of open saloons ended in Sumter.

Six days later, the *Watchman and Southron* commented that more liquor was in private homes, and more had been consumed each day under the new law, "than any time since there had been a Sumter County."

A county dispensary did not immediately open in Sumter, because the county Board of Control, E. M. Pitts, R. M. Wilson, and R. A. Frierson, did not at once decide to give the position of dispenser to W. H. Epperson, a respected man experienced in such business, whose petition for the job had 182 signatures, to 151 of Pete Thomas, the other applicant. Eventually, Epperson was appointed, and on July 8, the dispensary was opened in the Masonic Temple store, next door to the office of the *Watchman and Southron*.

Opinions on the dispensary varied among the temperance organizations of the day. The Good Templars of Sumter debated the resolution that "South Carolina knows her first disgrace in having her emblem, the palmetto tree, blown into the whiskey bottle," but apparently the resolution was not approved. The Woman's Christian Temperance Union favored the dispensary, in the main, as an approach to prohibition. One feature of the unpopular law won favorable comment in many quarters, namely, that freeholders of towns had local option on whether or not a dispensary would be established.

At Mayesville, E. D. Smith applied for the position of dispenser, but Dr. F. J. Mayes challenged three of the nineteen signatures on Smith's petition, one citizen withdrew his signature, and Smith's majority disappeared. The matter was postponed.

In August 1893, on affidavit of E. M. Pitts, chairman of the Sumter Board of Control, state constables raided Dave Morris' storeroom at the rear of the courthouse, and arrested Morris. As his stock was not on sale, citizens showed such indignation that Tillman's "spy", T. J. Jones, fled back to Columbia. Holloway, his companion, when boarding the train, was pelted with rotten eggs.

Some of the unpopularity of the dispensary was due to the methods which Tillman used for enforcement of the law. His constables were secret agents, not infrequently operating in disguise. Some posed as tourists; others, with blackened faces, as Negroes; a few really were Negroes. In some places, Tillman appointed local constables who were paid on a fee basis, from 25c a gallon for small captures of contraband, to $50 for a wagonload; and from $10 to $25 for evidence leading to a conviction. Search warrants served by the constables added to popular fury against them. Never before had the citizens of South Carolina been spied upon by their own state government, and many otherwise law-abiding citizens came to feel that defiance of the obnoxious law and its representatives, was a virtue. Illegal whiskey shops called "blind tigers" were soon flourishing, and in some places there was disorder culminating in fatalities.

The most spectacular of these clashes came in the spring of 1894, when a state constable at Darlington informed the governor that violations of the law were flagrant, and asked for aid. Three men were sent, and the four constables then began to serve search warrants on suspected places. Rumors soon spread that private homes would be searched, and armed men began to patrol the streets, with the avowed purpose of resisting any attempt to search residences. On Wednesday afternoon, March 28, the Darlington dispenser in alarm wired Tillman: "Constables raid. Armed men walking the streets swearing they will shoot." Another alarming telegram followed. These stirred Tillman to wire the Darlington Sheriff to preserve the peace; and to order Captain Henry T. Thompson of the Darlington Guards to place his company under orders of the sheriff.

The news of these orders added fuel to the flames. Angry citizens rushed the armory and seized the Guards' rifles, but upon Captain Thompson's immediate demand, they promptly returned the weapons. More telegrams flashed back and forth between Darlington and Columbia without clearing the situation. Tillman, convinced that a "Whiskey Rebellion" had begun, ordered a special train to carry the Sumter Light Infantry to Darlington, and telegraphed Captain Aaron Phelps: "Can your company be relied upon to uphold the law? A mob has taken possession of Darlington." The captain replied: "The Sumter Light Infantry will uphold the law." The wildest rumors immediately circulated in Sumter and throughout the state. Newspaper men and others went on the special train with the Sumter company. On the afternoon of Thursday, March 29, when they arrived in Darlington, the Light Infantry was met by the Darlington Guards, was hospitably received by the citizens, and spent a quiet night at the armory. On Friday morning, the governor, having learned that the situation was not serious, ordered the Sumter Light Infantry home.

Meanwhile, Chief Constable Gaillard and eighteen state constables had reached Darlington. Under orders of the governor, Captain Thompson swore out warrants for arrest of the men who had seized the rifles from the armory, including a warrant for his own brother. All submitted quietly to arrest. The Mayor of Darlington, hoping to avert further trouble, ordered the chief of police to accompany the chief constable on the last raid. In the afternoon, their work done, most of the constables were at the Cheraw and Darlington depot, waiting for the delayed train to arrive. On the other side of town, Chief Gaillard, three other constables, and Captain Thompson, were at the Charleston, Sumter and Northern station awaiting the outbound train.

While the constables were awaiting the overdue train at the Cheraw and Darlington station, quite a crowd had gathered around the depot, and although some of the bystanders were armed, they did nothing worse than heckle the departing officers. Had the train been on time, the Darlington raids might have been a closed incident. Unfortunately, as the long delay lengthened, two young men, with opposing views of the officers, got into a fight and were separated by the chief of police. One of them accused a constable of having helped his assailant. Frank Norment, an onlooker, is said to have cursed the constable, and although witnesses here differ in details of the affair, the fact is that Constable McLendon shot down Norment, and a general shooting ensued.

When it was over, Constable Pepper and two citizens were dead, McLendon was critically wounded, and Chief of Police Dargan and several citizens and constables had less serious injuries.

The infuriated crowd at once scattered to get arms and recruits. The constables, finding that McLendon was too gravely hurt to be moved, fled down the tracks and scattered into the woods and swamps. Telegrams carried the flaming news to all parts of the country.

Meanwhile, Chief Gaillard and his three companions had left Darlington on the train from the other depot, but at the nearby crossing of the two railroads, their train was riddled by a volley from the mob which had formed there to intercept the fugitives. When the party reached Sumter, there was a long wait for a connecting train. A Sumter citizen who happened to be on the train, invited one of the constables to go home with him for supper. When this hospitality became known, as it soon did, some of Sumter's wildly excited citizens held a mass meeting and made ready to deal severely with their townsman. As they moved in on him, he gave the Masonic signal of distress, and at once the Masons in the crowd surrounded him and quelled the mob.[4]

Tillman, in the meantime, had declared Darlington and Florence in a state of insurrection, and had seized the railroad and telegraph offices. Commandeering a train, he ordered three companies of Columbia militia and the entire Charleston brigade to Darlington. The Columbia companies refused to go, and Charleston brigade telegraphed: "The brigade will uphold and defend the honor of the state, but it will not lend itself to foment civil war among our brethren."

The governor's order to the Sumter Light Infantry to return to Darlington met with an inexplicable response. Members of the company met in their armory, and Captain Phelps then went down the lines advising each man to vote not to obey the order. The men unanimously voted not to go. The captain then met the special train from Columbia to Darlington, and reported himself for duty to Adjutant-General Farley, with the statement that his men had refused to go.[5] Editorial comment in Sumter supported the company's action.

By Saturday afternoon, companies of loyal militia from the Tillmanite counties began pouring into Columbia, and on Sunday, Tillman ordered to Darlington most of the twenty-seven

---

[4] H. G. Osteen, who was then reporting developments as they occurred.

[5] *Ibid.* The Sumter Light Infantry was disbanded by Governor Tillman's order, but was reorganized and served in the Spanish American War as a unit of the First South Carolina Regiment at Chicamagua, Tenn., and at Jacksonville, Fla., but did not go to Cuba. The officers were, L. S. Carson, captain; D. Harby Moses, first lieutenant; and Brainard D. Wilson, second lieutenant. At the close of hostilities in Cuba, Captain Carson was transferred to the regular army, serving in the Philippines and elsewhere until retired with the rank of colonel. The company also served in World War I, as part of the South Carolina National Guard in the Thirtieth Division, A.E.F., which won distinction in the heaviest fighting in northern France, breaking the Hindenburg Line. H. G. Osteen.

companies then at his disposal. As the train passed through Florence, the troops were jeered by an angry crowd, but when they reached Darlington, they are said to have been welcomed by the weary Darlington Guards and the anxious citizens, who dreaded any further violence.

Eventually, all of the fugitive constables straggled back to safety, and after a week of high tension, order was restored. Tillman dismissed a Columbia militia company from service, and ordered investigations, but although some trials were held, no one was punished. Thus ended the bloodiest chapter in the history of the state Dispensary.[6]

Tillman's admirers were delighted with his handling of the Dispensary War, as they called it, and the outcome apparently had little effect upon the political campaign of that year.

In June 1894, James E. Tindal of Pinewood, announced his candidacy for the governorship, upon Reform principles he had advocated for eight years. But he was too dignified and scholarly for the Reformers, and they did not support him. Of the other candidates, Tillman claimed neutrality between the favorites, William H. Ellerbe, a farmer, and John Gary Evans, a young lawyer of good family, and an effective speaker on Tillmanism, who had championed the dispensary.

Like most of the Conservative press, the *Watchman and Southron* refused to support a Conservative state ticket which was certain to be defeated, but it favored nominating a Conservative county ticket which could be elected. In the Democratic primary on August 28, the Sumter Conservatives successfully nominated a practically complete county ticket, including Altamont Moses as state senator; R. I. Manning, Frank Mellett, J. H. Wilson, A. K. Sanders, and C. L. Williamson for the House, and J. William Stokes for Congress. Gratified at this result, the editor announced "Our fight was finished on August 28."

With the aid of United States Senator Irby, John Gary Evans was nominated to succeed Tillman, and, unopposed by a

---

[6] For the Dispensary, see Wallace, *History of S. C.* III, 358-366,423; Simkins *Pitchfork Ben*, pp. 234-261; and John Evans Eubanks, *Ben Tillman's Baby: The Dispensary System of South Carolina* (privately printed, Augusta, 1951).

Conservative candidate, was elected governor. He was duly inaugurated in December, and, as was expected by everyone, the Tillmanite legislature promptly replaced General M. C. Butler of Edgefield by electing Tillman to his seat in the United States Senate. The Sumter delegation, with the exception of C. L. Williamson, voted for Butler.

Chapter XXVIII

BEN TILLMAN'S CONSTITUTION

After seven years of agitation for a new state constitution to disfranchise the Negro, Governor Tillman had finally forced through the legislature in 1892, a joint resolution for a referendum on the question of calling a constitutional convention.

The Conservatives opposed the convention for many reasons, some of which were factional, but others were sound and could not be refuted. The *Watchman and Southron*, pointing out that a constitution should be "the work of representatives of the whole people and not of a faction filled with rancour and hatred," opposed the timing of the call: "a Constitution should not be adopted while hate and partisanship are in the ascendency." Further, the editor argued, there was no valid reason for holding a convention: the pretense of eliminating the Negro vote without disfranchising any white man, was "based on a lie," because the federal constitution protects the Negro from discrimination. The fact also that Tillman, fearing the combined opposition of both Negroes and Conservatives, had decided to adopt the new constitution without ratification by the people, was "an outrageous assumption of power which the people should deny to any body of men." Finally, warned the editor solemnly, "The effects of a mistake in the selection of public officials are serious enough, but not permanent," whereas the constitutional convention "is absolutely supreme. It can adopt anything it may desire . . . and so frame it that it will be well-nigh impossible to undo the evil work. The results of a mistake . . . will be . . . as far as many of us are concerned, permanent."[1]

In the general election of 1894, returns from twelve of the fifteen precincts in Sumter County showed 879 votes against the convention, and only 437 for it. In the state at large, the vote was favorable, but by so narrow a margin, that a shift of less than a thousand votes would have reversed the result.

---

[1] *Watchman and Southron*, Oct. 31, 1894.

In preparation for the election of delegates to the convention, the legislature immediately enacted provisions which made registration by Negroes so difficult as to be all but impossible. In addition, Tillman even issued orders not to issue registration blanks to Negro applicants. As a result, only 10,000 Negroes succeeded in qualifying, and a Republican declared that "after unparalleled exposure, suffering and sacrifice," 100,000 Negroes remained unregistered.[2]

The Negroes had little or no leadership to oppose these tactics. In June 1895, John J. Dargan of Sumter went to Edgefield to try to organize them, but why he should have chosen Tillman's home county for this venture, is not clear. He was met by an Edgefield mob who told him, "We have got the Negro down, and by God, we are going to keep him down." When Dargan made an effort to speak, he was cursed and driven away with the ominous threat that if he resented the curses, the mob would cut out his "damned heart."[3]

As late as July, nothing was known by the people of the state concerning the issues to be settled at the constitutional convention, except that suffrage would be so regulated as to disfranchise as many Negroes as possible without disfranchising any white man. Woman suffrage was discussed by the Tillmanite leaders, who considered a plan for a property qualification of $200 for all white women; but this would have given urban women great power without doing anything for the majority of rural women. On the other hand, an educational qualification for all women would have enfranchised 40,000 or more new voters, but this was dismissed as "a dangerous experiment."

At a meeting in July at Hunter's Ferry in Barnwell, Tillman explained his position on Woman suffrage and Negro suffrage, both being closely associated in the male mind. After disposing of the 15th amendment to the federal constitution as an insuperable bar to any permanent plan for Negro disfranchisement, Tillman admitted that the effectiveness of his scheme for limiting Negro suffrage would depend upon white unity, and a discriminatory administration. "The Mississippi

[2] Simkins, *Pitchfork Ben*, pp. 289-290.
[3] *Ibid.*, p. 291.

constitution," he said, "provides that every voter must be registered and that the applicant must be able to read a clause in the constitution or be able to understand and explain it when read. The right to judge of the latter rests with the supervisors of registration . . . it is easy to see that the Negro could not understand, while the white man would . . . . Couple a provision forbidding registration after conviction for crime, and require the applicant to be also possessed of a good moral character, and you can see how many thousands of negroes will be disfranchised without fraud or without infringing on the 15th amendment."

If this scheme were not adopted, Tillman continued, "there is nothing else to do but have qualified women's suffrage and hide behind petticoats. I am perfectly willing to give the women of South Carolina the right to vote when they ask for it, but I don't believe they want it, and until they do ask for it, I prefer the other plan."

The number of delegates to the constitutional convention was to be the same as the number of members in the General Assembly. Tillman, perhaps realizing the need for the support of the Conservatives, agreed that an equal number of delegates should be elected from each faction. As the Tillmanites were in power, they saw no logic in this proposal, and Tillman repudiated it. Sumter County, however, put it into effect. At an all-day meeting in July at Armory Hall in the Sumter Masonic Temple, the Reformers agreed to work out with the Conservatives, who were also in session, a joint slate of six delegates, with three men from each faction. The Reformers, however, insisted that the slate should be voted upon in the primary. Colonel James D. Blanding promptly introduced a resolution not to submit Conservative chances to a "mongrel primary," because voters in that primary would be pledged to support "whatever undemocratic principles, Populistic schemes, fraudulent election devices, and suppression of higher education" might be incorporated into the new constitution. His resolution was approved.[4]

But before the midday recess, a committee of five was ap-

[4] *Watchman and Southron*, July 31, 1895.

pointed to confer with the Reformers and work out terms for an agreement. The Colonel, who saw no reason to compromise, became so irritated that he resigned his seat and went home. Near the end of the all-day session, the slate was agreed upon: *Conservatives*, R. D. Lee, lawyer of Sumter; J. H. Scarborough, farmer, near Bishopville; Thomas Boone Fraser, lawyer of Sumter. *Reformers*, G. P. McKagen, pharmacist of Sumter; Shepard Nash, clerk of court and farmer of Sumter; R. P. Stackhouse, farmer of Oswego. These were to be chosen in the general election for all delegates on August 20, 1895.

The extreme Tillman faction of Sumter County refused to support this ticket, however, and entered their own slate, which included D. E. Keels of Lynchburg and L. D. Jennings of Sumter. But the coalition ticket was elected.*

Of the total number of Convention delegates, 43 were Conservatives and 113 were Tillman's Reformers. Beaufort County elected an all-Negro delegation of five Republicans: former Congressman Robert Smalls; W. J. Whipper, whose election as judge in 1875 had helped to precipitate the Red Shirt Campaign; Thomas E. Miller, a pale mulatto lawyer and educator known as "Canary" because of his color; James Wigg, a merchant; and I. R. Reed, an attorney at law. From Georgetown came two white delegates, I. Harlston Read and E. F. Mathews; and one Negro, R. B. Anderson, a teacher. Conspicuous among the Conservatives was Ben Tillman's brother George, who in 1890 had broken with Ben when that leader endorsed Populism. Other prominent Conservatives were George Johnstone of Newberry, Theodore G. Barker of Charleston, John C. Sheppard of Edgefield, and D. S. Henderson of Aiken. The leading Reformers were the two United States senators, Tillman and Irby, and Governor John Gary Evans. There was no objection to dual office-holding in this Convention!

When the Convention met in Columbia at noon on September 10, 1895, Governor Evans was elected president. In his address to the Convention, he called attention to the governor's complete lack of constitutional powers to enforce the laws: "If we are to have a chief," said President Evans,

* H. G. Osteen.

"make him such; if a subordinate, define his province." He also urged that judges be elected by the people; and he pointed out that the legislature was "handicapped and burdened with the election of a multiplicity of officers."[5] Most of his suggestions were ignored.

Robert Aldrich of Barnwell introduced a draft of a constitution, which he moved should be printed and referred to appropriate committees. This was tabled, but his draft was referred to the Committee on the Judicial Department with instructions to refer various sections to the proper committees.

Although "the greatest resources of legal ability" have been conceded to the Conservatives, the leader of the Convention was Ben Tillman. He did not bring a draft of his constitution, but contented himself with the chairmanship of the Committee on Suffrage, for, said he, the disfranchisement of the Negro, was "the sole cause of our being here." Feeling the need for legal talent, he associated with himself on the Committee J. P. Kennedy Bryan of Charleston, who is credited with having drafted the provisions of the suffrage article so skillfully that they never have been nullified by the federal courts.

The Sumter delegates were assigned to the following committees: J. H. Scarborough, Committee on the Executive; R. D. Lee, Committee on Jurisprudence; G. P. McKagen, Committee on Eminent Domain; R. P. Stackhouse, Committee on Impeachment and Committee on Counties and County Government; Shepard Nash, Committee on Charitable and Penal Institutions; T. B. Fraser, Committee on Order, Style and Revision.

At the second day's session, the delegates fixed their compensation at two dollars a day and five cents a mile each way, coming and going. The record of this Convention for low cost, over-time work, and brevity of duration, has seldom if ever been surpassed.

A few petitions came to the Convention asking for improvement in the legal status of women. Senator Tillman himself

---

[5] *Journal of the Constitutional Convention of the State of South Carolina* (Columbia, 1895). This *Journal* and the Constitution itself, are the basic sources. An invaluable analysis and commentary is D. D. Wallace, *The South Carolina Constitution of 1895* (Columbia, 1927).

presented the memorial of Cora S. Lott of Johnston, who said: "Let our men give us the franchise, and the moral influence exerted by women will be the needful leaven which will permeate and make palatable what we now find a heavy loaf." Mrs. Sallie F. Chapin of Charleston, president of the Women's Christian Temperance Union, signed a petition, which, pointing out that "protection of the person of our women is not placed upon as high a plane as protection of their purse," asked that the age of consent be raised from ten years to eighteen.[6]

Tillman's plans for taking away suffrage from Negroes had been given wide publicity, and caused much anxiety among their leaders. On September 23, Thomas E. Miller of Beaufort presented to the Convention a petition from twenty Negro citizens of Sumter, protesting Tillman's suffrage plans: "the ballot," they said, "honestly regulated, is the safeguard of our American institutions." They urged that the words "who can read and explain the same (constitution) satisfactorily when read to him (an illiterate)," should be deleted, because for a "perhaps partisan" board of registration, such discretionary power would throw wide open "the floodgates of party discrimination, fraud and corruption." The petitioners asked that suffrage regulations be made "uniform, impartial, fair, and of an unchangeable and unequivocal standard."[7]

Signed by William T. Andrews, (a teacher who later edited and published the Negro newspaper, *The Defender*), William T. Smith, M. D., and eighteen other Negroes, the petition was referred to the Committee on Municipal Corporations and Police Regulations, who recommended that it be received as information. Although the word "satisfactorily" was deleted, the power of discrimination has been flagrantly exercised by Boards of Registration in favor of illiterate whites.

When the debates began on the floor of the Convention, the Negro delegates pleaded for fairness in applying the educational test for suffrage. They argued aloquently for giving to qualified Negroes a political voice. W. J. Whipper, who was conceded by Tillman to be "the ablest colored man" he had ever known, pleaded the Negroes' cause with such force and

[7] *Ibid.*, Sept. 23.
[6] *Journal of Convention*, Sept. 27, 19, 1895.

logic that the *Watchman and Southron* admitted he had the best of the argument. "It was the brawny arm of the negro," said Whipper, "that has cared for you in the cradle, made your harvests, protected you in your homes, and yet this is the man you propose to rob of his right to vote." He offered in place of Tillman's intricate scheme a simple educational and property test, and begged for standards other than the mere color of skin. His substitute received only the six Negro votes. Convention members listened to the logical pleas, but Conservatives and Tillmanites alike backed Tillman's plan. The argument which has rationalized their stand down to the present time, is that literate Negroes, voting as a racial bloc, would hold the balance of power between white factions, which would bid against each other for Negro support.

With the article on suffrage taken care of, Tillman's anti-Negro constitution needed other racial discriminations which would bypass the 15th amendment. So he provided that there should be separate schools for the races, without any requirement for compulsory attendance, or that school officials should impartially apportion school funds between the two systems. Tillman wanted the schools to exist for white children; in 1899 the Negro schools were receiving less than a third of the state's school money; a generation later, the share had shrunk to one tenth. Tillman did not foresee that in 1951, the state would be penalized for his unjust plans, which would bring down upon its people a $75,000,000 bond issue to build Negro schools, and a three per cent general sales tax upon food and the necessities of life, in the name of Negro education.

Another important racial mandate of the new constitution to be dealt with, was miscegenation. Both of the Tillman brothers knew personally of many families that were received as white people, but who had an invisible portion of Negro ancestry. When George Johnstone, the Conservative delegate from Newberry, proposed that no person with any fraction of Negro blood should legally marry a white person, the Tillmans saw the need for inserting into the constitution a definition, which defined a Negro as a person having 1/8 or more of Negro blood. Otherwise, said George Tillman, "respectable families in Aiken, Barnwell, Colleton, and Orangeburg would be denied the right to intermarry among the people with whom they are now associated."[8]

Robert Smalls proposed that a white man cohabiting with a Negro woman should be debarred from holding public office, and that the offspring of such a union should take the father's name and enjoy the right of inheritance. This was denied in favor of a prohibition of legal marriage between the races.

The remainder of Tillman's constitution was largely the same as the constitution of 1868, which it was replacing. From the declaration of rights were pruned the offensive sections which touched upon sore subjects, such as the prohibition of slavery, paramount allegiance to the United States, and the indissoluble nature of the Union. The article on the legislative department contained much extraneous matter, but continued intact the imbalance of the General Assembly in relation to the other two branches of the state government. Lip service was rendered to the American system of the separation of powers, but the automatic checks and balances were rendered inoperative. The dispersed executive branch was left without power to enforce law or to administer state business, and the judicial branch was subordinated to the General Assembly. In no important detail was the basic structure of the government altered from that ordained by the constitution of 1868. As David Duncan Wallace has said, the constitution of 1895 can be divided into two parts, "first, suffrage provisions; second, everything else."[9] Having accomplished this to Tillman's satisfaction, the Convention locked the door upon changes in his document by preposterous procedures for amendment. Understandably, the Negro delegates declined to sign the completed instrument.

After fifty-nine days of work, the constitutional Convention of 1895 adjourned at ten o'clock on the night of December 4. As already decided by Ben Tillman, his constitution would go into effect without ratification by the people. Architect of the framework of the new organic law, Tillman proudly hailed it as his monument. The verdict of the Charleston *News and Courier* was "The Convention has generally done

[8] Simkins, *Pitchfork Ben*, p. 305.
[9] Wallace, *Constitution 1895*, p. 33.

good work, and one that will in time redound to the credit of those who participated in it."

This verdict has not been sustained by history. The blunders in the constitution, however, should be viewed in the light of the fact that the men who sat in the Convention of 1895 had actually lived under the Reconstruction government that ruled the state by control of the Negro vote. James Morris Morgan, who experienced the indignities and injustices of those times has said: "South Carolina was the nearest approach to a hell on earth during the orgy of the carpetbaggers and negroes that ever a refined and proud people were subjected to."[10] His estimate has been confirmed by many.

Those who did not suffer under that tragic experience can now examine the situation as it was in 1895 with some degree of impartiality. A simple literacy test equitably applied, says Francis Simkins, would have excluded more than 13,000 illiterate whites and 58,086 Negroes; although about 75,000 literate Negroes might have been able to register, the whites would have retained a majority of 12,000 without fraud.[11] Tillman, however, looked very tenderly upon the illiterate whites, for it was by their votes, which he stirred from inertia, that he had risen to power.

Even a man who had suffered under Reconstruction argued for justice to the Negro. When the General Assembly was drafting new election laws in 1896, Joseph W. Barnwell said: "No people can long remain civilized to whom are presented the terrible alternatives of corrupt elections on the one hand or corrupt government on the other." He argued that 1/6 of the white voters and 2/3 of the black being illiterate, 85,000 whites and 44,000 blacks would be able to register, giving the whites a safe majority of 41,000 and leaving "no shadow of excuse for unfair or unjust laws." His "inopportune remarks" were scorned and his motion was tabled.[12]

For more than fifty-six years, Tillman's constitution has prevented enlightened consideration of the state's racial problem. Legalizing fraud in registration, it has also reduced official oaths to unashamed purjury, and made possible flagrant

[10] *Recollections*, p. 339.
[11] *Pitchfork Ben*, p. 295.
[12] Wallace, *History of S. C.*, III, 372.

corruption in elections. As Simkins puts it, "lawless force remains the ultimate arbiter of South Carolina color politics."[13] Says D. D. Wallace, "Whiteness of skin suffices to cover every blackness of character."[14] Tillman's constitution has sanctioned irresponsibility for the unfortunate children of mixed racial origin. It has permitted, if not fostered, illiteracy among citizens, and is directly responsible for discrimination in public education which has burdened the state with preposterous debt and improper taxation.

In the light of the record, Alexander Haskell's solemn words seem to have the ring of prophecy: "Tillman and his associates . . . have done more harm and brought greater sorrow on the State than the sword, or fire, or the hand of man in any shape, has ever before effected."

[13] *Pitchfork Ben*, p. 308.
[14] *History of S. C.*, III, 871.

CHAPTER XXIX

AFTERMATH OF 1895

The delegates who sat in the Constitutional Convention of 1895 could not foresee the paved roads, automobiles, radio, and network of telephones, which would soon bring all parts of the state within easy reach. So Tillman's constitution created one new county, and eased restrictions on the formation of others by reducing their minimum size from 625 square miles to 400, and the size of existing counties from 625 to 500 square miles. New counties would give more members to the state Senate, and perhaps more support from that body to the continuation of Tillman's program.

Steps were immediately taken for the formation of five new counties, one of which would be cut largely from Sumter. Tillman's support in Sumter County had been mainly from the north-eastern portion, within the bounds of old Salem County. This section now voted to leave Sumter, and, by act of the legislature in 1897, was made into Lee County, named in honor of General Robert E. Lee. The boundaries were surveyed, taking territory not only from Sumter but also from Kershaw and Darlington. County officers were elected and the legislative delegation was seated. But Darlington brought suit to contest the legality of the act, and it was annulled by the state supreme court on the ground that the election returns had not been attested by the commissioners of election.

Under the new constitution, no further effort could be made for four years, so not until February 25, 1902, was Lee County successfully established by an act that named W. A. James, J. E. McCutchen, W. R. Shaw, Edwin Wilson, W. M. Kelley, A. E. Skinner, A. M. Lee, A. Johnson, and J. F. Matthews, as commissioners to mark the boundaries and provide the courthouse and jail. The act mentioned natural boundaries along Lynches and Black rivers, Scape Oer and Sparrow swamps, Long and Screeches branches, but in the main, the limits followed old roads and artificial lines as surveyed in 1898 through the parent counties. The county-seat was Bishopville, an incorporated town of early origin which has been re-named about 1830 for Dr. Jacques Bishop, owner of the surrounding plantation. In 1914, a small area of Lee County was restored to Sumter.

The first county officers, elected in 1902, were: W. P. Baskin, clerk of court; J. Manley Smith, sheriff; J. T. Watson, coroner; J. O. DuRant, supervisor; John M. Smith, judge of probate; McDonald Davis, superintendent of education; T. G. McLeod, state senator; B. Frank Kelley and G. M. Stuckey, representatives. The governor appointed C. W. Woodham, auditor, and G. F. Parrott, treasurer. The first court, with Judge G. W. Gage presiding, opened on March 2, 1903, in the Opera House, which continued to be used as a courthouse until 1908, when the present building was erected on the square at the intersection of Main and Church streets, the former site of the Bishopville Hotel.

Thus, despite a homogeneous population with identical interests, Sumter County once more, as in 1855 when Clarendon was severed, lost a great part of its wealth, territory, and inhabitants.

Another change made by the constitution of 1895 has had far-reaching consequences. This was the provision in regard to the police powers of the legislature to regulate or to prohibit the manufacture and sale of alcoholic liquors, and was included because Tillman wished to protect his dispensary system with constitutional safeguards: the General Assembly "may authorize and empower State, County and municipal officers . . . in the name of the State, to buy in any market and retail within the State liquors and beverages in such packages and quantities . . . as it deems expedient: *Provided*, That no license shall be granted to sell alcoholic beverages in less quantities than one-half pint, or to sell them between sundown and sunrise, or to sell them to be drunk on the premises."[1]

The dispensary system degenerated into a hotbed of shameless corruption. In 1907 the state dispensary was abolished, and the continuation of county dispensaries was left to local option. Sumter closed its dispensaries in 1910.[2] In 1916, as the result of a statewide referendum, prohibition went into

[1] South Carolina Constitution of 1895, art. VIII, sec. 11.
[2] *Stat.* XXVI, 935.

effect with a gallon-a-month law, which later was changed to a quart a month for medicinal purposes. After three years of state prohibition, South Carolina ratified the national prohibition amendment, which was repealed in 1933. How well the state's constitutional limitations upon the sale of intoxicants are now being observed, the readers of this chapter may decide for themselves.

The effect of the constitution of 1895 upon the Negroes of Sumter should also be noted. Tillman's anti-Negro constitution could not prevent George Washington Murray from serving a second term in Congress. The career of this Negro serves as a fitting postscript to the story of his race in connection with Sumter's political history during the years after Reconstruction.

Born of slave parents near Rembert on September 22, 1853, Murray had his early education in the local public school for Negroes which was established soon after the War of Secession. Later he entered the University of South Carolina when it was opened to Negroes during Reconstruction. His own earnest efforts to get an education were generously aided by a half-brother, Prince James, who, though without education, bore an excellent reputation for intelligence and integrity. For fifteen years Murray worked simultaneously at teaching and farming. Out in his field at dawn, he followed his furrows until time to walk to school, several miles away. There he taught the swarming children the required number of hours, then hurried back to his farm to work until dark, and on moonlight nights for many more hours. He carefully saved the money he earned from these activities, and when a large plantation in the neighborhood was to be sold, he persuaded some thrifty Negroes to join him and succeeded in purchasing it on easy terms. He then divided the tract into small farms and shared them among the partners in proportion to the sums contributed, he, as promoter, obtaining quite a valuable share. Eventually Murray became the largest landowner in Sumter County.[3]

As time passed, Murray's leadership among the Negroes of his community began to extend into the political field; he be-

[3] MS news-story by H. G. Osteen, written at time of Murray's trial.

came prominent in Republican local and state conventions, and soon was sharing in the federal patronage. In 1890 he was made an inspector of customs at Charleston, and, as already related, in 1892 he campaigned as the Republican candidate against General E. W. Moise, and was given the certificate of election by the Tillmanites.

At that time Murray is said to have been the only member of his race in Congress. Otherwise he was not particularly distinguished, but he continued to save his money, and in his own right bought a large body of land in Sumter County.

A very black man, Murray was described by a reporter who knew him as "not an ordinary negro in appearance, intellectual ability, education, or attainments in the fields of politics and business, in both of which he has won more than the ordinary . . . success and prominence. He is tall, well built, carries himself erectly, and possesses a dignity of manner that is not made ridiculous by the pomposity so frequently displayed by the negroes who regard themselves as better than their fellows."[4]

When the constitution of 1895 was being drafted, Murray made great efforts, both in the state and in Washington, to prevent the inclusion of Tillman's suffrage clauses which would disfranchise Negroes. Some of his speeches are said to have been "intemperate and somewhat incendiary." He worked hard in all the counties to raise funds among the Negroes for fighting the suffrage clauses in the courts, and possibly he may have had some success. Be that as it may, Murray as Republican candidate for Congress contested the election of Colonel William Elliott to the 54th Congress, and served from June 4, 1896, until March 3, 1897.

Unable to run again under the Tillman constitution with any hope for success, Murray returned to the Rafting Creek community with a good deal of money. He purchased tract after tract of land, paying cash for what he could, and getting thousands of acres on credit, which he expected to liquidate by a sort of endless-chain plan, in which local Negroes would be the necessary links.

Soon after his election to Congress, Murray had acquired at $4 an acre, a large tract at the head of Rafting Creek in the

[4] *Ibid.*

High Hills near Sumter's Mount, a remote and uninhabited locality. This he cut into small tracts which he sold to Negroes on a lease-contract, under which the tenant would pay him stated sums for a term of years, at the end of which, if the contract had been complied with, he bound himself to give the tenant a title to the land. The annual payments when completed, would aggregate an average price of $9 an acre, plus interest at eight per cent. The contract required each tenant to reside on the land for the full term of years and to cultivate it according to "good husbandry." Failing to keep any of these agreements, the tenant would forfeit all payments he had made and must remove from the land.

Murray succeeded in settling a number of Negro families on his farms, despite the fact that the land was hilly, not very fertile, and at that time many miles from a railroad.

In 1897, Scipio Chatman or Chapman and his son James made an oral contract with Murray for a term of eight years, and in January 1898 entered into possession of twenty-five acres. The first payment was due and was paid in the fall of that year. The written lease-contract was executed at Murray's house on November 4, 1899, and was signed in duplicate by Scipio, one copy being for Murray and one for Scipio. Notes for the annual payments were signed by Scipio and also by his son James, who had accompanied him, and were witnessed by Marion W. Cato, a young white man, who was there to get from Murray a transfer and assignment of a contract for sale of land, made with Murray by Cato's father shortly before death. The transfer to Marion Cato was written on the back of the elder Cato's contract, and was signed and dated by Murray, November 4, 1899.

After the signing of the contract with Scipio Chapman, the Northwestern Railroad built a line through his farm. The Chapmans, however, had defaulted in their annual note payments, which they admitted, but they offered to pay all arrears. Murray brought suit to eject the Chapmans, and the Chapmans brought a counter suit at May term of court, 1903, to enforce his compliance with the lease-contract.

Murray introduced a contract executed on a printed form of white paper, which, he said, was the original instrument of

November 4, 1899. It bore the imprint of the *Freeman* Printing Company, and was identified as having been printed for Murray on February 16, 1900. Scipio Chapman presented his original contract on blue paper, signed in blue ink on November 4, 1899, four months before the white paper contract-form had been printed. Although both the contracts bore identical terms and dates, Murray was prosecuted for forgery at the May term of court 1905. Judge Purdy presided; H. D. Moise appeared for the prosecution, and Marion Moise for the defendant. The trial aroused intense popular interest.

Murray explained that an oral contract always preceded the written contract; and that when he signed a contract, he usually made a copy for himself by way of a record, and marked it copy. As this white contract was not so marked, he had assumed that it was the original. When the Chapmans defaulted on their notes and the railroad was built across their farm, he asked the Chapmans to turn over to him five acres, which they did; he had measured it and then laid it out into lots for a town. He left the Chapmans in possession and they were to pay him rent. He thought Mr. Miller of the *Freeman* office must be mistaken in the date of the printing of the white forms, as he had printed up several orders. Altogether, Murray had about 8,000 acres, had executed about 100 contracts, and had made titles for about 1,000 acres in compliance with terms of contracts which had been fulfilled.

The prosecution then brought out the fact that Scipio's name did not appear on Murray's white paper contract, which bore only the name of James, who had moved away and was not cultivating the land as required. The omission of Scipio's name was construed as evidence of Murray having forged the contract, for if James were the lessee, the right to evict him was clear, and Murray would recover the lands. Their increase in value was pointed to as the motive for the forgery.

The defense claimed that the charge of forgery was a conspiracy to ruin Murray, who had been lenient in waiting several years before taking action, and had given the Chapmans every chance to fulfill the terms of the contract.

Judge Purdy then charged the jury, who in less than an hour, brought in a verdict of guilty. Murray was sentenced to three years of hard labor on the county chaingang or in the penitentiary, and a fine of $250. His lawyer immediately gave notice of an appeal to the state supreme court, and Murray was released on bail of $2,000. In October 1905 the supreme court sustained the verdict of the circuit court, and the *Watchman and Southron* announced that Murray, "tearfully" asserting that he was "the victim of circumstances," had no idea of forfeiting his bail bond, but would serve his sentence. Mr. Marion Moise stated that he would seek to re-open the case, and failing in that, would seek a pardon from the governor for his client.[5]

Apparently Mr. Moise failed in both attempts, and Murray decided to forfeit his bond, for he went to Chicago. There, says the *Biographical Directory of the American Congress*, he engaged in literary pursuits and lecturing, became a delegate to several Republican National Conventions, and when he died on April 21, 1926, he was buried in Lincoln Cemetery.

As a further postscript, it may be said here that the most distinguished Negro of Sumter County is not a man and is not concerned in politics. She is Mary McLeod Bethune, born on July 10, 1875, in a three-room log cabin on a farm three miles from Mayesville, one of seventeen children of Sam and Patsy McLeod, former slaves. When the Presbyterian Board of Missions eleven years later opened a school for Negroes at Mayesville, Mary McLeod was one of the first pupils, daily walking the five miles back and forth between the cabin and the school.

On recommendation of her teacher, Miss Emma Wilson, Mary was awarded a scholarship to Scotia Seminary at Concord, North Carolina. Upon graduation, desiring to be a missionary, she received a scholarship to Moody Bible Institute, Chicago, where she was conspicuous as the only Negro student, and sang in the Institute's church choir.

Upon completion of her training, she applied for mission work in Africa, but there being no vacancy, she was sent to Haines Normal and Industrial Institute at Augusta, Georgia. Next she taught for two years in Sumter, where she was married to a fellow teacher, Albert Bethune.

[5] *Sumter Daily Item*, May 20, 1904; *Watchman and Southron*, May 25, 1904, Oct. 18, 1905.

After two years in Savannah, Georgia, and five years with a mission at Palatka, Florida, she arrived in Daytona in 1904, with a dollar and a half in her purse, and opened the Daytona Educational and Industrial Training School for Negro girls. That small venture has now grown into Bethune-Cookman College. Its founder's colorful career of successful work for the betterment of her race has brought her national fame and many honors. In 1931 Ida Tarbell listed her among America's fifty most illustrious women. In 1949 Rollins College, at Winter Park, Florida, awarded her an honorary Doctor of Humanities degree, the first, it is said, ever to have been conferred upon a member of her race by an institution in the south.

Young Negroes of today in Sumter County can obtain an education without the difficulties faced by Dr. Bethune. The public school system includes both elementary and high schools for Negroes. In 1908 the Negro Baptist Educational and Missionary Convention of the state founded Morris College[6], in the outskirts of the city of Sumter. Supported largely by contributions from Negro churches and fraternal organizations, it is free of mortgage debt, and offers opportunities for student self-help.

[6] For an interesting, but pessimistic, evaluation of Morris College, see Lewis K. McMillan, *Negro Higher Education in the State of South Carolina* (n. p., 1952).

Chapter XXX

COUNCIL-MANAGER GOVERNMENT IN THE CITY OF SUMTER

The city of Sumter was the first in the world to adopt a new, and until then, untried plan of government, which is now known favorably to students of political science as the council-manager form of municipal government. Its distinctive feature is the provision for a full-time, qualified manager to administer the costly and often complex business of a municipal corporation. The manager is employed by, and works under, the city council as a board of directors which is the policy-making body and makes all decisions.

From the time of its first charter in 1845, Sumter was governed by an elected council of five, an intendant and four wardens. In 1887 the charter of 1885 was amended to make the town a city, with a mayor and four aldermen. In 1894 the charter was again amended, to increase the number of aldermen to eight. These were elected at large by popular vote, but in practice an effort was made to elect two aldermen from each ward, although this did not always happen, and occasionally some wards had one alderman while others had three. This governmental plan served the purpose fairly well, but on the whole from a business standpoint was inefficient and haphazard. As time passed, politics in the usual sense crept into city government, and some favoritism was shown toward influential and aggressive interests. The natural result was dissatisfaction among many citizens.

As similar conditions existed in many of the larger towns of the United States, civic-minded citizens almost everywhere were seeking for a better system of municipal government, and there was widespread discussion of the problem in newspapers, periodicals and public forums. After the great hurricane and tidal wave of 1900 devastated Galveston, Texas, interest became focused on the unprecedented success and efficiency of the commission which was created to rehabilitate the city. That non-political commission spent many millions of dollars for repairs and new construction, including a great seawall for protection from future storms and tidal waves. The monumental task was completed with unexampled promptness and economy, and was a business-like achievement of arresting novelty in municipal affairs. Cities whose affairs were in a state of confusion and extravagance seized upon the idea of a non-political commission to administer municipal government as a business enterprise.

One of the first commission-form-of-government cities was Des Moines, Iowa, with a commission of four that administered city business on a departmental basis, with one commissioner in active control of each department, and all working under the whole commission as a policy-making body. The plan was reported as working well, was widely discussed, and was generally endorsed by authorities on city government. Other cities adopted the Des Moines plan or modifications of it.

The commission form of government a few years later aroused interest in South Carolina, and in 1910 the legislature passed an act for the especial benefit of Columbia, authorizing cities of more than 20,000 but less than 50,000 inhabitants to adopt a commission form of government, with a mayor and four aldermen, by vote of the qualified electors.

Meanwhile, in Sumter, sentiment for a change had grown considerably, and in 1911 came to a head. The Chamber of Commerce, which had just been re-organized and enlarged, and was full of enthusiasm, took the lead in giving direction to the sentiment for a more business-like town government. Dr. S. C. Baker was the dynamic president of the Chamber, and Arthur V. Snell was the executive secretary. A lawyer with experience in the Department of Justice in Washington, and in private practice in Oklahoma City, Mr. Snell had transferred his activities to chamber-of-commerce work both in Oklahoma City and Duluth. He attacked the municipal government problem with zeal and constructive intelligence, and made a searching study of all obtainable material on the subject, with special attention to the operation of the commission plan in cities which had adopted it.

A report that aroused interest concerned an experiment inaugurated in Stauton, Virginia, which had a mayor, and a council of two chambers similar to a state legislature, a system that was both cumbersome and inefficient. To remedy the situation, the Staunton Council, without change in the town charter and without a legislative act, employed a business administrator to manage the town's affairs and carry out the directions of the Council. When the Staunton plan had been in operation for more than a year with apparent success, the Sumter Chamber of Commerce, after consideration, invited Mr. Ashburne, the business manager of Staunton, to visit Sumter for a conference. Mr. Ashburne spent two days in Sumter, but gave little constructive information or advice. The pertinent fact that Staunton had a business manager instead of a political administration, impressed the Chamber of Commerce Committee, and resulted in a decision to frame an act authorizing Sumter to have the commission form of government.

The members of the committee appoined to draw up the bill were Dr. S. C. Baker, president of the Chamber, and Mayor L. D. Jennings, both ex-officio; Arthur V. Snell, C. M. Hurst, city clerk and treasurer; Davis D. Moise, H. G. Osteen, and possibly two or three others. The bill was largely the work of Mr. Snell, embodying what he had learned from his study, with suggestions from other members of the committee. As drawn, the bill provided for a special act for Sumter, and included all details of administration and a provision for submitting the plan of government to popular vote for acceptance or rejection, the issues being (1) for a commission of mayor and two councilmen, (2) for retention of the existing plan of a mayor and eight aldermen.

The proposed bill was placed with the Sumter county legislative delegation for introduction and passage in the General Assembly. Near the close of the session, no action having been taken, State Senator John H. Clifton discarded the bill proposed by the Chamber of Commerce, and offered in lieu of it a revised version of the Commission Form of Government Act previously enacted for Columbia. His bill contained the major features of the discarded bill, including the proposal for a city manager to be employed by and to work under the City Council, but extended provisions of the Commission Form of Government Act to cities of over 4,000 inhabitants, cities of over 10,000 but less than 20,000, and cities of over 50,000 but less than 100,000 and in certain cities therein named, the last category being the one applicable to Sumter.

The referendum was held in Sumter on the second Tuesday in June 1912, and the two questions presented were (1) Shall the City of Sumter adopt the Commission Form of Government? (2) Shall the City of Sumter adopt the Commission Form of Government with a city manager? The campaign preceding the election had been heated, for many preferred the existing form of government and were reluctant to commit the city to an untried experiment. But the plan for a manager was adopted by a substantial majority. The voters then faced another election on the second Tuesday in August for a mayor and two councilmen.

By general consent, L. D. Jennings, whose term as mayor had not expired, was proposed as the candidate for mayor. After much discussion and many conferences, C. G. Rowland and J. P. Booth were endorsed as candidates for councilmen. This was believed to be a happy solution of the problem, for Jennings was an aggressive progressive, Rowland was a hardheaded conservative economist and banker; and Booth, a successful businessman experienced in several lines, was expected to be a balance between Jennings and Rowland. All three were elected.

The new Council went into office, and the matter of first importance before them was the selection of the city manager. The news that Sumter had inaugurated an entirely new system of municipal government and would employ a business manager as administrator, had been widely publicized, and applications poured in. Secretary Snell was requested to screen the more than two hundred applications and select the twenty best prospects for City Council, which he did. Shortly thereafter, Council named the city manager, a Mr. Worthington, a young junior engineer in the construction department of the Atlantic Coast Line Railroad. He had no background of business or administrative experience, and was not among the applicants screened by Mr. Snell. As a matter of record, City Council had not considered any of those twenty applications, for when the package was returned to the Chamber of Commerce for filing, the seal was found to be unbroken.

City Manager Worthington took over his work. A competent engineer and of pleasing personality, he did not fit the job. Perhaps with a different type of council members, he might have grown into it and made good, but he never had a chance. Each of the three men on the council was an embryo city manager, with fixed ideas of his own, and in the diversity of opinion and multiplicity of council, there was confusion and lost motion. Mr. Worthington was given credit for an endeavor to do the best he could, but lasted barely a year.

The next city manager was W. F. Robertson, a construction engineer with several years experience as city engineer of a North Carolina town, and as manager of a construction company. Capable and energetic, he succeeded in bringing a degree of system into the city's affairs, as well as laying out and supervising the paving of Liberty Street. But he resigned after less than a year, in consequence of constant friction with the mayor, stating that his responsibility was so great and his authority so limited, in justice to himself he could not continue.

Following Manager Robertson came a succession of city managers, local men of diverse qualifications, with the exception of a business-efficiency expert brought to Sumter from Atlanta. He lasted only a few months, alleging too much overhead, too little authority, and no well-defined duties. The other managers mentioned above were all successful men in the businesses in which they had previously engaged: livestock selling, sawmilling, farming, etc. All worked hard and had certain accomplishments to their credit.

The first city manager who really pulled his weight on the job was Robert L. McLeod. He had the advantage of having served four years as councilman, several years as clerk of the board of county commissioners, and also as bookkeeper for more than one mercantile firm, and was the proprietor of a lumber-manufacturing and building-supply business. His administration, in cooperation with the City Council then in office, was constructive and successful. As the result of his handling of the city's financial affairs, which he had found in not too good shape, he was offered an important position with the South Carolina National Bank, which he accepted, and resigned as city manager.

For an interim of several months, the city was without a manager, until S. K. Rowland, a former insurance and real estate operator, was selected for the position, which he filled until elected city clerk and treasurer upon the death of R. B. Jennings.

At the same time, J. A. Raffield was elected city manager. He came to the job with many years experience as a railroad executive, eight years as city councilman, and four years as mayor. For fifteen or more years, Manager Raffield, though criticised at times, filled the position efficiently, and with exceptionally good judgment in suggesting a far-seeing program of development and improvement in all city departments. Some critics charged that he was not amenable to suggestions from the citizens. However, Mr. Raffield worked successfully with several succeeding Councils. The city manager is employed at the pleasure of Council and can be dismissed at any time he fails in his job or antagonizes Council. The conclusion of the writer is that the council-manager government in Sumter has been a success and proved its worth under the administration of R. L. McLeod, and more so under J. A. Raffield. That the record of the council-manager plan in Sumter has been high in the history of municipal government is evidenced by the more than a thousand cities and towns that have adopted it since Sumter pioneered with its design and adoption in 1912.

There has been only one basic change in the Sumter plan. In 1944, in response to sentiment for a larger council, sponsored largely by younger citizens who urged that it would be more democratic, a law increased the membership of Council from three to five. To the writer, the wisdom of the change is questionable, for the more members in the council, the more difficult it is to find qualified, civic-minded men willing to undertake this arduous and not always appreciated public service. It is always better for the office to seek the man than for the man to seek the office. In the early days of the council-manager government, candidates were brought out by unofficial committees, after conferences and a caucus of citizens, who endeavored to find candidates who would render non-partisan and unselfish service. This practice worked well, as the record shows, and should be revived. The efficiency of any government, and especially the council-manager form, is dependent upon the vigilant and sustained interest of the citizenry. Good government can be had if the citizens demand it, by an active and organized attention to the election of all public officials.

A retrospective survey of Sumter since the inauguration of the council-manager plan reveals that there has been steady progress in administrative technique and material development.

In 1912 Sumter had a city-owned water system; an adequate sewerage system for the needs of the community at that time; an inadequate and rundown electric-light-and-power system, privately owned by a Philadelphia corporation and operated under a ten-year franchise; and only a few paved blocks on Main Street and a few hard-surfaced sidewalks.

When the power company's franchise expired, it was not renewed, and the city purchased the physical property, paying far more than it was worth. Embarking upon a program of municipal ownership, the city was bonded up to the legal limit, to build a new powerhouse and to install a 1000-horsepower turbine generator as a supplement to a 500-horsepower generator of the old plant. Within a year the plant was overloaded, and the city was without financial resources to increase its production of current. Already bonded at that time beyond its legal limit, the city had $220,000 in notes in New York banks that were clamoring for payment — in the midst of the depression that hit the South in the early 1920's. To add to the gravity of the situation, the distributive system of the power plant was in an advanced state of dilapidation, no repairs having been made, for the money from the bond issue and the notes had all been spent in paying for the old plant and building the monumental powerhouse on South Main Street.

The general dissatisfaction with municipal ownership resulted in a political upheaval and the election of a new mayor and a new Council. The new administration solved the power problem by selling the power plant to the Carolina Power and

Light Company of Raleigh, North Carolina, for $650,000, which paid off the bonded and floating debt incurred on the power plant and left a surplus of about $165,000.

The Carolina Power and Light Company guaranteed to supply Sumter with all the power it could use for all purposes, to re-build the distributive system, and to give as low rates then and in future as might be in effect in any town served by the company. This guarantee had been fulfilled to the letter. The manufacturing development in Sumter since 1926 has been largely due to the good supply of electricity available at reasonable rates. This accomplishment can justly be credited to the council-manager government.

Both the water system and the sewage-disposal system have been vastly enlarged to keep pace with the growth of Sumter. Streets and sidewalks have been paved under a program inaugurated in 1915, and still goes forward as the town grows. Best of all, the town has been kept on a safe financial basis. There have been reductions in the tax rate several times since 1912, and, until recently, no increase in the levy. Altogether, the council-manager plan has been a good thing for Sumter.[1]

Forty years after Sumter led the way with the council-manager plan, the voters of the city approved another innovation, and, by a heavy majority, elected Miss Martha Priscilla Shaw as their first woman mayor.

---

[1] With the addition of a few dates and legal details from the South Carolina *Statutes*, this chapter is an edited version of an address made in 1951 by H. G. Osteen, a former member of the committee that drew up the original bill for the Sumter council-manager plan.

Chapter XXXI
OLD GARDENS AND A BIT OF GOSSIP

The gardens of Sumter long have been famous, but little is known of them in colonial times. The earliest found on record was at the rectory of St. Mark's, which in 1767 had both a garden and an orchard. Very near both the Santee and the Wateree rivers, which abounded in fish and wild fowl, the rectory, said the vestrymen, was a place where a gentleman might "lead an easy and comfortable, contemplative life."[1] But the first rector, the Rev. Thomas Morgan, instead of life found death from malaria within two weeks; and the next rector, the Rev. Charles Woodmason, prudently went to live in the High Hills. So the garden at the rectory soon perished.

Although most of the earliest and handsomest gardens seem to have been in the High Hills, there was none as long as summer houses and shooting boxes were the prevailing habitations, and only after permanent homes of prosperous families were built, did gardens become numerous.

At the entrance to the High Hills, William Richardson in 1773 settled Bloom Hill plantation. Evidently he chose the name to suggest flowers, for he immediately began making ready a garden for his Charleston wife. His letters to her told of its progress, and he described one of the garden walks as bordered with pinks and "rosaries" — an old name for rose bushes — which promised, in time, to be very pretty. The industrious gardener, Losia, credited with knowing his business, was probably Irish, for he had a spiteful Irish wife and was addicted to drunkenness. His time was not wholly given to flowers, however, for, said Mr. Richardson, the garden had upwards of two thousand cabbage plants in "very pretty order" as well as salads in abundance, radishes in great perfection, scallions, leaks and parsley in plenty, and beans of different sorts in great abundance. Besides, there were cucumbers, muskmelons, watermelons, cherries, peaches and

[1] To Bishop of London, Apr 20, 1767, cited in Cook, *Rambles*, p. 199.

plums; and Richardson asked his wife to send peas for planting and some celery seed.² When the war of the Revolution began a few years later William Richardson went into the American army; troops of both sides frequently were marching up and down the highway by Bloom Hill and the garden probably ceased to flourish.

William Richardson's oldest child, Ann, grew to womanhood during those troubled years, and in 1787 she was married to William Mayrant. They made a garden at their home, Ararat, now called Argyle, near Stateburg; and also a sort of kindergarten, for to their marriage were born thirteen children! In the spring of 1812, William Mayrant was a candidate for Congress against John Kershaw and Charles Richardson, and out of the campaign there came a curious lawsuit. James B. Richardson, campaigned vigorously for his brother Charles on a remarkable platform: John Kershaw, he said, had received an appointment from John Adams, and hence was a Federalist; while William Mayrant was crazy; so the only man fit for election was his brother Charles Richardson, who was duly elected. William Mayrant then brought suit against James B. Richardson for slander. Mayrant lost his case, however, for the court declared that every man had a right to judge and give an opinion of a candidate's fitness; a mere opinion that his mind was impaired by disease would excite compassion for a misfortune, and did not reflect shame or disgrace upon him.³

In the next Congressional campaign two years later, William Mayrant was elected to Congress and took his family to Washington. He became deeply interested in the manufacture of cotton, and resigned his seat before the expiration of his term to become one of the pioneer cotton-factory men of Sumter. While he was in New York purchasing machinery and making arrangements for his factory, although then twenty-eight years since his marriage, he was writing like a lover to his "Dearest lovely wife", in whose "enchanting fascinating company" he had been so happy, of his longing for their morning walk together in the garden at Ararat, "and that Sweet communion of thoughts" which they there generally enjoyed.⁴

2 "Letters of William Richardson", *SCHGM*, XLVII, 8, 9.
3 H. J. Nott and D. J. McCord, *Reports*, I, 848.
4 "Two letters by William Mayrant on His Cotton Factory," *SCHM*, LIV, 5.

Perhaps the most notable garden in the High Hills was the one at Home House, where lived Thomas Sumter Jr., and his charming French wife, Natalie Delage. As a child refugee from the bloody French Revolution, she had been educated in New York. Young Mr. Sumter had met her there as a lovely school girl at the home of the Prevost family. Their romance ripened soon after on shipboard, when he was on his way to Paris as secretary of the American legation under Livingston, the American minister, in whose care Natalie was returning to France to find her mother. Mr. Sumter aided her in the quest, and having obtained her mother's consent, he and Natalie were married in Paris. As a bride, Natalie bought seeds from a French nurseryman for her garden in the High Hills, and twenty-one years later, when she returned to France for a visit to her mother, she made arrangements with the same nurseryman to supply herself and Mrs. William Anderson every year with seeds and trees.

In her own small person Natalie was a forerunner of our great national department of agriculture, which now collects and experiments with plants from every part of the world. In her Home House garden she gathered plants not only from her beloved France, and from Italy, homeland of her son-in-law Joseph Binda, but also from remote Java, as well as from Brazil, where for more than ten years she was with her husband, then American minister at the court of Portugal. In Brazil Mrs. Sumter made a garden, and we find her writing to Mrs. Mary Hooper in Stateburg, to send garden seeds in her letters — honeysuckles, camomile, white and yellow jasmines, lilacs, wallflowers, strawberries, and pits of cherries, apricots and nectarines. In return, Natalie offered to send her friend some "Eiotrope" seeds derived from a single seed she had obtained in Philadelphia, and which had produced some five hundred flourishing descendants in the congenial soil and climate of Brazil.

Natalie Sumter also kept up a lively exchange of seeds and plants with her South Carolina neighbors and friends, from Camden to Charleston. Her diary during the last year of her life mentions sending fifteen kinds of seeds to Mrs. Canty, and a "load of rose cuttings" to Mrs. Robert Marion DeVeaux at The Ruins. The diary is almost a gardener's calendar, for on nearly every page appear the current events of a garden which was then the sole pleasure of the frail little widow.

For the delicate plants of the Home House garden, Mrs. Sumter had a greenhouse which was large enough to house an orange tree. The garden was so extensive that she sometimes rode around it on horseback, with one of her sons, DeLage or Sebastian, walking beside her. A year later, when she was too weak for horseback, she rode in her little carriage or little cart to see the work of her servants. Matilda, Delia and Charlotte helped in the garden, but Hampton seems to have been the gardener, although one day when Mrs. Sumter was busy with her sweet roses, he trimmed her grape vines so disastrously that she recorded, "they are done." On another sad day, when Mr. Gifford whom she had cared for through an attack of cholera, tried to help in the garden, she found him pulling up all her pomegranates.

At no time does her diary mention camellias or azaleas, but Home House garden had bowers and hedges, lemons, black-okra-seed cotton, and brown cotton. The diary also mentions a "plant from Java" and a Java blue pea, jasmines, rose geraniums and ivy geraniums, tea roses, a button rose, "banseka rose," the white and yellow banksias, dahlias, sweet olive, violets, cactus, a night-blooming jasmine, fushsias, box, the double pink oleander, dogwood, magnolia, elms, and a French peach. The last entry in the diary shows the unselfishness of its writer: "I sent by Sebastian the only bunch of my french grapes to Julia Mitchell who is very ill."

In the summer of 1841, during her last days, Natalie Sumter went into her garden looking for a place to be buried. She found none that pleased her, and decided that her children might put her where they pleased, provided it was not in the enclosure she had made around the graves of her husband and his parents. In the will she made at the time, she asked to be buried on the outside, to the east, and expressed the hope that her children would "be able one day to build a little chapel, ten feet by twelve."

When Natalie died in August that summer, her wishes were faithfully carried out, and her children built the little chapel, ten feet by twelve, which stands today as her memorial. Her garden and her home have vanished.

Close by the Sumters' Home House, was the famous garden at Acton, of the Cleland Kinloch family. Named for Acton Park in England, near Chester, this garden was probably laid out in 1807 by Cleland Kinloch of Georgetown, when, on his return from Europe, he completed his summer mansion on a Stateburg hilltop. The grounds at the front of the house sloped down to a terrace, bordered with trees along the roadside. The formal garden was at the rear, where the level ground was laid out in squares, bordered by clipped hedges and intersected by walks. Within the squares were roses, shrubs, and many flowers. As was the custom of the time, some of the squares contained vegetables; and one was for a labyrinth. There was also a lovers' lane, a green tunnel, formed by interlacing branches of mock orange trees.

When Cleland Kinloch became a widower, his sister, Mrs. Mary E. Huger, crippled with rheumatism, presided over his household with the assistance of a white housekeeper, and mothered his children: Isabella, the twin boys Francis and Cleland, and Harriett. On the death of the elder Cleland Kinloch in 1823, his brother Francis enjoyed a life-tenure of Acton for three years. Only two of Cleland Kinloch's children survived, Francis, who resided in Florence, Italy; and Harriett, who became the wife of Henry Middleton. They sold Acton to Samuel E. Nelson, who made it his home until his death there in 1852. Later, Acton became the home of Mrs. Harriott Horry Ravenel, and still later, it passed into the possession of a daughter of John J. Dargan. The handsome house was accidentally burned in 1911, and the garden has reverted to wild woods.

Near Stateburg was another notable place, known to this day as The Ruins, bought by General Sumter after the Revolution. The garden and grounds probably were developed long after General Sumter sold the place in 1802 to John Mayrant, brother of William Mayrant of Ararat. During the Revolution, John Mayrant had been a midshipman on board the "Bon Homme Richard", under John Paul Jones, who is said to have thought highly of him. In the battle with the "Serapis", John Mayrant received a wound in his leg, which disabled him for three months. Later he became a lieutenant under Commodore Gillon, on the frigate "South Carolina."

After fifty years of married life, most or all of which was spent at their Stateburg home, John Mayrant's wife, Isabella, died. The old man then went to live with his sons in Alabama, Mississippi, and Tennessee, one of whom sold the place to Willis W. Alston.

Willis W. Alston was a schoolmaster, and he converted the property into the Hawthorndean Seminary for young ladies, but two years later he sold it to John H. Colclough. After six months ownership, Colclough sold the place to young Robert Marion DeVeaux, whose attractive wife, Videau Marion, was a daughter of Colonel Richard Singleton. It was probably this properous young couple who planted the garden and developed the handsome grounds. A tradition says that it was they who gave the name to the place, which was quite run down when they purchased it. While they were getting it ready for occupancy, going there back and forth each day from Colonel Singleton's house, they would talk about what they were doing at "the ruins". Under their fostering care, not only was the place lovely to behold, but it produced fine peaches and figs, and enormous bunches of hothouse grapes. It was to Mrs. DeVeaux that Natalie Sumter mentioned sending a load of rose cuttings. Unfortunately, Robert Marion DeVeaux died young; but he left his widow with ample means for rearing and educating their three children.

The home of Mrs. DeVeaux's father, Colonel Richard Singleton, was one of the most famous in the Sumter District. His cotton plantations near Manchester on the road to Charleston, comprised some 12,000 acres. His mansion house was set back in a park of fifty acres, separated from the highway for miles by hedges of hawthorn, and fences concealed by brilliant roses, perfuming the air. Formal gardens, in charge of an English gardener, surrounded the house. The trees of the park were planted in rows, which radiated from the house in the center like the spokes of a wheel. Between the house and the highway was an oval race-course measuring a mile, and the Colonel could call to his jockeys from his pillared portice, where cement lions crouched at the head of the steps. A traveller who passed by in 1830 has recorded that "the house, the gardens and the hedges of roses, it yields to none."[5]

[5] Mrs. Ann Royall, cited in Reniers, *Springs of Virginia*, p. 51.

Like so many of the home-loving citizens of Sumter District, Colonel Singleton expressed his love for the place by naming it "Home". There his youngest daughter Sarah Angelica was married on November 27, 1838, to Abraham Van Buren, eldest son and private secretary to President Van Buren. The clergyman who officiated at the splendid wedding, the Rev. Augustus L. Converse, eleven years later also became a son-in-law of Colonel Singleton, when he married the wealthy young widow, Marion DeVeaux of The Ruins. Thereby hangs a tale, for that marriage, in a very different way, was as interesting as Angelica's.

Mr. Converse, a northern man with a wooden leg, was the rector of the Episcopal Church in Stateburg, and taught the local school. His wife, Mary Ann Kellogg, died in 1848, and the following year he married Marion DeVeaux, she being then thirty-three years old, and he, fifty-one. Under the law of that time, the property which she had inherited from her first husband, as well as the plantation and slaves which had come to her from her father, would become the property of her second husband, unless a marriage settlement conveyed it to trustees to hold for her. At the time of the marriage, with the consent of Mr. Converse, a marriage settlement was duly signed and her trustees were appointed. Later, however, Mrs. Converse revoked the settlement and signed a deed which gave Mr. Converse a share in her property, with the proviso that if he should survive her, he was to have it for life. The immediate result was that the reverend gentleman went on a rampage, for he slapped his wife's face, and knocked down her two daughters. The climax came on a rainy night in January 1854, when he abused the poor lady so dreadfully that, bruised and bleeding, she escaped from the house and hid with one of her daughters in the cotton-house. When Mr. Converse sent for hammer and nails to nail up the door, they once more fled, and hid in a cotton field, in the rain, until the dusk of evening, when they were rescued by a neighbor and carried to safety across the river. There the unhappy lady took up residence at her True Blue plantation, in St. Matthew's Parish.

Mrs. Converse was a woman of spirit and pride, and she did not bear "her wrongs with lamb-like patience and meekness," but applied to the court of equity at the May term in Sumter for permission to resume the name of her first husband, and to exclude the second husband from all rights in her property. Chancellor Dargan refused, however, on the ground that the couple later might be reconciled, and it would be wrong for the court to put any bar in the way.

Legally, therefore, all the rents and profits from her property had to be paid to Mr. Converse, and as she had no voice in his disbursements, Mrs. Converse appealed her case. But the decree of the lower court was confirmed, and her only relief was an order that Mr. Converse should give her half of the income! It is pleasant to know that one judge, John Belton O'Neall, drafted a dissenting opinion. He held that the deed by which she gave Mr. Converse a share should be regarded as procured by force, unless the husband could prove it was free and voluntary — that the burden of proof was on him, not her: "The sad events of January 1854, have separated forever, these unfortunate people. . . .He has no claim to the bounty of his wife; *he ought not to live upon it.*" But only two judges concurred in this opinion, and the appeal was dismissed.[6] Truly, in those days, a husband and wife were one person and that person was the husband!

There were famous gardens, too, on Black River. Twelve miles south of Sumter in the fork of the river was the 3000-acre plantation of M. H. Plowden. When he advertised it for sale in May 1857, he described it as one of the prettiest pineland places in Sumter District, unsurpassed for health, good water, fruit and vine orchards in full bearing, two vegetable gardens, and a fine flower garden, with many choice selections of shrubbery and flowers.

East of the river near the Clarendon line, was Rollindale plantation, containing more than 2000 acres owned by the George W. Cooper family. The extensive gardens were laid out by a professional gardener. The two-story house on a brick basement had an ell at the rear in which was the dining-room, said to have been large enough to seat more than fifty people. Staffed with some eight servants, including a coachman and an assistant coachman, the house was approached

---

[6] J. S. G. Richardson, *Equity Reports*, IX, 535-571.

from the highway by an S-shaped avenue,[7] which had been laid out on the theory that mosquitoes would be thus prevented from finding their way in from the swamp to torment the family.

Adjoining the churchyard of Salem Black River Church, was the equally well-known Coldstream plantation of the Witherspoon family. Robert Witherspoon, a prominent citizen of Williamsburg, had purchased this plantation in 1813 from Captain John B. Anderson, who had inherited part of it from his grandfather, David Anderson, one of the earliest settlers of Sumter District, and donor of the land on which the original Salem Church was built. Like David Anderson, Robert Witherspoon was a good Presbyterian, and he gave additional land to the church to enlarge the cemetery. He named his plantation Coldstream, a name derived from the little town in Scotland, where, in 1659, General Monk had raised the famous Coldstream regiment of Foot Guards, in which a Witherspoon ancestor is said to have served. After the death of his first wife, Janet James, Robert Witherspoon married Elizabeth, daughter of Colonel Thomas McFadden, who contributed to the purchase price of Coldstream the value of the lands he had expected to leave his daughter. Colonel McFadden was one of the wealthiest men of Sumter District, and when he died in 1824, he bequeathed his daughter Elizabeth Witherspoon a fourth share of his books, as well as a legacy in cash.

Robert and Elizabeth Witherspoon are said to have begun a beautiful garden at Coldstream. When Robert died in 1837 at the age of seventy-one years, he left Coldstream to his wife and two sons, the younger, Hamilton G. Witherspoon, then a boy eleven years old. In 1849 Hamilton brought his bride to Coldstream, and employed a German gardener who brought the garden to its highest perfection, a perfection which escaped the havoc of Potter's Raid, and continued into the twentieth century. As described by Miss Hamilton Witherspoon, in the *Century Magazine* of August 1909, a visitor, opening the latticed gate from the avenue at the front of the house, would have seen:

---

[7] Description from H. G. Osteen, who knew the place.

OLD GARDENS AND A BIT OF GOSSIP 419

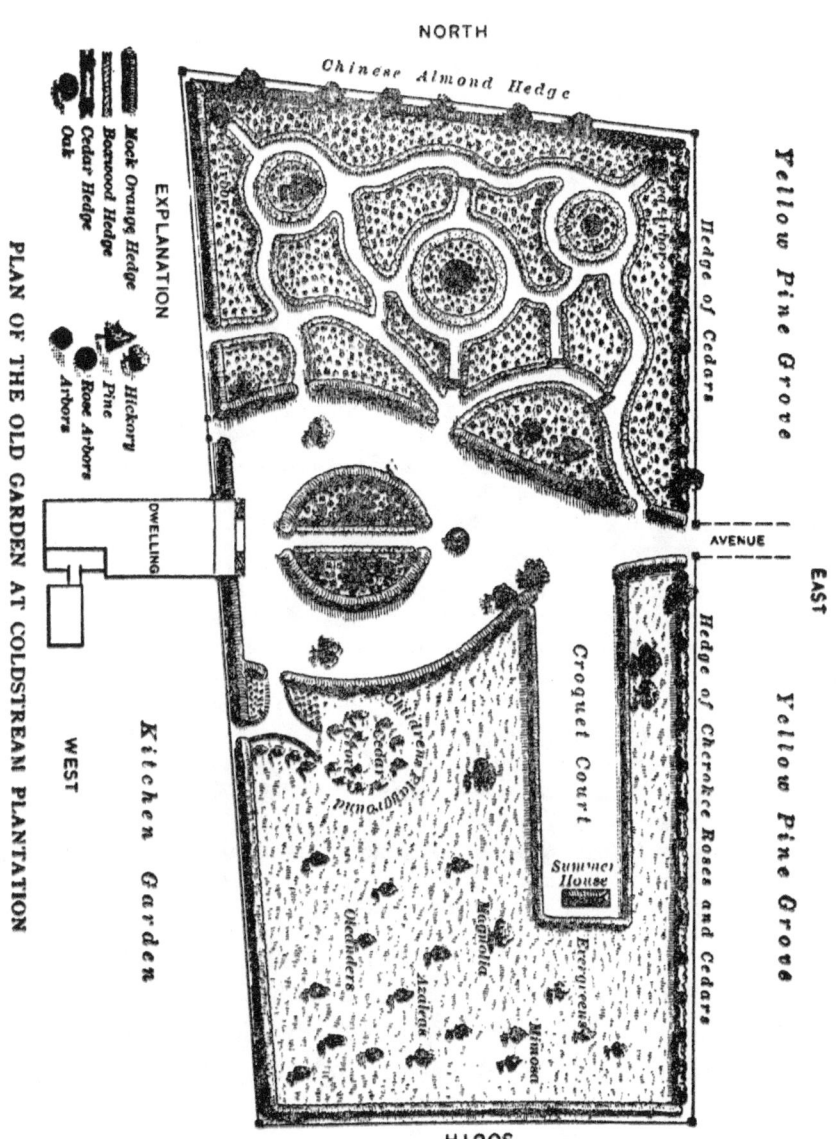

PLAN OF THE OLD GARDEN AT COLDSTREAM PLANTATION

A circle of evergreens spanned by two evergreen arches, making the driveway to the door and forming the garden's center. Walking beneath the arches, he discovers a broad, box-bordered pathway, inclosing beds fragrant with magnolias, oleanders, camellias, tea-olives, lilacs, gardenias, and laurestinus. Here year after year birds nest in trellises covered with white and yellow Banksias, and the airy wings of butterflies flutter over a tangle of moss-roses.

To the left of this central circle, in the southeastern part of the garden, there is a leafy hedge, trimmed like a wall, ornamented with rounded posts of evergreens at regular spaces. At the eastern end of this wall is the croquet-lawn. . . .

The western end of the evergreen wall terminates in an arch through which there is a glimpse of a circular grove of cedars, which is the children's playground. . . .

West of the cedar grove is another tall hedge, twice the height of the tall gardener. This divides the garden of flowers from the gay kitchen garden, where figs, raspberries, and strawberries share honors with an unending sequence of vegetables. There herbaceous borders of the beds exhibit a variety of rich hues the year around; and beyond the kitchen garden is the old Dutch oven, the fortress-like walls of which have withstood earthquakes, bearing testimony to work well done.

The northeastern end of the garden is the social center of the household. The broad walks, one of its main features, wind among flower-beds of geometric designs (ellipses, oblongs, quincuzes, lozenges, circles and triangles) and are bordered with box, *Euonymus*, imperial fleur-de-lis, old-fashioned scented violets, tea plants, *Yucca filamentosa*, and mockorange. The pathways are arched by drooping *Spirea*, and delicate tendrils of yellow jasmine have woven themselves from tree to tree. Under sheltering deodars, laurels, and magnolias are cozy nooks, and easy chairs and benches invite to reading and contemplation. Beyond a snowy mound of pearl *Banksias* the path makes a sudden turn, and there, walled in by Chinese almonds, is the green little tea-arbor.

After the death of Miss Hamilton Witherspoon in 1911, the home site of Coldstream was sold to a cotton planter, who cut down the trees and ploughed up the garden for a cotton field. The old house has fallen into ruin, but still stands in lonely desolation.

There were also many lovely gardens in the town of Sumter. A visitor who came in 1853, signing himself "Scribler", wrote the *Watchman* that "A taste for flowers obtains among the residents, and it will in a few years . . . well deserve the appellation of the 'Town of Roses!'" Strangely coincident, at the very time that "Scribler" was making his prophecy, Commodore Perry was in Japanese waters and had already begun the proceedings which opened the ports of Japan to the world. As an indirect result, Sumter, instead of being the "Town of Roses", has become the "Town of the Japanese Iris Gardens," and is equally well-known for its fine camellias.

The garden of Mrs. Franklin Israel Moses, in the block east of Main Street and north of Republican, now Hampton Avenue, was one of the handsomest in the town, and had a greenhouse in which she grew delicious pineapples for several years. Her gardener was a German, Christian Sanders, a native of Hamburg. He purchased eleven acres nearby from William Haynsworth, and opened the first plant-nursery ever to be in the town. Secession and the war came soon after, and ruined his business. In January 1866, his stock of fruit trees, ornamental shrubbery, flowering shrubs, and rose bushes, was sold at auction at the courthouse, along with his dwelling, furniture, orchard, horse, cow, hogs, wagons and flower pots. Christian Sanders and his wife, Louise, returned to Charleston, where he died in 1872, leaving a reputation as good citizen, "valued for his industry and his probity."

Mrs. James Harvey Dingle was another Sumter woman who took great joy in her flowers, and grew many varieties in the fine hedged garden which faced Sumter Street near the railroad. She and her husband, known as "Uncle Harvey" to everyone, had no children, and, like Mrs. Moses, were devoted members of the Methodist church. During Potter's Raid, their home was taken possession of by the invaders; and after their deaths, the place was sold to the railroad as a site for warehouses.

The home of Colonel James D. Blanding, on what is now West Hampton Avenue, facing Blanding Street, also was embellished with a handsome garden. A circular driveway brought visitors through the formal garden in front. The fine shrubbery completely concealed the house from direct view, for it was a riot of roses, camellias, arbor vitae, and a tremendous wisteria with an 8-inch trunk. Later, when the place was sold, the new owner cut away the garden. Eventually, the house was rolled further down the street, and the Blanding lot is now lovely Memorial Park.

The three-acre garden of A. A. Solomons, in the square where the present courthouse now stands, was one of the show places of the town, featuring camellias, banana trees, ferns and geraniums, with an orange tree in the center of the conservatory.

Swan Lake, the famous Japanese iris garden, has been developed by H. C. Bland into a place of fabulous beauty, and given by him to the city of Sumter for the free enjoyment of the public. Originally owned by the old Bradford family, who made it a well-known mill-site, it passed out of that family in 1877, when sold to Andrew Jackson Moses by Gabriel Wesley Bradford, the surviving executor of Robert Bradford, whose will had been probated in 1850. The subsequent transfers need not be cited here, but in 1908 it was held by Marion Moise, trustee for the Sumter Land Company, who divided it into lots. In 1927, the mill pond, and later some additional lots, were conveyed by F. M. Cain to H. C. Bland, who, with the artistry of genius, has made it the Mecca for annual visits from thousands of flower-lovers.

In 1947 another iris garden of rare beauty was opened on a commercial basis by Dr. and Mrs. J. Ralph Dunn at Dundell, in the High Hills, on the site of old Marden plantation of Chancellor Thomas Waties. Like the Swan Lake garden, its beauty is further enhanced with azaleas and camellias.

The garden of Mrs. Walter C. White at Stateburg is notable. But the modern gardens of Sumter County are so numerous, that a whole book might be required even to mention their names!

CHAPTER XXXII

PAINTERS AND PAINTINGS

The people of Sumter County in general have expressed their love of beauty more in gardens than in painting and sculpture, but nevertheless the county is not without an art history.

The earliest homes of course, lacked both gardens and works of art, but with prosperity and comfortable homes, came also a desire for home decoration. During the early 1800's prints seem to have been popular. Mrs. Margaret Vaughan, widow of Henry Vaughan, from his estate of some $40,000, received among other things, a print of the Washington family valued at twelve dollars, and four other prints valued at twenty-five dollars. The inventory of James H. Montgomery in 1814, amounting to more than $22,000 listed "House Pictures" and frames valued at eleven dollars. John Monk's effects as produced in 1828 by Rachel Haynsworth Monk, administratrix, and appraised at nearly $14,000 included six pictures valued at eight dollars, and three others in black frames. Captain George Cooper of Rollindale plantation, who died in 1829, leaving an estate of almost $55,000, had eight pictures, but only the frames were valued, and they at just two dollars.

Family portraits have always been popular, and perhaps one of the earliest painted in Sumter District was a small self-portrait done by Chancellor Thomas Waties (1760-1828), of Marden, Stateburg, who also painted a miniature of one of his daughters. These are now owned by Mayo Rees, a descendant, who also has artistic talent and has taught art in a number of southern colleges. Born and reared in Stateburg, she now lives at Crescent Beach, where she paints in oil and water colors. She has copied several family portraits from Sumter District, among others a portrait of Colonel Orlando Savage Rees (1796-1852) of Stateburg, for whom Orlando, Florida, is said to have been named. The original portrait is not signed or dated, but from the youth of the subject, it must have been painted about 1817. At that time John Tolman was advertising in the *Camden Journal* as a portrait painter, who would not receive pay for his work unless it gave perfect satisfaction. A New England artist, he also painted in Charleston.

Portrait painters travelling the "Great Road" between Camden and Charleston, made it possible for Sumter people to acquire family portraits, for doubtless these artists stopped along the way, especially in Manchester and Stateburg. An interesting but primitive old painting in very poor condition, is a portrait of Mrs. Rebecca M. (Pitts) Loring of Stateburg, wife of Daniel Loring from Massachusetts, which is now owned by Mr. Loring Lee of Sumter. After Loring's death, she married again twice and died at the early age of thirty-seven. From her apparent age in the portrait and the dates of her marriage settlements, the painting must have been done in the early 1800's.

William Kenedy Barclay, a well-known young Charleston artist, a pupil of Thomas Sully, was painting in Camden in 1837. His "admirable" portrait of Thomas Salmond of Camden, was done to hang in the cabin of the river steamer, "Thomas Salmond"[1] which plied between Camden and Charleston, making regular stops at Sumter's Landing.

In 1838 James DeVeaux, another young Charleston artist of great promise, having done a fine portrait of John Laurence Manning in New York, was invited to Milford, the Manning home in the Sandhills, to paint other members of the family. There "he remained until the winter of 1839, fully occupied, and turning off from his easel many of his best portraits, enjoying himself in a delightful society, which appreciated him highly . . . ."[2]

A third Charleston artist, Thomas Wightman, "highly promising pupil of the celebrated portrait painter Inman," was painting during the winter and spring of 1841 in Camden, Bennettsville, and Cheraw.[3] It is not improbable that he, as

---

[1] *Commercial Courier*, Camden, Sept. 30, Oct. 7, 1837. James McGibbon advertised in the *Camden Journal* during the winter of 1829-30, to paint landscapes and portraits in Camden and vicinity. On March 14, 1835, a "Mr. Gardner" was noted in the *Camden Journal and Southern Whig* as exhibiting his paintings.

[2] Robert W. Gibbes, *A Memoir of James DeVeaux of Charleston, S. C.* (Columbia, 1846), p. 41.

[3] *Farmer's Gazette and Cheraw Advertiser*, Feb. 4, Mch 3, Apr. 7, June 23, 1841.

well as Barclay and DeVeaux, may have executed some orders for well-to-do patrons in Sumter District.

Miniatures also were in high favor. Mrs. Catherine Ladd, who taught in the Bishopville Academy in 1835, was advertised by the principal as excelling "in painting Landscapes in Oil colours and Miniature painting on Ivory."[4] Later, Mrs. Ladd settled in Winnsboro, and she is said to have designed the first Confederate flag.

Young ladies who were educated in ante-bellum schools were expected to be "accomplished" and some of them were. Mary Hooper Anderson of Stateburg, who married Frederick L. Childs, inherited an interest in art from her father, Dr. William W. Anderson, whose drawing of Chancellor Waties from a miniature is said to be excellent. Among Mrs. Childs' paintings which are treasured by her descendants, are a portrait, now owned by St. Julien R. Childs of Charleston, and two pictures of Marden, Chancellor Waties' home.

Some painters combined their art work with surprising crafts. Isaac B. Alexander, jeweller and silversmith of Camden, in 1841 also repaired guns and pistols as well as "other work in the Smithing business," but when required, he painted "likenesses and miniatures as heretofore." Perhaps he is the same young "Mr. Alexander" whose "beautiful specimens of miniature painting" were praised in the Camden *Commercial Courier* in 1838, for their "delicacy of finish and accuracy of expression, many of them will bear comparison with the products of much older artists. . . ." In 1862, during the many shortages of the war years, a Dr. I. B. Alexander in Camden was offering to alter kerosene, camphene or oil lamps, so as to burn a substitute made from rosin and turpentine, called Terebene, "the best light now used in the Confederacy."[5]

Equally versatile, a native of Charleston but a resident of Sumter, was advertising in the *Watchman* in 1852. He was Charles W. Davis, "a young man of much genius and taste," who donated to the Charleston Fair a plan of Charleston and Savannah cut from paper, a wooden chain cut from a solid

---

[4] *Camden Journal and Southern Whig*, Jan. 24, 1835. Her husband, George Ladd, also painted portraits and miniatures. See sketch of Mrs. Ladd in *DAB*.

[5] *Commercial Courier*, Camden, Apr. 21, 1838; *Camden Journal*, June 2, 1841; T. J. Kirkland and R. M. Kennedy, *Historic Camden* (Columbia, 1926), II, 323.

block with a penknife, and "several Beautiful Specimens of Painting in Water and Oil Colors." In the latter branches, he wished to give lessons, but apparently failed to get pupils, for the next year he was advertising that he would be happy to do engraving at the store of C. T. Mason, jeweller. Later, at E. Sommers' Clothing Emporium, Mr. Davis was asking for fancy painting, lettering, "Architecturing or the repairing of Accordians, Flutenas, etc." Soon after, as a "Daguerrean Artist" he was taking daguerreotypes on metal at the "Sign of the American Flag." There he worked out for himself a method of making ambrotypes, which are taken on glass, but his were so light in weight that they could be "sent by mail without extra postage." He also specialized in stereopticon pictures, which then were found on every "parlor" table for the entertainment of visitors. By experiments he developed an original method of "Mirroring and Graining" his ambrotypes so as to make the pictured objects stand out in bold relief. The next year he invented an ambrotype clock-dial, taken upon mica instead of glass, which could be fitted into an old clock at little cost or effort. Some of Davis' advertisements indicate that he used original methods in that field also. After the fall of the Confederacy, he married Mrs. Laura Lamb of Union in 1866, who predeceased by fifteen years his death in 1890.[6] Both are buried in Sumter.

Many itinerant portrait painters were visiting the town of Sumter during the 1850's, usually coming in the autumn, when cotton crops had been sold and money was available. J. S. Wear took rooms at China's Hotel in 1852, and advertised as both a "Portrait and Daguerrean Artist." The next year George W. Fitzwilson exhibited his paintings at the grand jury room in the courthouse. Charles H. Lanneau, "superb Portrait Painter" and daguerrean from Charleston, in 1855 at China's Hotel, tried to stimulate his business with the slogan "Death is abroad and may take away your friends at any moment." On his return in 1856, he opened his gallery at the rooms of Charles W. Davis.[7]

One itinerant artist, "Mr. Prescott" reversed the usual

---

[6] *Watchman*, Nov. 6, 1852; Apr. 29, 1853; Jan. 5, 1855; May 28, 1856; Mch 4, Apr. 8, Dec. 28, 1857; Sept. 21, 1858. *Sumter News*, June 28, 1866. Epitaphs, cemetery, Sumter.
[7] For Wear, *Watchman*, Sept. 11, 18, 25, Oct. 2, 16, 1852. For Fitzwilson, *ibid.*, Oct. 14-28, 1853. For Lanneau, *Ibid.*, Oct. 31, Nov. 7, 1855; Nov. 26, Dec. 3, 1856.

order, and came to Sumter for the three spring months of 1858. Apparently he did a good business. After painting what were said to be excellent likenesses of the Rev. Donald McQueen, Colonel Montgomery Moses, the late Colonel John B. Miller, Dr. James Haynsworth, and un-named "others," Prescott departed "to complete some orders in Virginia, from whence he will proceed to Montreal, C.E., by way of Niagara and the Lakes." Possibly he was the artist Plumer Prescott, who was born in New Hampshire in 1838.[8]

During these years, a "Mr. Carter of Virginia", a tubercular artist, came to Sumter for his health and opened a studio. At least one of his portraits can be identified, Emma Spears, aged sixteen, the adopted daughter and niece of Mr. and Mrs. Thomas Jefferson Coghlan. The young girl had been very ill and was not expected to recover, but she did,[9] and Mr. Carter's charming portrait of her is now owned by her daughter, Miss Louise Whittemore of Sumter.

Many portraits by these and other artists probably were acquired by Sumter families, and although their number has been reduced by the fires which have destroyed so many old homes, a survey might yet bring to light some which could be identified.

The artist who has painted more portraits of Sumter people than any other, was William Harrison Scarborough, from Tennessee, who, in 1837, was invited by Colonel John B. Miller to visit his home, Corn Hill plantation near Sumter, and paint members of the family. The visit resulted in the artist's marriage to sixteen-year-old Miranda, one of the Colonel's seven attractive daughters. The *Watchman* of January 6, 1858, published a letter from Scarborough, then in Paris, to a member of the family, telling in great detail of his European trip, and of a visit to an art show, where treasures from all over England could be seen for a shilling. For several days he remained there, studying the painting and sculpture of old masters and modern artists, and acquiring knowledge which he put to good use in his own work. Among the many who sat for him in Sumter for their portraits, were John B. Miller

[8] *Watchman*, Mch 17, 31, Apr. 14, 28, 1858. His identity was suggested by Ethelwyn Manning, librarian of Frick Art Reference Library, Jan. 6, 1945.
[9] Information from Louise Whittemore.

and others of his large family, Judge and Mrs. John Smyth Richardson, William S. G. Richardson, Judge and Mrs. Franklin I. Moses, Franklin Moses Mikell; Mrs. S. R. Chandler, who later sat for him as Mrs. Baker; Dr. W. W. Anderson, Dr. Thomas W. Baker, Bishop William Capers, and Mrs. W. F. B. Haynsworth.[10]

Sumter's first native artist of note, was Albert Capers Guerry, born and reared at Stateburg, a nephew of Bishop William Capers. After being a student at St. John's College, Spartanburg, he received art instruction in New York from the well-known artist, John B. Irving, Jr., of Charleston. On November 28, 1867, Guerry was married at the Church of the Holy Comforter, Sumter, by the Rev. L. F. Guerry, to Miss Gertrude Wilson, who is said to have been the daughter of an English artist. Mr. J. Harvey Wilson of Mayesville, later reared one of Albert Guerry's children.

Guerry's studio was in a cottage in the yard of T. J. Coghlan's residence on Main street. The Church of the Holy Comforter now stands on the site of this cottage, which has since been rolled back to face on East Calhoun street, and, with extensive additions, it later became the parsonage of the church.

In 1868, Guerry's "Village Dreamer" was exhibited in Sumter at the photographic gallery of Wilder and Wheeler, and later was announced as being shipped to connoisseurs in the North, under the direction of John B. Irving, Jr. Guerry's portrait of the Rev. Donald McQueen also received favorable notice from the Sumter press. But unfortunately, the times were desperately hard, especially for artists, and Albert Guerry by temperament was unsuited to the strain of providing for a family. All accounts agree that Mrs. Guerry and the children suffered from actual hunger. Mr. T. J. Coghlan came to the rescue by advancing them groceries from his commissary, and then collected his compensation by having Guerry paint his and Mrs. Coghlan's portraits, as well as a portrait of Bishop England, which now hangs in the library of the Bishop England High School, Charleston. Guerry is said to have had

---

[10] Helen Kohn Hennig, *William Harrison Scarborough, Portraitist and Miniaturist* (Columbia, 1937), *passim*.

some musical talent, and to have played the fiddle for his friends at dances. Later he removed to Washington, where he painted celebrities, and eventually, after a not too happy life, he went to Atlanta, where he died. He is buried in Washington, Georgia.[11]

One of the earliest art shows on record in Sumter occurred at the Sumter Light Infantry Bazaar, in December 1890, when the "Art Gallery", in charge of Mrs. S. C. Baker, offered to art-lovers an exhibit of twenty-eight pieces of statuary, and one hundred and eight paintings, all entries being listed by title and artist.

Among the Sumter artists of the twentieth century who have won recognition, are Elizabeth White, who has studios in Sumter and Charleston; and, more recently, Charles Mason Crowson, who lives and works in Columbia. Miss White has made a name as an etcher, but works extensively in oil, water colors, and crayon, chiefly on landscapes. It was at her suggestion that the Sumter Art Association was formed in November 1925, when an exhibit of the work of Mrs. Edna Reed Whaley, was being held in Sumter at the Junior High School. The Association is small but active. During the first week in May 1947, it held a notable art show in Sumter, at which was shown the work of more than fifty painters, all of whom were born or domiciled in the county. Among the latter was Walter W. Thompson, born in Florida of Virginia and Massachusetts ancestry, but then residing at Road's End in the Dabbs' settlement, near Salem Black River. He died in April 1948.

Charles Mason Crowson is a great-grandson of Charles T. Mason, the inventive Sumter watchmaker and jeweller, who perfected a non-magnetic watch and an electric burglar alarm, both of which he pattented and sold. Mr. Crowson is also the grandson of Charles T. Mason, Jr., inventor of a successful mechanical cotton-picker and other notable inventions. In 1950, using the well-known bust portrait by Rembrandt Peale, Mr. Crowson painted a full-length portrait of General Sumter, which now hangs in the Sumter Courthouse. He works

---

[11] Information is from various sources: *Sumter News*, Nov. 30, 1867; Dec. 3, 1868; Mch 18, Apr. 15, 1869; Miss Louise Whittemore; H. G. Osteen; Sumter Art Association.

exclusively in oil, and accepts only portrait work, usually painted from life.

At the Sumter Art Show of 1947 was exhibited the work of Corrie McCallum, a Sumter girl, the wife of the artist William Halsey of Charleston. Also shown were a number of paintings by Carl Eugene Mittel, who studied at the Yale Art School. His nudes, said to be very fine, were not shown, probably because the show was held in the Sunday School Building of Trinity Methodist Church.

CHAPTER XXXIII

MUSIC AND THE STAGE

Although Sumter had no ante-bellum theatre, some of its citizens were probably among the wildly enthusiastic audiences in Camden in 1830, when the celebrated Clara Fisher played there for a week. Many pious church-members of that day still felt that the stage was a corrupting influence, which should not be encouraged among the godly. But the people of Sumter seem to have always enjoyed music without any qualms of conscience. The inventory of Dr. William F. Bradberry in 1819, included a violin and a German flute. Later, among the effects of well-to-do Isaac Michau, was a piano. John Haynsworth was another early piano-owner, and W. W. Brunson bequeathed to George W. Loring, his violin and a "Flute that his mother gave me years ago." Local music teachers and visiting singers, from time to time gave concerts in Sumterville; and in 1832, Mr. and Mrs. Samuel Weir of the Female Academy, gave a concert in the courthouse. Music was always in the curriculum of the girls' schools.

The Sumter Brass Band, chartered in 1848, has been mentioned. In the summer of 1851, Mr. Cuttino, apparently a travelling teacher of singing, advertised for his class in vocal music to meet at the Male Academy. The next year the Swiss Bell Ringers gave a "chaste, select and novel" entertainment at the remodeled jail, which had become the Town Hall. Parrow and Company's Great Southern Ethiopian Burlesque Opera and Ballet Troupe, in May 1854, performed for two evenings in their own "capacious pavilion," accompanied by a brass band. But the musical event of that year and later, were the concerts given by a young singer from Columbia, Ellen Brennan, "The Carolina Mocking Bird," whose visits to friends in Sumter already have been mentioned.

In the memorable year 1855, two child-prodigies billed as the "Infant Drummer" and the "American Mocking Bird", gave two concerts at the courthouse. J. C. Witherspoon, in his music class, taught the Baptists, Methodists, and Presbyterians to "sing scientifically" with such success that a concert of vocal music was given at the Baptist Church. And two blind musicians who had been trained in New York, when on their way to take positions in a girls' seminary at Decatur, Georgia, gave a vocal and instrumental concert, alluding with pride to the fact that both their first and their last public appearances were at Sumter.

The musical sensation of the following spring was a week of performances by the Lilliputian Musicians, five little Negroes who had created quite a furore the previous year when they had been taken on a tour of the Southern states by their master, Colonel James B. Richardson, of Momus Hall in the Sand Hills. Their story was told in an earlier chapter.

After the close of the war, a "Mr. Gruber and lady" came from Columbia in the summer of 1866, and gave a program of music and tableaux, assisted by Mr. Gayle of Sumter on the violin, and Mr. Lucas on the flute. In September, Sallie Poole and Adele Durban, assisted by several unnamed gentlemen, had a concert at the courthouse for the benefit of a disabled soldier. Thereafter amateur concerts, tableaux, and minstrels were announced from time to time for various worthy causes.

In 1871 a milestone in Sumter's music history was reached, when H. M. C. Kopff, a German music teacher, organized a brass band of eighteen pieces, and also the Sumter Orchestra. Mr. Kopff taught a number of musical instruments and tuned all the pianos in town. His band was quite international in its charter members, who included B. R. Nash, a capable businessman from North Carolina; M. F. Hewson, an Englishman who had come to town with the garrison; Jerry Croghan, an Irishman; Fritz Bultman, a German shoemaker, who had emigrated to Charleston after four years service in the army of the King of Hanover, and then served the Confederacy for another four years; J. C. Herrington, who seems to have been a native of the county; and A. Morris, a Jewish barkeeper.

Sumter's first theatre was on the second floor of the Town Hall, which was completed in 1872 by private capital. For a few weeks this theatre was called the Sumter Opera House, but in May 1873, it became Music Hall, under the management of J. W. Spalding of the Wilmington Theatre. The Town Council purchased a set of scenery painted in Wilmington, the garden scene of which was said to possess "peculiar merit." Under Spalding's management, professional engagements seem to have been few, but in January 1874, Mrs. James Oate's Operatic Troupe performed the first opera ever heard in Sumter, "creating quite a furore."

At some time during these years, young Joseph Physioc, son of J. E. Physioc then living in Columbia, began playing small parts in various visiting plays, and thus entered upon a distinguished stage career. The Physioc family moved to Sumter, probably during the Hampton administration. On July 3, 1881, Joe Physioc played at Music Hall in his benefit performance of the comedy *For Love of Gold,* and introduced "Emmet's 'Mountain Guide,' . . . Knight's beautiful 'Lullaby,' . . . 'The Famous Dude Song' and Banjo specialties." Mr. and Mrs. Theo Starke of Columbia volunteered their services for the occasion, and a complimentary hop was scheduled to follow the performance.

Joe Physioc was a versatile youth, possessing among other gifts, a "wonderful tenor," and his artistic talents were recognized by a barn-storming actor named Theodore, who taught him to paint scenery. Eventually, with his beautiful sister Mollie, Joe went North with a stock company, and in a varied and successful career, he won both fame and wealth as an actor, a designer of magnificent stage settings, and a mural and watercolor artist.

Joe's younger brother, Master Bob Physioc, won a skating tournament at Music Hall in 1884, as "first skater." During that year and the next, Joe, who was then with the Madison Square Theatre Company, and his sister Mollie, were mentioned many times in the local newspapers as visiting in Sumter. In March 1889, all three of the gifted young Physiocs came to Sumter professionally, with the Jessica Thomas Troupe for an engagement at Music Hall. Bob played a too-difficult role as tutor in *Asmodeous,* a play which forbade "good acting in any one," said the *Watchman and Southron,* but he redeemed his reputation in *Child of the Regiment.* Another local member of the same troupe was Emily Vivian, this apparently being the stage name of Lela Edwards.

When the troupe returned for a second engagement the following May, in the *Pearl of Savoy*, the audience was disappointing, for the young men of the town had spent all their money the previous day. The *Watchman and Southron's* discerning critic, in a detailed estimate of each performer, said of Joe Physioc that he had "not discovered the difference between an American buffoon and a French peasant. He lacks study, not ability."

During the 1880's, under the management of D. J. Auld, Sumter's postmaster, many high class attractions were booked for Music Hall, especially in the year 1886. The most notable was the prima donna Clara Louise Kellogg, who had been born in Sumter in 1839, when her parents were teaching at the Academy.

Having achieved an international reputation, Kellogg in 1886 was making a tour of the Southern states, but she did not allow sentiment for her birthplace to interfere with her financial arrangements, and she consented to give one concert in Sumter for a sum which Manager Auld described as large but attainable. Nearly two hundred reserved seats were sold at $1.50, and general admission was set at one dollar.

On the evening of February 3, 1886, Kellogg sang to a "crowded house, the largest possibly ever gathered" in Sumter. The music critic of the *Watchman and Southron*, distrusting his own ability to appraise the technicalities, rather tepidly had "no doubt that it was perfectly delightful," but noted that the diva was "fair, fat and forty . . . in the comparative degree. Her voice was exceedingly sweet, especially in the lower tones. . . . Mr. D. J. Auld has earned the thanks of the music lovers of Sumter." During an intermission, some young men with enthusiasm for the return of the home-town girl who had made good, are said to have gone backstage with an offering of champagne, which the singer so much appreciated, that she had some difficulty in completing her program.

Not long after the concert, an estimate of Kellogg from a prominent stage-manager was quoted in the local news: "Her avarice, vanity and coldness have been her chief impediments throughout her public career. They destroyed her chance of becoming one of the most popular women in the world, for she was one of the most perfect vocalists that ever appeared before the public."

Other attractions at Music Hall in the same month with Kellogg, were Katie Putnam and her comedy company, which played to a full house that was well pleased; and the Bijou Opera Company, which performed *The Mikado* to an appreciative audience. Later, an excellent Star Opera Company gave two performances.

The professional players during this time were in competition with local amateurs who probably were inspired by the work of the professionals. Under the direction of W. C. Kops, the Sumter Amateurs put on *Above the Clouds*, to help get uniforms for the Sumter Light Infantry, and later took their show to Manning. Several married couples appeared in a play called *Married Life*.

In 1887, the comedy *The Kansas Immigrants*, under the direction of Bartow Walsh, son of the judge of probate, filled Music Hall with a capacity crowd, which also was favored with tableaux directed by Miss Claude Girardeau. Later, a drama called *Comrades*, directed by Mrs. C. G. Bacot, drew a large and appreciative audience to Music Hall. Two weeks later, the Sumter Operatic Troupe rendered *Trial by Jury*, an operetto which "completely took the hearts of all present by storm," and the reporter hoped that the troupe would organize on a permanent basis. Miss Mary Girardeau, one of the principals of Eclectic College, wrote a cantata which was set to music by W. L. Johnson of Spartanburg, and was performed in Sumter in May, also at Music Hall.

The Monte Cristo Company in March of that year gave a professional performance which "took immensely" but the critic found the fourth act unpleasantly startling to those who did not favor a scene which smacked of the "Paris code of morals." In December the Marion Fleming Troupe brought a musical extravaganza called *The Brook*, which kept the audience laughing, and seems to have merited no adverse criticism.

During the winter season of 1888, the Rose Osborne Comedy Company, rated first class by the Sumter critic, in three performances at Music Hall in February, brought a repertoire that included a "great society play, *Forget me not*," and the finest orchestra ever heard in Sumter.

For the latter part of February, a very different type of entertainment was booked, Mrs. Belva Ann Lockwood, for her lecture, "Across the Continent and what I saw." Known as "Queen of the American Bar," this unusual lady, after being twice widowed, became at the age of forty-nine, the first woman admitted to practice before the United States Supreme Court. She also was the first woman to be a candidate for the presidency of the United States, having been nominated in 1884 and 1888 by the National Equal Rights party. General admission to her lecture was only thirty-five cents, but bad weather and some disapproval of the speaker, combined to keep people away. Despite the small audience, Mrs. Lockwood spoke for an hour and forty minutes, and although Manager Auld lacked a third of the sum he had guaranteed, he paid her in full. Not to be outdone, Mrs. Lockwood then stayed over to give another lecture for his benefit! The weather, however, would not cooperate, and again there was a very small audience. But, said the critic of the *Watchman and Southron*, she excelled the previous night's performance with her "Social and Political Life in Washington," one of the best he had ever heard, and those who had stayed away because of Mrs. Lockwood's women's rights ideas "would have heard nothing offensive or contaminating." Mrs. Lockwood refused to accept a cent of the proceeds.

Apparently this was one of the last attractions brought by Manager Auld, for he resigned this season. But in December 1888, after his resignation, two minstrel shows and *Peck's Bad Boy* filled engagements at Music Hall.

In February 1889, the Sumter City Council signed a three-year lease of the hall with J. A. Schwerin and P. P. Gaillard, under the firm name of J. A. Schwerin and Company, at a rental of three hundred dollars a year, from which two hundred dollars was allowed the first year for repairs. Once again the name of the little theatre was changed, and Music Hall became the Academy of Music.

Schwerin's first bookings were bad, and the local critic rated Mugg's Landing Company as a mere Bowery show. The next also was a dismal failure, and hope was expressed that Mr. Schwerin would "improve his taste. . . . There was a time within the past few years, when the stage here was occupied by the Madison Square Companies. When we had such plays as 'The Orphans,' 'Hazel Kirk,' etc. But we must now listen to second class minstrels or admire. . . . Concert Hall girls or do without the theatre altogether." His words were heeded, and soon after, the Prescott and McLean Company treated a large audience to a good performance of *Pygmalion and Galatea.*

During the summer of 1890, the lessees made extensive changes at the Academy of Music. Fifty electric lights, an inclined floor, and seven tiers of noiseless opera chairs with hatracks, were installed. The stage was remodeled, with a box on either side, and two hundred and fifty pieces of scenery. The drop curtain, painted by Eugene Cramer of Columbia, showed a view of Lake Como nestled among the hills of Italy. The capacity of the theatre was increased from four hundred to seven hundred.

The season opened in the fall with Hoyt's *Three Fast Men.* Favorable press notices were given performances by Hi Henry's Minstrels, Rose Osborne in the society play *Satan*, and Amy Russell in *Life in the Metropolis.* Schwerin and Company were congratulated. In January 1891, a large and appreciative audience braved a cold rain to see Dan Packard in *The Boomer.* Walter Lawrence played the title role in Aiden Benedict's *Fabio Romani* Company. The New York Theatre Company in a week's engagement, presented among other plays, *Master and Man*, and *The Galley Slave.* Madame Frye's Concert Company, all women, sponsored by the Masonic Temple Company of Sumter, charmed a good audience. Al Field's Minstrels followed. During Lent, Alberta Gallatin's Company drew the largest houses of the season with *As You Like It, Romeo and Juliet,* and *The Hunchback.* In March came J. W. Carner in *Rip Van Winkle;* and Adele Frost in *Ingomar* and *Virginia.* In August two concerts by the Golde Opera and Concert Company were noticed as "musical treats."

Encouraged by success, Manager Schwerin during the summer added a gallery to the Academy of Music. The new season opened on September 26, 1891, with the Barlow Brothers Operatic Minstrels, but the high-sounding name meant nothing, for it proved to be so like other minstrels "as not to demand further mention" from the disappointed critic. In October, *Jim the Westerner,* a society play, "captivated the entire audience." John Palmer's dramatization of *The Last Days of Pompeii* was rated as only "tolerable." Other bookings were: *A Breezy Time;* Milton Noble in *Sire to Son;* the Duncan Clark Minstrels; and the Cleveland Minstrels, which were "good in every respect." Elfin Star Company made a favorable impression with *Passion's Slave, Lady Audley's Secret,* and *Little Lord Fauntleroy,* in which last, little Mary Rowe captivated the largest audience of the week-long engagement. Gus Homer's Own Company with *Hit or Miss, Michael Strogoff* and a new play each night for a week, was rated a fine company.

In January 1892, came *A Social Session,* a humorous farce; and home talent in the Home Circle Minstrels, which sold out the house. In February, Janauscheck proved to be excellent in *Harvest Moon.* The Harry Lindley show, *Cynchea, the Queen of the Gypsies,* was the worst of the season, until a minstrel the following week turned out to be "the greatest fraud" ever in Sumter, and the unfortunate manager took an early train out the next morning, leaving his company stranded!

The tragic end of the Academy of Music came soon after the opening of the next season. About nine o'clock on the night of Friday, December 9, 1892, while the Chick Company was giving a performance, fire broke out in a dressing room. There was a momentary halt among the actors, who immediately resumed their roles, when Manager Schwerin appeared on the rear of the stage, and quietly announced that the building was on fire but in no immediate danger, and requested the audience to leave without hurry. The curtain was lowered, there was little confusion, and all got out safely.

But the scenery blazed like tinder, and flames engulfed the stage so quickly, that most of the actors escaped with only the costumes in which they were playing; one lost diamonds and $400 in cash. The Chick Company's loss was $1,500. Several stores also burned, and, as the goods which were saved from the fire were ruined by rain, the total loss was $70,000. This of course did not include the loss of all the town's official records, which were in the Town Office on the second floor of the building. Characteristically, the story of the disaster carried the announcement that the burned district would be rebuilt immediately.

The corner stone of a new City Hall-Opera House was laid December 27, 1893, and it was soon erected on the same site. Sumter continued to enjoy theatricals until the traveling road-shows were forced out of business by the competition of moving pictures.

After the second World War, a group of Sumter citizens, in the fall of 1948, organized the Sumter Community Theatre, with H. Glen Oetgen as president. The following April, 1949, James D. Moos of Louisiana, was engaged as director, and a new era of theatrical history came to Sumter.

CHAPTER XXXIV

WRITERS AND WRITINGS

The genius of the people of Sumter County has found comparatively little expression through literary channels, although the founding of the Sumterville Circulating Library Society in the summer of 1809, indicates that the community has long possessed readers with definite literary interests. William Gilmore Simms, who knew Sumter through his friend Maynard Richardson, stated in his *Geography* of the state in 1843, that Sumter District had "more than the usual share of taste for arts and literature. Some of her more wealthy planters appropriate large sums for these objects. Collections of pictures are forming, and the private libraries are frequent and select."

The earliest literary effort from the region to be printed, was probably the essay on the "Influence of Religion on Civil Society," published shortly after the Revolution, by the Rev. Thomas Reese of Salem Black River, and rated "an honorable testimony to posterity of the literature of Carolina in 1788." It was so highly regarded by theologians, that Princeton University, where the author had graduated twenty years earlier, conferred upon him the degree of doctor of divinity, said to have been the first such honor ever bestowed upon a Carolinian.

Francis Kinloch, who inherited from his brother Cleland Kinloch a life-interest in Acton at Stateburg, had literary and artistic tastes, as attested by his library of 1,115 books at Acton. He also did some writing. His *Eulogy of George Washington* was published in Georgetown in 1800, and reprinted in New York in 1867. His "Letters from Geneva and France" first appeared in 1808 in *Port Folio*, a Philadelphia periodical, and in 1819 was published in Boston as a two-volume book.

A very valuable historical work from Sumter District, published in 1821, was *A Sketch of the Life of Brig. Gen. Francis Marion and a History of his Brigade* . . . . by Judge William

Dobein James, of Brookland, Stateburg. The author was the son of Major John James of Williamsburg, and, as a lad of seventeen years, had served with his father and older brother, Captain John James, under General Marion. Judge James, therefore, had a firsthand knowledge of the events in which he had participated. Besides, he had a collection of contemporary letters for reference, many of which he published in the appendix. Elected a chancellor of the court of equity in 1802, he was transferred twenty-two years later to the law bench. Unfortunately, by this time he had become a notorious alcoholic, and in 1828 he was impeached, and removed from the bench. He died at Brookland on June 4, 1840.

In the field of legal writing, two publications are from the pen of John B. Miller. The first is *A Collection of the militia laws of the United States and South Carolina, that are of force. . . .*, printed in 1817, in Columbia, by D. and J. J. Faust. The appendix to this small book gives more than a hundred pages of pertinent cases, and eight indexes which testify to Mr. Miller's systematic and orderly mind. The other publication is *Instructions for Guardians and Trustees,* an 8-page pamphlet, printed in 1847, but which does not name the place or printer.

A noteworthy book to be credited to Sumter, is *Western Africa: Its History, Condition, and Prospects*, by the Rev. John Leighton Wilson, who, born and reared near Mount Zion Church, had served almost twenty years as a missionary in that then unknown continent. This encyclopaedic little book, published in New York in 1856, was an invaluable standard reference in its day, and still possesses historical value.

But it is in the old newspapers of Sumter that the names and works of local writers are most abundantly evident. Maynard Davis Richardson, son of Judge John Smyth Richardson, and remembered as the editor of the *Southern Whig,* died in 1830 at the age of twenty, with a reputation for intellectual gifts and literary promise which might have materialized had he lived. As a studious boy at Bloom Hill, with very weak eyes, he was forbidden by his mother to do any reading, but he moved his books into an old carriage in the garden, and there each day he read to his heart's content until sundown. A graduate of the South Carolina College at the age of eighteen, he collaborated with William Gilmore Simms to begin a newspaper in Charleston, the *Evening Gazette,* which "deservedly expired after one or two spasmodic gasps." Upon Richardson's untimely death, Simms collected and anonymously published his writings, as *The Remains of Maynard Davis Richardson, with a Memoir of his Life,* which is said to have been Simms' first prose effort, and bears evidence of the truth of the statement.

When the *Sumter Gazette* began publication, it apparently had some hope of printing books. In January 1831 Francis Bremar was advertising that book-binding in all its branches was carried on at the printing office, but no Sumter imprints of that period have as yet come to light. *The Black River Watchman,* in its first issue on April 27, 1850, advertised that both book and job printing of every description would be executed with neatness and dispatch at its office, but no books from its presses are known to exist.

The columns of Sumter's ante-bellum newspapers, however, reveal abundant evidence of local poetic ambitions. Numberless contributors developed a knack for rhyme and rhythm, very far-fetched sometimes; but almost all these modest people hid their identities behind pen names or initials. Some stanzas were witty, but most were lugubrious, and often stilted or grandiloquent. Very few of the contributors showed genius, but many of them knew their classics. "Homer's Ghost," "Juvenis," "Orion," "Roland," "Fides," "Felix Gossamer," "Peter Pindar," "Karloman Christie," "Susan Singledoom," "Ellie Claremont," and a host of other unkowns from all over the district, showered the printer with their offerings. "Gleaner" wrote short stories for both the *Banner* and the *Watchman.*

Few of these pen names can now be identified. "Clio" was a very secret name used by the Rev. James H. Thornwell during his brief sojourn in Sumterville in 1832, when he was writing for the Unionists against Nullification. "Philippon" was John J. James, "a man of learning and talent," son of Judge James and a graduate of West Point. He studied law and began a successful practice in Sumter District, but he, too, became an alcoholic, and eventually drifted into teaching.

During 1853, he contributed to the *Watchman* four articles on reminiscences of West Point. The next year, three articles appeared on European subjects; and in 1855, a series of eight articles on the Revolution were published from "the collection of the late Judge James." On January 19, 1856, John J. James, "aged about fifty-five years," died at the residence of Mr. Lawrence Spann near Stateburg.

Only one pen name of a woman has been identified. Mrs. Elizabeth Ann Chambers, daughter of the Rev. Hartwell Spain of the Sumter Methodist Church, made quite a name for herself as "Lizzie Clarendon," contributing stories, articles, and poems to the *Southern Christian Advocate*, the *Home Circle*, the *Columbia Times*, and many other periodicals. Born in 1827, she entered school at the age of six and mastered the spelling book in one week. Most of her schooling was in Columbia, under a Mrs. Martin, perhaps Mrs. M. Martin of the Columbia Female Seminary. At the age of sixteen, Elizabeth Ann Spain began her literary career, when her first effort was sent by her brother-in-law to the *American Courier* in Philadelphia, to which she became a regular contributor. After her marriage, she went with her husband to Florida, where her health was ruined by malaria. The *Sumter Banner* printed her story, "Circumstantial Evidence," and reprinted her "Domestic Troubles," from the *South Carolinian*. The *Watchman* published a few of her poems: "Memory — A Sketch;" "The Christmas Gathering," reprinted from the *Southern Sun;* "A Bride's Departure," and "I Would Not Live Always." Her writings conformed to the standards of the day, and she was rated "among the first female writers of the South." On December 12, 1857, she died suddenly of pneumonia at her father's home in Sumter, and was buried in the cemetery on Oakland Avenue, leaving a four-year-old daughter and a son of two months. Her "Literary Remains" were collected for a memorial volume, but were accidentally destroyed by fire before publication.

Of those who signed initials, W. H. A. R. proved to be W. H. A. Richbourg, of Rafton Creek, who during 1855 and 1856 kept the *Watchman* well supplied with his verses.

Among those who signed their own names, were Mrs. F. A.

Canfield, who contributed "The Humming Bird and the Wren;" a Miss Spann, who wrote "The First Kiss;" and Carrie J. McIntosh, who sent among many others: "Heaven," "The Dead Brother," "A Wife to her Absent Husband," "Moonlight Musings," and "Lines" on a boy of eight years leaving his mother and sisters "to seek work among strangers."

Dr. R. Augustus Bethune of Sylvan Retreat, Bradleyville, wrote odes, character sketches, articles on Temperance, some of which he signed "Dr. Patrick," and short stories. After a trip to the West in 1855, he located at Plowden's Mills, where, as was then customary, he opened his own drugstore. He married a daughter of Matthew P. Mayes of Mayesville. In 1874, he and his family were living in Ashley County, Arkansas.

Another contributor who used his own name was J. R. Chandler, who signed an epigram on "Civilization and Art:"

> When Eve through early Eden moved
>   And tuned her maiden voice
> It was not strange that Adam loved,
>   He'd only Hobson's choice.
> And when ten girls are found at home
>   With chance for scarce two men,
> Not idle grace, not linnet's hum
>   Will catch the beaux to make them come,
> Each girl must BUSTLE then!

A great many original stories and a few short-length novels were printed in the ante-bellum newspapers, which gave belles-lettres a place of honor on the front page. During the years that John Witherspoon Ervin was teaching in Sumter, he contributed much to the *Black River Watchman*, of which he was a founder, and also editor from April 27, 1850 until November 18, 1851. In June 1852, he sold his interest in the paper and gave his full time to teaching.

One day Ervin's wife happened to see in a Columbia newspaper an offer of a $100-prize for an original story. With eager faith in his genius, she begged him to compete. "I could not have been more astonished," he later wrote in his Journal of Thoughts and Events, "had she asked me to journey to the

Alps to gather an eidel weiss. But she was very persistent, and I had to give a reluctant consent to try. In the course of a week ... my story was completed, and copied as time permitted. My wife read it over with delight and pronounced it a story that would win. It consisted of some 13,000 words. I sent it to the publishers without much hope of its success, and when a week or two later I saw the titles of more than sixty competing stories published, I felt a pity for my wife. The stories were put into the hands of a committee to decide and award the prize. That committee consisted of Colonel John S. Preston, who became a General during the Confederate War; of Wade Hampton, afterwards a great cavalry leader; and of Mr. Arthur, of Columbia, a man of fine literary attainments. ... One morning about a month afterwards my wife opened the paper and announced much to her joy and my surprise that the prize had been awarded to me. The story entitled *A Shot in Time* was considered a great success."

In August 1854, Ervin's *Michael Allscot; or The Shot in Time,*" a tale of Marion's men, won a first prize of $75, and was reprinted in the *Watchman* from the *Columbia Banner*. In July 1857, the *South Carolinian* republished it again from the *Columbia Banner*, so the story must indeed have been a success! In 1855 the *Darlington Flag* reprinted from the *Sumter Banner*, "that beautiful episode 'The Serpent's Spell.' " The next year, Ervin's "Silver Shot or the Autossee Chief," a novel in thirty chapters, appeared in the *Watchman*, and was reprinted in the *Newberry Mirror*. It, too, proved popular, and in 1857, the *Watchman* issued a prospectus for its publication in book form, but this apparently did not materialize. Four of Ervin's short stories appeared in the *Watchman's* columns that year: "The Brothers;" "Archibald Kerr, 'The Scout of the Swamp,' " in four chapters; "Our Old Townsman, A Village Tradition," in two chapters; and "Morpeth in Muddleton." He also won a prize of $40 from the *Darlington Family Friend*, for his "Tracking the Forgers," in four chapters. Mr. Ervin left Sumter that year and removed his family to the new village of Manning, where he took charge of the grammar school, and edited the *Clarendon Banner*.

In addition to fiction, Ervin wrote a number of poems; and

some excellent descriptive editorials apparently came from his pen. In the spring of 1857, one of his admirers, writing in the Charleston *Daily Courier,* rated Ervin "one of the most successful and experienced of our young writers, and, after Simms, one of the most devoted students of our traditional resources of romance and local novelettes."

Writers were then beginning to realize that they ought to find inspiration in scenes and experiences which they knew first-hand. A letter to the *Watchman* in March 1856, signed "Adolens", counseled Southern writers to turn away from foreign scenes to the opportunities in America, "a home for literature in all its rich luxuriousness. . . . How many have given the true features of the Southern life? . . . Not one. Mrs. H. B. Stowe in 'Uncle Tom's Cabin' is perhaps as near the truth as any other . . . and . . . she is as far from truth as the father of lies. . . ."

Early in the twentieth century, Kate Furman of the Privateer section of Sumter County, very literally wrote from materials at home. From the old papers and account books of her ancestor, William Murrell, she wrote a delightful article, "An Oldtime Merchant of South Carolina", which appeared in the sixth volume of the *Publications of the Southern History Association.* Even more valuable was her "General Sumter and his Neighbors," in the same volume.

McDonald Furman also felt an urge to literature. In 1891 he tried his hand at short stories, "The Mystery Explained," and "The Tumbler of Blood," both of which were published in the *Watchman and Southron.* He also was interested in the Catawba Indians, and in the people of mixed Indian blood, known in Sumter as the Red Bones; and from time to time he contributed short articles on them to the same paper and perhaps to others.

During the same period, Mrs. Lee C. Harby, sister of Mrs. Altamont Moses, was contributing to magazines various local and historical sketches, fiction and biography. Her novel, "Judy Robinson, Milliner," was published in *Godey's Magazine* in 1893, and was described in the *Watchman and Southron* as "a fresh bright story," with bits of description that were "gem-like in beauty."

The peerless letter-writer of Sumter District was the witty and charming Natalie Delage, wife of Thomas Sumter, Jr. Her letters were justly compared by Aaron Burr to those of the celebrated Lady Mary W. Montague, of England. Mrs. Sumter's friends also appreciated her wonderful letters. Those which she wrote to Mrs. Thomas Hooper and Mrs. W. W. Anderson in Stateburg, were carefully preserved, and a century after Natalie's death, they were published in Columbia in 1942, by Mrs. Walter C. White, of Stateburg and Gates Mills, Ohio, as *Fifteen Letters of Nathalie Sumter.*

Shirley Carter Hughson, son of Dr. J. S. Hughson of Sumter, made a valuable addition to the early history of South Carolina in his book, *The Carolina Pirates and Colonial Commerce,* published in 1894 by Johns Hopkins University. After a brief career as a newspaperman, Hughson startled his friends by retiring to an Episcopal monastery.

Very few reminiscences by Sumter citizens have been published. After the fall of the Confederacy, the Rev. W. W. Mood wrote a number of articles on his own experiences and those narrated by other participants in the war, but all were published in periodicals: the *Southern Christian Advocate,* the *Watchman and Southron,* the Sumter *Freeman,* and the Manning *Enterprise.* Fortunately, Mr. Mood clipped and collected his articles into scrapbooks, which are now owned by Miss Emma Mood of Sumter, and in this unified form they are a mine of interesting and valuable information.

Although Major John A. Leland was not a native of Sumter, he has a place among Sumter writers because he was principal of the Sumter Male and Female Public School in 1879, when his *Voice From South Carolina* was being printed in Charleston. This little book tells of the Major's experiences during Reconstruction, and gives an account of the Red Shirt campaign which restored home rule to the state. Especially valuable are the excerpts from the author's journal, pertaining to his imprisonment when arrested on a charge of Ku Klux conspiracy and murder.

Pertinent portions of the published reminiscences of Bishop William Capers, the Rev. James Jenkins, and of Edwin J. Scott already have been cited in earlier chapters of this book.

A not too well-known pamphlet of reminiscences owes its origin to one who was not a writer, Robert W. Andrews, who earned a reputation as a long-distance pedestrian traveller, and when on his journeys, always made a practice of calling at newspaper offices. In his ninety-seventh year, on a trip to Boston, Andrews interested a journalist, Malton Downing, who from the old man's conversation, preserved his reminiscences in a very readable pamphlet which was published in Boston in 1887, by E. P. Whitcomb, as *The Life and Adventures of Capt. Robert W. Andrews, of Sumter, South Carolina, Extending over a Period of 97 Years*. Andrews was a keen observer with a remarkable memory, and although of limited education, he was accurate in stating what he knew. During his youth, he was haled into court several times for various offenses, and his honesty is attested by the public records, which show that he always pleaded "Guilty as charged." From his pamphlet, the reader gets a picture of Sumter District almost from the time of the Revolution through Reconstruction, as seen through the eyes of a plain man. Born near Stateburg July 4, 1790, he died October 11, 1894.

One other small volume of reminiscences has appeared, *Life on the Old Plantation in Ante-Bellum Days or a Story Based on Facts* published in Columbia in 1911, by the author, the Rev. I. E. Lowery. Born of mulatto slave parents in 1850, on the plantation of John Frierson on Pudding Swamp, near Mayesville, Lowery wrote of log rollings and other typical events of plantation life of the Negroes, before and after emancipation.

Two biographies from Sumter authors are worthy of note. The first is the *Life of Richard Furman*, published in Greenville in 1913. Although the author does not reveal himself, the biography is believed to have been written by Wood Furman, Dr. Richard Furman's son, and it was edited and supplemented by Harvey T. Cook. The second is the *Biography of Isaac Harby, with an Account of the Reformed Society of Israelites of Charleston, S. C.*, by L. Clifton Moise, youngest son of General Edwin W. Moise. It was published in Columbia in 1931.

Genealogies have proved to be the most popular subjects for Sumter writers: *The Belser Family of South Carolina*, Sumter, 1941, by W. G., J. E., and I. F. Belser; *Haynsworth-Furman and Allied Families*, Sumter, 1942, by Hugh Charles Haynsworth; five pamphlets on the McFadden family of varying titles, by A. L. Blanding, M.D.; *A Genealogical Record with Reminiscences of the Richardson and Buford Families*, printed in Macon in 1906, by Elizabeth Buford Richardson; *Singletons of South Carolina . . . Hartsville*, 1914, by Virginia Eliza Green Singleton; and *Family Album: The Moods of Charleston and Related Families*, published in Atlanta in 1943, by Thomas McAlpin Stubbs. Mr. Stubbs has also contributed articles to several periodicals, and is the author of *Early History of Sumter Churches* (a pamphlet illustrated by Elizabeth White), and *A History of Claremont Lodge No. 64 A.F.M. and Affilliated Lodges*, both of which were published in Sumter in 1950. His wife, under her maiden name of Beatrice Jeffords, has written a successful murder mystery, *Small Town Murder*, published in New York in 1941.

The distinguished novelist, Julia Peterkin, whose *Scarlet Sister Mary* won the Pulitzer Prize as the best novel of 1928, also has family roots in Sumter, for her father was the beloved Dr. Julius Andrew Mood of Sumter. Despite his busy life as a physician, his literary gifts found expression in a number of editorials, and addresses, notably his address on George McDuffie, whose grave is in the Singleton cemetery in Poinsett Park.

In the field of verse, there have been very few local books. In 1882, William G. Kennedy published in Sumter a volume entitled, *Ichabod; or, The Glory of the South has Departed: and other Poems*. Mrs. Octavia Harby Moses, wife of Andrew Jackson Moses, used to write verses to her many children. After her death, the family collected these into a volume which was published in 1915, *A Mother's Poems*, which contains also a memoir. A small volume, entitled *Dreams and Purple Horizons*, was published in Columbia in 1933, by the author, Mrs. Elizabeth Kerrison Ricker, much of whose verse has appeared in the Sumter and Charleston newspapers.

A clever curiosity in this field was the *Wooden Works of Thomas Anonymous*, published in 1904, by Thomas Childs. The verses, with illustrations, were printed on thirty wooden pages, held together in walnut covers by two brass rings, and the booklets were offered for sale at the "Backwoods Bindery" in Sumter. The last page, typical of the others, reads:

> The Tale End
> The reader's mental blindness
> All authors apprehend
> Else why should they in kindness
> Append the phrase "The End."

Mr. Childs had other original ideas and a few years earlier he is said to have been planning to set up a plant to make golf sticks from persimmon trees.

For another sample of local humor, we are indebted to Mary Hughes Girardeau, a veteran teacher of Sumter, who has left an amusing record of her pupils' misinformation, called *Pupils' Potpourri*, a pamphlet which was printed in 1902 in Columbia.

Among modern free lance writers should be mentioned Vivian Mordaunt Moses, who for several years in New York was contributing poems, stories, and articles, to various publications. But, he says, his marriage brought the need for greater security, and he "ran to cover" with the moving picture industry, taking a position as a scenario writer. Now he is advertising manager for one of the large producers.

James McBride Dabbs, author and former college professor, but now farming his ancestral acres on Black River, has contributed to many periodicals. His most recent publication is the excellent historical introduction for *Pee Dee Panorama*, published by the University of South Carolina Press.

A massive volume on a bird is *The Pigeon*, by Wendell M. Levi, who served as first lieutenant, in charge of the pigeon section of the United States Signal Corps, during the first World War. Privately printed for the author in 1941, with 785 illustrations, this authoritative book has been sold in sixty-seven foreign countries as well as in America.

Of the numerous pamphlets which have originated in Sumter are several on the history of religious bodies: *History of the First Baptist Church, Sumter, S. C., 1813-1938*, by **Dr. and Mrs. C. C. Brown**, published in Sumter in 1938; *An Historical Sketch of Methodism and Roll of Methodist Preachers stationed on the Santee Circuit and Sumter Station* . . . by D.

James Winn, Sumter, 1938; *The Church of the Holy Cross*, by John Rutledge Sumter, Sumter, 1930; and *The Early Minutes of the Sumter Society of Israelites*, by Herbert A. Moses, Sumter, 1936.

Other more or less historical pamphlets are: *Sumter County Economic and Social*, Columbia, 1922, by Ralph H. Ramsey and A. H. Green; *The Rhyme and Reason of American History*, Sumter, 1928, by Marion W. Seabrook; *Some Old Stateburg Homes*, Sumter, 1934, by John Rutledge Sumter; *Stateburg and its People*, Sumter, 1922, by Thomas S. Sumter; *Some Interesting Facts in the History of Sumter County*, Sumter, 1921, by H. L. Scarborough; *Abstract of Moore Records of South Carolina*, Columbia, 1931, by Janie Revill, who also is the author of a number of other genealogical pamphlets and of *Aunt Jane's Little Rimes for Little Folks*, 1948; *Historic Sketch of Sumter County Game and Fish Association*, 1945; *The Past Blows by on the Road to Poinsett Park*, and *After Glow*, by Josie Platt Parler.

In the field of school textbooks is J. J. Dargan's *School History of South Carolina*, published in Columbia in 1906. Another is *Little Clusters: A Mixed Method for Beginners*, by Lucie Bragg Anthony, M. D., supervisor of Sumter County colored schools, for whom it was printed in 1925. The "Foreword" by the Rev. J. Bentham Walker, is endorsed by J. H. Haynsworth, county superintendent, H. G. Osteen of the county Board of Education, and others.

THE NEWSPAPER PRESS OF SUMTER[1]

Of Sumter's first newspaper, *The Claremont Gazette*, nothing is known except that in November 1786, copies were received by *The Charleston Morning Post* from the Rev. Richard Furman,[2] who was then the pastor of the High Hills Baptist Church, Stateburg.

During the early decades, official advertisements for Sumter District were published in the *Camden Journal*. On November 29, 1828, the *Journal* carried in its columns "Proposals for publishing at Sumterville, S. C. on the 1st day of Jan. 1829, a New Weekly Journal to be entitled The Sumter Union, and Constitutional Advocate." As the Nullification controversy was then under way, the title suggests that the new weekly might be expected to be Unionist in sympathy. Whether this paper appeared as scheduled is not known, but if it did, it had a brief career.

A year later, on December 19, 1829, the *Camden Journal* advertised "Proposals for publishing at Sumterville, a New Weekly Journal, to be entitled The Sumter Gazette, and Constitutional Advocate. . . . as soon after the commencement of the new year, as the necessary material can be obtained. . . . J. S. Bowen, Sumterville, Dec. 12, 1829."

James S. Bowen, who signed this advertisement, was the publisher and possibly a printer; the owner of the press was D. W. Sims. Backed by Dr. Jacques Bishop as his security, Bowen acquired the press from Sims for two promissory notes, each for $246, and on February 4, 1830, he gave Dr. Bishop a mortgage on the equipment.[3]

On Saturday, February 13, 1830, the *Camden Journal* announced that the first issue of the *Sumter Gazette* had been received on the night of February 11: "It is published in Sumterville, and bids fair to attain great respectability." Further-

---

[1] For a more detailed account, see Thomas McAlpin Stubbs, "The Fourth Estate of Sumter, South Carolina", in *The South Carolina Historical Magazine*, October 1953.
[2] Brigham, *op. cit.*
[3] Records of Sumter County.

more, "the editorial matter is well written. The gentleman who is understood to have charge of this department is a scholar, of great reading and extensive information." By the end of May, however, the scholar had been replaced by "a correct and intelligent man." In July 1831, Bowen was still the publisher.[4]

An issue of the *Sumter Gazette and Constitutional Advocate*, dated apparently in late December 1831,[5] was described as a five-column folio, "published every Saturday by J. Hardman, at Three Dollars per annum, payable in advance or Four Dollars if delayed to the end of the year," and containing little local news. In the local items, however, was a notice of the formation of a law partnership by the brothers Franklin and Montgomery Moses.

The owner and publisher of the paper, "J. Hardman", may have been John Hemphill, a young lawyer from Chester, who had come to practice in Sumter. A graduate of Jefferson College, and a hot Nullifier, Hemphill, like the two preceding editors of the *Gazette,* seems to have withheld his name from publication for some time. Maynard Richardson, editor of the Unionist organ, the Sumterville *Southern Whig,* which made its appearance on January 26, 1832, wrote[6] two months later: "We are conscious of a feeling of degradation in stooping to notice the low and malignant sling in the last Sumter Gazette .... We withdraw our charge of its Editor being *incognito*. ... We have, however, stripped him of his mask ... unmuffled the 'Great Unknown' — and lo! stands revealed John Hemphill ... sole Editor and conductor of that immortal sheet, the Sumter Gazette." Despite this revelation, Hemphill did not begin to print his name as editor until September[7] of that year.

It was about this time that the press of the *Southern Whig* came near to issuing a literary review. Maynard Richardson had persuaded his college friend, James H. Thornwell, to lo-

---

[4] A copy of the *Gazette* of July 14, 1831, is fully summarized in the *Sumter News,* Aug. 7, 1873.

[5] This copy of the *Gazette* was left at the office of the *Watchman and Southron* by R. M. Jones, and was described in that paper Feb. 24, 1892.

[6] March 29, 1832.

[7] Stubbs, *op. cit.*

cate in Sumterville, where Thornwell taught a private class, and under the name of "Clio" contributed articles to the *Whig* and other publications. The two young men planned to establish a literary fortnightly, to be called *The Southern Essayist*, to be printed on twenty octavo pages of fine paper, carrying reviews, poetry, moral and philosophical essays, and perhaps other literary productions, all to be original.[8] But Richardson died suddenly in October, and the plan died with him.

After Richardson's untimely death, the *Whig* was edited by William Haynsworth until 1833. Purchased by the Camden Journal, it was merged with that paper as *The Camden Journal and Southern Whig*.

With the quieting of excitement after the tariff compromise of 1833, the *Sumter Gazette* suspended publication. What became of its equipment is not known to this writer. But twelve years later, a two-column tabloid called *The Sumter Gazette* was published in Sumterville by George W. Hopkins, editor and proprietor. Its career was brief and only about two dozens issues seem to have appeared.[9]

Despite the failure of the second *Gazette,* or perhaps because of it, a new weekly was launched the next year, 1846, *The Sumter Banner,* by William J. Francis, owner and publisher, and Andrew H. Buchanan, editor. This was a full-sized newspaper, and despite financial and other difficulties, met the needs of the community. Buchanan's successors in the editorial chair were successively: Francis M. Adams, M. M. Noah, Jr., Richard M. Dyson, James S. G. Richardson, W. F. B. Haynsworth, John T. Green, J. R. Logan, and John Smyth Richardson, Jr., all of whom except perhaps Logan, were lawyers.

In 1849, commenting on the fourth anniversary of the *Banner*, Publisher Francis reminded his readers that it had not been his lot "to have a place near the seat of power . . . where we can be the first to catch the shadows of coming events," nor "to sit by the enchanted wire of the Electric Telegraph and echo for the magic whisperings from distant climes;" but rather, in the peaceful retirement of village life, he had "to keep an unpretending chronicle of those local events, which...

[8] Palmer, *Life of Thornwell*, p. 93.
[9] Mr. Herbert A. Moses owns No. 12, June 4, and No. 19, July 23, 1845.

come home to . . . us all." He then announced the purchase of a new press, largely on credit, and gently reminded those who had forgotten to pay him, that he was dependent upon them to meet his payments.

This eloquent plea should have brought results. But competition appeared, and in April 1853, the press and all equipment were levied on as the property of W. J. Francis at the suits of E. M. Anderson and J. S. G. Richardson, Jr. Again in July of the same year, seven acres of land, two printing presses and all printing materials were advertised to be offered at the sheriff's August sale, at the suits of other creditors. Finally, in January 1854, William Lewis and John S. Richardson, Jr., purchased the entire interest of Francis.

Shortly after the *Banner* celebrated its fourth anniversary by the purchase of a new press, a rival paper, *The Black River Watchman*, had begun publication on April 27, 1850. The publishers were John F. DeLorme, and Allen A. Gilbert, the latter a tall, religiously inclined, rather silent young printer, just twenty-one years of age, with a shock of black hair and an impediment in his speech. The editors were Thomas Boone Fraser, a lawyer, and John Witherspoon Ervin, an imaginative and literary young schoolmaster.

After five years of rivalry, the two newspapers were merged, and on July 13, 1855, appeared as *The Sumter Watchman*, a weekly paper which was destined to a long life. The new owners were Allen A. Gilbert and John S. Richardson, Jr., both of whom doubled as editors, with the assistance of John R. Haynsworth and L. L. Fraser, Jr.

Soon after the merger, a new figure appeared in the printing office, a small twelve-year-old boy, Noah Graham Osteen, who came from a farm on the waters of Black River, as an apprentice to learn the printer's trade. After several months on trial, unpaid, for Mr. Gilbert hesitated to accept such a small boy, the printers signed his articles of apprenticeship, agreeing, in return for five years service from the boy, to teach him the trade, to give him bed and board and twenty-five dollars a year for the first two years, and fifty dollars a year for the ensuing years. As the five years were to be computed from the date of signing the articles, the boy served nearly five and a half years. Destined to a long career as a Sumter publisher, he spent many of his ultimate ninety-three years in connection with the *Watchman,* which he eventually owned. His address before the South Carolina Press Association,[10] in July 1906, has preserved much of this history of the Sumter press.

Soon after young Osteen entered the office of Gilbert and Richardson, a new partner appeared on the scene, Horatio Lincoln Darr, an experienced and "swift" printer from Charleston, who soon bought out Richardson. A short, florid, very energetic and rather talkative man of thirty years, Darr had a fringe of red hair, restless blue eyes, and a passion for keeping ahead of his work. He and Gilbert were not only partners and good printers, but also brothers-in-law, for they married two sisters, of the Flowers family.

In December 1859, the *Watchman* announced the advent of a rival, *The Sumter Dispatch,* which would begin in January with W. J. Francis and W. M. DeLorme, Jr., as proprietors and printers, and Thomas Waties Dinkins, a young lawyer, as editor. To meet the competition, Gilbert and Darr made their *Watchman* a tri-weekly.

Editor Dinkins soon entered the Confederate service and was sent to Richmond. The *Dispatch* lasted less than two years, and was bought by Gilbert and Darr. As young Osteen had just completed his apprenticeship, they sent him to Conway with their new purchase, to publish the first weekly in that section of the state, *The Horry Dispatch,* which lasted only until August 1862, when Osteen went to Columbia.

War conditions also affected the *Tri-Weekly Watchman,* for Allen Gilbert went into the Confederate service and became a captain of artillery. The paper, however, continued until April 1865, when Potter's raiders issued their single-issue *Banner of Freedom* in the *Watchman's* office, then wrecked the press and scrambled the type. Darr went to Kingstree.

When Captain Gilbert returned to Sumter after the war, he repaired the press at the railroad shops and revived the *Watchman,* in partnership with his brother-in-law, T. E. Flowers, who bought out Darr. A year later, Horatio Darr

---

[10] It was published in the *News and Courier,* July 20, 1906. He also made an address on the same subject to the Sumter Rotary Club about 1911.

returned to Sumter, and on May 31, 1866, began publication of *The Sumter News,* edited by Frank Moses, Jr. In September of that year, Darr took into partnership young N. G. Osteen, who had now married and brought his family to Sumter. Darr and Osteen were bitterly opposed to the vindictive radical Republican party then in control of Congress, and when Editor Moses went over to that party at its inception in South Carolina, they let the young man go.

A succession of editors followed Frank Moses. W. H. Johnson, principal of the Sumter Academy, served for a few months, until he accepted a position at the Peabody School in Mount Pleasant. Thomas Waties Dinkins succeeded him, with Sarah Ann (Moise) Dinkins, his wife, in charge of "News and Belle Letters." When Dinkins died in June 1868, his "talented widow" was retained, and Edwin W. Moise, whose views coincided with those of the *News'* publishers, prepared the political articles for her. When she returned to Charleston with her three little boys, the next editor was Lemuel Bingham Gay. A native of Massachusetts, Gay had given up law for teaching, and after four years in the Confederate army, had come to a school in Sumter. He proved to be a fearless and independent editor, but died suddenly in November 1871, of apoplexy. Gay's succesor was William G. Kennedy, a bent-over cripple, who walked with the help of two canes, but whose fearless and outspoken editorials made the *Sumter News* a powerful weapon against the radical Republicans.

During these dark years of reconstruction, *The Sumter Watchman* was being edited by Allen A. Gilbert, who believed that collaboration with the Republicans was the wiser course. Under the state law of 1870, the *Watchman,* like most of the newspapers of South Carolina, was given a contract for official printing. The state treasurer's report for 1872 shows that for advertising the Acts, the *Watchman* was paid $1,644, a substantial sum in those lean times! Papers which accepted such contracts were regarded as being subsidized to support the Radical administration. A similar contract was offered to Darr and Osteen, who, however, would not accept without assurance that it would not involve the sacrifice of their "loyalty to the state and its people."

At the suggestion of Editor Kennedy, the name of *The Sum-*

ter *News* was changed on August 14, 1873, to *The True Southron*. Because of his precarious health, Kennedy, after almost four years service, from December 7, 1871, to July 8, 1875, yielded the editorial chair to J. J. Dargan, who vacated it seven months later for "strictly private" reasons. For the next four months, Charles H. Moise was editor.

In 1879, the Ladies Monumental Association of Sumter began to publish a small four-page paper called *The Fair Enterprise* to raise funds for their Confederate monument.[11]

The partnership of Gilbert and Flowers continued until ended by the death of the latter, when Gilbert decided to enter the Methodist ministry, and sold the *Watchman* to Guignard Richardson. Richardson continued publication with J. J. Dargan and M. H. McLaurin until 1881, a year also marked by dissolution of the firm of Darr and Osteen. Darr sold his interest in the *Southron* to W. D. Blanding, and Osteen turned over his share to his stepson, D. B. Anderson. Osteen then formed a new partnership with the Rev. C. C. Brown and bought the *Watchman*.

Darr also took a new partner, P. E. Parmalee, a native of Pennsylvania, and together on August 1, 1881, they launched *The Sumter Advance*, a four-page, six-column weekly, which appeared every Saturday. When Parmalee died four years later, Darr took as partner his own son, Horace Darr.

Another noteworthy event of 1881 was the appearance of a fourth newspaper, *The Spirit of the Times*, published by Charles H. DeLorme. Faced with so much competition, Brown and Osteen decided to meet it by consolidating the *Watchman* with the *Southron*, which then became *The Watchman and Southron*. *The Spirit of the Times*, after several changes of ownership, was purchased by Horace Darr and removed to Manning, to become *The Manning Times*.[12]

After the death of Horatio Lincoln Darr in June 1888, *The Sumter Advance* was published for several years by Horace Darr, who eventually sold it to the Rev. S. A. Nettles. He sold the paper to J. M. and A. W. Knight, who enlarged the plant, re-named the paper *The Sumter Herald*,[13] and published it

[11] Stubbs, *op. cit.*
[12] Address of N. G. Osteen to Sumter Rotary. Stubbs, *op. cit.*, says it was finally acquired by Harry J. Haynsworth, a lawyer, who took the paper to Manning and began the *Manning Times*.
[13] N. G. Osteen, address to Sumter Rotary.

until it ended on January 10, 1952. F. Jenkins Knight, editor of the *Herald,* is a grandson of Horatio L. Darr.

Another member of the family, Miss Mary M. Darr, was Sumter's only woman publisher. In January 1882, she began a monthly called the *Sumter Mirror,* which ended the following December.[14]

At the time of the consolidation of the *Watchman* with the *Southron* in 1881, the state was in a serious economic plight, and Ben Tillman's ideas were beginning to take shape. *The Watchman and Southron* never accepted Tillman's leadership, and opposed him as consistently as it had the radical Republicans. During these years, N. G. Osteen wrote some strong editorials, and his sentiments were shared and voiced by the part-time editors he employed: Dr. Julius A. Mood, David B. Anderson, W. F. Rhame, W. J. Beard, W. H. Ingram, Mark Reynolds and finally, Hubert Graham Osteen, his son, who had grown up in the printing business and became editor on September 1, 1891. The Rev. John Kershaw also, from time to time contributed editorials as part payment for the printing in the office of the Watchman and Southron, of the Episcopal Church monthly which he founded, called *The Diocese.*[15]

A temperance organ called *The Broad Axe,* described as a neatly printed 4-page paper, was being published in Sumter in 1891, sponsored by the Independent Order of Good Templars.[16]

In the same year, Edwin F. Miller and John J. Dargan began publication of *The Freeman,* a weekly which came out every Friday. Mr. Dargan, two of whose nine daughters assisted him with the printing, was an advocate of woman suffrage. He engaged a suffrage leader, Mrs. Virginia Durant Young, a native of Marion, who published her own paper in Allendale County, to conduct a woman's department in *The Freeman.* In 1896 the editors of the paper were Edwin F. Miller and C. M. Hurst. *The Freeman* ended in 1906.

On October 15, 1894, "on an ebb tide of panic and depression", Hubert G. Osteen hopefully launched *The Daily Item,* Sumter's first daily, a small four-column paper of four pages, which carried only local news and came out every afternoon

---

[14] Stubbs, *op. cit.*
[15] H. G. Osteen. For Dr. Mood's editorials, *see* T. A. Stubbs, *Family Album* (Atlanta, 1943), p. 99.
[16] *Watchman and Southron,* Apr. 29, 1891.

except Sunday. The venture was so well supported by the people of Sumter that today the *Item* is a full-sized standard newspaper.

Another hopeful venture of the same publishers was *The South Carolina Tobacconist*, a weekly, which began on February 25, 1896, with Hubert G. Osteen as managing editor and J. A. Brogdon as assistant editor. The *Tobacconist*, however, made no money and ran only about a year.[17]

A rival of the *Daily Item* soon appeared. Edwin F. Miller, J. H. Darr, and J. B. Miller, formed an Evening News Company, and on May 20, 1895, published *The Evening News* with the announcement that it would be issued every afternoon except Sunday. It lived only about one month. Nine years later a second *Evening News* was issued. The Freeman Publishing Company, with R. F. Haynsworth as president, Edwin F. Miller as general manager, and Hugh C. Haynsworth as editor, published the first issue on December 1, 1904. It continued to appear daily except Sunday, until 1906, when it ended along with *The Freeman*.

A very young publisher entered the field some months before the second *Evening News* was born. J. Edwin Brunson, a schoolboy carrier of *The Daily Item*, a son of Joel E. Brunson, issued *The Monthly Chronicle* on May 1, 1904, priced enticingly at twenty cents a year, ten cents for six months, and five cents for three months. "The Chronicle is worth the price," gravely said *The Watchman and Southron*, "and we wish Edwin success." The wish came true, for Edwin Brunson later became editor of *The Greenville News*.

As the *Daily Item* soon outgrew its elder, the venerable *Watchman and Southron*, that honored weekly ended its career in 1931, after an existence of more than eight decades during which it chronicled and preserved for posterity an invaluable record of events in Sumter. When the *Item* was ten years old, it acquired its first linotype machine in 1904 and its publishers were incorporated. In 1916 the paper became a member of the Associated Press, and in 1929 the full leased-wire, teletype-printed news service was installed. Disaster struck on June 18, 1921, when the plant of the *Item* was totally

---

[17] Issue number 1, owned by H. G. Osteen, who gave additional information.

destroyed by fire. All of the early files, as well as files of the *Watchman and Southron* prior to 1915, were lost.

During the ensuing month, the *Item* was printed in Orangeburg, Editor Osteen going there daily on the morning train, and returning to Sumter on the evening train. At the end of thirty days, "business was resumed at the old stand in a new building, with entirely new and modern equipment." After the second World War, when Hubert Duvall Osteen was released from the Air Force, he took over the active management of the business, and his father retired, although remaining president of the company.

Several Negro newspapers have been established from time to time in Sumter. In the early 1880's, a Radical organ, *The Vindicator*, published by Sam Lee, had a brief career.[18] In the mid 1890's *The Journal of Progress*, edited by the Rev. C. C. Scott, with the Rev. W. G. Deas as business manager, was being printed in the office of *The Herald*.[19] On October 21, 1909, *The Samaritan Herald*, a weekly that was also printed in the Herald office, was "re-established" by the Rev. J. McKenzie Harrison, a grandson of the Ellison family of Stateburg. Another Negro newspaper, *The Defender*, also printed in the Herald office, was published and edited by William T. Andrews, a Negro lawyer and teacher, who married a daughter of Sam Lee and was principal of a school in Sumter. He removed to Baltimore about the time of the first World War. His son, Robert T. Andrews, is said to have studied law at Columbia University and later to have represented Harlem in the New York legislature.[20]

The only Negro woman publisher seems to have been Emma Wilson, whose flourishing school at Mayesville she hoped would be another Tuskegee, and whose most famous pupil was Mary McLeod Bethune. During the school session for some eight or ten years after the beginning of this century, she published a small monthly of from four to eight pages, about eight inches by fifteen in size, printed by the Osteen Printing Company. It is recalled that she had quite a hard time paying for it, but always managed to meet the printing bills.

[18] George B. Tindall, *South Carolina Negroes 1877-1900* (Columbia, 1952) p. 149.
[19] Stubbs, "Fourth Estate", *loc. cit.*
[20] H. G. Osteen.

Chapter XXXVI

SILK CULTURE[1]

For a number of years, at rather widely separated intervals, silk was produced with some success in and around Stateburg and Sumter, but at no time was it more than a very minor industry, scarcely beyond the experimental stage. Parson Woodmason evidently had it in mind when he desired to introduce mulberry trees into St. Mark's Parish, but he had long since departed from South Carolina when the idea was finally realized.

In 1825 Natalie Sumter, General Sumter's daughter-in-law, then on a two-year visit abroad, wrote from Paris, "Do tell Dr. Anderson that I have a great wish we should make our fortune either with the silk worms or gossamer ... but I don't know how to set about it." Apparently she found out how, for after her return to America she was in the business of raising silkworms.

At Marden near Stateburg, her neighbors, Anna and Mary Waties, also raised silkworms, and reeled off the raw silk from the cocoons. In 1829 they won a large silver teapot as a premium from the Charleston Agricultural Society, for the best quarter-pound of silk. In 1830 they were producing silk in commercial quantities, which was vouched for by some coach-lace and fringe manufacturers of Philadelphia, as "equal in quality to any imported silk floss." The next year, the Waties sisters were exhibiting in New York, where they were awarded a silver medal at the fair of the American Institute "for a beautiful Specimen of Raw Silk."

The Misses Waties' small nephew, Thomas Sebastian Sumter, was allowed to help with their silk business, and in his old

[1] This chapter has been compiled from: White, ed., *Fifteen Letters*; Sumter, *Stateburg and its People*; *Camden Gazette*, Apr. 24, 1830; *Farmer's Gazette and Cheraw Advertiser*, May 29, Nov. 1840; *Watchman and Southron*, Jan. 9, Apr. 17, May 1, 1883; Feb. 19, 1884; July 31, 1885; Apr. 27, 1887; June 13, 1888; Apr. 17, Nov. 20, 1889. Mrs. Beatrice Converse, of Sumter, owns the engraved silver teapot and the medal won by the Misses Waties.

[462]

age, he wrote an account of it, some of which is summarized below.

In April when the leaves were beginning to show on the white mulberry trees, the eggs of the silk moth were taken from cold storage, where they had been kept all winter. Looking like millions of little specks, on small pieces of cardboard about the size of visiting cards, they were placed on trays in a room of even, moderate temperature, and in a few days little black worms would begin popping out. Each morning after the dew had dried, and again in late afternoon, mulberry leaves were gathered in baskets and strewn over the little worms, which ate them ravenously. In about two weeks, the worms had reached the molting season, and would lie dormant as if dead for a time and then shed their skins. Now of a gray color and very vigorous, they grew rapidly and shed their skins several more times. When about an inch long, the worms would begin to move their heads from side to side, seeking a corner in which to spin the cocoons. This was the time to supply them with twigs or paper cones. Having selected one of these, the worm, moving its head from side to side, would begin enclosing itself in a mass of silk, at first quite transparent, and its work could be seen until gradually the small spinner inside was hidden. When completed, the cocoon was about the size of a pigeon's egg, and contained 120 yards of silk filament. Each cocoon that was to be used for silk, was pierced with a fine needle to kill the chrysalis within, for if it developed and burst out of the cocoon, the silk fibre would be spoiled. The pierced cocoons were then immersed, a few at a time, in a basis of warm water to dissolve the sticky substance binding together the fibres, which then floated off on the surface and were gathered on broom straws. Next, each strand of silk was wound on a spool of shuck, and later the silk from the spools was joined and looped into hanks, ready for processing into silk fabrics by a manufacturer.

Although plantation-made looms with hard, polished dogwood shuttles, were still in common use at that time, they probably were used only for the weaving of coarse fabrics of cotton, wool or linen. The famous colonial silk dresses of

Elizabeth Lucas Pinckney were woven from her own South Carolina raw silk when she carried it to Europe.

Silk culture continued to be a subject of interest, and in 1837 William Ellison, of Fairfield District, published a notice to silk culturists of the state that, if assured of a demand, he could supply them with from fifteen to twenty thousand Chinese mulberry trees.

Two years later, Mrs. Eleanor Spann began the silk business with 500 worms from eggs that had been carefully selected in France and Italy for Mrs. Natalie Sumter. Mrs. Spann's address was given as Sumterville, so probably she was not Mrs. Sumter's partner. From the 500 worms she produced the following season fifty bushels of cocoons, and both she and Mrs. Sumter had quantities of eggs for sale. In 1841 Mrs. Spann expected to feed a million worms, and so confident of success was she, that she offered to furnish a dwelling, eggs, and 20,000 trees to a competent silk culturist who would bring the proper machinery and workers to operate it: "I would ask nothing the first year," said her advertisement, "but that he would instruct myself and one or two servants how to manage the silk, and convert the cocoons into a salable article."

Cotton was selling in 1840 at from four to eight cents a pound, and planters were feeling the pinch, but they did not emulate Mrs. Spann's efforts to find a new staple. Nor did she find a silk culturist to accept her offer. Undaunted, she went ahead with whatever instruction she could find in books and periodicals. Some of her silk was reeled "on the Piedmontese reel, some on Brook's reel, and some on the common clock reel," and was spun into excellent silk thread "by a negro woman from the cotton field" under Mrs. Spann's direction. Encouraged by these achievements, she planned to extend her operations the next season. The editor of the *Farmer's Gazette and Cheraw Advertiser,* from whose columns this account is taken, expressed the opinion that South Carolina had more cause to be proud of this enterprising woman than of ten thousand daughters "whose chief pride it is to thumb a piano, or to skip across a dancing room."

Mrs. Spann in February 1841 offered silkworm eggs for

sale at ten dollars a dozen, and for less if in quantity. Mrs. Sumter died during the ensuing summer, and apparently this venture in the production of silk came to an early end soon after.

The next chapter in the story of silk culture opened forty years later, at the close of the year 1882, when ten Sumter women gave public notice that they would apply for a charter as the Sumter Silk Association. The members were Hattie DesChamps, Mary Jackson, Isabel Moise, Celeste Hughson, Isabel D. Moses, Sarah A. Harvin, Mary China, Ann E. Tradewell, Augusta Solomons, and Dulce Moise, of whom Mrs. Z. P. Moses was president, and Mrs. Harvin was secretary. The sincerity of their efforts was evidenced when they purchased not only a supply of silkworm eggs and mulberry trees, but also some land near the town as a site for the business. Apparently the idea for the enterprise was suggested by Colonel M. B. Hillyard of Mobile, who had been visiting Mr. Moses and was then organizing silk associations in the South, from Virginia to Texas.

By April 1883, the ladies' Cocoonery was in operation, with a surplus of eggs, cocoons, and mulberry trees being offered for sale. On May 1, the *Watchman and Southron* gave its readers a detailed description of the Cocoonery, then in the residence on Washington Street "lately occupied by Mr. Murray." The Association engaged Miss Eliza Chandler to feed the worms, and to be at the Cocoonery from ten o'clock in the morning to three in the afternoon, during which hours the public was invited to see the entire process of the work at a dime each. A reel was purchased, as planned, for unwinding the silk from the cocoons after the larvae within had been killed by steam. In July Mrs. Z. P. Moses had some beautiful specimens of reeled silk.

Two years later the *Watchman and Southron* was asking what had become of the Sumter Silk Association, and apparently, either from diappointingly inadequate profits, or because of the very disagreeable smell from the dead larvae, the Association had disbanded. Its president, however, Mrs. Z. P. Moses, seems to have continued in the business, and in the summer of 1888, she had 20,000 worms, raised from eggs furnished by the United States Department of Agriculture, to whom in return she was ready to ship six pounds of silk cocoons and a lot of eggs. The Department was trying to foster the industry by also offering to buy silk when made. The following year, Mrs. Moses was again noted in the news as having "adhered to her experiment with an enthusiasm worthy of any cause, and now has the satisfaction of raising about 25,000 silk worms every year. The product of the cocoons are disposed of satisfactorily, and Mrs. Moses continues her fascinating industry with gratifying results." However, according to Mr. Herbert Moses, who remembers the business, the most impressive feature was its dreadful odor!

Chapter XXXVII
THE TURKS

Up in the High Hills between Stateburg and Dalzell, is a community of dark-skinned farming people known as the Turks, whose obscure and undocumented origin has long been a subject of speculation. Numbering more than three hundred persons, living within a radius of ten miles, they are among the oldest inhabitants of Sumter County, their arrival having coincided with the coming of General Thomas Sumter to the Hills soon after the Revolution.

The first Sumter ancestors from whom the Turks are believed to be descended, are said to have been two followers of the General in his campaigns, the one a certain Joseph Benenhaley, the other a man called Scott, supposedly a Frenchman under an assumed name. A confused tradition connects them, either as victims or crew members, with a pirate ship which landed them at Charleston, where they enlisted under General Sumter. Scott is said to have the General's bugler; and after the war, as bugler for the Claremont Troop, he blew the cavalry calls at the regular musters and Washington Birthday parades. He is further said to have been a tailor by trade, and to have been entrusted by Mrs. Natalie Sumter with the cleaning of her silk dresses, which he accomplished with the oil-free root of a yucca. Benenhaley is said to have been the General's scout[1], and as his name is evidently Moorish in origin, he is probably the reason for the local name of Turk.

In 1790 "sundry free Moors, subjects of the emperor of Morocco; and resident in this state," petitioned the legislature that in case any of them should be haled into court for any fault, they might "be tried under the same laws as the citizens of this state ... and not under the negro acts." The committee to whom was referred this petition, reported it favorably on the ground that "persons who were subjects of the emperor of Morocco, being free in this state are not triable by the law

---
[1] Unsigned article, Columbia *State*, Mch 18, 1928.

for better ordering and governing of negroes and other slaves."[2] It is possible that the Sumter Turks had some connection with these Moroccans.

Apparently some free Moors did enter or attempt to enter the state as bond servants, possibly from a northern port, for by a law of 1792, the legislature declared that no Moor bound to service for a term of years should be brought into the state by land or water from any other state.[3]

The first Joseph Benenhaley married a white woman named Miller, according to their blue-eyed granddaughter, Mrs. Mary Ann Benenhaley Oxendine. She also said that her own mother was a daughter of Scott,[4] the bugler.

General Sumter settled the families of Scott and Benenhaley upon his lands, but, if either he or his descendants ever gave them a deed, apparently it was not recorded. For many generations the land was held in common, and yielded a more or less meagre living for all the Turks, who intermarried through the years and gradually increased. Holding themselves aloof from Negroes, and segregated by long custom from the whites, the Turks occasionally married outside of their community. One of the earliest of such alliances was with an Oxendine, a name which appears on records in Charleston County from 1767 until 1797,[5] and is said to be common among the Croatans of North Carolina. Mary Ann Benenhaley, who married her first cousin Oxendine, said that his father came from North Carolina and married her mother's sister, a daughter of Scott, the bugler. Scott married a woman named Sallie. Other family surnames among the Turks now are Chavis, Lowry, Hood, Ray, and Buckner.

There is a story that a Turk woman once married a Negro, and was at once ostracised by her people. When she died, her body was carried to the Turk's church for burial, but was refused permission either to enter the church or to be buried in the churchyard. She was then taken to the Negro church at Stateburg, but again was turned away, because she was not

---

[2] Journal House of Representatives, Jan. 20, 1790, cited by W. D. Workman, *News and Courier*, Feb. 13, 1951.

[3] *Stat.* VI, 431.

[4] *State*, Mch 18, 1928.

[5] *St. Philip's Parish Register 1754-1810*, pp. 308, 309, 328, 329; will of John Oxendine, 1797, Probate Court, Charleston.

a Negro; and finally, she was laid away in a plantation grave.[6]

The Turks have embraced the Baptist faith, and in early days were members of the High Hills Baptist Church, which then seated three racial groups: the Turks on the left, the other whites on the right, and the Negroes in the gallery. When the Turks became too numerous for the High Hills Church, they built their own, Long Branch Church at the head of Pocotaligo River, and employed a white minister. One of their former pastors, Dr. J. H. Mitchell now of Greenville, has noted the reference in Cervantes' *Don Quixote* to "Cid Hamet Benengeli, an Arabian Historiographer," and pointed out that the pronunciation of this name is exactly the same as that of the Sumter family of Turks,[7] thus adding one more evidence of their oriental origin.

The Turks have always been eligible to serve on juries. There is an old story credited to Colonel James D. Blanding, that when the right of two Turks to perform this duty was challenged once in a magistrate's court, General Sumter was sent for to say whether they were white men. The General is said to have walked over to the challenged men, and shaken hands with them, an act which satisfied everyone that he did not regard them as being of the Negro race. The Turks have always voted in the Democratic primaries, from which until recently, Negroes have been excluded.

In the War of Secession, the Turks served with white soldiers as white men. Seven of them were Benenhaleys: Warren and Dick, in Captain R. M. Cantey's company of Kershaw's brigade, were killed; John enlisted in a Marlboro company. Tom, Charlie and Jake served in Captain P. P. Gaillard's company of Hagood's Sharpshooters, and Winfield in Captain Spann's company. Of all, only Tom survived.[8] In both the First and the Second World Wars the Turks served with white soldiers.

Until recent years, the Turks had their own separate schools, one near Stateburg with a white teacher, and the other near Dalzell with two teachers, thus adding to the racial

[6] *State*, Mch 18, 1928.
[7] *Baptist Courier*, Apr. 1, 1943, p. 7.
[8] T. S. Sumter, *Stateburg and its People*, p. 44.

and financial problems of Sumter County. Apparently these two schools were consolidated into one in the outskirts of Dalzell, with three white teachers. This school made some effort to prepare pupils for high school, but was not accredited for college entrance. In 1950, therefore, the Turks asked the trustees of Hillcrest High School to admit their children, but the trustees refused. The Turks then brought suit in the federal district court in the names of Herbert Ray, Henrietta B. Ray, Henry Benenhaley, and Dallis H. Benenhaley. The trustees were named as defendants, but did not contest the suit, and without a legal battle the Turks won their case. In 1951 for the first time, the children of this voluntarily segregated community were enrolled in classes along with their white neighbors.

Always a law-abiding people, the Turks of Sumter County are said to be singularly lacking in "spontaneous joy. They wear, one and all, the air of patient and unquestioning acceptance of life as they find it."[9]

[9] *State*, Mch 18, 1928.

CHAPTER XXXVIII

INVENTORS AND INVENTIONS

Sumter County no doubt, has had inventors from the beginning, but the earliest of whom record has been found was Thomas Sumter, Jr., General Sumter's only son. In a letter dated October 25, 1809, from Germantown, Pennsylvania, the inventor's wife, Natalie, wrote that Mr. Sumter was head and ears in machinery, "he has invented a writing press that has succeeded — now a vat that has succeeded also, and he is busy about the cotton press, all of them on the same plan of wedges." With true wifely confidence, she was sure that "Mr. S. will make a fortune with all his machines and we will be rich enough when we get amongst all our friends."[1] Sad to say, her hopes were never realized.

Another early and also unremunerated inventor was Jeptha Dyson, who, in 1848, invented and patented for his Fulton cotton factory, a device for cleaning the teeth of the main card cylinder while it revolved. Previously, the teeth would be clogged, thus necessitating four 15-minute stoppages of the machinery each day for cleaning the teeth. Dyson sold his patent to Mason and Wright of Philadelphia, but it was infringed upon in England and he reaped no benefit. He died in poverty in Columbia in June 1881, and was buried in Trinity churchyard.[2]

In 1853 the Sumter *Watchman* carried several notices of Major Joseph S. Bossard as the inventor of an intricate machine, which was expected to prove of great importance in the South and Southwest, for it could gin cotton, grind corn, and pound the husks from rice. Operated by animal power, it could be run on either steam or water power. When a single process was performed at a time, one horse-power was adequate; if all three were simultaneous, five horse-power was necessary. The machine had been in successful operation on

[1] White, ed., *Fifteen Letters*, p. 52.
[2] *True Southron*, June 14, 1881, from *Columbia Register*, June 5.

Maj. Bossard's plantation for some time when he exhibited a model of it at the first Sumter Agricultural Association Fair.[3]

Five years later Bossard obtained a patent. The rice-pounding section of the machine was described as "a novel arrangement of arms attached to a horizontal rotating shaft for elevating the pestles." The next year, in a letter to the *Watchman*, he mentioned several flattering notices he had received of his invention, among them one from Glasgow, and another from the patent office at Lincoln's Innfield, London; he also stated that the American Institute had invited "this humble offspring of the interior of Sumter" to be exhibited at the Chrystal Palace. In December 1859, it was on display at the Charleston Institute Fair.

Before the War of Secession, several plantations of Sumter District were equipped with machines of an origin now unknown, which were described as ginning and spinning cotton. During that war, they were in active use and did good service. Locally, for the want of a better name they were called spinning jennies. In the spring of 1880, an imperfect specimen about forty years old, from the estate of Colonel John B. Moore, was on exhibit at the jewelry store of Charles T. Mason, who was anxious to obtain a better one to which he would attach an electric motor. Some weeks later, another machine of the same make but in better condition, was brought to him from the plantation of L. L. Fraser, Sr., of Mechanicsville. This one was estimated to be about fifty years old, but Mr. Mason said that both machines embodied several features which had been patented as new in recent years, and they "killed" a patent for the Clement attachment. A number of the machines were said to be then in the county.[4]

Charles T. Mason and his son of the same name, were Sumter's pre-eminent inventors. The elder Charles, son of the Rev. Thomas Mason, was born in Darlington District in 1829, grew up in Camden, and in 1850 settled in Sumter, where he carried on a jewelry and watch-repair business for almost forty years.

In 1858 Mason's jewelry store was equipped with a brilliant gas light system, invented by his neighbor, A. Hauser. The

---

[3] *Watchman*, Oct. 21, Nov. 11, 1858.
[4] *True Southron*, Mch 9, Apr. 6, 1880.

lowcost gas was generated from any kind of grease, "putrid or otherwise," by a "gasometer", for which Mason and Hauser obtained a patent. During the summer, Hauser put on the market his fruit cans, for the perservation of fruits and vegetables by his vacuum process for exhausting the air from the cans.[5]

Much of Mason's time was given to the study of electricity. During the 1860's he was superintendent of the telegraph service of the Confederate States, and manufactured in Sumter all of the instruments for that service. In 1869 he patented an electric alarm for banks. He also invented a number of improvements in various electrical devices, among them a way to non-magnetize watches, which he sold to the Waltham Watch Company. He also is said to have made a very early electric motor. But like many other men of genius, Mason was ahead of his time, and his monetary returns were small. After a long illness, he died on June 20, 1893, at the age of sixty-four years, survived by his second wife and nine children.[6]

Charles T. Mason, Jr., inherited his father's gifts, but was financially more successful. As a boy of fourteen years, he built a complete working model of a horizontal steam engine of the locomotive type, for which he received, in 1869, a silver medal at the Fair of the Agricultural and Mechanical Society of South Carolina. Under the caption "A Remarkable Boy Mechanic," the story was carried in the *Sumter News* on December 21, 1871, taken from the *Scientific American*. At the age of sixteen, Mason went to work in the machine shops of George Page and Company of Baltimore, where he remained two years. He then became department foreman at Farquhar's Agricultural Works in York, Pennsylvania. On returning to Sumter, he worked in a sawmill and cotton-gin until injured in a serious accident, and on recovery, he returned to the North.

Later, Mason came back to Sumter and equipped his own machine shops, which were said to have been the best south of Philadelphia. The lathe, planing machine, drill and other tools were power driven. He aided the Sumter Electric Light Company in perfecting that system, and he supplied the technical

[5] *Watchman*, Feb. 10, Aug. 18, 1858.
[6] *Watchman and Southron*, June 21, 1893.

knowledge for installing Sumter's telephones. From his invention of an artificial leg, he made enough money to finance his cotton picker, which removed cotton from the boll "with the seeming intelligence of a human being." James S. Richardson of Greenville, Mississippi, the largest cotton planter in the world, spent two days in Sumter as the guest of Mason to investigate the merits of the cotton harvester, and gave an order for several. The Mason Cotton Harvester Company was organized to manufacture the machine, which was expected to harvest 4,000 pounds of seed-cotton a day, and to be priced between $350 and $500. But the younger Charles Mason, like his father, was ahead of his time. A surplus of human labor was then available, and the mechanical harvester would have brought hardship to the Negroes of the South. Modern cotton harvesters are said to operate on the same principle as Mason's.

After abandoning the cotton picker, Mason began to manufacture telephones, for which he invented devices which did not infringe on Bell patents but did the same work. He founded the Sumter Telephone Manufacturing Company, chartered September 29, 1899, which eventually employed 400 persons and built up a worldwide trade. The company was bought by the Splitdorf Magneto Company of New Jersey, who closed the plant in the early 1920's. Mason also invented a magneto to be used in stationary gas engines and automobile engines.[7]

After the electric light system was installed in Sumter, E. Cardarelli invented in 1891 a crane for lowering the carbon street lights, in which new carbons had to be installed every day, and raising them back into position. His contract with a northern factory to manufacture the crane gave him a royalty of fifty cents each, but apparently something happened, for the following year a Sumter group chartered the Cardarelli Electric Light Crane Company, with a capital of $6,000. Officers were H. Harby, president; Charles T. Mason, Jr., vice-president; and Aaron Phelps, secretary.[8]

An interesting Sumter inventor was Harmon Moise, a son

---

[7] *Ibid.*, Oct. 30, 1883, for sketch; other notices, June 9, 1885; Jan. 13, 1887; Nov. 20, 1889. Additional information from H. G. Osteen.
[8] *Watchman and Southron*, June 17, 1891; May 4, 1892.

of Charles H. Moise. Highly intelligent, Harmon Moise was a lawyer and a surveyor, but, like many other inventors, he was usually in debt, and certain that he would make a million dollars from his inventions! His bicycle coaster-brake, which he sold for $500 is still in production. He also invented an automatic shift for typewriters, and a clearview attachment for windshields. His most successful and profitable invention was a valveless, automatic vacuum sewer-flushing tank, which he experimented with in Sumter and sold to the city.[9]

Charles Mason's cotton harvester probably inspired ideas for other cotton machines. The *Watchman and Southron* on April 4, 1894, congratulated George W. Reardon on having made arrangements with Thomas Bailey and Company to manufacture his Reardon cotton chopper, and introduce it into South Carolina, Georgia and Florida.

Necessity, however, has always been the most fruitful mother of invention. In the summer of 1880 Ervin Brunson built a homemade steam engine in Sumter which certainly showed evidence of inventive genius. Using the flue of an old locomotive, he plugged the two ends and completed his engine with parts from an old sewing machine. Strange to say, it worked like a charm![10]

[9] *Stat.* XXVI, 1132; other information from H. G. Osteen.
[10] *True Southron*, Aug. 10, 1880.

CHAPTER XXXIX

AN ECONOMIC RETROSPECT

A survey of the economic development of Sumter County necessarily includes the history of its banking facilities, although the early efforts to that end were failures. In 1850, the Bank of the State of South Carolina established a local office in Sumterville, with Montgomery Moses as agent. Three years later, James D. Blanding was the Sumter agent for the Bank of Camden. Charters for a local bank were issued in 1852 and 1856, but the promoters could not raise sufficient capital. During Radical rule, John W. Dargan, as assistant cashier, was in charge of a Sumter branch of the Citizens Savings Bank from 1871 until 1873, when the Columbia "Ring" of the Republican administration obtained an injunction against the bank, closed its doors, and liquidated its assets. Dargan then tried to organize a national bank for Sumter, but was unable to secure the necessary capital.[1] The hard times of the early 1880's, especially "the year of calamity," emphasized the great need for a local bank, to supply credit to hardpressed planters and the businesses which were dependent upon their prosperity.

In 1883, local men in Sumter subscribed $50,000 as capital, and in October, with fifty percent of the capital paid in, the subscribers organized and elected directors for a bank. On the first day of January 1884, the National Bank of Sumter opened on Main Street next to the old courthouse. The president was R. M. Wallace, a native of York; and the cashier was Charles E. Bartlett, son of the Rev. Lyman Bartlett.

The bank prospered. The annual report of 1887 showed a net profit of seventeen percent, and, in the three years it had been operating, not a dollar had been lost. In August, however, Sumter was stunned by the news that the cashier had absconded. A few days later the bank examiner reported the loss of the entire capital, $50,000; the surplus and profits,

[1] *True Southron*, Aug. 14, Dec. 4, 25, 1873; Jan. 8, June 4, Aug. 6, Sept. 3, 1874.

$11,000; and more than $18,000 additional, making a total of nearly $80,000 for which the stockholders were liable. Comparatively little was salvaged from the wreckage: the cashier's property, and his account of $4,181.07, with H. Clews and Company of New York, were attached; and a verdict for $10,000 was rendered against his bondsmen.[2]

Undaunted, the people of Sumter immediately went to work, and by October had subscribed $18,000 toward the capital for another bank. Andrew Simonds, a Charleston capitalist, took the remainder of the $50,000 capital stock, saying that a half million dollars would be available if needed. In mid-November, 1887, the Simonds National Bank opened in Sumter. This bank, said the *Watchman and Southron*, "while a totally different institution, may yet be regarded as the phoenix from the ashes of the defunct National Bank of Sumter."[3] Later known as the First National Bank, it was acquired by the South Carolina National Bank and became one of that chain. Neill O'Donnell, president of the First National, became manager, and at his death, was succeeded by R. L. McLeod.

In 1888 Sumter acquired the Bank of Sumter, distinctly a home institution, organized locally with a capital of $50,000, which became a depository for state, county, and city funds. Officers were W. F. B. Haynsworth, president; Marion Moise, vice-president; and A. White, Jr., cashier.[4] The bank prospered and increased its capital fivefold. After the first World War, it was bought by the People's National Bank of Charleston, and when that bank closed in 1932, the Sumter depositors recovered only a fraction of their accounts.

Several local banks were organized in the early 1900's, two of which had to close their doors during the great depression of the 1930's, namely, the Sumter Trust Company promoted by I. C. Strauss, and The People's Bank, organized by B. C. Wallace and L. D. Jennings.

The Sumter Savings Bank, chartered September 19, 1901, with Horace Harby as president, and George L. Ricker, as

[2] *Watchman and Southron*, Sept. 25, Oct. 9, 1883; Jan. 13, Aug. 24, 31, 1887; May 30, 1888.
[3] *Ibid.*, Oct. 3, Nov. 2, 1887; Nov. 20, 1889.
[4] *Ibid.*, Nov. 20, 1889.

cashier, had a capital of $25,000,[5] which was increased to $150,000 when it became the City National Bank. During the depression of the 1930's it was liquidated and paid all depositors in full, but the stockholders lost heavily.

A contemporary bank which did not close during these hard times was the Farmers Bank and Trust Company, organized by Charles G. Rowland in 1905, with a capital of $60,000. This bank, with a greatly increased capital, is still flourishing, under the present name of The National Bank of South Carolina.[6]

John J. Riley and S. L. Roddey organized in 1923 the Permanent Building and Loan Association. Federalized in 1935 as the First Federal Savings and Loan Association, it has financed the construction of hundreds of homes in and around Sumter.

Another vital factor in the economic development of Sumter has been its position as a railroad center. The decade of the 1880's brought Sumter County much closer to other parts of the state by greatly improved transportation facilities. Many railroad lines were projected and hopefully chartered, but money was very hard to get, and few of the lines materialized. Early in the decade, the Central Railroad built a branch between Sumter and Lane's, a station on the ante-bellum Northeastern Railroad, and thus gave Sumter a shortened route to Charleston. The close of the decade saw two more short lines completed. The first was a part of the Manchester and Augusta, known as the "M and A", extending from Sumter to Denmark, with the terminal objective Augusta, where it would connect with the Georgia Central. This line gave a direct route to Orangeburg and Denmark, and brought to Sumter some of the trade that had formerly gone by water to Charleston. The other short line was the Charleston, Sumter and Northern Railroad from Pregnall's, by Eutawville and Summerton, to Sumter. Later, this was extended through Darlington and Bennettsville to Gibson, North Carolina. Eventually the road went into bankruptcy and was acquired by the Atlantic Coast Line during the 1890's.[7]

---

[5] *Stat.* XXIII, 1324. Later history of this and other banks, is from H. G. Osteen.
[6] *Stat.* XXV, 455; *Daily Item*, May 17, 1950.
[7] "Sumter and its Roads," *Watchman and Southron*, Oct. 22, 1890; May 6, 1891.

AN ECONOMIC RETROSPECT 479

A queer story of a lost train belongs to this period. On a Friday night in January 1892, the train for Columbia left the Sumter depot as usual — and disappeared! The dispatcher in Wilmington was frantic, for Sumter reported that the train had left, and Wedgefield reported that the train was not in sight. How could a whole train disappear in an open stretch of only ten miles? The explanation was that a switch had been left open on the "M and A" line, and when the train pulled out of the Sumter station, it ran full tilt down the wrong track. Ten miles from Sumter the brakeman yelled "Wedgefield," the train stopped, and the passengers got out, to find themselves in the woods of Privateer! The train crept slowly back to Sumter, with one man walking ahead and another behind, each with a lantern, to signal any train approaching from either direction. Happily, none approached.[8]

In those days, the Sumter passenger station was on Dingle Street above the present freight depot, and freight was then being handled at the old location between South Main and Manning Avenue, at the end of South Main.

In 1882 the Sumter and Wateree Railroad Company was chartered by D. J. Winn, A. J. China, J. D. Graham, H. Harby, A. White, J. D. Blanding, M. H. McLaurin and associates, to build a short line from Sumter to a convenient point on the South Carolina Railroad. On the same day, the town of Sumter was authorized to issue $15,000 in seven percent coupon bonds to aid construction; but nothing further was done. Renewed and extended in 1894, the charter again lapsed without action. Under a new charter issued in 1898, to J. D. Blanding, Altamont Moses and others, a 16-mile branch was built from Sumter to Sumter Junction, on the abandoned roadbed of the Wilmington and Manchester. Completed on August 7, 1899, the branch immediately became part of the Southern Railway system, which had shortly before acquired the old South Carolina Railroad.[9]

Promoted the same year by Thomas Wilson of the Wilson and Summerton Railroad, a direct line was authorized from Sumter to Camden, and the stockholder's of the Wilson road changed its name to the Northwestern Railroad. This road

8 *Ibid.*, Jan. 20, 1892.
9 *Stat.* XVII, 884, 933; XXI, 1059; XXII, 950; Derrick, *S. C. Railroad*, p. 272.

had originated in 1888, when Thomas Wilson, a lumberman, chartered and built a logging road from his mill on the Central Railroad to Summerton. When the Atlantic Coast Line acquired the Charleston, Sumter and Northern Railroad, formerly the Eutawville Railroad, it transferred to Thomas Wilson the section which connected Summerton with Sumter.[10] As the town of Sumter had donated the site of the depot to the Charleston, Sumter and Northern Railroad, the Atlantic Coast Line refunded to the town the sum of $1800, which had been originally paid by Sumter for the terminal site. During the great depression of the 1930's, the branch line up to Camden was abandoned, and at the same time the Southern Railway abandoned the 16-mile branch on the roadbed of the old Wilmington and Manchester.

Another short line during the 1880's developed from the lumber business when a big sawmill at Atkins was repeatedly moved back into the pine forests until it reached Bishopville. This logging road became the Bishopville Railroad for regular service, with two trains a day in charge of a two-man crew: a white engineer-conductor, who stopped the train when he took up tickets, and a Negro fireman-porter. The story goes that the former fell in love with a woman in Sumter, and when his daily runs were over, he, knowing the schedules on the main line between Atkins and Sumter, would ride his engine into Sumter, park it on a siding, and go a courting. Later in the evening, he would slip his iron horse back to Atkins, ready for the next day's run.

The last railroad to be built into Sumter was the Seaboard Airline. In February 1912, the Sumter Board of County Commissioners was authorized by a special law to turn over to the city clerk and treasurer of Sumter the sum of $12,000 to assist the city and county "in furthering their railroad facilities and connections."[11] As a result of this cooperation, the Seaboard extended a branch line from McBee, down through Hartsville and Bishopville to Sumter.

These later railroads, like the earlier ones, caused some shifts in population, and developed new communities around their stations. The largest, perhaps, is Pinewood, southwest

---

[10] *Stat.* XX, 81; XXIII, 257; *Watchman and Southron*, Oct. 22, 1890.
[11] *Stat.* XXVII, 964.

of Sumter on the Atlantic Coast Line railroad. This incorporated town is said to have been called originally Pine Log by the Negroes who worked there in a logging camp. Only three miles from St. Mark's church, Pinewood has absorbed the old Fulton community, and Fulton has reverted to a cross roads. Rimini, on the edge of the river swamp, was named by the Coast Line officials, perhaps for a place in Italy.

Six miles northeast of Sumter, when old Bethel became a station on the Charleston, Sumter and Northern, promoters of that railroad renamed it Oswego, apparently for the town of that name in New York. Although the railroad has been dismantled, Oswego remains as an unincorporated community. On the same railroad, St. Charles became the new name for Mount Clio. Elliotts was named before the Charleston, Sumter and Northern was built.

Hagood on the old Camden Branch, now the Southern railroad, was once called Sander's station, but in Governor Hagood's administration was renamed in his honor. When Tom Wilson built his railroad through Providence, he discarded that name and called it Dalzell for a friend, and the next station Borden for another friend. Rembert, three miles from Hagood, also developed after the coming of the railroad.

When automotive transportation showed the necessity for paved roads, Sumter was one of the first counties in the state to undertake a county-wide system of hard-surfaced highways. The first step was to amend the state constitution so that the constitutional limit on bonded indebtedness should not apply to Sumter. Then, under a carefully drawn special law of 1920, the county held a referendum, which approved the issue of $2,500,000 in bonds for construction of paved roads. This project was to be handled by a commission of six men, L. D. Jennings, G. A. Lemmon, J. P. Booth, J. B. Britton, Stanyarne Burrough, and S. A. Harvin, each of whom was bonded for $5,000, served without compensation, and was prohibited to "employ in any capacity any person related by blood or marriage to any member of the Commission within the sixth degree."[12] Later, the commission was enlarged to nine members, and two additional bond issues in 1923 and 1924

[12] *Stat.* XXXI, 1726, 1658-1662.

increased the total amount to $4,000,000 for hard-surfaced county highways.

Within the next few years more than a hundred miles of paved roads radiated from the city of Sumter to the county limits, giving the county what was believed to be at that time the most complete county highway system in the United States.

Sumter County also sponsored the construction of a highway across Wateree Swamp and the erection of a bridge at Garner's Ferry to provide direct connection with Columbia. Federal aid financed half the cost of the bridge, and Sumter and Richland counties shared equally the other half. As most of the causeway through the swamp lay on the Sumter side of the river, Sumter paid the greater part of the cost of building it.

The present State Highway Department had been created in 1920,[13] the same year that Sumter began its county-wide road system, but at first the state department was an engineering agency, largely, for statewide planning in cooperation with county highway departments. After the state undertook construction of highways, it began in 1925 to incorporate portions of the Sumter County paved roads into the state system, and to reimburse the county in part for the cost of construction.[14]

In 1883 the town of Sumter had ten miles of elevated sidewalks, made of rammed clay and held in shape by wooden curbs. The roadways between the sidewalks "were sand or mud according to the weather." On Main Street some of the merchants laid brick sidewalks in front of their stores, but there was not an all-weather crossing until the Ryttenbergs built one of brick, from their store corner to the City National Bank opposite. Some relief came during the administration of Mayor W. B. Boyle, when Main Street was paved with brick from Canal to Bartlett, at a cost of more than $25,000. After the Council-Manager government was adopted, a citywide program of paving was inaugurated in 1915, and completed in 1922. Since then, street paving has kept pace with the growth of Sumter.

[13] *Stat.* XXXI, 1072, replacing an earlier department created in 1917, *Stat.* XXX, 320.
[14] *Stat.* XXXIII, 1193; XXXIV, 875.

Agitation for the lighting of the streets began in the poverty-stricken days after the fall of the Confederacy, when the *Sumter News* on November 1, 1866, recommended that the Sumter town council should light the streets, as lamps for "kerosene or American fluid" could be procured at little cost. Eventually, kerosene lamps enclosed in glass to protect them from wind, were installed on posts ten feet high, and a town lamp-lighter made his evening rounds.

The Sumter Electric Light Company was chartered on July 30, 1889, by R. M. Wallace, president; A. J. China, vice-president; D. J. Auld, secretary-treasurer; Charles T. Mason, Jr., electrician, and R. D. Lee. Capital stock was authorized at $10,000, but 130 shares were sold at $100 each. The company built near the depot, and installed two engines, one of 50-horse-power, the other of 35-horse-power, which would feed thirty-five arc lights of 2,000 candle-power, and 500 incandescent lamps. The arc lights were contracted for by the city at $3,000 a year, and if found to be insufficient, could be increased forty percent without over-taxing the engines. The limit of the incandescent lamps could not be increased, and two hundred lights were engaged by individuals.

On the evening of November 1, 1889, about a hundred young people stood in the streets to witness the "strange and novel spectacle" when the lights were turned on for the first time. Not until two months later was the cotton factory lighted.

The story of how the city later purchased and tried to operate a power system has been told in the chapter on Council-Manager Government.

During the 1880's, the water supply of Sumter came from sixteen open fire-wells in various parts of the town, and five driven wells, but a system of water-works had been under consideration for some years. In 1887 the Town Council had signed a contract with W. A. Jeter and E. A. Boardman of Macon, Georgia, and their associates, under the name of the Sumter Water Works Company, but Jeter and Boardman failed to keep their contract. Next, H. D. Garden of Boston entered into negotiations, and a special election was called for January 9, 1889, on a $30,000-bond issue for cost of construction, but it failed to carry by 71 votes. In February 1891, another abortive contract was made. Finally, in April 1892, a new contract was signed with the American Pipe Company of Philadelphia, who promptly began laying the water mains, and building the pumping station on the northern extension of Church Street.

Shortly after a state law of 1896 authorized cities and towns to issue bonds, if necessary, to acquire water works and electric lights, the city of Sumter purchased the water system from the American Pipe Company, at a price which was believed to have been more than twice the original cost.

At a special election in December 1906, the citizens of Sumter approved a bond issue of $50,000 for sewerage.

From these comparatively small beginnings have now grown, through a series of bond issues, completely modern and municipally-owned systems for almost unlimited water supplies and scientific sewage disposal. During the great depression of the 1930's the city of Sumter cooperated with federal relief programs to extend the street paving, and improve facilities for drainage.

Sumter's telephone service was begun by local enterprise, when Albertus Brown, and Dr. S. C. Baker, with a capital of $2,000, were chartered on March 11, 1891, as the Sumter Telephone Company. Still in operation, it has changed hands several times, and is now believed to be owned by the Telephone Bond and Share Corporation, a holding corporation. The Sumter telephone directory includes South Carolina Continental Telephone Company listings for Bishopville, Lamar, Manning and Summerton.

With a population now of almost 60,000 persons, more than ninety-nine percent of whom are native born, Sumter County has more than 3,000 farms and is still an important agricultural area. Of the farm operators, more than half are tenants, and almost three-fourths are Negroes. For many decades cotton was the staple crop, and now the annual yield is more than 30,000 bales. In 1896 the Pudding Swamp Tobacco Warehouse Company and the Sumter Tobacco Board of Trade were chartered, both located in the city of Sumter. During the 1920's the Sumter County Chamber of Commerce was subsidized by county appropriations to aid in paying for the services of a land settlement agent in procuring new settlers and instructing farmers in tobacco farming, grading and marketing. Now more than two million pounds of tobacco are marketed annually, with the result that sections which once were considered too poor for farming are now prosperous.

The value of livestock on Sumter farms is more than $2,000,000, and more than a million gallons of milk are produced. Fruits, nuts, cereals, and a wide variety of vegetables are marketed, as well as poultry and eggs. The Palmetto Pigeon Plant, said to be the largest in the world, does an extensive business in the shipment of dressed squabs.

In recent years, manufacturing has begun to assume major importance in the economic life of the county, particularly in the vicinity of the county seat. This phase of Sumter's history, perhaps, should begin with the ante-bellum brickyard in the outskirts of Sumter on the Mayesville road. Evidently it was there from the beginning of the town, for the bricks in the old courthouse built by Robert Mills are said to have come out of a big hole that used to be just beyond Turkey Creek. The name of the earliest known owner was O. C. Hulbert, who, in the 1850's ground his clay by mulepower, dried his bricks in the sun, and burned them in an open kiln.

After the War of Secession, Hulbert's Brickyard was owned by Rush Chandler, who sold a half interest to J. Ryttenberg and Sons, who later acquired the other half. Upon the death of Henry Ryttenberg in 1901, it was inherited by Irving A. Ryttenberg, who was then living in New York. He came here to Sumter and is said to have removed his silk hat and Prince Albert coat, put on overalls, and learned to make brick.

A peculiarity of the brick made from the local clay was the uncertainty of their color. After Irving Ryttenberg acquired full ownership, he experimented, and produced from pulverized bricks a product which he called "Airedale" bricks, which were said to be "So Darned Ugly, They Are Beautiful." Well advertised, they found favor with architects of that day, and were shipped to some twenty-three states, the District of Columbia, and even to Canada. They now may be seen in the front wall of the Kress store on Main Street in Sumter. But apparently the demand decreased later, and the Sumter Brick Works are said to have closed after the wage-and-hour law went into effect.

Another Sumter enterprise of the old days was the Curtis Carriage and Buggy Shops, which during the 1870's stood at the corner of Main and Dingle streets. These shops employed about a dozen workmen, who produced from raw materials very highgrade custom-made carriages, buggies and wagons. Dating from the same decade was the old Sumter Marble Works, whose memorials still preserve the names of many former Sumter citizens.

During the years that cotton was the staple crop, the town of Sumter, with its good railroad connections, was a busy cotton market and shipping center. In 1881, the brick walls of the Bellemont Cotton Manufacturing Company began to rise near the Wilmington, Columbia and Augusta tracks, with five cottages nearby for the workmen's families. When it began operation, the charter was approved, naming the promoters as D. J. Winn, W. D. Blanding, A. S. Brown, H. Harby, Joseph H. Earle, and R. P. Monaghan. With a capital of $40,300, and run entirely by steam, the factory employed only thirty-seven hands. An early annual report showed that it had consumed 375,000 bales of cotton, produced 350,000 pounds of yarn, operated 1,984 spindles, and declared the first year a three percent dividend. Suspended in 1884, the factory was leased by other persons and reopened as the Sumter Cotton Factory. In 1885, with twelve new homes for workers, it was running day and night.

A report on Sumter's industries in 1884, compiled by H. F. Wilson for the *News and Courier*, shows that besides the one cotton factory, the county had 73 flour and grist mills, 31 lumber mills, and 10 turpentine establishments, the last-named capitalized at a total of $10,000, and producing annually 600 barrels of turpentine and 3,000 barrels of rosin, valued at $15,000. The total capital invested in all amounted to $350,000, producing an annual value of $672,000, and employing 213 whites, 390 Negroes, a total of 603 persons.

Among the local firms chartered in 1890 were: the Sumter Ice Manufacturing Company by Eugene H. Moses and Joshua

H. Harby, with a capital of $10,000; the Sumter Land Improvement Company by William M. Graham and John P. Coffin, capitalized at $100,000, to deal in real estate, "lay out town sites," and build houses; and the Sumter Compress and Warehouse Company by A. J. Clark, N. O'Donnell, W. M. Graham, A. S. Brown, Abe Ryttenberg, and R. D. Lee, with a capital of $30,000.

Industrial progress continued with the advent of the Sumter Cotton Oil Company, now the Southern; Witherspoon Brothers Coffin Company, Sumter Machinery Company, Williams Veneer Mill, Sumter Roller Mills, Sumter Veneer Mills, Sumter Fertilizer Company, B. L. Montague Company, Sumter Hardwood Company (Korn Industries), and many others.

After the city of Sumter contracted with the Carolina Power and Light Company for unlimited supplies of power, a campaign was launched for advertising Sumter's advantages. In 1929 the county approved $1,500 to the Board of Trade, provided the city gave a like amount, for attempting to secure new industries.

Among the many enterprises that have added to the industrial wealth of Sumter may be mentioned: the Williams Furniture Company and its many subsidiaries, Nu-Idea Furniture Company, John Evans Manufacturing Company for truck trailers, Polly Prentiss for tufted bedspreads; Sumter Textile Mills, specializing in pants cloth; Rose Knit Hosiery Mills; Norwood Manufacturing Company, for furniture; Sumter Venetian-Blind Factory, the Harvin Packing Company, Tuxedo Feed Mills; and Segalock Fasteners, Inc., for zippers.

In addition to many other commercial businesses, there are at least six large bottling companies, one of which has in its plant an attractive, air-conditioned community center, where many of the local organizations hold regular meetings.

After the second World War, according to a survey by the Preparedness for Peace Commission,[15] the manufacturing plants in Sumter county had an increase of $83,934 in the first year of peace. During the last year of the war, thirty-nine plants had an annual production valued at $14,997,281, as compared with forty-three plants in 1940, with an annual

---

[15] *Daily Item*, Mch 8, 1945.

production valued at $8,333,118. The annual production for each employee in 1945 was $3,335. The thirty-nine plants of that year were diversified among twenty-two classifications. Recent figures indicate that capital invested in factories other than lumber exceeds $10,000,000.

The timber resources of Sumter have always been large, and even now almost half of the area of the county is in forests. In 1947 the pine saw-timber was estimated at 120,-000,000 board feet. The production of pulpwood in 1948 was nearly 19,000 cords, valued at $184,000; and the production of lumber in 1946 was more than 45,000,000 board feet, valued at nearly $3,000,000. So large is the volume of business handled by the great lumber companies that have headquarters in Sumter, but which own forests from Florida to Virginia and even in Central America and the Philippines, that Sumter has been called the capital of the lumber industry.

CHAPTER XL

RECENT PROGRESS

The recent years of Sumter's history have been crowded with achievement and change. Two World Wars, in which Sumter's sons and daughters participated with courage and devotion, have brought far-reaching consequences. The memory of those who died in the first World War is literally kept green in Sumter's lovely Memorial Park. The roll of those who perished in the second World War is recorded in white marble on the county courthouse grounds. Shaw Air Force Base of the second World War, is named in honor of Lieutenant Ervin D. Shaw, the first Sumter County pilot to die in combat in the first World War.

The miles of rolling countryside now behind the wire of Shaw Base had been fertile farm lands from the beginning of the county. In the spring of 1940, a group of Sumter citizens agreed that their county would be a good location for an Air Force training field. During the summer, the City and County of Sumter in consultation with engineers, obtained options on a suitable site of about 3,000 acres, and then sent a delegation to Washington to offer it to the United States for an airfield. The government, however, took no action. After several more fruitless trips, in the spring of 1941 a Sumter delegation went to Montgomery, Alabama, and obtained approval from the commander of the Southeastern Air Training Command. His endorsement soon brought governmental action.

The city and county then purchased the lands, paid for the destruction of crops, the moving of a church, the construction of an entrance road, the right-of-way for a railroad spur and a sewer line, and bought additional land for a radio station and the necessary housing — all at a cost which totaled some $180,000. The entire site they leased to the United States for ninety-nine years at a rental of one dollar a year.

Construction was immediately begun and the field was completed almost over night. During the next four years the training program at Shaw sent out a class of cadets every five weeks. Towards the end of the war, Shaw trained Allied bomber pilots and crews for France, Turkey and China. The tremendous wartime garrison brought a heavy influx of service men's families to Sumter and strained the housing facilities of the city. But these problems were met and Sumter grew. After the war, some of the military personnel became citizens of Sumter.

Many of Sumter's nurses served in the armed services. The Sumter Training School for Nurses was chartered on January 23, 1901, with a capital of $50,000, Robert O. Purdy, president, and Van Talbery Hofman, secretary. The training of nurses, however, preceded the chartered institution and began in two small private hospitals. The Baker-Dick Infirmary, founded about 1894, by Dr. S. C. Baker and Dr. A. C. Dick, was a 10-bed institution on West Hampton street between Sumter and Washington. The Mood Infirmary was also a 10-bed private hospital, founded shortly after the Baker-Dick Infirmary, by Dr. Julius A. Mood. Each infirmary had a training school for its nurses, taught by Dr. Mood and Dr. Baker. In 1897 Dr. Mood employed Mrs. Anna Simpson as his first superintendent of nurses.

In 1908 Dr. Baker and Dr. Dick and their associates, built a new infirmary which they called Sumter Hospital, a private institution built without aid from any outside agency. This building later was to become the Negro wing of Tuomey Hospital. In 1913 the Mood Infirmary was consolidated with Sumter Hospital.

Meanwhile, in 1897, Timothy J. Tuomey had died, leaving a will which provided for the establishment of Tuomey Hospital, to which after the death of his widow, the bulk of his large estate should go as an endowment. When Mrs. Tuomey died in 1909, she bequeathed an additional $35,000 to the hospital funds.

The Tuomey Board of Trustees, in August 1913, purchased the Sumter Hosiptal and changed the name to the Tuomey Hospital. The hospital's School for Nursing was established the next year, and in 1916 a Nurses' Home was built. With aid from the Duke Foundation, the central brick building was erected in 1930.

At the death of Neill O'Donnell, one of the Tuomey Hospital trustees, in 1937, a bequest of $400,000 was added to the endowment. The next year, with help from the Duke Foundation, a new Nurses' Home was built and named for Mrs. Neill O'Donnell. In 1945, assisted by a federal grant and city and county contributions, the maternity wing was added.

Among other bequests of public-spirited citizens to the hospital, should be mentioned $25,000 for general purposes in 1924, by Dr. Edwin R. Wilson, son of Thomas Wilson, the wealthy lumberman.

Another memorial to the philanthropy of a generous Sumter citizen is the Crosswell Orphanage, established and endowed under the will of John K. Crosswell, who died in 1929. Primarily for the orphans of Sumter County, the orphanage also receives children from other counties. The trustees named in the will were J. H. Strong, C. B. Yeadon, John J. Riley, H. H. Bruner, and their successors, with other trustees to be named by Sumter City Council and the County Board of Commissioners. The orphanage is on a 130-acre tract, which gives ample space for poultry, dairy and truck farms for the children and the administrative staff housed in the four brick cottages. The assets of the orphanage in 1950 were estimated to exceed a million dollars.

The first farm agent, Luther Martin, in 1909 came to the John J. Dargan school at Stateburg, but after a few months he resigned on a plea of ill health, and returned to Georgia.

Early in October of the same year, J. Frank Williams took over the work. For one day a week he taught agriculture and supervised a demonstration plot for the school; for the other five days with a horse and buggy, he drove out over the county, visiting the farmers. He and his family resided in a house supplied by the school until 1911, when Acton house, then used by the school, was destroyed by fire. Mr. Williams then transferred headquarters to Sumter, and carried on his work under the Board of Trade.

The approach of the boll weevil from Mexico caused Congress to send Dr. Seaman Knapp to assist southern farmers in planning for other crops in the place of cotton. Money for this work was supplied by the Rockefeller Foundation until Congress provided for it at the outbreak of the first World War. In 1924 Mr. Williams resigned to devote his entire time to his own farms, and developed his handsome residence at Needwood. He was succeeded by J. M. Eleazer, who, after twenty-two years, was recalled to Clemson College.

In 1913 Miss Mary Lemmon became the first home demonstration agent, and began tomato club work in the county. Since 1919 the county has been making appropriations to assist the extension work now directed from Clemson and Winthrop. The large modern agricultural building, locally called "the Kremlin," on the Sumter courthouse grounds, attests the county's realization of the value of extension work. The farm agent now has two assistants, and the home agent one assistant. There are also Negro agents for the extension work with the Negro farmers and homemakers.

The present educational facilities for the children of Sumter, show perhaps a greater advance over those in 1868 than any other development in the county's history. During the War of Secession, teachers were called into the armed services and schools were closed. The severe curtailment of opportunities for schooling during and after the war is attested by the following from a Sumter boy, which appeared in the *Sumter News* of January 25, 1868. Apparently the printer may have supplied some punctuation.

> Dogs is usefuller as cats. Mice is afeard of 'em. Dogs follers boys and catches a hog by the ears. Hogs rarely bite. People eats hogs, but it is said, they and all other animals that doesn't chew the cud isn't clean ones. Dogs sometimes git hit with boot-jacks for barking of nites. Sleepy people git mad and throw 'em. Dogs is the best animal for man, they do for man more than grownd hogs or koons or even goats. Goats smell. The end.

St. Joseph's Academy had been founded during the war by the Sisters of Our Lady of Mercy when they took refuge in Sumter from the federal bombardment of Charleston. In 1862 they erected a two-story building on East Liberty street, and later they added wings and another story. Eventually all three stories were surrounded by wide piazzas. The first floor was used for classrooms, and could be thrown into one long hall by opening the folding doors. The second floor was for classrooms and residence, and the third floor was the dormitory for the boarding pupils. The grounds comprised six acres which had a vegetable garden, an orchard, and a playground. The report of the state superintendent of schools in 1881 showed that St. Joseph's had five teachers and sixty pupils. It was discontinued after the graded school system proved satisfactory.

Another well-known boarding school for young ladies was the Sumter Female Institute, opened in 1868 on the north corner of Calhoun and Washington streets by Mrs. L. A. Brown, a graduate of Harmony College, and Miss Eliza Cooper. The report of the state superintendent of schools in 1881 showed that the institute had seven instructors and 105 pupils, of whom five were males. It ended with the century.

The ante-bellum Sumter Academy was in operation during 1866 and 1867, with S. M. Richardson and W. H. Johnson as principals. Richardson resigned in October 1867. Johnson completed the fall term, and edited the *Sumter News* until January 1868, when he seems to have left Sumter. The next year he was teaching in Mount Pleasant.

In the autumn of 1867 Thomas P. McQueen and George Edward Haynsworth, the cadet who had fired the first shot of the Confederacy, had opened Festina Lente, a school for boys in Temperance Hall. When Messrs. Richardson and Johnson gave up the Sumter Academy, McQueen and Haynsworth applied for it. The trustees of the Sumter Academy met, and considered but took no action on the request of the late principals for reimbursement for their repairs on the old building. They agreed, however, that McQueen and Haynsworth should have the Academy for the year 1868, and in lieu of rent, should spend $25 for repairs. This was the last meeting of the Board, for soon after, the historic building was burned.

Among other private schools of the period were Mrs. Moise's Seminary, a boarding and day school; and a school for young ladies and children kept by Miss Eliza E. Cooper and Miss Lina A. Johnson.

There were several reasons for the numerous private schools. The state constitution of 1868 had required compulsory education of all children in public schools, but made no provision for separation of the races. The public schools in general were one-teacher institutions, miserably housed and poorly taught. Under the reconstructed government of the carpetbaggers and their associates, funds for the public schools mysteriously disappeared, and in 1873 many public schools had to close. Angry citizens held several meetings at the Sumter courthouse and demanded an accounting from the school commissioner and the district trustees, but received little satisfaction, and it was generally believed that the school-money had been stolen.

Among the Sumter public school teachers the next year were Miss Mary Girardeau for the Female White School, Miss M. R. Logan for the Male Primary School, the Rev. I. E. Lowery for the Colored Male School, and Miss M. E. Scott for the Colored Female School. In 1876 Miss Girardeau was still in charge of her school, with the Misses Hurst and Barrett as assistants. Captain G. A. Andrew was at the head of the Male White School. In June that year, Trustee C. M. Hurst reported at the citizens' meeting in the courthouse a balance of $225 in hand. He appealed for a 4-mill tax to build a schoolhouse for the white children, as such a building was essential to enable the white school to share in the Peabody Fund, which heretofore had been making possible much longer school terms for the Negro children than for the white. A 3-mill tax was approved, and a building for a Male-Female Public School was rented on West Hampton avenue. In 1879 the principal was Major John A. Leland, who had an honorary Ph. D. degree from Williams College. There he had been a pupil of the celebrated Mark Hopkins, a teacher of whom President Garfield once said that a log in the woods, with a student at one end and Mark Hopkins at the other, could be an ideal college. In 1880 a five-room school building was erected on East Hampton Avenue. When it was abandoned in 1888, J. Diggs Wilder was principal.

The area within the city limits of Sumter was made a school

district that year for the purpose of maintaining a system of graded public schools, on a tax levy not to exceed two mills. The new School Board included the mayor, ex officio, and four members, each to be elected from one of the four wards.

The first superintendent of city schools was J. B. Duffie of Columbia, a graduate of Union College. His assistant was Victor R. Pringle, and in addition there were four other teachers. The graded school opened on September 2, 1889, in the A. J. Moses home on Washington Street, with 500 pupils who were classified into nine grades. By making use of the basement, all were squeezed in, and one teacher was added. The taxpayers approved a $12,000-bond issue, and a brick school was erected and equipped on Academy Square at a cost of $17,000.

In June 1895 Mr. Duffie resigned, and was succeeded by S. H. Edmunds, a graduate of Davidson, and a former assistant in the Sumter high school department. His first assistant was D. L. Rambo, at a salary of sixty dollars a month, and the seven women teachers each received thirty-five dollars. In the fall of 1896 Miss Linnie McLaurin was elected as an additional assistant. She resigned the following spring, but returned in 1906 as the seventh grade teacher. When the Girls' High School was built in 1917, she became principal, a position which she held for twenty years; and when death ended the career of Dr. S. H. Edmunds in 1935, she became acting superintendent until March 1, 1936.

The forty years of Dr. Edmunds' administration brought many changes and tremendous growth and development in the Sumter city schools. At the time of his death on September 14, 1935, the enrollment was 3,898 pupils, with 92 teachers, and property valued at $417,950. Between the years 1891 and 1937, graduates of the high school numbered 2,632. Since those years the city school system has continued to grow in step with the population of the area it serves.

The successive superintendents since Dr. Edmunds have been W. F. Loggins, William Henry Shaw, E. R. Crow, and James D. Blanding. In 1939 the separate high schools for girls and boys were consolidated and the Edmunds High School was built with the addition of a PWA federal grant to a $140,000 bond issue, in all, about $260,000. The former Girls High School became Junior High School. In 1947 it was partially destroyed by fire, but it was soon remodeled and enlarged. A recent bond issue of $370,000 has provided funds for two new elementary schools; and an issue of $275,000 made possible another elementary school and various other improvements.

Linked with the schools in its origin, is an important cultural institution, the Sumter Carnegie Public Library on Academy Square, facing Liberty Street. In the autumn of 1890, efforts were begun for a library at the new graded school. Some gifts of books were made, and local "entertainments" provided money for the purchase of some books. In 1902 in answer to a plea of Superintendent Edmunds for a building program, Colonel Blanding suggested that perhaps funds might be obtained from the Carnegie Foundation if a school and a library were combined in the same building. But this proved to be impossible.

In 1915 the Carnegie Foundation agreed to grant $10,000 for a free library if the city council would provide annually $1,000 for its maintenance. This was readily arranged for, the school Board provided a site on Academy Square behind the Washington school, and in the summer of 1917 the library building was completed.

The importance of the library was greatly enhanced in May 1939, when it became by a special act, a county institution. Control was vested in a Board of seven members: two appointed by trustees of the city schools (district 17); one, by the city Council of Sumter; one by the Board of County Commissioners; one by the County Teachers' Association; one by the county Council of Farm Women; and one chosen by the Library Board itself from the City of Sumter. Each member serves a 4-year term, and the Board has "exclusive control, fiscal or otherwise," of the library's property, assets, and employees. An annual county tax of two mills provides funds, a portion of which is set aside each year in a reserve which is being accumulated for enlargement of the library building. The library now has more than 23,000 volumes, and sends out books by motor truck on a regular schedule to all sections of the county. The library also sponsors a Vacation Reading Club, and offers the Inter-library Loan service to its almost 4,000 members. The first trained librarian, Miss Jean D. Cochran, during her tenure, 1945-1949, had all of the books inventoried and re-catalogued.

The Library Board in 1944 decided to sponsor a history of the county, a project of which this book is the result. Four years later, by legislative act, the County Historical Commission was created to place markers at the many historic spots. In 1950, when Sumter held its sesqui-centennial celebration of the organization of the county, the first of a series of historical pageants was featured at the annual Iris Festival, and the Sumter *Item* issued a special edition, which carried to the public much of the history of the place and its people. So much interest in Sumter's history was stirred, that a County Historical Society was formed, which is now actively fostering historical enterprises. The prospects are bright that the records of Sumter will be preserved for a succession of future historians.

CONFEDERATE MONUMENT, Sumter; granite, showing 341 names, "Erected by the Women of Sumter District to their Confederate Dead." Corner stone laid May 6, 1874; shaft raised October 3, 1878; completed in 1888 (Sumter Daily Item staff photo).

ST. JOSEPH'S ACADEMY, Sumter, from woodcut in *Watchman and Southron*, 1889. (Sumter Daily Item staff photo).

THE SUMTER INSTITUTE, from woodcut in *Watchman and Southron*, 1889. (Sumter Daily Item staff photo).

MAGNETO FACTORY OF CHARLES MASON, Sumter. (Sumter Daily Item staff photo).

WASHINGTON GRADED SCHOOL, Sumter, built in 1891. (Sumter Daily Item staff photo).

MAIN STREET, SUMTER, before 1920, when cotton was king. (Sumter Dialy Item staff photo).

ST. ANNE'S ROMAN CATHOLIC CHURCH, Sumter, corner stone laid Nov. 28, 1909. (Sumter Daily Item staff photo).

MEMORIAL PARK, Sumter, showing dedicatory stone in foreground. Former site of Col. James D. Blanding's home. (Sumter Daily Item staff photo).

HOME OF COL. JAMES D. BLANDING, now rolled to the next block and remodeled. (Sumter Daily Item staff photo).

HORACE L. TILGHMAN FOREST TREE FARM, near Wedgefield.
(State Forestry Commission photo).

ROSEMARY LOOKOUT TOWER, Mancheter Forest. (State Forestry Commission photo).

EDMUNDS HIGH SCHOOL, Sumter. (Sumter Daily Item staff photo).

LINCOLN HIGH SCHOOL, Sumter. (Sumter Daily Item staff photo).

CROSSWELL ORPHANAGE. (Sumter Daily Item staff photo).

CARNEGIE PUBLIC LIBRARY, Sumter. (Sumter Daily Item staff photo).

TEMPLE SINAI, Sumter. This, the second building, was dedicated March 28, 29, 1913. (Sumter Daily Item staff photo).

THE SUMTER HOSPITAL, Sumter, now part of Tuomey Hospital. (Sumter Daily Item staff photo).

TUOMEY HOSPITAL, Sumter. (Sumter Daily Item staff photo).

THE LAKE, Poinsett State Park. (State Forestry Commission photo).

IRIS, SWAN LAKE GARDENS, Sumter. (Photo by Thomas L. Martin).

AIR VIEW, CITY OF SUMTER. (Sumter Daily Item staff photo).

ADDENDA
BIBLIOGRAPHY
INDEX

ADDENDA

I

GOVERNORS OF SOUTH CAROLINA
From within the limits of old Sumter District

James B. Richardson	1802-1804	John L. Manning	1852-1854
Richard I. Manning	1824-1826	Franklin I. Moses, Jr.	1872-1874
Stephen D. Miller	1828-1830	John Peter Richardson	1886-1890
John Peter Richardson	1840-1842	Richard I. Manning	1915-1919

Thomas Gordon McLeod 1923-1927

II

TENTATIVE LISTS OF SOME OFFICERS

Clerk of Court

John Horan	1800	G. S. C. DesChamps	c. 1856
William Brunson	1818	Lucius P. Loring	1866
Israel G. Mathis	1819	George W. Reardon	1868
Robert Bradford	1822	William H. Cuttino	1881
John N. Miles	1827	James D. Graham	c. 1888
Thomas J. Wilder	1831	Shepard K. Nash	
John M. Dargan	1835	Lauren I. Parrott	1904
James Parsons	1839	H. Lee Scarborough	1913
John M. Dargan	1843	R. Eugene Wilder	1930

Raymond D. Blanding 1942

Sheriff

Huberd (Hubert) Rees	1800	Julius T. Edwards, Negro coroner,	
John Conyers	1803	a respected "Hampton Dem-	
Ulysses Rogers	1803	ocrat," became acting sheriff	
Hartwell Macon	1811	when Sheriff Wilder died in	
Robert Bradford	1816	1881, and served until the vacan-	
William H. Capers	1820	cy was filled.	
Joseph Durant	1824	Robert W. Durant	1881
David Durant	1828	Marion Sanders	c. 1886
William G. Richardson	1832	E. Scott Carson	
Harvey Skinner	1849	George P. McKagen	
J. C. Rhame	1852	B. Gaither Pierson	
Thomas D. Frierson	1856	Henry W. Scarborough	
Samuel Watson	1860	William H. Epperson	1901
Thomas J. Coghlan	1868	John Knox Bradford	1909
John M. Tindall	1874	Charles M. Hurst	1918
Josiah Murrell Wilder	1881	George L. Mabry	1941

William J. Seale 1945
J. Byrd Parnell 1953

ADDENDA 517

Ordinary

William Taylor	1800	William Lewis		1836
William Potts	1815	Noah Graham		1860

Judge of Probate

Charles M. Hurst	1869	Thomas E. Richardson		1907
Sam Lee	1877	Eleanor S. Richardson		1933
Thomas V. Walsh	1878			

Treasurer

Thomas J. Coghlan	1869	D. E. Keels		1890
W. H. Gardner	1874	H. Lee Scarborough	c.	1900
John B. Johnston	1876	Timothy W. Lee		1905
W. F. B. Haynsworth	1877	B. C. Wallace		1907
Philip P. Gaillard	1886	Mrs. Maude Bateman White		1946

Auditor

J. N. Corbett	1869	J. Diggs Wilder	1905
Charles Spencer		Horace Harby	1910
W. R. Delgar		R. E. Wilder	1911
A. Brooks Stuckey		John B. Duffie	1930
Peter Thomas		Will J. Shaw	1949

School Commissioner

J. N. Corbett	1869	James T. Wilder	
Timothy J. Tuomey		John T. Green	1887
W. F. Rhame		B. D. Wilson	
J. Diggs Wilder		J. Edwin Rembert	
William Durant			

County Superintendent of Education

William P. Baskin		William O. Cain	1927
S. D. Cain		Buford S. Mabry	1947
J. Herbert Haynsworth	1911		

III

"BARONIES" OF SUMTER COUNTY

People who have had occasion to work with the old land records of Sumter County have sometimes been puzzled by the reference to "baronies", especially in citations of transfers and boundaries. A barony as specified in the Fundamental Constitutions of Carolina in the days of the Lords Proprietors, meant the landed estate of either a landgrave or a cassique, and consisted of 12,000 acres. Each landgrave (only one to be created in each county) was to own four baronies; and each cassique (only two in each county), was to have two baronies. The term barony, therefore, was a term restricted to an estate that went with the titles of landgrave and cassique.

As early as 1736, there were two so-called baronies granted in the future Sumter County, and both were on Black River. William Dry, captain of the Goose Creek militia, had one of these baronies but, having married a daughter of the first Governor James Moore. who had then settled in North Carolina, Dry sold his plantations near Charleston the next year and followed his father-in-law. As late as 1814, and even in 1826, Dry's Barony is referred to in Sumter Deeds. On the north side of Black River, apparently not far from Dry's Barony, was the other barony, granted the same year to John Fenwick, a great merchant and planter of Charleston, who eventually returned to England. Fenwick's Barony is cited in a Sumter deed of 1829, and the accompanying plat shows a "New Cut Road from the fork of Black River into the Salem Road".

After the Revolution, many very large grants of land were made by the State of South Carolina, and although titles of nobility could not exist then, the surveyors who laid out the new grants, and the lawyers who drew deeds for sales of the lands in the grants, continued to use the term "barony". General Sumter's grant for 14,288 acres, a part of which is now in the City of Sumter, was called a barony in a deed of 1806. John Reardon's Barony was cited in 1801, when Roger and Sylvester Dunn sold 850 adjoining acres to Henry Dunn of Darlington. Nearby was John Cassels' Barony, granted in 1791 for 10,000 acres on Lynches river. Fullwood's Barony, also in Salem County, was cited in a deed of 1806 for land which touched on the 14,900 acres granted in 1791 to Robert Fullwood. Another well-known tract in Salem County near Coldstream plantation, was Baker's Barony, which was cited in a deed of 1829 as being claimed by Robert Tomlinson.

The reason for so many grants of such great size after the Revolution probably stemmed from the desire of the legislature to place vast areas of public lands in private hands so as to be able to collect taxes from them. The land-grant law of 1791 temporarily reduced the fee for acquiring public land from ten dollars to one dollar for 100 acres (*Stat.* V, 168, 169), and hence a number of the "baronies" on Black River were granted at that time.

SELECTED BIBLIOGRAPHY

PUBLIC RECORDS

State of South Carolina, Columbia.
  Secretary of State, MS grants and plats.
  Archives Department, MS Council journals.
  General Assembly, *Reports and Resolutions; Statutes at Large.*
SumterCounty, courthouse.
  Clerk of court, MS plats; mesne conveyances; court records; miscellaneous records.
  Probate court, MS wills and inventories.
Sheriff, MS sales and receipts.

PRIVATE RECORDS

Sumter, Natalie Delage (Mrs. Thomas, Jr.). Fragment of MS Dairy. South Caroliniana Library, University of South Carolina.
Sumter Art Association, MS minutes.
For family papers, *see* "Author's Preface."

NEWSPAPERS

The Camden Gazette.
The Camden Journal.
The Southern Whig, Sumter.
The Black River Watchman, Sumter.
The Sumter Banner.
The Sumter Gazette.
The Sumter News.
The True Southron, Sumter.
The Watchman and Southron.
The Sumter Daily Item.

MAPS

Map of South Carolina, MS, February 1770. Survey by Tacitus Gaillard and James Cook. South Carolina Historical Society.
South Carolina and a Part of Georgia. By John Stuart. London, 1780.
The Seat of War of the Revolution in the Southern States. ...In William Johnson, ... *Life ... of Nathanael Green.* ...
Sumter District. Surveyed by S. H. Boykin, 1821. In Robert Mills, *Atlas of the State of South Carolina.*
... Field of Operations of the 54th Mass. Regt., 1863-1865. By James B. Gardner. In L. F. Emilio, *History of the Fifty-Fourth Regiment.* ...
Map of Sumter County. ...1878. From Railroad and Private Surveys. By M. H. McLaurin.
General Highway and Transportation Map Sumter County, 1938. By State Highway Department and U. S. Department of Agriculture, Bureau of Public Roads.

SELECTED BIBLIOGRAPHY

PRINTED SOURCES
primary and secondary

Allen, Walter. *Governor Chamberlain's Administration in South Carolina.* . . . New York, 1888.
Andrews, Robert W. *The Life and Adventures of Capt. Robert W. Andrews of Sumter, South Carolina.* . . . Boston, 1887.
Belser, W. G., J. E., and I. F. *The Belser Family of South Carolina.* Sumter, 1941.
Biographical Director of the American Congress, 1774-1927, Washington, 1928.
Blanding, A. L. *The McFaddin Dedication,* vol. V. Clinton, 1937.
Boddie, W. W. *History of Williamsburg.* Columbia, 1925.
Brooks, U. R. *South Carolina Bench and Bar.* Columbia, 1908.
Brown, Dr. and Mrs. C. C. *History of the First Baptist Church of Sumter.* Sumter, 1938.
Burgess, James M. *Chronicles of St. Mark's Parish.* . . . 1731-1885. Columbia, 1888.
Capers, William. "Autobiography." See Wightman.
Cook, Harvey T. (ed.). *A Biography of Richard Furman.* Greenville, n. d., (1913).
Coxe, Elizabeth Allen. *Memoirs of a South Carolina Plantation During the War,* n.p., 1912.
Dalcho, Frederick . . . *the Protestant Episcopal Church in South Carolina.* Charleston, 1820.
Daughters of the Confederacy. *South Carolina Women in the Confederacy.* 2 vols. Columbia, 1907.
Davis, Henry E. *The Williamsburg Presbyterian Church, Kingstree, S. C.* n. p., 1936.
Davis, Matthew L. *Memoirs of Aaron Burr.* . . . 2 vols. New York, 1837.
Derrick, Samuel M. *Centennial History of the South Carolina Railroad.* Columbia, 1930.
Drayton, John. *A View of South Carolina.* Charleston, 1802.
Drayton, John. *Memoirs of the American Revolution.* 2 vols. Charleston, 1821.
DuBose, H. C. *Memoirs of Rev. John Leighton Wilson.* . . . Richmond, 1895.
Earle, Joseph H., *Memorial Addresses on the Life and Character of,* Washington, 1898.
Elzas, Barnett A. *The Jews of South Carolina.* Philadelphia, 1905.
Emilio, Luis F. *History of the Fifty-Fourth Regiment of Massachusetts Volunteer Infantry, 1863-1865.* Boston, 1894.
Eubanks, John Evans. *Ben Tillman's Baby: The Dispensary System of South Carolina.* Augusta, 1951.
Gregorie, Anne King. *Thomas Sumter.* Columbia, 1931.
Haynsworth, Hugh Charles. *Haynsworth-Furman and Allied Families.* Sumter, 1942.
Henry, H. M. *The Police Control of the Slave in South Carolina.* Emory, Va., 1914.

Hooker, Richard J. *See* Woodmason.
Howe, George. *History of the Presbyterian Church in South Carolina.* 2 vols. Columbia, 1870.
Irving, John B. *The South Carolina Jockey Club.* Charleston, 1857.
James, William D. *A Sketch of the Life of Brig. Gen. Francis Marion.* . . . Marietta, Ga., 1948.
Jarrell, Hampton M. *Wade Hampton and the Negro.* Columbia, 1949.
Jenkins, James. *Experience, Labours and Sufferings of Rev. James Jenkins.* . . . n. p. 1842.
Johnson, Joseph. *Traditions and Reminiscenses, chiefly of the American Revolution in the South.* Charleston, 1851.
Johnson, William. *Sketches of the Life and Correspondence of Nathanael Greene.* . . . 2 vols. Charleston, 1822.
Kirkland, Thomas J. and Kennedy, Robert M. *Historic Camden.* 2 vols. Columbia, 1905, 1926.
Lander, Ernest M., Jr. *See* Mayrant.
Lockwood, Thomas P. *A Geography of South-Carolina.* Charleston, 1832.
Lowery, I. E. *Life on the Old Plantation.* Columbia, 1911.
McCord, David James. *See* Nott.
McGill, Samuel D. *Narrative of Reminiscences in Williamsburg County.* Columbia, 1897.
Mayrant, William. "Two Letters by William Mayrant on his Cotton Factory, 1815." Edited by Ernest M. Lander, Jr. In *The South Carolina Historical Magazine*, LIV (1953).
Meriwether, Robert L. *The Expansion of South Carolina 1729-1765.* Kingsport, 1940.
Mills, Robert. *Atlas of the State of South Carolina.* Columbia, 1938.
Mills, Robert. *Statistics of South Carolina.* Charleston, 1826.
Moses, Herbert A. *The Early Minutes of the Sumter Society of Israelites.* Sumter, 1936.
Moultrie, William. *Memoirs of the American Revolution.* . . . 2 vols. New York, 1802.
Nott, Henry Junius and McCord, David James. *Reports of Cases Determined in the Constitutional Court of South Carolina.* I. Columbia, 1820.
O'Neall, John B. *Biographical Sketches of the Bench and Bar of South Carolina.* 2 vols. Charleston, 1859.
Palmer, B. M. *The Life and Letters of James Henley Thornwell.* . . . Richmond, 1875.
Pringle, Elizabeth W. Allston (ed.). *The Register Book for the Parish Prince Frederick Winyah.* Baltimore, 1916.
Ravenel, Beatrice St. Julien. *Architects of Charleston.* Charleston, 1945.
Reniers, Perceval. *The Springs of Virginia.* . . . Chapel Hill, 1941.
Richardson, Francis D. *Memoirs of Friars Point, Miss.* n. p., 1930. Courtesy of Allen Jones, Esq., Hendersonville, N. C.
Richardson, James S. G. *Equity Reports,* IX. Charleston, 1858.
Richardson, William. "Letters of . . .". *S. C. Historical Magazine*, XLVII.
Scarborough, H. L. *Some Interesting Facts in the History of Sumter County.* Sumter, 1921.

Scott, Edwin J. *Random Recollections of a Long Life, 1806-1876.* Columbia, 1884.

Simkins, Francis B. *Pitchfork Ben Tillman: South Carolinian.* Baton Rouge, 1944.

Simkins, Francis B., and Woody, Robert H. *South Carolina During Reconstruction.* Chapel Hill, 1932.

Simms, William G. *The Life of Francis Marion.* New York, 1844.

Simms, William G. *The Remains of Maynard Davis Richardson with a Memoir of his Life.* Charleston, 1833.

Singleton, Virginia E. Green. *Singletons of South Carolina.* ... Hartsville, 1914.

The South Carolina Historical Magazine. See Mayrant; Richardson, William.

Stubbs, Thomas M. *Family Album: The Moods.* ... Atlanta, 1943.

Sumter, Natalie Delage (Mrs. Thomas, Jr.). *Fifteen Letters of Nathalie Sumter.* Introduction and Notations by Mary Virginia Saunders White. Columbia, 1942.

Sumter, John R. *Some Old Stateburg Homes.* Sumter, 1934. *Church of the Holy Cross.* Sumter, 1930.

Tarleton, Banastre. *A History of the Campaigns of 1780 and 1781, in the Southern Provinces.* ... Dublin, 1787.

Townsend, Leah. *South Carolina Baptists 1670-1805.* Florence, 1935.

United States. ... *Official Records of the Union and Confederate Armies.* 130 vols. Washington, 1880-1901.

University of South Carolina. *Alumni Directory.* Columbia, 1926.

Wallace, David Duncan. *South Carolina: A Short History 1520-1948.* Chapel Hill, 1951.

Wallace, David Duncan. *South Carolina Constitution of 1895.* Columbia, 1927.

Wallace, James A. *History of Williamsburg Church.* ... Salisbury, N. C., 1856.

White, Mary Virginia Saunders. See Sumter, Natalie Delage.

Wightman, William M. *Life of William Capers ... including an Autobiography.* Nashville, 1858.

Williams, Alfred B. *Hampton and His Red Shirts.* Charleston, 1935.

Winn, D. James. *An Historical Sketch of Methodism. ... Sumter Station.* Sumter, 1918.

Woodmason, Charles. *The Carolina Backcountry on the Eve of the Revolution: The Journal and Other Writings of Charles Woodmason, Anglican Itinerant.* Edited with an Introduction by Richard J. Hooker. Chapel Hill, 1953. Transcripts of Woodmason's letters from the Library of Congress, and of his Journal from the Institute of Early American History and Culture, are cited in the *History of Sumter County*, which was in press when *The Carolina Backcountry* was published.

Woody, Robert H. See Simkins.

INDEX

Abbitt, Thomas, 11.
Abbott, Dr. Henry T., 369.
Abett (Abbott?), 13.
Abolitionists, 143-144, 244, 247, 248.
Academies, 63, 91, 176-182, 184-192.
Academy Green, see Academy Square.
Academy Grove, see Academy Square.
Academy Square, 185, 203, 320, 495, 496.
Academy of Music, 436, 437, 438-439.
Acton, 414, 440.
Adair, John, 62.
Adams, Francis M., 99, 190, 454.
Agricultural fairs, see Fairs.
Agricultural Extension: home demonstration, 492; farm demonstration, 491-492; Negro work, 492.
Alabama Railroad, 157.
Alcoholic beverages, see Temperance movement; Dispensary system.
Aldrich, Alfred P., 357, 364.
Aldrich, Robert, 364, 388.
Alexander, Isaac B., 425.
Alexander, John, 256, 331.
Alexander, Nathaniel, 60.
"Alhambra," ship, 158.
Allegiance, oath of: to S. C., 42; to George III, 44.
Allen, A. F., 155.
Allen, S., 155.
Allison, Andrew, 13.
Alston, Willis W., 179, 188, 415.
"American Mocking Bird," 431.
American Pipe Company, 484.
American Revolution, 36-54.
Anderson, 12.
Anderson, A., 155.
Anderson, David, 10, 11, 27; in Cherokee War, 32.
Anderson, David B., 458, 459.
Anderson, E. M., 455.
Anderson, Ellen, 167.
Anderson, John B., 418.
Anderson, Mary, 167.
Anderson, R. N., Negro, in constitution convention, 387.
Anderson, Richard H., 253, 277.
Anderson, Dr. W. W., 135, 161, 282, 366, 428.
Anderson, Mrs. W. W., 447.
Anderson, William, 61, 91.
Anderson, Dr. William W., 253, 425.
Andrews, G. A., 494.
Andrews, Robert, 66.
Andrews, Robert T., Negro, 461.
Andrews, Robert W. 119, 122, 123, 135, 213; death of, 448; Hampton parade, 346; Life and Adventures of, 448; omnibus, 171; Potter's raid, 261, 262; pedestrian, 120, 448; teamster, 128, 130.
Andrews, W. J., Negro, 331.
Andrews, William T., Negro, 389, 461.
Anthony, Dr. Lucie Bragg, Negro, 451.
Appomatox, 262.
Ararat plantation, 267, 411.
Argyle plantation, 267, 411.
Armstrong, 12.
Armstrong, George, 60.
Armstrong, James, 11, 60.
Arson, 312, 332, 333, 348.
Art, in Sumter, 423-430; shows, 429, 430.
Arthur, T. S., 445.
Asbury, Francis, 64.
Ashburne, city manager, Staunton, 404.
Ashley, Citizen Josh, 372.
Ashmore, John Durant, 242.
Association for Defense, 40.
Association for Defense of Southern Rights, 161.
Atlanta, 157.
Atlantic Coast Line Railroad, 478, 480, 481.
Auld, D. J., 434, 436, 483.
Auld, Dr. Isaac, 182.
"Australia," river boat, 238.
Ayllon, Lucas d', 5.

Bachouse, J. A., 182.
Bacot, Mrs. C. G., 435.
Bailey, R. W., 181.
Baker, Abner, 102.
Baker, Bill, 102.
Baker, George, 102.
Baker, R. C., 232.
Baker, Dr. Samuel Chandler, 258, 403, 404, 484, 490.

Baker, Thomas, 96, 178.
Baker, Thomas M., 154, 252.
Baker, Dr. Thomas W., 428.
Baker, William, 263.
Baker, William Furman, 150.
Baker-Dick Infirmary, 490.
Ball alley, 217.
Ball battery, 217.
Ballard, John, 226.
Ballards, the, 68.
Ballroom, at Big Home, 209, 221.
Bank of Sumter, 477.
Bank of the State of South Carolina, 199, 241.
Banks, 241, 242, 317, 476-478.
Banks, William, 177.
Banner of Freedom, The, 266.
Barclay, William Kenedy, 424.
Barfield family, 268.
Barfield, Thomas W., 248.
Barker, Theodore G., 387.
Barnwell, Colonel John, 7.
Barnwell, Joseph W., 392.
Barrett, 331.
Barrett, Miss, 494.
Barrett, Edward, 177.
Barrett, James, 104.
Barrett, William G., 190-91.
Barrett's schoolhouse, 185, 191.
Bartlette, 200.
Barlett, Mrs. Agnes White, 191.
Bartlett, Charles E., 476, 477.
Bartlett, Edward, 94.
Bartlett, Julius Lyman, 94, 191, 316, 476.
Bartlett, Mrs. Leonora, 170.
Bartlett's Female Academy, 191.
Baskin, W. P., 395.
Bateman, Briant, 142.
Bateman, E. H., 326.
Battery, *see* Ball battery.
Bawling Jenkins, 193.
Bazaar, 429.
Beard, James, 121.
Beard, W. J., 459.
Beasts, *see* Wild beasts.
Bee, Robert, 258, 266.
Beekman, Bernard, 13.
Beekman, John, 13.
Bell, John, 249.
Bell, W. K., 123.
Bellemont Cotton Manufacturing Company, 486.
Bells Mill plantation, 115.
Belser, Irvine Furman, *The Belser Family of South Carolina*, 448-449.
Belser, J. Edwin, *The Belser Family of South Carolina*, 448-449.

Belser, Captain L. H., 147, 169.
Belser, W. Gordon, *The Belser Family of South Carolina*, 448-449.
Belser residence, Manchester, 170.
Benbow, 12.
Benbow, Gershon, 61.
Benbow's Pit, 21.
Benenhaley, Dallis D., 470.
Benenhaley, Henry, 470.
Benenhaley, Joseph, 467, 468.
Benet, W. Christie, 364.
Bennett, Samuel, 31.
Berger, Monsier A., 222, 278, 330.
Bertrand, race horse, 215.
Berwick, James, 31.
"Best Friend", locomotive, 163.
Bethel Baptist Church, 64.
Bethel Methodist Church, 480.
Bethune, Albert, Negro, 400.
Bethune, Mrs. Mary McLeod, Negro, 400-401, 461.
Bethune, Dr. R. Augustus, 444.
Bethune-Cookman, College, 401.
Big Home plantation, 9, 22, 45, 47; life at, 209, 221.
Billiards, 186, 216.
Bills of credit, 56.
Binda, Joseph, 412.
Birch, Mrs. Mary, 205.
Bird, Friendly, 100.
Bishop, Dr. Jacques, 177, 452.
Bishopville, 147, 194, 240, 394.
Bishopville Academy, 177.
Bishopville Giant, 314.
Bishopville Hotel, 395.
Bishopville Opera House, 395.
Bishopville Railroad, 480.
"Black Code", 276, 280.
Black Jack, a horse thief, 214.
Black Jamey Pearson, *see* Pearson, Black Jamey.
Black River Cavalry, 201.
Black River Road, 121.
Black River Watchman, The, 455.
Black, Washington, 104.
Blackwell, John C., 125.
Bland, H. C., 422.
Blackwell, M. J., 125.
Blanding, Dr. A. L., 449.
Blanding, James D., 107, 149-150, 165, 226, 236, 286, 315, 334, 369, 469, 479; "deal," 358; garden, 421; resolution, 386-387; war service: Confederate, 252, 254-256, Mexican, 154. 159.
Blanding, James D., 495.
Blanding, Mrs. Leonora McFaddin, 159.

INDEX

Blanding, W. D., 355, 458, 486.
Bligh, Bridget, 104.
Bligh, John, 104.
Bligh, Pat, 104.
"Blind tigers," 379.
Bloc voting, 357, 390.
"Bloody shirt," 344.
Bloom Hill, plantation, 16, 37, 42, 43, 53, 54, 66, 410-411.
Blueford plantation, 217.
Board of Trade, 487, 491.
Boatner, Jacob, 90.
Bochat, William H., 195.
Bodiford, William, 248.
Bogan, 331.
Bogart, Peter, widow of, 170.
Bogin, 264.
Boll weevil, 491.
Bolters (Republican), 319, 320.
"Bon Homme Richard," 65, 414.
Book store, 231.
Boom: Sumterville, 99, 105, 241; Sumter, 317.
Boone, Thomas, Governor, 34.
Booth, J. P., 405, 481.
Booth, James, 311.
Boozer, Lemuel, 285.
Border Ruffians, 236.
Borough, James, 48.
Burrough, Stanyarne, 481.
Bossard, 15.
Bossard, Dr. J. J., 253, 263, 355.
Bossard, Joseph S., 180, 311; confederating plan, 233-234; invention, 471-472.
Boundaries, of Sumter County, 4.
Bowen, Mrs. Frances, teacher, 177, 184.
Bowen, James S., 148, 452, 453.
Bowen, William H., 134, 177.
Bowles, H. E., 191.
Bowman, Peyton G., 363, 364.
Bowman, Peyton G., Jr., 363.
Bowman, W. A., 364.
Boyce, W. W., 228.
Boyen, M., 275.
Boykin, S. H., 178.
Boykin, Samuel, 131.
Boykin's Mill, 269.
Boykin's Millpond, tragedy at, 249.
Boyle, W. B., 482.
Bracey, Mrs. Charlotte Waties, 68.
Bracey, William, 112.
Bracey, Dr. Xenaphon, 68.
Bracy, J. H., 330.
Bradberry, Dr. William F., 431.
Bradford, Gabriel Wesley, 243, 422.
Bradford, H. N., 226.
Bradford, Nathaniel, 180.

Bradford, Richard, 31.
Bradford, Robert, 65, 184, 422.
Bradford Springs, 114, 122, 124.
Bradford Springs Female Academy, 181, 182.
Bradford Springs Female Institute, 183.
Bradford Springs Female Institute Company, 182.
Bradley, 12, 147.
Bradley, John, 32.
Bradley, James, 11, 42, 54, 57; deceived by Tarleton, 45-46; his slaves, 131.
Bradley, Joseph, 11.
Bradley, Matthew, 46.
Bradley, Samuel, 11.
Bradley, Samuel, 171.
Bradley, Samuel J., 169.
Bradley, Thomas, 46.
Brailsford, A. Moultrie, 211.
Brailsford, Robert, 174.
Branding, 199.
Brass Band, Sumter, 127, 196, 220.
Bratton, John, 357, 368.
Breckenridge, John C., 249.
Bremar, Francis, 442.
Brennan, Ellen, 220, 431.
Brewington Road, 208.
Bribery, 310, 319, 325; of the press by Radicals, 323, 327, 457; by Tillmanites, 373.
Brick Bat Club, 223.
Brickyard, 102.
Brisbane, Adam Fowler, 66, 121.
Brisbane's Ferry, 121.
Brissenden, Henry J., 222.
Britton, Henry, 181.
Britton, J. B., 481.
The Broad Axe, 459.
Broadway, Nicholas, 13.
Brock, Charles, 195.
Brock, J. C., 231.
Brogdon, J. B., 232.
Brogdon, M. T., 232.
Bronson, Horace W., 181.
Bronson, W., 186.
Brookland, 194, 441.
Brooks, Preston S., 239-240.
Brooks, William Middleton, 122.
Brooks' Inn, 122.
Brown, Lieut. Colonel, 261.
Brown, A. S., 486, 487.
Brown, Albertus, 484.
Brown, C. C., 450.
Brown, Mrs. C. C., 450.
Brown, John, raid, 248.
Brown, John Joe, 314.
Brown, John Lem, 314.

Brown, Mrs. L. A. 493.
Brown University, 63.
Brown, J. W., 162.
Brownfield, R. J., 358.
Bruce, W. C., 283.
Brumby Family, 112.
Brumby, Robert H., 112.
Bruner, H. H., 491.
Brunson, Daniel, 10.
Brunson, David, 10.
Brunson, Ervin, 475.
Brunson, Isaac, 10, 24, 100.
Brunson, Isaac, Jr., 10.
Brunson, J. Edwin, 460.
Brunson, James, 13.
Brunson, Joel, 460; "Sumterville," 100-105.
Brunson, John, 223.
Brunson, Joshua, 10.
Brunson, Josiah, 10.
Brunson, M. A., 188.
Brunson, Mrs. Mary, 10.
Brunson, Matthew, 10.
Brunson, Moses, 10.
Brunson, Susan E., 191.
Brunson, Susannah, 10.
Brunson, W. H., 191.
Brunson, William J., 100.
Brunson, William L., 93, 142, 184.
Bryan, J. P. Kennedy, 388.
Buchanan, Andrew, 263.
Buchanan, Andrew H., 454.
Buford, Abraham, 44.
Buford, Mrs. Elizabeth, 247.
Buford, Jefferson, 236.
Bultman, Fritz, 432.
Burch, W. P., 330.
Burgess, 12.
Burgess, J. C., 232.
Burgess, Joseph C., 232.
Burgess, Samuel A., 232.
Burgess, W. B., 248.
Burgess, William A., 232.
Burial: Indian, 6; Negro, 145, 315.
Burr, Aaron, 447.
Burrows, J. B., 282.
Bus, see Omnibus.
Butler, A. P., 344.
Butler, Andrew Pickens, 239.
Butler, Anthony, 68.
Butler, M. C., 312, 342, 383.
Butler, Mrs. Mary Ann James (Moore), 68.
Butler, P. M., 126.
Byrd, William Friendly, 143.

Cain, 12.
Cain, F. M., 422.

Cain, R. B., 226.
Cain, sheriff, Orangeburg, 335.
Cain, William, 160.
Cainhoy massacre, 348.
Caldwell, Colonel, 261.
Caldwell, James, 222.
Caldwell, James M., home burned, 267.
Calhoun, John C., 152, 154, 235.
Calico ticket, 357.
Camden, 46, 48, 53, 55.
Camden Branch Railroad, 164-165, 269, 317.
Camden District, 30; counties in, 59.
Camden Journal, 149, 454.
Camp Branch, 7.
Camp Hunt, 214, 330.
Camp meetings, 223-225, 330.
Camp Sumter, 155.
Camps, Indian, 7.
Campbell, Mrs., teacher, 180.
Campbell, Alexander, 31, 169, 267.
Campbell, Mrs. E. S., 267, 331-32.
Canals, 64.
Canby, E. R. S., 286.
Canfield, Mrs. F. A., 444.
Cannon, Daniel, 13.
Cantey, John 24, 59.
Cantey, Joseph, 9, 22, 24.
Cantey, Josiah, 9.
Cantey, William, 24.
Cantey, Zachariah, 180.
Cantey's Tavern, 123.
Capell, Augustus, 268.
Capers, Gabriel, 176.
Capers, William, 128-129, 210, 224, 428, 447.
Capers, William T., 177.
Capps, John, 11.
Card playing, 216.
Cardarelli, E., 474.
Cardarelli Electric Light Crane Company, 474.
Cardoza, F. L., 323, 327.
Carlisle, James, 330.
Carner, J. W., 437.
Carnes, J. A., 281.
"Carolina Mocking Bird," 220, 431.
Carolina Power and Light Company, 409, 487.
Carpenter, Richard Brinsley, 312, 333.
Carpetbagger, 308, 310, 319, 320.
Carson, L. S., 381, note.
Carter, Mr., of Virginia, artist, 427.
Carter, James R., 180.

INDEX 527

Carter, Robert, 13, 39.
Carter, William, 11.
Cassels, Benjamin, 11.
Cassels, Henry, 11.
Cassels, John, 90.
Cassels, William, 11.
Castles, 12.
Catawba path, 8, 9, 12, 14, 45, 55, 119, 121.
Catawbas, 4, 7, 119, 446.
Cater, Edwin, 183.
Cater, Mrs. Edwin, 183.
Cater, R. B., 235.
Catlie, 12.
Cato, Marion W., 398.
Cato's Spring, 175.
Cattle, 9, 20; on tracks, 168.
Central Railroad, 479, 480.
Chamberlain, Daniel H., 310, 336-337; administration, 338, 341, 343, 344, 348-351.
Chambers, Mrs. Elizabeth Ann (Spain), 183, 443.
Chandler, Daniel, 225.
Chandler, Eliza, 258, 465.
Chandler, Isaac James, 258.
Chandler, J. R., epigrammatist, 444.
Chandler, Mrs. Mary Jacqueline, 257-258.
Chandler, R. A., 248.
Chandler, Rush, 485.
Chandler, Samuel Rembert, 205, 226, 257; trust funds, 258.
Chandler, Thomas, 61.
Chandler, Mayes, and Company, 172.
Chapel of ease, St. Mark's, 31.
Chapin, Mrs. Sallie F., 389.
Chapel: in will of Mrs. T. Sumter, Jr., 413; Rembert's, 65.
Chapman, James, Negro, 398-399.
Chapman, Scipio, Negro, 398-399.
Chapultepec, 159.
Charleston plate, won by Sumter's mare, 37.
Charleston, siege of, 43, 259, 492.
Charleston, Sumter and Northern Railroad, 478, 480, 481.
Charleston Volunteers, Palmetto Regiment, 155.
Charlotte Railway, 168.
Chateau de Plunderville, 324.
Chatman, Scipio, see Chapman, Scipio.
Cherokees, 32-35, 42.
Cherry Vale, 98, 275.
Chestnut, James, 347.
Chester, Mrs. J., 97.

Chester, John F., 114.
Chester Company, Palmetto Regiment, 155.
Chickering piano, 179.
Childs, Mr., 311.
Childs, Frederick L., 425.
Childs, Mrs. Mary Hooper Anderson, 425.
Childs, St.Julien R., 425.
Childs, Thomas, *Wooden Works*, 449.
China, Dr. A. J., 262, 265, 479.
China, Alfred, 122, 123.
China, John, 123.
China, Mary, silk business, 465.
China's Hotel, Sumterville, 123, 151, 155, 160, 426.
China's Inn, Stateburg, 122.
Cholera, 413.
Church choirs, 219-220.
Church of the Holy Comforter, 247, 428.
Church of the Holy Cross, see Claremont Episcopal Church.
Churchill plantation, 215.
Circuit courts, 30.
Circus, 218.
Citizens' Savings Bank, 476.
City Hall and Opera House, built, 439.
City National Bank, 478, 482.
Claremont Academy, 63, 91.
Claremont County, 3, 59-60.
Claremont Depot, 170-71.
Claremont Episcopal Church, 65, 135.
Claremont Gazette, 62-63, 452.
Claremont Lodge, 222.
Claremont plantations, 59, 60.
Claremont Society, 63.
Claremont Troop, 202, 203, 229, 341, 467.
Clarendon County, 3, 59, 61, 131; cut from Sumter District, 4, 118, 231-232.
Clarendon Depot, 164.
Clarendon, Earl of, 59.
Clarendon Orphan Academy, 176.
Clarendon Orphan Society, 175.
Clarendon Troop, 202.
Clarendon Vigilante Society, 141.
Clark, A. J., 487.
Clark, J. A., 223.
Clark, Mrs. Mary McKagen, 265.
Clark, W. J., 195.
Clark, William, 97.
Clarke, James, 31.
Clarke, Samuel, 31.
Clarke, William, 188.

Clarkson, Bowen, 103.
Clarkson and Brunson, 231.
Clemson College, 366.
Clemson, Thomas G., 364.
Clifton, John H., 404.
Cochran, Jean D., 497.
Cockerell, A. G., 177.
Cockeroft, Miss C. R., 173.
Cockfighting, 216.
Coffin, John P., 487.
Coghlan, Mrs. Penelope Sledge, 98.
Coghlan, Thomas Jefferson, 281, 282, 283, 427, 428; advertisements, 99, 115, 166, 223; birth, 98; county commissioner, 350, 353; constitution convention, 284, 285; defeated, 322, 357; intendant, 197; sheriff, 311, 315, 321; temperance, 196, 197; treasurer, 317-318, 322; tramway, 330-331; opposes Moses, 320-321; on Republican slate, 344-345.
Coghlan and Gay, 171.
Cohen, Esdaile P., 94.
Coit, George E., 177.
Coit, W. H., 177.
Colclough, Alexander, 59.
Colclough, Captain Alex., 261.
Coldstream plantation, 10, 136, 208, 418; garden, 420; garden plan, 419.
Cold Water Army, 160, 195.
Cole, David, 173.
Coleman, coroner, Orangeburg, 335.
Coleman, Fley, 188.
Colleton Gazette, cited, 323, 324, 325, 327, 328.
"Columbia Ring," 310, 318, 323, 333, 373, 476.
Commander, W. H., 372.
Community Room (Carolina Coca-Cola Bottling Company), 487.
Compton, Mrs. Jane, 123.
Concerts, 185, 219.
Concord Church, 7, 258.
Condy, Thomas D., 155.
Confederate Monument, 185, 458.
Congarees, 8.
Congress, first provincial, 39, 40; second provincial, 41.
Conjuration, 144.
Conley, George, 66.
Conner, General James, 346.
Connors (Conyers?), Colonel, 261.
Constabulary, state, 313, 314, 377, 378, 379-382.
Constitution, South Carolina: of 1776, 41; of 1778, 43; of 1790, 59; of 1865, 275; of 1868, 284-85; 310-11; of 1895, 384-393.

Continental Association, 39.
Contract, labor, with freedman, 274, 278.
Convention, constitutional of 1868, 284-285.
Convention of the People of South Carolina, 162.
Converse, Augustus L., 135, 416-417.
Converse, Mrs. Marion Singleton DeVeaux, 416-417. *See also* Mrs. Robert Marion DeVeaux.
Converse, Mrs. Mary Ann Kellogg, 416.
Conway, A., 223.
Conyers, 12.
Conyers, Captain, 51.
Conyers, Daniel, 112.
Conyers, J. J., 232.
Conyers, James, 174.
Conyers, James, Jr., 174.
Conyers, John, 174.
Conyers, John, 188.
Conyers, Mrs. Mary, 112.
Cook, Harvey T., 448.
Cook, James, 10, 12, 121.
Cook, John, 13.
Cook, Joseph B., 177.
Cook, Samuel, 31.
Cook's Mount, 5.
Cooke, J. D., 152-153.
Cooke, T. H., 349.
Coolican, P. O., 222.
Cooper, E. M., 367.
Cooper, Eliza, 493, 494.
Cooper, George, 90, 423.
Cooper, George W., 208, 417.
Cooper, J. M., 371.
Cooterboro, 194.
Copeland, Ripley, 195.
Coquina, 16.
Corbett, J. N., 311, 326, 328, 334.
Corbin, David T., 308, 320.
Cordes, Francis, 9.
Corn cribs, of Santees, 5-6.
Corn Hill plantation, 427.
Cornwallis, Lord, 45, 46, 47, 54, 57.
Coskrey, James, 95.
Costumes, pioneer, 20-21. *See also* Fashions.
Cottage Level, Alston's school, 179.
Cotton, 108-110, 484; effect of war, 130; factories, 108, 116-118, 486; market, 485; prices, 110, 130, 165, 228, 231, 464; seed-cotton traffic, 313, 314; value of crop, 242.
Cotton gins, 109, 134.
Coulter, James, 113.
Coulter, Mrs. Susannah, 113.

INDEX

Council-Manager government, 402-408.
County courts, 58-61, 70.
County government, 310-311.
Courcier, John M., 116.
Coursay, Mary de, 95.
Courthouse, Sumter, 90, 96, 265.
Courtney, Ezra, 64.
Courts: circuit, 30; closed, 57; county, 58-61, 70; magistrates, 22. *See also* Magistrates.
Cox, Mrs. Elizabeth Allen (Sinkler), *see* Sinkler, Elizabeth Allen.
Craig, John Davis, cabinetmaker, 277.
Cramer, Eugene, 437.
Crane, Noah, coach builder, 223.
Craven, Thomas, 13.
Craven County, 22-23.
Crawford, John, 24.
Crawford, Thomas, 13.
Credit system, *Watchman and Southron* on, 361.
Creydon, Lucas, 95.
Crime, among freedmen, 311, 318.
Cripps, John Splatt, 59.
Croatans, 282.
Croghan, Jerry, 432.
Croghans, the, 331.
Crop failures, 359.
Cropping, of ears, 199.
"Cross Jordan," 344, 348.
Crosswell, A. G., 177.
Crosswell, John, 113.
Crosswell, John K., 491.
Crosswell Orphanage, 491.
Crow, E. R., 495.
Crownson, Charles Mason, 429.
Cummings, Dr. Samuel M., 124.
Curtis Carriage and Buggy Shops, 486.
Cuttino, singing teacher, 431.
Cypress, use of, 17.

Dabbs, James McBride, 450.
Dalzell, 467, 481.
Dancing, 221-222, 229.
Daniels, Hopkin, 195.
Dargan, chief of police, Darlington, 380.
Dargan, Alice, 13.
Dargan, Mrs. Ann, 12.
Dargan, G. W., 417.
Dargan, Jeremiah, 30.
Dargan, John, 12-13.

Dargan, John Julius, 343, 366, 367, 368, 414; accused, 354; candidate, 345, 354; duel, 355-356; feud, 357; editor, 458, 459; effort to organize Negroes, 385; representative, 355; school, 491; textbook, 451.
Dargan, John William, 237, 239, 317, 346, 476.
Dargan, Mary, 13.
Dargan, Timothy, 12.
Darlington, 166.
Darlington Depot, 168.
Darlington Guards, 379, 380.
Darlington riot, 379-382.
Darr, Horace Laidler, 458.
Darr, Horatio Lincoln, 278, 456, 457, 458, 459.
Darr J. H., 460.
Darr, Mary M., 459.
Darr, Susan E., 247.
Darr and Osteen, 278, 332.
Darrington, John, 178.
Davis, Charles W., 425.
Davis, E. B., 201.
Davis, James, 59, 90, 175.
Davis, Mrs. Laura Lamb, 426.
Davis, Lemuel B., 112.
Davis, McDonald, 395.
Davis, Potts, 263.
Davis, William Ransom, 62, 131.
Davis home, Springhill, 268.
Dean, James I., 283.
Deas (Dees), 12.
Debating societies, 223.
DeBerry, W. H., 173.
Debtors, 198-199, 229, 243, 278.
DeKalb, Baron, 44.
DeKalb Guards, Palmetto Regiment, 158.
Delany, Martin F., 336, 344.
DeLeon, Harmon, 266.
DeLorme, 15.
DeLorme, Charles, 236, 262.
DeLorme, Charles H., 458.
DeLorme, John F., 455.
DeLorme, Thomas Murritt, 259.
DeLorme, W. M., 248.
DeLorme, William, 188.
Dennis, John E., 165, 177.
Dennis, J. M., 177, 236.
Dennis' Tavern, 123.
Depot, Sumter, 171, 261, 330, 479, 480.
Depot Lane, Manchester, 170.
Depressions, economic, 164, 165, 184, 228-229, 241-242, 408, 477-478, 484.
DesChamps, the, 15, 147.

DesChamps, G. S. C., 176, 248.
DesChamps, Hattie, silk business, 465.
DeSaussure, Henry W., 216.
DeVeaux family, 209.
DeVeaux, James, 424.
DeVeaux, Robert Marion, 415.
DeVeaux, Mrs. Robert Marion, 412, 417.
Dick, Dr. A. C., 490.
Dick, Dr. T. M., 94.
Dickerson, Prince, 326.
Dickey, 12.
Dickey, James, 61, 114.
Dickey, Richard, 215.
Dickey, Thomas E., 114.
Diggs, Mrs. 124.
Dingle James Harvey, 167.
Dingle, Mrs. James Harvey, 167, 421.
Dingle's Mill, battle of, 262-263.
Dinkins, John, 44.
Dinkins, Joseph, 188.
Dinkins, Sam, 44.
Dinkins, Mrs. Sarah Ann Moise, 284, 457.
Dinkins, Thomas Waties, 188, 191, 248-249, 284, 456, 457.
Dinkins, Tyre J., 123.
Dinkins' Mill, 269.
The Diocese, 459.
Dispensary system, 376-382, 395.
Diston, R., 173.
District Eastward of Wateree, 39, 42.
Divorce, 212.
Dobbin, Alexander, 112.
Dobbin, Mrs. Leah Conyers, 112.
Dogs, school boy on, 492.
"Dog trot", 17.
Doherty, E. C., 279-280.
Dority, John, 195.
District court, for trial of Negroes, 276, 311.
Douglas, Stephen A., 249.
Dow, John, 95.
Downing, Malton, 448.
Doyle, Colonel John, 51, 52.
Drake, Scarborough, 158.
Drayton, William Henry, 40.
Drovers, 123.
Drunkards, sold, 196.
Dual government: county, 350-351; state, 349-350, 352.
Dual office-holding, 311.
DuBose, 15, 147.
Dubose, Elisha, 11.
DuBose, Julius J., 181; attack on, 182.

DuBose, Mrs. M. E., 181.
DuBose, Samuel, 217.
Duel: Cash-Shannon, 357; Dargan-Earle, 355-357; Hemphill-Levy, 152-153; unknowns, 245.
Duffie, J. B., 495.
Dugan, Thomas, 96, 184.
Duke, Foundation, 491.
Dully, Lawrence, 13.
Dun, —, 11.
Dunbar, Sergeant, 261, 262, 263.
Duncan, George, 102.
Duncan, Tom, 102.
Duncan, William, 101-102.
Dunlap, Samuel, 54.
Dunn, Burrel, 195.
Dunn, J. Ralph, M.D., 422.
Dunn, Sylvester, 32.
Dunndell Gardens, 422.
DuPree, James, 185.
Durant, A. W., 173.
DuRant, Eugene W., 7.
Durant, Dr. James, 177.
DuRant, J. O., 165.
DuRant, J. O., supervisor Lee County, 395.
Durant, John, 355.
Durant, R. W., 173.
DuRant, Dr. Robert R., 162.
Durant, S. P., 173.
Durant, Thomas M., 254.
DuRant home, 208.
Durban, Adele, 432.
Dwyer, James, 180.
Dwyer, Samuel, 180.
Dyall, Thomas, 11.
Dyson, Jeptha, 117, 165, 471.
Dyson, Rev. Jeptha, 135.
Dyson, Mrs. Martha Manning, 117.
Dyson, Richard Manning, 117-118.
Dyson's factory, 117.

Earl Joseph, 13.
Earle, Joseph Haynsworth, 343, 354, 371, 486; attorney general, 362; duel, 355-356; feud, 357; governorship, 365, 368; relations with Tillman, 362, 366, 371-372.
Earthquake, 362; effects in Sumter County, 363.
Ecija, Francisco de, 5.
Eclectic College, 435.
Edgefield, in Hampton campaign, 343, 348, 349; mob, 385.
Edgehill Academy, 178-79, 210.
Edmunds, Samuel H., 495.
Edmunds High School, 495.
Edwards, Julius, 377.

INDEX   531

Edwards, Lela, 433.
Eight box election law, 358.
Eleazer, J. M., 492.
Elections system, 201. See also Primary party elections; Eight box election law.
Electric lights, Sumter, 483.
Electric power, Sumter, 408-409.
Ellerbe, R. G., 330.
Ellerbe, William H., 382.
Elliott, Robert Brown, Negro, 319, 321, 338.
Elliott, Samuel, 13.
Elliott, Thomas, 13.
Elliott, William, 397.
Elliotts, 481.
Ellis, Joseph, 199.
Ellison, Billy John, 136.
Ellison, Eliza Ann, free person of color, 134.
Ellison, Mrs. Matilda, free person of color, 134.
Ellison, Mrs. Patricia, 135.
Ellison, Reuben, free person of color, 136.
Ellison, William, of Fairfield, 464.
Ellison, William, free person of color, 134-136, 236.
Ellison, William, Jr., a free person of color, 135.
Emerson, Mrs., lecturer, 244.
England, John, 428.
English, Harrison, freedman, 275.
English, J. W., 177.
English, Julia, freedman, 275.
English, Thomas R., 162, 250, 281.
English's Cross Roads, 172.
Enrollment, citizen, 1868, 275, 283.
Epperson, W. H., 378.
Ervin, Hugh, 11.
Ervin, John Witherspoon, 137, 188, 223; editor, 227, 229, 230, 455; feud, 188, 227; writings, 444-446.
Esaw-Captain Jack, 7.
Estelle Troupe, the, 219.
Etiquette, 213.
Eutaw Springs, 54.
Eutawville Railroad, 480.
Evans, John Gary, 382-383, 387-388.
Evening News, The (Haynsworth and Miller, 1904), 460.
Evening News, The (Miller and Darr, 1895), 460.
Evening News Company, 460.
Examination execises, public, 179, 183, 186, 188.
Explorers, *see* Ayllon; Ecija; Lawson; Lederer; Pardo.

Extra, Watchman, 249, 354.

Fabib, G. C., 263.
Factories, early, 108, 116-118.
Fahm, a private, 263.
Fair Enterprise, The, 458.
Fairs, agricultural, 226, 359.
Fairfield District, 109, 230. See also Winnsboro.
Farley, adjutant and inspector general, 381.
Farms, Sumter County, 484-485.
Farmers' Alliance, 366.
Farmers' Association, Sumter, 360.
Farmers' Bank and Trust Company, 478.
Fashions, 204-205. See also Costumes.
Federal troops, 251, 343, 348, 349, 350, 352, 353. See also Garrisons; Negro troops.
Feeny, Thomas, 311, 331.
Fenn, James M., 185-187.
Ferriter, J. H., 282, 285, 286, 311, 331, 349.
Festina Lente, 493.
Feud, 357, 364.
Fiddles, 19.
Fire, 264, 265, 276, 332; in jail yard, 106; Manchester, burned, 170; Academy of Music, 438-439; wild fires, 229-230. See also Arson.
Fire engine, 107.
Fisher, Clara, 431.
First Federal Savings and Loan Association, 478.
First National Bank, Sumter, 477.
First-and-skull fights, 150.
Fitzwilson, George W., 426.
Five Forks, 172.
Fives, a ball game, 216-217.
Flag, Confederate, 252; Palmetto Regiment, 159; The Sumters', 155-56; South Carolina, 252.
Flagatruce, race horse, 37.
Flax, 20.
Fleming, Julius, J., 189, 321.
Fletchall, Thomas, 40, 41.
Floggings, 192, 199.
Florida, 43, 49, 58.
Flowers, Jim, 101, 103.
Flowers, T. E., 278, 456, 458.
Flowers, Tom, 101, 103.
Folsom, Franklin, 188.
Food, pioneer, 20, 38.
Ford, Mr., 144.
Fork Lake, 7.

532 INDEX

Fort Dearborn, 130.
Fort Sumter, 252.
Fort Watson, 50, 52, 53.
Fort Wiley, 130, 195.
Francis, William J., 248, 454-455, 456.
Fraser, Major C., 50-51.
Fraser, Ladson L., 177, 472.
Fraser, L. L., Jr., 223, 455.
Fraser, Robert, 177.
Fraser, Thomas Boone, 162, 260, 320, 333, 339, 346; delegate to constitution convention, 387, 388; editor, 455; state senator, 354.
Frazier, William, 314.
Fredericksburg, 8, 9, 12.
Free Masons, Ancient, 143, 222; temple, 378, 386.
Free Negroes, ante-bellum, 131-136, 161.
Free School Commissioners, 175.
Free School law, 175.
Free School System, 201.
Freedman's Bureau, 273, 281, 283, 284, 311, 319.
Freeman, Michael, 112.
The Freeman, 459.
Freeman Publishing Company, 460.
Freeman Printing Company, 399.
Friendship Academy, 177.
Frierson, 12.
Frierson, Aaron, 32.
Frierson, John M., 112.
Frierson, J. N., 275, 280, 282, 286, 353.
Frierson, John, of Pudding Swamp, 11, 18.
Frierson, John: as a slaveholder, 138-139; contracts with freedmen, 274-275.
Frierson, J. G., 216.
Frierson, R. A., 378.
Frierson, Mrs. Sarah Conyers, 112.
Frierson, T. D., 241.
Frost, Adele, 437.
Frost, William, 13.
Fugitive Slaw Law, 233, 235.
Fullwood, James?, 139.
Fulton, 117, 179, 481; post office, 124.
Fulton factory, 118.
Fulton Jockey Club, 214.
Funerals, 210-211.
Furman, Dr. J. H., 360.
Furman, John, 150.
Furman, Josiah, 63, 66.
Furman, Kate, 446.
Furman, McDonald, 446.
Furman, Rev. Richard, 31, 41, 57, 63, 64, 452.

Furman, Wood, 13, 14, 31, 54, 60, 121; teacher, 174.
Furman, Wood, grandson, *Life of Richard Furman*, 448.
Furman Academy, 178.
Furman University, origin, 178.

Gaillard, 15.
Gaillard, chief state constable, 380, 381.
Gaillard, H. A., 356.
Gaillard, P. P., 436.
Gaillard, Tacitus, 10, 12, 121.
Gaillard v. *McCoy*, 91.
Gaillard's Cross Roads, 366.
Gaillard's Ferry, 121.
Gallagher Brothers, 377.
Gambell, 12.
Gamble, John, 54, 59.
Gambling, debts uncollectible, 216.
Gamecock, *see* Sumter, General Thomas.
Gang: boys', 359-360; Joe's Gang, 144; Murrell Gang, 143.
Gantt, Richard, 194.
Garden, Mrs., 101.
Garden, Alester, 185.
Garden, Ally, 101.
Garden, Fanny, 101.
Garden, Hugh, 101.
Garden, Hugh R., 256, 279.
Gardens, 410-422.
Garden's Battery, 256, 262, 279.
Gardner, W. H., 322, 326, 328, 332, 334.
Garner's Ferry, 482. *See also* Brisbane's Ferry.
Garrison, Brother, circuit rider, 69.
Garrisons, federal: in state, 276; in Sumte, 272, 273, 309, 311, 315-16, 432.
Garrot, Jacob, 199.
Gary, Mart, 342, 371.
Gaskins, Amos, 47.
Gates, General Horatio, 44, 45, 46.
Gay, Lemuel Bingham, 316, 457.
Gay, William M., 179.
Gayle, Ambrose, 90.
Gayle, C. D., 118.
Gayle, Caleb, 31.
Gayle, Christopher, 31, 44.
Gayle, John 3, 90, postmaster, 124.
Gayle, Josiah, 31, 46, 90.
Gayle, Preston, 188.
Gayle, Sarah, 90.
Geissendanner, John, 24, 26.
Genet, Citizen, 119.
Giddens, Jacob, 195.
Gifford, Mr., 413.

Gilbert, Allen A., 280, 281, 456, 457; appearance, 455; enters ministry, 458; war service, 278, 456; YMCA delegate, 246-247.
Gilbert and Darr, 266, 278.
Ginnings, see Jennings, Daniel.
Gins, see Cotton gins.
Girardeau, Claude, 435.
Girardeau, Mary Hughes, 435, 450, 494.
Girardeau, W. H., 326.
Gleaves, Richard Howell, mulatto, 282, 319, 327, 336, 337.
Glebe: St. Mark's, 25; Scots', 12, 13.
Gold rush, 115, 160-161.
Golden Mortar, 115.
Good Templars, 378, 459.
Gordon, 12.
Gordon, Captain, 54.
Graham, James D., 256, 369.
Graham, J. D., 479.
Graham, Noah, 183.
Graham, Robert F., 335.
Graham, William M., 487.
Grange, 359.
Great Falls, 64.
Great Road, 36, 119, 121.
Greeleyville, 120.
Green, A. H., 451.
Green, Ellis C., 326.
Green, Dr. Henry D., 250, 343.
Green, John T., 228, 274, 321, 336, 337.
Green Swamp chapel, 65.
Greenbacks, 272, 361.
Greene, General Nathanael, 52-54; headquarters, 53, 54.
Grimes, James, 11.
Gregg, G. C., 226.
Groggery, 122, 194.
Grooms, Moses, 155, 156.
Guardians, for free Negroes, 133, 135.
Guerry, Albert Capers, 428.
Guerry, Mrs. Gertrude Wilson, 428.
Guerry, L. F., 428.
Gypsies, 243-244.

Habeas corpus, suspended, 315.
Hagen, Dennis, grantee, 13.
Hagood, 481.
Hagood, Johnson, 357.
Hail, 122.
Hall, John, 158.
Halsey, William, 430.
Hamburg, 156; riots, 342, 343.
Hammett, J. B. N., 223, 236.
Hammett, Mrs. J. B. N., 191.

Hammond Guards, Pametto Regiment, 155, 157.
Hampton, Wade, 342, 445; campaign of 1876, 343-349; inaugurated, 350; reelected, 355; U. S. senator, 355, 357, 371.
Hampton Day, 346-347.
Hampton oak, Sumter, 347.
Hanging, public, 318.
Hangman's tree, 60.
Hanks, L. B., 104.
Harbun, C. N., 263.
Harby, name taken by some of A. J. Moses family, 341.
Harby, Horace, 474, 477, 479, 486.
Harby, Joshua H., 486-487.
Harby, Mrs. Lee C., 446.
Harby, Walter I., 364.
Hardman, J., see Hemphill, John.
Hardy, Daniel, 211.
Hardy, Mrs. E. Lemon, 211.
Harllee, W. W., 165.
Harmony Female College, 183; destroyed, 184.
Harney, Mrs., 331.
Harrel, William, 263.
Harper, Mrs. Frances Ellen Watkins, Negro, 281.
Harris, Isaac R., 113.
Harris, William, 162, 225, 226.
Harrison, James, 14, 17.
Harrison, J. McKenzie, 136, 461.
Harrison, Tory brothers, 45, 46, 51, 57.
Hart, John, 109.
Hart, Oliver, 40.
Hartley, Dr. James, 66, 180.
Harvey, 12.
Harvin, S. A., 481.
Harvin, Sarah H., silk business, 465.
Harvin, William N., 195.
Harvin Packing Company, 487.
Haskell, Alexander C., 369.
Haskellites, address, 369, 393.
Hats, 204.
Hauser, A., 472-473.
Hauser's steam mill, 331.
Hawthorndean Seminary, 179.
Hayes, Rutherford B., 352, 354.
Hayes - Tilden presidential campaign, 345.
Hayne, Henry E., 327.
Haynsworth, Bill, 48.
Haynsworth, Major Billy, 101; marriage of, 103.
Haynsworth, Mrs. Elizabeth (Davidson), 14.

Haynsworth, Mrs. Elizabeth (Hesse), 14, 20.
Haynsworth, George Edward, 190, 251; 493; killed, 363-364.
Haynsworth, Henry, 14, 125.
Haynsworth, Hugh Charles, editor, 460; genealogist, 449.
Haynsworth, Dr. James, 96, 184, 185, 219, 427.
Haynsworth, Dr. James L., 106, 223.
Haynsworth, J. H., 451.
Haynsworth, John, 14, 15, 431.
Haynsworth, John F., 105, 329.
Haynsworth, John R., 455.
Haynsworth, Mrs. Maria Morse, 103.
Haynsworth, R. F., 460.
Haynsworth, R. R., 232.
Haynsworth, Richard, 14, 20.
Haynsworth, Richard P., 162.
Haynsworth, Mrs. Sarah Elizabeth Morse, 94.
Haynsworth, Mrs. Sarah (Furman), 14.
Haynsworth, Stephen, Negro, 266.
Haynsworth, William, 94, 114, 165, 185, 247, 421.
Haynsworth, William F. B., 175-176, 197, 241, 254, 276, 353, 372, 454, 477.
Haynsworth, Mrs. W. F. B., 428.
Headquarters: General Greene's, 53, 54; General Potter's, 264.
Heiti, Miss, music teacher, 184.
Hematite, 16.
Hemphill, John, 151, 184; duel, 152-153; editor and publisher, 453.
Henderson, D. S., in constitution convention, 387.
Henderson, Matthew, 61.
Henson, Archie, 58.
Heriot, R. L., 314.
Herring, William E., 61.
Herrington, Giles M., 195.
Herrington, J. C., 432.
Hewson, M. F., 331, 432.
Hibernian Society, Charleston, 327.
Hicks, John B., 211.
High Hill Tavern, 40, 48, 58, 62.
High Hills Baptist Church, 31, 57, 64, 469.
High Hills of Santee, 3, 5, 6, 8, 44. settlement of, 12-14, 24; summer resort, 31.
Hill, Jesse, 232.
Hill, Jonathan, 11.
Hill, Josiah, 31.

Hillyard, M. B., 465.
Hilton, William, grantee, 13.
Hinckley, Samuel L., 94.
Hindenburg Line, 381, note.
Hines, David, 232, 233.
Hissett, Ebenezer, 31.
Hobkirk's Hill, battle of, 53.
Hodges, Joshua, 66.
Hoff John, 93.
Hofman, Van Talbery, 490.
Holaday, Mr., 116.
Holliday, July, freedman, 279.
Holloman, E., 314.
Holloway, state, constable, 378.
Hollyman, H., 195.
Holt, Miss A., 186.
Holy Comforter, *see* Church of the Holy Comforter.
Home Guard, 256.
Home House, 128, 412; garden, 412-413.
Home plantation, 120, 211, 266, 415-416.
Hooper, Mrs. Mary, 66, 412, 447.
Hooper, Thomas, 66, 70.
Hooper's Bridge, 66.
Hoopskirts, 205.
Hope, John, 10.
Hope, Lewis D., 127.
Hopkins, George W., 454.
Hopkins, Mark, 494.
Horan, John, 62, 63, 91.
Horne, a blacksmith, 69.
Horry, Hugh, 50.
Horry, Peter, 51.
Horry Dispatch, The, 456.
Horse racing, 37, 38, 39; Stateburg, 65, 214-215; Sumter, 330.
Hort, Mary, 182, 191.
Hospitality, pioneer, 16-17.
Hospitals, Confederate, 258.
Houghton, W. C., "fire king", 218.
Houston, C. J., Negro, 324, 338.
Howard, Dr. Eli, 66, 124.
Howard, Dr. Joseph, 31, 66.
Howell, Bryant, 248.
Howell, Richard, 31.
Hoyt, Bill, 104.
Hoyt, Freeman, 94, 104, 223, 272, 307, 343.
Hoyt, Mary, 309.
Hoyt, Oliver, 272.
Hoyt, Ransom, Negro carpenter, 266.
Huck, *see* Huyck.
Hudson, W. S., 223, 226.
Huger, Francis, 59.
Huger, Mrs. Mary E., 59, 414.
Hughs, Thomas, 11.

INDEX

Hughson, Celeste, silk business, 465.
Hughson, Dr. J. S., 447.
Hughson, Shirley Carter, 447.
Huguenots, 15, 340, 345.
Hulburt, Mrs. Annette, 105.
Hulburt, O. C., 102, 105, 105, 485.
Hulburt's Brickyard, 102, 485.
Humbert, county treasurer, Orangeburg, 335.
Hummel, Madame, 183.
Humphries, Thomas, 176.
Humphries, William, 63.
"Hundred Days," the, 254.
Hunter, Henry, 13.
Hunting: camp hunt, 214; Santee method, 6; squirrels, 213-214; wild cattle, 213.
Hunting Boxes, 31.
Hurley, Tim, 335, 345.
Hurst, Miss, 494.
Hurst, C. M., 283, 404; editor, 459; probate judge, 351; teacher, 191; trial justice, 344; trustee, 494.
Hurst, Mrs. C. M., 191.
Hutchings, Thomas, 116.
Huyck, Christian, 44.
Hyrne, Henry, 13.

Illiteracy, 309; freedmen, 274-275, 357, 358; pioneer, 21, 175; Tillman era, 389, 392, 393.
Indians, 3-7, 52, 119, 446. *See also* Cherokees.
Indigo, 13, 20, 56.
Industries, Sumter County, 3, 485-488. *See also* Factories.
Inglis, John A., 187.
Ingram, W. H., 459.
Insanity, 182, 200-201.
Insurrections, slave, 133.
Internal improvements, federal, 146.
Ioor, Mrs. Frances (Guignard), 59.
Ioor, George, 59, 63.
Irby, John L. Manning, 367, 371, 382, 387.
Irving, John B., Jr., 428.
"Isabel," a ship, 115.
"Isis", river boat, 317.

Jackson, Andrew, 152.
Jackson, Mary, silk business, 465.
Jackonborough Assembly, 54.
Jacksonville, post office, Sumter District, 125.
Jail, Sumter, 241; built, 90, 171, 277; burned, 265, 276, 332; debtors', 142, 198; fire at, 106-107; town hall, 171, 265.
James, Mrs. Anne, 13.
James, Burwell, Negro, 282, 285.
James, Francis, 14.
James, John, 14, 31, 39, 122.
James, John, Jr., 31, 122.
James, John of the Lake, 41.
James, Captain John, son of Major John James, 441.
James, Colonel John, 54.
James, Major John, 41, 49, 50, 441.
James, Subaltern John, 41, 58.
James, John Ervin, 90.
James, John J., writer, 442-443.
James, John M., 123.
James, Matthew, 41, 175.
James, Prince, Negro, 396.
James, Sherwood, 14, 122.
James, Sherwood, Jr., 14.
James, W. A., Jr., 367, 394.
James, William D., 13, 41; death, 441; impeached, 194; life of Marion, 440-441.
James, William H., 216.
James' High Hill Tavern, 122.
James Hill plantation, 253.
James' Oldfield, 53.
Jameson, Mrs. Mary (Cantey), 35.
Jamestown, French, 15.
Jamesville, 121, 124.
Jefferson, Mrs., Stateburg, 210.
Jeffords, Beatrice, 449.
Jenkins, Mr., 183.
Jenkins, James, 68, 96, 193-194, 447.
Jennings, Daniel, 31.
Jennings, Henry, 132.
Jennings, L. D., 387, 404, 405, 477, 480.
Jennings, R. B., 407.
Jennings, Tyre, 124.
Jerks, the, 224.
Jessica Thomas Troupe, 433.
Jervey House, Sumter, 364.
Jews, come to Sumter, 94; in duel, 152-153.
Jews harps, 19.
Joe's Gang, fugitive slaves, 144.
John Evans Manufacturing Company, 487.
Johnson, A., 394.
Johnson, Andrew, 272, 276, 280, 286.
Johnson, David, 160.
Johnson, James M., 283.
Johnson, Jane, 259.

Johnson, Dr. Joseph, 259.
Johnson, Hannah, 259.
Johnson, Lina A., 494.
Johnson, Mark, 130.
Johnson, R. B., 252.
Johnson, Thomas Nightingale, 175.
Johnson, W. H., 190, 284, 457. 493.
Johnson, W. L., 435.
Johnson, William, 13, 55.
Johnson, William E., octoroon, 282, 284, 285, 321, 326, 336, 344, 345.
Johnson v. *Coulliette*, 91.
Johnston, John B., 338, 353.
Johnston, Thomas Brent, 311, 338, 345, 349, 366.
Johnstone, George, in constitution convention, 387, 390.
Jones, fireman, 249.
Jones, B. F., 372.
Jones, G. C., 115.
Jones, J. Blanding, 263.
Jones, John D., 142.
Jones, John Paul, 65, 414.
Jones, R. M., 203.
Jones, Samuel, 11.
Jones, T. J., state canstable, 378.
Jones, Thomas, 13.
Jonnes, Baron des, 35.
Jordon, Ku-Klux ox, 314.
Journal of Progress, The, Negro newspaper, 461.
Jousting, 203.
Judd's Friend, 33-35.
"Judge Dogberry," 319.
Judge of probate, 61, 91, 258.
June and Walker, store, 201.
Junior High School, Sumter, 496.
Justice of the peace, 22-23. *See also* Magistrates.

Kangaroo ticket, 249.
Kansas Assciation, 236-239.
Kansas Ball, 237.
Kansas Emigrants, 235-240.
Kansas Immigrants, The, 435.
Keels, Ezekiel, 283.
Keels, D. E., 364, 367, 387.
Keels, Isaac, 139.
Keels, Jacob, 355.
Keels, John R., 363-364.
Keels, William, 139.
Keen, Dr. Peter, 66.
Keith, Tom, Negro, 318.
Kelley, B. Frank, representative Lee County, 395.
Kelley, W. M., 394.
Kellogg, Clara Louise, 187, 434-435.
Kellogg, George, 186, 187, 188.
Kellogg, Mrs. George, 186.

Kendrick, J. R., 190, 191.
Kennedy, F. H., 280.
Kennedy, J. D., 356.
Kennedy, Thomas, 11.
Kennedy, William G.: editor, 316, 326, 333; 457; poem, 449; Rose Hill, 325.
Kershaw, Ely, 39.
Kershaw, J. B., 347.
Kershaw, John, 411.
Kershaw, Rev. John, 459.
Kershaw, Joseph, 31, 39, 42, 54.
Ketchum, Taylor, and Company, 172.
Kimball, Frederick, 59.
Kincaid, James, 109.
Kings Mountain, 47.
King George III, 33-34.
Kingstree, 8, 9, 15.
Kinloch, Cleland, 56, 414.
Kinloch, Francis, 56, 414, 440.
Kinloch, Francis, Jr., 414.
Kinloch, Isabella, 414.
Kinney, John, 104.
Kinney, Ned, 104.
Kirby, John, 225.
Knapp, Dr. Seaman, 491.
Knight, A. Wilkes, 458.
Knight, F. Jenkins, 459.
Knight, John M., 458.
Knight of Snowden, 215.
Knights of Clarendon, 202.
Knights of Jericho, 197, 228.
Knighton, Thomas, 13, 31.
Know Nothing Party, 228.
Knox, J. Johnston, 321.
Kolb, fire chief, 170.
Kopff, H. M. C., 329, 432.
Kops, W. C., 435.
Korn Industries, 487.
Ku-Klux Klan, 313-15, 447

Labyrinth, at Acton, 414.
LaCoste, family, 147.
Lacy, Edward, 59, 62.
Ladd, Mrs. Catherine, 177, 425.
Ladies' Monumental Association, 458.
Lafar and Dick, 171.
Lancaster, 60.
Lane, Edward, 31.
Langley, Mrs., teacher, 176.
Lanneau, Charles H., 426.
Lansdell, Mrs. Emilie Brumby, 103.
Lansdell, Robert, 142.
Lansdell, William Mitchell, 103.
Laris, 12.
Lassiter, James, 331.
Laurens, Henry, 41, 131.

Law, Jared, 236.
Lawlessness, backcountry, 27.
Lawrence, Walter, 437.
Laws, George, 225.
Laws, Henry, 225.
Laws, William, 225.
Lawson, Ben, Negro, 281.
Lawson, John, explorer, 4-6.
Lawson, John, magistrate, 59.
Lawton, Miss, teacher, 191.
Leary, W. B., 189.
Lebos Island, 158.
Lederer, John, 4.
Lee, A. M., 394.
Lee, Eli, 177.
Lee, Colonel G. W., 260.
Lee, Joseph, 54.
Lee, Light Horse Harry, 52.
Lee, Loring, 97.
Lee, R. D., 343, 483, 487; in constitution convention, 387, 388.
Lee, Sam, octoroon, 282, 284, 285, 319, 321, 345; "deal," 358; probate judge, 350, 351, 353, 354; publisher, 461.
Lee, Samuel J., 327.
Lee County, cut from Sumter County, 4, 394-395.
Leland, John A., 447, 494.
Lemon, Alexander, 139.
Lemmon, G. A., 481.
Lemmon, Mary, 492.
Lemon, Miss E., 211.
Lenoir, Isaac N., 179.
Lenoir, W. R., 200.
Levy, Chapman, 153.
Levy, Mordecai M., 152.
Levy, Wendell M., 450.
Lewis, Joseph, 188.
Lewis, Robert, 11.
Lewis, Shady, *see* Shady Lewis.
Lewis, William, the ordinary, 101, 196, 197, 223, 455.
Liberty Tree, Charleston, 13, 55.
Library society, Stateburg, 63-64; Sumterville, 93-94, 440.
Lilliputian Negro Band, 220-221, 432.
Limbaker, Sinclair, 180.
Lincoln, Abraham, 249.
Lincoln, Benjamin, 43.
Lincoln, H. D., 263.
"Little Dublin," 331.
Little, Samuel, 39, 59.
Livestock, 485. *See also* Cattle.
Lizardo, 158.
"Lizzie Clarendon," *see* Chambers, Mrs. Elizabeth Ann (Spain).

Lockwood, Mrs. Belva Ann, 436.
Lodebar Academy, 176.
Lodebar camp ground, 223.
Logan, J. Richardson, 454.
Logan, John Richardson, 223.
Logan, Miss M. R., 494.
Logan, Margaret Young, 346, note.
Loggins, W. F., 495.
Log-rolling, 18-19.
Long, Joseph H., 189, 247, 263.
Long, Mrs. Susan E. (Darr), 247.
Long, Reuben, 90, 178.
Long Branch Baptist Church, 469.
Loocock, Aaron, 39, 42.
Looters, Potter's, 264-265.
Lopez, Moses, 94.
Loring, Daniel, 112, 424.
Loring, George W., 431.
Loring, Lucius, P., 112.
Loring, Mrs. Rebecca Pitts, 112, 424.
Loryea, A., 170.
Lott, Cora S., pleads for suffrage, 389.
Lowery, 12.
Lowery, Irving E., Negro author, 18-19, 139, 144, 274, 448; teacher, 494.
Lowery, James, 61, 131.
Lowery, Dr. Robert, 113.
Loyalists, banished, 42, 48, 57, 59; return, 58. *See also* Tories.
Luckey, John, 236.
Lumber Industry, 488.
Lyceum, 330.
Lynchburg, 7, 51, 200, 225. chartered, 173; origin of, 172; post office, 172-73.
Lynchburg Academy, 173.
Lynchburg Female School, 173.
Lynching, Tillman's stand, 370, 375.
Lyon, Major, 124.

McBride, James, 208.
McBride, S., 165.
McCallum, H. B., 311.
McCallum, Corrie, 430.
McCants, J. J., 190.
McCants, Jane, 92, 181.
McCants, T. J., 286.
McCauley, Dr. James, 162.
McClendon, James, 236.
McConnico, Christopher, 117.
McConnico, William, 31, 59, 117.
McCord's Ferry, 54.
McCormick, James, 40, 48.

McCoy, Charles, 11.
McCoy, Charles, 263.
McCoy, Elijah, 60.
McCoy, Mina (Minor?), 142-143.
McCoy, Samuel, 11.
McCoy, William, 11.
McCreight, Captain, 134.
McCullum, James, 177.
McCutcheon, J. E., 394.
McDonald, John, 90.
McDonnell, John, 92.
McDowell, James, 188, 215.
McDuffie, George, 147, 148, 449.
McElween, Thomas, 61.
McFaddins, the, 147.
McFaddin, J. J., 232.
McFaddin, Mrs. Leah, 136.
McFaddin, Thomas, 12, 60, 418.
McFaddin home, 208.
McFarland, A. J., 175.
McGhee, Mrs., 104.
McGill, Samuel, 193, 210.
McGirt, Daniel, 49, 58.
McGirt, James, 13, 24, 49.
McGirt, Mrs. Priscilla Davison, 49.
McGowan, Theodore, 189.
McGregor, Lieutenant, 261.
McIntosh, Carrie J., 444.
McIntosh, James G., 173.
McIntosh, John, 11.
McIntyre, George F., 327-28, 336.
McJunkin, Samuel, 48.
McKagen, Mrs., 261, 264, 265.
McKagen, G. P., delegate to constitution convention, 387, 388.
McKagen, Mrs. Fannie, 261, 265.
McKagen, Isaac, 249, 259.
McKay, Lieutenant, 52.
McKay, William, 27.
McKellar, J. J., 283, 285.
McKellar, James, 95.
McKelvey, James, 13.
Mackey, Albert Gallatin, 284, 285.
Mackey, E. W. M., 344, 349, 358; miscegenator, 374.
Mackey, Mrs. Victoria Alice Sumter, 344, 374.
Mackey House of Representatives, 349, 350.
Mackey, Thomas J., 334, 338, 344, 350, 352.
MacKinney, 12.
McKnight, Mr., 116.
McKnight, Robert, 174.
McLaurin, Mrs. Agnes D. (Chandler), 258.
McLaurin, Catherine Louisa, 267.
McLaurin, D. B., 101, 123, 167, 267.
McLaurin, H. W., 116.
McLaurin, Linnie, 495.
McLaurin, M. H., 458, 479.
McLaurin residence, Manchester, 170.
McLaurin's Hotel, 123.
McLelland, John, 90.
McLeod, Mose, 314.
McLeod, N. S., 372.
McLeod, Mrs. Patsy, Negro, 400.
McLeod, R. G., 195.
McLeod, Robert L., 406-407, 477.
McLeod, Sam, Negro, 400.
McLeod, Thomas Gordon, 225.
McLeod, Thomas Gordon, state senator, Lee County, 395.
McLeod, W. J., 173.
McLendon, state constable, 380.
McLeroth, Major, 49, 50.
Macnair, John, 63, 108.
Macnairs, the, 65.
McQueen, Donald, 264.
McQueen, Rev. Donald, 330, 427, 428.
McQueen, Thomas P., 171, 190, 493.
McQueen, W. A., 261.
McTyeire, H. N., 330.
MacWhorter, George C., 177.
Mabry, J., 230.
Macon, Warner, 123.
Macon's Hotel, 123.
Magee, William, 92.
Magistrates, 70, 309. *See also* Justice of the peace; Trial justices.
Magnolia Farm, 155.
Magrath, A. G., 269, 272.
Maham, Hezekiah, 52.
Mahon, Patton, 48, 58.
Mail service, 124-127, 166.
Major, Dr. L., 143.
Malaria, 25, 92, 113, 166, 205, 410, 443.
Manassas, first battle of, 254.
Manchester: 68-70, 112, 122, 142, 200; abandoned, 316; ball battery, 217; "city", 170; fire, 170; Masonic order, 222; post office, 124; Potter's raid, 265, 266, 267, 269; Unionists, 147.
Manchester and Augusta Railroad, 478.
Manget, J. R., 191.
Manheim's, 377.
Manning, Colonel, 144, 148.
Manning, John Laurence, 141, 161, 162, 165, 232, 276; at Secession Convention, 250; on Potter's raid, 269-271; family portraits, 424.
Manning, Laurence, 65, 70, 117.

INDEX 539

Manning, R. I., 372, 382.
Manning, Richard I., 232.
Manning, Mrs. Richard I., 269.
Manning, Mrs. Susannah (Richardson), 65.
Manning, Wade Hampton, 352.
Manning, courthouse town, 232, 262, 445.
Manning Times, The, 458.
Mansfield, La., 180.
Manufacturing, 3, 485-488. *See also* Factories.
Manumissions, 131, 132.
Marden, 68, 422, 462.
Marion, Francis, 41, 44, 46-53; commissioned, 45.
Marriage settlement: Converse-DeVeaux, 416; Pitts-Loring, 424.
Marshall, John, 39.
Martin, Luther, 491.
Martin, William, 59.
Mason, Charles T., 104, 331, 426, 429, 472-473.
Mason, Charles T., Jr., 429, 473-474, 483.
Mason, Rev. Thomas, 472.
Mason Cotton Harvester Company, 474.
Masons, *see* Free Masons.
Masonic Temple, 378, 386.
Masonic Temple Company, 437.
Massey, William, 42.
Matthews, J. F., 394.
Maverick, Samuel, 112, 113.
Maverick, Samuel Augustus, 113.
Mavericks, origin of term, 113.
Mayes, F. J., 372, 378.
Mayes, Mrs. Henrietta Shaw, 172.
Mayes, Dr. Junius Alcaeus, 172, 253.
Mayes, Mrs. Martha Bradley, 172.
Mayes, "Squire" Matthew Peterson, 172 250, 444.
Mayesville, 4, 127, 177, 259; origin of, 172; Potter's raid, 265.
Mayrant, Mrs. Ann Richardson, 411.
Mayrant, Charles, 169, 184, 276, 286, 353.
Mayrant, John, 65, 96, 170, 414-415; first cotton crop, 109; slaves, 131.
Mayrant, Samuel, 150, 309.
Mayrant, William, 70; case, 411; factory, 116, 411; garden, 411; plantation, 267.
Mays, Dr. Samuel, 61, 66.
Means, John H., 161.

Mechanics Library, 223.
Mechanicsville: appeal to Negroes, 311-12; political meeting, 320, 321.
Medals, Mexican War, 159-60.
Medicine shows, 218-219.
Medicus, 197.
Meeks, Matthew, 177.
Melicher, Oswald E., 183.
Mellet, C. S., 154, 167.
Mellett, Frank, 371, 372, 382.
Mellett, Mary (Brunson), 10.
Mellett, Peter, 11, 13, 31, 92; in Cherokee War, 32.
Mellett, Dr. Robert Sydney, 253.
Mellette, James, 117.
Mellette, John, 48.
Mellichamp family, 259.
Melrose plantation, 14; house, 17, 36, 208.
Memminger, C. G., 189, 242.
Memorial Park, Sumter, 422, 489.
Meriwether, McKie, 342.
Mexico City, 159.
Meyers, Fed, 123. *See also* Myers.
Meyers' Hotel, 100, 123.
Michau, Isaac, 431.
Middleton station, 166.
Middleton Depot, 269.
Middleton, Mrs. Harriett Kinloch, 414.
Middleton, Henry, 414.
Midway plantation, 53, 92; house burned, 259.
Migration, *see* Western migration, Kansas Emigrants.
Miles, James, 13.
Milford, 269-271, 424.
Militia, 129; at Dingle's Mill, 260-263; Negro, 312-313, 338, 342, 347; organized, 352; system, 23-24, 201-202. *See also* Patrol system, Rifle Clubs, Volunteer companies.
Miller, Charles, 222.
Miller, C. W., 163, 185.
Miller, Edwin F., 459, 460.
Miller, J. B., publisher, 560.
Miller, Dr. J. I., 115.
Miller, John Blount, 92-93, 175, 184, 185, 200, 223, 427; gives lot, 185; publications, 441.
Miller, Jonathan, 177.
Miller, Mrs. Mary C. Murrell, 92.
Miller, Dr. S. H., 173.
Miller, Stephen D., 113, 146, 147, 148, 200, 222; ball player, 217.

Miller, Thomas E. ("Canary"), Negro, in constitution convention, 387, 389.
Miller, William (Buck), 150.
Mills, J. A., 353.
Mills, Mrs. Martha Elmira (Wilson), 205.
Mills, Robert, 96; courthouse, 96, 485.
Mills, William Elias, 120, 226; sketch, 205, 206.
Mine Hill, 116.
Minstrel shows, 219, 432, 436, 437, 438.
Minute Men, 249-50.
Miscegenation, 344, 374, 390.
Mitchell, 12.
Mitchell, Rev. J. H., 469.
Mitchell, John, 13.
Mitchell, Julia, 413.
Mitchie, Kenneth, 13.
Mitchum, Eleonor, 212.
Mitchum, Jesse, 212.
Mittell, Carl Eugene, 430.
Mobile, 157.
Moffatt, John, 59.
Moise, Mrs., seminary, 493.
Moise, Charles H., 340, 346, 353, 458, 475.
Moise, Davis D., 404.
Moise, Dulce, silk business, 465.
Moise, Edwin Warren, 277, 326, 352, 448, arrives, 272; builder, 317; candidate, 343; editor, 278, 287, 457; lawyer, 274, 317; party leader, 320, 372, 373, 375; orator, 286, 334, 340.
Moise, H. D., 399.
Moise, Harmon, 474-475.
Moise, Isabel, silk business, 465.
Moise, L. Clifton, *Biography of Isaac Harby*, 448.
Moise, Marion, 399-400, 422, 477.
Momus Hall, 215, 220, 221, 432.
Moise and Lee, 364.
Monaghan, Dick, 331.
Monaghan, R. P., 331, 486.
Monk, John, 178, 423.
Monk, Rachel Haynsworth, 423.
Montagu, Lady Mary Wortley, 447.
Montague, B. L., Company, 487.
Montgomery Artillery, 157.
Montgomery, James H., 423.
Montgomery, Leonora Gamble, 132.
Montgomery, Samuel, 175.
The Monthly Chronicle, 460.
Mood, Emma, 447.
Mood, Dr. Julius Andrew, 449, 459, 490.

Mood, William W., 99, 135, 167, 279; Potter's raid, 269-271; reminiscences, 447.
Mood Infirmary, 490.
Moore, Dick, Negro, 261.
Moore, Isham, 31, 48, 58, 63, 68, 70; slaves, 131.
Moore, John, 217.
Moore, John B., 472.
Moore, John J., 225.
Moore, J. Sinkler, 115.
Moore, L. R., 217.
Moore, Mark, 175, 176.
Moore, Mary Ann James, 68.
Moore, Matthew S., 216.
Moore, Dr. Matthew S., 253.
Moore, William, 31.
Moos, James, D., 439.
Moran, Myles, 331.
Moravians, 119.
Morgan, Alonzo, 102.
Morgan, Caroline, 102, 175, 191.
Morgan, David, 11.
Morgan, Eddie, 102.
Morgan, Gilbert, 183.
Morgan, Gilbert, Jr., 183.
Morgan, Henry, 102.
Morgan, James Morris, 392.
Morgan, Jesse, 94, 102, 229, 247.
Morgan, John, 11.
Morgan, Margaret, 183.
Morgan, Thomas, 25, 410.
Morning dram, alcoholic, 193.
Morris, A., 432.
Morris, Dave, 377, 378.
Morris College, 401.
Morse, Agur T., innkeeper, 114, 123.
Morse, George B., 115.
Morse, Mrs. Grace, 114.
Morse, Josiah, 114.
Morse, Mrs. Nancy, 114.
Morse, Sarah Elizabeth, 94.
Morse's tavern, 114, 151.
Morton, Oliver P., 344.
Moses, Altamont, 104, 286, 372, 479; elected to House, 369; to state Senate, 382; home, 264.
Moses, Mrs. Altamont, 446.
Moses, Andrew Jackson, 126, 241, 261, 266, 277, 422, 449; family change name, 341; home, 160, 495; losses in Potter's raid, 264.
Moses, Mrs. Catherine Esther, 104.
Moses, Claremont, 104, 188.
Moses, D. Harby, 381, note.
Moses, Eugene H., 486.
Moses, Frank, 104.

Moses, Franklin Israel, 107, 146, 155, 160, 202, 236, 281, 315, 316, 428; chief justice, 308, 321, 323, 335, 342, 347; Claremont Troop, 202, 341; comes to Sumter, 94, 95; Congress, candidate, 228; death, 352; delegate, 162, 275; Ervin feud, 188, 227; home, 325, 421; judge, 276, 308; legislator, 169, 227, 275; L.L.D., 326; partnership, 95, 227, 453; rivalry, 227; scalawag, 308; secessionist, 248, 251; trustee, 185, 227.
Moses, Franklin Israel, Jr., 95, 188, 274, 315, 316; delegate, 284-285; editor, 278, 280, 281, 283-284, 457; elected judge, 339, 348; first speech, 203; governor, 323-328, 333, 335-337; home, 325, 362, 371; pardons, 337; political campaign, 320-322; private secretary, 251, 252; Speaker, 309, 310, 319; war record, 252.
Moses, H. C., 327.
Moses, Herbert A., 451, 466.
Moses, Isabel D., silk business, 465.
Moses, Mrs. Jane McLellan, 95, 282, 421.
Moses, John, 13.
Moses, M. B., 327, 344.
Moses, Meyre, 104, 188.
Moses, Minie, 104.
Moses, Montgomery, 103-104, 162, 165, 197, 241, 276, 476; Democrat, 286; impeached, 341; partnership, 95, 227, 453; portrait noted, 427; Radical Republican, 309.
Moses, Mrs. Octavia Harby, 254, 257; verses, 449.
Moses, Perry, 126, 219.
Moses, Robert, 13.
Moses, Rosalie, 215.
Moses, Vivian Mordaunt, 450.
Moses, Zalegman P., 160, 188, 195, 327.
Moses, Mrs. Z. P., silk business, 465-466.
"Mosesism", 333, 336.
Moultrie Guards, Palmetto Regiment, 155.
Mounds, Indian, 6, 7, 52.
Mount Clio, 481.
Mount Clio Academy, 177.
Mount Hope plantation, 9, 22.
Mount Pleasant, 457.
Mount Zion: community, 205, 275; church, 441.
Muckelveeny, 12.

Muldrow John J., 177.
Muldrow, Thomas W., 275.
Muldrows, the, 147.
Muleedy, Thomas, 95.
Mules, 111, 155, 273, 320, 331.
Munds, J. T., 231.
Murphrey's Cross Roads, 172.
Murphy, M. J. M., 158-159.
Murray, 12.
Murray, George Washington, Negro, 366, 367; nominated for Congress, 373; seated, 375; sketch of, 396-398, trial of, 398-400.
Murrell Gang, slave-stealers, 134, 143.
Murrell, Mrs. Louisa, 148, 178, 210.
Murrell, Louisa Blanche, 179.
Murrell, Mary, 109.
Murrell, William, 60, 63, 70, 109, 446.
Music, 19, 219-221, 431-432.
Music Hall, 329, 339, 345, 432, 436.
Mustaches, 205.
Mutiny, Palmetto Regiment, 157.
Myddleton, Charles, 65.
Myers, Fed, 100. *See also* Meyers, Fed.
Myers' Tavern, 100, 123.
Myers, William M., 217.

Nail, W. F., 238.
Nash, B. R., 432.
Nash, Shepard, delegate to constitution convention, 387, 388.
National Bank of South Carolina, 478.
National Bank of Sumter, 476-477.
National Equal Rights Party, 436.
Neason, John J., 313-14, 321.
Needwood, 492.
Negro Baptist Educational and Missionary Convention, 401.
Negro, constitutional definition of, 390.
Negro troops, 260, 264, 265, 267, 269-270, 352.
Neilson, Dorcas, 41.
Neilson, Jared, *see* Nelson, Jared.
Neilson, John, 10.
Neilson, Matthew, 24.
The Neilsons, 20.
Nelson, Jared, 12, 30, 66, 121.
Nelson, Jared J., 162, 232.
Nelson, John, 188.
Nelson, P. H., 237, 239.
Nelson, Samuel E., 414.
Nelson's Ferry, 14, 20, 35, 42, 50, 121.

Nepotism, of Tillmanites, 371.
Nettles, Hezekiah, 212.
Nettles, S. A., 458.
Nettles, William, 162.
"New Deal," of 1880's, 360.
New England Emigant Aid Society, 236.
New Englanders, in Sumter, 94.
Newman, John, 11.
Newman, Wade, 263.
Newspapers: bribed by Radicals, 323, 327, by Tillmanites, 373.
Ninety Six, 40.
Ninety-Six Boys, Palmetto Regiment, 155.
Noah, M. M., Jr., 454.
Nominations, national 1860, 249.
Norment, Frank, 380.
Norris, W. J., 123, 238.
North Britain Tract, 12, 13.
Northeastern Railroad, 260, 478.
Northwestern Railroad, 398, 479-480.
Norton, Mrs. Sarah, 101.
Norton, Tim, 101.
Norwood Manufacturing Company, 487.
Notasulga, 157.
Nu-Idea Furniture Company, 487.
Nullification, 97, 146-152, 181; ordinance, 151-152.
Nursery, for plants, 247.

Oate's Mrs. James, Operatic Troupe, 433.
O'Brian, Mrs. 104.
O'Brian, Catherine, 104.
O'Brian, Johannah, 104.
O'Cain, William G., 114.
O'Connor, 331.
O'Connor, Michael P., 347.
O'Donnell, Dennis, 331.
O'Donnell, Neill, 477, 487, 491.
O'Donnell, Mrs. Neill, 491.
O'Donnell, Pat, 331.
O'Donnell's, 377.
O'Hara, Miss H., 186.
O'Hara, W. J., 186.
O'Neall, John Belton, 191, 202, 417.
Odd Fellows, 223, 228.
Oetgen, H. Glen, 439.
Old Bull, 179.
Old castle, see Edgehill Academy.
Old Hop, 32.
Old Tory road, 214.
Omnibus, 171.
Orangeburg Female College, 246, 316.

Orange Grove plantation, 181.
Oranges, hothouse: Stateburg, 413; Sumter, 422.
Ordinance: Nullification, 151-152; Secession, 250, 264.
Ordinary, see Judge of probate. See also Taverns.
Orr, James, L., 275, 278, 308, 319.
Orr, James L., Jr., 372.
Osborne, Charles, 174.
Osborne, Rose, 435, 437.
Osteen, Hubert Duvall, 461.
Osteen, Hubert Graham, 404, 451, 459, 460, 461.
Osteen, Noah Graham, 18, 266, 278, 312; apprentice, 455; editor, 373-374, 459; publisher, 456, 457.
Osteen Printing Company, 461.
Oswego, 481.
Otacite Ostenaco Skiagunsta, see Judd's Friend.
"Othello," a ship, 115.
Owens, Mrs. E., 191.
Owens, W. W., 232.
Oxen, 330-331.
Oxendine, Mrs. Mary Ann Benenhaley, 468.

Packard, Dan, 437.
Palmer, Joseph, 62.
Palmetto Battery, 256.
Palmetto Pigeon Plant, 485.
Palmetto Regiment, 154-160; second Palmetto Regiment, 252.
Pamperya, Lieutenant, 261, 262, 263.
Panic, financial, see Depressions.
Pardo, Juan de, 4.
Pardons: Chamberlain's, 338; Moses', 337; Scott's, 310.
Parker, John, 177.
Parler, Mrs. Josie Platt, 451.
Parmalee, P. E., 458.
Parrott, G. F., 395.
Parsons, James, 184.
Patrol system, for control of slaves, 140-141.
"Patrick, Dr." 197, 444.
Patrons of Husbandry, 359.
Patterson, Dr., teacher, 63, 180.
Patterson, "Honest" John, 319, 338.
Patton, Robert, 39, 42.
Paxville, 282.
Peabody Fund, 494.
Peace and Harmony Convention, 372.
Peale, Rembrandt, 429.
Pearson, Mrs., 180.

INDEX

Pearson, Black Jamey, 131.
Pearson, William, 131.
Peaseley, William, 25.
Pen names, of Sumter writers, 442.
Penitentiary, 200, 278, 284.
Pennington, Kenneth, 364.
People's Bank, 477.
Pepper, state constable, 380.
Perry, Benjamin F., 161, 272, 276, 336.
Permanent Building and Loan Association, 478.
Perry, John, 180.
Peterkin, Mrs. Julia (Mood), 449.
Pettigrew, J. E., 366.
Phelps, Aaron, 379, 381, 474.
Phillips, Hiram, 329.
Physioc, Bob, 433.
Physioc, J. E., 433.
Physioc, Joseph, 433, 434.
Physioc, Mollie, 433.
Pickens, Francis W., 251, 252.
Pickpockets, Indian, 5; American, 232.
Pierson, Benjamin, 124, 180.
Pillory, 60, 199.
Pinckney, Charles, 13.
Pinckney, Mrs. Elizabeth Lucas, 464.
Pinckney, Thomas, 129.
Pine Log, 481.
Pinewood, 4, 117, 368, 480-481.
Pitts, E. M., 378.
Pitts, J. D. M., 226.
Pitts, Jeremiah, 66, 112.
Pitts, Mrs. Valentine, 112.
Place, Samuel, 281, 311.
Platt, Simon, 140.
Player, Chris, 139.
Player, Jack, 139.
Player, Robert, 61.
Player, Thomas, 11.
Plenipo, race horse, 65.
Plowden, 12.
Plowden, M. H., 417.
Plowden's Mills, 177, 444.
Poinsett, Joel R., 161.
Poinsett State Park, 14, 449.
Polecat, 7.
Polly Prentiss, 487.
Poole, Joseph, 24.
Poole, Sallie, 432.
Population, Sumter County, racial, 3, 484.
Porcher, Dr. Francis Peyre, 253.
Porcher, Peter, 9, 10.
Posey, Ben Lane, cited on Mexican War, 156, 157.
Post offices, Sumter District, list of, 127.

Postell, James C., 177.
Potter, Edward E.: headquarters, 264; raid, 260-271, 421.
Potts, John J., 184.
Potts, R. G., 173.
Powell's Tavern, 65.
Preparedness for Peace Commission, 487.
Prescott, Plumer, 427.
Prescott and McLean Company, 437.
Pressley, Benjamin C., 357.
Pressley, Colonel James F., 261, 263, 268.
Preston, John S., 445.
Preston mansion, 324-325.
Prevost family, 412.
Primary, party elections, 354, 355, 365.
Prince Frederick's Parish, 24.
Pringle, Elijah, 226.
Pringle, Victor R., 495.
Prison bounds, 198.
Prison reform, 198-200.
Privateer, 363, 479.
Privateer Rifle and Vigilance Company, 248.
Proctor, Miss, teacher, 185.
Prohibition, 376, 395-396.
Providence, 95, 481.
Providence camp ground, 223.
Provost court, 273-274, 275, 276, 280.
Public road, first in Sumter County, 8; on Black River, 11.
Pudding Swamp Tobacco Warehouse Company, 484.
Pugh, E. J., 226.
Pugh, Ezra, 162.
Pulitzer Prize, 449.
Pumpkin, a free Negro, 132.
Punishments, 199-200.
Pur——, John, 31.
Purdy, Robert O., 399, 490.
Purvis, H. W., 327.
Putnam, Katie, 435.

Race riots, 342, 344, 345, 348.
Race track: Stateburg, 65; Richardson, 66; Singleton, 65; Sumter, 102.
Raffield, J. A., 407.
Raft, the, 7.
Rafting Creek, precinct, 369.
Rafton Creek Acadmy, 179.
Ragin, Henry Lawrence, *see* Thomas, Henry Ragin.

Railroads, 105, 137, 156, 157; charters, 163; early lines, 163-173; schedule, 168, later lines, 492-496.
Ralle (Rawl?), 12.
Ram, hydraulic, 183.
Rambo, D. L., 495.
Ramsay, David, 193.
Ramsey, Ralph A., 451.
Ramsey, Dr. W. A., 170.
Ramsey, W. Warren, Negro, 282, 321.
Ramseys, the, 68.
Ransier, Alonzo J., octoroon, 312.
Ravenel, Mrs. Harriott Horry, 414.
Rawdon, Lord, 44, 45, 46, 50.
Ray, Henrietta B., 470.
Ray, Herbert, 470.
Reardon, George W., 285-86, 326, 331, 350; cotton chopper, 475.
Reconstruction: congressional, 280-287; presidential, 275-276.
Records: early public, burned, 91; Sumter District, hidden, 261, damaged, 277; town of Sumter burned, 439.
Recreation, 19, 216-219. *See also* Log-rolling, Sports, Tournaments.
Red Bones, 282, 446.
Red Shirt campaign, 344-348, 447.
Reed, I. R., Negro in constitution convention, 387.
Reed, Jacob Pinckney, 339.
Reeder, William, 263, 266.
Reeish, W. H., 349.
Rees, Mr., 214.
Rees, Benjamin, 48.
Rees, Huberd, *see* Rees, Hubert.
Rees, Hubert, 63, 90, 91.
Rees, John W., 117.
Rees, Mayo, 423.
Rees, Orlando Savage, 423.
Rees, Roger, 13.
Rees, William, 31, 40, 43, 48, 58.
Reese, David, 61.
Reese, Joseph, 30.
Reese, Thomas, 57, 64, 440.
Reforms, 193-203.
Refugees, Confederate, in Sumter, 259.
Registration, of voters, 386, 389, 392. *See also* Enrollment.
Regulators, 29-30.
Reid, Merrick, 374-375.
Rembert, Abijah, 31.
Rembert, Andrew, 15, 31.
Rembert, Caleb, 180.
Rembert, Dr. Edward J., explanation of farmers' plight, 361.
Rembert, James, 63, 177.
Rembert, James E., 225, 359.
Rembert, J. J., 226.
Rembert, James W., 135.
Rembert, S., 180.
Rembert, Samuel, 225.
Rembert Hall, 63, 64.
Rembert's, 129, 177.
Rembert's academy, 177.
Rembert's Chapel, 65.
Rembert Settlement Temperance Society, 194.
Remonstrance, from the backcountry, 28.
Report: on county offices, 328; on schools, 175.
Republican Party, 228.
Revill, Janie, 451.
Revolution, *see* American Revolution.
Reynolds, James, 21.
Reynolds, Dr. Marcus, 253, 282; quoted, 341.
Reynolds, Mark, 459.
Reynolds, Samuel, 21.
Reynolds, W. L., 162.
Rhame, Mrs. Ellen S., 114.
Rhame, Joseph F., 114.
Rhame, L. F., 232.
Rhame, Captain Levy, 147.
Rhame, William F., 355, 459.
Rhett, Lieutenant, 271.
Rhett, Alfred, 252.
Richardson, Arthur, 31.
Richardson, Dr. C. H., 223.
Richardson, Charles, 131, 411.
Richardson, Mrs. Dorcas (Neilson), 41.
Richardson, Edward, 37.
Richardson, Eleanor, 211.
Richardson, Eleanor S., 211, note.
Richardson, Elizabeth Buford, genealogy, 449.
Richardson, Mrs. Elizabeth Sinkler (Manning), 211, note.
Richardson, Francis, 110.
Richardson, Guignard, 356, 458.
Richardson, James Burchell, 133, 144, 175, 215.
Richardson, James B., 220-221, 411, 431.
Richardson, James S., of Mississippi, 474.
Richardson, James S. G., 333, 454.
Richardson, James S. G., Jr., 455.
Richardson, John Gaulden, 110-111.
Richardson, John Peter, first governor of name, 90, 148, 162, 175, 236.

Richardson, John Peter, second governor of name, 363, 366, 369; marriage, 211.
Richardson, Judge John Smyth, 66, 94, 128, 148, 150, 151, 180, 428.
Richardson, Rev. John Smyth, Sr., 185, 196, 223, 226; in War, 253.
Richardson, John Smyth, Jr., 246, 339, editor, 454-455; legislator, 279; party activities, 280, 281, 286, 334; war record, 252, 254.
Richardson, Julia, 211.
Richardson, Mrs. Louisa Blanche Murrell, 179.
Richardson, Mrs. Margaret DuBose, 111.
Richardson, Martha, 41.
Richardson, Mrs. Martha (Gaulden), 110.
Richardson, Maynard Davis, 150, 440; death, 152; editor, 151, 453-454; sketch, 441-442.
Richardson, R. C., 162.
Richardson, Richard, 9, 22, 24, 25, 65; delegate, 39, 42; in Cherokee War, 32; Snow Campaign, 41.
Richardson, Richard, Jr., 9, 39, 41, 54, 59, 175.
Richardson, S. M., 190, 493.
Richardson, Thomas E., 274.
Richardson, Willard, 210; career, 178-79.
Richardson, William, 16, 37-39, 41, 42, 54, 60, 66, 410-411.
Richardson, William E., sheriff, 142.
Richardson, William S. G., 428.
Richardsons, "foot" and "head", 221.
Richbourg, Claudius, 15.
Richbourg, Mrs. Honoria, 181.
Richbourg, John S., 195.
Richbourg, W. H. A., 443.
Ricker, Mrs. Elizabeth Kerrison, 449.
Ricker George L., 477.
Ricker and Ferriter Building, 331.
Ricker, E. P. & Company, 377.
Ridgill, J., 212.
Rifle Clubs, 334, 347.
Riley, John J., 478, 491.
Rimini, 481.
"Ring doves," 318, 332.
Rings, rule for wearing, 213.
Riots, 348; Bowman-Keels, 363-364; Darlington, 379-382. See also Race riots.
Rip Raps plantation, 208.
Rivers, William James, 330.
Road duty, 301.

Roads, 120-121; early petition for, 11; paved roads, 481-482. See also Brewington road, Catawba Path, Old Tory road.
Road's End, 429.
"Robert Martin," steamboat, 169.
Roberts, John, 46.
Roberts, John M., 64, 103, 178.
Roberts, William, 11.
Roberts' Academy, 178, 210.
Robertson, David G., 313, 314.
Robertson, D. J., 286.
Robertson, Matthew, 31.
Robertson, T. J., 285, 313.
Robertson, W. F., city manager, Sumter, 406.
Rocky Mount, 64.
Rocky Mount junction, 166.
Roddey, S. L., 478.
Rollindale plantation, 208, 417-418, 423.
Roman Catholic Church: at Providence, 95; Sumterville, 96.
Ronzoni, Miss, Italian teacher, 184
Rosa, D. D., 189.
Rose, Daniel, 92, 93, 94, 222.
Rose, Mrs. Elizabeth Singleton, 92.
Rose, Henrietta Elizabeth, 94.
Rose Hill, 325.
Rose Knit Hosiery Mills, 487.
Rosin, 486.
Ross, Isaac, 39.
Ross, J. M., 372.
Ross, James, 11.
Rowland, Charles G., 405, 478.
Rowland, S. K., 407.
Royall, Mrs. Anne, 120.
Ruffin, Abram, Negro, 343.
Ruffin, Archibald R., 114, 123.
Ruffin, Edmund, 249-250.
Rugeley, Henry, 59.
Ruins, The, 62, 179, 412; garden, 415; history of, 414-415; life at, 210.
Russell, Amy, 437.
Russell, George, 12.
Russell, Thomas B., 188.
Rutledge, Andrew, 13.
Rutledge, Mrs. Ann, 138.
Rutledge, John, 43, 53-54.
Rutledge, R. K., 178.
Ryttenburg, Abe, 487.
Ryttenburg, H., 314.
Ryttenburg, Henry, 485.
Ryttenburg, Irving A., 485-486.
Ryttenburg, J., and Sons, 485.

St. Charles, 205, 481.

St. Joseph's Academy, 259, 492-493.
St. Mark's Parish, 14, 17, 20, 21, 24-31, 37, 66. church, 24, 26, 56, 65; glebe, 25; rectory, 24, 410.
St. Paul's Academy, 177.
Salem County, 3, 61, 91, 394.
Salem Presbyterian Church, Black River, 27, 57, 63, 136, 418.
Salem, town of, 61.
Salem Troop, 202.
Salem Vigilant Association, 141.
Salmond, Thomas, 424.
Samaritan Herald, The, Negro newspaper, 461.
Sanders, A. K., 371, 382.
Sanders, Bartlett, 225.
Sanders, Christian, 247, 421.
Sanders, George, 13.
Sanders, Mrs. Louise C., 247, 421.
Sanders, William, 59, 122.
Sanders' station, 481.
Sandville Academy, 176.
Santee Circuit, organized, 65.
Santee Jack, 6-7.
Santees, 4, 5, 6, 7.
Saucy Jack, an Indian, 35.
Sawmills, early, 17, 35.
Saxton, Rufus, 273.
Scalawag, 308, 310.
Scarborough, H. L., 451.
Scarborough, J. H., in constitution convention, 387, 388.
Scarborough, Mrs. Miranda Miller, 427.
Scarborough, O. C., 367.
Scarborough, W. D., 355, 369, 372.
Scarborough, William Harrison, 427.
Schools, 96, 97, 170, 173, 174-192, 492-496.
Schwerin, J. A., 436.
Scots' Glebe, 12, 13.
Scott, a bugler, 467.
Scott, Edwin J., 193, 204, 447.
Scott, James, 63.
Scott, Joseph C., delegate to "Peace and Harmony" convention, 372.
Scott, Miss M. E., 494.
Scott, Robert K., 281, 285, 310, 312, 322, 347.
Scott, William, 30.
Scott, Winfield, 158.
Scott's Tavern: Manchester, 122; Sumterville, 91.
"Scribler," 420.
Scrip, Sumter County, 309, 334.
Seaboard Airline Railroad, 480.
Seabrook, Marion W., 451.
Seabrook, Whitemarsh B., 200.

Secession: sentiment in 1850, 161, 162, 235; S. C. Convention, 250.
Segalock Fasteners, Inc., 487.
Settlers, of Sumter County, 3, 8-21.
Sewerage, Sumter, 408, 409, 484.
Shady Lewis, 101, 273.
Shaw, Archibald J., 339, 342, 351; death of, 355.
Shaw, Ervin D., 489.
Shaw, H. G., 367.
Shaw, Martha Priscilla, 409.
Shaw, William Henry, 495.
Shaw, W. R., 394.
Shaw Air Force Base, 489-490.
Shell, G. W., 367.
Shell Manifesto, 367.
Shepherd, Alexander, 13.
Sheppard, John C., nominated, 372; in constitution convention, 387.
Sherman, W. T., 259.
Shiloh Methodist Church, 139.
Shot Pouch Camp, 155.
Shower bath, 179.
Siamese Twins, 218.
Sickles, Daniel E., 278, 283.
Sidewalks, Sumter, 482.
Silk culture, in Sumter, 462-466.
Silliman, Alexander, 64.
Simkins, Francis Butler, 392.
Simmons' Ferry, 121.
Simms, William Gimore, 152, 440.
Simonds, Andrew, 477.
Simonds National Bank, Sumter, 477.
Simpson, Mrs. Anna, 490.
Sims, D. W., 452.
Sims, Henry, 13.
Singleterry, 12.
Singleton, Mrs., keeper of a groggery, 194.
Singleton, Alberry L., 351, 354.
Singleton, Christopher, 13.
Singleton, Jake, 332.
Singleton, John, 367, 369.
Singleton, John, 53, 61, 92; home burned, 259; slaves, 131.
Singleton, Mrs. Mary (James), 14.
Singleton, Matthew, 14, 17, 31, 36, 39, 40, 42, 63.
Singleton, Richard, 120, 147, 211; death of, 169; plantation, 120, 215, 415-416; racing stud, 215.
Singleton, Robert, 31, 65.
Singleton, Sarah Angelica, wedding, 211, 416.
Singleton, Mrs. Virginia Eliza Green, *Singletons of South Carolina*, 449.
Singletons, the, 68.

Singleton stud, 215.
Singleton's mill, 50, 53.
Sinkler, Elizabeth Allen, 209.
Sioux, 4.
Skeletons, Indian, 6.
Skinner, A. E., 394.
Slave trade, 39, 133.
Slavery, 136-145; effect of cotton on, 109-110; emancipation sentiment, 110, 131-132.
Slaves, 10, 13, 14, 15, 16, 106; law for fugitives, 233; slave gangs, 109, 131.
Smallpox, 50, 250.
Smalls, Robert, Negro, 320; in constitution convention, 387, 390.
Smiley, James E., 282, 285.
Smith, Arthur, 224.
Smith, Benjamin, 31.
Smith, Ellison Durant, 369, 378.
Smith, J. J. Pringle, 259.
Smith, J. Manley, 395.
Smith, John M., 395.
Smith, L. T., 115.
Smith, Michael, 24.
Smith, Mrs. S. K., 191.
Smith, William T., M.D., Negro, 389.
Snell, Arthur V., 403, 404.
Snow Campaign, 41, 57.
Soldiers' Relief Associations, 257.
Solomons, A. A., house, 171, 264; garden, 422.
Solomons, Augusta, silk business, 465.
Solomons, Augustus, 266.
Solomons, J. T., 326.
Solomons, Mark, 94.
Solomons, S. S., 167.
Sommers, E., 426.
Somsinson, see Tomlinson.
Sons of Temperance, 195, 196, 228.
Sophy, 106.
South Carolina Conference, 330.
South Carolina Continental Telephone Company, 484.
South Carolina National Bank, 477.
South Carolina Railroad, 164, 479.
South Carolina Tobacconist, The, 460.
South Mount, 148.
Southern Rights Convention, 161.
Southern Railway, 479.
Southern Whig, 151, 453, 454.
Spain, Aimee, 192.
Spain, Alberta, 264.
Spain, Albertus C., 154, 155, 162, 223, 227, 236, 250, 264.

Spain, E(lizabeth), 183. *See also* Chambers, Mrs. Elizabeth Ann (Spain).
Spain, Rev. Hartwell, 191, 443.
Spalding, J. W., 433.
Spanish-American War, 381, note.
Spann, Miss, 444.
Spann, Andrew, Negro carpenter, 266.
Spann, Mrs. Charles, 95, 181.
Spann, Mrs. Eleanor, silk business, 464-465.
Spann, James G., 147.
Spann, John, 90, 91.
Spann, John R., 199, 215.
Spann, Lawrence, 448.
Spann, Mrs. Louisa (Chandler), 258.
Spann, Mike, 150.
Spann, Willis, 135, 142.
Sparrow, Henry, 11.
Spears, Anderson, 103.
Spears, Emma, 427.
Spears, Mason, 66.
Spencer, Elisha, 172, 173.
Spirit of the Times, The, 458.
Sports, 213-217.
Spring Hill, 268.
Sprott, Joseph, 195, 232.
Stackhouse, R. P., delegate to constitution convention, 387, 388.
Stage, The, see Theatre.
Stagecoach, accidents to 125, 127.
Stamp Act, 36.
Stancill, Mrs. Charles, 346, note.
"Star of the West," 251.
Starke, Theo, 433.
State Hospital for Insane, 200.
Stateburg, 41, 60, 63, 66, 171, 268; factories near, 108, 116; founded, 62; plan of, 67; Nullification, 147.
Stateburg agricultural association, 225.
Stateburg Jockey Club, 65, 214.
Statesburg, race horse, 65.
Stations, railroad, 169-173, 480-481.
Steele, John, 13.
Stewart, Miss, teacher, 63.
Stewart, M. F., 367.
Stewart, Thomas McCants, Negro, 345, 367.
Stiles, Mrs. Amelia Rosamond, 191.
Stiles, Copeland, 191.
Stiles, Sarah, 191.
Stobo, Archibald, 13.
Stocks, for culprits, 60.
Stokes, J. William, 382.
Stokes, R. M., 226.

Storry, Charles, 11.
Stowe, Harriet B., 446.
Staightouts, address to S. C. democracy, 368-369.
Strauss, I. C., 477.
Strauss & Co., 377.
Street Lights, 483.
Stringham, Gilbert, 13.
Stringham, James, 13.
Strong, Mr., teacher, 190.
Strong, J. H., 491.
Stuard, John, 13.
Stuart, John, see Stuard.
Stuart, Mrs. Susanna Marion Heriot, 179.
Stuart, William Keating, 179.
Stubbs, Thomas McAlpin, writings, 449 452, note.
Stubbs, Mrs. Thomas McAlpin, see Jeffords, Beatrice.
Stuckey, G. M., representative, Lee County, 395.
Stuckey, Hardy, 177.
Stuckey's Tavern, 185.
Stukes, William, 48, 58.
Suares, J. E., 311, 326, 331.
Suder, A. W., 312, 326.
Suffrage, 276, 282; Confederate officers debarred from 280; granted to freedmen, 280, 286; Negroes debarred, 385, 388, 389-390, 397; women suffrage, 385-386, 389, 459.
Sugar, 20.
Suggs, Miss Catherine, 140.
Sully, Thomas, 424.
Summer Resorts, 31, 180-181, 205.
Summerton Academy, 178.
Sumner, Charles, 239-240.
Sumter, Francis, 154, 158, 159.
Sumter, John, brother of General, 62.
Sumter, John Rutledge, 451.
Sumter, Mrs. Mary Cantey (Jameson), 35, 109.
Sumter, Mrs. Natalie Delage, 95, 110, 465, 467, 471; garden, 412-413; letter writer, 447; silk business, 462, 464; slaveholder, 137-138.
Sumter, Sebastian, 154, 161, 413.
Sumter, General Thomas, 15, 30, 37, 39, 180, 429, 467, 469; ball player, 217; Cherokee campaign, 42; commissioner, 59; in Congress, 63, 128, 129; county named for, 3, 89; death, 151; debtor, 199; dinner party, 128; elected general, 44; enterprises, 62; grants, 61; homes, 35, 42, 44, 50; Nullification, 148-149; rescues family, 50; retires, 129; state senator, 54; Snow Campaign, 41; War of 1812, 12, 128-129; youth, 32-35.
Sumter, Thomas, Jr., 90, 122; diplomat, 412; inventor, 471.
Sumter, Mrs. Thomas, Jr., see Sumter, Mrs. Natalie Delage.
Sumter, Thomas Delage, 149, 413.
Sumter, Thomas Sebastian, 451, 462.
Sumter, Victoria Alice, 344, 374.
Sumter, William, 129.
Sumter Academy, see Sumterville Academy.
Sumter Advance, The, 458.
Sumter Agricultural Association, 225, 233, 472.
Sumter Art Association, 429.
Sumter Banner, 159, 454-455; editorial on temperance, 195.
Sumter Bible Society, 223.
Sumter Brass Band, 127, 196, 220, 329, 431, 432.
Sumter Brick Works, 486.
Sumter Carnegie Public Library, 496.
Sumter: city of, 4, 402, 489; charter, 402; Potter's raid, 264-266. *See also* Sumterville.
Sumter Colegiate Institute, 191, 249.
Sumter Community Theatre, 439.
Sumter Compress and Warehouse Company, 487.
Sumter Cotton Factory, 486.
Sumter Cotton Oil Company, 487.
Sumter County, area, 4; general view of, 3, 4; industries, 485-488.
Sumter County Chamber of Commerce, 484.
Sumter County Historical Commission, 497.
Sumter County Historical Society, 497.
Sumter County Sesqui-centennial celebration, 497.
Sumter courthouse: first, 90, 91; second, 96, 484; third, 422, and *frontispiece.*
Sumter Daily Item, The, 459-460; fire destroys, 460-461.
Sumter Dispatch, The, 248-249, 456.
Sumter District, origin, 3, 70, 89-90.

INDEX 549

Sumter Electric Light Company, 472, 483.
Sumter Fantastic Company, 223.
Sumter Female Institute, 493.
Sumter Fertilizer Company, 487.
Sumter Gazette, The, 452, 454.
The Sumter Gazette and Constitutional Advocate, 452-454.
Sumter Hardwood Company, 487.
Sumter Herald, The, 458.
Sumter Hospital, 490.
Sumter Hotel, 245.
Sumter House, 123.
Sumter Ice Manufacturing Company, 486.
Sumter Institute, college for men, 258.
Sumter Junction, 479.
Sumter Juvenile Debating Society, 189.
Sumter Land Company, 422.
Sumter Land and Improvement Company, 487.
Sumter Light Infantry, 379-380, 381 and note; bazaar, 429; benefit play, 435.
Sumter Machinery Company, 487.
Sumter Marble Works, 486.
Sumter Military, Gymnastic and Classical School, 96.
Sumter Mirror, The, 459.
Sumter Negro Band, 377.
Sumter News, 278, 457.
Sumter Opera House, 432.
Sumter Operatic Troupe, 435.
Sumter Park and Agricultural Association, 359.
Sumter Riflemen, 202, 203.
Sumter Roller Mills, 487.
Sumter Savings Bank, 477.
Sumter Silk Association, 465.
Sumter Telephone Company, 484.
Sumter Telephone Manufacturing Company, 474.
Sumter Textile Mills, 487.
Sumter Tobacco Board of Trade, 484.
Sumter Town Hall, *see* Town Hall.
Sumter Training School for Nurses, 490.
Sumter Trust Company, 477.
The Sumter Union and Constitutional Advocate, 452.
Sumter Veneer Mills, 487.
Sumter Venetian-Blind Factory, 487.
Sumter Volunteers, 252, 256.
Sumter Watchman, The, 266, 278, 455-456.

Sumter Water Works Company, 483.
Sumter and Wateree Railroad Company, 479.
Sumter's Ferry, 121.
Sumter's Hotel, 122.
Sumter's Landing, 179.
Sumter's Mount, 398. See also South Mount.
"Sumters, The," Company A, *see* Palmetto Regiment.
"The Sumters'" flag, 155.
Sumterville, 90-107; chartered, 97; name changed, 107, 232; named, 124; nullification, 147. railroad's effect, 171.
Sumterville Academical Society, 185, 187.
Sumterville Academy, 180, 185-190, 227, 431, 493.
Sumterville Baptist Church, 96, 103.
Sumterville Circulating Library Society, 93-94, 440.
Sumterville Female Academy, 184.
Sumterville Gazette, 148, 151.
Sumterville Jockey Club, 214.
Sumterville Mechanics Association, 223.
Sumterville Methodist Church, 96.
Sumterville Presbyterian Church, 96, 181.
Swamp Fox, 45.
Swan Lake Gardens, 65, 422.
Swimming Pens, 177.
Swiss Bell Ringers, 431.

Tableaux, 432, 435.
Tabernacle camp ground, 224.
Talbert, W. Jasper, 375.
Tanyard, Morgan's, 102-103.
Tariff of Abominations, 146.
Tarleton, Banastre, 43, 45-48.
Tate, Matthew, 65.
Taverns (ordinaries): Bradford Springs, 181; Manchester, 68, 122-123; Stateburg, 122; Sumter, 91, 100, 123, 151.
Tax unions, 334.
Taylor, 12.
Taylor, Mrs. Jane (Chandler), 258.
Taylor, Governor John, 146.
Taylor, Samuel P., 195.
Taylor, T. B., 172.
Taylor, Thomas, 59.
Taylor, William, 90, 91, 124.
Tebout, Tunis, 13.

Teicher, Francis Alexander Maximilian, 367.
Telegraph, 230, 454, 472; Sumter office, 251.
Telephones, in Sumter, 474, 484.
Telephone Bond and Share Corporation, 484.
Temperance Hall, Sumter, 196, 197, 226; title to, 197.
Temperance movement, 193-198.
Tennent, William, 40, 41.
Terebene, 425.
Terry, Mrs., 167.
Terry, Jo, 31.
Theatre, The, 431-439.
Theus' academy, 97.
Theus, Major W. R., 96, 178.
Thirtieth Division, A.E.F., 381, note.
Thomas, Henry Ragin, 360; active Tillmanite, 362, 367, 368; appointed, 371; demurs to "Peace and Harmony", 372.
Thomas, Martha Wright, 259.
Thomas, Pete, 378.
"Thomas Salmond," steamer, 424.
Thompson, Henry T., 379, 380.
Thompson, John, 104, 219, 247; death of, 263.
Thompson, Waddy, 149.
Thompson, Walter W., 429.
Thornton Academy, 179.
Thornwell, James H., 184, 212, 246 442, 453-454; on Secession Convention, 250.
Tillman, Benjamin Ryan, 360-369; governor, 370-382; his state constitution, 384-393; his methods, 360, 373; his program, 361, 371; railroad pass, 370; trustee of Clemson College, 364.
Tilman, George, defeated by Tillmanites, 375; in constitution convention, 387, 390.
Timber, 488.
Timberlake, Henry, 32-34.
Timmons Town, 201.
Tindal, James Ezra, candidate, 368, 374, 382.
Tindall, John M., 322, 326, 344, 350, 351, 354.
Tisdale, C. L., 239.
Tobacco, 20, 212-213, 484-485.
Token, for slaves to commune, 136.
Tolman, John, 424.
Tomlin, Hiram, 174.
Tomlinson, 12.

Tomlinson (Somsinson), Arthur, 11.
Tomlinson, Reuben, 319.
Tomotley, 33.
Tories, 40, 45, 46, 47, 48, 49, 51, 57.
Tornado, 231.
Tournament, 179, 215, 273.
Town Hall: first, 229, 237, 248, 431; second, 329-30, 432; city hall, 439.
"Town of Roses," Sumter, 106, 420, 421.
Townsend, Charles Pinckney, 237, 238, 239.
Townships: Fredericksburg, 8, 9; Williamsburg, 8, 9.
Tradewell, Ann E., silk business, 465.
Trial justices, 318, 328, 344, 363.
True Blue plantation, 416.
The True Southron, 332; for "straightout" ticket, 341; merged with *Watchman*, 458.
Tucker, William, 13.
Tuomey, Timothy J., 329, 350, 366; endowment, 490.
Tuomey, Mrs. Timothy J., endowment, 490.
Tuomey Hospital, 115, 490-491.
Turkeys, wild, 7.
The Turks, 467-470.
Turpentine, 486.
Turquand, Paul, 26.
Tuscaroras, 7.
Tuxedo Feed Mills (Early & Daniel Company), 487.
"Two-pen" house, 17.
Tynes, Colonel, 47.

Ugly, race horse, 65.
Uncle Tom's Cabin, 235, 244, 446.
Union League, 283, 313.
Union Reform Party, 312.
Unionists, 147-151, 228, 284.

"Validating Bill", 320.
Van Buren, Abraham, 211.
Van Buren, Martin, 211.
Vassar, Eli, 248.
Vaughan, Henry, Jr., 132, 423.
Vaughan, Henry, III, 216.
Vaughan, Mr. Margaret, 423.
Velocipede, 312.
Venable, N. E., 170.
Venison, Indian barbecue, 6.
Venning family, 259.
Vesey, Denmark, 133.

Vigilance, Committee of, 161.
Village, Indian, 7.
The Vindicator, Negro newspaper, 461.
Vivian, Emily, 433.
Volunteer companies, *see* Claremont Troop, Clarendon Troop, Knights of Clarendon, Salem Troop, Sumter Riflemen, Sumter Volunteers, The Sumters.
Voodoo, *see* Conjuration.

Wagon trade, 119, 120, 130, 164, 277.
Walker, Rev. J. Bentham, 451.
Walker, Thomas, 37, 38, 39.
Walker, William, 232, 244-245.
Walker, Zach, Negro, 326, 350.
Wallace, B. C., 477.
Wallace, David Duncan, 391, 393.
Wallace, R. M., 476, 483.
Wallace, William Henry, 349.
"Wallace House" of Representatives, 349, 350.
Walsh, Bartow, 435.
Walsh, T. V., 355.
War materials, centered in Sumter, 259-260.
War of 1812, 128-130.
War with Mexico, 154-160.
Wardle, Mr., 116.
Waring, Benjamin, 108; slaves, 131.
Warren, John, 11.
Washington, William, 45.
Washington Light Infantry, Palmetto Regiment, 155.
Washington Race Course, 156.
Watchman and Southron, The, 458, 459, 460; files destroyed, 461.
Water system, Sumter, 408, 409, 483-484.
Wateree Junction, 267.
Waterees, 4-5, 7.
Waties, Mr., 125.
Waties, the Misses, 125.
Waties, Anna, 462.
Waties, Mary, 462.
Waties, Thomas, 68, 422; self portrait, 423; miniature, 425.
Waties, Thomas, Jr., 177.
Waties, Dr. Thomas, 68.
Ward's Tavern, 122.
Wasserman, Miss, teacher, 183.
Watson, Mrs., 167.
Watson, Alexander, 143.
Watson, J. T., 395.
Watson, John, 142.
Watson, Colonel John, 50-52.
Watson, Mag, 167.
Watson, William, 13.
Watson's Inn, Manchester, 123.
Wayside Homes, 257.
Wear, J. S., 426.
Webb, John, 11.
Webb, William, 100.
Weddings, 211.
Wedgefield, 316.
Weinberg & Company, 377.
Weir, Samuel, 185.
Weir, Mrs. Samuel, 185.
Welch, Michael, 101.
Welch, N. D., 181.
Welch, William, 54.
Wells, Miss S. M., 191.
Memyss, Major James, 45, 55.
West, *see* Western migration.
Westbury, J. W., Negro, 283, 312, 349, 354.
Westberry, Rufus, 350.
Westberry, William, 11.
Western migration, 110-116, 153.
Weston, Jonathan, farm, 206-208; plan, 207.
Whaley, Mrs. Edna Reed, 429.
Wheeler, R. E., 248.
Whildens, 259.
Whipper, W. J., Negro, 310, 339, 340, 342; in constitution convention, 387, 389-90.
Whipping post, 60, 199.
"Whiskey Rebellion," 379.
White, A., 128, 477, 479.
White, Elizabeth, 429.
White, Grier, 188.
White, James, Negro, 266, 281.
White, J. B., 281.
White, James Grier, 174.
White, Leonard, 165, 191.
White, Leonard, Jr., 115.
White, Mrs. Walter C., 422, edits *Fifteen Letters of Nathalie Sumter*, 447.
White, Haynsworth, and Co., 171.
White's Mills, 166.
Whittemore, Benjamin Franklin, 345.
Whittemore, Louise, 427.
Wigg, James, Negro, in 1868 convention, 387.
Wightman, Thomas, 424.
Wigs, 204.
Wild beasts, 6, 7, 8, 21, 23.
Wilder, J. Diggs, 494.
Wilder, J. M., 355.
Wilder, Joseph, 188.

Wilder, Thomas J., 184.
"W. W. W.," (William W. Wilder?), 116.
Wilder and Wheeler, 428.
Wiley, J., 321.
Willard, A. J., 352.
"William Bradstreet," river boat, 157.
Williams, Alfred B., 347.
Williams, J. Frank, 491, 492.
Williams, Thomas, 184.
Williams' Furniture Company, 487.
Williams' Old Field, 12.
Williams' Tavern, 122.
Williams Veneer Mill, 487.
Williamsburg Township, 8, 9, 24.
Williamson, C., 314.
Williamson, C. L., 382, 383.
Willow Grove, 51-52, 172.
Wilmington, Columbia, and Augusta Railroad, 316, 317.
Wilmington and Manchester Railroad, 165-173, 479, 480.
Wilson, 12.
Wilson, Augustin, 199.
Wilson, Brainard D., 381, note.
Wilson, Edwin, 394.
Wilson, Dr. Edwin R., 491.
Wilson, Emma, Negro, 400, 461.
Wilson, H. F., 486.
Wilson, Hosea, 283.
Wilson, Jesse, 199.
Wilson, J. Harvey, 428.
Wilson, J. H., 367, 382.
Wilson, John L., 95.
Wilson, John Leighton, 253, 275; *Western Africa*, 441.
Wilson, John T., 199.
Wilson, R. M., 367, 373, 378.
Wilson, Robert, 11.
Wilson, Roger, 61.
Wilson, S. E., 165.
Wilson, Taylor, Negro, 318.
Wilson, Thomas, 61.
Wilson, Thomas, 479-480, 481, 491.
Wilson, W. W., 177.
Wilson, William, 11, 39.
Wilson and Summerton Railroad, 479.
Windham's Hotel, 123.
Wingate, William, 263.
Winn, D. James, 262, 451, 479, 486.
Winn, Richard, 59.
Winnsboro, 47 59, 60.
Winthrop Training School, 370.
Wisacky, 194.

Witchcraft, 60.
Withers, Potter, 282.
Witherspoon, A. G., 226.
Witherspoon, Mrs. Elizabeth McFaddin, 418.
Witherspoon, Miss Hamilton, 418, 419.
Witherspoon, Hamilton G., 418.
Witherspoon, Dr. J. B., 184, 281, 326.
Witherspoon, J. C., 431-432.
Witherspoon, Jack, Negro, 281.
Witherspoon, Mrs. Janet James, 418.
Witherspoon, John, Jr., 61, 90.
Witherspoon, Robert, 10, 136, 418-419.
Witherspoon, Dr. Samuel W., 150, 162.
Witherspoon Brothers Coffin Company, 487.
Wolf pits, 21.
Wolfe, Charles Wesley, 223, 244.
Woman's Christian Temperance Union, 378, 389.
Women: Confederate work, 257; legal status of, 388-389, 416, 417.
Woodham, C. W., 395.
Woodland plantation, 128.
Woodmason, Charles, 11-12, 24, 26, 27, 31, 462; cited, 15, 16, 17, 20, 21, 28-30, 36-37, 198, 410.
Woods, 12.
Woodville Academy, 178.
Woodville, Mississippi, 111.
Woodward, T. W., 356.
Wooten, 263.
World's Fair, Paris, 232, 233.
World War I, 381, note; 489.
World War II, 489.
Worsham, P. S., 232.
Worthington, first city manager, Sumter, 405-406.
Wright, 12.
Wright, Jonthan Jasper, Negro, 347, 349.
Wright, Dr. T. W., 20.
Wright, William, 13.
Yeadon, C. B., 491.
"Year of calamity," 359.
Yemassee War, 7.
Youmans, L. W., 372.

Young, Ben, 63.
Young, Henry, 124.
Young, Mrs. Virginia Durant, woman suffrage leader, 459.

Young Men's Christian Association, 246-247.
Zippers, 487.
Zoar Academy, 191.

www.ingramcontent.com/pod-product-compliance
Lightning Source LLC
Chambersburg PA
CBHW020631300426
44112CB00007B/86